Criminal Justice in China

Criminal Justice in China

An Empirical Inquiry

Mike McConville
Faculty of Law, The Chinese University of Hong Kong

and

Satnam Choongh
No 5 Chambers, Birmingham

Pinky Choy Dick Wan, Eric Chui Wing Hong, Ian Dobinson and Carol Jones

Edward Elgar
Cheltenham, UK • Northampton, MA, USA

© Mike McConville 2011

All rights reserved. No part of this publication may be reproduced, stored in a retrieval system or transmitted in any form or by any means, electronic, mechanical or photocopying, recording, or otherwise without the prior permission of the publisher.

Published by
Edward Elgar Publishing Limited
The Lypiatts
15 Lansdown Road
Cheltenham
Glos GL50 2JA
UK

Edward Elgar Publishing, Inc.
William Pratt House
9 Dewey Court
Northampton
Massachusetts 01060
USA

A catalogue record for this book
is available from the British Library

Library of Congress Control Number: 2010939219

ISBN 978 0 85793 190 0 (cased)

Typeset by Servis Filmsetting Ltd, Stockport, Cheshire
Printed and bound by MPG Books Group, UK

Contents

Acknowledgements   vii

1	Introduction	1
2	Sources of police cases	26
3	Police powers in relation to detention and arrest	40
4	The construction of the police case	66
5	Pre-trial preparation of prosecutors	106
6	Pre-trial involvement of judges	144
7	The construction of the defence case	165
8	Trial procedure, rules, setting and personnel	191
9	The trial: case file analysis	234
10	The prosecution observed	261
11	The defence at trial observed (1)	292
12	The defence at trial observed (2)	316
13	Trial outcomes observed	351
14	The process and the system	377
15	Conclusion	425
Appendix 1	Chinese criminal procedure: an overview	455
Appendix 2	A note on research methodology	462
Appendix 3	Case file analysis schedule	475
Appendix 4	Courtroom observation schedule	489
Appendix 5	Interview schedule for judges	491
Appendix 6	Interview schedule for prosecutors	493
Appendix 7	Interview schedule for defenders	495
Appendix 8	A note on administrative punishment in China	497

Bibliography   507
Index   543

Acknowledgements

This study arises out of a long-term research project which has had several homes and the support of many friends. The magnitude of the task set at the outset was ambitious enough but the project grew as the field work developed and became sustainable only with help, support and encouragement from many individuals and institutions.

The overall ambition of the research was to provide a rich description of China's criminal process in action in a way that would better inform those who have responsibility for its structuring and management, those who work in it on a daily basis and those interested in the process of law reform. The research set out to correct an over-emphasis upon purely procedural law by looking at the whole process and those engaged in it through a widespread empirical engagement with the system as it operates in everyday cases. It was and is intended to contribute to dialogues about China rather than in any way to foreclose discussion.

No research project can be comprehensive, the more so in a country as large as Mainland China, but empirical research can often provide an account that transcends the knowledge and experience held by individuals who work within the system by identifying interrelationships and, hopefully, picking out the principles and values that represent the glue that keeps the whole process together.

In many jurisdictions today, the process of reform of the law and its institutions and the questioning of existing arrangements has given more significance to research. The current project seeks to advance this process on the basis that a rational engagement with reform should proceed from a fuller understanding of the whole system and that a basic requirement of informed change is that the system itself should be self-aware. It is indeed difficult for those who work within a complex system to comprehend the whole and see how component parts inter-relate and interact and it is heartening that we received co-operation from so many working within China's criminal justice system. Much more needs to be done but we hope that this project will advance knowledge of China and act as a spur to others better placed to intervene in intelligent debates about the way forward.

This research attempts to offer a broad factual basis for better understanding a highly complex criminal justice system through recourse to empirical and verifiable data and, as will become clear, through giving prominence to the voices of those who work within it. We emphasize that our research is intended to give a holistic view of the system and to the views and opinions of those who work within it: the focus is not on individual or atypical criminal cases but on the routine everyday case that confronts the courts.

The origins of the project on which this book is based go back many years to days at Warwick Law School when Professor Geoffrey Wilson and I thought that it really was worth knowing more about China not for what we could get out of it by way of overseas student fees but because of the intellectual challenge posed by comparative scholarship which in our understanding sees law and the study of law as about the quality of life rather than confined to seeing it in terms of procedural technicalities or simply as one method for settling disputes. Throughout the long years that have passed since then, Geoffrey and his wife Marcia encouraged me and gave me confidence that it could be done despite the inevitable and many setbacks along the way.

The core of the project has been primarily located at The Chinese University of Hong Kong, Faculty of Law under a team led by Professor Mike McConville having initially started life at the School of Law, University of Warwick, continued later at the School of Law, City University of Hong Kong. Each of these institutions has played a key role in helping the research and providing ancillary resources at times of need.

The individuals who provided constant support for the project at The Chinese University of Hong Kong were: Dr. Eric Wing Hong Chui (now based at the University of Hong Kong); Alice Chan Ka Yee; and Paul Leung Po Sang (now barrister-at-law in private practice in Hong Kong). Eric helped with the training of the researchers and provided general support at all stages. Paul provided all-round research assistance until he left to take up practice at the Bar. Alice has been with the project from the outset and undertook almost every task associated with a major field endeavour and did so with unflagging energy and good will.

I wish to thank all my colleagues at The Chinese University of Hong Kong: they have provided continuing and unstinting support throughout in all sorts of ways. Some require special mention. Professor Eva Pils was a constant source of knowledge and inspiration, and selflessly provided detailed comments on an early draft when she was under great time pressure herself. Eva has been an admirable colleague and a fountain of knowledge about Chinese law and this project owes a great debt to her. Professor Lutz-Christian Wolff continually updated me on developments in China and on the latest views of participants in various discussion forums and reassuringly said on many occasions, 'One day you will finish it'.

Nothing could have been achieved without the wonderful backroom support the Faculty of Law at The Chinese University has provided. Mrs. Diana Ying, Faculty Planning Officer, was always on hand to help and support in every way possible. John Bahrij, our Law Librarian, sought to help at every stage and was able to trace even the most obscure source. At an earlier stage, Helen Suen of The City University of Hong Kong also helped and gave support to the project.

A special word of thanks goes to Choy Dick Wan Pinky (now based at the University of Hong Kong) who undertook detailed research of Mainland law and scholarship, drafted countless memoranda and notes, as well as undertaking some of the labour involved in initially sorting out the massive data-set. We were indeed most fortunate to have had Pinky as our principal research officer.

Others closely involved with the project at various stages were: Professor Carol Jones (who helped draft the initiating grant application and spent a great deal of time training individual researchers) and Professor Ian Dobinson (who assisted with the training of researchers as well as providing help and guidance on other aspects of the project) who were core members of the planning team. Both have been friends and colleagues and in that capacity have been unswerving in selflessly offering their support and advice on the many occasions where their help was needed. Professor Satnam Choongh (also at The Chinese University of Hong Kong) joined the project after the field-work was completed and was a great source of inspiration in the early write-up phase, providing initial drafts of a number of chapters and giving general support elsewhere.

The project was undertaken with the encouragement and advice of friends and partners from Mainland China. Their commitment to law reform in China is of long-standing and it has been a privilege to work alongside the leading academics in Chinese Criminal Procedure Law. None of this research could have been achieved without their help.

Special thanks go to our three researchers. Their efforts in the field were unyielding despite the novel challenges presented and the occasional obstacles placed in their path. As faithfully as they could, they implemented the research instruments and used ingenuity in adjusting to new environments. They took the novel challenges presented by fieldwork in China in their stride and stuck to their task whatever the difficulties encountered. Their work will, we hope, inspire others in Mainland China to undertake similar research projects so that information on the functioning of the Chinese legal process in general becomes richer.

In addition, we are grateful to those judges, prosecutors and lawyers who provided direct or indirect support to this research. In doing so, they wanted to assist in gaining a richer understanding of what they see as the real issues of the criminal justice system so that those who know China well can better address the problems they confront. We hope that they will fully appreciate our gratitude and understand that we are unable to mention their names and affiliations.

Among those who provided general and administrative support to the research are Eastman Chan and Stephanie Tam who have been a joy to work with as they struggled uncomplainingly with endless drafts, a task made more rather than less difficult by the invention of word-processing.

Our thanks also go to the whole team at Edward Elgar Publishing Ltd. In particular, Tim Williams was committed to the project as soon as it came to his notice and he has given unfailing support and displayed unflagging optimism throughout production of the book. John-Paul McDonald patiently answered all our questions and gave us latitude when it was most needed and Rebecca Hastie, Jack Webb, Emma Gribbon and Laura Seward helped see the manuscript through to completion.

All works of this kind depend upon the personal and moral support of those who are close to you. In this regard, I had the unqualified support, love and friendship of my late colleague Professor Chester L. Mirsky and his wife Gloria. They saw value in the enterprise and spurred me on whenever I met a problem or offered encouragement whenever I became dispirited. I am forever in their debt.

This book could not have been written without the love, understanding, forbearance, support and friendship of my wife, Sonia McConville. She has been at my side from the very beginning and showed unflagging support over the many years it has taken to see it through including acting as proof-reader and style-guide.

In a project of this kind and dealing with a subject that is fraught with all sorts of challenges, the usual disclaimers need reinforcing. The views expressed in this book are those of the project team alone and are not to be taken as the views of any others who have assisted in the project or have given support and encouragement to the research enterprise.

1. Introduction

In this book, we examine from an empirical standpoint how the modern criminal justice process in China is functioning and the implications this might have for our understanding of system change. The political, economic and social transformations that have taken place in China over the last half century have had a major impact upon the methods, institutions and mechanisms used to deal with alleged criminal infractions. Although the period after the founding of the Republic in 1949 was marked by a state-driven, class-based ideology focusing episodically upon 'enemies' of the state and 'counter-revolutionaries' without the discipline of a system of criminal procedure, symbolized by arbitrary detentions, torture and summary justice[1] (at its height during the notorious Cultural Revolution, 1966–1976, when formal institutions themselves were abolished), from the introduction in 1979 of a Criminal Procedure Law and its successor in 1996 there has been a process of building formal criminal justice institutions and procedures which represent, at least to some degree, a break from the past and which outwardly resemble institutions and procedures in societies based on the rule of law. In this book we analyse the extent to which these changes to the formal legal structure have resulted in changes to the law in practice.

We begin by briefly describing the main features of China's criminal justice process, its institutions and its procedures as they bear upon public, as opposed to private, prosecutions.

THE CHINESE CRIMINAL PROCESS IN OUTLINE[2]

Investigations into reported crime are conducted by the police (*Gong'an*) or Public Security Bureau (PSB). This is the body which is responsible for deciding whether an incident is or is not a crime and for collecting any and all evidence relevant to the resolution of the matter. If it is not considered a 'crime' the police may either take no further action or they may consider that some official action against an individual is still merited utilizing for this purpose various administrative powers described in more detail in Appendix 8 which include detention and 're-education through labour' (*laodong jiaoyang*).

If the police decide that the matter is a crime, they should file the case. They have

---

[1] The starting point of serious inquiry into China's criminal justice system is the pioneering work of Jerome Cohen (1968) who can rightly be said to be the father of the academic study of China's criminal justice system. As Cohen makes clear, there were significant differences in the state's position in regard to law and its institutions over this period which witnessed, among other things, the 'Anti-Rights campaign' and the 'Hundred Flowers Blooming' period. See also Lubman (1969).

[2] See Appendix 1.

powers to detain any suspect and carry out investigative actions such as search of the person or property and may seize relevant material or documentary evidence. If the police decide that it is necessary to detain the suspect, they may submit the case to the People's Procuratorate (*Renmin Jianchayuan*) and request approval to arrest. If arrest is approved, the police have powers to release the suspect or to detain the suspect (with maximum detention periods fixed by law) while evidence is collected.

Once a case goes forward for prosecution, it is handled by the Procuratorate. The Procuratorate has powers to interview the criminal suspect and, where they deem the evidence deficient, may ask the police to undertake 'supplementary investigation'. In the event of a prosecution, it is the responsibility of the Procuratorate to draw up a Bill of Prosecution detailing the charges levelled against the criminal suspect and to present the case to the People's Courts (*Renmin Fayuan*).

As set out in Table 1.1, less serious cases will be dealt with in a Basic Court.[3] Basic Courts are normally located in counties, municipal districts and autonomous counties. Crimes of a more serious character are heard in Intermediate Courts,[4] which are established in capitals or prefectures at the provincial level. Except in certain summary cases, the court sits as a collegial bench (*heyi ting*) and in theory reaches a decision collectively, although in practice the case will be handled by one of their number, referred to herein as the case-responsible judge (*chengban faguan*).[5] Additionally, there is in each court institution a presiding judge (*shenpanzhang*) who may also be the case-responsible judge in an individual case.

In major (*zhongda*) or complex (*yinan*) cases,[6] the case may be passed for advice or decision after the court hearing to the adjudication committee (*shenpan weiyuanhui*) which comprises the President of the Court, Vice-Presidents and the Heads of the Divisions[7] and senior judges. Where this occurs, the decision of the adjudicative committee must also in practice be approved by the head of the division and thereafter by the President of the Court. In practice, the case-responsible judge at the trial will, in this highly bureaucratic setting, defer to his or her superiors.

In parallel with the courts, the Chinese system has political-legal committees at each level. The Party's political-legal committee (*zheng-fa weiyuanhui*) supervises and directs the work of the police, procuratorate and the courts and can involve itself in law enforcement, court procedure and individual case adjudication. The political-legal committee is usually headed by the local chief of police and includes the deputy party-secretary in charge of political-legal affairs, the President of the court, the head of the procuratorate

---

[3] Criminal courts in China are organized at four levels: Basic Court; Intermediate Court; Higher Court; and the Supreme People's Court. Except for the Basic Court, all courts have both original and appellate jurisdiction.

[4] The Court also has an appellate jurisdiction none of which are included in our study.

[5] Technically, power and responsibility is vested in the 'court' not in individual judges. For this reason, members of the court (such as presidents and division chiefs) have a legitimate right to take part in or review draft opinions before they are released.

[6] These will typically include cases involving the death penalty, corruption and bribery cases, economic crimes involving deceit or corruption, cases that might have a major social impact and politically-sensitive cases (including Falun Gong cases).

[7] Courts in China are organized into separate divisions to deal with different categories of case such as civil, criminal, economic and administrative.

Table 1.1 Criminal jurisdiction of different level courts in China

Type of Court	Location	Criminal Jurisdiction
Basic People's Courts	In counties, municipalities, autonomous counties, and municipal districts. A basic people's court may set up a number of people's tribunals (*renmin fating*) according to the conditions of the locality, population and cases. Judgments and orders of these tribunals have the same effect as judgments and orders of the basic people's courts.	• All first instance ordinary criminal cases, except those that fall under the jurisdiction of courts at the higher levels as stipulated by the Criminal Procedure Law, other laws or decrees; • Minor criminal cases that do not need to be determined by trials; • Directing the work of the people's mediation committees.
Intermediate People's Courts	They are established in prefectures of a province and municipalities	• Cases of first instance as assigned by laws and decrees; • First instance cases transferred from the basic people's courts; • Appeals and protests against the judgments and orders of the basic people's courts; • First instance counter-revolutionary cases and cases endangering State security; • Cases punishable by life imprisonment or death penalty; Criminal cases in which the offenders are foreigners; and • Protests lodged by the people's procuratorates in accordance with judicial supervision procedures.
Higher People's Courts	Established in provinces, autonomous regions, and municipalities directly under the Central Government.	They have jurisdiction over first instance major criminal cases that 'pertain to an entire province (or autonomous region or municipality directly under the Central Government)'. Their jurisdiction includes: • First instance cases transferred from the lower courts; • Appeals and protests against the judgments and orders of the lower courts; • First instance cases as assigned by laws and decrees; and • Protests by the people's procuratorates in accordance with judicial supervision procedures.
Supreme People's Court	The highest court in China.	It has jurisdiction over first instance major criminal cases that 'pertain to the whole nation'. Its jurisdiction includes:

Table 1.1 (continued)

Type of Court	Location	Criminal Jurisdiction
		• Interpretation of laws; • First instance cases as assigned by laws and decrees; • Appeals and protests against the judgments and orders of the Higher People's Courts; • Protests by the Supreme People's Procuratorate in accordance with judicial supervision procedures; • Supervising the work of the lower courts; and • Approving death sentences.

Sources: Chapter 2 of the *Organic Law of the People's Court of the People's Republic of China*, and Chapter 2 of Part One and Article 199 of *the Criminal Law of the People's Republic of China*.

and the heads of other ministries or state bureaucracies, such as public security, state security and justice. The desirability of the continuation of the adjudicative and political-legal committees as China develops has been placed on the basis that 'there may still be a need for adjudication committees in courts where the level of [judicial] competence remains low, or for political-legal committees to ensure that judicial decisions keep with macro-level development goals and that the court has the resources and competence to provide an effective remedy in cases that are often the result of systemic shortcomings in the economy or social welfare system . . .' (Zhu Suli, 2010). Where the political-legal committee becomes involved, the decision-making is more complex and the ultimate decision may take the form of a directive.[8] As Ira Belkin (2007) succinctly put it: 'Suffice it to say that judicial, prosecutorial and police decisions in the criminal justice system in China are very much part of a larger political process that is extra-judicial and is not transparent.'

An adverse decision of the collegial bench may be the subject of an appeal (*shangsu*) by the defendant or a 'protest' (*kangsu*) by the procuracy to a court at the next higher level. Appeals and protests are heard by Higher People's Courts which are located in provinces, autonomous regions and municipalities directly under the Central Government.

Provision has been made for expediting first instance trials in certain cases. Summary Procedure, under which the trial will be conducted by a single judge, may be applied where the defendant is pleading guilty and the offence charged does not carry more than three years' imprisonment. Simplified Ordinary Procedure, which may be used in certain

---

[8] Randall Peerenboom (2010b) states that the intervention of the political-legal committee 'does not necessarily dictate the outcome of the case' but rather 'it recommends action to the court': p. 80. Our discussions with judges in China suggest rather that where the political-legal committee takes a view, that view is dispositive. No judge that we have spoken to has indicated that he or she would be able to disregard intimations from the political-legal committee whether framed as a recommendation or as a directive.

cases where the defendant is pleading guilty, allows the court (which normally is provided only with the 'major evidence' by the prosecutor) to read all evidence in advance of trial. These two trial forms are dealt with in greater depth in Chapter 8 *infra*.

BACKGROUND TO 1996 CRIMINAL PROCEDURE LAW: THE 1979 CPL REFORMS

The introduction of a new Criminal Law (CL) and Criminal Procedure Law (CPL) in 1979 was seen by many as constituting a welcome break from a past marked, even discounting the Cultural Revolution, by arbitrariness in decision-making, torture of suspects and 'demonstration trials' in which the outcome had already been decided:[9]

> [B]efore the promulgation of the Criminal Law, we depended on criminal policies in convicting someone of crimes and meting out punishment. We made decisions at our discretion, and the work was strongly characteristic of rule by man. Under such circumstances, the promulgation of the Criminal Law put an end to an era in which there was no law to go by. . . .

Similarly, Wang Hanbin (1996), in welcoming the 1996 CPL reform stated:

> We have made significant amendments to the various stages of criminal proceedings, including investigation, prosecution, and adjudication. This is a major development toward protecting the legitimate rights of the parties concerned. The amendments accord greater protection to citizens' rights and interests under the criminal procedure system and are conducive to correctly meting out punishment for criminals. They address, in a more explicit, concrete, and scientific manner, the issues of how public security organs, procuratorates, and law courts should divide their responsibilities and cooperate and restrain each other.

The police, procuratorate and the courts became responsible for different stages of the criminal process, investigation, prosecution and trial working together under the principle of 'mutual co-ordination and restraint' (*huxiang peihe, huxiang zhiyue*).

The starting point of the criminal process was the apprehension of the suspect by the police. In the immediate past before the 1979 Criminal Procedure Law (CPL), the police powers in this regard were almost untrammelled and they were unrestricted as a matter of practice.[10] The 1979 CPL imposed a requirement that, in order to obtain approval for arrest from the prosecutor, the police had to satisfy a high standard namely to show (Article 40) that the 'main facts of the crime have been already clarified'. There was limited provision to detain 'an active criminal or major suspect' prior to arrest where, for example, the individual was in the process of committing a crime, was identified as having committed a crime by a victim or witness or there was a likelihood that he or she would destroy or falsify evidence (Article 41). Following such detention, the police had a maximum of seven days in which to apply to the procuratorate for permission to arrest

---

[9] Zhang Huanwen, a National People's Congress Deputy, cited by Turack (1999), p. 50.
[10] During the Cultural Revolution (1966–1976) political mobilization through the 'mass line' dominated such that official agencies, including the police, were effectively destroyed. See, Cai Dingjian (1999a).

after which the procuratorate were given up to three days to decide whether or not to approve (Article 48). Additionally, once an arrest had been approved, the total period over which a suspect could be held in custody (including any period covered by pre-arrest detention) was limited to two months, extendable in 'complicated cases', by a further month only upon approval of the procuratorate at the next highest level (Article 92(1)).

Given such a relatively restrictive framework, however, the police continued the practice of widespread resort to detention by utilizing powers outside the 1979 CPL and not requiring the approval of the procuratorate, in particular, the administrative power of 'shelter and investigation' (*shourong shencha*).[11] Even this power, limited as it was to three months' detention, was routinely flouted and the police were able, without external supervision, to utilize detention in order to secure confessions. Further powers could be invoked 'according to the circumstances of the case' (Article 38, 1979 CPL) including 'taking a guarantee and awaiting trial' and 'supervised residence'. The objective of the police was to secure confessions under the prevailing ideology of 'leniency for confessions; harshness for resistance' (*tanbai congkuan; kangju congyan*).

On transfer of the case to the procuratorate, Article 97, 1979 CPL provided that the procuratorate had up to one month to decide whether to initiate a prosecution, extendable by two weeks in 'major' or 'complicated' cases. Throughout this time, the suspect would remain in custody and the detention could be further extended by the procuratorate requesting the police to undertake 'supplementary investigation'. Although such an investigation was time-limited to one month, no limit was placed upon the number of such requests that the procuratorate could make.

Following the initiation of proceedings against an accused and transfer of the case to the court, the court would constitute a 'collegial panel' to try the case. The opening of the hearing was not the occasion to inform the court about the charge and evidence: that had already occurred. In advance of trial, the collegial panel would meet to discuss the case and reach a decision on both the nature of the offence and sentence. 'It was normal practice in China that a case was decided before a trial and that those who tried the case might not have the power to make the decision' (He, 2009, p. 319).

The court had to try the case unless there was not 'clear and sufficient evidence' to support the prosecution: if that happened, the court would remand the case to the procuratorate for supplementary investigation. Where it considered that no criminal punishment was necessary, the court could ask the prosecutor to withdraw the case. In cases where there was any doubt or uncertainty, a people's court could undertake its own inquest, examination, search, seizure, crime scene visit and expert evaluation. In short, it was the judge who, through pre-trial investigation, decided on the facts and the law. 'As a matter of law, no court would open a court session if the collegial panel was not certain about the facts, the offence and the sentence' (Fu, 1998, p. 32).

The result was: 'verdict first, trial afterwards (*xian ding hou shen*)'.[12] But, as we have noted, the verdict itself was not necessarily the verdict of the court. The collegial panel

---

[11] See, for a fuller account and sources, Hecht (1996a), pp. 20 ff.
[12] Various popular sayings encapsulated this arrangement. 'The police cook the rice, the prosecutor delivers the rice and the court eats it.' Another, on the same lines: 'The prosecutor reads the paper, the defendant's lawyer reads the paper, and the judge has already made up his mind.'

was a subordinate institution and cases were commonly discussed with the adjudication committee or after referral by the Presiding Judge or Head of the Unit through consultation with a higher court. In cases which were considered sensitive, Party officials and other political figures would need to be consulted or would determine the decision through the political-legal committee.

It follows that there was limited role for the defence lawyer because a challenge to the case was not simply a challenge to the investigator or the prosecutor but to the court which had already formed a concluded view before the trial. The role of the defence lawyer (then a state employee) was to plead mitigating circumstances or help 'educate' defendants as to the error of their ways. If the lawyer wished to argue innocence, this could be done generally only with the prior permission of the government (Gelatt, 1991). In 1983, the Standing Committee of the National People's Congress promulgated a 'decision' (the so-called 'September 2 Decision') which effectively took away a defendant's right to a lawyer in death penalty cases by abolishing the requirement to notify the defendant of the institution of trial. Defence lawyers were subject to harassment by the government and, in 1983, were extraordinarily made part of the prosecution team in the 'strike hard' (*yanda*) campaign against crime (on 'yanda' campaigns, see Tanner, 1999 and Trevaskes, 2007a). The malign influence this had on the public image of defence lawyers continued for some years.

By virtue of Article 110, 1979 CPL, under which the Bill of Prosecution would be delivered to the defendant 'no later than seven days before the opening of the court session' and the defendant informed of the right to appoint counsel, lawyers could not be involved in a case until a week before the trial at the earliest. In practice, lawyers often had far less time to prepare: whatever the complexity of the case or the volume of documentation involved,[13] lawyers were not accorded access to the records of the collegial panel (which had already determined the offence and punishment) or to evidence uncovered by the court's investigation. There was no concept of pre-trial disclosure: the duty on the prosecution being to deliver the file and evidence to the court. Occasionally informal meetings occurred between lawyers and prosecutors to identify issues in dispute and, where there was convincing counter-evidence, the prosecutor and judge could be saved from public embarrassment by withdrawing the case.

Under the 1979 CPL, the trial judge was the dominant figure who opened the session, announced the subject matter of the case and introduced the participants. After the prosecutor read out the Bill of Prosecution (including the facts, the offence and the punishment sought), the trial judge questioned the defendant (the prosecutor could also question the defendant with the permission of the judge). By Article 116, 1979 CPL the judge and prosecutor questioned any witnesses or read out testimony of those witnesses not in court, read out conclusions of expert witnesses and documentary evidence. In the absence of prosecution witnesses (the norm), there was little the defence could do.

By Article 115 of the 1979 CPL, the parties and defence lawyers could ask the case-responsible judge to question the witnesses or expert witnesses or ask permission to put their own questions directly. The court was empowered to stop defence questioning if it

---

[13] Provision was made to allow a lawyer to apply for delay of the trial in complex cases where the time was inadequate but these were rarely granted: Zhou (1994) cited in Fu Hualing (1998).

considered this irrelevant. The court additionally had, by virtue of Article 117, discretion whether to allow the defence to call its own witnesses.

> Given the fact that a case was decided before the trial, the trial could only be a ritual, with the parties knowing that any input would be too little and too late. (Fu, 1998, p. 39)

Most defence lawyers at this time worked in state-owned firms and were government employees: their status was low and their motivation lower.

THE CRIMINAL PROCEDURE LAW, 1996

The 1996 Criminal Procedure Law (CPL) was introduced at a time of optimism over the direction of the reform of criminal justice in China with Chinese academics and others persuaded that reform was indeed moving in the direction of greater transparency, an enhancement of the role of the defence and prosecution lawyers and a removal of the 'decision first' thinking that had marked the earlier era.[14] It was understandable, therefore, that the rays of hope in the 1996 CPL would attract particular interest from commentators. Writing of the 1996 CPL, Fu Hualing (1998) provided an early overview of the changes that were introduced:[15]

> In many respects the [CPL] introduces important changes to the previous procedures and significantly redistributes the existing division of powers within the criminal justice system. It restricts police power and the prosecution's discretion. It enhances the position of the court and differentiates the roles of judges. It also offers more protection for the rights of the accused and enhances the position of defence lawyers in the criminal process in substantive and procedural aspects. Consequently criminal lawyers are expected to play a more active and meaningful role in criminal law. (p. 31)

Similarly, Carol Jones (2005), in reviewing developments from 1949 to 1999, underlined the advances made but sounded a warning about what was happening in practice:

> The 1996 CPL did introduce a number of improved due process rights and made the trial system more adversarial. It abolished 'verdict first, trial second' (a person could be convicted only *after* a trial). It also enabled legal representation at an earlier stage in the criminal process, gave lawyers a bigger role at trial and made the initial stages of the process (where the suspect was in police custody) more transparent and accountable to law. However, since 1997, the number of defendants being represented by a lawyer has declined, mainly because of the harassment lawyers experience when they try to use their new powers. (p. 201)

The promise was that China had taken the first step towards the introduction of an 'adversary' system of trial. As Amanda Whitfort (2007) put it:

---

[14] In addition to the 1996 CPL, other major reforms to the Chinese criminal justice system at this time included the Judges Law (1995), Procurators Law (1995), Police Law (1995), Administrative Penalty Law (1996) and the Criminal Law (1997).

[15] The quotation omits the reference to Article 12 of the 1996 CPL which provides that no one is guilty of a crime without a people's court rendering a judgment according to law.

Many of the reforms contained in the 225 articles of China's Criminal Procedure Law of 1996 were intended to introduce aspects of the adversary system of justice to the prevailing system, which although not inquisitorial, *per se*, had European civil law at its roots (citation omitted).

As Jonathan Hecht (1996a) noted at the time of its passing, the 1996 CPL, whatever the motivations and intentions underlying it (as to which see, Hecht, 1996a and Fu, 1998), had an impact in at least four major areas of the criminal process: pre-trial detention; the right to counsel; prosecutorial determination of guilt; and the trial process.

So far as police detention powers are concerned, the 1996 CPL imposed some restrictions. The powers of the police to 'take a guarantee and await trial' and 'supervised residence' were restricted to certain types of criminal and time limits were imposed (one year limit on 'taking a guarantee and awaiting trial' and six months limit on 'supervised residence': Article 58(1)). Further, by omitting mention of 'shelter and investigation' from the 1996 CPL, the power was formally abolished. However, the new law extended police pre-arrest detention powers in ways which effectively restored them by other means. For example, Article 61, 1996 CPL provided that the police could detain individuals who 'do not tell their true name or place of residence or whose identity is unclear' as well as to individuals who the police 'strongly suspected' of wandering around committing crimes or forming bands to commit crimes. Further, the circumstances justifying a two month extension of pre-arrest detention was extended by Article 126 to include 'major, complicated cases where the scope of the crime is broad and gathering evidence is difficult', and, by Article 127, an additional two months (giving a total of seven months) could be added for any crime punishable by ten years or longer.

Articles 140(2) and (3), 1996 CPL significantly altered the power of the procuratorate to extend an arrested person's stay in custody by repeated recourse to requests to the police for 'supplementary investigation' by limiting such requests to a maximum of two. On the other hand, the period within which the procuratorate had to decide whether or not to authorize arrest was extended from three to seven days (Article 69(3)).

The former practices under which courts themselves engaged in pre-trial investigation by remanding the case to the procuratorate for supplementary investigation (Article 108, 1979 CPL) and had their own power to discover facts (Article 109, 1979 CPL) were abolished in a reform that was seen to shift the burden of investigation and the adduction of evidence away from the court to the procuratorate:

> These changes shift the burden of leading evidence from the court to the procuratorate. Accordingly, the procuratorate alone will be responsible for the validity of the evidence, and the court will no longer examine the evidence prepared by the procuratorate before trial. If this procedural reform is faithfully executed, judges may become neutral arbitrators, who decide a case according to whatever evidence is given in court. (Fu, 1998, p. 44)

For many commentators, the 1996 CPL enhanced the position of the court in criminal proceedings and thus allowed defence counsel to play a more active and meaningful role. It was considered that the 1996 reform had altered the dynamics of the trial so that in future the prosecution would bear the burden of proof (He, 2009, p. 304; and Zhang and Hao, 2005, pp. 97–99).

In cases in which the prosecution decides to institute a prosecution, the new law changed the position with regard to the transfer of evidence. The former practice under which all evidence was transferred to the court was considered to create such bias in the mind of the judges that there could not be a fair trial: the 'first impression', it was said, 'would be the strongest'. Accordingly, Article 150, 1996 CPL provided that the prosecution would not transfer all the evidence but instead the court would try a case where a Bill of Prosecution includes the alleged criminal facts and has attached a list of evidence, names of witnesses and photocopies or photographs of the 'major' evidence.

The 1996 CPL was also seen, by virtue of Article 149, to increase the powers of the collegial panel. Under Article 149, a collegial panel has the right and duty to render a decision after trial. If the panel is unable to make a decision on a complex and important case after a trial, it should submit the case to the adjudication committee for consideration and decision. This was seen (Fu, 1998) to effect two important changes: the collegial panel itself, not the President of the court, is to initiate the process of referring a case to the adjudication committee for decision; secondly, such a referral occurs only after a trial is completed:

> The reform of trial procedures will improve the quality of legal representation before and during a trial. Right to counsel is extended to the investigative stage. . . . At the investigative stage, an accused may retain a lawyer to provide legal consultancy. At the prosecution and trial stages, a defendant may retain a lawyer for criminal defence. (Fu, 1998, p. 44)

At the investigative stage, by virtue of Article 96, 1996 CPL a lawyer can be a legal 'representative', represent the suspect or lodge a complaint and to apply for bail (a provision subsequently amended by an Interpretation so that a lawyer could, in theory, represent a client following the first police interrogation); at the prosecution or trial stage, a lawyer has the right to read and copy case files, interview witnesses and the victim.[16]

THE IMPACT OF THE 1996 CPL: THE PROMISE

There is no question that the introduction of the 1996 CPL was seen by many commentators as ushering in the start of a new era in Chinese criminal justice by introducing some concepts familiar to Western jurisdictions and more clearly resembling an adversarial than an inquisitorial trial model.[17] Professor Randall Peerenboom (2006) provided an overall assessment of the reforms in this way:

> One of the most significant reforms in criminal law was the transition from an inquisitorial system to a more adversarial system in the mid-1990s. In an inquisitorial system, a judge or prosecutor carries out the pre-trial investigation; detention periods tend to be long, with little role for the lawyer, who is often limited to brief visits with the accused after the initial questioning; at trial, the judge actively pursues the truth by questioning witnesses and overseeing the production of evidence. The process is structured as a search for truth conducted by impartial officers of the state. In contrast, in an adversarial system that process is structured as a contest between the parties. Judges are not involved in police investigation; lawyers play a much larger role both

---

[16] These rights, as we shall see, have been formally extended by the 2007 Lawyers Law.
[17] It is interesting to note that in 1992, Italy also sought to incorporate adversarial features into its then 'pure' inquisitorial system in order to increase transparency and improve efficiency. For an early evaluation of the problems involved, see Pizzi and Marafioti (1992).

before and during the trial; and the judge serves as a passive umpire during the proceedings. (p. 844)

To similar effect, Jonathan Hecht (1996a) wrote:

> [The reform] demonstrates that China has begun to reorient its basic approach to criminal justice away from a dominant preoccupation with social control toward a somewhat greater concern for the protection of defendants' rights. It also sets a stricter standard against which government actions, including those that contravene the CPL itself, can be judged. (p. 79)

Similarly, Jennifer Smith and Michael Gompers (2007) stated:

> In many respects, the 1996 reforms to the Criminal Procedure Law represent China's transition to a more adversarial based system, one in which the prosecution and defense play active roles in the pursuit of truth, and the judiciary serves a more neutral and independent role in administering the law. (pp. 111–112)

This overall assessment broadly reflects that of many other commentators. In their view, the central problem of the reform programme has been that 'implementation has proven exceedingly disappointing'.[18] Thus, Professor Albert Chen (1998) writing shortly after promulgation of the 1996 CPL signalled the general concern:[19]

> [G]iven the severe shortage of professionally qualified judges, lawyers, procurators and other personnel involved in the operation of the Chinese legal system today, given the complex interaction between party organs and members on the one hand and law-related institutions and personnel on the other hand, and given the lack of a tradition, custom or habit of abiding by the law on the part of government, party, police and even judicial officers, there is a significant gap between the law-in-the-books and the law-in-action, between enacted rules and actual practice, and between the officially professed ideals and objectives of the legal system on the one hand and on the other hand, its practical management, operation and impact on those who come into contact with it. (p. 152)

Professor Chen went on to point out that the written rules were by no means meaningless and the 'gap' identified would shorten as more legally trained people are recruited into the system as its operators and as the officially endorsed ideology of socialist legality penetrates more deeply into the consciousness of officials and citizens alike.

Overall, then, the 1996 CPL was seen as a welcome and radical departure from earlier law. It appeared to have abolished the discretionary power of the police to detain criminal suspects under their administrative powers ('shelter and investigation') and placed pre-trial detention within a legal framework; specific (though extendable) time limits for pre-trial detention were set out and made subject to prosecutorial supervision; police powers of arrest, search and questioning of suspects became subject to tighter prosecution

---

[18] Peerenboom (2006), p. 845. Commentators here are not concerned with defining 'law' or, necessarily, advancing a positivistic view of law as a collection of codes, statutes, ordinances or other authoritative texts but rather with examining whether the (perceived) promises in the actual wording of the 1996 CPL, such as the introduction of a presumption of innocence (on which, see text *infra*), are given meaning in the day-to-day operation of the courts.
[19] See, to like effect, the Third Edition of this book (Hong Kong: LexisNexis, 2004) at p. 202.

control; accused persons were given the right to meet a lawyer at an earlier stage (including in the police station); the role of the prosecutor at trial was expanded; defence lawyers were to be given access to the prosecution case and witness lists; they were also to be allowed to prepare their own case, carry out their own investigations, call witnesses at trial and cross-examine prosecution witnesses.

A key change was said to be the introduction of a 'presumption of innocence'. Before 1997, trials could open only once the court was satisfied of the guilt of the accused, established by the prosecution or court *before* trial ('verdict first, trial afterwards'). After the 1996 CPL, commentators pointed to the fact that the guilt/innocence of the accused was to be established *at* trial. The presumption of innocence was thought[20] to be encapsulated in Article 12, 1996 CPL which provides:

> No person shall be found guilty without being judged as such by a People's Court according to law.

For some, the reforms heralded the introduction of elements of the adversary system into the criminal trial. Judges were to adopt a more supervisory rather than direct, interrogatory, role.[21] Daniel Turack (1999), for example, commented:

> [T]he Law of Criminal Procedure makes the criminal trial more adversarial. The court no longer conducts or participates in any pre-trial investigation. It is the Procuratorate that is responsible for the validity of the evidence and for carrying the burden of proof. (p. 53)

Writing of the changes introduced by the 1996 CPL, Daniel Turack (1999) said[22] that as well as intended to prevent the abuse of judicial power and to constitute the cornerstone in administering the PRC's criminal justice system, they also 'complement the principle in the new [CPL] that a person is deemed innocent until proven guilty by the courts'.

THE LEGAL IMPACT OF THE 1996 CPL: THE BACKGROUND CULTURE

A basic theme in much of the writing about the 1996 CPL has been the concern that ingrained habits and attitudes of state officials – police, prosecutors and judges – might subvert the reforms such that 'the gap' between the law and practice might grow in the short term and might be difficult to close in the long term. In this regard, Fu Hualing's (1998) assessment was as follows:

---

[20] See, for example, the commentators referred to by Hecht (1996a) at p. 43, fn. 155.

[21] As will be discussed in Chapter 6, *infra*, many inquisitorial systems are based upon a division of responsibilities in which investigating judges are not involved in the determination of guilt or innocence at trial.

[22] *Ibid.*, at p. 54. For a salutary corrective, see Dobinson (2002). While some commentators applauded the abolition of crimes of 'counter-revolution', Dobinson describes how the new law simply re-classified these as crimes endangering national security so that, because of the elasticity of the term 'national security', 'successful prosecution could even be easier under the new provisions' (*ibid.*, at p. 27).

> Given the substantial changes made in the Amendment, one cannot help being cynical that the law in practice will definitely be different from the law in the book. How can it be possible for the police to accept genuine external review of arrest after nearly 50 years' practice of unsupervised arbitrary detention? How can a Chinese judge become accustomed to adversarial proceedings overnight after being an investigator/inquisitor throughout his career as a judge? . . .
>
> [G]iven the ingrained pattern of practice in China's criminal justice system, the practical impact of the Amendment in protecting the right to counsel will be limited. Efforts to amend the law will not alone guarantee the protection of rights. (p. 48)

To the same effect, Jonathan Hecht (1996a) in a wide-ranging and perceptive overview of the 1996 CPL wrote:

> Since the revisions are intended to change ingrained patterns of behavior by law enforcement officials, it seems likely that the gap between the law and the practice of criminal justice in China will actually grow wider, at least in the short term. (p. i)

Similarly, Jennifer Smith and Michael Gompers (2007) stated that:

> The greatest obstacle that China faces in achieving lasting reform is not in legislating new laws, but in implementing them. Implementation of laws will entail not only institutional capacity building and training for legal professionals, but a redefinition of the roles of lawyers, judges, prosecutors and police officials within the criminal justice system. (p. 114)

Underlying these assessments is a view that the relevant legal actors and institutions are somehow autonomous although lacking capacity or being victims of long-standing culture. Perhaps it is sufficient to note at this point that an analysis which leaves out of account a Party-centred state and its relevance to the 'autonomy' of subordinate institutions lacks persuasiveness.

THE LEGAL IMPACT OF THE 1996 CPL: THE LEGAL REALITY

Randall Peerenboom (2006) has issued some cautionary words to any who embark upon an assessment of the state of China's criminal justice system today:[23]

> [C]omparing China against standards of legal systems in the United States or Europe, or worse yet against an idealized version of those legal systems or the utopian, perfectionist requirements of human rights activists,[24] will result in bitter disappointment about the lack of rule of law in China. (p. 842)

---

[23] Having said that, Peerenboom adds: 'But one cannot compare China's legal system against the standard of other developing states without feeling positive about Chinese accomplishments to date.' *loc. cit.*

[24] We would only comment here that it may be thought inappropriate to criticize 'human rights activists' for 'utopianism' or 'perfectionism' given the reality of Chinese criminal justice. External activists adopt various strategies in an effort to highlight deficits without necessarily any expectation that their proposals are going to be adopted immediately. To restrict a reform agenda to that which might be achievable runs the risk of buttressing the very thing that you believe should be overhauled or discarded. At any rate, the applicability of the remark to those activists within China

We echo those words but think that it is important to go further and, in particular, to avoid some of the weaknesses of 'the gap' problem well-known in socio-legal literature.[25]

While some commentators have viewed the 1996 CPL reforms in very positive ways and at the same time recognized substantial shortcomings in the lived experience of suspects, defendants and lawyers, it would not be appropriate to adopt an analysis which presented the issue as a simple 'gap' problem between the law in the books and the law in practice. As, in different ways, McBarnet (1981), McConville, Sanders and Leng (1991), and Dobinson (2002) have emphasized, the problem with law reform (and law reform expectations) is that 'the law' (or, at least, specified legal rules) is often not as supposed and 'the gap' may well be between practice and an *imaginary or idealized* state of the law (or 'legal rhetoric'). A common misreading is to assume that new laws import what Packer (1968) termed 'Due Process' values in place of 'Crime Control' values when, in reality, no such change may have occurred.

Thus, although '*shelter and investigation*' was formally removed by Article 69, 1996 CPL and applauded by many commentators as a progressive step, the police were in fact accorded extended powers to detain. The seven days previously allowed were extended to 30 days and the period allowed for the prosecutor to decide whether to authorize arrest extended from three to seven days (giving a total of 37 days); noting that time began to run only from when a person's identity had been established. Extensions beyond 30 days can also be sought in 'major' or 'complex' cases. As Carol Jones (2005) notes, the police do not have to *abuse* the law to detain suspects for long periods, 'all they have to do [is] *use* it'. In this analysis, 'due process' is seen to be *for* 'crime control'.

Professor Jones (2005) further points out that the criminal process only ever applied to one-third of all offenders; two-thirds being dealt with under police administrative powers which give the police almost unfettered discretion to process individuals for alleged infractions short of 'crime' (see, further, Appendix 8 *infra*). Moreover, the 1996 CPL did not prohibit successive use of the various powers of extra-judicial detention. Additionally, as Dobinson (2002) shows, although 'counter-revolutionaries' was dropped, its replacement 'endangering state security' broadened the capacity of the state to suppress dissent so that individuals may be dealt with by 'Re-education through Labour'.

We emphasize again that our overall purpose is not to measure 'the gap' between the law-in-the-books and the law-in-action but to place our findings in a broader socio-legal framework. This includes an understanding of *case construction* on the part of the prosecution and defence, including the roles of the police and the courts; and an explication of the link between law and society in the particular context of China.

At the heart of case construction is the understanding that legal actors seek to achieve a particular outcome by utilizing the *legal form* (see Cicourel, 1968). 'Cases' are not pre-formed but rather are the product of decisions taken by the various parties who are

---

who conduct their lives under circumstances the oppressive and dangerous character of which outsiders cannot even imagine is questionable.

[25] The revival of interest in research on the sociology of law from the 1960s generated many studies which demonstrated that the effects of normative legal rules or administrative guidelines on human behaviour were indirect and that the impact could be understood only by examining the way in which the rules and guidelines were affected by the social environment. This approach rested upon a number of contestable assumptions, on which see Nelken (1981).

involved in the event which gives rise to the criminal complaint and thereafter process it. This study concentrates solely upon those cases which are constructed to fall within the criminal sphere from the initiating complaint through to disposition. In this process, case construction is an ongoing task of the actors involved (complainants, witnesses, police, prosecutors, judges, defence lawyers and defendants) but one which renders down the complexities of human interaction into relatively simple 'factual' accounts which fits the relevant legal category – 'Guilty' or 'Not Guilty' of an offence known to law.

CRIMINAL CASES

The focus of the research is only upon criminal cases decided in the Basic Courts or the Intermediate Courts. This has a number of important implications. First, as we have briefly mentioned, the focus is upon *crime* rather than more minor acts, categorized as 'unlawful', which fall within the administrative jurisdiction of the police. Crime in this setting is restricted to acts which, under the Chinese understanding, endanger society with serious circumstances or consequences. The distinction between 'administrative offences' and 'crimes' is, however, arbitrary[26] and the police are accorded almost unfettered discretion to deal with individuals through the 'administrative' system of 'penalties'.

Second, the focus on crime invokes a particular species of law in China and our insights are not necessarily applicable to the general state of law or law reform in China. It is fundamental to an understanding of criminal justice in China that the 1996 CPL was enacted for a prescribed purpose, as set out in Article 1:

> . . . of ensuring correct enforcement of the Criminal Law, punishing crimes, protecting the people, safeguarding State and public security and maintaining socialist public order.

This objective is further underscored by Article 2, 1996 CPL:

> The aim of the Criminal Procedure Law of the People's Republic of China is: to ensure accurate and timely ascertainment of facts about crimes, correct application of law, punishment of criminals and protection of the innocent against being investigated for criminal responsibility; to enhance the citizens' awareness of the need to abide by law and fight vigorously against criminal acts in order to safeguard the socialist legal system, to protect the citizens' personal rights; their property rights, democratic rights and other rights; and to guarantee smooth progress of the cause of socialist development.

As these provisions make clear and as Fu Hualing (2003) observes, crime in China 'is seen not simply as a violation of criminal law but also as a political challenge to the role of

---

[26] For illustration of the magnitude of discretion, under the Security Administration Punishment Regulations, 1986, 'Whoever disturbs social order, endangers public safety, infringes upon citizens' rights of the person or encroaches upon public or private property, if such an act constitutes a crime according to the Criminal Law of the People's Republic of China, shall be investigated for criminal responsibility; if such an act is not serious enough for criminal punishment but should be given administrative penalties for public security, penalties shall be given according to these regulations.' It should be noted that, many of the 'rights' incorporated into the 1996 CPL (whatever their actual value to the individual) are not available to an individual subject to this administrative system of penalties.

the Chinese Communist Party (CCP) and to the socialist system'.[27] In the light of this, it is necessary to confine our study to its proper domain and not draw assumptions about other areas of Chinese law which may need to be viewed through a different lens.

Thirdly, for the reasons stated by Peerenboom (2006), in seeking to explain why lawyers have been routinely denied access to their clients, prosecutors have refused to provide defence lawyers access to the whole dossier, defence counsel are unable to question witnesses because they do not appear at trial and the high confession rate results in lawyers seeking of leniency, crime in China requires a special understanding:

> [W]hat distinguishes criminal law from other areas of law is the lack of public support for criminal law reforms; the majority of the citizenry sees such reforms as harming, rather than furthering, their interests. At the same time, there is little political support for criminals. The government has responded to the fears of the public by acceding to demands to crack down on crime. Thus, interest group politics explain much of China's harsh approach to crime, much as they account for the war on crime in other states. (p. 846)[28]

We will discuss the overall relevance of Peerenboom's explanation in due course but for the present we can note that, at the same time as the 1996 'reform' was in process, China was able to launch another 'strike hard' (*yanda*) campaign designed to underscore the certainty and celerity of punishment under which thousands of individuals were subject to arbitrary arrest, compulsory interrogation and show trials, with many incarcerated individuals suffering execution (Shu, 1996; Tanner, 1999; and Note, 1985). Subsequent campaigns have been launched when the State feels that it needs to address 'problems', as by establishing 'social hygiene' in advance of major events such as the Beijing Olympics in 2008 or in dealing with ethnic unrest in Xinjiang.

A NOTE ON PREVIOUS RESEARCH

There has been a substantial body of research into the legal reforms in China over the past 50 years and scholars have advanced various accounts at a theoretical level in an effort to explain what has happened. While early research had to rely upon studying China 'at a distance' (Whyte, 1983), more recently scholars from Western countries and, increasingly from within China, have been able to secure access for research through interviewing individuals and analysing materials derived from courts and other institutions within Mainland China itself. The following account is indicative only and much other research is discussed at relevant points later in the text.

Lu and Miethe (2002) sought to examine the impact of legal representation on pre-trial and sentencing decisions in a sample of 237 theft cases drawn from one district court. They found that there was substantial under-representation, with only some 20

---

[27] See also, Michelson (2008) whose analysis showed significant increase in criminal-related matters in the Lawyer Bao columns coincident with 'strike hard' campaigns.

[28] The claim that the government responds to public demands to crack down on crime seems to invert the reality, namely that public perceptions of crime are largely a creation of government propaganda which also constructs 'public concern' at times of its choosing, a factor not unique to China.

per cent of defendants having the benefit of a defence lawyer. The presence of a lawyer did not appear to affect decisions on pre-trial detention or the sentences imposed. Decisions on pre-trial detention were based on such factors as seriousness of offence, confession, residential status and education, while sentencing was based upon offence seriousness and multiple offending rather than whether the defendant was represented by counsel. They also found, however, that although defence lawyers have not been a major social force in affecting case outcomes, where they advance defences which do not challenge the legitimacy of the system (such as a defence based on character), the defence is more likely to be affirmed by the court. By comparison, where the defence challenges the system by, for example, challenging the 'facts' presented by the prosecution, the court is unlikely to accept the defence. They concluded that defence lawyers in China were, nevertheless, 'moving toward more aggressive and effective defence' (at p. 278).

In an extension of their study, Lu and Miethe (2003) took a sample of 1009 criminal cases before and after the reform and analysed the relationship between confessions and disposition. They found that most cases (79 per cent pre-1996 and 67 per cent post-1996) included a confession by the defendant. Confessions deemed to express real remorse were awarded more lenient sentences in line with China's policy to reward repentance.

In a study restricted to death penalty cases, the Max Planck Institute (2006) undertook interviews with 25 defence lawyers in Beijing and Guizhou, all of whom had a formal legal education with a degree from a law school, specialized in criminal cases and had at least five years professional experience. Additionally, the researchers analysed 322 case files drawn from four Intermediate Courts across China. The research concluded that during the investigative stage defence lawyers have a marginal role: at first instance trial their influence is modest and at the appeal stage such limited influence is mostly informal and based on out-of-court communications with the judicial organs.

In analysing lawyers' representation of criminal suspects and defendants in the lawmaking and implementation of China's CPL since 1979, Liu and Halliday (2009) examined: (i) archival materials on the history of the reform process; (ii) online ethnographic data from a nationwide Internet forum hosted by the official *All-China Lawyers Association*; and (iii) in-depth interviews with lawmakers and practitioners in the criminal justice system (lawyers, police, procurators, judges and legal academics). Bearing in mind that the Internet forum used by Liu and Halliday (2009) is subject to official censorship, their analysis showed that, notwithstanding this and other possible constraints, lawyers using the forum spoke in a forthright manner on a range of topics including the courts, the police and the absence of the rule of law or democracy (see also, Halliday and Liu, 2007). Overall they found that the basic procedural rights of criminal suspects and defendants are poorly protected and that defence lawyers face considerable obstacles in representing their clients.

Lu and Drass (2002) found that residential status (being a local or a migrant) significantly affected pre-trial detention (but not sentencing outcome). Migrants received pre-trial detention at a rate of 92 per cent compared to local residents at 62 per cent.

Research on sentencing (Lu and Drass, 2002; Lu, Liu and Crowther, 2006; and Lu and Liang, 2008) has found that, in general, the principal determinant of sentencing, across a wide range of offences, is offence severity.

Pitman Potter (1999) in a wide-ranging review of legal reforms, whilst pointing to positive aspects, underscored a general problem of implementation in the face of reduced technical competence and corruption. William Alford's work on Chinese lawyers analysed the burgeoning numbers, problems in their education, ethical understanding and the recourse by some to bribing judges (Alford, 1995). Susan Trevaskes (2003) has described how sentences were often announced at mass rallies and Lu and Miethe (2007) has reported that capital offences tend to be committed by young males of low social status. Sida Liu's study of a lower court in Hebei Province shows how judicial day-to-day work is only loosely coupled with the formal roles of judges and that the judicial decision-making process is contingent upon the historical origins of the judiciary, administrative influence, and the legal consciousness of local communities (Liu, 2006).

All research is subject to limitations and the existing literature on China is no exception. Perhaps the most important limitation is that we lack systematic and comprehensive national statistics on criminal cases in China and existing data are neither reliable nor accessible (Lu and Kelly, 2008; Dicks, 1995). Many scholars (e.g., Lu and Miethe, 2002) have been forced to rely upon a local source, or upon selective criminal cases made public and accordingly, as the researchers acknowledge, the cases may not be typical having been in all likelihood presented to showcase the system and 'educate' the public (Lu, Liu and Crowther, 2006).

Nonetheless, what has been achieved to date is impressive and we are indebted to all those who have in different ways sought to throw light on an area of great social importance to the people of China. What we have attempted, to add to the growing literature, is a more systematic and comprehensive study than has hitherto been attempted.

PRACTICE AND THEORY

Much of our ultimate interest is on understanding and explaining the criminal justice system in theoretical terms, but we do not shy away from policy considerations. This project has relevance to those monitoring the operation of the current law and assessing what is needed to enable those charged with its operation to fulfil the aims of the legislators and/or law reformers. The findings will hopefully provide a better understanding of the obstacles to change as well as the areas of greatest default. To better enable criminal justice actors to operate the system and meet the new expectations placed upon them, many donor organizations and countries have offered China assistance, particularly in the area of capacity-building. While some of the early assistance focused on law reform, more recent initiatives have involved practical training programmes for judges, prosecutors and police officials, some of which has been delivered out-of-country. Attempts have also been made, for example, to show Chinese judges and officials how trials work in the Anglo-American system of criminal justice, how to better understand the implications of allowing torture and how to imagine and provide for its eventual removal from the process and how to re-align the training of police officers and re-fashion working relationships between police and the procuratorate. Our project has relevance to identifying areas where assistance can be more effectively targeted in the future.

In practical terms, the project has sought to create a detailed mapping of criminal justice through observing courts at work and interviewing key actors involved in the day-to-day running of the courts. Among its tangible outcomes, the project sought to:

(1) provide an empirical account of the practices of criminal courts in relation to the organization and management of court cases;
(2) provide a factual account of the daily workings of the 1996 CPL to guide future reform debates;
(3) afford a more objective means of evaluating the nature, reliability and persuasiveness of the evidence that constitutes the case for the prosecution;
(4) examine the extent to which there is unmet legal need in criminal justice;
(5) establish a factual basis for initiatives involving the rights of individuals and the responsibilities of officials in the criminal justice system;
(6) enable more precise targeting of aid and assistance by development agencies; and
(7) introduce a more rigorous empirical research tradition into Mainland Chinese scholarship and policy-making.

There has been much talk of an 'adversarial system' being introduced into China in place of its inquisitorial system.[29] It is not the purpose of this research to advocate the introduction of an adversary model or to compare it with an inquisitorial model but rather to examine the quite separate question whether claims made that the 1996 CPL introduced greater adversariness into China have any foundation in reality.

We would also point out that, as we mention at various stages in the text, many of the features which are evident in the Chinese system are not necessary features of 'inquisitorial' systems as is often implied by commentators. Thus, for example, significant continental European systems are marked by an independent judiciary, the presumption of innocence, the principle of orality at the hearing, with the burden of proof clearly placed upon the prosecution (Delmas-Marty and Spencer, 2005).

Increasingly, for both inquisitorial and adversarial systems to operate successfully there is broad consensus that a number of things need to be in place, as conveniently set out in the European Convention on Human Rights, particularly Article 6:

1. In the determination of his civil rights and obligations or of any criminal charge against him, everyone is entitled to a fair and public hearing within a reasonable time by an independent and impartial tribunal established by law. Judgment shall be pronounced publicly but the press and public may be excluded from all or part of the trial in the interest of morals, public order or national security in a democratic society, where the interests of juveniles or the protection of the private life of the parties so require, or the extent strictly necessary in the opinion of the court in special circumstances where publicity would prejudice the interests of justice.

---

[29] There are in fact very different principles and practices evident in systems that fall within the broad inquisitorial family. Moreover, inquisitorial systems do not necessarily operate in the way people imagine or, indeed, in the way that they are usually portrayed. See, for example: Hodgson (2006). The same caveats need to be entered in respect of 'adversarial' systems.

2. Everyone charged with a criminal offence shall be presumed innocent until proved guilty according to law.
3. Everyone charged with a criminal offence has the following minimum rights:
   (a) to be informed promptly, in a language which he understands and in detail, of the nature and cause of the accusation against him;
   (b) to have adequate time and the facilities for the preparation of his defence;
   (c) to defend himself in person or through legal assistance of his own choosing or, if he has not sufficient means to pay for legal assistance, to be given it free when the interests of justice so require;
   (d) to examine or have examined witnesses against him and to obtain the attendance and examination of witnesses on his behalf under the same conditions as witnesses against him;
   (e) to have the free assistance of an interpreter if he cannot understand or speak the language used in court.

Thus, the principle of 'equality of arms' demands that those without sufficient funds to hire a lawyer be granted legal aid. A trial with adversarial elements also assumes the presence of adversaries – another issue we explore is whether accused persons have ready access to a defence lawyer and/or the attitude of the local legal professionals to becoming involved in criminal defence work. The project also seeks to determine how lawyers become involved in defence work, as, for example, by nomination/selection by the accused or by court assignment. Even where lawyers are ready and willing to act, a further question is whether they can mount an effective defence, i.e. do they have the resources and know-how required to investigate and construct a case for the defence?

Similarly, the 1996 CPL seemingly requires prosecution lawyers to play a more adversarial role. A further question is whether and how far prosecutors have been able to meet these requirements. Is there evidence in their performance that they have received training in evidence presentation and advocacy? Are they aware of the rules/practices regarding disclosure of prosecution evidence and if so, what (if anything) hinders adherence to such rules?

Finally, the 1996 CPL is said to have altered the role of the judiciary. One question this project addresses is whether and how judges in China's courts have adapted to their new environment and is there evidence in their performance that they received and benefited from judicial training, for example, in the conduct of trials? Has the production of evidence in open court led to the development of judgments based on judicial reasoning?

OUTLINE OF FIELDWORK

Our analysis arises from a long-term study of those aspects of the system to which we were able to secure access. For reasons which are well-documented, the collection of data outside of those provided through official channels is fraught with difficulties and, as we shall see, along with others before us, the information to which we could obtain unmediated access was not unrestricted.

Beginning in 1994, following an invitation to Mike McConville by the doyen of Chinese Criminal Procedure, Professor Chen Guangzhong,[30] to attend a conference to discuss possible reform of the 1979 Criminal Procedure Law, exploratory overtures were made to see whether it would be possible to launch an empirical project to look at what would happen after reforms were put in place. After protracted discussions, the research started in 2001 and continued in the field until 2006, with limited follow-up visits taking place from 2007 to 2009.

The kind of data we set out to collect includes such items as: whether the defence had been given reasonable time to prepare case/access to prosecution file; the length of time the suspect had been held in detention pre-trial; whether or not the accused was represented by a lawyer; whether oral evidence from witnesses was led in court or whether the case was a 'paper trial' only; how many witnesses were called, to what did they testify, whether they were cross-examined and by whom; whether questioning of prosecution witnesses by the defence indicated that the defence lawyer had prepared a foundation for the questioning; whether the defence produced witnesses and if so how many; whether they were cross-examined and if so, on what basis; whether any of the parties produced tangible evidence, forensic evidence or expert witnesses and if so how such evidence was presented and dealt with at trial; whether the case was subject to adjournments and if so how many/how long; whether the trial judge(s) adopted a supervisory or interrogatory role at trial; the length of the trial itself; whether the court had a system for summoning witnesses, and if so, how this operated; what involvement the judge had in the trial, e.g. by ruling on questions of admissibility and by questioning witnesses; how and what judgment was delivered and whether reasons were given.

The research sought to examine across China the working practices and philosophies that underpin China's two principal criminal courts: the Intermediate People's Court (which deals with more serious first instance trials of criminal offences) and the People's Basic Court (which deals with less serious crimes). Ultimately, we were able to look at 13 courts throughout China including large cities, county areas, developed and less-developed regions (further details are provided in Appendix 2). This cannot be said to be completely representative of practices across the whole of China, but we are satisfied that the sites represent a fair cross-section and include some of the biggest and most influential areas of the country as well as regions that are less developed and cannot be expected by reason of their local economies to be concurrent with latest legal thinking.

In each site, we sought access to case files relating to at least 50 of the most recently-completed first instance cases,[31] to observe whatever trials were being conducted during the currency of the site visit, and sought semi-structured interviews with Judges, Prosecutors and Defence Lawyers (further details of our research instruments are set out in Appendices 3–7). We were indeed fortunate that we were given unmediated access to the case files and to all court cases that we were able to observe during the research periods. In general, we were successful in securing interviews with key state justice system

---

[30] Professor Chen Guangzhong was then President of The China University of Political Science and Law in Beijing and, as China's leading scholar on criminal procedure was an active voice in promoting reform prominently through a symposium held in 1991 the papers of which were published as Chen (1992).
[31] We did not include appellate cases which can be heard in the Intermediate Court.

actors although, not unexpectedly, approaches to a few individuals for interviews were declined. We also undertook interviews with defence lawyers although they proved a more elusive target, either because few were to be found in the environs of the court or because they had little time or inclination to give the research priority in their lives. It was not possible, because of the arrangements that we had made, to interview any defendants, a limitation that we hope will be made good by others.

Entry into each site was preceded by informal approaches made by Chinese colleagues to key personnel to pave the way for our field researchers. What must be borne in mind at all times is that a lot of data that would be of interest and relevance to an understanding of China's legal system are regarded as sensitive or beyond sensitive. It is remarkable that we were able, through the good offices of our Chinese colleagues, to obtain access in the way that we did. Fortunately, their extensive network created the opportunities for us in all of the areas for which we had expressed a preference. Despite those helpful introductions, a great deal rested on the skills of our researchers in gaining actual access and in putting into effect the research instruments. Without their field work skills none of the research could have gone ahead.

In each site, we extracted data from the case files held by the court on a systematic basis through a *Case Analysis Form* (see Appendix 3) which had been prepared through a process of discussion with experts in Chinese criminal procedure. A major advantage of this approach is that, by concentrating on recently-completed files, the danger of file-corruption, whether by intention or because of the researcher-effect, is avoided. A major disadvantage is that the files were prepared for other purposes and accordingly data relevant to our inquiry might not be included in the files at all or not recorded systematically from region to region.

In each site we undertook a semi-structured analysis using a *Court Observation Form* (see Appendix 4) and applied this to any first instance trials that were being processed by the courts during the currency of the research. The strength of this approach includes the fact that none of the key actors (prosecution, defence or court) could prepare in advance for the presence of the researcher and, indeed, some (such as defence counsel) were unaware of the identity of the researcher.[32] The disadvantages include the fact that we could not thereby draw a random sample of cases nor could we guarantee to know the outcome of cases observed since the judgment might be given after an adjournment and our departure from the field site (see Appendix 2).

Our interviews with key justice personnel were entirely dependent upon the agreement of the individuals we approached. It was not possible to draw a sample from within each group: the researchers had to be content with establishing a long-term relationship of trust with individuals and persuading them to agree to an interview. We were conscious that, without formal approval, our approaches could place individuals at personal risk and, despite undertakings of confidentiality and anonymity, this doubtless contributed

---

[32] It is possible that some of the parties who had given consent (usually, the Presiding Judge) could have adjusted their behaviour in the presence of the research. For reasons which will become clear, we do not think that this, if it occurred at all, had any significant impact upon the research. At least we are confident that, after a short period in the field, our researchers came to be accepted by the participants so that little 'presentational' data were offered as against 'research data' that we were trying to collect.

Table 1.2   Fieldwork data from 13 sites

	Case File Analysis	Courtroom Observations	Interviews with Judges	Interviews with Prosecutors	Interviews with Lawyers
Site A	157	10	10	15	10
Site B	141	22	14	18	7
Site C	153	10	4	5	6
Site D	70	15	6	6	6
Site E	65	16	7	7	7
Site F	65	20	7	5	7
Site G	70	33	5	5	4
Site H	53	10	6	7	4
Site I	70	12	2	0	5
Site J	60	19	8	8	6
Site K	70	15	4	4	5
Site L	100	25	11	11	11
Site M	70	20	4	5	5
Total	1144	227	88	96	83

Table 1.3   Fieldwork data from different level of courts

	Basic Court			Intermediate Court	
	Case File Analysis	Courtroom Observations		Case File Analysis	Courtroom Observations
Site A	157	10	Site E	65	16
Site B	141	22	Site H	53	10
Site C	153	10	Site I	70	12
Site D	70	15	Site J	60	19
Site F	65	20	Site K	70	15
Site G	70	33	Site L	100	25
Site M	70	20	–	–	–
Total	726	130	Total	418	97

to the fact that a few declined our invitation. Mostly, however, they agreed to be interviewed although, understandably, this sometimes took place away from the work site in restaurants or other social settings where privacy was more likely to be secured.[33]

An overview of the data underpinning our research is set out in Tables 1.2 and 1.3.

We again stress the limitations of this research. Professor Donald Clarke (2003) has rightly cautioned the research community about the care needed in gathering empirical

---

[33] This is far from unusual as a research experience. Indeed, a great deal of valuable qualitative research has been gathered in informal settings. See, for example, Flood (1983).

research data and the importance of appreciating the limitations of data in respect of the complexities of the Chinese legal system:

> What we already know, in the form of reliable data, about the Chinese legal system is not much. Useful data are not generally available, and the available data are not very useful. (p. 165)

In part, therefore, the present research is an attempt to respond to this deficit in knowledge of Donald Clarke's further injunction that:

> ... a priority in an empirical research agenda at this stage of our understanding should be further study of the actual functioning of China's various legal institutions so that we have a better idea of what questions to ask. (p. 181)

The reader should be clear, therefore, that this book does not aspire to be definitive or predictive: what it tries to do is provide as rigorous an account as was possible in the circumstances facing the research. It deliberately chose to paint a broad picture and in consequence it does not offer a close study of any local court with its specific culture[34] nor does it document the plight of suspects, individual defendants, individual lawyers or 'activists' (see Human Rights Watch, 2008; Savadove, 2006; Wang, 2006; and Cohen and Chen, 2010a and 2010b).

It does, however, attempt to go beyond a study of 'the rule of law' and similar abstractions, responding to Randall Peerenboom's critique of research in China (Peerenboom, 2006):

> Scholars must complement studies relying on abstract variables like rule of law with specific studies that break these variables down into more discrete institutions and practices. Separate studies should focus on each of the major actors: the judiciary, prosecutors, police and correctional officers, and other legal professions ... (p. 863)

We will return in the concluding chapter to wider implications of our study but note at this point that criminal justice writing on China has given rise to contrasting explanations at the level of meta-theory. Thus, for example, Pitman Potter (2004) in reviewing the major contributions of Stanley Lubman (1999) and Randall Peerenboom (2002) summarizes the contrasting positions of two broad schools of thought thus:

> Lubman suggests that Communist Party dominance constrains the role of law to such an extent that China cannot be said to have a legal system. Peerenboom suggests that the economic reforms undertaken since the later 1970s, coupled with changing popular expectations, will require the party to rely increasingly on law and thus lay the foundation for a recognizable rule of law system. (p. 468)

In different ways, nonetheless, all these writers remind us of the relationship between law and underlying social norms and practices and the fact that for many people '... the

---

[34] The importance of social connections in China may be a large factor in conditioning the operation of general rules and regulations at the locality. See, for example, Gold, Guthrie and Wank (2002) suggesting that legal reform remains conditional on local culture.

meaning of law still depends on conditions and outcomes of performance in practice' (Potter, 2004).

STRUCTURE OF THE BOOK

We begin our account with the way in which allegations of crime come to the notice of the police, whether by citizen-report or by pro-active detective work on the part of the police (Chapter 2). In Chapter 3, we examine the various powers available to the police to gather evidence, detain and question suspected individuals. We then, over the next two chapters, look at the way in which the case for the prosecution is assembled by the police (Chapter 4) and the procuratorate (Chapter 5) in advance of the trial. In Chapter 6, we examine what, if anything, judges do before the trial given that they have now been assigned a more neutral role in the re-structured criminal process. In Chapter 7, we turn to the preparations defence lawyers make before trial. In Chapter 8, we describe in outline how trials are set-up in the Chinese process, including the physical lay-out of courts, the rules that govern proceedings and the personnel of the law. We then turn in Chapter 9 to the findings arising out of our case file analysis of the court records in some 1144 cases. After this, we turn our attention to first instance trials that we observed (227) during our fieldwork and describe the activities of the prosecution (Chapter 10) and defence (Chapters 11 and 12) in that regard. In Chapter 13 we examine the outcome of trials that were observed in terms of such matters as whether the judgment was immediate or delayed, whether the prosecution was able to establish its case and for which offence and, if so, with what outcome in terms of sentence. Chapter 14 attempts to examine the institutions of criminal justice and their relationship to one another. In Chapter 15, we draw together our findings and make an assessment of the criminal justice process as a whole.

2. Sources of police cases

INTRODUCTION

This chapter discusses our findings on how and by whom crime is discovered and reported to the police and other law enforcement agencies; the nature of that crime by offence category; how and by whom suspects are identified; and the profile of suspects in terms of gender, age, occupation, education, employment and migrant/non-migrant status.

The information was extracted from a total of 1144 completed first instance case files drawn from 13 research sites, the target number for each site being at least 50, the actual number of case files analysed in each site ranging from 53 (Site H) to 157 (Site A). The cases analysed in the study had reached the point of final disposal at varying times between 2002 and 2006. Each case file was composed of a number of folders, and although the number of folders varied from site to site, the information recorded in the files was broadly consistent across sites. Each of the files included an evidence folder which recorded matters such as who reported the crime, how the suspect was apprehended, the identity of the suspect (including matters such as age, gender, education, employment status etc.), and the offence or offences with which the suspect was charged.

As explained in Chapter 1, formal charging and prosecution is not the only route open to the police once they discover or have brought to their attention a crime or potential crime. In cases involving crimes of public disorder, offences against the person, offences against property and acts impairing social administration, the police (and indeed other administrative organs such as tax and land administration authorities) have a fairly broad discretion to dispose of cases via a range of administrative punishments, including detention. These 'administrative' cases are not reflected in the data that we collected, because our data are based upon cases that were prosecuted and which passed through the formal criminal court process.

REPORTING OF CRIME

In China, as in most other jurisdictions, primary responsibility for detecting crime, identifying offenders and deciding what charge or charges, if any, should be preferred against the suspect lies with the police (Chen Weidong, 2002, p. 112). These responsibilities are prescribed by the Criminal Procedure Law and Police Law of the People's Republic of China. Zhou (1998) has estimated that 85 per cent of criminal cases are investigated by the police.

In other countries the allocation of responsibilities in this way has led to an assumption in the public mind that the police discover and detect crime largely on their own initiative, using specialized training and knowledge. In fact, this widely held view is contradicted by a wealth of research findings. Research studies in the UK, USA and Germany, for example, have found that the police are essentially reactive in nature, heavily reliant on information provided by the public.[1] So, for example, in England, Bottomley and Coleman (1976) found that the police discovered only around 13 per cent of all the crimes in their sample of cases. This general picture was subsequently confirmed by a number of other studies, including those by Chatterton (1976), Mawby (1979), and Steer (1980). American researchers (see, e.g., Sellin and Wolfgang, 1964; Black, 1970, 1971; Greenwood, Chaiken and Petersilia, 1977; and Vera Institute, 1977) have similarly found that in the overwhelming majority of cases crimes are brought to the attention of the police by citizens, and are not discovered as a consequence of police patrols, surveillance or other investigative methods. In Germany, less than 5 per cent of criminal cases are directly initially discovered by the police (Song and Wu, 2002, p. 277).

We found that, as in many other countries, the police in China play a relatively subsidiary role in the discovery of crime. Of course, this is not to imply that the police role in resolving the crime after it is first reported is unimportant although we do know from substantial criminological research that pure detective work on its own solves (or is needed to solve) relatively few crimes. The aphorism, 'if you tell the police who did it they will catch the culprit; if you don't they won't', is a general truism and emphasizes the need to be realistic about the capacity of the police, unaided by the citizenry, to solve crime. The picture emerging from our research is shown graphically in Figure 2.1.

As Figure 2.1 shows, of the 1078 cases in our sample where information was known, 392 (36.4 per cent) were reported by the victim, 172 (16.0 per cent) by the victim's family and 232 (21.5 per cent) by other civilians. In brief, on the basis of our sample, at least 74 per cent of crimes are first reported by the public. Even if it is assumed that the 5.6 per cent of cases (60) in which the information was provided by another suspect were cases where the information was discovered as a result of police intervention (for example by police interrogation of an accessory), the police were responsible for initially identifying only around 20 per cent of the crimes in our sample. Although there were some variations across the 13 sites as to the percentages of cases attributed to reports by, for example, victims,[2] when the three categories of victim, victims' families and third parties were combined the picture was broadly consistent across sites in that in all sites these three categories accounted for between approximately 60 and 95 per cent of all cases. To put it another way, at none of the sites did police initial detection of crime (i.e. on-the-spot detection by police plus police detection after investigation) exceed 25 per cent[3] and it is likely that, as elsewhere, in most of these cases the police were led to the suspect by information supplied by the public.

---

[1] Reiner (2000) has described public involvement as the 'prime determinant of success' in detecting crime, pp. 118–119. See also Ashworth (1994), p. 4.

[2] So, for example, the highest percentage of cases reported by victims was in Site M (74 per cent) and the lowest in Site E (12 per cent).

[3] The highest figure (24 per cent) for these two sources combined was at Site A. At all other sites it was well below 20 per cent.

28   *Criminal justice in China*

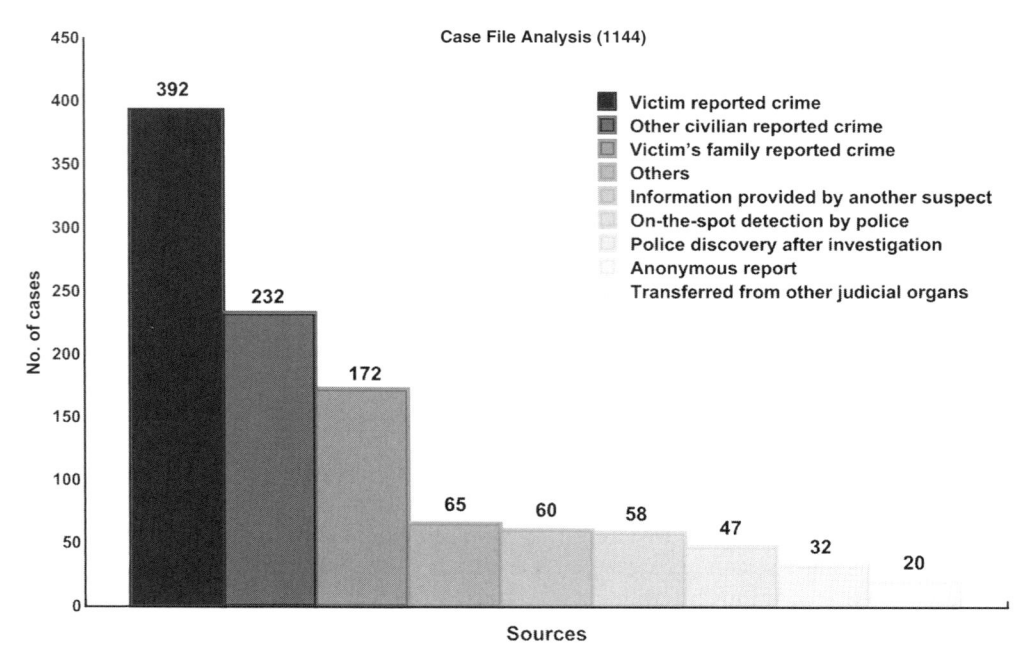

Case File Analysis (1144)

Bar chart showing number of cases by source:
- Victim reported crime: 392
- Other civilian reported crime: 232
- Victim's family reported crime: 172
- Others: 65
- Information provided by another suspect: 60
- On-the-spot detection by police: 58
- Police discovery after investigation: 47
- Anonymous report: 32
- Transferred from other judicial organs: 20

Figure 2.1   How did the offence(s) come to the attention of the police – 13 sample sites

Table 2.1   Offence type in case file sample

Offence Type	Percentage
Crimes of property violation	45.0
Crimes of infringing citizens' right of person and democratic rights	24.7
Obstructing administration of public order	16.6
Disrupting the order of the Socialist Market Economy	6.2
Embezzlement and bribery	4.1
Crimes of endangering public security	3.3
Impairing interests of national defence	0.1
Crimes of dereliction of duty	0.1

CHARGING AND OFFENCE TYPE

In almost all cases (91 per cent) defendants faced a single charge in the Bill of Prosecution. There were only 93 cases (8 per cent) in which defendants faced two charges, and only 9 cases involving three charges. This meant that the sample as a whole contained 1255 charges and, as can be seen from Table 2.1, the most common types of offence were crimes against property, crimes against the person and public order offences.

Generally speaking, crimes involving offences against the person were likely to be more serious than other crimes. More of these types of cases were dealt with by the

Intermediate Courts than by the Basic Courts (46 per cent of the Intermediate Court case load comprised such cases, compared with only 15 per cent in the Basic Court). Property crimes, such as theft, tended to predominate in the Basic Courts (almost 50 per cent of the Basic Court case load comprised such offences).[4]

IDENTIFICATION OF SUSPECTS

Researchers in the United Kingdom and the United States have found that the police rely heavily on the public not only for the initial discovery of crime but also for information leading to the identification of suspects.[5] McConville and Baldwin (1981), for example, took a 500-case sample in Birmingham (UK) and found that in almost 47 per cent of cases the suspect was either caught in the act by the victim or other civilian, or named or otherwise directly identified to the police by the victim or other witnesses. Research conducted 10 years later by McConville, Sanders and Leng (1991) found an even greater role played by the public in identifying suspects: in 58 per cent of their cases the suspect was apprehended or identified directly as a result of the efforts of the victim or other civilians. In a sample of 1080 cases, the police either witnessed the offence, saw the suspect at the scene or apprehended the suspect following a stop in only a quarter of cases (McConville, Sanders and Leng, 1991, p. 19).[6]

In the present study, we found that the role played by victims and others in identifying the suspect, by either naming them or providing a specific description, was as significant in China as it is in the UK. As Table 2.2 demonstrates, 33 per cent of the suspects in our sample were identified in one of these two ways.

This figure of 33 per cent is lower than the 47 per cent and 58 per cent identified in the above UK studies, but a closer analysis demonstrates that the difference is not as marked as appears from the raw statistics.

Firstly, McConville, Sanders and Leng's (1991) figure of 58 per cent included cases in which the suspect was caught in the act by the victim or other civilian. In the present study, 26 per cent of suspects were caught in the act. Although our Case File Analysis Schedule did not differentiate between suspects caught in the act by the police and those caught in the act by victims/civilians, we conducted a manual check of the information recorded within the Schedules for one site to discover the circumstances in which individuals were caught in the act. For the purposes of this exercise we chose Site D (which had the highest percentage of 'caught in the act' cases). We found that the suspect had been

---

[4] The break-down of offence type varied (sometimes significantly) as between the various research sites. For the reasons explained in Appendix 2, this was to be expected and could not be controlled for under the case collection methodology adopted in this research which was to take the most recently-completed cases in each research site.

[5] It goes without saying that 'identification' in this context simply refers to how particular individuals are drawn to the attention of the police so that they are taken into custody as a criminal suspect. It does not follow that the individual in question was 'correctly' identified because we do know from a long line of research both that identification evidence is often unreliable and that many miscarriages of justice result from misidentifications. See, for example, Loftus (1979); Wells and Olson (2003); Cutler and Penrod (1995); and Roberts (2004).

[6] A similar situation obtains in the United States – see, Vera Institute (1977).

Table 2.2 How the suspect was identified

	BC 7 Sites		IC 6 Sites		All Sites	
Caught in the act	217	33.6	52	13.4	269	26.0
Directly identified by victim/witness	113	17.5	79	20.4	192	18.6
Description provided by victim/witness	73	11.3	76	19.6	149	14.4
Police stop and search	154	23.9	110	28.4	264	25.6
Forensic identification	5	0.8	2	0.5	7	0.7
Transfer from another region/state body	2	0.3	8	2.1	10	1.0
Police discovered the suspect through interrogation	46	7.1	31	8.0	77	7.5
Police discovered the suspect through other means	14	2.2	13	3.4	27	2.6
Voluntary surrender	21	3.3	17	4.4	38	3.7
Not known	81	–	30	–	111	–
Total	726	100.0	418	100.0	1144	100.0

caught by the police in only 30 per cent of the cases recorded under this category. These were predominantly drugs cases, where the police in effect discovered the crime and the offender as part of the same policing act (usually a stop and search or surveillance operation). Assuming this 30 per cent figure is broadly the same for the sample as a whole, this means that the suspect was caught in the act by the victim or civilians in 18 per cent of the cases for which we have information. When these cases are added to the cases in which the suspect was identified either directly by the victim/civilian or as a result of a specific description provided by the victim/civilian, the public role in identifying suspects increases to 51 per cent.

Secondly, the statistics gathered from our Case File Analysis revealed that, compared with the UK research findings, there was a high incidence of suspects being identified through police stop and search (25.6 per cent in our sample compared with 16.9 per cent in McConville and Baldwin (1981) and 12.4 per cent in McConville, Sanders and Leng (1991)).[7] We were also concerned about the variations in the percentage of suspects recorded across the 13 sites as having been identified through police stop and search. These varied from as high as 60 per cent (Site K), 56 per cent (Sites I and J), and 53 per cent (Site F) to as low as 0 per cent (Sites E and H), 1 per cent (Site L) and 4.6 per cent (Site G). These variations could not be explained by reference to offence category. So, for example, the samples for both Sites C and F included a similar proportion of cases dealing with crimes of property violation, crimes against the person and public order offences (the three most common types of offence). Yet the proportion of suspects identified through police stop and search contrasted sharply, with 52.5 per cent of suspects

---

[7] The figure for McConville, Sanders and Leng (1991) is the sum of two categories: 'suspect apprehended after police stop' and 'police see suspect at crime scene'. These were combined in the earlier McConville and Baldwin (1981) study under the category 'police caught defendant in possession of stolen goods or other suspicious circumstances'.

being identified through this method at Site F but only 16.7 per cent at Site C. Similarly, with the Intermediate Court sample, Sites E, H and K had a similar offence profile for these three types of offence, yet while no suspects were identified by police stop and search at Sites E and H, over 60 per cent were identified through this method at Site K.

We therefore carried out a closer analysis of the case files for Sites F and K.[8] An examination of 18 of the 32 case files at Site F which recorded that the suspect had been identified through stop and search showed that in all 18 cases the crime had in fact been reported by the victim or the victim's family, and that 17 of the offences were offences of theft, swindling or robbery. It is very unlikely therefore that these suspects were *first* identified through police stop and search – the overwhelming probability is that the victim either named the suspect or gave a description which allowed the police to find and detain the suspect.[9]

The case files revealed some clear cases of inaccurate recording, supporting the thesis that the researchers had made too liberal a use of the 'stop and search' category. So, for example, at Site F a case of 'intentionally destroying property' which was reported by the public was recorded as one where the suspect had been identified through a police stop and search. There were also a number of multi-defendant cases at both Sites F and K in which it was clear that the police had been led to the first defendant as a result of precise information provided by the public, and that the remaining suspects had been captured as a result of the first suspect apprehended naming or identifying them during police interrogation. At Site K a suspect was recorded as having been identified through a police stop and search when the offence was one of rape reported by the victim with discrete information.

By way of summary, therefore, it is clear that a high proportion of the 26 per cent of cases in which the suspect was said to have been identified through police stop and search were in fact cases where the suspect had been first identified as a result of information or description provided either by the victim or other members of the public. Once these recording errors are properly accounted for, it becomes clear that the public role in identifying suspects in China is very similar to that recorded in the UK and other Western countries.

We found that the percentage of suspects in our sample identified as a result of police interrogation (e.g. where a person already in custody named an accomplice) was, at 7.5 per cent, almost identical to the percentage in McConville and Baldwin's 1981 study (7.6 per cent) and broadly similar to McConville, Sanders and Leng's 1991 study (5.4 per cent). However, it must be acknowledged that the 7.5 per cent recorded in the present study is probably an underestimate, as when we read the files for Sites F and K we discovered that a fairly significant number of suspects identified through police interrogation had wrongly been categorized as having been identified through police stop and search. As with criminal cases in the UK, suspects were very rarely linked to the crime through forensic evidence (0.7 per cent) or other forms of police forensic investigation (2.6 per cent).[10]

---

[8] An inspection of some other sites revealed similar findings.

[9] It would appear that the fieldwork researchers recorded these cases as 'stop and search' cases because that was the immediate cause for the suspect being detained or arrested, when the purpose of the question was to ascertain whether the suspect had been *identified* as a result of public assistance and information or as consequence of police investigation.

[10] McConville and Baldwin (1981) found that forensic evidence 'was rarely important' (p. 148).

This broad picture was corroborated by our courtroom observations. Although we did not have detailed information in some sites because, for example, they had not been observed by our principal researchers and we had accordingly less qualitative material, it is clear that there was little difficulty in identifying the defendant in many cases because, for example, good information had been supplied by the public, the defendant had been captured by the victim or caught by the masses after a hue and cry. Moreover, of the 99 cases involving personal offences (murder, robbery, bodily injury, sexual offences and kidnapping), only 32 (32 per cent) involved a defendant–stranger relationship. There was a much lower proportion in homicide cases in which, where the relationship was clearly established in court, only 5 (16.6 per cent) out of 30 victims were strangers to the defendant, the major portion (66.6 per cent) being acquaintances, with the residue (16.6 per cent) being family/relatives. The identity of the defendant was also readily established in other cases where there was a prior relationship with the victim, as in blackmail, fraud and bribery cases as well as in traffic offences where suspect and victim remained at the scene.

PROFILE OF SUSPECTS

The profile of suspects in our sample confirmed what has long been known in the UK and the USA about the make-up of the suspect population, namely that they are as a generality unskilled, unemployed males with little or no formal education.[11]

The overwhelming majority (89 per cent) of suspects in our sample were male; more than three-quarters (78 per cent) were unemployed; almost 80 per cent were described as 'unskilled'; and only a quarter had been educated beyond junior middle school (with only 8.3 per cent educated at college level or above). This is similar to the findings by some Chinese researchers. For example, in the survey conducted by Lin, Zhang and Huang (2009), 88.8 per cent of offenders were male and 11.2 per cent female; most offenders were unemployed or had no stable job prior to being in custody. Of their 2620 research sample, 84.6 per cent of offenders received education to junior middle school (junior middle school 49.9 per cent, primary school 28.7 per cent, illiterate 6 per cent), with 12 per cent receiving high school or three-year vocational school, and only 0.8 per cent university. In line with research in other countries, the suspect population in our sample for the most part comprised younger males, with 60 per cent aged between 16 and 30. More detailed information on some of these aspects of suspect profile is shown below.

A. Age of Suspects – Total Sample[12]

Figure 2.2 shows that the largest age group was between 18 and 25 (34.3 per cent). The second largest group was those aged between 31 and 40 (26.3 per cent), and about one-fifth were aged between 26 and 30 (20.9 per cent). The combined total of suspects under 18 and those over 50 amounted to less than 10 per cent of the sample.

---

[11] See Box (1981). McConville, Sanders and Leng (1991) found that 86.4 per cent of their adult sample and 88.3 per cent of their juvenile sample were males (*ibid.*, at p. 17).

[12] Age was not known in nine cases.

Sources of police cases 33

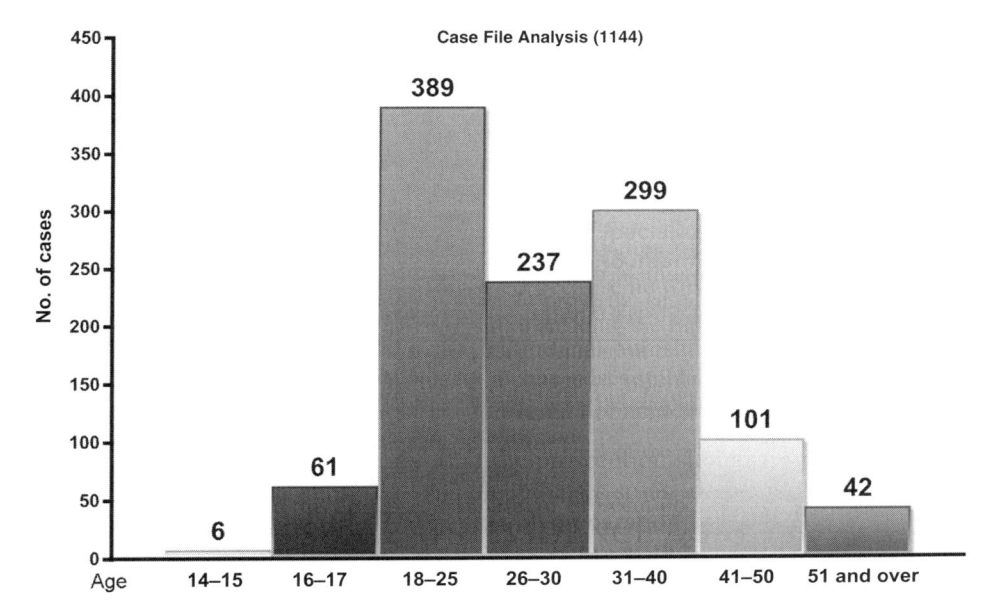

Figure 2.2 Age of suspect – 13 sample sites

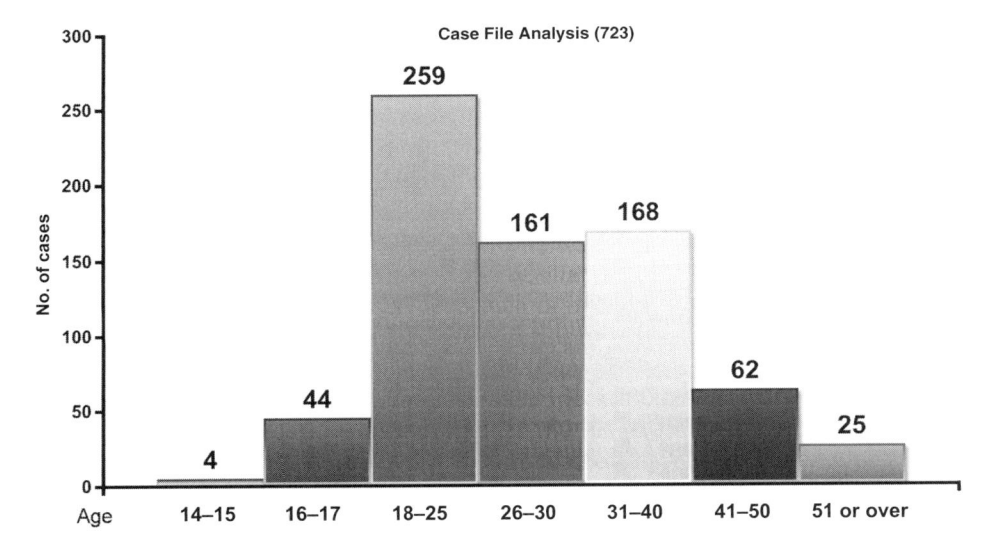

Figure 2.3 Age of suspect – 7 sample BC sites

B. Age of Suspects – Basic Court Sample

Figure 2.3 shows that the age profile of suspects appearing before the Basic Courts was very similar to the age profile of the sample as a whole.

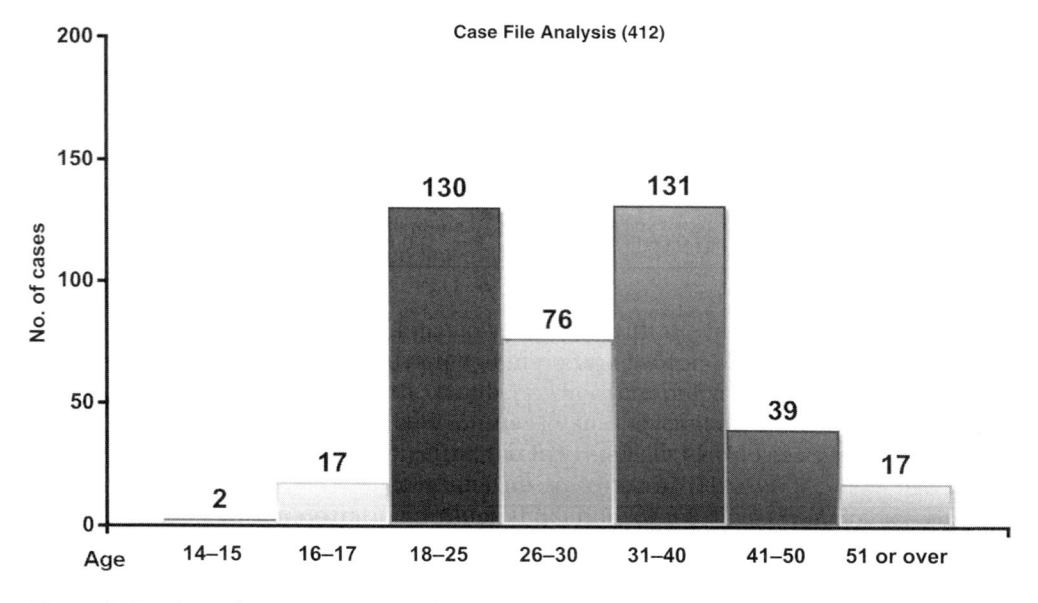

Figure 2.4   Age of suspect – 6 sample IC sites

C. Age of Suspects – Intermediate Court Sample

The age profile of those appearing before the Intermediate Courts was slightly different from the age profile of the suspects in the sample as a whole. Although the largest age group remained the 18 to 25 year olds, there were more suspects aged between 31 and 40 (31.8 per cent).

D. Age of Suspects – Representation of Young Offenders

As shown by Tables 2.3 and 2.4, the percentage of young offenders in our sample (i.e., those aged between 18 and 25) was broadly similar to the national percentage of such offenders.

E. Education of Suspects[13]

As Figure 2.7 illustrates, almost half of suspects were educated only to junior middle school level. Less than 10 per cent of suspects had studied to college or postgraduate level, and a small minority (3.2 per cent) had received no formal education. The vast majority (79.6 per cent) of suspects were unskilled or semi-skilled (10.8 per cent) with less than 10 per cent falling into the skilled or professional category.

---

[13] Educational attainment was not known in four cases.

Table 2.3 No. of young offenders (national figures) (1997–2008)

Year	No. of Young Offenders (Age) Under 18	18–25	Total	Total No. of Offenders	Percentage of Young Offenders in the Total No. of Offenders
1997	30 446	168 766	199 212	526 312	37.85
1998	33 612	174 464	208 076	528 301	39.39
1999	40 014	181 139	221 153	602 380	36.71
2000	41 709	179 272	220 981	639 814	34.54
2001	49 883	203 582	253 465	746 328	33.96
2002	50 030	167 879	217 909	701 858	31.05
2003	58 870	172 845	231 715	742 261	31.22
2004	70 086	178 748	248 834	764 441	32.55
2005	82 692	203 109	285 801	842 545	33.90
2006	83 697	219 934	303 631	889 042	34.15
2007	87 506	228 792	316 298	931 745	33.95
2008	88 891	233 170	322 061	1 007 304	31.97

Source: China Statistical Yearbook (2009).

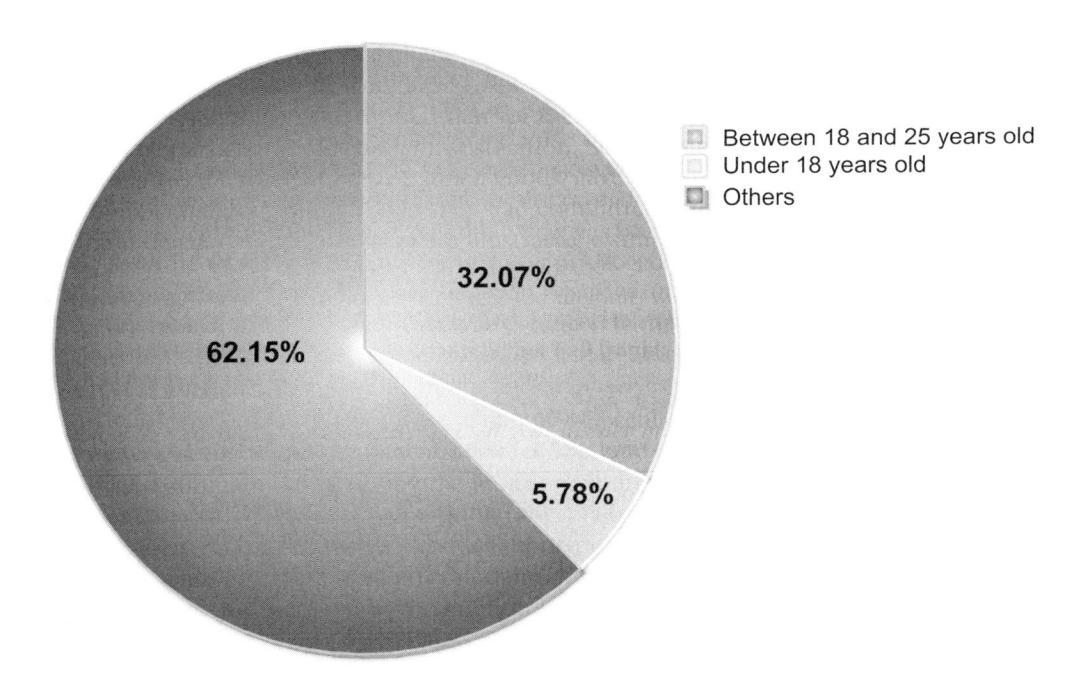

Sources: China Law Yearbook (1999–2006).

Figure 2.5 No. of young offenders (1997)

Table 2.4 No. of young offenders (13 sample sites)

	No. of Young Offenders (Age)			Total No. of Offenders	Percentage of Young Offenders in the Total No. of Offenders
	Under 18	18–25	Total		
BC Sites	48	259	307	726	42.3
IC Sites	19	130	149	418	35.6
Total	67	389	456	1144	39.9

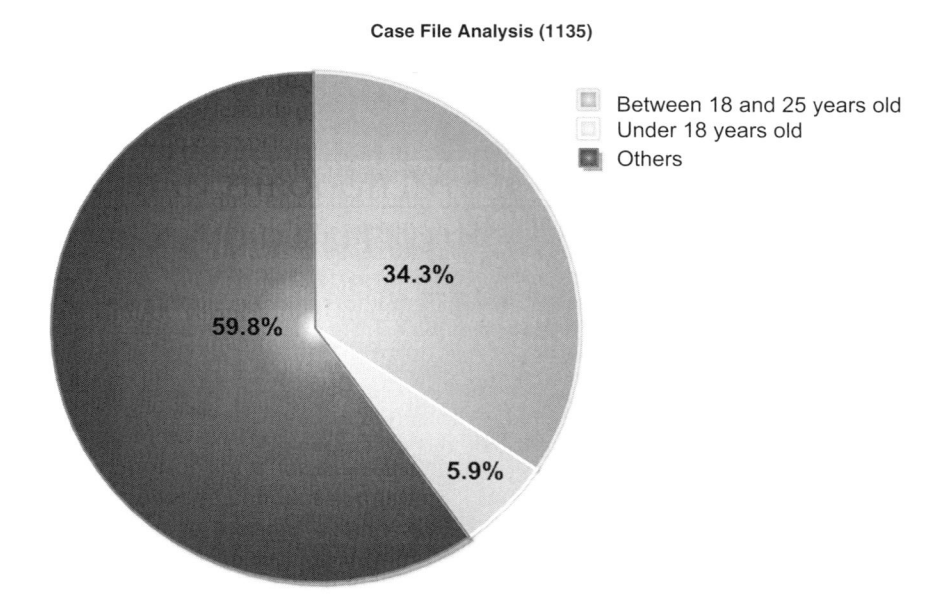

Case File Analysis (1135)

- Between 18 and 25 years old: 34.3%
- Under 18 years old: 5.9%
- Others: 59.8%

Figure 2.6 No. of young offenders – 13 sample sites

F. Residential Status of Suspects[14]

In our study internal migrants formed the majority of those who found themselves before the criminal courts, a factor which is totally absent in Western studies of the criminal justice process where there is no *hukou* system of household registration.[15] As measured across the 13 sites as a whole, we found a 44.5 per cent to 55.5 per cent split between local and migrant suspects respectively. However, as Table 2.5 illustrates, this percentage split varied significantly as between sites. So, for example, as Table 2.5

---

[14] Residential status was not known in 13 cases.
[15] On the issue of internal migrants in China, see Bakken (1998); Bakken (2000); and Cindy Fan (2008).

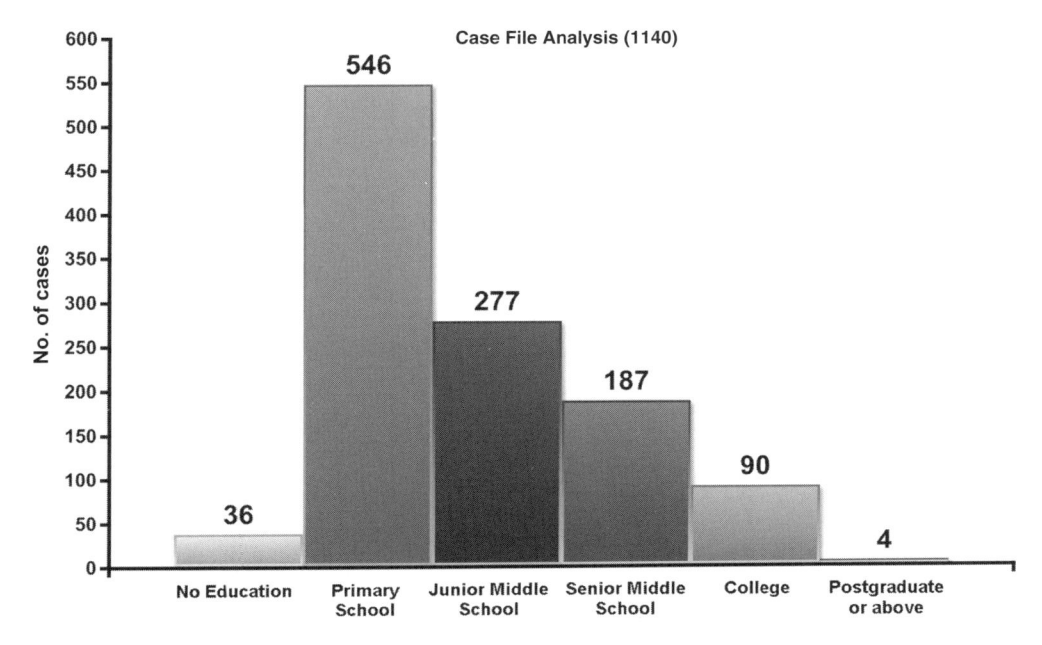

Figure 2.7 Education of offenders – 13 sample sites

shows, migrants accounted for only 15 per cent of the sample at Site E, but 93 per cent at Site J.[16]

CONCLUSION

There is a striking similarity between research findings in the UK and USA and those of the present study in terms of how crimes come to the attention of the police, the nature of those crimes, how suspects are initially identified and the gender and socio-economic make up of the suspect population. The overwhelming majority of crimes come to the attention of the police because they are reported by victims, their families or other members of the public. As in England and Wales and the United States, the vast majority of crimes fall into three broad categories: crimes against the person (i.e. crimes of violence such as robbery, assault and kidnap); crimes against property (principally theft and deception); and public order offences.

Although it is difficult to make direct comparisons with studies elsewhere because of the different categories used in the various research studies, it is fairly safe to conclude

---

[16] In Zhangjiagang, among the 4840 suspects between 2005 and 2007, the majority (3641, or 79 per cent) were migrants: See Dong (2008), p. 26. According to a survey in three grassroots courts (one in central Shanghai, another in an area between the city and the rural area, and the last one in a suburb) of Shanghai, of the 7006 defendants who were investigated for criminal liability in trials at first instance between 2005 and 2007, some 66.8 per cent (4083) were migrants. See Chu (2009), p. 76.

Table 2.5 Residential status of case file defendants

Residential status	Site A n	Site A %	Site B n	Site B %	Site C n	Site C %	Site D n	Site D %	Site F n	Site F %	Site G n	Site G %	Site M n	Site M %
Local	60	40	58	41	70	46	16	23	32	49	26	39	34	49
Migrant	90	60	83	59	82	54	54	77	33	51	41	61	36	51
Not known	7	–	0	–	1	–	0	–	0	–	3	–	0	–
Total	157	100	141	100	153	100	70	100	65	100	70	100	70	100

Residential status	Site E n	Site E %	Site H n	Site H %	Site I n	Site I %	Site J n	Site J %	Site K n	Site K %	Site L n	Site L %	BC 7 sites n	BC 7 sites %	IC 6 Sites n	IC 6 Sites %	Total 13 Sites n	Total 13 Sites %
Local	55	85	16	31	32	46	4	7	39	56	61	61	296	41.4	207	49.8	503	44.5
Migrant	10	15	35	69	38	54	56	93	31	44	39	39	419	58.6	209	50.2	628	55.5
Not known	0	–	2	–	0	–	0	–	0	–	0	–	11	–	2	–	13	–
Total	65	100	53	100	70	100	60	100	70	100	100	100	726	100.0	418	100.0	1144	100.0

that, as in England and the USA, the police in China are reliant on the public to initially identify suspects. Our research revealed that the majority of suspects are caught because the victim or members of the public catch them in the act, they are directly identified by the victim/public or the victim/public provides a description which allows the police to readily locate and arrest the suspect.

As we would expect, only a minority of suspects are identified through classic police investigative techniques such as police interrogation of co-suspects, stop and search and forensic examination. Although our figures probably under-recorded the number of suspects identified through police interrogation, it is relevant to note that many of those who reveal information about their accomplices during police interrogation were themselves captured as a result of public initiatives. This demonstrates at the least that the public in general have confidence in the police as the agency that can best deal with serious criminal matters.[17]

Finally, the preponderance of those who become police suspects in China and end up being processed through the criminal courts are migrants and, like their counterparts in the West, young, unemployed, unskilled and relatively uneducated men.

---

[17] We can, of course, provide no information on unreported crimes.

3. Police powers in relation to detention and arrest

INTRODUCTION

The purpose of this chapter is to explain the powers granted to the police to detain, arrest and interrogate suspects, to grant bail or to impose residential surveillance pending further investigation or trial. This is followed by a presentation of the data gathered by this and various other studies in order to throw light on how, in practice, the police utilize their powers in the investigation of crime and the collection of evidence in respect of those who are suspected of criminal involvement.

It should be noted that the research methodologies used in the present study focused on extracting data from 'dead' case files, observing trials, and interviewing prosecutors, defence lawyers and judges. The principal advantages and disadvantages of adopting this approach are set out in Appendix 2. A major advantage of using 'dead' files is that they cannot be 'doctored' so as to influence the research. One of the drawbacks of this approach is that our knowledge of the decisions taken by police and suspects and the reasoning underlying those decisions is restricted. Our researchers were not positioned within police stations and our data are reliant upon what official actors within the criminal process chose to record within the case files.[1] We do not deal with wider police powers (as to which see Ma Yue, 2003) such as those relating to the search of persons and premises and the power to seize material evidence since we had neither direct access to the police nor indirect knowledge of how such powers are exercised in practice nor do we have direct information on extra-legal detention of significant individuals (usually Party members) under the practice known as *shuanggui*.[2]

PROCEDURES, POWERS AND RIGHTS AT THE POLICE STATION

Under international covenants, the rights of suspects are accorded special importance. For example, Article 9(3) of the International Covenant on Civil and Political Rights states that:

---

[1] Nevertheless, what was recorded was done in accordance with routine practices and without knowledge that the files might be accessed subsequently by researchers.
[2] *Shuanggui* or 'double requirement' is used to place individuals in designated locations at designated times outside any protection afforded by the 1996 CPL.

... anyone arrested or detained on a criminal charge shall be brought promptly before a judge or other officer authorized by law to exercise judicial power and shall be entitled to trial within a reasonable time or to release. ...

Once a criminal suspect has been identified, as Ma Yue (2003) describes, the police have five types of compulsory measures at their disposal:

(i) **Summons** – the suspect can be compelled to appear for examination (interrogation) (Article 50, 1996 CPL), a procedure sometimes referred to as 'forced appearance' or *juchuan*. Article 92, 1996 CPL also permits the police to interrogate the suspect at his or her residence. Under this procedure the 'time for interrogation ... shall not exceed 12 hours' and a 'criminal suspect shall not be detained under the guise of successive summons or forced appearance'. This latter power known as *Chuanhuan* is not officially regarded as a form of detention but may be used by the police and amounts to summons.[3] In addition, lien (*liuzhi*) can be applied before detention or summons according to the *Police Law*.[4]

(ii) **Bail/Guarantor** – rather than holding the suspect in custody, the police 'may' allow him or her to obtain bail pending trial (*qubao houshen*) provided (a) the alleged crime is one punishable by public surveillance, criminal detention or supplementary punishment or (b) they would be given fixed term imprisonment at least and release on bail or under residential surveillance would not 'endanger society' (Article 51, 1996 CPL). The 1996 CPL establishes a right on the part of suspects, their relatives or their legal representatives to apply for a guarantor pending trial (Article 51). The guarantor must be able to satisfy certain conditions, which include having no involvement in the current case and having a fixed domicile and steady income. Rather than providing a guarantor, the suspect may be ordered to pay guarantee money (Article 53). Where bail is granted it is granted subject to conditions (such as not leaving the city or county without permission or not interfering with witnesses or not destroying

---

[3] For example, the Shanghai lawyer Zheng Enchong, who has lived under house arrest since his release from three years in prison on 2 June 2006, was reportedly 'summoned' to appear in a police station for the 76th time as of 3 January 2009: Chinese Human Rights Defenders (CHRD) (2009). In addition, the police may 'invite' individuals for a 'chat' or to 'drink tea' in order to warn against the pursuit of certain activities (including engaging in rights-defending) which may not lead to extended detention but are reminders of the tenuous nature of the individual's personal security and liberty (*ibid.* at p. 37).

[4] Articles 8–9, People's Police Law of the People's Republic of China. According to this law, if a person seriously endangers public order or constitutes a threat to public security, the police may forcibly take him/her away from the scene, detain him/her in accordance with law, or take other measures as provided by law; interrogate and search the person suspected of having violated the law or committed a crime. After interrogation, the person may be taken to a public security organ for further interrogation upon approval of this public security organ, if he or she is: (1) accused of a criminal offence; (2) suspected of committing an offence at the scene; (3) suspected of committing an offence and being of unknown identity; (4) carrying articles that are probably obtained illegally. The interrogated person may be held for up to 24 hours but in special cases this may be extended to 48 hours upon approval by the public security organ at or above the county level. Zuo Weimin (2007) found that the police in Sichuan often used the lien (*liuzhi*, compel to stay) before detention or summons. See also Xie and He (2010).

or falsifying evidence). A breach of these conditions will lead to the confiscation of guarantee monies and may involve the imposition of other conditions such as writing a statement of repentance, providing another guarantor or being subjected to residential surveillance or arrest (Article 56, 1996 CPL). The period for which a suspect can be kept on bail pending trial must not exceed 12 months, and investigation, prosecution and handling of the case must continue during that period (Article 58). This provision is available to the police to restrict people who are not charged with an offence in cases where there is insufficient evidence to justify arrest.

(iii) **Residential Surveillance** – as an alternative to granting bail, the police may subject the suspect to residential surveillance (*jianshi juzhu*). The circumstances in which residential surveillance is available, and the conditions the suspect must observe under residential surveillance if he or she is to avoid arrest, are similar to those governing bail (Articles 51 and 57). Those with no fixed abode (typically, migrants) must remain at a residence which has been 'designated' and, in contradistinction to bail, there is no right to *apply* for residential surveillance. The period for which a suspect can be kept under residential surveillance pending trial must not exceed six months, and investigation, prosecution and handling of the case must continue during that period (Article 58, 1996 CPL). It is quite clear that this provision is intended to allow the police to restrict the liberty of individuals against whom there is insufficient evidence to justify arrest (Article 65, 1996 CPL).

(iv) **Detention** – In China 'criminal detention' (*xingshi juliu*)[5] precedes 'arrest' (*daibu*) and is not an arrest in law. In order to make an arrest, the police must secure approval from the people's procuratorate (see below). The legal position regarding detention can be summarized as follows:

a. Article 61, 1996 CPL provides that the police may 'initially detain an active criminal or major suspect' if any one of a fairly wide-ranging set of conditions is met. These conditions include where a suspect is preparing to commit a crime, is in the process of committing a crime, is discovered immediately after committing a crime, is identified as having committed a crime by a victim or an eye witness, has criminal evidence found on his or her person or at his or her residence, does not tell his or her true name and address and his or her identity is unknown[6] or is strongly suspected of committing crimes from one place to another, repeatedly, or in a gang.

b. When detaining a person, the police must produce a 'detention warrant' and within 24 hours inform the suspect's family or work unit of the fact of and reasons for detention and the place of custody unless there is no way of notifying them or to do so would hinder the investigation (Article 64, 1996 CPL).

c. Having decided to detain a suspect, the police must interrogate him or her within 24 hours (Article 65, 1996 CPL).

---

[5] Individuals may also be subject to administrative detention (*xingzheng juliu*) by the police exercising powers under the administrative system.

[6] For individuals who do not tell their true name and place of residence or whose identity is unclear, the period for detaining them after arrest starts being calculated only from the time their identity is clarified (Article 128, 1996 CPL). This allows for indefinite detention until their identity is clarified.

d. If interrogation reveals that he or she should not have been detained, he or she must be released and issued a 'release certificate' (*ibid.*).

e. If the police 'find it necessary to arrest a detainee' when sufficient evidence is still lacking, they may grant bail or impose residential surveillance whilst continuing their inquiries (Article 60, 1996 CPL).

f. If there is evidence to arrest but the suspect is seriously ill, pregnant or breast feeding her own baby the police may grant bail or impose residential surveillance rather than resorting to arrest (Article 60, 1996 CPL).

g. *Requests for arrest* – If the police deem it necessary to arrest a detainee, they must within three days apply to the procuratorate for authorization to arrest. An arrest may be effected in the case of a suspect or defendant 'in respect of whom there is evidence to prove the facts of the crime and who could be sentenced to a punishment of not less than imprisonment' and where the adoption of other measures (such as residential surveillance) would be insufficient to prevent the occurrence of danger to society and where, accordingly, it is necessary to arrest.[7] In 'special circumstances' (which are not defined) the police are allowed to extend the period for submitting a request for arrest by one to four days (i.e. giving a maximum of seven days). The period for submitting a request for arrest may be extended to 30 days where a major suspect is involved in committing crimes in various locations, repeatedly or in a gang (Article 69, 1996 CPL). In cases directly accepted by the procuratorate,[8] the decision on arrest must be made within ten days of detention, with an ability to extend this period by one to four days in special cases (Article 133, 1996 CPL).

h. Once the police have submitted a request for arrest, the procuratorate has seven days in which to approve or reject the request.[9] If the request is rejected, the police must release the suspect unconditionally or, if the conditions for bail or residential surveillance are met, they can release the suspect subject to one or other of these measures (Article 69, 1996 CPL).

i. These powers of detention are supplemented by a parallel administrative system of justice operated by the police under the Police Law 1995. Article 9 of this law grants the police a broad power to interrogate those 'suspected of having violated the law or committed a crime' for 24 hours, and this period may be extended to 48 hours by the public security organ at or above county level.

(v) **Arrest** – arrest having been authorized:

a. The suspect's family or unit must be informed within 24 hours of the reasons for the arrest and the place of custody except where such notification would hinder the investigation or there is no way of notifying them (Article 71, 1996 CPL).

---

[7] The standard has been lowered from that prevailing under the 1979 Criminal Procedure Law which required that the facts had to have been clarified prior to arrest.

[8] Such cases are restricted to those falling within Article 60 and Article 61(4) and Article 61(5) where arrest or detention of the criminal suspect is necessitated.

[9] There is provision in the law (Article 75, 1996 CPL) for the suspect or relative or defence lawyer to request the lifting of any coercive measure that has been applied beyond the permissible time limit.

b. Interrogation must commence within 24 hours, and the suspect immediately released and issued a release certificate if it transpires that he or she should not have been arrested (Article 72).
c. If further time is needed to complete the investigation, the police can release the suspect on bail or place him or her under residential surveillance (Article 74, 1996 CPL).
d. If the police or procuratorate decide to hold the suspect in custody following arrest, they can do so for two months, plus an additional month for complicated cases subject to approval by the procuratorate at the next higher level (i.e. three months in total) (Article 124, 1996 CPL).
e. An extension of a further two months may be obtained from a procuratorate of provincial or above status in grave and complex cases in outlying areas where travel is difficult, or which involve gangs, or where the crimes have been committed in various locations and collection of evidence is difficult (i.e. five months in total) (Article 126, 1996 CPL).
f. Article 127 provides that for offences carrying a sentence of ten years or more, a further two month extension may be granted by a procuratorate of provincial level or above (i.e. total seven months).
g. Article 75 provides that if the compulsory measure adopted (detention, arrest, bail or residential surveillance) exceeds the time limit prescribed by law, the defendant, his or her lawyer or family 'shall have the right to demand cancellation of the compulsory measures'. The court, procuratorate and the police are then obliged to cancel the measure in question.
h. However, there is also provision for indefinite detention without trial for 'particularly grave and complex' cases subject to application by the Supreme People's Procuratorate and approval by the Standing Committee of the National People's Congress (Article 125, 1996 CPL).

Whether it is the police or the procuratorate who have carried out the investigation, both are subject to the rule that having concluded their investigations they must decide whether the suspect ought to be prosecuted. If they decide that 'the suspect's criminal responsibility should not have been investigated' they must dismiss the case, release the suspect and (in the case of the police) inform the procuratorate which authorized the arrest (Article 130, 1996 CPL). If they wish to prosecute, they must (in the case of the police) submit the case file, the evidence and a written recommendation for prosecution to the procuratorate at the same level for examination and decision (Article 129, 1996 CPL). In cases directly investigated by the procuratorate, the procuratorate having made the decision that prosecution is justified, must initiate a prosecution in a People's Court (Article 141, 1996 CPL).

THE PROBLEM OF PRE-TRIAL DETENTION

A. Existing Literature and Data

There is no right to bail in China. Many suspects have historically been detained in custody pending trial subject to 'investigative detention', a provision which appears to have been without limit. Today, conditions in detention centres may be appalling and there has been official recognition of the concerns which have arisen as a result.[10] As has been periodically reported, extra-judicial detention is also deployed at politically sensitive and other times with some citizens held in 'black jails' (Anderlini, 2009; Hartley, 2007; and Jacobs, 2009). Thus, a defendant called Wu Liusuo in Henan, in a murder case, was reportedly arrested in 1984 and had not received a final judgment by August 1998, which meant that he had been subjected to 14 years' detention (Chen Yongsheng, 2004). In addition, in practice, the investigation organ sometimes fails to inform the families of suspects of the decision to detain within 24 hours as required by Article 64(ii), 1996 CPL (Wang Xin'an, 2004). In this section we look at the issue of pre-trial detention and try to deal both with detention beyond the legal time limits and detention which may be for proper or improper purposes within the allowable time limits.

A range of estimates of the incidence of extended detention beyond the legal time limits has been reported at both national and local level. *Xinhuanet* reported that according to statistics maintained by 'authoritative departments' there were 50000 to 80000 suspects subjected to extended detention each year from 1993 to 1999.[11] The *Legal Daily* reported that as of 15 August 2003, 7415 persons were being subjected to extended detention in the public security organs in China: of these, 6982 had been detained for less than one year after the expiration of the statutory time limit for detention, 369 persons had been detained for one to three years beyond the statutory time limit, and 64 persons had been detained for over three years following the expiration of the statutory time limit (Zhai Huaimin, 2003). According to a survey of 720 dossiers (951 suspects) provided by the public security bureaus of eight districts and counties in a city used for annual evaluation and selected intentionally to highlight positive aspects, 41.5 per cent of suspects suffered from extended detention (Zhang Chao, 2010). Of the extended detention cases, the longest was three years and 155 days involving some 400 extensions to effect detention beyond the required period.

The statistics should be viewed with caution. Thus, the police can side-step the time limits by 'creative' use of the rules. A commentary in the *People's Procuratorial Semi-Monthly* reported that in some cases suspects were granted residential surveillance after the expiration of the period of criminal detention, but re-arrested a few days later and placed under detention once more. Alternatively, the police have been known to release suspects 'unconditionally' after expiry of the detention time limit, only to re-arrest them immediately after their release (Wang, Han and Bi, 1999). And individuals may be held in 'black jails', facilities which are not officially acknowledged to exist.

Extended periods of both pre- and post-arrest detention have attracted criticism in China from both official and non-official sources (Sun, 2000; Chen and Song, 2000). At a conference in 2000 examining the implementation of the CPL, the Chairman

---

[10] A run of unexplained deaths in centres managed by the Ministry of Public Security in 2009 led the Supreme People's Procuratorate to launch an initiative designed to secure appropriate management of centres. See, 'Top Prosecuting Body Starts Jail Safety Drive After Inmate Deaths', *South China Morning Post*, 21 April 2009.

[11] 'Sunshine Detention: Public Security Organs, Procuratorates and the Courts are Taking Actions', *Xinhuanet*, available at <http://www.humanrights-china.org/china/rqgz/rd20031114.asp>.

of the Standing Committee of the National People's Congress (NPC) recognized the problem,[12] and similarly the Chairman of the Committee for Internal and Judicial Affairs of the NPC was quoted as saying that: 'A number of cases in which the persons concerned have been detained for years remain unresolved. Moreover, after old cases of extended detention are straightened out, new ones have emerged, and cases of extended detention in disguised form have also increased.'[13] Despite this, the practice continues. The main themes and concerns which emerge from the literature can be summarized as follows:

(i) The police routinely use the exceptional power granted under Article 69 to detain for up to 30 days (Lu Weiju, 2004). Scholars and lawyers in Shanghai and Beijing interviewed by *Human Rights in China* revealed that the power to detain a suspect for the maximum of 37 days was invoked by the public security organs in all detention cases,[14] a view that many scholars in China have voiced in academic journals;[15]

(ii) A commentary in the *People's Procuratorate* reported that some judicial organs apply the special 30 day detention period to all migrants, even to those who have worked and lived in the local jurisdiction for a long time and also to suspects who have committed more than one crime without regard to whether they satisfy the test of being a 'major suspect' (the requirement under Article 69, 1996 CPL) (Wang, Han and Bi, 1999);

(iii) A commentary in the *Guangming Ribao* and *Legal Daily* attributed the problem to the mentality of police officers who fail to appreciate such concepts as rule of law and fairness towards suspects (Guo Qing, 2001; Zhu Guobin, 2004; Cui Shixin, 2000);

(iv) Some cases of extended detention occur not because the police need more time to investigate, but because the initial apprehension of the suspect was unjustified and prolonged detention is used simply to keep an aggrieved individual in check (Guo Qing, 2001);

(v) Some police forces, rather than filing one application for arrest for all counts of crimes involved in a case, apply for arrest for each count separately thereby 'justifying' a re-calculation of the permissible detention period. Others falsely claim that the further counts have been discovered during the course of the investigation, thereby 'entitling' them to recalculate the detention period from the alleged date of discovery of the further offences (Zhang Lizhao, 1999). Others readily resort to the excuse that the case is complex, or involves travel over large areas (Jiang Xianyong, 2004);[16]

(vi) Requests by the procuratorate for supplementary evidence caused by police

---

[12] 'Top legislator on implementation of the Criminal Procedure Law', *Xinhua News*, 20 November 2000.
[13] 'China's assembly hears of torture, irregular judicial procedures', *BBC Monitoring Asia Pacific*, 29 December 2000. See also Sun Changyong (2009) at pp. 28–29.
[14] Chen Weidong (2001).
[15] See for example Chen Ruihua (2001); Cui Min (1998).
[16] See also, Tan Hua (2010); Ai Jianguo and Junying Yan (2006); Liu Lina, Ying Wang and Jing An (2010); Sun Changyong (2009); and Yang Cheng (2007).

investigative failings or incompetence inevitably lengthens the period of time for which the suspect is held in detention and may, indeed, be used for this purpose (Xiong Jiangning, 2001);
(vii) One major problem arises out of the internal police performance indicators which are closely connected with the welfare, promotion and even continued employment of the police officers involved. These include such matters as the detection rate and percentage of procuratorial approvals of arrest. For example, crimes involving the death of the victim must be detected within a certain period. Against such a background, there is strong incentive to detect cases by using detention to obtain confessions;[17]
(viii) Once extended detention is utilized, the system does not possess an efficient method for challenging or rectifying the decision (Chen Ruihua, 2001).

On 12 November 2003, the Supreme People's Court, Supreme People's Procuratorate and the Ministry of Public Security jointly issued the *Notice Concerning the Strict Enforcement of Criminal Procedure Law and Serious Rectification and Prevention of Extended Detention* ('*Notice*'). The *Notice* pointed out that extended detention had not been effectively eliminated in many areas and set out five tasks for the personnel of the courts, procuratorates, public security organs, military courts and procuratorates of the People's Liberation Army, and the Defence Department of the General Political Bureau to improve the situation regarding extended detention:

1) To pay equal attention to both substantive law and procedural law and respect the legal rights of suspects/defendants;
2) To strictly observe the time limits for detention as set out in the CPL, and prohibit the abuse of measures such as supplementary investigation, withdrawal of prosecution and change in jurisdiction over the case to extend the duration of detention of suspects/defendants;
3) To use bail or residential surveillance if the relevant conditions are satisfied;
4) To ensure that the judicial organs check and balance each other;
5) To punish those involved in imposing extended detention on suspects/defendants.

There is no reliable information on the impact of this *Notice* on the ground although some studies claim that efforts have been made to clear backlogs (e.g., Zhong Shikai, 2004; and Ding Xingyu and Xiangqiang Lu, 2004).

B. Our Qualitative Research Data

Our survey of judges, prosecutors and defence lawyers revealed that extended detention remains an issue and, subject to the important caveat that qualitative interview material might generate some self-serving responses and material that relates more to how respondents would like their world to be than to how it actually is, for some it remains a 'problem'. A judge from Site D (D-K-03) mentioned extended detention as an ongoing

---

[17] Zhang Ying and Shang Xidong (2009), p. 141.

problem, and some prosecutors we interviewed (e.g. in Site K, prosecutors K-W-01 and K-Z-02; and in Site D, prosecutor D-K-01) stated that they would check, during the stage of examination for prosecution, whether there had been extended detention. One prosecutor from Site F (F-N-04) suggested that in some cases he might decide not to prosecute if a defendant had already been subjected to a period of extended detention though no concrete example was offered of any occasion on which this had in fact been done.

In our research study, a lawyer from Site E (E-L-04) said that he always asked his clients whether they had been subjected to extended detention and, if they had, he would file a petition or complaint on their behalf. Another defence lawyer (Site E, Defence lawyer in E-L-05) was less optimistic in terms of what he could do for those subjected to extended detention. He said he would visit such suspects more often, check on their health and keep their families informed, but that none of this helped to bring the case to trial earlier. A lawyer from Site F (F-N-04) stated that he had secured a judgment from the court that his client had been wrongfully detained for 56 days in one province. Although the lawyer added that the procuratorate made it difficult for his client to actually enforce the judgment, it suggests that at least some lawyers are pushing the authorities to comply with the rules on detention.

There is some evidence of top-down pressure to eradicate cases of extended detention. A prosecutor from Site H (H-S3-003) disclosed that the number of extended detentions was used as an index to assess their work performance. In fact, during the currency of the research one of the leaders of the Supreme People's Court visited one of our research sites to investigate and 'resolve' cases of extended detention in the province and there was considerable concern within the procuratorate that an adverse report would be filed following the visit, local officials conceding privately to us that some cases had been subject to unacceptably prolonged delays spanning years.

Among respondents in the research sites, there were differences of opinion as to whether the authorities had been able to rein in excessive use of extended detention. A lawyer from Site D (D-K-01) (who blamed both the police (PSB) and the procuratorate for extended detention) said that although the problem had been serious in the past it had improved considerably in recent years:

> *Site D-KM-01:* Extended detention is a problem. This was a big problem several years ago but it is better now.

However, another lawyer in Site E (E-L-03) suggested that the situation had not improved:

> *E-L-03:* . . . in practice extended detention at each stage is serious, most of which exceeds two months. They can change the time of detention in the legal document. This is why the Supreme People's Court, Supreme People's Procuratorate and the Ministry of Public Security jointly issued a document to demand that courts, procuratorates and the public security organs eliminate cases of extended detention.

As to the causes of extended detention, some of our respondents identified reasons similar to those highlighted in the literature reviewed above. So, for example, a prosecutor from Site C (C-B3-04) pointed to shortcomings in the initial police investigation which can sometimes lead to the procuratorate ordering one or possibly two supplementary investigations, a process which extends detention. Another in Site A (A-B1-02) pointed to communication problems between the various state organs, giving as an example the decision by a court to adjourn the trial: unless the court informs the prosecution at an early stage, the likelihood is that the procuratorate or police will simply hold the defendant in custody until the new trial date.

C. Time Lapse Between Initial Detention and Application for Approval of Arrest: Our Quantitative Data

As explained above, the 1996 CPL allows suspects to be held for extensive periods of time during the investigative stage of the criminal process. Although pre-arrest detention is limited to three days in ordinary cases, it can extend to seven days in 'special circumstances' and 30 days if the case involves a 'major suspect' who is suspected of having committed offences in several locations, repeatedly or in a gang.

In our sample, we found only a tiny percentage of cases (2 per cent) in which the police made an application for approval of arrest within the three days laid down in Article 69, 1996 CPL for ordinary cases. The percentage of cases in which the police made their application for approval of arrest within the seven days allowed in 'special circumstances' (Article 69) was similarly small (3 per cent). Compliance with these time limits was slightly lower for the Basic Court sample (1.3 per cent and 2.3 per cent respectively) than it was for the Intermediate Court sample (3.1 per cent and 4.1 per cent respectively).[18] However, we cannot read too much into this counter-intuitive finding given that the police managed to make a decision on prosecution within three and seven days in only 50 of the 1000 cases in which the relevant data were available. In the vast majority of both Basic Court cases and Intermediate Court cases (74 per cent and 63 per cent respectively) the police took between eight and 30 days to apply for authorization of arrest.[19] In approximately one-fifth of Basic Court (20.2 per cent) and Intermediate Court cases (19.4 per cent) the police took up to 12 months to make an application for authorization of arrest. In one Basic Court case and in four Intermediate Court cases no application was made for up to two years, and in a further four Intermediate Court cases no application had been made even after two years had elapsed from the date of first detention.[20] These data are set out in more detail in Tables 3.1–3.3.

We will deal with bail/residential surveillance later but note here that few get either with the consequence that most suspects are held in custody.

---

[18] Zhang Chao (2010) found that in 14.5 per cent of the cases following detention, the procuratorate did not make a decision within seven days as allowed by law after receiving the investigation organ's request for arrest or there was no clear record in the dossier.

[19] Under Article 69, 1996 CPL the time limit for submitting a request for examination and approval may be extended to 30 days in cases involving 'a major suspect involved in crimes committed from one place to another, repeatedly, or in a gang. . . .'

[20] See also Wang Xin'an (2004) who found that of the 128 defendants surveyed, 21 per cent had a custody period after criminal detention of less than 14 days, while the majority (62 per cent) were detained between 15 and 37 days, and 17 per cent had been detained for 38 days or more.

Table 3.1 Period between date of first detention and application for approval of arrest: Basic Court

	Site A		Site B		Site C		Site D		Site F		Site G		Site M	
Within 3 days	2	1.6	2	1.5	0	0.0	1	1.6	0	0.0	4	6.3	0	0.0
3–7 days	0	0.0	9	6.9	3	2.4	3	4.8	0	0.0	3	4.7	7	15.6
8–30 days	35	28.5	111	85.4	117	92.1	56	88.9	54	88.5	46	71.9	35	77.8
31 days to less than 1 year	86	69.9	8	6.2	7	5.5	3	4.8	7	11.5	11	17.2	2	4.4
1 year to 2 years	0	0.0	0	0.0	0	0.0	0	0.0	0	0.0	0	0.0	1	2.2
Over 2 years	0	0.0	0	0.0	0	0.0	0	0.0	0	0.0	0	0.0	0	0.0
Not known	34	–	11	–	26	–	7	–	4	–	6	–	25	–
Total	157	100.0	141	100.0	153	100.0	70	100.0	65	100.0	70	100.0	70	100.0

Table 3.2 Period between date of first detention and application for approval of arrest: Intermediate Court

	Site E		Site H		Site I		Site J		Site K		Site L	
Within 3 days	1	1.7	0	0.0	0	0.0	0	0.0	0	0.0	1	1.0
3–7 days	25	42.4	6	16.2	5	7.4	1	1.7	4	5.8	16	16.3
8–30 days	29	49.2	27	73.0	46	67.6	27	45.0	61	88.4	58	59.2
31 days to less than 1 year	2	3.4	4	10.8	15	22.1	32	53.3	3	4.3	20	20.4
1 year to 2 years	1	1.7	0	0.0	1	1.5	0	0.0	0	0.0	2	2.0
Over 2 years	1	1.7	0	0.0	1	1.5	0	0.0	1	1.4	1	1.0
Not known	6	–	16	–	2	–	0	–	1	–	2	–
Total	65	100.0	53	100.0	70	100.0	60	100.0	70	100.0	100	100.0

Table 3.3 Period between date of first detention and application for approval of arrest: all cases

	BC 7 Sites		IC 6 Sites		Total 13 Sites	
Within 3 days	9	1.5	2	0.5	11	1.1
3–7 days	25	4.1	57	14.6	82	8.2
8–30 days	454	74.1	248	63.4	702	69.9
31 days to less than 1 year	124	20.2	76	19.4	200	19.9
1 year to 2 years	1	0.2	4	1.0	5	0.5
Over 2 years	0	0.0	4	1.0	4	0.4
Not known	113	–	27	–	140	–
Total	726	100.1	418	99.9	1144	100.0

D. Time Lapse Between Date of Arrest and Transfer for Prosecution: Our Quantitative Data

Our researchers gathered data on the time that elapsed between the arrest of a suspect and the date at which the case was transferred by the police to the procuratorate. These data demonstrate that in a minority of cases (15.8 per cent) the police make a decision within the two month custody time limit prescribed for 'ordinary cases'. The percentage of cases in which the decision was taken within two months was higher in the Basic Court sample (19.1 per cent) than in the Intermediate Court sample (10.1 per cent), which may be explained by the greater complexity and seriousness of cases in the Intermediate Courts. One-third of cases took between two and three months to be transferred to the procuratorate; almost 40 per cent of cases took between three and five months, and 8.3 per cent took five to seven months (the percentage of such cases in the Intermediate Court sample being much higher at 13.1 per cent than in the Basic Court sample at 5.6 per cent). In the Intermediate Court sample, four suspects had to wait between one and two years following their arrest before their case was transferred to the procuratorate and two suspects had to wait for over two years. The data are set out in more detail in Tables 3.4–3.6.

E. Time Lapse After Transfer for Prosecution: Quantitative Data

Once a case is transferred to the procuratorate further delays may occur in the processing of the case and hence in the delay for the suspect. We looked at whether requests by the procuratorate for supplementary investigation are a regular occurrence, and thus another possible cause of extended detention. The data are set out in Table 3.7.

The data demonstrate that supplementary investigation is requested in one-third of all cases in which the file records the relevant information. Supplementary investigation was requested in a higher proportion of Intermediate Court cases (43 per cent) than Basic Court cases (29 per cent). The high proportion of cases in which the procuratorate find it necessary to request supplementary investigation supports the view that there is a need

Table 3.4 Period between date of arrest and transfer of case to procuratorate: Basic Court

	Site A		Site B		Site C		Site D		Site F		Site G		Site M	
Less than 2 months	24	16.9	18	14.0	23	18.5	4	6.3	20	32.8	8	13.1	26	40.0
2 to less than 3 months	63	44.4	57	44.2	19	15.3	18	28.6	11	18.0	27	44.3	18	27.7
3 to less than 5 months	45	31.7	46	35.7	74	59.7	38	60.3	23	37.7	18	29.5	20	30.8
5 to less than 7 months	5	3.5	8	6.2	6	4.8	1	1.6	7	11.5	8	13.1	1	1.5
7 months to less than 1 year	5	3.5	0	0.0	2	1.6	2	3.2	0	0.0	0	0.0	0	0.0
1 year to less than 2 years	0	0.0	0	0.0	0	0.0	0	0.0	0	0.0	0	0.0	0	0.0
Over 2 years	0	0.0	0	0.0	0	0.0	0	0.0	0	0.0	0	0.0	0	0.0
Not known	15	–	12	–	29	–	7	–	4	–	9	–	5	–
Total	157	100.0	141	100.0	153	100.0	70	100.0	65	100.0	70	100.0	70	100.0

Table 3.5 Period between date of arrest and transfer of case to procuratorate: Intermediate Court

	Site E		Site H		Site I		Site J		Site K		Site L	
Less than 2 months	1	1.7	0	0.0	5	7.4	0	0.0	5	7.7	27	31.0
2 to less than 3 months	26	43.3	6	16.2	0	0.0	1	1.7	54	83.1	46	52.9
3 to less than 5 months	29	48.3	27	73.0	41	60.3	27	46.6	4	6.2	13	14.9
5 to less than 7 months	2	3.3	4	10.8	16	23.5	25	43.1	1	1.5	1	1.1
7 months to less than 1 year	0	0.0	0	0.0	4	5.9	4	6.9	0	0.0	0	0.0
1 year to less than 2 years	1	1.7	0	0.0	1	1.5	1	1.7	1	1.5	0	0.0
Over 2 years	1	1.7	0	0.0	1	1.5	0	0.0	0	0.0	0	0.0
Not known	5	–	16	–	2	–	2	–	5	–	13	–
Total	65	100.0	53	100.0	70	100.0	60	100.0	70	100.0	100	100.0

Table 3.6 Period between date of arrest and transfer of case to procuratorate: all courts

	BC 7 Sites		IC 6 Sites		Total 13 Sites	
Less than 2 months	123	19.1	38	10.1	161	15.8
2 to less than 3 months (Complicated cases)	213	33.0	133	35.5	346	33.9
3 to less than 5 months (Grave and complex cases)	264	40.9	141	37.6	405	39.7
5 to less than 7 months (Cases carrying 10 yrs or more)	36	5.6	49	13.1	85	8.3
7 months to less than 1 year	9	1.4	8	2.1	17	1.7
1 year to less than 2 years	0	0.0	4	1.1	4	0.4
Over 2 years	0	0.0	2	0.5	2	0.2
Not known	81	–	43	–	124	–
Total	726	100.0	418	100.0	1144	100.0

Table 3.7 Prosecutor requested supplementary investigation

	BC 7 Sites		IC 6 Sites		All Sites	
Yes	169	28.6	148	43.4	317	34.0
No	422	71.4	193	56.6	615	66.0
Not kown	135	–	77	–	212	–
Total	726	100.0	418	100.0	1144	100.0

to enhance police investigatory and evidence-gathering skills (see also, Zuo, Ma and Hu, 2007).[21]

Article 140, 1996 CPL requires that supplementary investigation be completed within one month, and states that 'supplementary investigation may be conducted twice at most', a limitation introduced by the 1996 CPL to stop the practice of suspects being held indefinitely under the guise of supplementary investigation. Our data show that in a quarter of those cases in which supplementary investigation is requested it is requested twice. As Table 3.8 shows, the proportion of cases in which it is requested twice was higher in respect of the Basic Court sample (29 per cent) than the Intermediate Court sample (20 per cent).

It is clear from the above that the combination of the various stages of detention from initial apprehension to the application for approval of arrest, from arrest to transfer for prosecution, and from delays after transfer, all contribute to prolong the total period of detention. Setting aside wholly unlawful detentions the number of which cannot be determined, in the absence of a right to bail and with a porous set of legal provisions

---

[21] The investigation and prosecution departments may also borrow time limits from each other, the investigator commonly pays little attention to returned cases and some take no further action. See, Xu Meijun (2009), p. 28; Ji Gang and Jing Liu (2006), p. 91; Hu Zhifang and Zhihui Hu (2009), p. 70; Sun Xiaoyu (2009), pp. 28–29; Cheng Fei and Cheng Ming (2006), p. 6; Ma Jingrui, Xuemei Jin and Heng Liu (2005), p. 80; and Ru Yaguo (2007), p. 65.

Table 3.8 No. of supplementary investigations conducted per prosecutor's request

	BC 7 Sites		IC 6 Sites		Total 13 Sites	
One	83	70.9	57	80.3	140	74.5
Two	34	29.1	14	19.7	48	25.5
Not Known	52	–	77	–	129	–
Total	169	100.0	148	100.0	317	100.0

Table 3.9 The outcome of the police's request for the authorization of arrest

	BC 7 Sites		IC 6 Sites		Total 13 Sites	
Approved	474	99.6	381	99.0	855	99.3
Disapproved	2	0.4	4	1.0	6	0.7
Not known	250	–	33	–	283	–
Total	726	100.0	418	100.0	1144	100.0

which confer considerable discretion on state actors, extended detention is a common feature of Chinese criminal justice in both serious and non-serious cases.

OUTCOME OF APPLICATIONS FOR APPROVAL OF ARREST: OUR QUANTITATIVE DATA

As explained above, having interrogated the suspect the police must decide whether they wish to arrest the suspect. If so, they must make an application to the procuratorate for authorization of arrest. In China, there is a common tendency among state agencies to place more emphasis on fighting crime and mutual co-operation rather than upon legality, human rights and mutual supervision. Accordingly, arresting before investigation and using arrest to replace investigation has been abused (Zhang and Qu, 2010).

In our sample we had a sizeable number of cases (283) in which the file did not reveal the outcome of the police's request for authorization of arrest.[22] In those cases in which we could obtain this information we found that the procuratorate withheld approval for arrest in only six out of 861 cases. The details are set out in Table 3.9.

These findings are echoed in the Chinese literature. For example, between 2003 and 2009, the police of Hedong District, Tianjin requested approval of arrest in respect of 3328 suspects and the procuratorate approved the arrest in 3037 instances: 91 per cent on average and 93 per cent in respect of migrants (Liu and Zhang, 2010; and Chen Junmin, 2010).

A more detailed examination of the six cases in our sample in which authorization

---

[22] Obviously, this is simply a recording artifact because it is clear that the application for approval was granted in almost all cases. In Site D, for example, all cases were recorded as 'not known'. Sometimes, the police also applied conditional approval of arrest.

of arrest was withheld revealed that in one of these cases the suspect was granted bail while the police continued with their investigations. In another approval was withheld because the procuratorate considered the offence 'minor'. However, the case made its way into the court files because the suspect, who was sentenced to reform by 're-education through labour' for the minor offence, fled from the institution, was caught, and his arrest later approved. The third was a case in which the police persuaded the procuratorate to approve arrest on a second request. In two cases the police overturned the initial decision to disapprove on a review under Article 70, 1996 CPL. Accordingly, disapproval of arrest remained extant in only one case (on the basis that the facts were unclear, the evidence insufficient and it was not clear who out of a number of suspects had done what).

As with many of the provisions of the 1996 CPL, the porous character of legal provisions leads to a great deal of uncertainty as to when approval ought to be given or withheld. Article 68, 1996 CPL provides little guidance, simply stating that the procuratorate should make the decision 'according to the circumstances of the case'. In addition, as a performance indicator, an internal control has been placed on the disapproval rate (Tang Liang, 2004). The rate of procuratorial approval of arrest and public prosecution after review are put into an evaluation performance index with the result that the arrest standard, 'if it is necessary to arrest', is not respected. Within the procuratorate, the rate of approval of arrest is also set as an important performance indicator, the non-prosecution rate being required to be controlled at a fixed percentage (Liu, Qi and Zeng, 2008; Sun Changyong, 2009).

Despite this, there is evidence that disapproval of arrest varies from area to area.[23] Disapprovals appear to arise from the fact that some procuratorates apply too high an evidential threshold (Ma Haixian, 2003). Some procuratorates appear to believe that if they approve arrest but the suspect is later not prosecuted this will in and of itself prove that the arrest was wrongful, leading to liability to pay compensation (Gao and Wu, 2001). In support of this explanation Gao and Wu (2001) point to a reply provided by the Office of the Compensation Committee of the Supreme People's Court to a query raised by the Higher People's Court of Shaanxi Province in November 1998, in which the former wrote:

> If the procuratorate decides not to prosecute or withdraw the case on the ground that the facts of the case are unclear, or there is insufficient evidence, then it would imply that it failed to ascertain the facts of the crime allegedly committed by the suspect in accordance with the Criminal Procedure Law. Thus, the approval of arrest by the procuratorate in this kind of case should be considered as approving the arrest of a person against whom no facts of crime have been found, hence the procuratorate should pay the suspect compensation according to Article 15 of the State Compensation Law.

Our interviews with prosecutors and judges revealed at least some evidence that there was a failure by certain actors in the criminal process to understand that approval of arrest was not the same as deciding that a prosecution ought to be initiated or that there was a reasonable prospect of conviction. Thus, a prosecutor from Site J (J-S4-08) stated that

---

[23] A report by the People's Procuratorate of Sichuan Province showed that in 2000 it disapproved 7708 applications out of 44763. Work Report of the Sichuan Province People's Procuratorate, *Sichuan Ribao* (*Sichuan Daily*), 19 February 2001. A survey by Chen Weidong between April and December 2000 reported a disapproval rate in Yantai City of between 10 and 20 per cent, Chen Weidong (ed.) (2001). Gao Jingfeng and Hongmei Wu (2001) found that in some provinces the disapproval rate rose to as high as 49 per cent during certain periods.

in order to avoid bearing responsibility for creating liability for state compensation as a result of inability to prosecute a suspect for whom it has approved arrest, the procuratorate simply raises the standard of evidence needed to approve arrest to that required to initiate prosecution.

THE QUESTION OF BAIL AND RESIDENTIAL SURVEILLANCE

One of the most important tasks for defence lawyers at the outset of a case is to try to secure bail for their clients. The grant of bail is consistent with the view that no person should be detained unless he or she has been found guilty, better enables the preparation of the defence and allows the citizen to remain in employment (Raifeartaigh, 1997; King, 1981; Hucklesby, 1994; and Burrows, 2000). Against this, of course, bail might enable a person to abscond, interfere with potential witnesses, destroy evidence, commit further offences or otherwise obstruct the course of justice. A mass of literature has been produced in China on how the police exercise their discretion in practice. This literature is contradictory and confusing but the main concerns and findings are set out below.

A. Success Rate for Bail is Too Low

Unlike in the UK or USA, where there is a right to bail (Toborg, 1994; Choongh, 2002), in China whether bail is granted is purely a matter of police discretion. This has led many to argue that the police routinely deny bail granting it only in exceptional cases (e.g. where the suspect is seriously ill, pregnant or a breast-feeding mother: Cui Min, 1998; Su Xiaochuan, 2001). In the absence of systematic and reliable statistics, piecemeal studies have reported wildly varying success rates. So, for example, some lawyers and procurators have reported that in their sample of cases bail was never granted (Wang Guangjing and Longtian Wang, 1998a) whereas others have reported a rate as high as 40 per cent (Wang Chunwang, 2000; and Tang Liang, 2001 who reported a success rate of 37 per cent). The survey by Jiang Shimei and Xing Hong (2008) on the operation of the bail by the police in one district showed that only 139 out of 1636 suspects/times were granted bail (8.5 per cent) between 2006 and 2007.

In general, juvenile offenders are more likely to be granted bail and female offenders' rate of approval of bail appears higher. According to Liu, Qi and Zeng (2008) in the Haidian District of Beijing around 30 per cent of juvenile suspects obtained bail; and more than 32 per cent of female offenders (the adult male rate being around 16–21 per cent) were granted bail between 2004 and 2006. Moreover, the rate of non-local suspects who obtained bail was 14 per cent on average between 2004 and 2006, which was dramatically lower than that of local suspects (40 per cent) a finding supported by other studies (Dong Qihai, 2008; and Ma Lifeng, 2009). Despite some experiments aimed at raising the bail rate in some areas in China,[24] the rate in general remains low because, from the

---

[24] Starting in 2006, Zhangjiagang Municipal Procuratorate expanded the scope of bail application for migrant suspects from minor offenders charged with such minor offences as theft, minor injury and traffic crime to adult offenders charged with serious offences such as rape and robbery

police perspective, granting bail increases the prospects of suspects absconding[25] or withdrawing their confessions,[26] or committing offences on bail thus leaving the police open to internal punishment and external criticism for having granted bail.

B. Bail is Granted Inappropriately

Alongside the charge that the police do not grant bail frequently enough is the concern that bail is often granted in cases where it is inappropriate to do so. Thus, for example, according to a report by the Political and Legal Committee of the Chinese Communist Party (CCP) Committee of Hubei, between 1997 and 1999 authorities across three provinces in Hubei granted bail inappropriately to 1396 individuals, many in cases where accomplices had already absconded and where many of those granted bail also absconded (Li Jiya, 2001). In similar vein, a survey of six counties of Jiangsu Province reported that in some cases bail was granted as a face-saving exercise by the police when they could find no evidence against suspects or because they had encountered difficulties in concluding an investigation (Gu, Wang and Tan, 1999; see also Hu Guojian, 2004). Release on bail may also assist the police in meting out punishment whilst reducing the risk of being sued for false imprisonment (Cohen, 2009c). Cohen points out that a release may be negotiated between the detainee and the investigator by, for example, signing a 'confession' that will protect the captors against a lawsuit or by promising to abandon the conduct that gave rise to the detention.

C. Bail is Used for Material Gain/as Private Favour

There are reports that in some cases the police grant bail to supplement their budget and in other cases because of personal connections. So, for example, Chen Lianyi (2000) from

---

who might be sentenced to a penalty of more than three-years fixed-term sentencing, so long as they could meet the bail conditions and it loosened the requirements relating to guarantors. To promote effective monitoring of bail, the procuratorate set up risk assessment and prevention mechanisms and reinforced supervision after bail and case-handling officers would not be investigated for liability if bail was granted by law. Following this, the rate of non-approval of arrest went up to 5.9 per cent in 2007 from 1.5 per cent in 2005. See Dong Qihai and Qingfeng Zhang (2008).

[25] Wang Gao (2000); Fang Sheng, Jiang Lian and Xing Hong (1997); Zeng Yabo (2001); Song Yinghui and Luo Haimin (2007). All suspects, especially migrants, are considered a high risk if they are likely to face a custodial sentence upon conviction: Wang Minyuan (2003). Bail-jumping figures do not suggest a large problem in all areas. For example, in Zhangjiagang of Jiangsu between 2005 and 2007, of the 873 suspects given non-custodial measures, only seven jumped bail, including four from other provinces, two from other cities of Jiangsu Provinces and one from Zhangjiagang: Dong Qihai and Qingfeng Zhang (2008), p. 99. By contrast, between 2004–2006 there was a higher rate (between 8 and 11 per cent) of bail-jumping in Haidian District: Liu Zhongfa, Jinsong Qi and Jingyin Zeng (2008); Guang Yan (2007), p. 211.

[26] If given bail, suspects may withdraw their confession, collude with other suspects or witnesses, or even influence witnesses' court appearance. For instance, in the cases where suspects confessed before bail in Haidian District Procuratorate of Beijing in 2005, 3 per cent of suspects withdrew their confessions or witnesses changed their testimony, sometimes significantly, which led to the prosecution's withdrawal of the prosecution: Liu Zhongfa, Jinsong Qi and Jingyin Zeng (2008); Guang Yan (2007).

the Procuratorate has written that in cases involving matters such as financial fraud, false invoices of value-added tax, abduction of women and counterfeiting trademarks, the police will grant bail regardless of whether it is appropriate to do so, presumably because they believe suspects in such cases are in a position to pay.[27]

D. Law Governing Bail is Vague/Misunderstood

A body of evidence, mainly anecdotal in quality, suggests that legal provisions governing bail are often misunderstood. This is perhaps not surprising, given that Article 51, 1996 CPL confers a discretion but provides no guidelines on how that discretion ought to be exercised (it states that bail or residential surveillance 'may' be granted, 'according to the circumstances of the case'). While Article 51 states that there are conditions which must be fulfilled before bail can be granted (one of which is in itself vague – the suspect would not 'endanger society'), it is not clear whether satisfaction of these conditions is sufficient, or whether it is necessary but not sufficient in the sense that even where the conditions are satisfied the police may decline bail 'according to the circumstances of the case'. A further layer of complexity is added by Article 60 which provides that if a 'criminal suspect . . . who should be arrested is seriously ill or is a pregnant woman or a woman breast-feeding her own baby' he or she 'may be allowed to obtain' bail. At the same time, some academics have argued that the position is made more complex still by Article 38 of the *Rules of Supreme People's Procuratorate* which prohibits the grant of bail in cases where the alleged crime caused 'serious danger to society', and Article 64 of the *Procedural Rules of the Public Security Organs in Handling Criminal Cases* which states that bail may not be granted to recidivists, principals in crime syndicates and those who self-harm to avoid investigation (Hu Guojian, 2004).

Given this complex position the police also struggle to understand the circumstances in which bail may be granted. It has been reported that in many provinces the police mistakenly believe that bail can be granted only to the seriously ill, pregnant women and breast-feeding mothers (Xie Cheng, 2004), or only if the suspect provides both a guarantor and bail money (Chen Jianxin, 2002a). There also appears to be confusion over the duration of bail, despite Article 58 of the CPL stipulating that bail should not exceed 12 months. Xie Cheng (2004) from the Wenzhou Public Security Bureau reported that this had led the police, the procuratorate and the court to believe that each of them could bail the suspect for 12 months cumulatively. Somewhat bizarrely, other police forces believed that having granted bail they could not terminate it within 12 months (i.e. that if granted, bail had to last a minimum of 12 months).

---

[27] The allegation that personal connections play a part in the decision making process was reported in *Renmin Jiacha* 20 'Problems with bail' (September 1997). There is also anecdotal evidence that the families of (non-political) criminal suspects in detention may be asked to pay 'thank-you-money' to the police for the decision to release on bail.

E. Internal Evaluation Mechanism is Problematic and Risk Prevention Systems are Missing

The current internal performance evaluation mechanism started in the 1990s within the investigation organ increased the personal risk to case-handling officers should bail be granted. For example, if the suspect commits another crime on bail or escapes from control, case-handling officers will face consequences – punishment through internal performance evaluation, their bonus might be deducted, their authority might be reduced and their promotion might be hindered (Song Yinghui and Haimin Luo, 2007; Liu Zhongfa, Jinsong Qi and Jingyin Zeng, 2008; Dong Qihai and Qingfeng Zhang, 2008; Sun Changyong, 2009). If the consequences are serious, case-handling officers might be dismissed or even prosecuted for criminal liability, negligence or abuse of power. Moreover, there are reports that the legal provisions governing bail can be considered largely irrelevant because courts and chief procurators have been known to issue edicts banning the use of bail in all or certain categories of case (Li Jiya, 2001).

F. Internal Bureaucratic Approval Process Discouraged Police to Grant Bail

Apart from the unreasonable internal evaluation system, the internal approval for bail pending trial is a bureaucratic nightmare for the police. For instance, the police need to first submit the report for approval to the department head, and then the deposit guarantee for bail will be paid to a special account in the local financial department after holding the receipt of deposit issued by the police, which requires formalities from five departments and their leaders concerned. After trial, such a procedure will be gone through for a second time. This has weakened the incentive for case-handling officers to grant bail (Liu, Qi and Zeng, 2008).

G. Residential Surveillance

Although the provision on the location of residential surveillance is not clear in Article 57, 1996 CPL, the investigation organ often misuses this measure to deprive suspects or defendants of personal freedom (Zhang Rujin, 2009; Qian Xuetang, 2005). For example, according to a survey in a local public security bureau, of the 603 suspects who were granted residential surveillance, 588 (97.5 per cent) in fact stayed in the detention centre, while only 15 (2.5 per cent) were able to stay at home (Chen Jianxin, 2002a).

Those subject to this surveillance cannot leave the designated place, nor can they meet their lawyers or family members (Qian Xuetang, 2005). Lan Jian (2000) commented on residential surveillance as follows:

> (1) (the police) put the 'residence' of residential surveillance into the police office, detention centre or designated rooms; (2) put suspects in a study class for self-reflection, suspend work and do not let them go back home; (3) although suspects were granted residential surveillance, they were not allowed to go outside the room; and (4) suspects bear the costs and may be moved to a designated guesthouse or hotel.

In practice, suspects given residential surveillance are commonly put in a designated place, such as a hotel or inn, or in a self-constructed 'work station', some even in the 'black house' of the police station (Zhou Wei, 2000).

For the police bail pending trial has a number of advantages over residential surveillance: first, it is felt to be safer to require a guarantor. Second, when suspects on bail escape or commit suicide or destroy the evidence, the suspects rather than the police will be regarded as responsible; whereas if it happens under residential surveillance, the officers may be held responsible for the consequences of such acts. Third, by granting bail pending trial guaranteed by money, the police and judiciary may have extra income by confiscating the guaranteed money (Jiang Yong, 2009).

UTILIZATION OF BAIL: OUR QUALITATIVE DATA

Many of the concerns set out above over the granting of bail were echoed by judges, prosecutors and defence lawyers whom we interviewed. So, for example, some lawyers and judges complained that bail was being granted inappropriately, that this led to defendants absconding and was a restraint on defendants being granted bail. This view was expressed by a judge in Site D (D-K-02), two prosecutors in Site B (B-B2-09 and B-B2-02) and a judge from Site B (B-B2-14). Another prosecutor from Site B (B-B2-02) revealed that this had led prosecutors to ask the police not to grant bail. A prosecutor (B-B2-06) and a judge (B-B2-14) from Site B suggested that measures had to be taken to prevent defendants from jumping bail, and suggested that one solution would be to increase the liability of guarantors. When asked what improvements might be made at the pre-trial stage, a judge from a big city put the matter as follows:

> *C-B2-14:* 1. Bail by providing a guarantor in fact is not useful. Why? Firstly, it has little credibility in the eyes of society . . .; second, the situation regarding employment is looser today because the dependence on and control of the units has been reduced; third, family relationships have been weakened; fourth, guarantors are basically not required to undertake any responsibility; they will only be held criminally liable for the offence of concealing if they intentionally conceal the defendant, but there is no way to prove this in practice. Therefore, if bail by providing a guarantor is going to be used, the liability of the guarantor must be increased. 2. There are also many problems with the system of cash bail; in fact it also fails to prevent defendants from absconding. Currently, the amount of bail money normally is between RMB 2000 to RMB 3000, and in practice bail is often granted in cases involving property infringements, injuries and traffic accidents. Many involve incidental civil actions and normally we need to conduct mediation regarding the civil action. Once the mediation is conducted and the suspect discovers that the compensation in the civil action is RMB 50 000 or RMB 80 000, he may decide to jump bail and forfeit the bail money. 3. The public security organs' supervision over bail is inadequate.

Defence lawyers told us that while they would ask suspects whether they would like to apply for bail, it was difficult to apply for bail either at the investigative stage (e.g. Site E, E-L-05; Site J, J-S4-03; Site F, F-N-04 and Site A, A-B1-09) or at the stage of examination for prosecution (e.g. Site G/H, G-S1-006; Site J, J-S4-03 and Site D, D-K-04). One lawyer from Site G/H (I-S3-008) said that he would make an application for bail only if there was a chance of success, but he had found that bail was not granted in serious cases. Similarly, two lawyers from Site D (D-K-04; D-K-05) said that they would consider making an application for bail only in less serious cases. One of these (D-K-04) went on to add that most of his bail applications were rejected, suggesting that even in less serious cases the success rate is very low. Indeed, complaints about the low success rate for bail applications were widespread amongst defence lawyers. For example, two Site G/H lawyers (G-S1-001 and G-S1-004) said that almost all bail applications they had made were unsuccessful; one lawyer in Site G/H (G-S1-003) said that over 90 per cent of the bail applications were unsuccessful while another lawyer in Site G/H (G-S1-002) said the failure rate was as high as 99 per cent.

As in the research studies summarized above, some of our respondents also blamed the low level of bail on the ambiguities of the law. One lawyer in Site G/H (G-S1-004) complained that the right to apply for bail was an empty promise because there was no restriction as to the circumstances in which a bail application should be approved or rejected. Another (Site E, E-L-05) argued that the current bail system was arbitrary and effectively a black-box. The allegation of the system being a black-box was also reflected in the observation of one lawyer (Site GH, G-S1-006) that the police never provided a reason for rejecting bail applications.

One of the reasons for the low success rate, and indeed for the reluctance of defence lawyers to even apply for bail, may be that the police prefer to set cash bail rather than accept a guarantor. A lawyer from Site L (L-X-09) was of the opinion that bail was normally in the form of cash bail, whilst a Site D lawyer (D-K-04) went so far as to say that 99 per cent of the grants of bail were in the form of cash bail. Two lawyers from Site A and Site J stated that, while many judicial organs only accepted the provision of bail money rather than guarantors, some requested both guarantors and bail money.

Alongside the complaints about the low success rate for bail applications lawyers argued that the decision on bail was influenced by factors such as enmity between judicial personnel and particular defence lawyers, the status, wealth and/or connections of the suspect, and the desire of judicial personnel to cover up mistakes:

Site G, G-S1-04: Sometimes, it is agreed internally, but the reply to the lawyer is still one of disapproval, mainly because the persons in charge of the case don't want the lawyer to have a psychological advantage; they consider that lawyers would take advantage and raise their fees.

Site I, I-S3-04: Some criminal suspects will apply for bail, especially in economic cases. These criminal suspects had high status before being detained. They have some social relationship, so it is comparatively easier [to obtain bail].

Site F, F-N-04: In my opinion, nobody can successfully obtain bail through formal procedures. It's better if you have relationships. The reason why suspects in crimes of corruption or misappropriation of public funds find it easier to obtain bail is that they are personnel of the government. They have special relationships.

Site H, H-S2-002: Sometimes judicial personnel themselves invite an application for bail because the evidence in the case is insufficient, and [the judicial personnel] are afraid of having trouble because the allegation [of a criminal offence] would not be substantiated.

Finally, in common with the earlier studies referenced above, we also found evidence in our interviews that the police, prosecutors and courts misunderstood or misapplied the rule that bail could not exceed 12 months. A prosecutor from Site B (B-B2-08) said that he had observed situations in which the three institutions had each imposed successive 12 month periods of bail, thereby extending the duration of bail duration from one year to three years and undermining the protection of the suspects' legal rights.

UTILIZATION OF BAIL: OUR QUANTITATIVE RESEARCH DATA

Our researchers examined the case file to see whether the defendant was recorded as having applied for bail during the investigative stage. The results are set out in Table 3.10 and the outcome of bail applications is set out in Table 3.11.[28]

Two matters emerge from these tables: firstly, the vast majority of suspects are recorded as not having applied for bail, and secondly, those who are recorded as having applied for bail almost invariably succeed in securing bail. Only 13.8 per cent of suspects in the Basic Court sample are recorded as having applied for bail, the percentage recorded as having applied in the Intermediate Court was even lower at 6.0 per cent. In the Basic Court sample 98 per cent of those who are recorded as having applied managed to secure bail (92.8 per cent) and in the Intermediate Court sample all of those who are recorded as having applied managed to secure bail.

In one respect, these figures are consistent with other research (e.g., Lu and Drass, 2002) and with the observations of defence lawyers in our interview sample that bail is more likely to be granted in less serious cases. While the overall recorded success rate for bail was approximately the same in the two samples, in the Intermediate Court sample the police made slightly greater use of residential surveillance reflecting the more serious nature of the offences tried in the Intermediate Courts.

Table 3.10   Applications for bail

	BC 7 Sites		IC 6 Sites		Total 13 Sites	
Yes	96	13.8	21	6.4	117	11.4
No	600	87.2	307	93.6	907	88.6
Not known	30	–	90	–	120	–
Total	726	100	418	100	1144	100

Table 3.11   Outcome of bail applications

	BC 7 Sites		IC 6 Sites		Total 13 Sites	
Bail granted	90	97.8	17	100.0	107	98.2
Bail application rejected	2	2.2	0	0.0	2	1.8
Not known	4	–	4	–	8	–
Total	96	100	21	100	117	100

---

[28] Table 3.11 excludes 14 cases in which the police subjected the suspect to residential surveillance. In total, there were five such cases in the Basic Court of which two were for between 8 and 37 days, one was over three months but less than one year and in two cases the duration was not known. Altogether there were nine such cases in the Intermediate Court of which five were for between 8 and 37 days, one for between 38 days to less than three months, two were between three months and less than one year and in one case the duration was for a period of two years or over.

As Table 3.10 shows, since over 87 per cent of suspects in the Basic Courts and over 93 per cent in the Intermediate Courts did not apply for bail all but a minority of defendants in our sample were held in custody pending trial. Overall, therefore, our data support the widely held view amongst scholars, lawyers and commentators in China that the police rarely grant bail and most suspects are held in custody while the police carry out their investigations or as the case proceeds to trial (Song and Luo, 2007; Jiang and Hong, 2008, pp. 31–32; Liu, Qi and Zeng, 2008; Dong Qihai (2008); Yang Jun (2009); and Chen Junmin, 2010).

What is not explicable on these figures is why so few suspects apparently apply for bail when the success rate for those who do apply is so high. The explanation probably lies in the fact that in cases in which bail is granted the file records the fact of grant. In other words, bail applications are almost invariably only recorded when they have been successful. The overwhelming likelihood is that where a suspect was not granted bail the file would not record whether an application was made and was, accordingly, recorded by our researchers as 'no bail'. The two case files which record that bail was refused are exceptional in this regard: in one instance, no further information was given, the other simply stating that the conditions for bail had not been met.

Overall, bail does not appear to be granted as a result of an application by the suspect or his lawyer,[29] but rather because the police decide for their own reasons that it is appropriate to grant bail (and, indeed, residential surveillance). In any event, the likelihood of suspects and legal advisers taking the initiative at police stations in China is low. As demonstrated in Chapter 4 *infra*, most suspects are of low educational attainment and unlikely, without legal assistance, to know that they can apply for bail.

Further, one matter which suspects are likely to be aware of is that bail will not be granted unless they or their family can put up bail money. The case files did not systematically record whether bail was granted on condition of paying bail money or providing a guarantor, but in those cases where the files made reference to bail money (23 cases) considerable sums were deposited (the lowest sum was RMB 2000 in two cases, the highest RMB 30000, with about one-third of cases attracting bail money of RMB 5000). Given the social status of the vast majority of defendants (unskilled or semi-skilled with more than three-quarters unemployed) bail was out of their reach simply on financial grounds.

We looked to see whether the decision on bail and the imposition of residential surveillance was determined by gender or residential status. There was no positive correlation with gender: of those cases in which bail/residential surveillance was granted/ imposed and where gender was known, 87 per cent were male and 13 per cent female, which was broadly in line with the overall male/female split in the sample as a whole (89 per cent/11 per cent). The results are set out in Table 3.12.

By contrast there was a positive correlation with residential status. Although migrants comprised over 55 per cent of the overall sample, of those defendants who were granted bail or had residential surveillance imposed and whose residential status was known, only

---

[29] However, it should be noted, that the presence of a lawyer may prolong detention probably because the police feel it necessary to take extra steps to counter any possible challenges that may be advanced by the lawyer: Lu Hong and Kriss Drass, *op. cit.*, at p. 84.

Table 3.12 Results of applications of bail or residential surveillance (gender)

	BC 7 Sites		IC 6 Sites		Total 13 Sites	
Male	83	83.8	26	86.7	109	84.5
Female	16	16.2	4	13.3	20	15.5
Not known	2	–	0	–	2	–
Total	101	100.0	30	100.0	131	100.0

Table 3.13 Results of applications of bail or residential surveillance (residential status)

	BC 7 Sites		IC 6 Sites		Total 13 Sites	
Local	71	72.4	17	56.7	88	68.8
Migrant	27	27.6	13	43.3	40	31.3
Not known	3	–	0	–	3	–
Total	101	100.0	30	100.0	131	100.0

32 per cent were migrants.[30] The greater relative incidence of locals being granted bail/residential surveillance was true in respect of all of the individual sites where there were sufficient numbers granted bail/residential surveillance to make a meaningful comparison. The overall results are presented in Table 3.13.

Migrants are even less likely than locals to secure bail/residential status probably because they are less likely to be able to raise bail money and less likely to be able to secure a guarantor with a fixed domicile and steady income as required by Article 54 of the 1996 CPL. Additionally migrants or 'peasant workers' (*nongmingong*) suffer widespread social discrimination, social and cultural marginalization.[31]

CONCLUSION

The police or PSB in China has at its disposal a vast array of powers which can be utilized in the investigation of crime and the collection of evidence in regard to those suspected of involvement in criminal activity. It is also clear that the police use these powers not only to the full extent permitted by law but where they feel it necessary or useful beyond

---

[30] See also, Lu and Drass (2002) who found, in a study of 212 non-violent theft cases committed by male offenders and handled by a district court in a midsized city in China in 1999, that transients received longer pre-trial detention than did residents, although the sentence dispositions did not appear to have been harsher.

[31] See, for example, *The Children of Migrant Workers in China*, China Labour Bulletin available at http://www.china-labour.org.hk/en/node/100316 (last viewed 22 May 2010). The report documents the plight of migrant children who because of their 'inferior' status attend sub-standard schools and illegal clinics and routinely suffer institutionalized discrimination. See also, Wang Feiling (2004); Eva Pils (2007a).

and occasionally far beyond what is legally permitted. Suspects are routinely subjected to detention to the full extent allowed by law and in many cases beyond the periods allowed by law and few secure either bail or residential surveillance at any stage in the process. The figures show that the vast majority do not apply but of the minority who do, most get it. In terms of the low application rate this is most likely because there is simply no prospect of bail. As has been shown, in only about one per cent of cases where the suspect has been detained by the police is there an application for approval of arrest within three days and in fewer than ten per cent is the application made within seven days. Delays at this stage of the process are not the end of the matter because these are followed by further delays after approval of arrest and prior to transfer to the procuratorate. And thereafter additional delays occur when the case is in the hands of the prosecutor. The cumulative impact of the addition of delay upon delay is not mitigated by the use of bail (which was granted at some point to only 107 suspects) or residential surveillance (which was imposed on only 14 suspects) so that almost all suspects initially detained by the police remain in custody throughout the pre-trial process. While the negative impact of this upon the lives of suspects and their ability to construct a defence cannot be directly measured by this research, the extent to which the use of these powers is productive in terms of gathering incriminating evidence from suspects themselves and from other potential sources is the subject of the next chapter.

4. The construction of the police case

In constructing the case for the prosecution, the police (PSB) in China, like those in Western countries, employ a variety of methods to collect evidence that would be admissible at trial or useful to their general investigatory and crime control role. As we have seen, the PSB have extensive powers to enable them to detain suspects and keep them in custody for this purpose. Given the negative view of 'criminals' and the view widely held in China that the 'confession is king' (*kougong shi zhengju zhi wang*), it is not surprising that the PSB spend significant efforts in questioning suspects with a view to gaining a confession and other crime-relevant information. Beyond this, the PSB have wider investigative powers including the power to stop and search individuals, to search premises, engage expert witnesses and gather information from victims and witnesses. In this chapter we document the ways in which the PSB utilize these powers with a view to constructing the case for the prosecution.

THE SOURCES OF EVIDENCE

Article 42, 1996 CPL makes clear that a wide range of information is included within the definition of 'evidence':

> All facts that prove the true circumstances of a case shall be evidence.
> Evidence includes the following seven categories:
> 1. material or documentary evidence;
> 2. testimony of witnesses;
> 3. statements of victims;
> 4. statements and apologia of the crime suspects and defendants;
> 5. conclusions of expert witnesses;
> 6. written records of inquests and examination; and
> 7. video and audio materials.
> Any of the above-listed evidences must be verified to be true before it can be used as the basis for settling the case.

Article 43, 1996 CPL further provides that those responsible for collecting evidence (Judges, Prosecutors and PSB) should do so in a lawful manner and, in particular, that no recourse should be made to torture:[1]

---

[1] It will be noted that there is no provision in the 1996 CPL which specifically provides for the exclusion of illegally-obtained evidence. We discuss later the introduction in 2010 of new rules regarding the exclusion of illegally-obtained evidence in criminal cases which, however, are not expected to substantially change the situation on the ground.

> Judicial, procuratorial and investigating personnel must, in accordance with the statutory procedures, gather various kinds of evidences that can be used to prove the guilt or innocence of crime suspects and defendants and the gravity of the crimes. It shall be strictly forbidden to extort confessions by torture or to collect evidences by coercion, inducement, deceit or any other unlawful means. It must be guaranteed that all citizens who are involved in a case or who have information about the case to objectively and fully provide evidence, and with the exception of special circumstances, they may be brought in to assist the investigations.

As we have already seen, the PSB have in practice unmediated access to suspects, may detain them for long periods and subject them to repeated questioning. We describe below what we were able to learn about the evidence-gathering function from the official records. We emphasize once again our reliance upon the official records and our inability to directly observe the most critical phase of evidence-acquisition, namely police interactions with suspects in a custodial environment. Having said this, there is no obvious reason why a prosecution file would fail to record such matters as whether a defendant sought to retract a confession alleged to have been made at the police station and, certainly, prosecutors had no opportunity to 'doctor' the files because of the way in which we drew the samples.

For completeness sake, we should note that in China the PSB have the major duty to investigate *crime*, not simply to gather evidence against the suspect as mandated by Article 89, 1996 CPL:

> With respect to a criminal case which has been filed, the public security organ shall carry out investigation, collecting and obtaining evidence to prove the criminal suspect guilty or innocent or to prove the crime to be minor or grave . . .

Because the sample was drawn from prosecuted cases, we are not in a position to provide a complete account of the extent to which the police seek or obtain evidence of innocence as a generality. What we can say is that, in cases which are prosecuted, the PSB concentrate on accumulating evidence which tends to incriminate the suspect rather than producing a 'balanced' dossier and that this picture is confirmed by our observation of live trials.

INTERROGATION OF SUSPECTS: ACCESS TO LEGAL ADVICE

Article 96, 1996 CPL provides that 'after the criminal suspect is interrogated by an investigative organ for the first time or from the day on which compulsory measures are adopted against him, he may appoint a lawyer to provide him with legal advice and to file petitions'. It further provides that if the suspect is arrested, his appointed lawyer 'may apply on his behalf for obtaining a guarantor pending trial'. This leaves unclear the point at which the suspect can appoint a lawyer. As explained earlier, forced appearance and detention are defined as compulsory measures, and it would seem on the face of it therefore that a suspect is entitled to appoint a lawyer as soon as he or she is summonsed or detained. However, Article 96 also clearly implies that a lawyer can be appointed only *after* the first interrogation has been completed. This interpretation is supported by Article 33, which provides that a suspect has the right to appoint a defence lawyer 'from the date on which the case is transferred for examination before prosecution' (i.e. some time after interrogation has been completed and indeed after the police have decided that they have sufficient evidence to recommend prosecution). The new Lawyers Law (2007) simply confirms the position in law. As we shall see, the problems for defence lawyers have not been improved by the new legislation and, indeed, there is evidence that they have worsened (Donald Clarke, 2009a and 2009b). During the currency of the research, there were significant limitations placed upon the role that a defence lawyer could play during the police investigative stage:

> Firstly, Article 33, 1996 CPL makes it clear that the suspect need not be informed about his right to appoint a lawyer until his case has been transferred to the procuratorate for examination before prosecution. So, regardless of the debate about precisely when access to a lawyer is legally permitted, the reality is that many if not most suspects will not know that they can appoint a lawyer until the police investigation is complete.
> Secondly, Article 96, 1996 CPL states that in cases involving 'state secrets' (a term left undefined) the suspect can have access to a lawyer only with the prior approval of the police.
> Thirdly, the CPL does not grant the suspect a right to have his lawyer present during interrogation.[2]
> Fourthly, although the defence lawyer has the right to know the charges against his client and may meet with him in custody, the police have a right to be present during such meetings 'in light of the seriousness of the crime and where it [the police] deems it necessary' (Article 96).
> Finally, there is no absolute right to legal aid for those who cannot afford a lawyer. Article 34, 1996 CPL provides that if the defendant has not appointed a lawyer 'due to financial difficulties or other reasons' the People's Court 'may' designate a lawyer, but that applies only where 'a case is to be brought in court by a public prosecutor'. Even at this stage, appointment of a defence lawyer at State expense is mandatory only if the defendant is deaf, mute, blind, a minor or facing the death penalty.

It is important to note that there is under Chinese law no right to have a lawyer present during interrogation, and there are no rules regulating the duration of interrogation and entitlement to breaks, sleep and refreshments. As research on interrogation elsewhere has shown,[3] these factors too may play a part in the greater willingness of suspects to co-operate with their interrogators on terms acceptable to the interrogators. Available research suggests that defence lawyers are not present during the investigative stage in China and that lawyers are rarely involved at any stage, while the suspect is in detention the PSB routinely denying or delaying access on some pretext (Chen Weidong, 2001; Fan Chongyi, 2001). An examination of our case files supports this picture to the extent that there is not a single reference to lawyers being present at the early stages of the investigation or at police interrogations.

In Western jurisdictions the reliability of confession evidence has been the subject of much controversy, with allegations of police violence, mistreatment, trickery and fabrication regularly made and denied over the years (McConville and Baldwin, 1981, pp. 161–167). As we did not observe police interrogations we cannot comment on whether these sorts of practices are prevalent in China, but it is certainly the case that

---

[2] There have been experiments in this regard in some police stations studied by Professor Fan Chongyi.

[3] See, for example, Irving and Hilgendorf (1980); Gudjonsson and MacKeith (1982); Gudjonsson and Clark (1986); Gudjonsson (1992).

allegations of the type made in the West surface regularly in China. So, for example, Professor Fan (2001) reported a source as saying that 26 police officers were involved in the extortion of confessions through torture nationwide in the first half of 1997.[4] Chen's interviews of police officers revealed that many believed it perfectly legitimate to apply extreme pressure on suspects to confess.[5] As one officer put it, 'when the police cannot obtain confession by normal process, they may attempt to get it by torture. In practice, they succeed in detecting the case in that way; consequently, confession by torture has [an] exemplary role in detecting the case.'[6]

In practice, extortion of the suspect's confessions is deemed the most efficient and effective means in criminal investigation through which the police can also obtain clues for other evidence required for conviction, such as stolen property or goods, tools used for crime, etc. (Zhang and Shang, 2009). According to the 2620 respondents in a survey by Lin, Zhang and Huang (2009), 55.3 per cent claimed that they received direct and 60.1 per cent indirect torture by the police; 6.9 per cent said that they suffered from direct and 11.2 per cent indirect torture by prosecutors. Zuo Weimin, Jinghua Ma and Jianping Hu (2007) found that greatest emphasis upon obtaining a confession occurred early in the investigation. In practice, because direct use of coercive force may be exposed and give rise to corresponding disciplinary punishment, other non-violent means such as sleep-deprivation, punishment by standing in stress positions, withdrawal of food or not allowing access to the toilet or humiliating the suspect in other ways are more common. In addition, some investigators adopt a 'wheel-war style' to continuously interrogate the suspect, as there is no specific provision or restriction on the length of each interrogation (Sun Changyong, 2009, p. 489). One scholar commented on current Chinese criminal procedure as follows:

> After the investigation organ obtains some clues about the crime, it will interrogate the suspect immediately and then collect evidence through clues obtained from the suspect's statement. If other evidence collected is different from what the suspect said in the confession, they will continue the interrogation. The whole criminal investigation in general centres on the suspect's confession . . . Such an investigative mode is characterized by [a number of] features: First, it is deeply affected by the confession-oriented thinking . . . that is, the case cannot be deemed to be detected without the suspect's confession. Second, the investigation process operates in a closed

---

[4] See also, Fan Chongyi (2008a). Fan attributes reliance on oral confessions to a number of factors including the low quality of judicial officers and primitive investigative techniques.

[5] There is nothing surprising about this and many equivalent examples have been identified historically in Western literature on police interrogations running from the infamous 'third degree' in nineteenth-century America to equally discomforting techniques employed in the UK up to and during the 1970s as attested to by the investigations into bomb outrages on mainland England and the activities of the (later disbanded) West Midlands Serious Crime Squad.

[6] Chen Weidong (2001). One commentator also attributes torture to the various pressures imposed on investigating officers. In order to evaluate police performance at the grassroots level, there is an internal performance evaluation system including the detection rate and the percentage of procuratorial approvals of arrest submitted by the police. The police in China are not only responsible for criminal investigation but also social security and order. The pressure to resolve cases involving death within a certain period and the evaluation indexes are closely connected with the welfare, promotion and even future of the police involved. Against such a background, the police feel that it is relatively simple to detect cases through obtaining confessions. See Zhang Ying and Xidong Shang (2009).

environment.... Third, it adopts the method of concluding the case if 'information of the three pieces of evidence are the same', that is, if the suspect confesses and two witnesses testify to what the suspect confessed, then everything is considered alright and the investigation focuses on using the confession to look for testimony. Fourth, the quality of the investigation cannot be safeguarded, as it is a common phenomenon for the accused to change their confessions or testimonies in the proceedings.

As later chapters will reveal, some of the suspects in our sample complained that they had been subjected to violence by the police and sought to reject confessions that had been attributed to them by the police or retract confessions that had been, they said, extracted by torture.

INTERROGATION OF SUSPECTS: CONFESSION EVIDENCE

Interrogation of the suspect must be by no fewer than two investigators (Article 91, 1996 CPL). The suspect must be given an opportunity to 'state the circumstances of his guilt or explain his innocence', the interrogators have a right to ask questions, and the suspect has a duty to answer those questions 'truthfully'. His or her only right to refuse to answer is in respect of any questions that are irrelevant to the case (Article 93, 1996 CPL). Formally, the suspect has a right to check the record of interrogation, to make additions or corrections to it, and if he or she acknowledges it as an accurate record he or she must sign or affix his or her seal to it. The investigators must also sign the record. The suspect can if he or she chooses write a personal statement, and if the investigators think it necessary they can ask him or her to write a personal statement (Article 95, 1996 CPL).

Although Article 42, 1996 CPL appears to contain a rule to the effect that truthfulness is the sole test of admissibility ('All facts that prove the true circumstances of a case shall be evidence'), Article 43, 1996 CPL states that it is 'strictly forbidden to extort confessions by torture and to collect evidence by threat, enticement, deceit or other unlawful means'. Indeed, it is a criminal offence for a judicial officer to extort confessions by torture from a suspect or defendant, or to use violence to extort testimony from a witness.[7] Article 61 of the *Interpretation of the Supreme People's Court on Several Questions in the Implementation of the Criminal Procedure Law of the People's Republic of China* (SPC Interpretation) provides that:

> ... If after investigation and verification, it is proved to be true the testimony of a witness, the statement of a victim, or the confession of a defendant was obtained by using torture to coerce a statement, or by threatening, fraudulent inducement, deceiving, and other illegal means, such testimony, statement, or confession shall not be used to determine a case.[8]

A similar provision can also be found in Article 265 of the *Rules of the People's Procuratorate on Criminal Procedure* (SPP Rules). Further, if the procuratorate discovers

---

[7] Article 247 of the Criminal Law provides that: 'Any judicial officer who extorts confession from a criminal suspect or defendant by torture or extorts testimony from a witness by violence shall be sentenced to fixed-term imprisonment of not more than three years or criminal detention.'

[8] The translation of this provision is extracted from Wei Luo (2000).

that the testimony, confession or statement is obtained by unlawful means, according to Article 265 of the SPP Rules, 'it shall raise an opinion of rectification. At the same time, it shall request the investigative organ to send another investigator to re-investigate the evidence.' If it considers it necessary, the procuratorate may even conduct the investigation by itself, or 'return the case to the investigative organ for supplementary investigation according to law'.

The 1996 CPL further provides that credence shall not be readily given to oral statements and that a defendant cannot be found guilty if there is 'only his statement but no evidence'.[9] Article 46, 1996 CPL also provides that a defendant may be convicted if the evidence is sufficient and reliable, even without his statement.[10] Interestingly, it is also provided that the testimony of a witness may be used as a basis in deciding a case only after the witness has been questioned and cross-examined by both sides, that is, the public prosecutor and the victim as well as the defendant and defenders (Article 47, 1996 CPL).

Research conducted as far back as 1967 in the USA suggested that 80 per cent of all crimes were solved as a consequence of the suspect confessing under police interrogation, that a confession, once secured, almost guaranteed conviction, and that many cases were reliant on confession evidence to secure a conviction (Zimbardo, 1967). Since then numerous commentators in the UK and USA have drawn attention to the central role played by police interrogation and confession evidence in both the detection of crime and the identification and eventual conviction of suspects.[11] In the UK, despite official efforts to restrict arrest to those occasions on which it is 'necessary' to do so, the UK police detain and interrogate almost all suspects (McConville, Sanders and Leng 1991). The percentage of suspects making a full or partial confession in police interrogation has been reported as 60 per cent (Softley, 1980), 68 per cent (McConville and Baldwin, 1981), 54 per cent (Sanders et al., 1989) and 75 per cent (Evans, 1992).[12]

It has been suggested that interrogation and confession is prized by the police not only for its utilitarian value in securing convictions, but also because, for police officers themselves, it re-enforces a belief in the correctness of their investigation, their judgment,

---

[9] Article 46, 1996 CPL. Rules recently issued by the principal criminal justice bodies, including the Supreme People's Court, the Supreme People's Procuratorate and the Ministry of Public Security, reiterate that illegal evidence includes statements by criminal suspects or defendants obtained through such means as coerced confessions as well as witness testimony or victim statements obtained through violence or threats; and that oral evidence so obtained may not serve as the basis for conviction. See http://www.duihua.org/hrjournal/evidence/rules_criminal.htm.

[10] There have been occasional attempts to acknowledge the problem of coerced confessions but these have not been systematically pursued. See, for example, a report that a People's Procuracy in Fushun City in Liaoning Province attempted to stop this practice by an internal directive ordering its officials (prosecutors) to entirely disregard any statements obtained from suspects in police detention, a ruling that implies knowledge of the routine application of torture: *China Daily*, 10 February 2002 at http://www.legaldaily.com.cn/gb/content/2002-02/10/content_31946.htm. However, the police see the defendant's statement as valuable in most cases. On oral statements, see Sun Changyong (2009), pp. 491–498.

[11] Mawby (1979); Softley (1980); Bottomley and Coleman (1976); McConville and Baldwin (1981); Wrightsman and Kassin (1993).

[12] Softley (1980); McConville and Baldwin (1981); and Sanders et al. (1989).

their efficiency and their 'knowledge' of crime.[13] This observation is supported by the fact that confessions are sought regardless of the fact that they may not be necessary to the prosecution case (McConville and Baldwin, 1981), and despite the fact that confessions in serious criminal cases in the UK may often be disputed at trial and may accordingly jeopardize an otherwise sound case because juries may be sceptical of the process that has given rise to the confession.

In the present study in China we found that the percentage of those who are recorded as having made a full or partial admission[14] during police interrogation was significantly higher than that in the UK. Across the 13 sites as a whole, we found that denials at the police station featured in only around 3 per cent of cases, and this percentage was unaffected by seriousness of offence (the figure was broadly similar for Basic and Intermediate Courts). Further, the percentage making a full or partial confession (at around 95 per cent) was broadly the same across all 13 research sites. This is in line with research undertaken by Liu Fangquan (2007) who found a confession rate in three sites ranging from 95.1 per cent to 100 per cent, with most suspects admitting the crime at the time of first interrogation varying between 79.8 per cent and 95.5 per cent in the three sites. For 112 suspects in the 80 criminal cases handled in one district the average time of confession in flagrant crimes was 69.9 minutes, while that in non-flagrant crimes was 153.3 minutes (Liu Fangquan, 2007).

In short, it can be said that the criminal justice system of China is, according to our study and that of Chinese researchers, one in which all suspects are interrogated by the PSB in circumstances of secrecy and almost all suspects are recorded by the police as having wholly or partially admitted guilt at the first stage of the criminal process. Our statistics are presented in Tables 4.1–4.3.

Further analysis reveals that the PSB and prosecutors do not rely on a single confession/ statement from a defendant. Instead, it is police practice to subject the suspect to multiple interviews, to make a record of each interview[15] and to submit in evidence the various confession statements that have been extracted through this process. As was explained to us by a Chinese expert:[16]

> In China, after a suspect has been detained, he or she will be interrogated for a number of times by the investigators, unless the case is minor. Each time, what the suspect says will be recorded by the police in handwritten form. So what we call the 'result' of each interrogation is the 'defendant's confession'. If the suspect is interrogated six times, then we will say 'the defendant made six confessions' or 'there are six copies of the defendant's confession'. Sometimes, if the

---

[13] Pepinsky (1970); Lambert (1970); McConville and Baldwin (1982); McConville, Sanders and Leng (1991) pp. 65–67.

[14] A statement was recorded as a 'partial admission' where some element of an offence was not included. For example, in a murder case, if the suspect admitted striking the victim in the course of a dispute but did not state explicitly that this was done with intent to kill this was categorized as a partial confession.

[15] We have no means of knowing whether records are made of all interrogations or whether, as was frequent in England and Wales before the advent of tape- and video-recording at police stations, the police undertake off-the-record interviews with suspects which are not officially documented. The occurrence of such practices would merely add to the number of encounters between police and suspects. See, also, Zuo Weimin (2008).

[16] Private communication.

Table 4.1 Outcome of interrogation: Basic Courts

	Site A		Site B		Site C		Site D		Site F		Site G		Site M	
Full confession	121	81.8	121	91.7	108	87.8	70	100.0	64	98.5	64	92.8	68	97.1
Partial admission	16	10.8	9	6.8	12	9.8	0	0.0	0	0.0	2	2.9	2	2.9
Denial	11	7.4	4	1.5	3	2.4	0	0.0	1	1.5	3	4.3	0	0.0
Not known	9	–	9	–	30	–	0	–	0	–	1	–	0	–
Total	157	100.0	141	100.0	153	100.0	70	100.0	65	100.0	70	100.0	70	100.0

Table 4.2 Outcome of interrogation: Intermediate Courts

	Site E		Site H		Site I		Site J		Site K		Site L	
Full confession	61	93.8	52	98.1	65	92.9	52	88.1	68	97.1	94	95.0
Partial admission	4	6.2	0	0.0	3	4.3	3	5.1	1	1.4	4	4.0
Denial	0	0.0	1	1.9	2	2.9	4	6.8	1	1.4	1	1.0
Not known	0	–	0	–	0	–	1	–	0	–	1	–
Total	65	100.0	53	100.0	70	100.0	60	100.0	70	100.0	100	100.0

Table 4.3   Outcome of interrogation: all cases

	BC 7 Sites		IC 6 Sites		All Sites	
Full confession	615	90.8	392	94.2	1007	92.1
Partial admission	40	5.9	15	3.6	55	5.0
Denial	22	3.3	9	2.2	31	2.8
Not known	49	–	2	–	51	–
Total	726	100.0	418	100.0	1144	99.9

Table 4.4   Average number of confession statements in prosecution case

Research site and court level	Average number of confession statements included as part of the prosecution case
Site M: Basic Court	3.6
Site F: Basic Court	3.9
Site E: Intermediate Court	5.0
Site K: Intermediate Court	5.2

case is complicated or the defendant is an experienced guy, he may not tell the police all the facts of the crime at one time. Sometimes he may admit to the police his crime in six interrogations, either telling the same facts in six interrogations or saying some part of the criminal facts at each interrogation. And also, sometimes, he may confess and tell the police about his crime in four interrogations, he may refuse to admit the crime in the other two interrogations. On quite a few occasions, the suspect refuses to admit all the criminal facts at the beginning but finally admits them.

We found in our research that this pattern was repeated in all research sites. By way of illustration, we set out in Table 4.4 the average number of confession statements derived from police interrogations and relied upon by the prosecution in four randomly-selected sample research sites.

In these four sites, the highest number of confession statements submitted in a single case was 11 which occurred in two separate homicide cases. Although classified by prosecutors as 'confessions', it is clear as indicated above that there is, through repeated encounters with the suspect, a process of extracting information that the prosecution needs to establish its case so that some statements may contain denials or only partial admissions. It is also clear that the process can give rise to contradictory statements which may prove to be a point of attack by the defence at trial.

The other point that is of significance is that the role of the PSB in extracting the statement is invisible. The process by which information is elicited from the suspect is not revealed because the statements do not disclose, for example, the nature and number of questions put to the suspect. Nor, of course, do the disembodied statements disclose anything about the psychological condition of the suspect or the environmental circumstances governing custodial detention.

As stated above, not all 'confessions' made by the defendant were full and frank

Table 4.5 Questioning the confession attributed to the defendant

	BC 7 Sites		IC 6 Sites		All Sites	
Yes	18	5.8	60	17.3	78	11.8
No	294	94.2	287	82.7	581	88.1
Not known	300	–	45	–	345	–
Sub-total	612	100.0	392	100.0	1004	100.0
By defendant	12	80.0	44	73.3	56	74.7
By others	3	20.0	16	26.7	19	25.3
Not known	3	–	0	–	3	–
Sub-total	18	100.0	60	100.0	78	100.0

admission of responsibility. As our case file analysis (CFA) showed, the statement sometimes sought to specify the defendant's role in the crime, to mitigate his or her involvement or to advance some claim of reduced responsibility. Thus, for example, in J-CFA-S4-032/33, the statements in a homicide case were made to admit that the defendants were part of the group involved in the incident but additionally to assert: (i) that they were not the principal offender(s); (ii) that another person had gathered the group together, assigned each party a role in the crime and prepared the crime weapons; and (iii) that they were not the individual(s) who actually killed the victim but were involved merely as accessories. Similarly in F-CFA-N-07, on a charge of robbery contrary to Article 263 of the Criminal Law, the second defendant admitted that he had been present when the first defendant had carried out a robbery. However, he claimed that the robbery had not been, for his part, premeditated, that he was unaware that his co-defendant carried a knife and that he had not stolen anything from the victim. In other words, in these and many other cases, the officially-described 'confessions' could often be better described as 'statements' made by or attributed to the suspect at the police station.

In addition, it is important to note that occasionally there were contradictions in the files between (i) confessions made to the police and (ii) statements made by defendants later in the process, because at some point, when appearing before the prosecutor or in the course of the trial, defendants sought to retract or qualify the earlier confession or made a clear claim of innocence inconsistent with the earlier statement. This not only shows that defendants do seek to withdraw statements made at the police confessions but also that prosecutors do, at least occasionally, record the accounts of defendants in the files. We set out in Table 4.5 the occasions on which defendants directly challenged the accounts attributed to them in the police station.[17]

Because of the greater seriousness of the charges and greater lawyer involvement, defendants in the Intermediate Court more frequently contested their police station confession as compared to the Basic Court where there was a comparative under-representation by lawyers. Having said this, there was an unexpectedly high level of

---

[17] There were many other instances in which the defence at trial was of a character which could not be reconciled with the alleged confession at the police station.

disputes over police confessions in two of the Basic Courts (Court A and C), both of which were located in a major northern city.[18]

In addition, we can note that, notwithstanding the custodial isolation of the suspect in police hands, a small number of suspects (31 or 2.8 per cent) refused to make any confession and instead made a denial. We do not have enough detail about these cases to explain the actions of the suspect. The charges covered a broad spectrum of offences from rape through robbery, swindling, extortion, possession of counterfeit money to theft and contractual fraud. The suspects, with one exception, were males, largely poorly educated, unskilled and unemployed, a majority of whom (54.8 per cent) were migrants. In a few of these cases, the suspect did not dispute the factual circumstances but argued that the occurrence in question did not amount to a criminal offence. Thus, for example, a female suspect was stopped and searched by the police on the basis that she was engaging in 'suspicious behaviour'. On searching a bag in her possession they found various compact discs, leaflets and similar material. The police charged her under Article 300 of the Criminal Law which provides: 'Whoever forms or uses superstitious sects or secret societies or weird religious organizations or uses superstition to undermine the implementation of the laws and administrative rules and regulations of the State shall be sentenced to fixed-term imprisonment of not less than three years but not more than seven years; if the circumstances are especially serious, he shall be sentenced to fixed-term imprisonment of not less than seven years.' It is clear that the PSB must have been keeping the suspect under surveillance for activities connected with the Falun Gong. The suspect, who was convicted at trial, did not dispute that the items found were hers but argued that this was not criminal. Similarly, in several cases (e.g., A-CFA-B1-25 and I-CFA-S3-42), the suspect argued that the activity of which complaint was made was contractual not criminal.

In all denial cases except two, the suspect was convicted at trial. In exceptional cases the procuratorate decided that there was inadequate evidence to proceed and reverted the matters back for police action. One, B-CFA-B1-100, involved proactive action on the part of the police in stopping a young (27-year-old) migrant on suspicion of contractual fraud. In the absence of additional evidence, the matter was sent back for police action. Similarly, in B-CFA-B1-154, the police, acting on a civilian complaint, detained a 57-year-old migrant on suspicion of swindling, contrary to Article 266 of the Criminal Law. Because the evidence was deemed insufficient, the case was returned to the police for withdrawal.

We also examined the related but separate question whether defendants maintained complete innocence at the Debate Stage in court, notwithstanding that they had made a confession at the police station. The results are set out in Table 4.6.[19]

So far as possible, our researchers noted what was annotated in the case files[20] in regard

---

[18] This did not appear to be a function of legal representation.

[19] The results include all cases, including the many cases where there was no information on this issue.

[20] In a couple of instances, the researcher came across no such annotations or did not record any that were encountered. The information recorded in one court sample (Site B) was uniformly scanty across the field work. In this site, there was no record of defendants disputing police confessions or alleging torture.

Table 4.6 Defence claimed complete innocence in court at Debate Stage

	BC 7 Sites		IC 6 Sites		All Sites	
D submitted a statement claiming complete innocence	27	4.4	12	3.1	39	3.9
Total	612	–	392	–	1004	–

to disputing the police station confession but oftentimes the annotations were simply aide-memoires, acting as no more than a simple record of the fact of challenge rather than a detailed account of it.[21] It should also be noted that the record was made only where the defendant explicitly withdrew the confession or alleged police torture. By contrast, there were many other cases where the defence, without explicitly withdrawing the confession, made claims of innocence or advanced arguments which were inconsistent with all or parts of the confession. These latter cases are not included in Table 4.7. Nor, should it be added for completeness, are those cases in which the defendant did not challenge what was in the statement because he or she had, through the interrogation process, come to internalize what was said, whether accurate or not, and accept it as a 'factual account' of what had happened.[22]

As can be seen, the files provide some, albeit limited, information on the reasons why defendants directly challenged the confession made at the police station. The files indicate that in five cases, defendants claimed that they were not fully apprised of the contents of the statement that they had signed either because they had not read it or were reliant on the police as to the content of what they were signing because they were illiterate. Others argued that they had been tortured (8), suffered prolonged interrogation (3), were induced by the police (2), made the confession while 'fearful' (1) or had written out the statement as dictated by the police (1). These findings are noteworthy because, as we shall see in more detail later, there are considerable disadvantages to any defendant who challenges the prosecution and, in particular, a greater risk in claiming that they had been abused whilst in police custody.

In many other cases, the defendant did not withdraw the police station confession but qualified it at trial, usually for the purpose of persuading the court that his or her role in the crime was relatively minor or that there were mitigating circumstances. Thus, for example, at the police station the defendant in K-CFA-W-51 is recorded as having admitted a charge of robbery contrary to Article 263 of the Criminal Law but stated at trial that, 'I didn't participate in premeditating the crime, nor did I hold any knife or tie up any of the victims';[23] in K-CFA-W-65, the defendant is recorded as having confessed to

---

[21] In the three courts where data were collected by researchers from the procuratorate there was a tendency to record the fact of a challenge without providing further details.

[22] This is a not-unimportant category of suspect/defendants because the 'coerced-internalized' confession is attested to in the psychological literature and there are instances in which innocent defendants have gone through their trials without contesting the confession attributed to them.

[23] Article 263 requires only that the robbery be carried out by 'violence, coercion or other methods' with exposure to aggravated sentencing if, for example, a gun is used: there is no provision expressly related to knives.

Table 4.7 Case file analysis: defendant challenges a police station confession at the trial

Site	Case No.	D's Info and Charge	I. Interrogation	II. Prosecution Stage	III. Trial	IV. Trial – Debate
A (A-CFA-B1-1)	10	D(M), 45, unemployed, C: kidnapping	Full confession	Confirmed his confession	D challenged his confession: 'The defendant denied the truthfulness of his earlier confession.' 'The defendant claimed that he had not been at the crime scene.'	D made a statement claiming complete innocence (no remarks). *D was convicted of kidnapping, sentenced to 12 years' imprisonment and he lodged an appeal. Appeal dismissed and decision sustained.
A (A-CFA-B1-1)	11	D(F), 18, attendant, privately retained defender, C: robbery	Full confession	Confirmed her confession	D challenged her confession: 'New statements as to parts of the facts were given.'	No information. Convicted: 6 months' imprisonment.
A (A-CFA-B1-1)	12	D(M), unemployed, privately retained defender, C: robbery	Full confession	Confirmed his confession	D challenged his confession: 'New statements as to parts of the facts were given.'	No information. Convicted: 2 years' imprisonment.
A (A-CFA-B1-1)	14	D(M), 20, unemployed, C: robbery	Full confession	Confirmed his confession	D challenged his confession (no remarks).	No information. *D was convicted of robbery and he lodged an appeal. Appeal dismissed and decision sustained.

A (A-CFA-B1-1)	15	D(M), 18, attendant, privately retained defender, C: robbery	Full confession	Confirmed his confession	D challenged his confession (no remarks).	No information. *D was acquitted, reason: Not guilty in law 'The circumstance of the crime was minor.'
A (A-CFA-B1-1)	87	D(M), 23, unemployed, C: trafficking in narcotic drugs	Full confession	Withdrew his confession	D challenged his confession (no remarks).	D made a statement claiming complete innocence (no remarks). D's final statement 'Didn't traffic in narcotic drugs.' *D was acquitted, reason: Not guilty in law. 'The evidence was insufficient and the charge was not substantiated.'
C (C-CFA-B3-3)	111	D(M), 31, unemployed, privately retained defender, C: blackmail	Full confession	Confirmed his confession	D challenged Co-D's confession: 'The defendant challenged that part of defendant Yang's confession that related to him.'	D made a statement claiming complete innocence: 'The defendant Liu didn't participate in the second, fourth and eighth cases, and there was no evidence to prove the seventh case. The first, third and fifth cases were simply civil disputes and didn't constitute the offence of extorting money and property by blackmail, therefore the allegations against the defendant Liu could not be substantiated.'

Table 4.7 (continued)

Site	Case No.	D's Info and Charge	I. Interrogation	II. Prosecution Stage	III. Trial	IV. Trial – Debate
D (D-CFA-K)	32	D(M), 37, Farmer, privately retained defender, C: fraud	Full confession	Confirmed his confession	D challenged his confession: 'The defendant challenges his statement of confession and thinks that he didn't know he was swindling in the hospital. The defence lawyer thinks he saw one copy of the defendant's confession only, so he challenges the content of the defendant's confession. The defender thinks that this evidence can only prove that the defendant came and talked about the swindle.'	No information. *D was convicted of fraud and he lodged an appeal. Appeal dismissed and decision sustained.
D (D-CFA-K)	42	D(M) 37, privately retained defender C: illegal possession of drugs	Full confession	No information	D challenged his confession: 'The defendant said that what he said before was not true, because he made up the story. The defender thinks the panel should consider what the defendant said in the trial is true.'	No information.

F (F-CFA-N)	1	D(M), 49, Businessman, no defender C: Swindling	Full confession	No confession	D challenged his confession: 'The defendant argued that this was not the truth.'	No information. *D's final statement: 'I didn't deceive. There was nothing wrong for me to receive money for helping in applying for visas. Among the money I received, 20 000 Yuan was lent to me by Ms Zhou. I hope the court could pay attention to the facts.' *D was convicted of swindling and he lodged an appeal. Appeal dismissed.
F (F-CFA-N)	21	D(M), 22, Staff, 2 privately retained defenders C: Taking advantage of one's position to unlawfully take possession of property	Full confession	Confirmed his confession	D challenged his confession on the grounds of police torture. 'I didn't give the mobile phone to the second defendant. Also, I didn't have a share of her money.' *D challenged material/ documentary evidence produced by the prosecution 'I was taken to the public security organ by the victim. I was forced to confess.' The defendant produced a shirt with holes in it and blood-stains which he said were caused by rubbing of the handcuffs.	Court said that the production by the prosecution of the body check report by the detention centre, report of document examination and the statement of a witness who was locked up in the same cell as the defendant proved that the public security organ did not use torture to extract the confessions.

81

Table 4.7 (continued)

Site	Case No.	D's Info and Charge	I. Interrogation	II. Prosecution Stage	III. Trial	IV. Trial – Debate
M (M-CFA-Y)	45	D(M), 34, Farmer, no defender C: Intentional injury	Full confession	Confirmed his confession	D challenged his confession: 'The police station designed this written record for me. As to the second written record, I signed on it without reading the content.' Judge: Why didn't you read it before signing? Defendant: Officer Wang was very polite, so I signed it. Prosecutor: You had been asked whether your previous confessions were true and you had been saying that they were true. Defendant: The first written record was written by me while I was feeling dizzy, during this period I was beaten, I could not move.	No information.

E (E-CFA-L)	3	D(M), 33, unemployed, privately retained defender, C: Offence of obstructing official functions	Full confession	Confirmed his confession	D challenged his confession.	No information.
E (E-CFA-L)	8	D(M), 40, unemployed, privately retained defender, C: intentional harm	Full confession	Confirmed his confession	D challenged parts of his confessions: 'Some of the statements are not true.'	No information.
E (E-CFA-L)	50	D(M), 41, unemployed, privately retained defender, C: transporting, selling and making the drugs	Full confession	Confirmed his confession	D challenged his four statements of confession: 'The fact is not clear, and the police induced my confession.'	D made a statement claiming partial innocence: 'It is not true to charge that I trafficked drugs on many occasions. I didn't buy all the drugs in the last crime. I bought 25 grams, and the other defendants took the rest away. I was present in making the drugs, but I did not participate in it.' Defender: The prosecution's charge is not admissible. The defendant bought the drug from LY City, and it was Mr. Liu instead of the defendant who made drugs.

83

Table 4.7 (continued)

Site	Case No.	D's Info and Charge	I. Interrogation	II. Prosecution Stage	III. Trial	IV. Trial – Debate
E (E-CFA-L)	51	D(M), 38, unemployed, privately retained defender, C: selling the drugs	Full confession	Confirmed his confession	D challenged his confession: 'The fact is not clear, and the police lured [induced] my confession.'	The defendant's statement in the police station was a negative answer to the charge, so the prosecution's charge does not meet the objective situation.
E (E-CFA-L)	52	D(F), 41, unemployed, privately retained defender, C: transporting, selling and making the drugs	Full confession	Confirmed her confession	D challenged her confession: 'I have never sold drugs.' The defendant argued that her confession had been extracted by police torture	No information.
						D made a statement claiming complete innocence: 'It is not true. The defence lawyer argued that the defendant's act was not a crime. The defendant did not conspire to commit the crime nor commit the crime. The defendant's signature was made by torture.'

84

E (E-CFA-L)	58	D(M), 32, unemployed, privately retained defender, C: intentional harm	Full confession	Confirmed his confession	D challenged his confession: 'When the police interrogated me, I was nervous and fearful, so I dare not say all I confessed was true. For example, the iron bar confessed in the first statement is not true. I did not do the act of stabbing the victim nor did I say so.'	D pleaded guilty at the debate stage: 'I am willing to accept legal responsibility.' Defence lawyer: The defendant should bear criminal responsibility suitable to his crime. 'I took the knife there not to plan to hurt the victim intentionally, but I was forced to take out the knife in the fight. I did not hurt others but to frighten them for the sake of self-defence. I didn't stab the victim actively but to confront with them passively, which is not true. That is also the reason why I did not want to sign my name in the written record of interrogation. I did not know the law, so I just thought I would compensate the victim's medical cost.'

Table 4.7 (continued)

Site	Case No.	D's Info and Charge	I. Interrogation	II. Prosecution Stage	III. Trial	IV. Trial – Debate
E (E-CFA-L)	64	D(M), 22, unemployed, privately retained defender, C: harbouring the suspect (Article 310 CL)	Full confession	Confirmed his confession	D challenged his confession:	D made a statement claiming complete innocence: 'The defendant's act did not constitute the offence of harbouring the suspect.'
H (H-CFA-S2)	2	D(M), 33, unemployed, privately retained defender, C: intentional injury	Full confession	Confirmed his confession	D challenged his confession: Defendant: I didn't say that. Judge: Did you see the signature at that time? Defendant: I didn't know, it was the public security officers who read to me. D argued that he had a quarrel with V, that V attacked him first.	No further information. Death penalty, suspended for two years. *D was convicted of intentional injury and he lodged an appeal. Appeal dismissed and decision sustained.

| H (H-CFA-S2) | 7 | D(M), 33, with job, privately retained defender, C: intentional injury | Full confession | Withdrew his confession | D challenged his confession: Prosecutor: Read out the confession statement of the defendant dated 30 June 2004. Judge: Defendant, do you object to the evidence mentioned above? D: They are not true. Judge: Defender, you may express your opinion. DL: D is an illiterate: he did not understand the content and facts in the written record. The defence lawyer objected that the confession statement of the defendant had not been disclosed to the defence before the commencement of the trial. Because of the defendant's illiteracy, there is doubt as to the reliability/value of his signing the confession statement. | Defence lawyer argued that the confession was unreliable. Convicted: 15 years' imprisonment. |

Table 4.7 (continued)

Site	Case No.	D's Info and Charge	I. Interrogation	II. Prosecution Stage	III. Trial	IV. Trial – Debate
H (H-CFA-S2)	29	D(M), 35, unemployed, court appointed defender, C: robbery	Full confession	Confirmed his confession	D challenged his confession: Defendant: I was forced to do so. Judge: Which of your confession statements are true? Defendant: The confession that I am now making in court is true.	Defence lawyer argued that the defendant played a minor role.
H (H-CFA-S2)	41	D(F), unemployed, court appointed defender, C: intentional injury	Full confession	Confirmed her confession	D challenged a factual element in her confession: 'When the security guard saw us, V had not seen the knife yet.'	No further information.

H (H-CFA-S2)	50	D(M), 50, Taxi driver, no defender	Full confession	Withdrew his confession: *D alleged police torture and provided written materials 'Beat me three to four times. They pulled my head to hit against the wall, didn't give me clothes to wear. The previous confessions were made because they beat me and forced me to confess. They didn't let me see the written record, and forced me to sign, including the time when they took a video-recording of me.'	D challenged his confession: 'After I was arrested, the public security organ forced me to confess by torture and used the confessions of the other two persons to incriminate me. No, they forced me to confess by torture.'	D made a statement claiming complete innocence: 'What the prosecution said is true, but they only reached that conclusion by logic but not based on facts. I was wronged by others without any knowledge of it. Shen X had been planning the robbery and theft, but I was forced to bear all the responsibilities….'

Table 4.7 (continued)

Site	Case No.	D's Info and Charge	I. Interrogation	II. Prosecution Stage	III. Trial	IV. Trial – Debate
I (I-CFA-S3)	31	D(M), 40, Hong Kong businessman and political figure in PR China C: Bribery (Article 389, Criminal Law)	Full confession	Confirmed his confession	The defendant challenged the factual basis of the prosecution case. The defendant said that he had written the confessions under the dictation of the officer in charge of the case and after several days and nights without sleep. The defence lawyer raised technical objections to the evidence adduced. The defence lawyer said that it was unrealistic to argue that the defendant could have made a confession in the same words as the person said to have taken the bribe because the confession of the defendant had been made one year after the statement taken from the other person.	No further information. The court rejected the account of the defendant, returned a verdict of guilt and passed a sentence of 18 months' imprisonment.

I (I-CFA-S3)	41	D(M), 35, Deputy manager of a company, privately retained defender, C: Smuggling ordinary goods [jointly charged with another]	Full confession	Confirmed his confession	D challenged his confession: 'I remain silent.' Defender: The defendant was permitted under special circumstances [to undertake the action complained of]; the defendant didn't know whether the [documents] were authentic or fake at the time of delivering the [items]. Defence lawyer argued that the defendant was merely a low-level (and under-educated) worker in the company and did not understand that the documents were being used for Customs' clearance.	D made a statement claiming partial innocence: '(1) In the course of my work, I had never heard the first defendant saying [anything about] smuggling by the company. (2) To my knowledge, the amendment of the [documents] was only an amendment to the unit that was used in calculating the quantity. (3) I didn't take the statements to deceive the Customs.' Convicted: 3 years' imprisonment, suspended for three years; tax evaded confiscated.

Table 4.7 (continued)

Site	Case No.	D's Info and Charge	I. Interrogation	II. Prosecution Stage	III. Trial	IV. Trial – Debate
I (I-CFA-S3)	49	D(M), 51, The person in charge of a company, privately retained defender, C: Swindling, contractual fraud	Full confession (6 statements)	Partly withdraw his confession	D challenged his confession: 'It was the police who told me to write down what they said.' Defence lawyer argued that the prosecution evidence was insufficient to establish swindling and that all that the case showed was a debt relationship.	D made a statement claiming complete innocence: 'I didn't swindle: my relationship with the victim was one of employer and employee; the motive was to ask me to help in dealing with the loan. I was framed. I argued that the 500 000 RMB between his company and me should be a debt dispute.' *D was convicted of swindling, contractual fraud and he lodged an appeal. Appeal dismissed and decision sustained.
I (I-CFA-S3)	54	D(M), 51, Secretary of the district CCP committee of a district, privately retained defender, C: Accepting bribes	Full confession	Confirmed his confession	D challenged various points within his confession and argued that a number of matters were not accurate and that assertions to the contrary needed to be verified.	*D was convicted of accepting bribes and he lodged an appeal. Sentencing amended from 11 years' to 10 years' imprisonment.

92

J (J-CFA-S4)	06	D(M), 24, unemployed migrant, privately-appointed defender, C: intentional injury	Full confession	No information	D challenged his confession. The defendant said that his confession was made under police torture.	The defendant said in court that the police had tortured him to confess to the time and place of the commission of the crime. The defence lawyer thought that the confession could not be the basis for deciding the case. Verdict: Guilty. Life imprisonment.
J (J-CFA-S4)	07	D(M), 25, unemployed migrant, C: intentional injury	Full confession	No information	The defendant said that his statement had been made under police torture.	No further information. Verdict: Guilty. Life imprisonment
J (J-CFA-S4)	10	D(M), 18, unemployed local, privately-appointed defender, C: intentional injury	Full confession	No information	D claimed innocence. Later, after being 'educated' by the judge, he confessed the facts little by little.	No further information. Verdict: Guilty. 3 years' imprisonment suspended for 4 years. Affirmed on appeal.
J (J-CFA-S4)	19	D(F), 28, unemployed local, C: intentional injury	Full confession	No information	The defendant withdrew her confession in court and the authenticity of her statements and the accuracy of the translation of her sign-language were disputed by the defence lawyer.	No further information. Verdict: Guilty.

Table 4.7 (continued)

Site	Case No.	D's Info and Charge	I. Interrogation	II. Prosecution Stage	III. Trial	IV. Trial – Debate
J (J-CFA-S4)	38	D(M), 30, unemployed migrant, privately-appointed defender, C: trafficking drugs	Full confession	No information	D claimed that he had been tortured by the police.	Verdict: Guilty.
K (K-CFA-W)	33	D(M) 34, unemployed migrant, C: intentional injury	Full confession	Confirmed confession	Denied involvement. 'The allegation is not true. I didn't chop anyone....I didn't enter the crime scene....I was scared at the time: I only said I chopped and injured others; in fact, I didn't chop anyone.'	Verdict: Guilty. 12 years' imprisonment. Sustained on appeal.
K (K-CFA-W)	43	D(M), 36, self-employed local, privately-appointed defender, C: intentional injury	Full confession	Confirmed confession	D withdrew confession.	Verdict: Guilty. Life imprisonment.

K (K-CFA-W)	44	D(M), 21, unemployed local, C: intentional injury	Full confession	Confirmed confession	D: 'Some of [the statements] are not true. I was interrogated by the police for a long time. I spoke some things wrongly.'	Verdict: Guilty. Life imprisonment.
K (K-CFA-W)	47	D(M), 20, unemployed local, privately-appointed defender, C: intentional injury	Full confession	Confirmed confession	D withdrew confession: 'I didn't stab the victim with a knife.'	Verdict: Guilty. 3 years' imprisonment.
L (L-CFA-X)	24	D(M), 36, unemployed local, C: rape and robbery	Withdrew confession: 'I didn't commit a crime. I never did anything illegal. The police beat me and I was forced to confess as they wanted.'	Denied confession: 'The charge is not true: I didn't rape any woman.'	D: 'Some of [the statements] are not true. I was interrogated by the police for a long time. I spoke some things wrongly.'	Verdict: Guilty.

Table 4.7 (continued)

Site	Case No:	D's Info and Charge	I. Interrogation	II. Prosecution Stage	III. Trial	IV. Trial – Debate
L (L-CFA-X)	57	D(M), 25, unemployed local, privately-appointed defender, C: rape and intentional injury	Full confession	Confirmed confession	D withdrew confession: 'After I was beaten by the police, I don't know anything. I didn't participate in the crime.'	Verdict: Guilty.

20 robberies and at trial added the minor qualification: 'I didn't touch the victim's waist with a knife in the fourteenth charge'; and in J-CFA-S4-11, the defendant qualified his confession to multiple robberies by stating that he had not taken part in the sixth robbery.

Of course, in the overwhelming majority of cases, the defendant did not challenge the police station confession which was reinforced by repetition at trial or by a plea for mitigated punishment. In F-CFA-N-015, for example, the defendant, having confessed at the police station, told the court: 'I know I was wrong. I hope the court can give lighter punishment'; in J-CFA-S4-05, on a charge of robbery, the defendant's account at trial was that the offence of robbery was committed because he was poor; in J-CFA-S4-58, on a charge of intentional killing, the defendant stated: 'I realize I had no sense of law following instruction [by the Judge]. I deserve a judicial punishment for my extreme act in violating the law'; and in K-CFA-W-13, on a charge of intentional homicide, the defendant underlined her earlier confession to intentional homicide telling the court: 'I urge the collegial bench to sentence me to death.'[24]

INTERROGATING SUSPECTS: EVIDENCE AGAINST ACCOMPLICES

In addition to securing confessions, early research in both the UK and USA has shown that police interrogation leads to suspects incriminating accomplices, although, for various reasons,[25] the extent to which this happens is not clear (McConville and Baldwin, 1981). In a USA study, Wald et al. (1967) found that police interrogation helped identify accomplices in 12 per cent of cases, and provided incriminating evidence against accomplices in 18 per cent of cases. The USA study by Witt (1973) similarly found that the police were able to secure evidence implicating others in approximately 12 per cent of the cases studied. Softley (1980) found that suspects 'gave information about other persons' in 43 per cent of cases. Although this is a significantly higher percentage than that found in the American studies, it is not known whether Softley's figure related specifically to accomplices, and if so, whether these were otherwise unknown accomplices, or indeed whether the information secured in this way was of material significance in any further police action.

In the present study we found that the incidence of suspects incriminating others was considerably higher than that reported in the USA or the UK.[26] This is exactly in line

---

[24] One can see a reflection of this in the 'leaked' excerpt of the transcript of Yang Jia's interrogation (arising out of the stabbing of six Shanghai police officers in 2008) which might explain in part why some defendants act in this way. According to the document leaked the police said during interrogation: 'Aren't you giving any thought to your family? Only if you comply with the government will the "Party and government" treat your family kindly.' (Yang Jia's mother had been locked up in a psychiatric hospital shortly after Yang Jia's detention.) See, http://news.boxun.com/forum,201005/boxun2010/130889.

[25] Apart from methodological difficulties in empirically quantifying such data, it may serve the interests of both suspects and police that information of this nature derived from informants or suspects does not enter the official records.

[26] For a case study involving accomplice evidence see, Simpson (2003) describing how police in Sichuan, having missed vital clues, eventually solved the murder of Shirine Harburn more than two

Table 4.8 Suspect incriminated others

	BC 7 Sites		IC 6 Sites		All Sites	
Yes	196	30.1	197	48.3	393	37.1
No	455	69.9	211	51.7	666	62.9
Not known	75	–	10	–	85	–
Total	726	100.0	418	100.0	1144	100.0

with expectations given that in China co-operation with the investigating authorities, as through voluntary surrender, confession or implicating accomplices, will lay a foundation for a lesser sentence. Although the numbers who were prepared to incriminate others varied (sometimes markedly) as between the 13 sites, overall around 30 per cent of the Basic Court suspects and almost half of the Intermediate Court suspects were recorded as having incriminated others. The results are presented in Table 4.8.

Some examples of co-operation through the supply of information about accomplices are set out below:

K-CFA-W-36: In a case of robbery contrary to Article 263 of the Criminal Law, the suspect made three confession statements to the police in the course of which he provided information implicating three co-defendants. In sentencing him, the Intermediate Court acknowledged his co-operation: 'The defendant has assisted the police in arresting the [three] co-defendants following his own arrest. He has meritorious performance; thus his punishment can be reduced according to law.'[27]

K-CFA-W-18: The police arrested X for possession of illegal drugs. In order to gain merit, X reported to the police the involvement of K-CFA-W-18 in the drugs trade. At the suggestion of the police during the investigation, X then telephoned K-CFA-W-18 and asked him to supply 2 kilos of heroin at a fixed price of RMB 220 per gram. As K-CFA-W-18 handed over the drugs, he was arrested by the police.

J-CFA-S4-32: The suspect, one of a group, was arrested on a charge of inflicting intentional injury contrary to Article 234 of the Criminal Law causing the victim's death. After being detained by the police, the defendant provided information which assisted the police in catching one of the others involved.

In a similar way, the information supplied by suspects led to the arrest of criminals other than their own accomplices.

---

years after the killing. A police informer overheard Li boasting that he had killed a foreigner. After arrest, Li implicated Mao whose DNA was then found to match blood stains on Harburn's clothes that had been extracted by police in the UK and brought to China two years after the killing.

[27] The Case Files provide evidence that the courts make a distinction between the supply of information about on the one hand accomplices or other criminals which has been verified and on the other that which the police have failed to substantiate. Thus, for example, in Site I, Case I-CFA-SY-045, where the defendant tendered information allegedly concerning the trafficking of drugs by others and sought credit for this, the court is reported to have responded: 'The police are carrying out investigations on this but, as it has not been proved to be true [yet], this would not count to meritorious performance.'

K-CFA-W-02: The defendant was arrested by the police on a charge of smuggling goods contrary to Article 153 Criminal Law involving a substantial evasion of customs duty. In sentencing the defendant, the Intermediate Court stated that the defendant was entitled to 'significant meritorious performance' in that he had reported smuggling by others and in consequence other crimes had been solved.

INTERROGATING SUSPECTS: EVIDENCE OF INVOLVEMENT IN OTHER CRIMES

American and British studies have found that suspects under interrogation, in addition to confessing their own crimes and incriminating others, sometimes provide other information to the police about their involvement in the crime under investigation (e.g. revealing the whereabouts of drugs or weapons), or provide information about their involvement in other crimes.[28] Whereas these studies found that few suspects provided such information (Softley (1980) reported a figure of 17 per cent but others have emphasized that such information is rarely provided and is usually fairly vague in nature),[29] in the present study we found that suspects in China were recorded as having routinely provided information about their involvement in crime. As Table 4.9 shows, almost 40 per cent of Basic Court suspects and almost 60 per cent of Intermediate Court suspects provided such information (although once again the percentages varied markedly across the individual sites for reasons we are unable to explain).

A closer look at the files of those cases in which suspects provided other evidence of their involvement in crime showed that for the most part this 'other evidence' related in fact to the particular crime under investigation. So, for example, suspects provided information as to the whereabouts of stolen goods, gave information about their motives and *modus operandi*, or admitted that they had committed similar crimes many times before without detection. The following are illustrative examples:

A-CFA-B1-040: The defendant, a 21-year-old migrant, was caught after the victim of a theft gave a good description of the offender to the police. In convicting him, the court acknowledged that the defendant had not only confessed but had frankly admitted to committing crimes that had not been discovered by the judicial organs.

Table 4.9 Suspect provided other evidence of his/her involvement in crime

	BC 7 Sites		IC 6 Sites		All Sites	
Yes	194	39.2	223	57.6	417	47.3
No	301	60.8	164	42.4	465	52.7
Not known	231	–	31	–	262	–
Total	726	100.0	418	100.0	1144	100.0

[28] M. Wald et al. (1967); Stephens, Flanders and Cannon (1972); Witt (1973); Irving (1980); Softley (1980).

[29] See, for example, Stephens, Flanders and Cannon (1972) and McConville and Baldwin (1981), p. 144.

A-CFA-B1-110: On a charge of robbery, the prosecutor told the court that 'the defendant had frankly confessed to other crimes of the same kind that the judicial organs had not discovered thus suggesting that he deserves a more lenient sentence.'

The greater tendency on the part of suspects in China to confess, provide evidence against others and to give other information about their involvement in the crime is also clearly related to the fact that, as explained above, there is no right to silence under Chinese law. In fact, suspects have a duty to answer questions 'truthfully', and may refuse to answer questions only if they are 'irrelevant to the case' (Article 93, 1996 CPL). Further, Article 68 of the Criminal Law of the People's Republic of China provides that defendants who perform 'meritorious service' by exposing offences committed by others are entitled to a lighter punishment, thereby providing suspects with an incentive to incriminate others.

POLICE INVESTIGATION: COLLECTION OF EVIDENCE OTHER THAN THROUGH INTERROGATION

As we have seen, Article 42, 1996 CPL provides for seven types of evidence, any item of which must be 'verified before it can be used as the basis for deciding cases' (although what is meant by verification is not addressed). The types of evidence listed are: material evidence and documentary evidence; testimony of witnesses; testimony of victims; confessions and exculpations of suspects and defendants; expert conclusions; records of inquests and examinations; and audio-visual materials.[30] The duty on the PSB is to collect and obtain evidence 'to prove the criminal suspect guilty or innocent or to prove the crime minor or grave' (Article 89, 1996 CPL).

The PSB power to conduct 'inquests or examinations of the sites, objects, people and corpses relevant to a crime' extends to assigning or inviting experts to carry out such investigations under their supervision (Article 101, 1996 CPL). All individuals and units have a duty to preserve the scene of a crime and to notify the police to send officers to hold an inquest (Article 102, 1996 CPL). Where the cause of death is unclear the PSB have the power to order an autopsy (Article 104, 1996 CPL), and they can conduct an examination of the suspect or the victim 'to ascertain some of his characteristics or physiological condition, or the circumstances of the injury' (Article 105). Suspects who refuse to be examined can be examined compulsorily (*ibid.*). The police have extensive powers of search, not only of the suspect's person, belongings or premises but also those of individuals suspected of hiding either the suspect or relevant evidence and may also search 'other relevant places' (Article 109, 1996 CPL). Article 112, 1996 CPL requires that during such searches the person to be searched 'or his family members, neighbours or other eyewitnesses shall be present at the scene',[31] and all individuals and units have a duty to hand

---

[30] According to research undertaken on 150 randomly selected cases in an unnamed site in China, Zuo Weimin (2008) found that the average number of pieces of written evidence per case almost doubled in 2004 as compared to 1984 and 1994 and the increase in evaluation conclusions and written records of investigations and examinations was even higher.

[31] Article 112 also provides that searches of women shall be conducted by female officers.

The construction of the police case 101

over to the police material evidence, documentary evidence or audio-visual material 'which may prove the criminal suspect guilty or innocent' (Article 110, 1996 CPL).

Article 115, 1996 CPL requires that all articles and documents seized be carefully and jointly checked by the police and eyewitnesses, listed and copies of the list be duplicated on the spot and signed and sealed by the police, the eyewitnesses and the holder, with a copy provided to the holder. Article 119 provides that 'when certain special problems relating to a case need to be solved in order to clarify the circumstances of the case, experts shall be assigned or invited to give their evaluations'. If the suspect or victim disagrees with the evaluation a supplementary expert verification or another expert verification 'may' be conducted if the suspect or victim submits an application requesting a second evaluation (Article 121, 1996 CPL).

In addition to interrogation, the police will in all jurisdictions, as a matter of standard practice, seek to secure relevant evidence by other means. Indeed, in China, as in other civil law jurisdictions, it is not possible to secure a conviction on the basis of a confession alone. Article 46, 1996 CPL expressly provides that 'stress shall be laid on evidence, investigation and study; credence shall not be readily given to oral statements. A defendant cannot be found guilty and sentenced to a criminal punishment if there is only his statement but no evidence.' Even in common law countries such as England and Wales, where there is no legal requirement that a confession be corroborated, research has shown that the police will search the suspect on arrest and they may, in addition, search the home or place of abode of suspects particularly in property-related offences. Search of the person on arrest is standard practice not only because it might uncover evidence relevant to the offence under consideration but also because the police have a duty to ensure that the suspect is not in possession of unlawful items such as drugs or offensive weapons (which, if present, may lay the foundation for other charges) or of offensive weapons or other items that could be used to cause harm to the police or the suspect himself or herself. Search of the individual's property is also common because, for example, it provides the police with an opportunity to trace stolen goods, locate the proceeds of crime or to find further evidence to determine whether the suspect is a user or dealer of drugs, an opportunist thief or a persistent predicate felon.

There is little doubt that search of the person on initial detention is also standard practice in China[32] but the case files appear to record such searches only where they produce evidence relevant to the offence which is the subject of investigation. Searches of the person are typically recorded in drug-related cases or in inter-personal offences where a weapon is involved, while searches of a suspect's place of abode occur most often where goods obtained by theft or deception are being sought. The total number of recorded searches of the person and of property, which no doubt understate the actual frequency, is set out in Table 4.10 and Figure 4.1.

Additionally the police in China utilize information gathered at the crime scene, post mortem examinations and various 'expert assessments/conclusions' relating primarily

---

[32] Despite the fact that the PRC Constitution, Article 37, provides that, 'No citizen may be arrested except with the approval or by a decision of a people's procuratorate or by decision of a people's court, and arrests must be made by a public security organ. Unlawful detention or deprivation or restriction of citizens' freedom of the person by other means is prohibited and unlawful search of the person of citizens is prohibited.'

Table 4.10 Search person and search property

	BC 7 Sites		IC 6 Sites		All Sites	
Search person	111	15.3	112	26.8	223	19.5
Search property	199	27.4	103	24.6	302	26.4

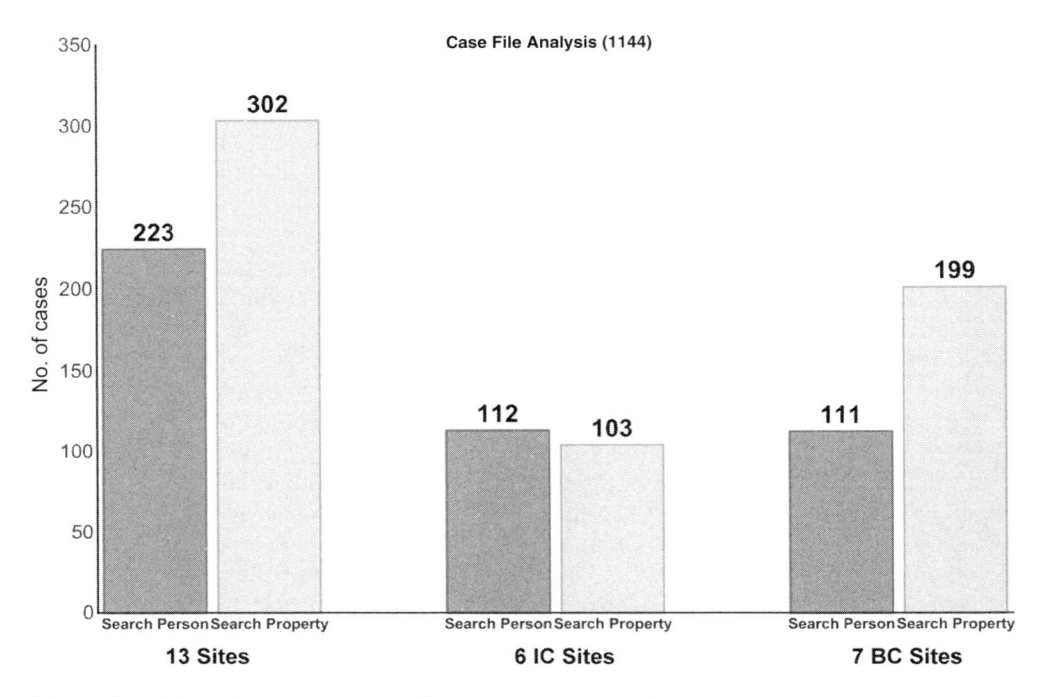

Figure 4.1 Searches of persons and property – 13 sample sites

to the value of stolen property. In cases where there has been death or serious injury, the police file will typically contain a crime scene report supported by diagrams and photographs. In homicide and other offences against the person, forensic reports will be submitted detailing the cause of death and the nature and extent of injuries supported by photographic evidence. These necessarily all become part of the police file whether or not the inquest or crime scene examination produces evidence linking the suspect to the crime. Indeed, in most cases, there is no forensic link to the suspect. Forensic examination of any kind is infrequent (except in drugs cases) but this may occur where the police are already satisfied that the case is being resolved successfully as, for example, in K-CFA-W-01:

> *K-CFA-W-01:* Following his detention, the suspect made a confession which led the police to the weapon said to have been used and the clothes worn at the time of the robbery for which the initial detention had been made. Following this, the police forensic team undertook a DNA examination to forensically link the suspect with the crime and additionally carried out a fingerprint examination of a Nokia mobile phone, the subject of the robbery.

Table 4.11 Means of collecting evidence other than interrogation

	BC 7 Sites		IC 6 Sites		All Sites	
Scientific investigation	179	24.7	116	27.8	295	25.8
Inquest and examination	217	29.9	295	70.6	512	44.8
Expert conclusion	331	45.6	223	53.3	554	48.4

Table 4.12 Means of collecting evidence other than interrogation

	BC 7 Sites	IC 6 Sites	All Sites
Search person	111	112	223
Search property	199	103	302
Scientific investigation	179	116	295
Inquest and examination	217	295	512
Others	46	150	196
Expert conclusion	331	223	554

Data on the utilization of non-confession evidence other than searches are set out in Table 4.11.

There was considerable variation from site to site in respect of scientific investigation, this being heavily utilized in three Basic Court sites (D, F and G) and two Intermediate Court sites (J and L) but otherwise rarely used. This appears to be more a function of police practice than basic capability because, for example, there were both great variations within a single city in this respect (Site G and Site H) and as between cities. Certainly, we can say that whilst the police in certain less-economically developed areas (such as Sites E and M) lacked state-of-the-art forensic equipment, others (such as Sites A, B, C and H) were highly developed cities in which the police did not lack modern equipment.

The overall detailed picture of the inclusion of non-confession evidence in police files is set out in Table 4.12.

Overall it is clear that, beyond the suspect, the police in China look for evidence from other traditional sources: victims; occurrence and post-occurrence witnesses; the crime scene itself; the instruments of crime; documents associated with the event in question; and the object of the crime. We are not able to assess the probative value of such evidence but our analysis demonstrates that the police in China gather such evidence in serious and non-serious cases alike. In the 65 cases examined in the Intermediate Court Site E, for example, the police presented at least 594 witness statements taken from 473 witnesses[33] together with 52 victim statements taken from 42 victims.[34] In addition, the police arranged for post mortem reports to be carried out on the victims in 39 cases, the

---

[33] We have discounted the duplication of statements in multiple defendant cases. However, our researchers failed to record the actual number of witness statements or witnesses in six cases.

[34] These statements were drawn from only 26 cases, the residue consisting of crimes in which the victim had been killed.

reports and ancillary photographs being a core part of the prosecution case file. The police also conducted crime scene investigations and made reports in 40 cases supported by 264 photographs; undertook fingerprint examinations (3); conducted DNA tests (3); analysed substances suspected to be drugs (6); carried out forensic examinations of weapons (4); prepared medical reports on the extent of bodily injuries (5); and prepared expert reports on the value of stolen or damaged goods (5). The extent and nature of this evidence collection was replicated in other research sites.

RECOMMENDATION FOR PROSECUTION

As explained above, if, having completed their investigations, the police conclude that the facts are clear and that there is sufficient and reliable evidence of guilt, they are obliged under Article 129, 1996 CPL to make a written recommendation to the procuratorate that the suspect be prosecuted. All of the cases in our sample were cases which proceeded to the procuratorate level. Accordingly it is no surprise that in all but one of our cases the police recommended that the suspect be prosecuted.[35]

If the police conclude that the suspect's 'criminal responsibility should not have been investigated' the police are obliged under Article 130, 1996 CPL to release the suspect 'immediately' and to issue a 'release certificate'. Article 130 also states that 'the People's Procuratorate which originally approved the arrest shall be notified' of this police decision.

The one case in our sample (H-CFA-S2-21, Site H) in which non-prosecution was recommended was treated by the police as falling within neither Article 129 nor Article 130.[36] It was a case in which the suspect voluntarily surrendered himself to the police and made a full confession to smuggling 'ordinary goods' contrary to Article 153 of the Criminal Law 1997. The suspect was a 34-year-old college educated professional male who fully confessed to the offence. It was therefore a case in which the facts were clear and the evidence reliable and sufficient, and accordingly under Article 129 the police had no discretion but to make a written recommendation for prosecution. However, they chose to recommend non-prosecution. Having done so, they did not treat the case as falling under Article 130, which would have required them to release the suspect, presumably because it was not a case in which investigation showed that 'criminal responsibility should not have been investigated'. Instead, the police took the middle course of

---

[35] The police may use administrative measures (e.g. Regulations of the PRC on Punishments in Public Order and Security Administration, Decision on Strictly Forbidding Prostitution) to dispose of some criminal cases. For example, in a district of medium-size in central and southern China neighbouring Guangdong Province in 2001, the police detained a total of 426 suspects, of whom 140 were arrested (33 per cent), 74 re-educated through labour (17 per cent), 182 granted bail pending trial (43 per cent), 18 given residential surveillance (4 per cent) with one (0.2 per cent) charge withdrawn. Suspects subjected to administrative measures do not enjoy the minimum requirements set out in the international covenants. See Tang Liang (2004). See also Huang Wensheng (2009); Fang and Wang (2009), pp. 112–119.

[36] Technically we could have excluded this case from our sample because our sample was drawn from prosecuted cases but this one file had been retained in the court files and was included by our researcher. We have reported what we found.

passing the case to the procuratorate but with a recommendation that the suspect not be prosecuted. The procuratorate interrogated the suspect[37] (who confirmed his confession) but ultimately exercised its discretion pursuant to Article 142, 1996 CPL not to prosecute on the basis that the crime was deemed 'minor'.[38]

As in common law countries, the police/prosecution sought to differentiate between alleged offenders on the basis of the degree of involvement in the offence and alleged culpability. In J-CFA-S4-50–53, on an offence of kidnapping by a group of defendants, the police drew a distinction between the principal offender (J-CFA-S4-50) who had initiated the kidnapping scheme and who had gathered the others together for this purpose and who should accordingly bear greatest responsibility, and the others who had taken, in varying ways, a lesser part. While the principal offender received a term of 13 years' imprisonment, the defendant who was least involved received only 4 years', the prosecutor indicating that he had given the first defendant information as to the whereabouts of the victim even though he had known what the principal offender intended to do. This pattern of differentiation was repeated throughout all research sites.

CONCLUSION

In constructing the case for the prosecution, the police in China employ a full range of methods to collect evidence for use at trial or as required as part of their general investigatory and crime control role. In discharging these functions, the police place heavy reliance upon their powers to apprehend and detain suspects with a view to obtaining confessions or other evidence useful in their general policing role. From the case file analysis it appears that the greatest concentration of police effort is upon securing a confession from those believed to be guilty of an offence and in this regard they appear to be remarkably successful. Such evidence is buttressed by resort to other standard investigative strategies including search of the person, search of property, seizing of real evidence, crime scene reports, expert evaluation of such things as drugs and the value of stolen or damaged goods. It is clear that, in so far as can be inferred from the case files,[39] the police, rather than gathering any and all evidence about the crime (as they are mandated to do), pack their files with as much evidence as possible against the suspect to support or be included alongside the confession which, in almost all cases, lies at the heart of the case for the prosecution.

---

[37] The suspect advised the procuratorate that he had hired a lawyer himself.
[38] Article 142 requires that the People's Procuratorate make a decision not to initiate a prosecution with respect to a case that is minor and the offender need not be given criminal punishment.
[39] An inspection of the files can only disclose what the police did and what they adduced as evidence. What it cannot do is provide information in regard to material evidence which the police failed to discover or having discovered it failed to preserve. As we shall see, prosecutors and judges are sometimes critical of police investigation skills and of their lack of professionalism.

5. Pre-trial preparation of prosecutors

INTRODUCTION

Once they have completed their investigations, the police in China transfer the case file to the procuratorate with a recommendation as to whether or not the suspect should be prosecuted. In our sample of cases the police recommended prosecution in all but one case.

In this chapter we set out the powers and duties of the procuratorate in China and, drawing upon our case file analysis and our interviews with prosecutors, provide an overview of what prosecutors do in practice. We examine the steps taken by the prosecutor to evaluate the strength and persuasiveness of the police case and any action that they take in this regard utilizing the powers invested in them by the 1996 CPL and other provisions.

THE PROCURATORATE: POWERS AND DUTIES UNDER THE 1996 CPL

As previously explained, if, having completed its investigation, the public security organ concludes that the facts are clear and the evidence 'reliable and sufficient', the security organ is mandated to make a written recommendation for prosecution and to transfer the case file and evidence to the procuratorate for examination and decision:

> Article 129, 1996 CPL: After a public security organ has concluded its investigation of a case, the facts should be clear and the evidence reliable and sufficient and, in addition, it shall make a written recommendation for prosecution, which shall be transferred, together with the case file and evidence, to the People's Procuratorate at the same level for examination and decision.

It is the duty of the procuratorate to decide whether prosecution should be initiated (Article 136, 1996 CPL). Article 138, 1996 CPL provides that the procuratorate must make a decision on prosecution within one month of receiving the papers from the police, with an extension of half a month permitted in 'major or complex cases'.[1] This time limit is subject to the power of the procuratorate to either request that the police carry out a supplementary investigation or to carry out such investigation itself (Article 140, 1996 CPL).

In examining the case, the procuratorate are directed by Article 137, 1996 CPL to 'ascertain' the following matters:

---

[1] If the case is transferred to another procuratorate the time limit is recalculated from the date of receipt by the receiving procuratorate.

1) Whether the facts and circumstances of the crime are clear, whether the evidence is reliable and sufficient and whether the charge and the nature of the crime has been correctly determined;
2) Whether there are any crimes that have been omitted or other persons whose criminal responsibility should be investigated;
3) Whether it is a case in which criminal responsibility should not be investigated;
4) Whether the case has an incidental civil action; and
5) Whether the investigation of the case is being lawfully conducted.

As part of the process of ascertaining these matters, Article 139, 1996 CPL directs that the procuratorate 'shall' interrogate the suspect and 'heed the opinions of the victim and of the persons entrusted by the criminal suspect and the victim'.

Having considered the evidence, the procuratorate has to decide whether or not to prosecute. Article 141, 1996 CPL provides that if (a) 'the facts of a criminal suspect's crime' have been ascertained, (b) the 'evidence is reliable and sufficient', and (c) the procuratorate considers that 'criminal responsibility should be investigated according to law', the procuratorate 'shall make a decision to initiate a prosecution and shall . . . initiate a public prosecution'. If the procuratorate decides not to prosecute, the decision has to be announced publicly and provided in written form both to the suspect and to his or her (work) unit (Article 143, 1996 CPL).

The existing literature on the role and practices of the procuratorate suggests that, in contrast with the decision to prosecute, the decision *not* to prosecute is more likely to lead to confusion and controversy. The confusion arises because there are a number of different provisions under which non-prosecution may be justified, and the relationship between the various provisions is not straightforward. The controversy arises because, unlike the decision to prosecute, the decision not to prosecute can be challenged by the victim or the victim's family, the police and even the suspect himself.

There are three broad categories of case in which the procuratorate may decide not to prosecute: 'decision not to prosecute because of doubts', 'decision not to prosecute relatively' and 'decision not to prosecute absolutely'. We explain below what is meant by each of these categories.

DECISION 'NOT TO PROSECUTE BECAUSE OF DOUBTS'

As mentioned above, Article 141, 1996 CPL states that the procuratorate 'shall' initiate a prosecution if, in addition to being satisfied in respect of other matters, it is satisfied that the evidence is 'reliable and sufficient'. The converse of this provision is that the procuratorate may decide not to prosecute if the evidence is not reliable or is incomplete. Although the procuratorate has the power under Article 140, 1996 CPL to require the police to carry out a supplementary investigation or to carry out such investigation itself if there are doubts relating to the evidence, such supplementary investigation must be completed within a month and cannot be conducted more than twice. According to Article 140, if, having exhausted the supplementary investigation route, the procuratorate 'still believes that the evidence is insufficient and the case does not meet the conditions for initiation of a prosecution, the People's Procuratorate may decide not to initiate a prosecution'. As one prosecutor we interviewed explained:

J-IP-S4-08 [Prosecutor]: Some suspects won't be prosecuted after arrest because of problems in the case. For instance, in an intentional injury case that I handled, the criminal suspect admitted that he injured the victim but after a photo-identification, the victim said it was not the criminal suspect who injured him. Since there was insufficient evidence, we decided not to prosecute the criminal suspect. Eventually, we released him on the ground that although he did participate in the event, he did not cause the injury.

The Supreme People's Procuratorate has supplied further guidance on what is meant by sufficiency of evidence through two publications issued in 2001 and later amended in 2007: 'Quality Standard for Decisions to Prosecute Cases by the Procuratorate (Trial Implementation)'; and 'Quality Standard for Decisions Not to Prosecute Cases by the Procuratorate (Trial Implementation)' ('the SPP rules').[2] These state that the quality of evidence is high if the facts can be proved through legal and valid evidence and without reliance on illegal evidence. Article 286 of the SPP rules states that evidence is 'insufficient' where there are doubts about the evidence and it is not possible to ascertain its truthfulness; there is insufficient evidence to prove the factual elements of the offence; there are inconsistencies in the evidence, or the evidence is capable of supporting possibilities other than guilt.

If the procuratorate decides not to prosecute because of doubts about the evidence, but further evidence emerges later in support of prosecution, the procuratorate has the power to initiate a prosecution at that later stage (Article 287, SPP Rules). It is this which probably explains the discretionary 'may' in paragraph 4 of Article 140, because if the evidence is insufficient and the case does not meet the requirements for initiation of prosecution it is difficult to see what choice the procuratorate has but to not prosecute. The discretion in paragraph 4 of Article 140 preserves the ability of the procuratorate to revisit the decision not to prosecute.

'DISCRETIONARY DECISION NOT TO PROSECUTE'[3]

This refers to a decision made by the procuratorate pursuant to a discretion found in the second paragraph of Article 142, 1996 CPL:

> With respect to a case that is minor and the offender need not be given criminal punishment or need be exempted from it according to the Criminal Law, the People's Procuratorate may decide not to initiate a prosecution.

This provision is replicated in Article 289 of the SPP Rules. The Rules provide further guidance to procuratorates as to the circumstances in which they may decide not to prosecute pursuant to this discretion:

1) The suspect is a minor or elderly, his malicious intent to commit the crime is relatively minor, and the harmful impact of the case to society is not serious;

---

[2] See also, http://cip.chinalawinfo.cn/law/137594/viewspace-2092; and http://vip.chinalawinfo.com/newlaw2002/SLC/slc.asp?db=chl&gid=66040.

[3] Sometimes referred to as 'not to prosecute relatively'.

2) The suspect has committed a minor crime as a result of a dispute between relatives, neighbours, schoolmates or colleagues, and he has admitted his guilt, apologized, made compensation, actively compensated the loss of the victim, has been forgiven by, or reached a settlement with, the victim, has been seriously performing the settlement agreement, and the harmful impact of the case to the society is not serious;
3) The suspect is a first-time offender and the offence is minor, and his malicious intent to commit the crime is relatively minor;
4) The suspect has committed minor crimes such as thefts occasionally because of inability to make a living, and he would not cause great harm to personal safety of others; and
5) The suspect committed a crime arising from a mass incident, and he was only an ordinary participant in the relevant incident.[4]

DECISION 'NOT TO PROSECUTE ABSOLUTELY'

The first paragraph of Article 142, 1996 CPL directs that the procuratorate 'shall make a decision not to initiate a prosecution' if the criminal suspect 'is found to be under one of the circumstances provided for in Article 15, 1996 CPL'. The circumstances provided for under Article 15 are as follows:

a. The act is 'obviously minor, causing no serious harm, and is therefore not deemed to be a crime';
b. The limitation period for criminal prosecution has expired;
c. A special amnesty decree has granted exemption from prosecution;
d. It is a crime that requires a complainant and there is either no complainant or the complaint has been withdrawn;
e. The suspect/defendant is deceased;
f. There are 'other laws' which provide an exemption from investigation of criminal responsibility.

As mentioned above, the decision not to prosecute may be challenged. If the police disagree with the decision they can ask the procuratorate to reconsider, and if this request is rejected they can appeal to the procuratorate at the next higher level (Article 144, 1996 CPL).

The victim is also given extensive rights to challenge a decision not to prosecute. By Article 145, 1996 CPL, the procuratorate has a duty to inform the victim in writing that it has decided not to prosecute, and the victim has seven days in which to present a petition to the procuratorate at the next higher level requesting that the latter initiate a prosecution. If the petition is rejected the victim can bring a lawsuit to a People's Court. If the court accepts the case, the procuratorate must transfer the case file to the court.

In a provision which at first sight seems odd, the 1996 CPL grants the suspect a right to appeal against a decision not to prosecute. Article 146 provides that where a decision is taken 'in accordance with . . . Article 142 . . . not to initiate a prosecution', the suspect may within seven days request the procuratorate to conduct a re-examination. The rationale behind this provision becomes clear once it is understood that a decision not to prosecute made pursuant to the second paragraph of Article 142 is based upon a finding that the case is minor or that the suspect is exempted from criminal punishment, *not* upon

---

[4] See *Fazhi Ribao* (Legal Daily), 15 August 2007.

a finding that there is no evidence to justify a prosecution. As Article 142 makes clear, a decision not to prosecute pursuant to this Article does not mean that the suspect escapes without penalty, for the procuratorate may decide that the suspect 'need be given administrative penalty or administrative sanction or his illegal gains need to be confiscated'. As summarized by Chow (2003, pp. 269–270), the power of the procuratorate to exempt defendants from prosecution in this way was 'subject to intense criticism within China because it suffered from many glaring deficiencies; the practice raised serious fairness and rule of law concerns because the procuratorate had the power to find a suspect guilty without a trial and before the suspect had been granted legal counsel'.

We did not seek to measure the overall frequency with which prosecutions were not proceeded with in these ways but occasionally in interviews with prosecutors (IP) the prosecutors volunteered such information and the reasons behind the decisions.

> *F-NN-01:* There were altogether 340 registered cases in [this] People's Procuratorate in our District this year of which 320 were prosecuted and sentenced with some 20 cases withdrawn because either (1) the facts were not clear and sufficient or (2) the circumstances were too minor to constitute a crime according to Article 15 of the CPL.

> *G-SH1-04:* Cases that are not prosecuted are very rare. I have not experienced any. Not prosecuting a case should be very rare; normally this method is not adopted . . . There has been no case returned to the police in recent years. It could be 'not to prosecute' if it is known that the court will not try the case [but] other methods can be found to solve a problem in relation to the police . . .
> Q: Why?
> A: Because you have to spend a lot of energy balancing the different relationships. For example, what can you do if the case cannot be prosecuted because there are problems? All cases have problems; none are perfect. Whether it is because of evidence or from the nature of the case, even sending the case back to the Public Security Bureau to undertake some supplementary investigation will be the subject of inspection.
> Q: Inspection by whom?
> A: Inspection by the internal inspectors [from inside the procuratorate] by the Supreme Procuratorate. The political-legal committee is appointed to do this in difficult cases. The quality of cases also needs to be inspected. . . . There is also a policy standard. For example, if cases inspected during the 'strike hard' period are returned by the court without trial, this would be your responsibility.

> *M-YK-03:* Few cases are not prosecuted. Such cases will be discussed by the prosecution committee and reported to the Upper Level. The Upper Level will examine these every year because of concern over abuse of non-prosecution.
> Q: Have you ever returned matters back to the [PSB] on a regular basis?
> A. Less in recent years. There is an internal regulation in the [PSB]: an investigator will have scores reduced if his case is returned.[5]

> *K-WZ-02:* Few cases are not prosecuted. Most are ones where it is hard to get evidence such as poisoning cases and selling drugs. Maybe a few in each year.

It must not be assumed that the decisions discussed above regarding non-prosecution are simply mechanical applications of established and clear rules. As we have indicated, much of the law in this area is obscure or discretionary. Additionally, as is clear from

---

[5] The reference here is to a case being returned to the PSB as a case not to be prosecuted.

the quotations above, such decisions affect the way in which prosecutors are themselves assessed, remunerated or promoted (non-prosecution is, in effect, a 'performance indicator') and the determination may be influenced by political and social factors. Importantly, given that the decision may be seen as a judgment upon the investigating police officer, the decision is usually not that of the individual prosecutor but is taken at a higher level within the procuratorate (Peng Jianmin, 2010; Yan Xiufang, 2009; and Li and Yang, 2009). Although the decision may be considered as bureaucratically inefficient (a point made by some prosecutors) it is also embraced by many prosecutors because it protects the individual prosecutor from criticism and adverse assessment. Thus, as the following prosecutors put the position:

L-IP-X-09: There are many shortcomings at present. For example, there is a system of running punishments for mistaken cases. Since 50 per cent of my opinions on cases are different from that of my section meeting, who is going to be liable for punishment? Now, the environment of law enforcement is bad: for example, the defendant's criminal act is minor but no-one dares to speak for the defendant in my section's meeting. If you speak for him, you will be suspected of having taken a bribe from the defendant. If the case is complicated, it will be decided by the political-legal committee.

H-IP-S2-02: In fact, prosecutors have no right to decide whether to prosecute or not. . . . This is not a decision of the prosecutor. Many cases . . . are decided by the chief prosecutor or the inspection committee. After the leader's decision, the decision has to be carried out. It still follows the old time administrative management system. The ratio of prosecuting is 100 per cent.

G-IP-S1-01: The decision to prosecute or not to prosecute is not decided by me. It is decided by (a) leaders – the chief prosecutor or very often the leaders in the unit; and (b) there is a three-tier level of approval which the prosecutor has to obey unconditionally. [The prosecutor illustrated this by reference to a co-defendant case in which the judge had one view and the prosecutor had another and, since both were in conflict with each other, 'the political-legal committee intervened and we could only withdraw our prosecution against the first defendant'.] The decision not to prosecute a big or important case has to be signed by the leaders and the political-legal committee.

J-IP-S4-06: There are many procedures in examination and prosecution. Efficiency in handling cases is low. We discuss the case together if there are different understandings as to the facts and the evidence. The decision of the majority will prevail over that of the minority. The decision will then be approved by the director of the department and the chief prosecutor. There are too many procedures and it takes a lot of time. Individual prosecutors like to discuss cases because they will not be investigated for responsibility if there is any mistake: the responsibility will be borne by all the prosecutors.

F-IP-N-05: I think that the decisions by the political-legal committee on whether some complicated cases should be prosecuted are not professional enough because some committee members lack experience in dealing with criminal cases. The work pressure is so great because of the system of investigation of responsibility in failed cases, periodic random selection and examination of our work and the statistics.

J-IP-S4-04: With respect to a case where more than two supplementary investigations have been conducted but the evidence is still insufficient, we will give up initiating the prosecution. There are two conditions: one is absolutely not to prosecute, if the circumstance is too minor to be a crime; the other is relatively not to prosecute. The latter is very common and it needs to be discussed in the department and reported to the Procuratorate Committee for discussion, approval and finally to write the written recommendation for non-prosecution and release the suspect.

F-IP-N-02: According to the Criminal Procedure Law the prosecution standard is 'the facts are clear and the evidence is sufficient and reliable'. But some cases do not meet this standard in practice. Cases with basically clear facts and basic evidence are also prosecuted; and cases with unclear facts and insufficient evidence after supplementary investigation are prosecuted. . . . Our task is completed if judges find defendants guilty. But if there is a verdict of innocence, we risk being investigated for having been responsible for handling a mistaken decision to prosecute. So we try to solve the problem internally through such methods as not to prosecute, withdrawal of prosecution and so on.

K-IP-W-03: I obey laws just as a soldier obeys orders. When my personal opinion is inconsistent with the collective decision, I will follow the latter. The prosecution standard is that cases shall be clear and without any doubt. The procedure for non-prosecution is very complicated and the person responsible will be suspected of not doing his best.

J-IP-S4-08: We will be investigated for responsibility for state compensation if the criminal suspect is wrongfully arrested. That is a big constraint on our work.

More generally, some prosecutors indicated that their work was subject to repeated interference at various levels. We shall see examples of this at various points but several respondents were quite clear about the impact this might have:

L-IP-X-05: At the start, I felt pleased with this job. I thought it was an honour to punish guilty people. There are too many cases which involve outside interference. Some leaders bring man-made interference. I feel unhappy over this problem and feel greater pressure especially in cases of innocence. I cannot handle the case completely according to the law. [When asked about further training opportunities, this prosecutor said: There are too many unfair things about my work, so I do not want to have further education [in law]. I want to learn Chinese and journalism instead.]

L-IP-X-07: [When asked what were the main problems he faced as a prosecutor] Some external pressures on my work in handling cases, especially from the leadership.

It is unclear whether such complaints as these arose because they were pressured into proceeding with cases that had evidence deficiencies[6] or whether the cases should have been withdrawn (in the view of the prosecutor) on policy grounds.

THE PROCURATORATE: PRE-TRIAL ACTIVITIES IN PRACTICE

Although Article 129, 1996 CPL provides that a procuratorate's examination for prosecution starts only after the public security organ has concluded its investigation and

---

[6] Prosecuting a case with evidence deficiencies would risk failure in court and hence criticism of the prosecutor unless there is confidence either that, despite the deficiencies, the court would convict or that in the event of an adverse decision, there would be no negative assessment of the prosecutor. However, a number of prosecutors said that cases were nevertheless prosecuted where they felt that the defendant was innocent and their superiors felt otherwise.

transferred the case file and evidence to it,[7] as disclosed in the following comments of two Site G prosecutors we interviewed, they started their work of examination for prosecution from the time they considered approving arrest:

> *J-IP-S4-05:* Actually we start the pre-trial review stage from the approval of arrest. We give the Public Security Bureau an investigation recommendation report. The Public Security Bureau also hopes we can be involved in the case earlier so as to make the transfer of cases easier.

> *J-IP-S4-08:* Actually our examination and prosecution work starts from the approval of arrest. We took the lead in implementing the experimental system of the integration of arrest and prosecution in our county, so we examine evidence strictly when approving the arrest of criminal suspects. . . . When we return the materials of approval of arrest, the Public Security Organ will carry out their one month's investigation. After that, they will transfer the materials they found to us for examination for prosecution.

Our interviews with 96 prosecutors and separate case file analysis revealed that the examination for prosecution stage of the criminal process is an apparently comprehensive affair in which prosecutors discharge numerous tasks.[8] They include such preliminary and fundamental tasks as ensuring that the procuratorate has jurisdiction to handle the case, administrative tasks such as arranging for an interpreter where necessary and core legal tasks such as researching the law and ensuring that the correct charges are preferred. We set out below some of the key tasks mentioned to us by prosecutors, together with supporting data collected on these matters through our case file analysis. Before doing so, however, it is necessary to indicate that, as some prosecutors told us (despite the possible dangers to themselves), decision-making in this setting cannot be understood in conventional Western terms as restricted to the weighing of evidence and considerations of articulated public interest criteria. As we saw above, in relation to the question of non-prosecution, decisions in China are taken within a bureaucratic and extremely hierarchical environment so that individual decisions may have heavy political and socio-cultural overtones which are determinative. Thus, for example:

> *D-IP-K-04:* If the case is assigned to me by a leader or if he gives me a direction on it, we may relax the evidence requirement but we will treat it carefully.

Against this background, we set out below the primary tasks prosecutors engaged in as they sought to strengthen or perfect the case for the prosecution.

---

[7] Article 129, 1996 CPL provides that:

> After a public security organ has concluded its investigation of a case, the facts should be clear and the evidence reliable and sufficient and, in addition, it shall make a written recommendation for prosecution, which shall be transferred, together with the case file and evidence, to the People's Procuratorate at the same level for examination and decision.

[8] This is in contrast to the findings of Zuo Weimin in an unnamed district in China: See, Zuo Weimin (2008). The study found that whilst the provincial procuratorate required that a suspect be questioned at the time of the decision to make an arrest, in practice this questioning often became a mere formality and that despite legal powers conferred by various provisions (such as Article 139, 1996 CPL and Articles 251, 252, 254–259 of the Criminal Procedure Regulations of the Supreme People's Procuratorate) procuratorial agencies rarely engaged in activities other than requiring investigation agencies to gather supplemental evidence.

INFORMING VICTIMS OF THEIR RIGHTS/IDENTIFYING ANY INCIDENTAL CIVIL CLAIMS/NOTIFYING AND LIAISING WITH RELEVANT PARTIES (E.G. VICTIM'S FAMILY, SUSPECT'S FAMILY AND/OR UNIT ETC.)

By Article 139, 1996 CPL, prosecutors must, when examining a case, 'heed the opinions of the victim and of the persons entrusted by the . . . victim'. When asked 'what did you do at the pre-trial stage?' 16 of the prosecutors we interviewed spontaneously mentioned that it was part of their remit to inform victims of their rights and two prosecutors emphasized that this was particularly important where an incidental civil action had been identified.[9] Others mentioned the importance of keeping the victim's family informed and receiving representations from parties involved in the litigation:

> *B-IP-B2-00:* Mainly the activities stipulated in law. To give greater explanation to the defendant and the family of the victim within the scope permitted by law. . . . Some defendants and the family members of victims whose education level is low and who lack legal knowledge, they can understand the law through contacting the prosecutor. The work of a prosecutor is not merely to obtain judgment; he should also discharge his responsibility to properly convince others.

> *D-IP-K-03:* In cases with victims, I have to inform the victim of his or her rights. In addition, I will ask questions of the victim if necessary.

> *M-IP-Y-05:* If it is a case of intentional injury and so on, I will inform the victims that they can lodge an incidental civil action.

Prosecutors sometimes made clear that there were limits as to what they could achieve in these respects:

> *E-IP-L-05:* I will listen to the opinions of the victims and the lawyers of both parties conditionally. I try my best to contact the victim's family but I have no other way if they fail to receive my notice because we are restricted by time limits.

Nonetheless, some prosecutors indicated to us in private that the family of victims could place substantial pressure upon the prosecutor and, unless they could be placated by the process, were a potential source of trouble for the prosecutor if they believed that justice had not been secured at trial, as by complaining to courts at another level or carrying out a campaign or by petitioning Beijing.

VERIFYING THE IDENTITY OF SUSPECTS, CHECKING THEIR CRIMINAL RECORDS, INFORMING SUSPECTS OF THEIR RIGHTS

Prosecutors seek to ensure that the suspect has been correctly identified, and research his or her criminal background to document whether he or she has an existing criminal

---

[9] Of course, many other prosecutors may not have thought it important to mention an activity that they are required by law to undertake so little can be read into the quantitative responses.

Table 5.1 D was recorded as having been informed by the prosecutor of his/her rights

	BC 7 Sites		IC 6 Sites		All Sites	
Yes	638	98.5	381	99.7	1019	98.9
No	10	1.5	1	0.3	11	1.1
Not known	78	–	36	–	114	–
Total	726	100.0	418	100.0	1144	100.0

record and whether there are any circumstances which by law would count towards mitigation of sentence. Although the 1996 CPL does not expressly impose a duty on the procuratorate to inform the suspect of his or her rights, some 33 of the 96 prosecutors we interviewed stated that during their pre-trial review they informed suspects of their rights. In some areas, a written statement of rights was said to be issued to suspects and some said that they required suspects to sign that they had been provided with a copy of their rights. As Table 5.1 illustrates, the case files we examined also recorded that prosecutors informed suspects of their rights in almost all cases.

The following cases illustrate the responses prosecutors gave in relation to the rights of suspects when asked in general terms about what they did at the pre-trial stage:

D-IP-K-01: [After reviewing the case papers] Then I will go to the detention house to interrogate the suspect, give him a letter relating to being a suspect or defendant and their rights and duties with the purpose of protecting his human rights and ask him to sign his name.

D-IP-K-03: [Having explained that the suspect would be interviewed] Our procuratorate began to send the suspect the Letter of the Suspect's Rights and Duties in 1999.

D-IP-K-04: I will interrogate the suspect once, which is a compulsory process. I will give the defendant a Letter of Rights and Duties and ask him questions about the course of the crime. ...

Where prosecutors mentioned that they had informed suspects of their rights, only in a few cases did they mention specific rights, such as the right to a lawyer (and in no case did they volunteer that legal advice would be free) as in the following example:

EIP-L-02: I will inform the suspect of my status and his or her rights such as the right to employ a lawyer, ask him about basic information such as when, why and where he or she was detained and arrested for what charge and some other questions in detail. After this verification, I will ask the suspect if he or she has anything else to tell me and if what he or she said today was true.

Our researchers also noted whether suspects were recorded as having asked for legal advice at the prosecution stage. As can be seen from Tables 5.2–5.4, as recorded in the case files, the request rate varied considerably as between the sites (for example, as high as 100 per cent at Site J and as low as 0 per cent at Site G),[10] but overall we found that around one-third (35.6 per cent) of suspects were recorded as asking for legal assistance

---

[10] It is probable that the prosecutors in Site G did not have a practice of noting any such request.

Table 5.2 Defendant recorded as requesting legal advice/defender: Basic Courts

	Site A		Site B		Site C		Site D		Site F		Site G		Site M	
Yes	48	33.3	45	32.4	9	7.4	5	83.3	24	36.9	0	0.0	13	21.3
No	96	66.7	94	67.6	113	92.6	1	16.7	41	63.1	17	100.0	48	78.7
Not known	13	–	2	–	31	–	64	–	0	–	53	–	9	–
Total	157	100.0	141	100.0	153	100.0	70	100.0	65	100.0	70	100.0	70	100.0

Table 5.3 Defendant recorded as requesting legal advice/defender: Intermediate Courts

	Site E		Site H		Site I		Site J		Site K		Site L	
Yes	28	43.1	15	28.3	34	48.6	31	100.0	36	51.4	22	78.6
No	37	56.9	38	71.7	36	51.4	0	0.0	34	48.6	6	21.4
Not known	0	–	0	–	0	–	29	–	0	–	72	–
Total	65	100.0	53	100.0	70	100.0	60	100.0	70	100.0	100	100.0

Table 5.4 Defendant recorded as requesting legal advice/defender: all cases

	BC 7 Sites		IC 6 Sites		All Sites	
Yes	144	26.0	166	52.4	310	35.6
No	410	74.0	151	47.6	561	64.4
Not known	172	–	101	–	273	–
Total	726	100.0	418	100.0	1144	100.0

at this stage.[11] The case file analysis data revealed that suspects charged with the more serious offences tried in the Intermediate Court are more likely to ask for legal advice (a request rate of 52.4 per cent) than those charged with offences tried in the Basic Court (a request rate of 26.0 per cent), as shown in Tables 5.2–5.4.

We also recorded whether those who asked for legal advice or a defence lawyer managed to secure one. Apart from Site G, in which there was no record of any request for legal advice,[12] we found that suspects were for the most part ultimately (by the date of the trial)[13] successful in securing advice or legal representation in those cases in which they requested it although it is clear that such assistance was not obtained at the prosecution stage.[14] Altogether, the success rate varied from 60 per cent (Site D) to 100 per cent (Sites A, M, H, I, J and K). Overall, almost 88 per cent of the suspects in the Basic Court sample and almost 98 per cent of suspects in the Intermediate Court who are recorded as having requested legal advice at the prosecution stage eventually managed to secure such assistance. More detailed data are presented in Table 5.5 (which deliberately omits Site G).

It was difficult to identify clear patterns in the 22 cases where despite a request for legal advice/defence lawyer having been made the defendant remained unrepresented at trial. Whilst a majority of these cases (63.6 per cent) involved migrants, a substantial minority (36.4 per cent) were locals. In seven of the migrant cases, the defendant stated that he/she had told the family of the arrest but the family had not hired a lawyer. There was a considerable variety of offences ranging from theft (6), to robbery (4), causing intentional injury (2), swindling, rape, harbouring a criminal, misappropriating public funds and drugs. Where known, sentences were often substantial. In the Basic Court cases (15), for example, whilst seven defendants were given a custodial sentence of between five months and one year and one received 18 months, others were sentenced to far heavier terms of

---

[11] In general, our inspection of the records simply recorded 'No' in answer to the question: 'Did the suspect request legal advice/defender?' but occasionally the file annotation might state: 'The defendant expressly gave up his right to a lawyer.'

[12] This would appear to have been a recording artifact of the case files rather than evidence that no suspect had eventually succeeded in securing the services of a lawyer.

[13] The files generally indicated that the suspect had eventually obtained the services of a lawyer. There was no indication that a lawyer had been supplied at the prosecution stage and, indeed, our interviews with prosecutors and defenders show that defence lawyers are not engaged, if at all, until close to the trial.

[14] Our schedule had sought to identify whether suspects had been granted access to a lawyer at this stage but we were unable to obtain such discrete information. From all the evidence we gathered, however, it is clear that lawyers were not present at the prosecution stage.

Table 5.5 Success rate in securing legal advice/defender

Site	Did not retain any defender	Retained defender	Not known	Total who requested advice
Site A	0	48	0	48
Site B	8	35	2	45
Site C	3	5	1	9
Site D	2	3	0	5
Site F	2	22	0	24
Site M	0	13	0	13
Site E	3	25	0	28
Site H	0	13	2	15
Site I	0	33	1	34
Site J	0	31	0	31
Site K	0	36	0	36
Site L	4	18	0	22
Total BC	18	126	3	147
Total IC	4	156	3	163
Total	22	282	6	310

three years, four years (2), five years, seven years, nine years and 13½ years. Illustrative cases drawn from our case file analysis (CFA) are set out below:

> *B-CFA-B2-132:* The suspect was a 19-year-old unemployed and unskilled migrant who was charged with robbery contrary to Article 263 of the Criminal Law. The principal evidence against the suspect was a confession made to the police and a statement supplied by a young boy who was alleged to be his accomplice. At the procuratorate, the suspect requested legal advice and stated that he had already informed his family but that they had not hired a lawyer for him. When the indictment was read at court, the defendant claimed that he did not participate in the robbery. Similarly, the defendant stated that he was not involved in the crime when the victim's statement was produced and when expert evidence as to the injuries was read. He was convicted and sentenced at the Basic Court to four years' imprisonment.

> *C-CFA-B3-052:* The suspect was a local male aged 31, unskilled and unemployed. He was charged with robbery and rape having entered a private house to steal then raping the woman occupant after threatening her with a knife. He made a full confession to the police. Despite having requested legal advice at the prosecutor's office, he remained unrepresented at trial. The defendant made no challenge to the prosecution evidence which consisted primarily of the reading of the victim's statement and expert conclusions on the real evidence. The defendant was sentenced at the Basic Court to 12 years' imprisonment for the robbery and three years for the rape, with a combined sentence of 13½ years' imprisonment.

Fewer details are available for Intermediate Court cases in which, with one exception where the sentence was suspended, all known sentences resulted in custodial terms.

EXAMINING THE LEGALITY OF POLICE ACTIONS

When interviewed, a number of prosecutors mentioned that they checked to ensure that the police had acted lawfully during the investigative stage. Examples given by prosecutors included checking to see whether evidence had been collected legally, whether there had been extended detention and whether the police had mistreated or tortured the suspect. So far as certain kinds of 'unlawfulness' are concerned, the prosecutors' principal concern was to ensure that all procedural requirements (such as having the correct date and signature on relevant case papers) had been complied with. In respect of police mistreatment, some of the prosecutors indicated that they would routinely ask the suspect whether the confession had been induced by mistreatment, while others suggested that they would investigate mistreatment only if the suspect himself alleged that he had been coerced to confess. In a number of cases, prosecutors indicated that, if any allegation of torture was made, they would look to the suspect to provide the necessary supporting evidence[15] and not take account of any torture if there was other evidence. Some voiced understanding of the police where torture had been used. The following are some examples of what prosecutors said about this issue in interviews with us:

E-IP-L-01: I will inform the suspect of his rights and duties, ask about his/her basic information, his/her opinions on the case and if he/she admits his/her crime. If yes, I will ask him/her to tell me the process and result of crime. In addition, I will ask the suspect if there was any torture during the police interrogation. In most cases, the answer is no. If he/she says 'yes', then I will ask when? where? who? how? and the condition of the injury. If the suspect's allegation is true, I will suggest that the police correct their action and conduct a new investigation. But this is quite rare in practice, since the police pay more attention to procedural requirements.

D-IP-K-04: I will give the defendant a Letter of Litigation Rights and Duties and ask him questions on the course of his crime, his criminal intention, if he has any circumstance of meritorious performance or voluntary surrender, how he was caught by the police and if the police extorted the confession by torture. If the suspect has signs of physical injury when he was put into the prison, there should be a record of it.

L-IP-X-03: Many defendants complain that confessions were extracted by torture when we question them. At the review stage, if the defendant claims that there was torture, we will check if there is but the answer is always negative.

L-IP-X-04: The aim and content of our interrogation [of the defendant] is quite different from the police. In general, most defendants withdraw their confession: the rate in drug trafficking cases is at least 90 per cent to near 100 per cent. We will ask them the reason. But so long as the evidence is sufficient, interrogating defendants is just a formality.

M-IP-Y-02: Then I will question the criminal suspect to verify his identity, criminal record, offending process, whether his confession was extorted by torture, whether he wants to withdraw confession and so on.

F-IP-N-01: Except for reading written materials, I interrogate criminal suspects and examine whether the criminal facts as stated in the Bill of Prosecution exist, whether the crimes were committed by the criminal suspects in custody, whether the evidence is sufficient and whether the police extorted confessions by torture.

---

[15] In talking to prosecutors, it was clear to us that none of them saw that it was realistic to pursue allegations of torture (which, if it occurred, often would have taken place many weeks earlier) and all operated on the assumption that any claim of torture would need to be established by the suspect producing evidence of torture.

> *Researcher:* If criminal suspects claim that the police extorted confessions by torture, what will you do?
> *Procurator:* Generally speaking, criminal suspects who are tortured to confess will raise this issue by themselves. I will see whether they have any evidence, listen to their explanation and that of the police. I will leave the allegation if there is other evidence to prove the facts of their crimes. I can understand investigators' work. Sometimes it is very difficult to solve a criminal case if investigators don't adopt certain measures in dealing with criminal suspects. But we cannot simply rely on defendants' confessions that are extorted by torture as the basis of prosecution.

> *L-IP-X-01:* If the defendant claims that the confession was extorted by torture, it is he who bears the burden of proof. If there is no other evidence, we will consider the claim in the whole case. For example, drug crimes. If he doesn't confess but we searched out the drug from his person or his home and the person who buys or sells him the drug can prove his crime, the fact of beating the suspect is normal, although we do not advocate doing this.

Our researchers checked the case files to see how often prosecutors recorded complaints from suspects that they had been tortured or mistreated by the police. We found that case files rarely included a record of such complaints. Six of the Basic Court files and eleven of the Intermediate Court files examined by our researchers (2 per cent of the total files examined) recorded that the suspect made a complaint of police mistreatment to the prosecutor (see also Lin, Zhang and Huang, 2009, p. 121). The details of such complaints (where the case file recorded details) are set out in Table 5.6.

EXAMINATION OF THE CASE MATERIALS

One of the major tasks prosecutors undertake is to examine the case materials to ensure that everything is in order to ensure a successful prosecution. When we interviewed prosecutors this was one of the functions mentioned most often, and it included a wide variety of tasks such as chasing the police for incomplete documentation, ensuring that exhibits had been transferred by the police, checking and correcting the classification of dossiers, ensuring that all relevant charges and/or suspects were included in the Bill of Prosecution, and eliminating from the charge sheet those whose alleged criminal responsibility did not need to be further investigated.

VISITING THE CRIME SCENE

During the course of our interviews, a few prosecutors told us that, as part of their pre-trial activities, they might visit the scene of the crime. Thus, for example:

> *E-IP-L-05:* Sometimes, if possible, I will go to the scene of the crime and have a look in order to exclude the possibility of other people having committed the crime, to have a clearer understanding of the case and to prevent some police officers from creating false evidence.

This was not, however, an activity that prosecutors in general appeared to undertake.

Table 5.6   Complaints recorded by prosecutor of alleged police mistreatment

Sites	Case No.	Details
Site C (C-CFA-B3) Basic	63	The public security organ applied violence.
	78	I told lies (admitted that I stole wine) because they hit me. The criminal investigation team hit me. They hit my body. No evidence (to prove that the criminal investigation team had hit me).
	131	Being beaten when telling the truth, would not be beaten when telling lies.
Site F (F-CFA-N) Basic	1	No information
	21	Provide written materials.
Site H (H-CFA-S2) Intermediate	26	No information
	50	Beat me three to four times. They pulled my head and hit it against the wall, didn't give me clothes to wear. The previous confessions were made because they beat me and forced me to confess. They didn't let me see the written record, and forced me to sign, including the time when they took a video-recording of me.
Site J (J-CFA-S4) Intermediate	45	No information
	46	No information
	47	No information
Site K (K-CFA-W) Intermediate	10	The criminal suspect said he had been beaten by the investigative personnel.
	11	The criminal suspect said he had been beaten by the investigative personnel.
Site L (L-CFA-X) Intermediate	4	They beat me in the prison, the person who beat me was called Mr X.
	24	I didn't commit a crime. I have never done anything illegal. The police beat me and I was forced to confess as they wanted.
	81	No information
	82	They did not give me any food. They beat me up.

EXAMINING THE LAW AND VERIFYING FACTS AND EVIDENCE

Our interviews revealed that prosecutors are concerned to ensure that they understand and correctly apply the relevant law. A number of prosecutors mentioned that they researched whether the crime charged was the most relevant and appropriate charge, and that they looked up relevant judicial interpretations where necessary. Some of the prosecutors we interviewed told us that given legal ambiguities and conflicting judicial interpretations they often struggled to determine which law to apply and how to categorize the case. The following is a typical remark highlighting the concerns prosecutors have about getting the law right:

A-IP-B1-10: [There is a] problem as to whether a crime was committed and whether the suspect should be charged with this crime or another. This is a problem facing every procurator. In addition to studying the case by oneself, the way to solve this problem is mainly to discuss the case in the chief prosecutor liaison meetings, or to report to the department head and the chief managing procurator. If the problem still cannot be solved after taking these actions, the case should be submitted to the procuratorial committee. But I mainly examine the cases by myself.

INTERROGATING THE SUSPECT

As explained above, the 1996 CPL expressly places a duty on the procuratorate to interrogate suspects. Thirty-eight (40 per cent) of the 96 prosecutors expressly stated that they would routinely interrogate the suspect although it is almost certain that all do. The reasons they gave for interrogation included verifying the facts and evidence contained in the case files; clarifying any doubts they had about the case; ascertaining whether there were any problems related to the suspect's confession statement; obtaining further information from the suspect about the crime; gauging the suspect's attitude towards his crime; and listening to any defence or explanation put forward. When interviewed, one prosecutor (F-IP-N-02) revealed that for him interrogating the suspect was particularly important when he had not had time to read the case files: 'If I don't have the time to read the case files, I will conduct an interrogation.' Another disclosed that suspects would be interrogated if they withdrew their previous confession, but this would only be a formality if there was sufficient evidence:

L-IP-X-04: When a suspect withdraws his previous confession, we will ask for the reasons. But so long as the evidence is sufficient, interrogating such suspects is just a formality.

F-IP-N-02: If there is no unusual circumstance, we will interrogate criminal suspects once. If the case is complex, there will be two or more interrogations.

J-IP-S4-02: After reading the files, I will interrogate the suspect and listen to his explanation. If he withdraws his confession, I will examine the credibility of his confession and decide whether his explanation is true or not by linking it with the file. Of course this phenomenon is very common; about 95 per cent of suspects agree with the indictment. It is normal that a suspect avoids the important and dwells on the trivial. Listening to his explanation is one thing: the key point is whether the evidence is sufficient.

Although the 1996 CPL provides an overall time limit for making a decision on prosecution, it does not stipulate a time period within which the procuratorate must interrogate the suspect once the case has been transferred to it. Our interviews with prosecutors revealed varying practices in this regard: a prosecutor from Site H (H-IP-S2-03) said that he would conduct the interrogation before he had even read what the suspect had said to the police, two prosecutors from Site D (D-IP-K-02 and D-IP-K-05) said they would interrogate within three days of the case being transferred to them, whilst a prosecutor from Site E (E-IP-L-05) revealed that he usually interrogated suspects one to two weeks after reading the case materials.

Practices also varied in respect of how many times prosecutors interrogated the suspect. Some of the prosecutors we interviewed stated that their normal practice was

Table 5.7 Number of times defendant was questioned by the prosecutor

	BC 7 Sites		IC 6 Sites		All 13 Sites	
Once	556	90.4	289	83.5	845	87.9
Twice	42	6.8	55	15.9	97	10.1
Three times	15	2.4	2	0.6	17	1.8
More than three times	2	0.3	0	0.0	2	0.2
Not known	111	–	72	–	183	–
Total	726	100.0	418	100.0	1144	100.0

to carry out one interrogation only, but that if the case was complicated they would interrogate more frequently, sometimes in excess of three times. A prosecutor from Site H (H-IP-S2-004) explained that much depended on the nature of the crime: in cases of violence he would normally interrogate only once, whereas in cases involving economic crimes he would carry out a number of interrogations. One prosecutor (L-05) said he would interrogate suspects before and after reading case materials. Four of our interviewees disclosed information relating to the duration of each interrogation, and their estimates ranged from 30 minutes to two hours and two hours to four hours.

Occasionally, prosecutors indicated that the interrogation of the defendant might be used to strike a bargain with the defendant:

> F-IP-N-02: Some cases have clear facts but lack evidence in some respect. In practice, we will plea bargain with the criminal suspect. In a case of appropriating public money, for example, in which the suspect embezzled RMB 3 million but the evidence we found made it difficult to prove all the facts. To save time and human resources and to improve efficiency, we would only prosecute him for the RMB 500 000 that we had verified.

Our case file analysis revealed that in 90 per cent of Basic Court cases and in 83 per cent of Intermediate Court cases the suspect was recorded as having been interrogated only once by the prosecutor. Suspects were interrogated twice in 7 per cent of Basic Court cases and in 16 per cent of Intermediate Court cases, the difference most likely explained by the more complex nature of Intermediate Court cases. Prosecutors recorded as having undertaken interrogations on three or more occasions were rarities. The detailed results of the analysis are set out in Table 5.7.

As earlier explained, only about 3 per cent of suspects in our sample were recorded as having made a denial at the time when they were interrogated by the police. A full or partial confession was a feature of almost 95 per cent of cases. Although four of the prosecutors we interviewed told us that withdrawal of confession by suspects was a common phenomenon, and that over 95 per cent of suspects made a different statement when interrogated by the procuratorate to that which they were recorded as having made when interrogated by the police, this was not borne out by our analysis of the case files.[16]

---

[16] This illustrates one shortcoming of attitudinal material. It is quite common for interviewees to misstate or misunderstand their own working world because their minds are concentrated upon the unusual rather than the common.

Table 5.8 Suspect's response to his/her confession

	BC 7 Sites		IC 6 Sites		All 13 Sites	
Confirm his/her confession	568	95.9	333	92.5	901	94.6
Withdraw his/her confession	12	2.0	10	2.8	22	2.3
Partially withdraw his/her confession	12	2.0	17	4.7	29	3.0
Not known	134	–	58	–	192	–
Total	726	100.0	418	100.0	1144	100.0

We found that almost 95 per cent of those who were recorded as having made a confession to the police were recorded as having confirmed that confession when interrogated by the procuratorate. Only 5.3 per cent of suspects were recorded as having sought to extricate themselves from the confession they had made to the police. This small percentage comprised those said to have made a full retraction (2.3 per cent) and those said to have only partially withdrawn their confession (3 per cent). The disparity between the records which revealed relatively few suspects retracting their statements to the police and the repeated assertions of prosecutors that suspects routinely retracted confessions is not something that our research is able to explain dispositively.[17] It seems plausible, however, in the light of our other informal discussions with respondents in China that retractions of confessions may be suppressed by excluding them from the case file.

According to prosecution case file records, the willingness of suspects to confirm their confessions was not significantly affected by whether the cases were Basic Court or Intermediate Court cases, and although there were some variations as between the sites these were not particularly marked (at four sites there was a 100 per cent confirmation rate, and the lowest confirmation rate at 85 per cent was at Site A).[18] The detailed figures can be seen in Table 5.8.

QUESTIONING VICTIMS

As explained above, the procuratorate is charged with the duty of ascertaining whether the evidence is reliable and sufficient for a prosecution, and whether the most appropriate charge has been selected by the police. In discharging this duty, prosecutors will normally need to question the victim or the family of the victim. In our interviews with prosecutors, as we have noted above, respondents occasionally[19] mentioned that they advised

---

[17] It is, however, common in field-work to find that respondents may be overly-influenced by exceptional occurrences which nevertheless cause them difficulty or concern.

[18] See, *Congressional-Executive Commission on China*, 2006 Annual report fn. 144 (2006), detailing a requirement by the Supreme People's Procuratorate to tape or record interrogations of criminal suspects in job-related crimes, such as bribery, corruption and dereliction of duty starting from 2006. However, one should note that the majority of cases are investigated by the police who are not subject to the same requirement.

[19] The failure to mention encounters with victims should not be accorded much weight given

Table 5.9 Issues on which victim was questioned

	BC 7 Sites		IC 6 Sites		All Sites	
Crime details	384	62.5	211	44.9	595	54.9
Own evidence	128	20.9	90	19.1	218	20.1
Preferred outcome	81	13.2	94	20.0	175	16.1
No victim identified	21	3.4	75	16.0	96	8.9
Not known	324	–	285	–	609	–
Total	938	100.0	755	100.0	1693	100.0

victims of their rights and also that they had, as in B-IP-B2-16: 'inquired of the victim and listened to his opinion on the handling of the case'. While most prosecutors gave no details of their interviews with victims, some told us that they were not simply seeking the victim's story but were also seeking to ensure that it fitted in with the other evidence, as in F-IP-N-03: 'I will examine witness statements to see whether the statement of the victim matches the defendant's confession, whether there is any contradiction, difficult or doubtful points.'

In reviewing the case files, some of the cases in our sample were ones where no victim was identified (or not available in homicide cases), and in many other cases (609) the file did not record any details relating to questioning of the victim or victims of the alleged crime. Where the file recorded details, we categorized what it was that victims were questioned about. As Table 5.9 shows,[20] in more than half of these cases victims were asked questions about the details of the crime, and in almost one-fifth of cases victims were asked questions regarding the evidence they had already provided to the police. In a significant percentage of cases (13.2 per cent of Basic Court cases and 20.0 per cent of Intermediate Court cases) victims were asked what they would prefer to see as the outcome of the case. This interest in the views, as opposed to the evidence, of the victim is most likely due to the provision in Article 139, 1996 CPL which obliges the procuratorate to 'heed the opinions of the victim' and, in and of itself, introduces into the equation the possibility of victims asserting pressure upon the prosecutor to reach a particular outcome. This, as we shall see, is a not inconsiderable matter so far as prosecutors are concerned.

REVIEW OF OTHER WITNESS STATEMENTS, MATERIAL EVIDENCE AND DOCUMENTARY EVIDENCE

In addition to questioning suspects and victims, the case files recorded that prosecutors review witness statements, as well as material and documentary evidence. As Table

---

that we did not specifically ask prosecutors to detail their contacts with victims. On the other hand, it is fair to say that the great majority of prosecutors did not stress this aspect of their responsibilities in our interviews.

[20] The table adds up to more than the total number of cases because the victim might be asked about more than one of the categories.

Table 5.10 Review of other witness statements, material evidence and documentary evidence

	BC 7 Sites		IC 6 Sites		All Sites	
Yes	534	94.8	385	100.0	919	96.9
No	29	5.2	0	0.0	29	3.1
Not known	163	–	33	–	196	–
Total	726	100.0	418	100.0	1144	100.0

Table 5.11 Questioning other witness statements, material evidence and documentary evidence

	BC 7 Sites		IC 6 Sites		All Sites	
Yes	19	5.4	51	32.7	70	13.8
No	334	94.6	105	67.3	439	86.2
Not known	373	–	262	–	635	–
Total	726	100.0	418	100.0	1144	100.0

5.10 shows,[21] this type of evidence review was recorded as having taken place in all the Intermediate Court cases and in 95 per cent of the Basic Court cases.

Our interviews with prosecutors revealed numerous examples of the types of evidence that fell to be reviewed at this stage. Prosecutors mentioned that they screened witness testimony to decide whether statements were consistent with each other; checked the authenticity of evidence; examined documents purporting to prove the identity and occupation of the suspect; assessed conclusions provided by experts; determined whether exhibits, documentary evidence and expert conclusions supported the police opinion, and compared the materials available at the transfer for prosecution stage with those submitted by the police during the stage of approval of arrest.

As Table 5.11 shows, in a small minority of cases (13.8 per cent) the procuratorate were recorded as having raised questions about the evidence that they had reviewed. The data demonstrate that the procuratorate are far more likely to adopt this course in Intermediate Court cases (32.7 per cent) than in Basic Court cases (5.4 per cent).

The questions raised by prosecutors revolved around the adequacy of the evidence, and usually called for further investigation to supplement or resolve inconsistencies in the existing evidence. In some cases the files stated that the prosecutor had called for further verification of documentation (criminal records, identification documents or household registration documents), and in others that he or she had carried out further investigation by speaking to additional witnesses or by carrying out further questioning of existing witnesses on specific points. Sometimes the questions raised were about procedural aspects of the case (e.g. bail) and whether the necessary documentation had been provided by the

---

[21] The table adds up to more than the total number of cases because the respondents could choose more than one option.

police. The following is a sample of comments noted down from the case file analysis by our researchers:

B-CFA-B2-15: Since a lot of witnesses were involved, therefore there were also many doubts, such as the person who had conducted the identification had not signed the relevant documents, no identification had been conducted in relation to some of the items, some of the victims had not been found, etc.

B-CFA-B2-19: The materials such as those concerning the bail of the suspects Wan and Li, the previous convictions of the suspect Gao, the investigation of the involvement in the procuring of prostitution by the suspects He, Zhang and Jiang, and materials proving the role of the suspect Li in the blackmail were lacking.

C-CFA-B3-132: Challenged the materials concerning the proof of release and previous conviction of one of the suspects.

H-CFA-S2-07: Conduct an examination of the crime scene: [for example, in one case I visited] a refuge house in a village where the victim lived (the place where the victim lived had already been demolished), and interviewed the family of the victim in order to understand the relationship between the victim and the defendant in this case. I verified the crucial witness ZXY; listened to the opinions of the family of the victim. The family of the victim requested that I punish the defendant and other criminals suspected for intentional homicide, who had not voluntarily surrendered themselves, requested the court to severely punish all the criminal suspects in this case and order them to compensate for the related loss (the bill of incidental civil action was submitted). I conducted a preliminary exchange of views on this case with the defence lawyers of the defendants over the phone.

H-CFA-S2-26: Interrogating three witnesses as to the situation at the time of when the crime happened again.

I-CFA-S3-46: Investigate the whereabouts of some of the illegally acquired money and the situation of the witness.

K-CFA-W-14: One of the criminal suspects had been beaten up by the victim and his wife before the occurrence of this case, thus an identification of the seriousness of the injury of the criminal suspect should be conducted. Looking at the course of arresting one of the criminal suspects to see whether it should be considered as voluntary surrender. The previous criminal records of two of the defendants should be verified and investigated. The family of the victim should be informed of the cause of death of the victim.

REVIEW OF COMPULSORY MEASURES

As noted in the previous chapter, the vast majority of suspects (87.2 per cent) are not recorded as having applied for bail or residential surveillance at the police investigation stage. This meant that all but 131 of the suspects in our sample were held in detention. Article 73 provides that if at any time the procuratorate finds that the compulsory measures adopted against a suspect or defendant are inappropriate, it must cancel or modify those measures immediately. We checked the case files to see if the procuratorate had changed the compulsory measures following interrogation of the suspect and review of the evidence.

Table 5.12 Prosecutor changed the compulsory measures

	BC 7 Sites		IC 6 Sites		All Sites	
Yes	11	1.9	3	1.0	14	1.6
No	562	98.1	295	99.0	857	98.4
Not known	153	–	120	–	273	–
Total	726	100.0	418	100.0	1144	100.0

Table 5.13 Change in compulsory measures: details

Cases	Case No.	Details
A-CFA-B1	24	Defendant was first charged with a traffic accident offence by the police and was granted bail. Prosecutor reviewed the case and amended the charge to the offence of using dangerous means to endanger public safety, in violation of Article 115 of the Criminal Law. Prosecutor changed the compulsory measures by arguing that bail was not enough to prevent the suspect from causing danger, arrest was suggested and the application for arrest was approved.
	56	Defendant was first detained before bail was granted.
M-CFA-Y	38	Bail changed to Criminal detention.
	39	Application for approval of arrest was submitted and was rejected due to insufficient evidence. Prosecutor changed the compulsory measure and granted bail for trial to Defendant. Defendant paid 3000 RMB as surety.
	43	Defendant paid 2000 RMB as surety and granted bail for trial.
	61	Defendant was granted bail. Prosecutor later changed the compulsory measure from bail to arrest.
	62	Defendant was granted bail. Prosecutor later changed the compulsory measure from bail to arrest.
H-CFA-S2	1	No details
	40	No details

As shown by Table 5.12, suspects in China continue to be held in custody following the transfer of their case to the procuratorate. We found that the procuratorate changed the compulsory measures in a mere 1.6 per cent of cases in our sample (11 Basic Court cases and three Intermediate Court Cases).

In the nine cases in which there was a procuratorate-initiated change in the compulsory measures, the change was not necessarily from detention to bail or residential surveillance. As the details in Table 5.13 evidence, in four of the cases bail was rescinded in favour of detention, and in one case detention was further formalized by the imposition of arrest.

There can be little question that prosecutors are predisposed to support the police. Once the police have made a determination of the custodial status of the defendant that status is very unlikely to change and prosecutors follow the police decision and are little influenced by other views including any advanced by defenders as the following prosecutor said in interview:

F-IP-N-05: Although we protect the rights of lawyers, in practice we still dislike them. Some of their rights are restricted. For instance, generally we won't agree with their requests to change compulsory measures.

SUPPLEMENTARY INVESTIGATION

In order to assist its preparation for trial the procuratorate may ask the police to carry out supplementary investigation. We saw in the previous chapter that the procuratorate asked the police to carry out supplementary investigation in a significant minority (34 per cent) of all cases, such requests being even more prevalent in Intermediate Court cases (43 per cent). In a quarter of supplementary investigation cases, the procuratorate requested such investigation on more than one occasion.

In addition, Article 140, 1996 CPL allows the procuratorate to carry out supplementary investigation itself, and six of the prosecutors we interviewed expressly stated that they would carry out their own investigations if they believed this was necessary and provided that they had the time to do so. Often we were told by prosecutors during interview that they were overburdened with cases and that they did not have time to do investigations themselves.

F-IP-N-01: It is very common to return files to the Public Security Bureau, maybe 20 per cent. It is relatively greater in crimes involving corruption in office, taking advantage of one's position. The criminal measures in bribery cases are secretive and it is hard to investigate and collect evidence. There are two circumstances in which supplementary investigation will be conducted: one is where the material is very simple and we investigate by ourselves. Of course, we try to avoid this situation. The other is where the supplementary materials are very complex in which case we list our opinions and return the files to the police or anti-corruption bureau for investigation.

J-IP-S4-02: At the time when the Approval of Arrest Department and the Prosecution Department were two separate offices, the returned cases were about 80 per cent. After the innovation of our Procuratorate of 'Who approves arrest will prosecute' the rate dropped to 20–30 per cent. Cases that do not accord with requirements will be returned in time. The return letter will list the reasons . . . giving advice.

J-IP-S4-03: If the facts are not clear or evidence is not sufficient, I will return the materials to the Public Security Bureau. It is very common. But we can only return twice.

The major reason for prosecutors conducting supplementary investigation by themselves instead of returning cases to police for supplementary investigation was because of what they saw as the poor performance of the police.[22] For example, a big city prosecutor said that:

---

[22] According to procurators, non-prosecution cases because of doubt mostly arise from the fact that the evidence in the cases transferred does not reach the requirement of public prosecution: (1) the investigators fail to collect evidence in a timely and comprehensive manner; and are excessively reliant on suspects' oral confessions. (2) The investigators fail to collect or consolidate the evidence with adequate measures. (3) The quality of supplementary investigation is poor because either nothing is done, or what is done does not follow the requirement set in the outline

A-IP-B1-05: Normally I am reluctant to return cases to the police; if their investigation is not good, I will investigate by myself; sometimes I will do the investigation together with the police.[23]

While the prosecutors are critical of the performance of the police, one prosecutor (F-IP-N-02) also admitted that, given the lack of relevant skills and equipment, the efficiency of prosecutors' supplementary investigation itself was often low.

As disclosed by some prosecutors,[24] the time limit of examination was another factor that would be taken into account by the prosecutors in deciding whether to return a case to the police for supplementary investigation, and the following comments of two prosecutors we interviewed clearly revealed serious concern over time limits:

D-IP-K: If I found there was any problem, I would call the police to supplement the required materials. If they could hand in the materials within several days, I would return the case. Otherwise, it may affect my time limit in handling the case.

H-IP-S2-03: We don't return cases for supplementary investigation because we don't have sufficient time, and we only ask [the investigative organs] to provide supplementary materials. If they can provide supplementary information, we will not return the cases to them, and 80 per cent of the cases need to be supplemented in such a way.

It is clear from our interviews that the supplementary information commonly relates to getting correct documentation, signatures, dates and to ensuring conformity with the evidential requirements set by the procuratorate. As disclosed by one prosecutor we interviewed (H-IP-S2-04), matters that needed to be supplemented included: information as to voluntary surrender; proof of the existence of a sufficient basis for the determination of the amount of loss etc. involved in the case; objective facts; changes in an expert conclusion; information as to the course of the crime; proof of identity; proof of report of crime by the defendant (because this involves meritorious performance of the defendant) etc. Another prosecutor (G-IP-S1-03) gave two further examples of matters that needed to be supplemented: evidence that could prove that the defendant should be given a lighter or heavier sentence or showing that the defendant was a recidivist. Another prosecutor (H-IP-S2-01) said information as to the course of crime is also a category of materials that may need to be supplemented.

K-IP-W-02: There is a difference in the standard of evidence [in the PSB]. Sometimes it is hard to communicate with them. For example, about the identity of the suspect they think that the identity is clear if they have his identity card. But you know there are many false identity cards so we ask the police to obtain an identity statement from the police station that the suspect belongs to. Even on this minor issue we still have disputes with the police.

L-IP-X-01: I will read the facts of the crime and evidence in the Bill of Prosecution and examine if any crime has been missed or if the source of evidence is lawful. For example, identification.

---

for supplementary investigation. (4) There is no effective countermeasure against the suspect's withdrawal of confession. See Chen and Jin (2008), pp. 61–62.

[23] Similarly, a prosecutor from the West (IP-XA-04) also said that he would conduct the investigation jointly with the police. One prosecutor (IP-BJ1-09) even said that the procuratorates directed the supplementary investigation of the police.

[24] E.g. L-IP-X-08; L-IP-X-09; L-IP-X-10; and E-IP-L-07.

The Ministry of Public Security requires that the number foils [on the parade] should be not fewer than seven or the number of photos should not be fewer than ten in identifying the suspect. But some public security bureaux at the district or county level use only five persons or seven photos. So we have to return the case. Another example is forensic appraisal. One forensic physician's signature is unlawful because two are required for forensic appraisal documents.

Many prosecutors, however, told us that, whilst they would have carried out supplementary investigation themselves, they returned cases to the police because they were under too much case pressure. Thus, for example:

> *J-IP-S4-05:* The work pressure is very high at the stage [of examination for prosecution]. To avoid extended detention of suspects, I usually work overtime. For cases with unclear facts and insufficient evidence we either return them for supplementary investigation or investigate ourselves. But because of staff shortages, the majority of these cases are returned for supplementary investigation.

At any rate, prosecutors tended to suggest that they exercised caution at this stage because of the consequences for themselves in making a wrong determination:

> *J-IP-S4-08:* If the evidence is insufficient, I will list an outline for supplementary investigation and return the materials to the [PSB]. The [PSB] can carry out supplementary investigation for one month. After receiving the supplementary materials, I can conduct an examination for one month. If there are still problems, I can return for supplementary investigation again. In other words, supplementary investigation can be conducted at most twice at the examination and prosecution stage. Anyway, I am afraid of making mistakes at this stage.

Prosecutors also understand that returning cases has potentially adverse consequences for the police as well as themselves and accordingly, to preserve good relations with the police, they are very reluctant to return cases for supplementary investigation:

> *M-IP-Y-01:* There is an internal regulator in the [PSB]. A police investigator will have his scores reduced if his case is returned. So we will not return as often as we could.

> *M-IP-Y-02:* The evaluation system in the procuratorate and the [PSB] is not in accordance with the legal order. The investigator will be penalized RMB 100 if the case is returned for supplementary investigation. If the prosecution is not the same as the final judgment of the court, we have scores deducted that are connected with bonus and evaluation.

Accordingly, apart from conducting the supplementary investigation themselves, another alternative to formally returning the case to the police for supplementary investigation is to request the police to provide the necessary supplementary materials. As one prosecutor (M-IP-Y-05) commented, calling the police and informing them of the materials that needed to be supplemented, was a more efficient method. Another prosecutor (H-IP-S2-007) also said that since returning cases for supplementary investigation could not help solve the problems in certain circumstances, she normally would conciliate with the police and ask them to provide the necessary materials. Some prosecutors we interviewed[25] also said they normally would simply ask the police to provide supplementary

---

[25] E.g., M-IP-Y-01; M-IP-Y-02; M-IP-Y-03; and B-IP-B1-13.

materials. Some other prosecutors[26] further disclosed that they would just phone the police or request the police officer in charge of the case to come to the prosecutor's office and ask them to provide supplementary materials. For these reasons, therefore, it is clear that the case files under-record the number of cases in which the procuratorate sought the assistance of the police in undertaking supplementary investigation.

It does not follow, however, that a request for supplementary investigation will result in action by the police. Pan Diaohua and Lai Daqing (2004) found that in practice the public security organs often fail to conduct the supplementary investigation as requested by the procuratorate. A similar view was shared by some prosecutors we interviewed (e.g. B-B2-06, B-B2-16, B-B2-13 and B-B2-04). Instead, the police either simply submit their Work Explanation (B-B2-03) or use failure to find the relevant evidence as an excuse for non-investigation (B-B2-04 and B-B2-06). As one prosecutor told us:

> *B-IP-B2-06:* As for the cases returned for supplementary investigation, the police will not do any investigation. They use failure to find the evidence as an excuse. The procuratorate lack effective supervision measures and the quality of supplementary investigation is not very high.

Wei Zujian (2000) even disclosed that sometimes the public security organs would re-submit cases that were returned to them for supplementary investigation to the procuratorates for examination for prosecution again without having done any of the supplementary investigation requested.

Even if supplementary investigation had been conducted by the police, the quality of the relevant investigation was often found to be very poor.[27] Pan and Lai (2004) also found that the original purposes of supplementary investigations were often not achieved, thus seriously affecting the quality of the cases, causing delay in litigation and wasting judicial resources.[28] Thus, the poor performance of the police increased the workload of the prosecutors, and this is clearly revealed in the following comments of a big city prosecutor we interviewed:

> *H-IP-S2-03:* After returning the case for supplementary investigation, I always need to call the police and do the necessary preparation in case they fail to provide the necessary supplementary materials. If the outcome of supplementary investigation is hopeless, I will report to the leader and leave them to do the communication with the police and to give suggestions.

One of the causes of this was the investigative officers' imperfect understanding of evidence requirements. For example, as Wei Zujian (2000) and Pan and Lai (2004)

---

[26] E.g., M-IP-Y-05; B-IP-B2-02; G-IP-S1-01; H-IP-S2-04; H-IP-S2-007; and E-IP-L-02.

[27] In the prosecutors' view, the purpose of investigation and prosecution are different: the purpose of investigation is to detect the case and conclude the investigation, so long as the case is transferred for review and prosecution, the investigation work in general is over. Currently, the police performance evaluation mechanism places emphasis on the rate of case detection and procuratorial approval of the arrest after police submission of the request and pays little attention to the conviction rate. If the evidence is not collected in a legal, timely and complete manner, the prosecution may have difficulty at trial. See Ji Gang and Liu Jing (2006), pp. 84–85.

[28] A similar view was expressed by Chi Weihui from the People's Procuratorate of Taijiang District of Fuzhou City of Fujian Province and Chen Lunzhao from the People's Procuratorate of Nanjiang County of Sichuan Province. Chi Weihui (2002); Chen Lunzhao (1999).

have argued that in some cases because of the investigative officers' ignorance of the importance of evidence, key evidence is not collected promptly in the course of initial investigations, thus causing defects in evidence from the very beginning; and when the cases are returned for supplementary investigations, time has passed and the exhibits might have already been lost or destroyed.[29] In some cases, the failure of the investigative officers to establish effective communication links with the victims or key witnesses after the latter had given their written statements would also make any subsequent supplementary investigation difficult, for it would be difficult for the investigative officers to find those witnesses and victims to help verify and provide evidence again (Wei Zujian, 2000).

Another reason for the poor quality of supplementary investigation was the inappropriate attitude of the investigative officers towards it. For example, Pan and Lai (2004) and Chi Weihui (2002) pointed out that some investigative officers tended to put much more weight on clearing cases and ignore the work of supplementary investigation.[30] Some prosecutors we interviewed[31] also said that the police failed to understand the necessity of supplementary investigation, and one prosecutor even said:

> *J-IP-S4-06:* The efficiency of returning a case for supplementary investigation is not high because the police think that a case is solved after the criminal suspect has been arrested and they have done something meritorious when they transfer the case for prosecution. Therefore, the police are not enthusiastic in doing supplementary investigation.[32]

As Pan and Lai stated, the investigative organs often believe that the procuratorates intend to cause them trouble by returning cases for supplementary investigation. As a result, in many cases, instead of seriously conducting supplementary investigation, the investigative organs often simply state that 'it was not possible to investigate thoroughly' or 'the suspects had already confessed', or simply produced some 'explanations'.[33]

In certain circumstances, the lack of communication between the procuratorates which requested supplementary investigation and the relevant investigative organ might also lead to the poor quality of supplementary investigation and repetitive supplementary

---

[29] Wei Zujian (2000); and Pan and Lai (2004). See also Chen and Jin (2008).

[30] See also Xu Meijun (2009), p. 28; Ji and Liu (2006), p. 91; Hu Zhifang and Hu Zhihui (2009), p. 70; Sun Xiaoyu (2009); Cheng and Cheng (2006), p. 6; Ma, Jin and Liu (2005), p. 80; Ru (2007), p. 65.

[31] For example: K-IP-W-01; K-IP-W-03; K-IP-W-04; J-IP-S4-05; and A-IP-B1-04.

[32] Similarly, a prosecutor (B-IP-B2-00) thus blamed the police for failure to pay enough attention to supplementary investigation.

[33] A similar view was expressed by Zhou Cuifang from the People's Procuratorate of Tongzhou District of Beijing City: Zhou Cuifang (2002). This kind of material titled 'Explanation of the Situation' was sometimes used at random in practice and many explanation documents were defective in form. The Explanation allows the investigators to cover flaws in the case dossier, which also opens up the opportunity of judicial corruption. The content of the Explanation of the Situation mainly includes such information as the process of catching the suspect, other suspects not caught at the time, the illicit property not available, jurisdiction, the offender's identity, statement that there was no torture in the investigation and whether the suspect voluntarily surrendered or had meritorious performance. See Li and Wang (2009); Huang Jie (2010); Fang Baoguo (2010), pp. 51–52.

investigations, thus delaying the conclusion of the cases.[34] One prosecutor we interviewed commented:

> *A-IP-B1-04:* The police do not understand the requirement of initiation of prosecution because of the insufficient communication between the prosecutors and the police and their different understanding and requirements of evidence.[35]

In view of the frequency with which prosecutors ask the police to carry out supplementary investigation, it is perhaps not surprising that many of the prosecutors we interviewed expressed extreme dissatisfaction with the standard of police investigative work. The following are a few examples of the many comments made by prosecutors about what they perceive as shortcomings in the way that the police investigate cases and compile the evidence:

> *L-IP-X-01:* The police fail to handle cases seriously; there is even a lack of basic evidence in some cases, even in murder cases.

> *L-IP-X-03:* Another problem involves carelessness in keeping evidence safe. Much evidence is lost, causing us serious embarrassment.

> *L-IP-X-04:* Handling cases unsystematically: this problem mainly happens at the basic court level; the performance of the basic level organs became poorer after adopting the system of combining detection and interrogation since many police do not know how to collect evidence according to the constitution.

> *A-IP-B1-10:* The problem of collecting evidence is very serious; there is often illegality in complying with the formal evidentiary requirements.

> *A-B1-12:* The police fail to preserve evidence properly during investigation.

> *B-B2-00:* The evidence collected by the police is not good enough, some helpful evidence is lost.

> *B-IP-B2-02:* There is great difficulty in supplementary investigation: evidence is needed at the initiation of a prosecution. The police are reluctant to do so: their work is not detailed enough; it is perfunctory.

> *B-IP-B2-03:* The quality of investigation of the police sub-bureaux is not strong enough: they miss the best time to conduct the investigation, thus resulting in some people failing to appear in court. The police fail to provide supplementary investigation as requested.

> *B-IP-B2-04:* The police inappropriately collect and secure exhibits, thus leading to defects and missing evidence; the witness statements collected by the police are insufficient and not reliable (for example the details as to the characteristics of the suspect may be crucial to the conviction).

---

[34] Pan and Lai (2004); and Zhou Cuifang (2002). Pan and Lai also argued that the two organs failed to cooperate with each other, and sometimes one might even try to shift the burden to the other.

[35] A prosecutor (SZ-04) also pointed out that, returning cases for supplementary investigation related to the different understanding of the evidence and facts among the police, procuratorates and judges, and it 'was difficult to set a unified standard'.

As to cases returned for supplementary investigation, the police fail to undertake the relevant investigation using failure to collect evidence as an excuse.

D-IP-K-04: The failure of the police to collect the evidence carefully thus making the evidence unusable. When the police do not collect evidence promptly this leads to the loss of evidence.

J-IP-S4-08: I am afraid that the evidence provided by the police is false or they use unlawful means to collect evidence, so I examine matters carefully.

J-IP-S4-05: In individual cases, even after having communicated with the investigative organs, the efficiency of solving the problems is still low. In this circumstance, I will submit the case to the leaders.

E-IP-L-02: The police still rely heavily on the defendant's confession and do not pay attention to collecting other evidence.

REPORT STAGE AND PREPARATION OF DOCUMENTATION FOR TRIAL

After studying the case in detail, prosecutors write a report on their examination and evaluation of the case. Prosecutors told us that these reports would include information about the suspect and victim, the compulsory measures adopted, the facts of the crime; an analysis of the relevant evidence; a report on the investigation process and its legality; the problems discovered during examination for prosecution; the prosecutor's opinion on whether the case should be prosecuted and if so what charge should be preferred; and a recommendation as to sentence.

For those cases which proceed to trial prosecutors are charged with preparing the necessary legal documentation for trial (the Bill of Prosecution, questions to ask the defendant at trial, lists of witnesses and affidavits, statements of experts, records of inquests and documentation to assist in the debate stage of the trial).

THE PROSECUTION REVIEW PERIOD

Article 138, 1996 CPL provides that the procuratorate must make a decision on prosecution within one month of receiving the papers from the police, with an extension of half a month permitted in 'major or complex cases'.[36] This time limit is subject to the power of the procuratorate to either request that the police carry out a supplementary investigation or to carry out such investigation itself (Article 140). If a case goes back for supplementary investigation that adds another month in the hands of the police and this power may be used, in collusion with the police, to extend detention in certain cases. On return to the prosecutor, the prosecutor has a further month (one and half months in serious or complex cases) for review; and the process can be repeated for one more time.

---

[36] If the case is transferred to another procuratorate the time limit is recalculated from the date of receipt by the receiving procuratorate.

Table 5.14 Interval of prosecution review

	BC 7 Sites		IC 6 Sites		All Sites	
Up to 1 month	372	62.6	102	29.1	474	50.2
1 month to 2 months	100	16.8	81	23.1	181	19.2
2 months to 3 months	53	8.9	61	17.4	114	12.1
3 months to 4 months	33	5.6	35	10.0	68	7.2
4 months to 5 months	13	2.2	50	14.2	63	6.7
5 months to 6 months	16	2.7	11	3.1	27	2.9
6 months to 1 year or over	7	1.2	11	3.1	18	1.9
Not known	132	–	67	–	199	–
Total	726	100.0	418	100.0	1144	100.0

Table 5.15 Outcome of the prosecution review

	BC 7 Sites		IC 6 Sites		All Sites	
Prosecute	676	95.5	413	99.3	1089	96.9
Not to prosecute	32	4.5	3	0.7	35	3.1
Not known	18	–	2	–	20	–
Total	726	100.0	418	100.0	1144	100.0

Accordingly, the review process can take up to five months in ordinary cases or up to six and a half months in complex cases. Our analysis of the case files showed that while most cases did not reach the maximum review period allowed, in a small number of cases the maximum was reached or exceeded as shown in Table 5.14.

OUTCOME OF EXAMINATION FOR PROSECUTION

We checked all the case files to examine the outcome of the review process. As Table 5.15 shows, in almost all cases in our sample (96.9 per cent) the procuratorate decided that the suspect should be prosecuted. There were only three cases in the Intermediate Court sample where the procuratorate decided not to prosecute. The non-prosecution rate was higher in the Basic Court sub-sample (32 cases out of 708 in which the outcome was known), but even so remained below 5 per cent.

We further examined those cases which were prosecuted to ascertain how frequently the process of examination for prosecution led to a change in the charge from that preferred by the police when it initially submitted the case to the procuratorate. In a total of 61 cases the files did not reveal whether the suspect was prosecuted (20) or, if prosecuted, whether the charge was amended by the procuratorate (41). As seen in Table 5.16, of the remaining 1048 suspects, 976 (93 per cent) were prosecuted on the same charge as that recommended by the police. In summary, therefore, it can be said that almost all suspects who the police recommend for prosecution are prosecuted, and almost all are prosecuted on the charge or charges as initially framed by the police.

Table 5.16 Decision on charge

	BC 7 Sites		IC 6 Sites		All Sites	
With the same charge	606	95.1	370	90.0	976	93.1
With amended charge(s)	31	4.9	41	10.0	72	6.9
Not known	57	–	4	–	61	–
Total	694	100.0	415	100.0	1109	100.0

Table 5.17 Reason for non-prosecution

	BC 7 Sites		IC 6 Sites		All Sites	
Insufficient evidence	4	12.5	0	0.0	4	11.4
Article 15 of CPL	2	6.3	0	0.0	2	5.7
Prosecution's discretion/minor offences	10	31.3	3	100.0	13	37.1
Other (e.g. transferred to procuratorate in other district, out of jurisdiction, etc.)	16	50.0	0	0.0	16	45.7
Not known	0	–	0	–	0	–
Total	32	100.0	3	100.0	35	99.9

For the small minority of cases in which the procuratorate decided not to prosecute we examined the files to see whether they revealed the reasons underlying the decision. The results of this case file analysis are set out in Tables 5.17 and 5.18.

As these tables show, only four of the 35 non-prosecuted cases were eliminated on ground of insufficiency of evidence. In these four cases the files did not record details about the precise nature of the insufficiency, nor (save for one of the four cases) did we learn how the case was ultimately handled. The one case in which details were recorded revealed that it was returned to the police and then 'handled in other ways' (presumably through the system of administrative punishment). Two cases were recorded as falling under Article 15, 1996 CPL (i.e. 'not prosecute absolutely'), but apart from stating that the 'sub-bureau withdrew the case' the files did not reveal how or why the cases were deemed to fall under Article 15.

The main reason for non-prosecution recorded by our researchers from their analysis of the case files was that the case was deemed by the prosecutor to be minor (i.e. a decision to 'not prosecute relatively'). This accounted for 13 of the non-prosecuted cases, and was the reason for non-prosecution in all three of the Intermediate Court cases that were not prosecuted. In two of these three Intermediate Court cases the file recorded that 'the amount involved in the smuggling was so small that it was not enough to constitute a crime'. The files noted that these two cases were 'returned to the investigative organ for handling' (as explained above, a disposition under Article 142 does not mean that the suspect is necessarily exempted from punishment because the Article provides that if the procuratorate decides that the individual 'need be given administrative penalty or administrative sanction' it can make a suggestion to this effect and 'transfer the case to the competent organ for handling').

Categorization of these two cases under Article 142, together with the comment made

Table 5.18 Cases reference – reason for non-prosecution[1]

a. Insufficient evidence

Sites and Case No.			BC Court Sites	IC Court Sites
Site A (A-CFA-B1)	88,100,147,148		4	–
		Total		4

Details of Each Case

Sites and	Case No.	Details
Site A (A-CFA-B1)	88	No information – q.28 Returned to the public security organ for handling.
	100	No information – q.29 Returned to the public security sub-bureau for supplementary investigation and then handled in other ways.
	147	No information
	148	No information

b. Article 15 of CPL

Sites and Case No.			BC Court Sites	IC Court Sites
Site B (B-CFA-B2)	139,141		2	–
		Total		2

Details of Each Case

Sites and	Case No.	Details
Site B (B-CFA-B2)	139	No Information – q.28 The sub-bureau withdrew the case.
	141	No Information – q.28 The sub-bureau withdrew the case.

c. Prosecution's discretion/minor offences

Sites and Case No.			BC Court Sites	IC Court Sites
Site A (A-CFA-B1)	29,76,97,98,99,129,134,135,141,151		10	–
Site H (H-CFA-S2)	19,20,21			3
		Total		13

Details of Each Case

Sites and	Case No.	Details
Site A (A-CFA-B1)	29	Not to prosecute, reasons: had persuaded not to commit crime many times, and the circumstance was obviously minor.
	76	The facts of the crime had not been confirmed. – q.28 Returned to the investigative organ for handling.
	97	The act of the crime was obviously minor. – q.28 Not to prosecute, returned to the public security organ for handling.
	98	The act of the crime was obviously minor. – q.28 Not to prosecute, returned to the public security organ for handling.

Table 5.18 (continued)

Sites and	Case No.	Details
	99	The act of the crime was obviously minor. – q.28 Not to prosecute, returned to the public security organ for handling.
	129	The circumstance was minor and it would not be treated as a crime. – q.28 Returned to the public security sub-bureau for handling.
	134	The circumstance of the crime was minor, the defendant had a good attitude in confessing his crime and he had already reached an agreement with the victim. – q.28 The case was returned to the public security sub-bureau for handling.
	135	The circumstance of the crime was minor, the danger to society was small, the suspect and the victim had reached an agreement regarding civil compensation, the compensation had already been made, the suspect had a good attitude in confessing his crime. – q.28 The case was returned to the public security sub-bureau for handling.
	141	No information – q.28 The case was returned to the public security organ for handling.
	145	No information – q.28 The case was transferred to the Second Branch Procuratorate of the City Procuratorate for examination for prosecution.
Site H (H-CFA-S2)	19	The amount involved in the smuggling was so small that it was not enough to constitute a crime. – q.28 Returned to the investigative organ for handling.
	20	The amount involved in the smuggling was so small that it was not enough to constitute a crime. – q.28 Returned to the investigative organ for handling.
	21	Not to prosecute relatively, Article 142 of the Criminal Procedure Law (1996).

d. Other (e.g. transferred to procuratorate in other district, out of jurisdiction, etc.)

Sites and Case No.		BC Court Sites	IC Court Sites
Site A (A-CFA-B1)	23,38,80,81,82,89,125,127,131,143,144,145,153,154,155	15	–
Site C (C-CFA-B3)	174	1	–
	Total		16

Sites and	Case No.	Details
Site A (A-CFA-B1)	23	Due to the insufficiency of evidence, the public security organ granted bail to the suspect, but later that person had absconded, and he was not available to attend the trial.

Table 5.18 (continued)

Sites and	Case No.	Details
	38	Returned to the public security organ to withdraw the case, reason: bail was granted, and the whereabouts of the suspect was unknown, therefore there was no way to initiate the prosecution.
	80	It was learned from the person in charge of the case that the case was transferred to the Second Branch Procuratorate of the City Procuratorate for prosecution, the situation was unknown….
	81	It was learned from the person in charge of the case that the case was transferred to the Second Branch Procuratorate for examination for prosecution.
	82	It was learned from the person in charge of the case that the case was transferred to the Second Branch Procuratorate for examination for prosecution, thus the situation of prosecution and adjudication were not reflected in the case file, but the cover of the case file reflected that the defendant in this case was sentenced to 2 years' imprisonment with 2 years' suspended sentence after prosecution.
	89	The suspect was granted bail, he could not be arrested. – q.28 Returned to the public security organ for handling.
	125	The mediation was completed, the compensation for the injury had already been paid, the parties applied for non prosecution. – q.28 The public security organ withdrew the case.
	127	Not within the jurisdiction of this procuratorate.
	131	The two parties had reached a consensus, the suspect had a good attitude. Returned to the public security organ for handling.
	143	Not within the jurisdiction of this procuratorate. – q.28 The case was transferred to Another District Procuratorate for examination for prosecution.
	144	Not within the jurisdiction of this procuratorate. – q.28 The case was transferred to Another District Procuratorate for examination for prosecution.
	145	No information – q.28 The case was transferred to the Second Branch Procuratorate of the City Procuratorate for examination for prosecution.
	153	The case was transferred to Another District Procuratorate for examination for prosecution.
	154	The evidence was different and the suspect could not be arrested. – q.28 The case was returned to the public security organ for withdrawal.
	155	The public security organ withdrew the prosecution while the case was returned for supplementary investigation for the second time.
Site C (C-CFA–B3)	174	No information – The public security organ withdrew the case.

Note: 1. 'q.28' refers to Question 28 in the Case File analysis Form, Appendix 3.

on the file demonstrates that prosecutors have discretion when it comes to minor cases as to whether the case should be categorized under Article 142 or Article 15. The former provides for non-prosecution if the offence is 'minor', and the latter provides that innocence should be declared 'if an act is obviously minor, causing no serious harm, and is therefore not deemed a crime'. As there is no guidance as to when a crime is so minor that it is deemed not to be a crime (as opposed to minor but still worthy of administrative punishment), categorization appears to be arbitrary and the note in this instant case internally inconsistent (because if in these two cases the amount involved meant that the act could not constitute a crime it should have been categorized under Article 15).

The 13 Basic Court cases which were eliminated under Article 142 mostly recorded that 'the act of the crime was obviously minor' and the cases were referred to the PSB for handling. However, in one case the file recorded: 'The facts of the crime had not been confirmed: returned to investigative organ for handling.' This shows that rather than accepting that the case was one where there was insufficiency of evidence, the prosecutor decided instead to categorize the case under Article 142, thereby allowing it to be dealt with administratively under the guise that the case was minor.

The remaining 16 cases out of the 35 non-prosecuted cases (i.e. almost half of all the cases which did not proceed to prosecution) were not necessarily cases where the procuratorate, acting contrary to the police recommendation, made a positive decision not to prosecute on evidential, legal or policy grounds. In three of these cases the suspect had absconded whilst on bail, and the file simply recorded that for this reason the case could not proceed further. A further eight cases were transferred to the jurisdiction of another procuratorate and accordingly it was not known whether the suspect was prosecuted (with the exception of one of these cases, where the file recorded that the suspect was ultimately sentenced to two years' imprisonment with two years' suspended). A further three cases were noted as having been withdrawn by the police. In two of these cases the file gave reasons for this change of heart by the police. In one case the parties had mediated, the defendant had made recompense and the victims had petitioned for the defendant not to be prosecuted. In the other case the police withdrew the case when it was sent back to them for a second time for supplementary investigation.

In only two of these 16 cases was the decision not to prosecute initiated by the procuratorate. In one of these cases the file recorded that the parties had conciliated, the suspect 'had a good attitude' and the case was returned to the police for handling. In the other case the procuratorate appear to have directed the police to withdraw the case because of a fatal insufficiency of evidence ('the evidence was different and the suspect could not be arrested').

Our findings on the low rate of non-prosecution cases are reflected in other research and consistent with official policy in this regard. In general, the Chinese procuratorates have put crime control values as the key focus. In order to increase the rate of convicted cases and 'strike hard' against criminals, they have adopted a series of measures to control the rate of non-prosecution (Zhang and Zhong, 2007). For example, the Supreme People's Procuratorate, holding a cautious and conservative attitude, set up a system of non-prosecution evaluation and warning of non-prosecution rates in advance.[37] In

---

[37] Liu, Qi and Zeng (2008), pp. 112–113; Sun Changyong (2009), p. 83.

February 1998, the Supreme People's Procuratorate issued a normative document to require the procuratorates at all levels to strictly control the non-prosecution rate. After that, the non-prosecution rate at a national level fell to 2.5 per cent in 1998, 2 per cent in 1999, 2.4 per cent in 2000, 3 per cent in 2002, 2.8 per cent in 2003, and 3.3 per cent in 2004. Later, the Supreme Procuratorate in 2005 issued a document, *Trial Measures on the Evaluation of Cases Handled by the Procuratorial Organs*, to further specify 2 per cent or less as the rate of relative non-prosecution in ordinary criminal cases, 6 per cent or less in cases destroying social market economic order and 12 per cent or less in cases directly handled by the procuratorate (Liu and Yang, 2009).

As in our research, it is possible to see the major change in non-prosecution that the policies have effected. For example, before 1996 the non-prosecution rate was between 10 and 11 per cent (Li Sha, 2008). Subsequently, the non-prosecution rate in Jiangsu Province varied between 0.9 and 1.8 per cent over the years 2003 and 2006 (Li and Zhang, 2007) and in Guizhou it was less than 2 per cent (Peng, 2010). In 2006, a municipal procuratorate accepted cases involving 4650 suspects, while only 10 suspects (0.22 per cent) were not prosecuted (Li and Yang, 2009).

The main reason for the low rate of non-prosecution would appear to be the internal evaluation mechanism apart from internal policy. In some places, the public prosecution offices set the rate of non-prosecution as one of the 'five rates' (the rate of acquittal, case withdrawal, non-prosecution, success of protest and correction of wrong or retroactive criminal cases) in the performance evaluation mechanism.[38] Once the rate of non-prosecution exceeds the required percentage or if the decision is wrong, the procuratorate concerned will lose points in the performance evaluation, and the result may affect the award or punishment of the procuratorate at the higher level and local party committee.[39]

CONCLUSION

It is clear from the above that the primary consequence of the prosecutor's actions is to advance or shore up the case prepared by the police. Once a case is received with a recommendation for prosecution from the police, the procuratorate will generally move the case forward to trial. In this process, steps will be taken to ensure that the ancillary paperwork is accurate and in compliance with internal prosecution rules, that statements are signed and dated and that any and all exhibits are photographed and available for inspection by the court. If there are gaps in the evidence presented by the police when they recommend prosecution, either the police will be asked to respond (though they will rarely do so in a positive manner) or prosecutors might take steps themselves to make good any shortfall (though they are rarely successful in this regard).[40] Processing decisions within

---

[38] Huang and Chen (2006), pp. 68–69. Chen Weidong (2004), p. 261; Li Sha (2008), pp. 94–95; Tian Yuan (2006), p. 71; Li and Yang (2009), p. 111; Guo Youjia (2007); Liu and Yang (2009), p. 41.

[39] This was the part about which prosecutors complained in other studies. See, Li and Yang (2009), p. 111.

[40] The apparent contradiction between requesting supplementary evidence but continuing a prosecution even where no such evidence is produced can be explained in a number of ways. For example, the request may simply be a device to assist the police in prolonging detention rather than

the procuratorate are subject to a strict bureaucratic and hierarchical vetting regime which subordinates the role of individual prosecutors not only to the dictates of superiors but also to the decisions of committees which may in turn take into account social or political or personal considerations. Policy edicts and internal performance indicators further reduce the number of cases which might be discontinued. Essentially, the part played by the prosecutor at the pre-trial stage is to advance the case, as received and/or strengthened, to trial.

---

reflecting a genuine need for additional evidence. Further, as we shall discuss in Chapters 14 and 15, the procuratorate may itself be under pressure to proceed with a case notwithstanding some deficiencies in evidence.

6. Pre-trial involvement of judges

INTRODUCTION

Under the 1979 CPL the court had extensive pre-trial involvement in cases, with judges heavily involved in the consideration and investigation of cases prior to the opening of the trial. It was the duty of the procuratorate to send all case documents to the court, and it was the duty of the court to review and examine the case thoroughly in deciding whether the case should be accepted for trial, sent back with an order for supplementary investigation by the procuratorate, dismissed or sent back with a request that the case be withdrawn. As part of this process, judges were themselves empowered to conduct inquests, interrogations, searches and seizures, and obtain expert evaluations in deciding whether a case should be accepted for prosecution (Chow, 2003, p. 271).

This system of prosecutorial and judicial alliance was criticized for blurring the line between prosecution and adjudication.[1] In deciding whether to accept a case for trial the judiciary were obliged to ask whether the facts of the crime were clear and the evidence sufficient, and to make this determination on the basis of all the prosecution evidence, supplemented if necessary by further investigations ordered by the judiciary itself. As the standard for conviction was the same as that for deciding whether a case should be accepted (namely, whether the facts were clear and the evidence sufficient) it followed that there was a large element of predetermination on the part of the court as soon as the trial opened and a public perception that trials were in form only. Observers criticized the system as one which operated on the basis of 'decision first, trial later'.[2]

In line with changes in inquisitorial systems elsewhere,[3] this system was reformed by the 1996 CPL, and in this chapter we explain the rules that apply under this reformed process. We also report what practical involvement judges now have in the pre-trial process as disclosed by what judges told us when we interviewed them in private.[4] We

---

[1] E.g. see Sun Changyong (2009); Zuo Weimin et al. (2009); and Zhang and Hao (2005).

[2] E.g. Zuo Weimin et al. (2009); and Zhang and Hao (2005).

[3] There has been a tendency in other inquisitorial systems to reduce the role of the judge in the pre-trial phase with some jurisdictions limiting the judge to decisions concerning such matters as search/seizure warrants, arrest, pre-trial detention and bail. See, Langer (2004) who provides details of a number of countries such as Germany, Italy, Guatemala, Costa Rica, Venezuela and Chile: *ibid.*, at p. 27. See also, Esser (2004) who states that as the result of the reform of the criminal procedure law in Germany in 1975, 'the position of the investigating judge in cases of serious crime was abolished in favor of an unlimited competence of the public prosecutor to investigate during the pre-trial stage' (*ibid.*, at p. 118).

[4] We reiterate that in a number of instances, our researchers undertook interviews with judges in restaurants, tea-houses and other settings in which the judge felt more able to conduct such a conversation. In all cases, we were fully aware that judges experienced difficulty and felt concern over the extent to which they could be open with us on sensitive issues.

place these findings in the context of the criticisms and concerns that observers continue to voice about the pre-trial involvement of judges in the criminal process.

PRE-TRIAL PROCEDURE OF THE 1996 CPL

Article 150, 1996 CPL provides that the People's Court, having examined a case in which the procuratorate has initiated prosecution:

> shall decide to open the court session and try the case, if the bill of prosecution contains clear facts of the crime accused and, in addition, there are a list of evidence and a list of witnesses as well as duplicates or photos of major evidence attached to it.

The term 'major evidence' is defined in the *Interpretation of the Supreme People's Court on Several Questions in the Implementation of the Criminal Procedure Law of the People's Republic of China* (SPC Interpretation[5]) and in the *Rules of the People's Procuratorate on Criminal Procedure* (SPP Rules). According to Article 116 of the SPC Interpretation, 'major evidence' includes all evidence mentioned in the Bill of Prosecution and which also falls within any category of evidence listed in Article 42, 1996 CPL. Article 42, in turn, contains a comprehensive list of the types of evidence that are likely to feature in any trial (including all material and documentary evidence, testimony of victims and witnesses, confessions and exculpations of the defendant, records of inquest and examination and expert conclusions). Article 116 of the SPC Interpretation also includes within the definition of 'major evidence' all information that can be used to show that the defendant is a recidivist. Article 283 of the SPP Rules defines 'major evidence' as 'evidence that is crucial to the facts that are used to ascertain the elements of the crime and evidence that has significant impact on the determination of guilt and the sentence of the defendant'.

The net effect of these provisions is that the procuratorate may send to the court *all* the evidence that it has collated as part of its task of preparing the case for prosecution, and it can do this by simply mentioning it in the Bill of Prosecution and thus bringing it within the definition of 'major evidence', or it can do so by relying upon the definition under Article 283 of the SPP Rules. Moreover, Article 283 offers explicit legal justification for providing to the court only those parts of the evidence which tend to prove the guilt of the defendant. The provision states that if the major evidence is a piece of documentary evidence (such as a written statement, written record of the witness statement, victim's statement, confession of the defendant, or written record of expert evaluation) the procuratorate need only transfer a duplicate of that part of the evidence that can prove the guilt of the defendant.

Article 116 of the SPC Interpretation sets out ten items that the court has to examine after receiving the Bill of Prosecution transferred by the procuratorate, and it is clear from this list that the court could not discharge the legal obligations placed on it without access to all the evidence listed above. The ten items are as follows:

---

[5] Issued by the Supreme People's Court, Supreme People's Procuratorate, Ministry of Public Security, Ministry of State Security, Ministry of Justice and the Legal System Working Committee of the Standing Committee of the National People's Congress in 1998.

1) Whether the court has jurisdiction over the case.
2) Whether the identity of the defendant, the time and place of the occurrence of the alleged crime, the means to perpetrate the alleged crime, the facts and harmful consequence of the crime, the charge of the alleged crime, and other matters that may affect the determination of guilt and the sentence of the defendant are clear.
3) Whether the bill of prosecution has stated the kind of compulsory measures that have been imposed on the defendant, the place of detention, whether the defendant has been arrested, and whether the property of the defendant has been seized or frozen and the place where it is kept, and whether the name, address and correspondence details of the victim are attached to the bill of prosecution.
4) Whether the list of evidence that was collected before the initiation of prosecution is attached to the bill of prosecution.
5) Whether the duplicates or photos of major evidence that can prove the nature and circumstance of the crime alleged are attached to the bill of prosecution.
6) Whether the list of witnesses that have given statements before the initiation of prosecution is attached to the bill of prosecution.
7) Whether the name, address and correspondence details of the defender or *agent ad litem* are attached to the bill of prosecution.
8) Whether materials related to the incidental civil action are included in the case files.
9) Whether the duplicates of all the litigation documents relating to investigation and initiation of prosecution are included in the case files.
10) Whether any of the situations listed in Article 15(2) to (6) of the CPL 1996 apply in the present case (i.e. situations in which criminal responsibility is not to be investigated).

The failure by the procuratorate to provide the court with the documents and evidence listed in Article 150 does not mean that the court can reject the case. Article 37 of the SPC Interpretation provides that where the procuratorate fail to transfer any material the court may notify it to provide supplementary materials within three days of receipt of notification.

Additional guidance on how courts should approach the task of initial case examination is provided by Article 117 of the SPC Interpretation, which states that:

1) cases may be returned to the procuratorate if the court does not have jurisdiction or if the defendant has not been arrested;
2) the court may accept cases where the defendant has previously been found not guilty after trial if the procuratorate re-initiate a prosecution based on new facts and evidence;
3) unless supported by new facts and evidence, the court must not accept cases forwarded by the procuratorate where the court has already after examination requested that the case be withdrawn;
4) if the facts of a crime are clear and the evidence is reliable and sufficient the court should accept the case even if the true identity and address of the suspect is not known.

Article 118 of the SPC Interpretation provides that the court should make a decision on whether or not to accept a case for trial within seven days of examination for cases which are to be prosecuted under the Ordinary Procedure, and within three days for those cases which are to be prosecuted using the Summary Procedure.

Article 151, 1996 CPL prescribes a number of practical steps that a People's Court must take in respect of those cases which it decides to accept for trial. These steps include determining the members of the collegial panel that are to try the case; delivering the Bill of Prosecution to the defendant no later than ten days before the opening of the court session; informing the defendant that he may appoint a defence lawyer, or, where applicable, appointing a defence lawyer for him under legal aid; providing the procuratorate three days' notice of the time and place of trial; delivering summons and notifications to all relevant parties (including witnesses and experts); making an announcement, three days before commencement of trial, of the subject matter of the case to be heard in public, the name of the defendant, and the time and place of the court session. That all these steps have been taken must be entered into the written record, and signed by both the judges and the court clerk.

PRE-TRIAL JUDICIAL ACTIVISM

Our interviews with 88 judges revealed that judges undertook what at one level appear to be simply a variety of administrative steps to ensure compliance with Articles 150 and 151, 1996 CPL.[6] These steps included ensuring that the court had jurisdiction to hear the case; checking that evidence had been transferred from the police/procuratorate; verifying the identity and antecedents of the defendant; examining the Bill of Prosecution; determining whether the case was to be tried by Ordinary or Summary Procedure; fixing the time and place of trial; selecting the collegial panel; notifying defendants, defenders, victims and victims' families of the time and place of trial and ensuring that relevant documents (Bill of Prosecution, summons etc.) were served on them; notifying the defendant of his or her right to hire a defender or appointing one for him or her where the legal provisions required this; considering whether the compulsory measures imposed on the defendant needed to be changed; and ensuring that relevant property had been returned to victims or their families. Some judges described the pre-trial stage in these terms:

> *D-IJ-K-04:* First, I will read case files and review the case to see if it can meet the registration requirements. If yes, I will ask the internal secretary to register the case. Then, I will arrange for a court clerk to send the Bill of Prosecution and find out if the defendant will engage a lawyer. If the defendant wants to have a lawyer, I will help him or her to inform the agency regarding hiring a lawyer. After that, I will arrange the time of the court session ten days later. Three days before the session, I will also inform the prosecutors and the defence lawyer of the time to attend the court trial. Then, I need to read the Bill of Prosecution and files briefly and prepare the questions that I will ask during the trial. During this period, one important thing is to ask the defence lawyer to come and read case files. In addition, I will prepare an outline of the court session and get familiarized with relevant articles.

> *F-IJ-N-04:* When I receive a case, I will carefully read all the materials handed over by the Procuratorate to find out whether there is anything missing or mistaken in the Bill of Prosecution, including whether the facts are clear and the evidence is sufficient. I dare not be careless at all. There is accountability for both myself and other people. When I find any problems I usually communicate with prosecutors or discuss with my colleagues. Except for the substantive examination, I also attach importance to examining the procedure. I learned a hard lesson in hearing a criminal case in an incidental civil action. In the pre-trial stage I didn't notice that I hadn't delivered the *subpoena* to the plaintiff in an incidental civil action. After opening

---

[6] In some courts there was a system under which cases were initially received by a court filing section the clerks of which would often undertake basic administrative tasks such as filing the case, delivering relevant notices and arranging court sessions. The abilities of these clerks were sometimes called into question but we have no direct data on this stage of the process.

the court session I started to realize it. Then the plaintiff intended to complain. The head of the criminal court and I made an apology to them and opened another court session.

All these steps are to be expected given the duties that are imposed on the judiciary under the 1996 CPL. But the judicial role was not so limited and extended routinely to reading the evidence in the prosecution file and preparing for the trial:

> *J-IJ-S4-06:* When I receive a case, I will firstly read the Bill of Prosecution to find out whether there is sufficient evidence to prove the offence prosecuted and whether there is any doubt on the facts and evidence, so as to prepare myself to focus on some particular issues when adjudicating the case. If the case is complicated, generally I will prepare a question-outline to improve trial efficiency.

> *J-IJ-S4-05:* When I get the files, firstly I will study the case and how the police solved it, how the suspect was caught and his background, then I will study the suspect's crime and the main catalogue of evidence, and analyse whether the charge is tenable. I will list a question outline for the files. It's desirable if these questions are asked by the prosecutors or lawyers. But if not, I will supplement by further questioning. Generally speaking, I will introduce the case briefly to the other two judges in the collegiate panel in order to improve the efficiency of court. If there is any special and difficult case, pre-trial research is necessary. Of course that is not common.

What is of perhaps greater interest is that the discharge of their pre-trial tasks is not merely a paper-based exercise. As the interview extracts set out below demonstrate, many judges routinely leave the precincts of the court to physically meet defendants, victims and victims' families, and use this opportunity to actively engage in gathering information about the substance of the case prior to the commencement of the trial:

> *D-IJ-K-02:* If the defendant is not under detention, I have to contact him first.

> *D-K-06:* I check his place of detention; if the defendant was being granted bail, I will try to contact him . . . if there is also an incidental civil action, I also need to deliver the pleading to the defendant.

> *L-IJ-X-04:* I will also question the defendant when I deliver the Bill of Prosecution to him if I have questions.

> *E-IJ-L-06:* [I] . . . go to the detention centre to deliver both the Bill of Prosecution and the pleading of incidental civil action to the defendant.

> *D-IJ-K-05:* If the case involves an incidental civil action, I will also notify the victim whether the defendant is willing to have mediation.

> *K-IJ-W-01:* If the defendant is a minor, I have to meet with him first and then notify his legal representative: if he is a student, I need to go to his school to inquire about his behaviour in school.

> *L-IJ-X-02:* I ask whether he [the victim] is going to initiate an incidental civil action and whether mediation should be conducted before trial, to learn about their views as to how to punish the defendant.

> *D-IJ-K-06:* I question the defendant to learn about his views and whether his views are consistent with his confession statement.

A-IJ-B1-02: I will talk with minors based on the characteristics of the juvenile court, to understand their experiences, and even their family conditions.

E-IJ-L-01: I question the defendant to learn about his attitude in admitting his guilt.

E-IJ-L-02: I will check whether the defendant objects to the allegation stated in the Bill of Prosecution.

C-IJ-B3-07: Upon receiving the procuratorate's decision on initiation of prosecution, I will examine all the materials carefully, write a record of the examination work, the legal basis of the case according to the facts and the accusations, question the defendant, meet with the lawyers and prepare an outline of the adjudication.

G-IJ-S1-03: I will ask the defendant while delivering the Bill of Prosecution whether he admits his guilt and try to learn his views.

What the above extracts demonstrate is that the 1996 CPL has not had the effect of insulating judges from case preparation, and neither has it stopped them from conducting their own investigation and examination prior to the trial.[7] In discharging the various tasks that have been assigned to them under Articles 150 and 151, 1996 CPL judges can, and on many occasions clearly do, question both defendants and victims prior to the case coming to trial, and do so by visiting their homes or schools, meeting victims at court or, in the case of defendants, at their place of detention and interact with the prosecution, as the following extract from our interviews show:

E-IJ-L-01: I read case files and list the evidence. Then, I will list the problems I found when I read the case files. It is an old tradition for us to list out the problems to be investigated during the trial. This practice also helps us to become familiar with the case and see if the evidence is sufficient. For example, a murder case should have the following evidence: the defendant's confession, written record on the taking of evidence such as the lethal weapon, fingerprints, blood stains, written record on the identification of lethal weapon and fingerprints and the document on the conclusion of the material evidence, such as the victim's blood on the defendant's clothes. If the above-mentioned evidence is complete, this case would be simple for us to make a judgment. Sometimes, prosecution cases without sufficient evidence embarrass after the transfer. We have to suggest that the procuratorate withdraw the case before the opening of the court session. In addition, I have to deliver the defendant the Bill of Prosecution in person on most occasions in order to know the defendant's attitude toward the charge. Moreover, I will contact the defendant's family to make sure whether they want to employ a lawyer for the defendant; issue and send the notice of court hearing to the prosecutors and the defender. If the defendant is detained in a county, I will contact the local court and the judicial police to arrange the courtroom for the trial in order to save resources and reduce security problems.

---

[7] It is very likely that our data understate the extent to which judges involve themselves in pre-trial investigation because a number of judges, as our researchers noted, were very reluctant to talk about this issue and others did so guardedly. When asked how they prepared for trial, for example, some judges responded by asserting strict compliance with the 1996 CPL (e.g., B-IJ-B2-02 'I strictly follow the provisions of the Criminal Procedure Law to conduct preparation. For example, examination of jurisdiction, the content of the bill of prosecution, and whether the evidence has been transferred'; B-IJ-B2-04 'I will conduct the work of examination of filing a case and procedural examination after receiving the case, but I will not conduct substantive examination.').

This in itself means that the role of the judge is very different to the role played by judges in the common law adversarial system, where the judge is forbidden from having any communication with defendants, victims or witnesses outside of the courtroom. The judicial role in China also differs from that in many other inquisitorial systems which, although not precluding judicial involvement in pre-trial investigation have created detailed rules in an effort to ensure the presence of an individual free from bias and to protect against the problem of predetermination of guilt. Thus, for example, in Germany while the prosecutor in charge of the inquiry conducts the necessary investigation, certain measures may be undertaken only with the authorization of the judge but that judge (*Ermittlungsrichter*) is not the trial judge but one whose responsibility is to oversee (but not direct) the preliminary stages of the case (Juy-Birmann, 2005). Similar divisions of responsibility exist in other inquisitorial systems such as Italy, France and Belgium.[8]

Some Chinese judges are aware that their pre-trial actions in regard to investigation may influence their attitude towards the case, as for example the following judge sets out:

> *J-IJ-S4-04:* In this process, the relatives of the victim may visit me to report on the present situation of the victim, proposing an incidental civil action and asking the judge to punish the defendant severely. In this way, we can know more about the case on the one hand. On the other hand, we are human beings and we have feelings and sympathy for the weak. Maybe it would influence the outcome of the trial. Of course we must control ourselves and try our best to give the accused appropriate punishment. To assure equality of judicial justice, we try our best not to meet the victim.

The review undertaken by Chinese judges is also anticipatory, identifying areas of importance which they will need to cover if the prosecutor fails to do so:

> *F-IJ-N-01:* First, I will read the case files and review the evidence, which is the requirement of flow management, to check if the material is complete and the evidence is sufficient. If I think it is acceptable, I will take the defendant the Bill of Prosecution in person, ask him/her questions simply to know if he/she has any disagreement with the Bill of Prosecution, if she/he wants to employ a defence lawyer and the contact number. If there is an incidental civil action in the case, I will also give the defendant the civil complaint. In addition, I will send the plaintiff of the incidental civil action the Bill of Prosecution and inform him/her of the litigation rights and the required evidence. If the defendant's family encounters financial difficulty but the defendant may be sentenced to death, I have to find a legal aid lawyer for him/her. Then, I will decide the time and place of the court session, which should be ten days later. If the case involves legal aid, I will also copy and send the case files to the legal aid centre. After that, I will read the case files again, understand the case information in detail and list the question-outline for the trial in order to be completely prepared. From this year on, generally speaking, prosecutors have started to transfer the original copy of the case files. In the past, they might fail to transfer copies of some important evidence. Under such a situation, I had to ask them to complete it. Then, I will inform the parties concerned of the time and place of the trial three days in advance.

---

[8] Thus, for example, in Italy, the judge in charge of preliminary investigations (*guidice per le indagini preliminari*) and appointed to each court does not preside at the preliminary hearing, a function discharged by a different judge (the *guidice dell'udienza preliminare*): Perrodet (2005). There is also now a division of function in the French system where the *juge d'instruction* acts as investigator and judge but decisions on remand in custody are made by an independent judge (the *juge des libertes et de la detention*) and the hearing is before the *cour d'assises*: See, Dervieux (2005). A similar situation obtains in Belgium: Pesquie (2005).

This also illustrates that, if one purpose of the reform was to convert judges into neutral arbiters, this has not been achieved.

As the system for pursuing compensation for criminal injuries is combined into the formal criminal justice system, judges will frequently have substantial contact with both defendants and victims prior to the criminal trial in the context of resolving civil claims. This inevitably means that they must have access to and be familiar with much of the evidence which will ultimately feature in the criminal trial. The following extracts are examples of judges who, on being asked how they prepare for the trial, volunteered that they sought to resolve the civil action arising from the case file:

B-IJ-B2-01: Examine the jurisdiction, the content of Bill of Prosecution, whether the evidence has been transferred; based on the content of the Bill of Prosecution consider the major points that need to be examined during trial; refer to the relevant judicial interpretations for new offences; conduct mediation in personal injury cases, try to recover the loss for the victims.

B-IJ-B2-11; B-IJ-B2-14; L-IJ-X-07: Conduct mediation in personal injury cases, try to recover losses on behalf of the victim.

B-IJ-B2-10: Notify the parties, understand the case, handle civil compensation, conduct partial questioning, meet with the lawyers, make inquiries of the prosecutor in charge of the case or experts on relevant issues.

D-IJ-K-01: For private prosecution cases, mediation will be conducted before trial; for public prosecution cases, mediation will be conducted during the trial.

A-IJ-B1-01: I conduct mediation first in cases involving minor injury; in cases involving incidental civil action, I need to contact the victim first.

When asked to describe how they prepared for trial, many judges said that they read the case materials. Most amplified this only to say that they did so in order to 'learn the circumstances of the case' but others provided slightly more detail by saying that they read the materials to verify the confessions, testimonies and evidence, examine whether the facts of the crime alleged by the prosecution existed or learn the circumstances of the case and discover how the police solved the case and how the defendant came to be arrested. While most judges indicated that they routinely read the case materials, others suggested that they concentrated more on certain types of case or cases with certain features:

L-IJ-X-05: I read the case files in detail if the offence alleged is incompatible with the facts alleged.

A-IJ-B1-04: After the assignment of the case by the president of the court, the clerk and I will perform work such as delivery of Bill of Prosecution and notification of the defendant of his rights according to the provisions of the Criminal Procedure Law. I will examine the materials transferred by the procuratorate to see whether they are comprehensive, prepare a trial outline in order to discover the problems and find the objectives of the trial.

F-IJ-N-06: Everyone knows that I don't read case files before court sessions, because of my sufficient experience and my intention of avoiding forming a predetermination. My mind is very clear and I can find out problems in a short time. As for some important cases or cases with many files, I will study case files to have a clearer understanding of the trial.

B-IJ-B2-12: I conduct a detailed examination of the case before trial.

G-IJ-S1-03: If the defendant doesn't admit his guilt and if the case is complicated; but in some cases, even if the defendant has admitted his guilt, I still need to read the case materials.

G-IJ-S1-02: If the defendant has made a defence and explanation, I will read the facts.

A-IJ-B1-03: Firstly, I will examine the case files that were transferred by the procuratorate. Based on the circumstances of the case, I will look at the relevant laws and do some preparation regarding the legal basis.

One big city judge gave a detailed account of the approach to pre-trial preparation which she took, along with the clerk, and which she thought standard, in the following terms:

B-IJ-B2-14: Firstly, a judge will examine if there are any mistakes in the Bill of Prosecution, mainly to check whether there are any typing errors, grammatical mistakes and problems such as with information concerning household registration and age of the defendant. Then the clerk will be responsible for handling the procedure for any change in custodial arrangements (if it is a case in which the defendant was arrested), informing the defendant of his rights and responsibilities and delivering the Bill of Prosecution. Also, when a defendant requests a defence lawyer, the clerk will handle the relevant procedure. If the defendant is a minor, blind, deaf or dumb or if he may be sentenced to death . . . the clerk will need to appoint a defender for him. At this stage the judge will start to read the case file. He will read the investigative organ's case file for preliminary examination if the case is going to be tried according to summary procedure; he will read the duplicates of the major evidence as provided by the procuratorate if ordinary procedure is to be adopted. After that he will read the confession statements of the suspect and the statements of witnesses, examine whether there has been a failure to transfer any evidence or whether evidence that could confirm the case is lacking. For example, if some defendants in a case confessed frankly, then the judge has to see whether the interrogations were conducted by the investigative organ individually and, if so, which defendants were interrogated this way. In conclusion, preparation for trial is very burdensome: a judge is primarily responsible for conducting a substantive examination of the case, while the clerk is mainly responsible for clerical work. One point that needs to be added is that in a criminal case with incidental civil action, a lot of mediation work has to be undertaken in relation to the civil action before trial.

Judges were fully aware of the bias that reading the prosecution case file inevitably creates. As one big city judge put it:

A-IJ-B1-08: Before trial, a judge will mainly conduct an examination of the relevant materials that are provided by the procuratorate, but all the materials provided by the procuratorate are materials that prove the guilt of the criminal suspect: there are relatively few materials about the minor responsibility of the suspect. Materials that may involve the innocence of the suspect may not be provided.

Another judge indicated that in their region, although the procuratorate should transfer to the court copies of the 'major evidence', a full inspection of the files occurs in advance of trial even though this is not contemplated by the 1996 CPL and is, in the view of the judge, contrary to the law:

K-IJ-W-01: It takes different time and different energy to deal with different cases. Some simple cases can be scanned briefly; but some cases involving several defendants and involving several locations must be read carefully. I mainly read the written prosecution evidence to see whether the facts are clear, whether defendants admit crimes, whether there is any evidence to prove the defendant's confession, whether the crime charged is correct and so on. In fact, all files are sent to the court at the pre-trial stage. *This is against the law*. But there is not enough time, particularly in difficult and complicated cases. If judges do not examine case files carefully before trial, the trial efficiency cannot be ensured and the trial will even exceed the time limits. To process the case well, we have to do it (emphasis supplied).

A minority of respondents indicated that reading the case materials was not an important part of their trial preparation:

E-IJ-L-04: Only a rough review, no details will be examined before trial.

H-IJ-S2-01: Flip through the duplicates of evidence.

G-IJ-S1-02: If I have time, I will read the case materials, but if I don't have time, I will not do that until after the trial.

A-IJ-B1-09: I rarely conduct an in-depth substantive examination of the duplicates of the major evidence before trial.

As explained above, the object behind changing the rules governing pre-trial examination of cases by the judiciary was to remove the judiciary from the process of prosecution case preparation and construction. The idea, as commonly understood and explained in the Chinese literature, was that the 1996 CPL would limit the amount of information that was supplied to judges prior to the trial so that they would not, on the basis of the prosecution file, reach a predetermination or a bias in favour of the prosecution case.[9] Our interviews with judges revealed that, leaving aside the evidence gathered by judges through their own endeavours, the 1996 CPL has not succeeded in limiting the amount of prosecution evidence that is transferred from the procuratorate to the court prior to trial.

Before setting out illustrations from the relevant parts of our interview data, it is important to make the point that if the objective of reforming the 1996 CPL was to limit the amount of prosecution evidence that judges were allowed to view prior to trial, the legal provisions themselves have not been drafted so as to make this either obvious or inevitable.[10] As mentioned above, it is difficult to see how a judge can comply with Article 116 of the SPC Interpretation without a detailed understanding of all evidence in the case. A judge cannot, without access to the prosecution file, for example: decide whether there can be pre-trial mediation of an incidental civil claim; cannot check whether the identity of the defendant, the time and place of the occurrence of the alleged crime, the means to

---

[9] The reform on the transfer of case files was expected to have a number of virtues: (1) it would reduce the possibility of a judge's predetermination; (2) it would help enhance the defence and improve the balance between the defence and the prosecution; (3) it would strengthen the impartiality of the trial and improve the correctness of the judgment; (4) it would contribute to improving the professional quality of the judiciary. See also Liu Genju (1999). This also cannot be avoided before the trial in the cases heard in simplified ordinary procedure. See for example, Guo Zhiyuan (2007); Xu Meijun (2007); and Ji Xiangde (2006).

[10] Despite this, some judges believe that only a restricted file of evidence can be transferred to the court by the procuratorate and that a full-file transfer would be 'illegal'. See, for example, K-IJ-W-01 (above).

perpetrate the alleged crime, the facts and harmful consequence of the crime, the charge of the alleged crime, and other matters that may affect the determination of guilt and the sentence of the defendant are clear; and cannot decide whether the case falls under Article 15(2) to (6) of the CPL (i.e., various situations in which criminal responsibility is not to be investigated). In order to perform these tasks judges must, at the very least, have access to the witness statements.

Further, it is difficult to see how the 1996 CPL provisions could be viewed as restricting judicial access to the prosecution evidence, given the all-encompassing definition of 'major evidence', coupled with a provision allowing the procuratorate to forward only that part of the evidence which shows the defendant to be guilty, the latter provision, in and of itself, hardly serving the objective of preventing the risk of predetermination by the judge (see also Ye Qing, 2006). This provision alone demonstrates once again the point that attention needs to be given by reformers to what the law is rather than what it is thought to be. This provision, like so many others, is enabling rather than restrictive.

Finally, the 1996 CPL does not put in place a procedure whereby the examining judge is barred from conducting the trial (as happens, as we have noted above, in many other inquisitorial systems), a safeguard which would be expected if the aim was to prevent judges becoming unduly influenced by the prosecution case prior to trial.[11] In fact, it is almost routine practice in China for the judge who conducts the Article 150 pre-trial examination to act as one of the judges, if not the case-responsible judge,[12] in the trial itself.[13] As the interview extracts set out below demonstrate, the fact that the examining judge will in all likelihood conduct the trial[14] is one of the matters which drives judges to seek as much information about the case as possible prior to trial.

This tension between the stated objectives of the reform and the letter of the legal provisions has not been lost on legal commentators or judges in China. For example, Cheng Guoping (1998) pointed out that the 1996 CPL does not prohibit judges from carrying out substantive examination during pre-trial examination. According to Cheng, if the pre-trial examination was supposed to be confined to procedural examination, there would have been no need for the procuratorate to transfer duplicates or photos of the major evidence to the court. Li Jian (2003) has noted that restricting judicial access to the prosecution file could not have been intended, because (a) such restriction would hamper judicial control of procuratorates and the need for the judiciary to prevent procuratorates abusing their powers and (b) without conducting substantive examination, issues such as jurisdiction, withdrawal and matters relating to the incidental civil action could not be resolved before trial, and this would lead to inefficiency if trials had to be adjourned midway in order to resolve such issues.

Although we did not specifically ask judges what evidence they had access to prior to trial, it is clear from the responses given to the question of how they prepared for trial

---

[11] See, Chen and Liu Jihua (1998); Long Zongzhi (1998); Wei Hong (2000); Yang Zhengwan (1998); Wang and Yang (2002); Song and Chen (2002).

[12] See, Xiao Nianhua (1998). In our research, we found that cases did in fact 'belong' to one of the judges, that that judge undertook all steps relevant to the case and that the other judges for the most part were not actively engaged in the disposition of the case or any other aspect to do with it.

[13] See, Wang Yu (2002); Xiao Nianhua (1998); and Li Jian (2003).

[14] In a few instances, other judges undertook the initial review.

that many judges continue to have access to the entirety of the prosecution file, including the confession of the defendant and the prosecution witness statements:

B-IJ-B2-14: Look at the confession statements of the defendant and the witness testimonies.

K-IJ-W-01: Read the evidence, examine whether the defendant's confession is supported by evidence.

K-IJ-W-02: The defendant's confession statements must be read, especially if those are different from those alleged in the Bill of Prosecution and his defence.

D-IJ-K-01: Just a procedural examination, but after the case has been filed, the substance of the case also needs to be examined.

L-IJ-X-04: Check whether the evidence is concrete and whether there is any inconsistency in the evidence and whether the facts of the crime can be confirmed.

L-IJ-X-05: Read the major evidence to see whether it supports the prosecution allegation.

L-IJ-X-06: Check whether there is any problem with the major evidence, whether it can prove the facts of the crime alleged by the prosecution, and whether any evidence is missing.

In fact, as the following judges made clear, the judiciary and procuratorate continue to work together to ensure that the case is comprehensively prepared prior to trial and that the procuratorate view the judiciary as a source of information and guidance to assist them in putting together the prosecution case:

L-IJ-X-02: We mainly examine the major evidence, but if the case is complicated and there is insufficient budget and the prosecutor feels that it is burdensome to make copies, he may transfer the original materials to the court; or when the prosecution thinks there is insufficient evidence in the case, it will send the original evidence so as to exchange opinions with us.

B-IJ-B2-14: There is a conflict between judicial custom and criminal procedure law. For example, the procuratorate transfers material to the court and, after examination, it is discovered that the evidence regarding some aspects is lacking. The judge will ask the prosecutor in charge of the case to provide supplementary materials.

It can be seen, therefore, that not only are judges commonly given pre-trial access to all the information and evidence on which the prosecution rely for demonstrating the guilt of the defendant, but that judges continue to be actively involved in reviewing cases in partnership with the procuratorate with the objective of ensuring that 'the facts are clear and the evidence sufficient' prior to opening the court session and trying the case. This is also clear from the following interview extracts:

M-IJ-Y-02: I communicate with the prosecution if some materials are missing or if there are doubts.

M-IJ-Y-04: I inform the prosecution to rectify or provide supplementary materials.

A-IJ-B1-01: Normally I will conduct a paper examination of the materials concerning major evidence that was transferred to me so as to have a brief understanding of the case. Also, I will exchange opinions with the procurators in charge of the case regarding those problematic materials.

B-IJ-B2-10: I make inquiries of the prosecutor in charge of the case.

L-IJ-X-04: I communicate with the prosecution when I have questions or ask the prosecutor to provide supplementary evidence.

L-IJ-X-06: Request the prosecutor to provide supplementary evidence if some evidence is missing.

A-IJ-B1-06: In some cases, certain aspects of their facts are not very clear, some evidence is lacking. In these circumstances, I will find the prosecutor so as to learn more about the situation.

L-IJ-X-07: I will ask the prosecutor to provide supplementary materials if necessary.

F-IJ-N-03: I will communicate with the prosecution if the facts of the case are unclear, the evidence is insufficient or some key materials are missing; I will communicate with the prosecution promptly and ask them to provide supplementary materials.

F-IJ-N-04: I will communicate with the prosecution if I discover any problem while reading the case materials.

Some judges also mentioned that they communicated with the defence prior to the trial, but the research data does not make clear the purpose behind such contact. Some of the interview extracts with judges set out below suggest the purpose is limited to answering questions that the defendant or his defender may have, while others suggest that judges gather information from the defence:

H-IJ-S2-03: Communicate with the prosecution and the defence in complicated cases.

C-IJ-B3-01: Answer questions raised by the prosecution and the defence.

M-IJ-Y-03: Exchange opinions with the prosecution and the defence.

K-IJ-W-02: Communicate with prosecutors to ask for supplementary materials; meet with the defence lawyer to ask for supplementary materials.

E-IJ-L-04: Meet with the legal representative of the defendant if the defendant is a minor to learn about the defendant's situation.

Whereas in an adversarial system great care is taken to ensure that the judge (and even more so, the jury as fact-finder) hears only the evidence that emerges during the course of the trial in accordance with strict rules of evidence and procedure, under the Chinese system judges not only approach witnesses prior to the trial, but may also carry out their own legal and other research before the trial has commenced. One judge told us that he consulted experts prior to the trial (B-IJ-B2-10), three said that they familiarized themselves with the relevant law[15] and one said that he surfed the internet to look

---

[15] D-IJ-K-04; A-IJ-B1-03; and G-IJ-S1-01,

for information related to the case (J-IJ-S4-01). One judge said that this sort of activity was rare: 'If there is any special and difficult case, I may do research on the case before trial. But of course, that is not common' (J-IJ-S4-05). And judges were not blind to the consequences of their investigative activities: as one judge put it:

> *D-IJ-K-03:* First I will review the case to see whether it can meet the requirements of registration and jurisdiction. Then I will read the Bill of Prosecution to get myself acquainted with the defendant's status, the charge and relevant facts. After that I will read the evidence transferred by the procuratorate to see if there is anything that needs to be verified. This may give us the 'first impression being the strongest' but this is China's characteristic.

If the aim of the 1996 CPL was to change the nature of pre-trial examination from a substantive examination into a purely procedural examination (i.e. an examination designed to ensure only that the procuratorate had followed all relevant procedures and forwarded all documentation required by the court to organize the trial), this is an aim which has not been realized.

Having said that, it is also clear that a few judges expressed concern over their investigative roles and looked to a future in which they did not experience such role-conflict. The following exemplify this view:

> *D-IJ-K-04:* I don't think it is the judge's responsibility to review a criminal case. On the one hand it adds to the judge's workload; on the other hand, it gives the judge an opportunity to have the 'first impression being the strongest' when dealing with the case.

> *D-IJ-K-05:* When the case comes to the court and if I am responsible for the case, I will review it in procedural terms. Of course, I will have a general understanding of the evidence and details of the case. Then, I will decide if the case can be registered. Here, it is the judge in charge of the case to review the case. We have to admit that it may bring us the first impression being the strongest. But this is practical, since there are not enough judges here. . . . At present, we don't have enough judges to deal with the cases, so the judge is also responsible for reviewing the case. I hope that there would be a judge who is wholly responsible for the review in order to avoid the situation of 'the first impression being the strongest'. . . . The judge should not get involved in such matters as the service of the Bill of Prosecution, reviewing the case and informing parties concerned to attend the trial. The judge could hear the case directly, like judges in western countries. But it is impossible in reality.

We should note that it is fair to say that our interviews did reveal some judges who appear to have taken to heart the purported rationale of the new procedure, and who at least attempted to limit their pre-trial involvement so as to avoid developing a prosecution bias:[16]

> *F-IJ-N-06:* I don't read case files before trial because I am experienced and I don't want to form a predisposition before trial . . . but I will read case materials if the case is big or involves many files.

> *J-IJ-S4-01:* Because I am very familiar with various kinds of case, normally I do not read case materials because I want to prevent myself from forming a predisposition on the case before trial.[17]

---

[16] See also to the same effect: M-IJ-Y-02; M-IJ-Y-04; B-IJ-B1-04; B-IJ-B1-09; K-IJ-W-03; D-IJ-K-01; D-IJ-K-05; L-IJ-X-02; E-IJ-L-03; F-IJ-N-04.

[17] Even this judge added later in the interview when discussing relationships with the police and prosecutors: 'We will also ask the police to collect supplementary evidence occasionally.'

G-IJ-S2-04: Normally I don't read case materials unless the prosecutor asks me to do so.

Further, in respect of one court, the Presiding Judge indicated that she employed a procedure under which the Presiding Judge would become involved in detailed case review only in complex cases with other cases being referred directly to another judge after an initial screening:

D-IJ-K-02: When a case is transferred to the court, I will review the case to see whether it meets the case-filing standard. Then I will distribute the case to a judge according to his capacity or the specialism of the case. For example, if the case involves minor offenders, I will assign it to a female judge. If the case is of great importance or complexity, I will deal with it in person. When I review the case, I will see if the jurisdiction is correct, if the defendant's status is clear, if the defendant is in custody. If the defendant is not in custody, for instance on bail or residential surveillance, I will contact the defendant. If I can find the defendant, I will accept the case. Then I will read the Bill of Prosecution, get a general understanding of the case and see whether the charge is in conformity with the copies of the evidence. If yes, I will open the court session. During this period I will not review the sufficiency of the evidence in detail until trial.[18]

And in a few other cases, judges said that because of case pressure they did not evaluate a case on submission by the prosecutor but, as a matter of routine, accepted all cases for prosecution (and, after this, undertook detailed review to shore up the case or fill in any gaps in the prosecution case):

K-IJ-W-01: Nowadays, courts basically accept all cases sent by the procuratorates. It is against the law. But we don't have enough staff. We can't spare any time to examine cases carefully. Because we don't examine the details of the case materials when filing a case, some problems occur when the case is heard; for example, the defendant's identity is not clear, his age is not clear and so on. These problems waste a lot of time. Judges should focus on examining criminal facts when hearing cases.[19] The defendant's basic information should be clear when the case is filed. If it is not clear, the case should be rejected [at that stage].

L-IJ-X-01: The functions of the case-filing court have not been fully realized. As a result, the relevant workload has been imposed on the trial judge.[20] The examination by the case-filing court is not detailed.

Overall, it is clear that judges who do not conduct substantive examination of case materials before trials appear to be in the minority. As can be seen from the general thrust of the majority of interview extracts we have provided, most judges continue to conduct a substantive pre-trial examination under which they read the prosecution file, interrogate suspects, interview witnesses, consult experts, carry out legal research, and liaise with the procuratorate to ensure that any gaps in the evidence are made good prior to the opening of the trial. For example, a big city judge (B-IJ-B2-12) said he would conduct

---

[18] The judge went on to say that investigations would take place should the evidence appear deficient and an adjournment would be ordered to allow this.

[19] A similar view was shared by a judge from Site D (D-IJ-K-01). A judge from Site L (L-IJ-X-09) was of the opinion that delivery of the Bill of Prosecution and inquiring whether the victim is going to initiate an incidental civil action should be done by the case-filing court.

[20] A similar view was shared by a judge from Site D (D-IJ-K-04).

a detailed examination of the case before trial while another judge from the same locality (B-IJ-B2-13) said he would conduct pre-trial examination from both substantive and procedural aspects. A judge from a province (F-IJ-N-04) also said he would conduct substantive examination of the case during the stage of pre-trial examination. A judge from a big city (Site A) said he would read the case materials before trial though he believed that was in violation of the law and would affect his impartiality:

> *A-IJ-B1-02:* Although I should not read the case files before trial in order to ensure objectiveness and impartiality, I will still take a look at the case files. But by doing so, I will be affected by the prosecution case to a certain extent.

Other judges were equally open about reading the files before (and in a number of instances, after) the trial notwithstanding the risk of creating bias in their minds:

> *J-IJ-S4-02:* Usually I will read the case after I get the files, understanding the facts of the case and the catalogue of the main evidence, then analyse whether the facts fit the crime charged, e.g. in a corruption case, firstly I will see whether the money that the defendant embezzled is public money or not, whether the defendant is a State functionary or not, whether the evidence provided by the prosecutor is sufficient or not and so on. I will also list several questions on the paper. It's fine if these questions are asked by the prosecutors or lawyers. If not, I will ask myself. You know it's such a short time from when the judges get the files to open the court, from several hours to several days.
>
> Actually not too much can be done in such a short time. According to our trial regulations in criminal procedure, we don't need too deep an understanding, to avoid first impression being the strongest. What we read are just in favour of the accusing party. Frankly speaking, the files are not carefully read before the trial. Anyway we will do that after the trial. But there is an exception in some big cases. I hope the prosecutor would hand over the files as early as possible, so that we can prepare fully. Also I hope the original files would be given to judges before the trial.

> *K-IJ-W-04:* To control the trial better, I predict possible problems and carefully examine cases before hearing court. I examine whether the procedure is sufficient, such as whether young defendants have been assigned lawyers. Then I will examine whether the evidence is consistent with the criminal facts. Detailed criminal facts can be debated by two parties in court.

One judge (J-IJ-S4-07) openly disagreed with the argument that judges should not read the prosecution file, and argued that restricting judges to the duplicates of the major evidence was an unnecessary and unworkable rule:

> *J-IJ-S4-07:* We usually don't read the duplicates of case files transferred from procuratorates. Actually, it is a great waste . . . to transfer duplicates. There is nothing wrong in judges reading the original case files. The worry that judges would form a predisposition still exists because judges can read the duplicates. I would still prefer that procuratorates transfer all original case materials to the court.

Another big city judge (G-IJ-S1-005) said that *all* judges would read the case materials before trials, and the overall impression from our interview data is that the vast majority of judges view this as a normal part of their day to day work. It is perhaps not surprising, given the amount of pre-trial preparation that judges carry out in understanding and helping to augment the prosecution case, combined with the lack of any defence involvement that one judge felt that he was in a position to draft his judgment prior to the trial commencing:

D-IJ-K-01: For cases to be adjudicated according to summary procedure, I have to read all the case files beforehand so as to familiarize with the prosecution evidence and then present the evidence on behalf of the prosecution in the trial. Sometimes, I will prepare part of the draft of the judgment.

A few judges were fully aware of the unbalanced character of prosecution files and looked forward to a time when the procuratorate supplied a comprehensive dossier, including material that was beneficial to the defence, as for example in the following quotation:

A-IJ-B1-08: A judge should conduct the adjudication impartially, and the premise is the evidence that he can have access to should be comprehensive, including the evidence that can prove the guilt and the innocence of the defendant. I hope the procuratorate would provide the materials comprehensively.

REASONS FOR PRE-TRIAL JUDICIAL ACTIVISM

There can be little doubt that one of the main reasons why judges take such an active part in pre-trial case preparation is because the 1996 CPL and Article 116 of the SPC Interpretation place a number of duties on judges which they cannot discharge without a full understanding of the case. Thus, for example, one judge explained why he had to deal directly with the police:

J-IJ-S4-08: Judges and the police do not have any direct relationship under legal procedure. But we will directly telephone the police if any supplementary investigation is needed. This is because it is a judge's duty to examine the relevant facts and evidence; otherwise it will be hard for them to decide the case.[21]

In addition to this, the literature on this topic reveals other reasons why substantive examination has persisted.

Cheng Guoping (1998) argued that, given the poor quality of judges and lawyers in China, it is difficult for judges to discharge their duties if they do not carry out substantive examination of cases before trial, especially in complicated cases. Li Jian (2003) argued that, given the poor quality of judges, some courts (particularly those at the basic level) require the procuratorates to transfer all the case materials to the court, or request them to provide supplementary evidence before trial, so as to give judges a better opportunity to prepare for the trial. And Qin Zongwen (2001) has argued that if judges were not given any information about cases before trial, they might not be able to master the trial, resulting in litigation chaos and delay. According to Qin, the judicial practice of not giving judgment at the conclusion of the trial, but instead postponing judgment to allow time to understand the evidence *after* the trial, proved that Chinese judges were incapable of following and managing trials without an in-depth substantive examination of the case file prior to trial.

---

[21] The judge added: 'Additionally, given the time constraints, and it takes a long time to allow prosecutors to handle it, which will affect concluding the case, thereby judges have to contact the police directly. The police are very co-operative.'

This view gains some support from our interview data. Three judges (E-IJ-L-03, E-IJ-L-05 and I-IJ-S3-06) said that transferring only major evidence would be insufficient to allow judges to have a comprehensive understanding of the case before trial. The following comments of a lawyer we interviewed (F-IL-N-06) clearly showed that he considered that, as he saw it, the poor quality of most of the Chinese judges made substantive examination before trial a necessity:

> *F-IL-N-06:* Some judges don't read the case materials before trial, so they don't have a clear mind in adjudication and fail to master the focus of the trial, thus leading to arbitrariness on the part of the prosecution in producing evidence to prove the case. Of course, some experienced judges can identify the focus of the trial by simply reading the Bill of Prosecution. The original legislative intent is to avoid judges forming predetermination on the case before trial by reading the case materials. But a substantial number of our judges still fail to discover and solve problems within a short period of time.

Another judge (J-IJ-S4-02) suggested that the prosecution should transfer case materials to the court earlier in major and significant cases so as to give judges more time to prepare for the trial. He added that this sort of preparation was also necessary in cases where the judge had noticed an inconsistency between the facts of the case and the alleged offence (a view shared by another judge in the West of China (L-IJ-X-05)). One judge (K-IJ-W-01) told us that judges would normally conduct substantive examination in complicated cases. In his view this was in violation of the law, but necessary to guarantee judicial efficiency:

> *K-IJ-W-01:* In fact, all files are sent to the court at the pre-trial stage. This is against regular laws. But we don't have sufficient time to handle cases, especially for difficult and complicated cases. If judges don't examine files carefully before trial, trial efficiency can't be ensured and the legally prescribed time limit will also be exceeded. To handle a case properly, we have to do that.

Others told us that supplementary investigation initiated by a judicial request or conducted by the judge was necessary in order to ensure quality control and that the trial went smoothly and that there were no gaps in the evidence. Thus, for example:

> *F-IJ-N-07:* When I receive a case, I will read the case file to find out whether the facts and evidence the prosecution advance are in accordance with the crime charged, whether there are any doubts or whether anything is omitted. If there are any problems with facts or evidence I will make enquiries with the People's Procuratorate. If the problems are clarified the court session can be arranged: if supplementary investigation is necessary the court session will be deferred until the evidence is completed. As for the current situation, to guarantee the quality of the work of handling cases, it is impossible not to communicate with the People's Procuratorate.

As is apparent from a number of comments, judges were not unaware of the contradictions between what they understood to be the law and their own practice at the pre-trial stage. Some openly justified their conduct in terms of their co-operative relationship with prosecutors and the need to ensure, in their terms, an efficient process and the avoidance of public embarrassment. Thus:

> *B-IJ-B2-14:* [Explaining why the judge would ask the prosecutor to provide supplementary material to cover deficiencies in the evidence at the pre-trial stage] If the provisions of the Criminal Procedure Law are followed, the court can only adjudicate the case on the evidence

that has been transferred. The problem of evidence deficiencies would then be raised by the defence lawyer; then the prosecutor would provide supplementary materials. If the prosecutor failed to provide supplementary materials the defendant would be found not guilty. But by doing it in such a way, on the one hand a lot of time would be wasted and the court would have to open the court session again and again; and on the other hand, the face of the prosecutor and the court would be saved.

Others saw the issue as so obvious as to require no further justification, even though they were conscious of the gap between law and practice:

> *D-IJ-K-01:* I mainly review the evidence [pre-trial]. According to the law, my review only involves procedure. But if the court decides to accept the case, we will also review the substantive content. When reviewing the case, I pay special attention to the facts and the evidence.

According to a commentary in the *Journal of the Guizhou Ethnics Institute (Social Sciences Edition)*, courts asked procuratorates to transfer all the case materials to them before trial on the basis that the court considered that all the material constituted major evidence, thus making pre-trial examination under the 1996 CPL little different from that under the 1979 CPL (Yang Zhengwan, 1998). Commentators have further suggested that procuratorates do not turn down such requests, because they wish to preserve a harmonious relationship with judges.[22] As the following comment from one of the prosecutors we interviewed shows, this practice persists, and the procuratorate is sympathetic to judicial requests of this type:

> *A-IP-B1-03:* The reform of the new trial mode has both advantage and disadvantage. The advantage is that a higher requirement is set for prosecutors: it becomes more difficult for prosecutors to discharge their duties and they have to have a comprehensive understanding of the facts and evidence and to investigate the facts properly. But in China, we still lack a legal environment that exists in developed countries and the quality of our judicial personnel remains low, their methods of verifying evidence are unscientific. As a result, problems of changes in evidence often emerge during trials, and the court then needs to return cases for supplementary investigation. This results in many cases being unable to be decided and this is disadvantageous to crime fighting. For this reason, we should absorb the advantages of the mode of trial we had previously and allow judges to have some understanding of the case by reading the case files before trial.

Another reason that substantive examination persists is because cases tried under the Summary Procedure are tried by a single judge and Article 175, 1996 CPL provides that procuratorate need not send a prosecutor to be present at trial. This means that a judge examining the case pre-trial will be acutely aware that he or she will have two functions at trial: to adjudicate upon the outcome, and to present the prosecution case. Not surprisingly, this leads judges to believe that they must have mastery of the prosecution file before the trial opens. For example, two judges (D-IJ-K-01 and G-IJ-S1-001) said they would read the case materials in great detail in cases to be adjudicated according to summary procedure. Another judge (D-IJ-K-06) explained why this was so:

---

[22] See, Wang Yu (2002); Yan Ying (2001); and Qin Zongwen (2001). A similar view was expressed by Meng and Guo (2001). See also Sun Yuan (2009).

D-IJ-K-06: For cases adjudicated according to summary procedure, I will read the case files in great detail because I will be responsible for producing evidence to prove the case. But I personally think producing evidence to prove the case by judges is a violation of the Criminal Procedure Law.

As the above comment demonstrates, criticism of the philosophy underlying the 1996 CPL was by no means universal. A minority of the judges and prosecutors we interviewed adopted the stance that judges should not engage too closely at the pre-trial examination stage. A prosecutor from a big city (A-IP-B1-08) insisted that judges should not be allowed to read the case materials before trials, while some prosecutors (e.g. F-IP-N-05, A-IP-B1-08, A-IP-B1-13 and A-IP-B1-14) and judges (e.g. A-IJ-B1-07, A-IJ-B1-13, A-IJ-B1-14, L-IJ-X-06, L-IJ-X-07, L-IJ-X-09, E-IJ-L-03, and G-IJ-S1-001) we interviewed suggested that judges should, before trial, only be provided with the Bill of Prosecution, or as few case materials as possible:

D-IJ-K-01: I suggest that the reviewing work be undertaken by the court registrar and that the judge just directly opens the trial.

CONTINUED CRITICISM OF PRE-TRIAL JUDICIAL ACTIVISM

In view of the above findings, it should not come as a surprise that criticism persists in China of the pre-trial involvement of judges, and in particular of the close working of the judiciary and procuratorate.[23] For example, Xiao Nianhua (1998) has pointed out that the process is particularly unfair because there is little or no defence involvement at this stage, and judges who are to try the case see only those materials which prove the defendant's guilt. This, he argues, allows the prosecution to participate in the litigation process earlier than the defence. A similar view has been voiced by Wang and Yang (2002) who describe the arrangement as a form of privileged access by the prosecution to the adjudicating body.[24]

CONCLUSION

As we have seen, one proclaimed objective of the 1996 CPL reform of the rules governing pre-trial examination of cases by the judiciary, namely to remove the judiciary from the process of prosecution case preparation and construction and to turn the pre-trial stage into a purely procedural rather than substantive examination of the prosecution file, has not been achieved. The law is so framed that it actually permits what is thought by some

---

[23] Suo Zhengjie (1998); Long Zongzhi (1998); Wei Hong (2000); Wang Yu (2002); and 'Perfecting pretrial examination in criminal litigation', *Fazhi Ribao (Legal Daily)*, 7 November 2002.
[24] Wang and Yang (2002). A similar view was expressed by Xie Mangen (2004) from the Law School of the Xiangtan University who also pointed out that the defence could only be a passive recipient of information. It was even not allowed to express its opinions. For these reasons, it was difficult for it to have any effective impact on the trial. See also, Zhang and Ma (2003).

commentators to have been banned. Judges, with few exceptions, conduct substantive examination of case materials before trial under which they read the prosecution file, interrogate suspects, interview witnesses, consult experts, carry out legal research, and liaise with the procuratorate to perfect the prosecutor's case prior to the opening of the trial. As we explain, this in part is unavoidable given the structure of the rules, given the responsibilities placed on judges and given that in almost all instances the pre-trial review is undertaken by the judge who will oversee the trial. Beyond this, however, it is also clear that there remain key drivers that make this situation inevitable. While recognizing the risk that pre-trial engagement will create a predisposition in favour of the prosecution, judges, lacking adequate training, experience and confidence in overseeing trials, feel that it is necessary to become familiar with the case in advance of trial. Accordingly, they develop their own informal rules to deal with the situation. More significantly, judges see themselves as working with the procuratorate, as co-operative partners in constructing the case against the defendant, and readily join prosecutors in seeking to stop up any gaps in the prosecution case prior to the court hearing supplemented in some cases by reading the files and undertaking investigation *after* trial.

7. The construction of the defence case

The right to a fair trial is now widely accepted as a basic human right by the international community. In this context, fair trial rests upon the principle of 'equality of arms' which requires states to permit those accused of crime to defend themselves with the assistance of a lawyer of their own choosing or, where the individual is indigent, to have the state provide such assistance free of charge. As part and parcel of this right, accused persons and their lawyer must be accorded adequate time and facilities to prepare for their defence. Fairness at trial requires fairness at the pre-trial stage. Without adequate pre-trial preparation by the defence lawyer the trial will be a mere formality. In China, legal assistance for those charged with criminal offences is covered by Article 32, 1996 CPL which provides:

> In addition to exercising the right to defend himself, a criminal suspect or a defendant may entrust one or two persons as his defenders. The following persons may be entrusted as defenders:
> (1) lawyers;
> (2) persons recommended by a public organization or the unit to which the criminal suspect or the defendant belongs; and
> (3) guardians or relatives and friends of the criminal suspect or the defendant.

Persons who are under criminal punishment or whose personal freedom is deprived of or restricted according to law shall not serve as defenders.

The value of providing legal advice to criminal suspects may be thought to be too obvious to require explanation but it is critically important at all stages of the criminal process because of the differential in power between the individual and the state and because all criminal justice systems have been shown to be prone to egregious error in convicting people of crimes of which they were in fact innocent, error which may be reduced if the defence representation of suspects and defendants is an in-built requirement in the criminal process.

Just as the police are responsible for constructing the case for the prosecution, so the legal representative of the suspect/defendant would be expected to build the case for the defence (e.g., Ashworth and Redmayne, 2005; Bridges et al., 2000; Cape, 2006; and Ede and Edwards, 2008). In discharging this responsibility, the defence lawyer might be expected to engage in a variety of investigative tasks both reactive to the case for the prosecution and proactive in developing a defence theory and the evidence to support it.

These defence actions might include: advising suspects of their legal rights in advance of any police interrogation; being present at police interrogations to ensure that there was police compliance with the prevailing procedures and that any contribution that the suspect might make would be voluntary and not extracted by improper or illegal means; attending identification parades to ensure that these were properly conducted in accordance with rules and procedures designed to minimize the well-known risk of misidentification; in appropriate cases, visiting the scene of the crime; taking a formal proof of evidence from the defendant; tracing and interviewing potential defence witnesses; engaging expert witnesses to examine real evidence relied upon by the prosecution such as blood samples, ballistics material, DNA, fingerprints etc.; undertaking legal research; filing pre-trial motions; corresponding with prosecution officials and discussing relevant aspects of the case with prosecutors including problematic evidence and appropriate charges.

These powers and responsibilities typify adversarial systems of the common law but they are not necessarily features of inquisitorial systems which tend to repose these powers in the public parties (police, prosecutor and investigating magistrate). By contrast, 'private parties', including the accused and the defence lawyer only have the right to request that investigatory measures be undertaken (Dervieux, 2005).

We now turn to examine the extent to which defence lawyers in China were able to engage in acts of preparation in the defence of suspects and defendants. This part of our inquiry is derived from interviews undertaken with defence lawyers in our 13 research sites and is subject to the limitations we have earlier mentioned when discussing research methodology. The views of the defence lawyers are, of course, attitudinal in nature and for the most part were founded in their general experiences rather than arising out of a particular case. Again we remind readers that defence lawyers were cautious in what they said because they were speaking to 'outsiders' and because they work within a system in which the state retains a controlling interest over the activities of lawyers.[1]

We preface our discussion by reminding readers that a mass of evidence has depicted, through individual case study and in other ways, the plight of defence lawyers in China today and that many exceptionally brave lawyers have suffered greatly for standing up for the rights of individual citizens not only in criminal cases but in other areas of law, such as land rights and freedom of assembly, protest and religion (see, e.g., Ran Yanfei, 2009; Yu Ping, 2002; Cohen, 2003; and Pils, 2009a). There is also, however, evidence that lawyers have developed coping strategies and collective action in relation to state actors (Liu and Halliday, 2008).

ACCESS TO THE CLIENT ON INITIAL DETENTION

It is now generally accepted that the suspect is most in need of legal assistance when initially detained by the police and subjected to questioning, particularly when taken into police custody. In large measure this is because of the psychological pressures on suspects generated by isolation and confinement irrespective of police behaviour (Irving, 1980; Irving and Hilgendorf, 1980; Gudjonsson, 2002; Zuo Weimin et al., 2009; and Sun Changyong, 2009), a situation that is as applicable to China as it is to Western countries

---

[1] As Donald Clarke (2009b) points out, the state is able to dampen activism through formal and informal ways including de-licensing individual lawyers or firms or by failing to allow lawyers to pass the annual re-licensing process. Clarke discusses a number of cases including the suspension of Yitong, a Beijing law firm headed by the activist lawyer, Li Jinsong. Although re-opened after six months, the firm was weakened and a chilling signal given to other activist or potentially-activist lawyers. See also, Human Rights Watch (2008).

where these environmental effects upon the decision-making of suspects have been documented. Additionally, there is a need for legal advice because of the use by the police of interrogation tactics which are designed to extract a confession but which may infringe legal rules or moral values (McConville et al., 1994). The police culture which gives rise to this behaviour has been the subject of extensive research in Western countries (e.g., Wilson, 1968; Reiner, 1985; Banton, 1964; Manning, 1977; Chatterton, 1976; Ericson, 1982; Foster, 1989; Graef, 1989; McConville and Shepherd, 1992; Cape, 1997; Ashworth, 1996; Sanders and Bridges, 1999; Bridges et al., 2000) and there is reason to suppose that cultures bearing similar characteristics exist in police forces elsewhere.[2]

Empirical research on criminal justice has underlined both the importance of this stage of the criminal justice process and the difficulty that institutional actors, particularly the police, may have in changing their former, largely unregulated, practices. In England and Wales, for example, where Parliament has recognized the need to give both suspects and defendants rights from the outset of the criminal process,[3] research studies have shown that the police may not respect those rights and, moreover, defence lawyers may not supply the protection to suspects and defendants expected or needed. Thus, in England and Wales, where a suspect is initially apprehended and taken to the police station, that suspect should be detained in police custody only where it is 'necessary' to do so. Soon after the legislation came into effect, research demonstrated that detentions in custody were being routinely authorized rather than decisions being made on the sufficiency of evidence or the need to detain in custody (McConville, Sanders and Leng, 1991; McKenzie, Morgan and Reiner, 1990; Phillips and Brown, 1998).

Similarly, research has found that the police in England and Wales, though required under legislation to do so, often do not inform suspects of their rights or some of their rights. Thus, while suspects had the right to have someone informed of their detention, had a right to legal advice and that such advice would be free, independent and given in private, research showed that not all suspects were being advised of these rights and that police officers would use various 'ploys' to reduce the number of suspects requesting legal advice (McConville, Sanders and Leng, 1991; Sanders et al., 1989; Sanders and Bridges, 1991; and Choongh, 1997). Subsequent amendments to the relevant rules were intended to improve the situation of the suspect,[4] but official research revealed that although there had been improvement in some regards, less than three-quarters of suspects were told

---

[2] One reason for this is that the conditions which underlie police culture are of a generic kind: the sense of mission in police work; the view that 'rules' are there to be used in creative ways; the fact that as Wilson (1968) noted, within policing discretion increases as one moves *down* the hierarchy; and the fact that police work gives rise to an aggressive physical culture with particularly strong views about defined groups in society, such as minorities.

[3] The modern reform of police and prosecutors did not in fact take place until the mid 1980s. Until the introduction into law of the Police and Criminal Evidence Act (PACE) 1984, policing was in large part self-regulated with a set of judges' Rules as guides to good practice rather than as rules of law. See, McConville and Wilson (2002). Because it would not be appropriate to rely upon the police to decide who should get legal advice and who should not, in England and Wales the Police and Criminal Evidence Act, 1984 provides in section 58 that (1) A person arrested . . . shall be entitled, if he so requests, to consult a solicitor privately at any time. . . .'

[4] The changes were made in 1991 to the Codes of Practice issued under the Police and Criminal Evidence Act, 1984.

that legal advice was free, only just over a half (56 per cent) were informed that it was independent and very few at all were informed that such legal advice would be given in private (Brown, Ellis and Larcombe, 1993).

Similar problems have been identified in inquisitorial systems. Thus, for example, in France, as Jacqueline Hodgson (2005) has shown, the pre-trial investigative stage is dominated by the supervising *magistrate* with little space for the defence lawyer to operate. There, defence lawyers are denied access to the dossier of prosecution evidence and are absent during police interrogation of the suspect, although they are accorded a thirty minute consultation with the suspect detained in police custody. In the result, a number of researchers have described the role of the criminal defence lawyer within the French inquisitorial system as symbolic rather than real (Karpik, 1999).

Nor should it be assumed that the introduction of defence lawyers will constitute a 'good' in and of itself: whether lawyers benefit anyone and if so who is an empirical question. In this regard, empirical research has, once again, disclosed serious shortcomings among defence lawyers both in terms of the poor quality of pre-interrogation advice and in the paucity of protection offered to suspects during police interrogations (Roberts, 1993; Baldwin, 1993; McConville et al., 1994). Early research in England and Wales showed, for example, that lawyers often sent non-legally qualified individuals (junior clerks or retired police officers) to assist suspects arrested by the police (McConville et al., 1994; Roberts, 1993), that legal advisers were sometimes lacking the skills with which to properly advise their clients, might be unwilling to intervene to protect their clients during police questioning and even permitted oppressive questioning without protest or comment.[5] Subsequent research found improvements in many areas though still with problems at all levels (Bridges and Choongh, 1998).

In this regard, at the time of the main fieldwork the 1996 CPL did not provide a right of access to a lawyer at the point of detention but, under Article 33, 1996 CPL only at the stage when the case was transferred for examination before prosecution:

> A criminal suspect in a case of public prosecution shall have the right to entrust persons as his defenders from the date on which the case is transferred for examination before prosecution. A defendant in a case of private prosecution shall have the right to entrust persons as his defenders at any time.

Prior to the passing of this law, proposals to allow a suspect access to a lawyer at the investigatory stage were dropped after vigorous police opposition (Fu Hualing, 1998). What the 1996 CPL did allow (Article 96) was that a defendant could retain a lawyer as a 'representative' for limited purposes such as making a bail application after the police complete their first interrogation and assisting in drafting a petition or a complaint over illegal treatment.

It should be noted that, after the main fieldwork was completed, the formal legal

---

[5] See, for example, the notorious case of *R v Parris* (1992) 97 Cr. App. R. 92 in which the English Court of Appeal said that it was hard to conceive of a more intimidating and hostile approach by police officers to an interrogation of a suspect but which had all been conducted in the presence of the legal adviser (a solicitor of standing) of the suspect without any form of protest being entered, leading to the Court quashing the conviction based largely on confession evidence obtained through oppression.

position in respect of representation by lawyers changed as a result of the 2007 Lawyers Law which became effective on 1 June 2008. At first sight, the Law appears to have enhanced the rights of lawyers by providing for them to meet with clients without the need for judicial authority and without having their conversations with clients monitored by the police (*but only after the first police interrogation*), a provision that was not in force during the currency of our fieldwork.[6]

> Article 33: As of the date of first interrogation of or adoption of a compulsory measure on a criminal suspect by the criminal investigative organ, an authorized lawyer shall have the right to meet the criminal suspect or defendant and learn information related to the case, by presenting his lawyer's practicing certificate, certificate of his law firm and power of attorney or official legal aid papers. A lawyer who meets a criminal suspect or defendant shall not be under surveillance.

We should note that the effect of this new provision remains highly problematic because among other things it is, in several respects, inconsistent with the 1996 CPL. Although the revised Lawyers Law provides that a lawyer need only show the three certificates[7] to meet with the suspect after the first interrogation, the 1996 CPL requires that in cases involving 'state secrets' the lawyer must obtain the permission of the relevant institution (public security bureau or procuratorate).[8] Similarly, the revised Lawyers Law purports to prohibit the monitoring of lawyer–client encounters, but the 1996 CPL gives investigating officers the right to be present at such meetings when it is deemed necessary.[9] Once again we see that 'the law' is highly problematic and allows for differing interpretations and differing practices. Although there is some evidence that access in some areas is becoming easier, the overall picture is unclear.[10]

---

[6] But the police still retain discretion in this respect as, for example, by deciding that the matter in question or the stage of the proceedings qualifies as 'state secrets', thus entitling the police to withhold or delay access.

[7] The lawyer's licence; the certificate from the lawyer's firm; and a power of attorney or legal aid papers.

[8] According to Article 9 of *Law of the People's Republic of China on Guarding State Secrets* (2010), matters involving state security and national interests shall be determined as state secrets if release of such matters is likely to prejudice state security and national interests in the field of political, economic, national defence and foreign affairs, which shall include: (1) secrets concerning major policy decisions on state affairs; (2) secrets in the building of national defence and in the activities of the armed forces; (3) secrets in diplomatic activities and in activities related to foreign countries as well as secrets to be maintained as commitments to foreign countries; (4) secrets in national economic and social development; (5) secrets concerning science and technology; (6) secrets concerning activities for safeguarding state security and the investigation of criminal offences; and (7) other matters that are classified as state secrets by the state secret-guarding department. In addition, secrets of political parties that conform with the provisions of Article 2 of this Law shall be state secrets. In practice, 'state secrets' is an excuse broadly used by the investigation organ. See, for example, Zhong Jingmin (2008).

[9] Article 96, 1996 CPL. Chinese language discussions are available at http://www.chnlayer.net/ShowArticle.shtml?ID=20080604170328.htm; http://www.civillaw.com.cn/article/default.asp?id=48533.

[10] See, *Congressional-Executive Commission on China, Annual Report 2009* at p. 103 reporting on information derived by Congressional-Executive Commission on China staff from interviews with a lawyer in Beijing saying that for ordinary (*putongde*) cases access to detained clients was good but permission was still needed for state secret cases. Another report from Beijing, however,

Additionally, the new provision must be read together with Article 37 of the Lawyers Law and the continued existence of Article 306 of the Criminal Law (below) under which lawyers may be prosecuted if they put forward evidence which is inconsistent with the evidence advanced by the prosecutor (as, for example, a witness statement from Witness A which is at variance from the statement Witness A gave to the prosecutor).[11] As Teng Biao stated:[12]

> Article 37 of the newly revised Law on Lawyers, in particular, deserves attention. It says, 'The personal rights of a lawyer in practicing law shall not be infringed upon. The representation or defence opinions presented in court by a lawyer shall not be subject to legal prosecution, however, except speeches compromising the national security, maliciously defaming others or seriously disrupting the court order.'; [a trap for lawyers, in particular criminal lawyers].

The basis for this comment is that lawyers can still be open to prosecution for malicious libel under Article 306 of the Criminal Law (below) if they adduce evidence which contradicts that secured by the prosecution[13] and subject to the administrative punishment of licence revocation and other administrative punishments.[14]

It is not felt, accordingly, that this change has substantially affected the position as described in the current research (see further Cohen, 2005). Indeed, commentators have concluded that the situation for lawyers has in fact deteriorated since the new law (Chen Ruihua, 2005; Ji Xiangde, 2006), as Jerome Cohen (2009a) has noted:

---

claimed that one procuratorate in Beijing was not implementing the three certificates provision of the Lawyers Law; *ibid.*, footnote 207. The situation in many other areas showed no improvement: *ibid.*, p. 103.

[11] For a recent illustration of the dangers posed to defence lawyers, see 'Lawyer's arrest puts Chongqing justice on trial', Tuesday, 15 December 2009, *South China Morning Post* discussing the arrest of high-profile Beijing lawyer Li Zhuang following a claim by his client, Gong Gangmo (the alleged leader of a triad group accused of murders, loan-sharking and firearms offences), that Li had told him to say that his confession had been forced by the police.

[12] Teng Biao, originally published by the China Human Rights Lawyers Concern Group (http://chrlcg.Org/?p==206). The link also contains comments by Li Heping and Zhang Jiankang in separate pieces.

[13] The procuratorate is not only responsible for prosecuting the criminal defendant but also has standing to prosecute a lawyer exercising its supervisory role over the whole criminal process (Article 8, 1996 CPL).

[14] As set out in the Ministry of Justice Regulations on Administrative Punishment for Lawyers' Illegal Conduct, available in Chinese at http://www.legalinfo.gov.cn/moj/index/content/2010-04/09/content_2108824.htm?node=7346. See also, Cohen and Chen Yu (2010a) and at: http://www.usasialaw.org/?p=3536 discussing the case of defence lawyers Tang Jitian and Liu Wei who state that they were repeatedly obstructed by the trial judge in a 2009 trial concerning an 'evil cult' (Falun Gong) in addition to being filmed by an unidentified individual while trying to present their criminal defence. Mr. Tang and Ms. Liu, who were unable to practise from June 2009 when they were deemed to have failed their annual evaluation, were informed in April 2010 by the Beijing Judicial Bureau that they might be permanently disbarred for allegedly disrupting courtroom order and interfering with regular litigation process. The lawyers, having been unable to present their case as they wished, ultimately withdrew from the court in peaceful protest. At the Beijing Judicial Bureau hearing, the authorities reportedly pressed the pair's counsel not to represent them, causing one to drop out. Another was prevented from participating in the hearing.

The Law on Lawyers amended in 2007 seemed to promise greater autonomy to human rights lawyers. Yet their plight has actually worsened in the 20 months since the 17th Communist Party Congress. The reconfirmed Hu Jintao-We Jiabo leadership placed veteran Party officials, without legal education or experience, but with a strong police background, in charge of the Ministry of Justice and the courts as well as the Central Party Political–Legal Committee that instructs all legal institutions. These new appointees seem determined to eviscerate the country's 'rights lawyers' who constitute only a tiny fraction – perhaps one percent – of China's almost 150 000 licensed lawyers. Local officials under the Ministry of Justice, and the local lawyers associations they control, quietly press activist lawyers not to participate in a broad range of 'sensitive' matters or at least to follow their 'guidance.'

As discussed elsewhere, there is evidence to show that implementation of this law is at best patchy and that some procuratorates do not implement it at all. As in the UK, police have used various 'ploys' to delay or deny access to a lawyer. Thus, police and prosecutors have commented that 'the Law on Lawyers doesn't apply to us; it only regulates lawyers'.[15] The 2007 Lawyers Law, while seemingly offering greater autonomy to lawyers, defines lawyers in such a way as to re-emphasize the point that they are under state control, as Article 2 makes clear:

> The term lawyers as stated in this Law refers to practitioners who have obtained a law licence in accordance with law and who are engaged or appointed to provide legal services to clients.

The optimistic note struck in the definition that lawyers are individuals who 'provide legal services to clients' is modified by the provision relating to having obtained a 'law licence in accordance with law', a provision that would be unproblematic in countries subject to the rule of law but which, in China, gives authorities the power to de-licence at will rights-lawyers who pose a challenge to the interests of the party-state. Moreover, short of not renewing a licence, state institutions such as the police and procuracy are able, at will, to block criminal defence lawyers in this regard because, among other reasons, the Lawyers Law is in conflict with the 1996 CPL (Ran, 2009). Accordingly, despite the new Lawyers Law, the problems lawyers encountered before remain in full force so that informed commentators have concluded that the new Lawyers Law does not offer a glimmer of hope for new lawyers.[16]

Empirical work in China has concluded that the difficulty, indeed impossibility, of a lawyer who has been retained to act for a criminal suspect remains the biggest problem confronted by criminal defence lawyers. Thus, the survey of police station detention cells in Beijing's Haidian district by Chen Ruihua (2005) found that lawyers were able to visit only 14.6 per cent of detainees under investigation. A survey conducted by the Beijing

---

[15] See, 'Revisions a step forward but not enough', *South China Morning Post*, 30 October 2007 citing a lawyer, Mo Shaoping, who said that a police officer could say 'no' to a lawyer's request under the Lawyers Law claiming that the officer is not governed by industry-specific law.

[16] *Ibid.* at pp. 1014 ff. Ran (2009) collected cases involving 151 lawyers who had been detained, arrested or charged between 1984 and 2008 and reported that 89 were eventually found not guilty and five were found not guilty but sentenced to 'Re-education Through Labour' because 'the authorities wanted to punish them anyway' (at p. 1023). Ran concludes that the reasons for charging lawyers include: professional reprisal; abuse of power; legal misunderstandings by unqualified judicial officers; and the lawyer's own problems.

Lawyers Association (Liu and Zhang, 2005) showed that in more than one-third of cases (38.1 per cent) applications by defence lawyers for a meeting were rejected by the police at the investigation stage. When the police rejected the application, they gave no reason in 45.3 per cent of cases, used 'state secrets' as a justification in 28.7 per cent of cases, or gave other reasons (42.7 per cent) such as that case-handling officers were not available, that the case required the leaders' approval, that leaders were not in the office, that they (case-handling officers and their leaders) were too busy or that the lawyer would have to wait for a few more days. The survey also found that lawyers said that they could meet with their clients after some effort in 34.7 per cent of criminal cases represented. The investigation organ arranged the meeting within 48 hours as required by law for less than a quarter of suspects, arranged only one meeting with the suspect in half of cases represented, restricted the meeting time in most cases and the investigators were present in 55.4 per cent of the meetings; sometimes interrupting or even stopping the meeting.[17]

In our interviews with defenders, we sought to understand the role they played in practice at the pre-trial stage through three broad non-directive questions: 'Describe how you prepare for the defence'; 'Have you experienced any problems in this respect?' and 'What improvements would you like to see at this stage?' As a result, defenders described a number of problems that they encountered in seeking to represent those suspected of criminal offences.

A major problem confronting all defenders was the inability to gain access to the client in police custody.[18] This has a number of different aspects. The first, and most critical, is that no defender is given access to the client either before or during interrogation. Legal advisers are not informed that the suspect has been detained and they are not advised that an interrogation or series of interrogations is to take place. This means that the police have unmediated access to the suspect at the most critical point of the investigation.

A number of consequences directly flow from this situation. In the first place, there is inevitably a question as to the reliability of any confession obtained in these circumstances if only because a number of suspects will fall into the 'vulnerable' group so clearly identified in research studies.[19] This will include, for example, those of low intelligence, those who are suggestible, those who will do anything to escape what they perceive as unacceptable confinement, the young, the old and those already suffering psychological problems. It is well-known that the custodial environment is itself a major influence on the decision-making of suspects.[20] Added to this, many studies have shown that the police

---

[17] See also Ji (2006), p. 188 footnotes, where the six investigators were present in the lawyers' meeting with the suspects in a room less than ten square metres; Tang and Zuo (2007); Lian Yingting (2007); and Shen Shitao (2008).

[18] See also, Liu and Halliday (2009); and Cohen (2003).

[19] There is evidence that false confessions are likely to be produced when the police are themselves under pressure to solve a case and where there is little admissible or credible evidence against the suspect. See, for example, Ofshe and Leo (1997); and Brandon and Davies (1973).

[20] It has been long-established that some false confessions result more from internal psychological factors than by dubious or illegal police tactics: Borchard (1932). Borchard's sample was confined to cases in which the innocence of the wrongly convicted defendant had been authoritatively demonstrated as, for example, by subsequent discovery that the 'murder' victim was in fact alive or by the later arrest of the real culprit. See also, Brandon and Davies (1973); and Bedau and Radelet (1999).

commonly seek to manipulate the custodial environment to maximize pressure on the suspect with a view to obtaining a confession (Inbau, Reid and Buckley, 1962; Walkley, 1987; and Kassin and McNall, 1991). It is sufficient to remark in this context that allegations of police torture during interrogations are widespread in China and are accepted to occur in practice by judges and prosecutors in our interview sample.

It also follows that the defence lawyer, not being engaged at the outset and not having access to the client at the early stages of the police investigation, will be unable to make early preparation of the case. Vital information may be lost and opportunities to gather evidence missed. Indeed, the lawyer may be so ill-informed that he or she is rendered unable to make any effective progress with the case. Lawyers we spoke to freely acknowledged this core problem and recognized that their pre-trial role was virtually rendered nugatory given the constraints under which they operated.

I-IL-S3-03: There are many difficulties in meeting defendants at the investigation stage. Not much information can be read at the examination and prosecution stage. Even I hardly know the whole case after having accepted instructions for half a year. Sometimes I have no facts to tell the defendant's family. They will regard me as of poor quality and I am very embarrassed.

J-IL-S4-03: At the investigation stage, the suspect and the family are very nervous. They hope to get help from the law and get peace of mind because the investigation can extend up to four months. But it is very difficult for us to meet the suspect, so there is not much we can do.

M-IL-Y-04: It is very difficult to meet criminal suspects. According to law, lawyers must obtain approval to meet defendants in important, complicated cases and cases concerning state secrets. But no matter what the case, all meetings are examined for approval. Particularly in bribery and corruption cases, defendants are generally detained in some other place.[21] The meeting will not be approved even five days after I have presented the application. At that time, clients are very anxious and complain that lawyers do not know the case after such a long time. I can understand their feelings.

A-IL-B1-01: There is difficulty in meeting the suspect. This is particularly true at the investigation stage: the common excuse is that the person in charge of the case is not in the office. . . . On the other hand, the procedures for meeting suspects are not standardized. Each detention centre has its own procedure. . . . Lawyers find it difficult to prepare.

B-IL-B2-00: It is difficult to meet suspects during the investigative stage. . . . The investigators, prosecutors and adjudicators do not accept the idea that the suspect should be considered innocent before trial.

As a consequence of the fact that notification of detention is sometimes given with considerable delay, there are situations in which the lawyer retained by the family cannot even tell whether – let alone where – the suspect has been detained.

In the environment of the police station, it is the police who determine what 'the law' is and what 'the law' allows. In the understanding of the police, they have the authority and discretion to permit or deny whether a lawyer can see the suspect and, if so, under what

---

[21] This is a reference to 'black jails', 'special houses' and 'secret hotels' that are sometimes used for interrogation purposes.

conditions notwithstanding that defence lawyers may have a different understanding of their rights and of 'the law' in this situation.[22]

ACCESS TO THE CLIENT FOLLOWING POLICE INTERROGATION

Legal representatives of the suspect become involved in the criminal process, if at all, only after the police have conducted their interrogations or when they decide that access can be permitted.[23] In some sites, during our fieldwork, the lawyers were able to secure access to the suspect within two days of a request being made[24] but this was not the usual experience.

In most cases, the suspect was held at a detention centre and the lawyer, as the law and practice stood, required approval before any meeting with the client could occur. While approval was typically delayed as a tactic or because of bureaucratic procedures, a 'good relationship' with the police might secure speedier access as lawyers told us:

> *D-IL-K-04:* It is difficult to meet the suspect. The police do not follow the law. According to the law, the police should arrange the lawyer's meeting with the suspect within 48 hours of the application. But in fact this is impossible: we have to wait at least four or five days. They fear the lawyer may collude with the suspect.

> *B-IL-B2-01:* I am only allowed to meet the defendant once: I will encounter resistance when I request a second meeting.

> *A-IL-B1-09:* There is a restriction on the frequency of meetings [with the client]. Basically, the first meeting can be arranged within 48 hours [of the application] because the law expressly requires that but there are no such guarantees in respect of the second meeting; normally we are not allowed to meet with the suspect.

> *C-IL-B3-02:* I will only be allowed to meet the suspect if I am familiar with the police officer stationed in the detention centre.

Many lawyers complained that, in addition to the difficulty of securing access, the time available to see the suspect was very short and meetings would be subject to police monitoring:

---

[22] The ambiguity of the law in this respect in China (see, Liu and Halliday, 2009) finds resonance in legal provisions in England and Wales. See: McConville, Sanders and Leng (1991). See also, Liu (2001).

[23] Until the 1970s, this was very much the position in England and Wales. Prior to reforms introduced by the Police and Criminal Evidence Act, 1984, access to a suspect in police custody was a matter wholly determined by the police themselves. Few lawyers were able to gain such access.

[24] As our respondents made clear, access to clients in police custody was never easy to secure and practices varied from area to area and could be influenced by personal relationships or the lack of them. This echoes the findings of Liu and Halliday (2008) available at: http://ssrn.com/abstract=1296536. They found that in order to meet criminal suspects, lawyers had to find social connections with the police or even 'pay bills' for the officers at detention centres.

J-IL-S4-01: The rights of the lawyer cannot be secured. For example, the interview time is limited, only 20 minutes.

J-IL-S4-02: We can [now] meet the suspect within 48 hours after the request has been raised. However, during the meeting we are forbidden to discuss the case and our meeting continues under the watch of the investigator. I won't have any relationship with the suspect if I can't discuss the case; what else can we talk about?

B-IL-B2-02: I am only allowed to meet the defendant once and will encounter resistance if I request a second meeting. The duration of the meeting with the defendant is rather short: I am subjected to a time limit as set out by the detention centre.

Aside from any delay in meeting the suspect, lawyers made clear that they were limited in what could be said. Typically, this consisted of confirming that the suspect was willing to instruct the lawyer, advising the suspect on the nature of the alleged offence and asking whether the suspect had any complaints about police treatment during the investigation. Such interactions, as the lawyers conceded, hardly amounted to 'legal advice' and created little more than a contact point for the detained person for future reference.

I-IL-S3-05: I can only provide criminal suspects with legal consultation at the investigation stage. What we talk about is very limited when we meet criminal suspects, especially in political cases or cases of great social concern.

K-IL-W-01: At the investigation stage, though lawyers can be involved, we can do little. I am able to learn of some circumstances, provide defendants with some legal advice and inform them of their rights. . . .

K-IL-W-02: It is very difficult to meet criminal suspects. To be sure the situation is better than before but what I can do is very limited: just to know what offence the suspect is involved in, inform criminal suspects of their rights and responsibilities, provide legal advice and apply for bail. I have never appealed or accused [the police] because it is very difficult to collect evidence.

A-IL-B1-01: The duration of the meeting with suspects is rather short: they will arrange only 20 minutes but this is not enough for a discussion.

D-IL-K-01: If I get involved in the case at the police investigation stage, we will hand in the relevant formalities to the police. In the light of the Criminal Procedure Law, the scope of help we can provide for the criminal suspect is very limited because the nature of the case has not yet been decided by the police. We can only ask the criminal suspect if they want to appeal or complain or have received unfair treatment in the detention centre, for example a confession extracted by torture, and the name of the suspected offence.

D-IL-K-04: I don't know why it is difficult to meet the suspect. I have to look for the police officer in charge of the case on several occasions. Anyway, the police try to delay our request.

In very rare cases, the defence lawyer claimed that it was possible to perform some positive role in these adverse conditions particularly if the matter was not of a serious kind and if the police could be persuaded not to take the matter forward as a criminal prosecution:

D-IL-K-04: After meeting the suspect in the detention centre, if the suspect thinks that he is innocent or has made a false statement, I will look to the police to discuss whether there is any possibility of withdrawing the case. If the suspect's crime is not serious, I will try to persuade the police to see whether the suspect can be punished by administrative sanctions. But if the crime is clear, I have to wait for the case to be transferred to the procuratorate.

In general, however, lawyers indicated that they could make no useful contribution by early intervention in the case and that to pretend otherwise would be to deceive people. As one lawyer put it:

H-IL-S2-03: Legal consultation, application for bail, filing petitions on behalf of the defendant, are things that can be done by ordinary people: there is no need for us to do those things because we cannot conduct investigations, read the case files and ask about the circumstances of the case.

ACCESS TO CASE MATERIALS

It is essential that the defence lawyer gains an understanding of the prosecution case at the earliest point so that the lawyer can properly know how to respond. For example, the defence lawyer in England and Wales is entitled to know in general terms the case against the client at the earliest point (after initial apprehension of the suspect), can interview the client in depth and in private, may be present at interrogations and at identification parades and will have early access to case papers, thereby gaining a good (if not complete) understanding of the prosecution case as it develops.[25] This is not the case in China where a large body of literature reflects the problems that lawyers encounter in seeking access to case materials from the investigative or procuratorial organ when preparing for the defence (e.g., Fan, 2008b; Ji, 2006).

As our respondents made clear, lawyers in China are, in effect, working in the dark and are unable to confront in a meaningful way the case for the prosecution. Information about the prosecution case needed for a rational challenge is not made available at an early stage in the process: there is no system of formal disclosure of the prosecution case in advance of trial that would enable a defender to review the material and rationally respond to it. All lawyers agreed that no case-relevant information would be obtained from the police, as summed up by the following lawyer:

D-IL-K-03: During the investigative stage, the police do not allow us to read any case files so we can only ask the police for some information on the charge in the case. The police are unwilling to talk to us because they think that we are against them. The lawyer's status is low, so we have to bow and scrape wherever we go. The attitude of the police is not good at all so we feel that it is difficult to meet the suspect.

One illustration of the inherent problems to which such a system gives rise is the treatment of identification evidence tying the suspect to the offence. Study after study has demonstrated that eyewitness testimony not only plays a significant role in prosecution cases but also that it has played a significant role in miscarriage of justice cases. Indeed,

---

[25] This is not to suggest that all these rights are taken up by defence lawyers but the structure of the system would allow a conscientious defence lawyer to become familiar with the prosecution case at a very early stage in the proceedings and to have plenty of time to prepare a defence.

one study of wrongful imprisonment in England and Wales concluded that the commonest cause of miscarriages of justice was the unreliability of eyewitness testimony.[26]

Various steps have been taken to address this problem in England and Wales including the development of elaborate rules governing the holding of identification parades.[27] In England and Wales, it is common for the suspect's legal adviser to be present at such parades to ensure that the procedures are properly complied with and that the parade is conducted in such a way that there are no biases which might induce a potential eyewitness to wrongly identify the suspect. Although there remain substantial concerns at the reliability of identification evidence notwithstanding the new rules,[28] in China there are no discernible protective rules and no possibility of a defender intervening to ensure police compliance.

The first release of significant case-information comes at the review and prosecution stage when the prosecutor makes evidence available to the defender. This release or disclosure of evidence, however, is often not detailed enough to enable the defence lawyer to make significant progress on the case because what the prosecutor chooses to release is partial. Nor does such disclosure meet the requirements of a fair trial and the principles of natural justice now incorporated into international conventions such as the European Convention on Human Rights which provides in Article 6.3 (a) that everyone charged with a criminal offence has the right 'to be informed promptly, in language which he understands and in detail, of the nature and cause of the accusation against him'. The right to disclosure, again, is significant because experience in other jurisdictions has shown that non-disclosure of evidence has figured prominently in many miscarriage of justice cases (O'Connor, 1992; Corker, 1996; Niblett, 1997; Fisher, 2000; Leng, 2002; Redmayne, 2004). In China, as defence lawyers told us, even the belated disclosure at the review and prosecution stage was wholly inadequate and far short of that required by international standards:

J-IL-S4-02: The rights of the suspect cannot be guaranteed. . . . The files provided by the Procuratorate are not detailed enough. With only several pages copied from the thick file, lawyers cannot grasp the key points of debate.

L-IL-X-09: At the review and prosecution stage, if the acts of the suspect constitute a crime, the prosecutor will only give me a letter of recommendation. No other materials will be provided. We can exchange opinions with the prosecutor in charge on the alleged crime and facts, apply to meet the defendant and handle certain procedures. When I meet the defendant, I will ask his opinion on the letter of recommendation and conduct investigation if necessary. If the nature of the charge is not correct or the facts are not clear, I will give the prosecutor my letter of advice.

---

[26] Brandon and Davies (1973). The Criminal Law Revision Committee also concluded that mistaken eyewitness identifications were 'the greatest cause of actual or possible wrong convictions': Criminal Law Revision Committee (1971). See further, the *Innocence Project* at Cardozo University which has produced similar evidence following the exoneration by DNA evidence of wrongly convicted individuals: http://www.innocenceproject.org.

[27] See, for example, *R v Turnbull* [1977] QB 224 which set out circumstances in which a judge should warn the jury of the danger of relying upon identification evidence.

[28] The Devlin Committee long ago proposed that it should not be safe to convict upon eyewitness evidence unless the circumstances of the identification are exceptional or the eye-witness evidence is supported by substantial evidence of another sort: Devlin (1976). See also, Roberts (2004).

F-IL-N-02: The materials we can see at the pre-trial stage are very limited and most of them are duplicates of the main evidence in favour of the prosecution. After prosecution, the procuratorate transfer the duplicates of the main evidence to the courts but there is no clear definition of 'major evidence'. The procuratorate always transfer the materials that prove that defendants are guilty but do not transfer materials that prove defendants are innocent or guilty of a lesser crime. For instance, there are five copies of a defendant's statement of confession in the police station, but among them only three where the defendant admits the crime are transferred and the two that are not [confessions] are not transferred. It obviously does not benefit the defendant. The less information the defence lawyer has the worse the effect.

F-IL-N-03: In the examination and prosecution stage I will read files carefully and duplicate as many materials as possible to find doubtful points. Particular questions when I meet defendants are: 'Do you admit the prosecution?' 'What do you disagree with?' I will analyse deeply and even carry out an investigation if possible. Of course, the effect of investigations is not great because of the limited time, human resources and other factors.

M-IL-Y-05: The main problem is evidence. Lawyers have no investigation rights. They have to present defence opinions through reading files. But the evidence lawyers can read is very limited and there is not enough time to prepare; so it is hard for lawyers to prepare an effective defence. Lawyers should have safeguards to read all the evidence that prosecutors have.

C-IL-B3-03: We are unable to read some of the evidence before the trial. The procuratorate should transfer all the case material to the court including evidence that can prove the guilt or innocence of the defendant.

A-IL-B1-02: We have access to the files at too late a stage.

D-IL-K-01: Generally speaking we can get access to most case files at the procuratorate stage but prosecutors still keep some parts of the case files.

The defence lawyer is able to engage, if at all, in some form of preparatory work only just before the trial itself at which time the prosecutor deposits in the court the case papers. At this point the defence lawyer has access to the 'main evidence' that the prosecutor proposes to rely upon at trial. However, it does not follow that *all* evidence will be disclosed even at this stage. When disclosing evidence before trial, the prosecution mostly show only evidence favouring a conviction giving rise to what Chinese lawyers call the prosecution's 'evidence attack' (Zhen and Wang, 2007). While there are undoubted variations in the practices of prosecutors, defence lawyers made clear that the evidence submitted to the court was commonly incomplete and that key evidence could be introduced for the first time at the trial itself, thus making defence preparation impossible:

I-IL-S3-03: When the case is prosecuted in court, I can read files and duplicate relevant materials for deeper research.

M-IL-Y-01: In the procuratorate, I can only read prosecution opinions, expert conclusions and so on. In court, I can see all materials sent by the procuratorate. You know they are all duplicates of the main evidence in favour of the prosecution. The failure to master the case makes it difficult for lawyers to perform their function. Yesterday I tried to persuade a client not to employ lawyers and I refused two cases.

M-IL-Y-02: In the examination and prosecution stage, I can only read prosecutors' opinions and presumably know the responsibilities that the criminal suspect will have to assume. When the case is prosecuted in court, the materials I can read are still very limited. For example, there are five or six confessions by the defendant but only one or two confession records have been duplicated. Anyway, it is very hard to gain a comprehensive understanding.

M-IL-Y-05: The procuratorate will send duplicates of the main evidence to court at the prosecution stage. The main evidence is favourable to the prosecution. . . . Most evidence is announced in court one-off or selectively. Sometimes we find it very hard to accept.

D-IL-K-02: Even when we read case files in court, we find that some are not complete. Even the prosecutor does not know why. I don't know whether the missing parts of the file are advantageous to the defendant; but one thing is certain, it is at least not disadvantageous to the prosecution.

D-IL-K-05: When the case goes to the review and prosecution stage, I can mainly obtain the police recommendation for prosecution. . . . Actually, we should copy the case file at this stage but in fact we cannot. . . . In general we will copy case files in the court first and then decide if we will collect evidence. . . . During the review and prosecution stage, the prosecutors discriminate against lawyers. For example, they do not follow the Criminal Procedure Law and they do not allow lawyers to copy case materials thereby seriously impairing the lawful interests and rights of lawyers and the parties concerned. When the prosecutors transfer the material [to the court] they do not transfer materials such as those relating to deserving leniency or exemption from punishment.

E-IL-L-03: [At the review and prosecution stage] I still cannot decide my plan of defence since I cannot read the prosecution material. When the case comes to court, I will copy the files available. The procuratorate charge for photocopies is too high since, in general, the number of copies is not more than ten pieces but the procuratorate charges us RMB 50–100. In addition, the charge for photocopies in the Basic Courts is mostly between RMB 100–200, with an average of one RMB per page. The charge in the Intermediate Court is 0.5 RMB per page.

E-IL-L-05: When the case comes to the procuratorate, I can copy such materials as the detention and/or arrest warrant, photos, document on the expert's conclusion and written record of the site reconnaissance and gain a basic understanding of the case. . . . When the case comes to court, I can copy all the evidence and then meet the defendant with the doubts I have found in the files. . . .

F-IL-N-05: Some evidence is not shown until the court session opens. It is very hard for defenders to check the authenticity of the evidence without any preparation.

Accordingly, disclosure of evidence in China appears to be little more than a discretionary power in the hands of the prosecutor. Material may be disclosed to the defence at the review and prosecution stage, it may be withheld until the case is sent for trial or it may be kept away from the defender until the trial is in progress.[29] Further to this, judges may collect evidence *after* the court hearing.

---

[29] There is no information on a crucial aspect of this question, namely, the duty upon the prosecutor to gain access to information tending to exculpate the defendant and held by the police; or the parallel need to ensure that the police seek out such information. A difficulty is that, with the defender entering so late on the scene, there may be no stimulus to push the police into collecting such exculpatory material.

COLLECTION OF EVIDENCE: THE LEGAL FRAMEWORK

Irrespective of the problems of gaining access to prosecution materials, it might be thought that, once instructed or assigned to a case, the lawyer would be free to carry out such investigations as are deemed necessary, approach potential witnesses and collect any and all evidence that might be helpful to the defence. This impression is reinforced by the new 2007 Lawyers' Law which provides that:

> As needed by a case, an authorized lawyer may apply to the people's procuratorate or the people's court to gather, investigate and take evidence or apply to the people's court for notifying a witness to testify in court.
>
> Where a lawyer investigates and takes evidence on his own, he may investigate information related to the legal affairs handled from the relevant entity or individual, by presenting his lawyer's practising certificate of his law firm.

In fact, however, lawyers constantly expressed concern that they did not enjoy such freedom, that they would place themselves in danger if they did not exercise great care in this regard and that such concerns have continued despite the new law. The key problem resides in the 1997 Criminal Law, in particular, Articles 306 and 307:

> *Article 306:* If, in criminal proceedings, a defender or agent ad litem destroys or forges evidence, helps any of the parties destroy or forge evidence, or coerces the witness or entices him into changing his testimony in defiance of the facts or gives false testimony, he shall be sentenced to fixed-term imprisonment of not more than three years or criminal detention; if the circumstances are serious, he shall be sentenced to fixed-term imprisonment of not less than three years but not more than seven years.
>
> Where a witness's testimony or other evidence provided, shown or quoted by a defender or agent ad litem is inconsistent with the facts but is not forged intentionally, it shall not be regarded as forgery of evidence.
>
> *Article 307:* Whoever, by violence, threat, bribery or any other means, obstructs a witness from giving testimony or instigates another person to give false testimony shall be sentenced to fixed-term imprisonment of not more than three years or criminal detention; if the circumstances are serious, he shall be sentenced to fixed-term imprisonment of not less than three years but not more than seven years.
>
> Whoever helps any of the parties destroy or forge evidence, if the circumstances are serious, shall be sentenced to fixed-term imprisonment of not more than three years or criminal detention.
>
> Any judicial officer who commits any of the crimes mentioned in the preceding two paragraphs shall be given a heavier punishment.

So far as Article 306 is concerned, while the provision itself did not exempt lawyers' acting in good faith, it had a special deterrent role in discouraging active defence.[30]

---

[30] Many Chinese scholars, lawyers and some judges and prosecutors have called for abolishing this Article. See, for example, Chen Ruihua (2000a); Chen Ruihua (2005); Song (2005); Li Hong (2010); Zhang (2005); Zhang and Men (2007). See also Zhao Liming, available at http://www.law-lib.com/lw/lw_view.asp?no=6137&page=1; and Li Jian (2005). In 2003, more than 30 people's congress deputies signed a proposal to abolish Article 306 at the National People's Congress meeting. See 'Proposal on Abolishing Article 306 of the Criminal Law', 18 March 2003, available at http://

The impact of this 'Big stick', as it is commonly referred to must not be underestimated. Apart from leading to the arrest of many lawyers,[31] it acts as a uniform restraint on any proactive defence work[32] and many of those who have been vindicated after being charged under Article 306 have found it impossible to continue to practise professionally (Cheung Yiu-leung, 2009).

The constraints, it should be noted, are not ones which seek to secure that in defence of their clients lawyers should not engage in criminal, illegal or unethical behaviour. They are more widely drawn so as to encompass actions ordinarily associated with good investigative defence preparation. Indeed, so far as Chinese lawyers are concerned, there is a real threat that they could face criminal prosecution if they uncover evidence which is simply inconsistent with or contradicts that relied upon by the prosecution.

This could occur, for example, where a proof of evidence from a defendant or a statement taken from a witness is at variance with what the defendant or witness is said to have told the police because that could found an allegation that the lawyer had, for example, 'coerce[d] the witness or entice[d] him into changing his testimony in defiance of the facts or given false testimony'. Lawyers who propose to submit testimony which contradicts that of the prosecution may be told that they will be prosecuted if they go ahead and witnesses themselves may be advised to withdraw their statements. Indeed, the official pressure on lawyers in this regard has increased substantially since 2007.[33]

Accordingly, lawyers felt constrained in what they could do and, in general, did not

---

www.chinaelections.org/NewsInfo.asp?NewsID=22481. See also Liu and Zhang (2005) in which 42.2 per cent of lawyers said that the most important reason for their failure to collect evidence and investigate properly was because of fear of being investigated for criminal liability.

[31] Figures collected by the All-China Lawyers Association cited by Liu and Halliday (2009), at p. 932, disclose that over the years 1997–2001, some 142 criminal defence lawyers were arrested by the police and procuracy, among which 77 lawyers were illegally detained or even beaten and 27 cases directly concerned 'perjury'. Fu Hualing reports that, prior to 1997 prosecutions were mainly for covering up and malpractice for personal gain but that after the new Criminal Law was brought in (October 1997), prosecutions immediately switched to Article 306: Fu Hualing (2007) available at, http://papers.ssrn.com/sol3/papers.cfm?abstract_id=956500. Further information is reported in Human Rights Watch (2008).

[32] The 2007 Lawyers Law purports to give some protection to lawyers for good faith statements made in court by providing that liability in respect of the opinion of the defence lawyer in court 'shall not be subject to investigation' (Article 37). However, this provision does not apply to 'the endangerment to national security, malicious defamation to others, or serious disruption of court order' (*ibid.*). In a recent initiative, a Hunan lawyer, Yang Jinzhu, sought to collect signatures online for an appeal to issue a 'Judicial Interpretation' (by the SPC) of Article 306 in order to mitigate its adverse effects. However, Yang was threatened and told to stop these efforts. See, http://www.tianya.cn/publicforum/content/law/1/220655.shtml; see also, http://www.voanews.com/chinese/news/china/20100509-Chinese-lawyer-93227294.html.

[33] See, for example, Wang Heyan (2010). Discussing a new Ministry of Justice initiative asking bar associations across the country to initiate 'warning programmes' designed to avoid a repeat of an incident in a Chongqing trial involving Beijing lawyer Li Zhuang. Li was hired to defend Gong Gangmo, an alleged crime boss. During the trial, Gong alleged that Li had advised him to withdraw prosecution evidence. This eventually led to the detention, charging and conviction of Li for fabricating evidence and obstructing defence evidence. The Ministry's directive also stated that lawyers must 'help law authorities fight crime'. Academics have criticized this directive as having no legal basis and as contrary to the professional principles and duties of lawyers.

collect evidence from potential witnesses as lawyer after lawyer told us. The following are merely examples of the concerns and fears entertained by defenders in this regard:

I-IL-S3-04: At [the investigation] stage generally I will not collect evidence. On the one hand, it is because of professional discipline. I am not willing to have bad relations with the police. On the other hand, it is a great risk to do that. If I cannot guarantee my rights, how can I protect the rights of a criminal suspect? So it is better not to risk collecting evidence. I do not wish to be put into prison before the criminal suspect.

F-IL-N-06: Article 306 of the Criminal Law is a hanging sword for lawyers.

L-IL-X-10: In fact, the reason I seldom conduct investigation is the risk thereof. Because if the outcome of your investigation is not the same as that of the police, especially when there is a contradiction in the testimony of the same witness, a charge will await you – the crime of inducing the witness to change his testimony.

G-IL-S1-01: I do not provide evidence to prove the case. The longer I have worked, the less I dare to do that. I am afraid if I go to collect evidence. One witness was against my client; I went to look for him. He told me that the prosecutor had asked him to sign. After amending the content of the statement, the prosecutor went to look for him. He said it was the lawyer who asked him to make the change. Now I teach my students not to exercise this right. If you exercise this right, you will have great trouble.

E-IL-L-03: I seldom deal with criminal cases. According to a report, the lawyers in Beijing deal with 0.7 criminal cases on average in 2002. Why? Because of the high risk! Once you lose caution, you might be caught by the police under Article 306. For example, the first lawyer to be caught in Inner Mongolia was where the lawyer in one case suggested that the defendant's son collect evidence from the victim's work unit because he knew the risks of collecting evidence in person. But eventually, he was caught before he entered the court to defend the client because he had suggested collecting evidence which, in the view of the police, was not true. In one word, Article 306 is a sword hanging over the lawyer's head.

K-IL-W-05: Clients hope that I will collect evidence, but the lawyer's rights are too limited. It is especially difficult to collect evidence that is different from that collected by the investigators.

L-IL-X-04: The lawyer in a criminal case seldom conducts investigation because it causes trouble. What is more, it may contain certain risks. If he must conduct investigation he will adopt a careful method and will not collect evidence directly.

L-IL-X-08: The first problem is the difficulty in meeting the client. The second problem is that there is great risk in collecting evidence, especially when the prosecution witness has provided written evidence and your evidence is contrary to that of the prosecution. You are liable to perjury.

D-IL-K-05: I think that lawyers in China work well in criminal defence. But they are facing a bad environment. . . . Perjury in the criminal law, which is specially prepared for lawyers, brings more risk to lawyers in criminal defence. This is also the reason why lawyers do not directly come into conflict with the police and prosecutors.

D-IL-K-06: We are afraid of being involved in perjury which is provided in the Criminal Law.

M-IL-Y-01: It is very risky to investigate and collect evidence. So we are not willing to receive criminal cases.

The construction of the defence case

A-IL-B1-00: Lawyers cannot genuinely conduct a defence if Article 306 of the Criminal Law is not abolished.

A-IL-B1-01: I do not dare collect defence evidence. Article 306 of the Criminal Law is about falsifying evidence and obstruction of witnesses in giving evidence by defenders and legal representatives. They often make lawyers fall into the trap of litigants and nothing can be done.

A-IL-B1-09: If we are not careful enough, it is possible that we may be suspected of having fabricated evidence etc. I think that the lawyer's basic rights are violated.

B-IL-B2-04: It is difficult to collect evidence: the risk is very great.

D-IL-K-01: Whatever you plan as a defence, you need evidence. We find it very difficult to collect evidence because we cannot get evidence by ourselves or with the help of the court or the procuratorate.

F-IL-N-02: We need to be very careful when we collect evidence from witnesses to avoid them biting us in return. They tell lawyers the truth but later when prosecutors alter their statements they may speak through fear and even say that the former testimony has been schooled by lawyers. To avoid such possibilities, I will not collect witness statements if possible.

On the rare occasions where they engaged in evidence acquisition, they took steps to try to insulate themselves from such attacks and the risk of arrest and prosecution. Among the methods employed, defence lawyers ensured that any interaction with a potential witness took place in the presence of another lawyer; was recorded; or they simply asked the prosecutor or court to contact the witness rather than do so themselves. The following extracts from interviews with lawyers speak clearly of their strategies:

I-IL-S3-02: I take great risks in collecting evidence. If defendants make any unfavourable confessions at the trial stage, they will be considered as having been misdirected by the lawyer; so I require that there shall be two lawyers when they are collecting evidence.

K-IL-W-02: It is very hard to collect evidence. Lawyers are all concerned about the suspicion of false evidence, so they dare not collect evidence. But if there is any new evidence from a witness which can safeguard the rights of the defendant, I will request the Public Security Organ to collect evidence or apply to the court for the witness to attend court to give evidence.

K-IL-W-03: [Any] evidence collection shall be approved by the court. If it is a clue provided by criminal suspects or their family, I will directly go and find the relevant witnesses to orally understand the relevant information. I will not record the witness testimony on paper to avoid the professional risk caused by unstable testimony. If the witness is willing, it is better to arrange for the witness to give evidence in court.

G-IL-S1-02: [Explaining why the defence did not approach witness already contacted by the police or prosecutor] If what the witness tells the lawyer is inconsistent with what he told the procuratorate, the lawyer may be prosecuted for misleading the witness into giving false evidence.... Normally most of the witnesses found are family members and friends of the defendant. I'm also not willing to find more; I worry that something wrong will happen and I will be caught.

K-IL-W-01: It is very risky to investigate and collect evidence. I generally will not collect evidence. If witnesses are willing, I will arrange for them to provide testimony in court.

F-IL-N-05: To avoid the offence of giving false evidence, I usually let the court ask the procuratorate to collect evidence when necessary. If the procuratorate do not wish to do so and the evidence is very important for me, I will ask two lawyers to be present and record it by audio or video or find a notary to be present so that the evidence I collect is legal and I can also protect myself.

E-IL-L-07: There is a big loophole in the new criminal procedure. A lawyer may fall into that trap if he or she is not careful. For example, the problem of collecting evidence from witnesses or the victim. One lawyer from my firm was detained because of perjury and released later through special relationships.

For other lawyers, the restrictive legal background of Article 306 together with a legal practice which has never involved active defence preparation has resulted in a mindset which accords authority to the police in the gathering of evidence and which, in and of itself, relegates the lawyer to a passive role:

D-IL-K-03: According to the law, we can conduct investigations and collect evidence; but I will not do it actively because I do not know what I should collect. I think that the police collect almost all the necessary evidence. Many lawyers can only collect and provide evidence to indicate that the defendant does not have a criminal record.

E-IL-L-06: Though people mention the presumption of innocence, the evidence collected by the police mostly indicates the defendant's guilt. There is little evidence available for us to collect or it is not safe or convenient for us to collect it.

F-IL-N-04: We have to read the files provided by the procuratorate but the materials are fewer and fewer. Some materials that I have not seen before will be presented at court.

The overall result is that it is difficult if not impossible for defence lawyers to undertake the defence of a client. As one lawyer summed up the position:

F-IL-N-07: Lawyers are subject to many restrictions in exercising their right to investigate and it is hard for them to make an effective defence.

Although by law, lawyers may apply to the court to collect evidence this is rendered valueless in practice. For instance, according to a survey by Liu and Zhang (2005), only 6.9 per cent of the lawyers at the first instance trial stage who applied for the court's help gained approval; some 37 per cent of judges rejected their application to approach the victims' families and witnesses on the ground that it might affect the litigation; approximately 32 per cent of judges gave no reason; another 30.6 per cent saw no need for investigation; and 22.5 per cent thought that intervention by the lawyer would exaggerate the conflict (between the defendant and the victim).[34] In practice, accordingly, the process has hindered defence investigation and even helped the goal of conviction (Chen Ruihua, 1997).

---

[34] *Ibid*, at p. 17. A survey by Professor Zuo Weimin (2007) showed that evidence from lawyers constituted only around 1.0 per cent of the total evidence in the Basic Courts surveyed in Sichuan and that lawyers mainly concentrated on collecting evidence relevant to leniency in sentencing. See also Zuo Weimin et al. (2009).

WITNESS CO-OPERATION

On the face of the legislation, the impression would be that the production of witnesses at court in China would be routine. Article 47 of the 1996 CPL provides:

> The testimony of a witness may be used as a basis in deciding a case only after the witness has been questioned and cross-examined in the courtroom by both sides, that is, the public prosecutor and victim as well as the defendant and defenders, and after the testimonies of the witnesses on all sides have been heard and verified. ...

In practice, witnesses rarely appear.[35]

Even if Article 306 did not operate to deter defence lawyers from approaching potential witnesses, defence lawyers made clear to us that in the absence of a tradition of witness production at court, without an obligation to appear as a witness,[36] without guarantees of witness protection and because witnesses would fear retaliation or revenge for giving evidence, it is virtually impossible to produce witnesses for the defence.[37] Lawyers also said that, as they saw it, their own low status in the eyes of all official organs (police, prosecutors and judges) and their low standing in the eyes of the public, coupled with the absence of compulsory powers, inevitably resulted in non-cooperation of witnesses:

> *I-IL-S3-05:* It is very hard to require witnesses to attend court. There are no corresponding measures to protect witnesses. It is mainly a problem of social culture that people are unwilling to provide testimony in court.

> *J-IL-S4-04:* Witnesses for the other side do not co-operate with me in the investigation and collection of evidence. They are not willing to perform their duty to give testimony for fear of trouble and revenge.

> *L-IL-X-02:* There are some problems regarding investigation by lawyers. For example, some witnesses will refuse to co-operate and there is no compulsory measure.

> *B-IL-B2-06:* Witnesses refuse to co-operate.

> *F-IL-N-02:* It is very hard to investigate and collect evidence because those to be investigated are not always co-operative. You know, lawyers are not like the investigative organs that are guaranteed co-operation by coercion.

---

[35] A survey conducted by the Human Rights Research Centre of the Peking University Law School and published in 2005, produced a figure of witnesses appearing at trial in one in four criminal cases in Beijing: see, Cheung Yiu-leung (2009). Cheung's own examination of statistics for several provincial courts led to a calculation that the rate of citizen witnesses appearing in court was typically only five to ten per cent.

[36] Witnesses are under a duty to testify but there is no duty to appear at trial and no sanction for failure to appear.

[37] There have been reported cases in which witnesses were named by defence lawyers but not allowed to appear in court. This occurred, for example, in the case of the blind advocate, Chen Guangcheng, in which the lawyers named potential witnesses several of whom were not permitted to appear in court: available at, http://hrichina.org/public/contents/press?revision%5fid=31736&item%5fid=31723.

L-IL-X-07: Of the cases I have defended, no witness ever came to court to testify.

L-IL-X-10: When we discuss reasons for the low attendance rate of witnesses: first, the prosecutor may not welcome the witnesses' appearance in court; and secondly, the witness himself or herself may not like to attend the trial. It is better to provide compulsory rules in law that the evidence will not be recognized by the court if the defence lawyer does not accept the written statement of the witness.

M-IL-Y-04: It is difficult to investigate and collect evidence. There is no problem in requesting ordinary witnesses to describe the circumstances. But they will not allow lawyers to write it down and they do not want to give evidence in court. The police tell witnesses that if their testimony is different from the initial statement, they shall be providing false testimony; so witnesses are very nervous. If the witness is very important, I will communicate with the procuratorate and the court with the hope of verifying the facts and evidence together and let the witness go to court.

A-IL-B1-02: There is difficulty in collecting evidence: the relevant organs refuse to co-operate and it is also difficult to make an application requesting the police, the procuratorate and the court to carry out investigations.

E-IL-L-02: Right now, when we collect evidence, the witnesses will show no interest in us. We lack a relevant compulsory provision regarding witness testimony. . . . It is noticeable that there are many provisions in the legislation beginning with 'the lawyers should not'. . . .

E-IL-L-05: The biggest problem is the absence of witnesses from the court trial. In China, determination of guilt or innocence or sentence in all cases is dependent on written evidence. The witnesses are only willing to give a statement to the police instead of the court. This makes cross-examination of evidence in court a mere formality.

STATUS OF DEFENCE EVIDENCE

The rights of lawyers were further extended on 24 November 2003 when the Supreme People's Procuratorate issued its normative document entitled *Several Provisions of the Supreme People's Procuratorate on Preventing and Correcting Extended Detention in the Procuratorial Work*, which stated that: '. . . procurators should pay attention to listening to the views of lawyers and other defenders on adopting the measure of arrest. . . .' This provided an institutional basis for lawyers to present their opinions on the application of the measure of arrest (Xu and Cheng, 2008).

LAWYERS' REFORMS

Not unexpectedly, because of this restrictive regime lawyers frequently told us that they wanted major reforms introduced. Some of these concerns have been formally addressed in the 2007 Lawyers Law by removing the requirement for judicial approval and removing the monitoring of the lawyer–client meeting, though these are not universally respected, but the most crucial changes requested, including allowing access to legal advice prior to interrogation, have not been implemented.

Reforms proposed by lawyers concentrated on four main areas, all seen as crucial to the

The construction of the defence case

role of the lawyer in mounting a defence through pre-trial preparation or as necessary to give substance to the trial itself.

First, lawyers recognize that the unregulated nature of police interrogations make it impossible to know or discover the circumstances surrounding the obtaining of confession evidence. This is a matter of concern generally but also particularly in the light of what is seen as the widespread use of torture affecting the veracity of confessions and leading to unverifiable claims at trial as to what went on in the police station. Lawyers in China argue for their own presence at interrogations and the mechanical recording of police questioning of suspects, as the following examples illustrate:

I-IL-S3-01: When the investigative organ questions criminal suspects, they should inform the lawyers appointed [on behalf of the suspect] to be present. Otherwise, the interrogation would be unlawful. If the criminal suspect has not employed a lawyer, a lawyer appointed by a legal aid institution should be present. The lawyer's signature and views should be on the interrogation record. Normal interrogations should be conducted in the detention facility; otherwise it is easy to use torture to extort confessions.

I-IL-S3-02: It is very difficult to prove that confessions were extracted by torture. Actually, there are video records of the investigation process and physical examination records when the criminal enters the detention facility. But the relevant units are unwilling to supply these materials. I cannot take photos of criminal suspects when I meet them. To reduce the possibility of extorting confessions by torture, I suggest that the detention house be separated from the police organs.

K-IL-W-02: It is very hard to ensure the accuracy and authenticity of interrogation records made by investigators. It would be better to have audio or video recordings.

L-IL-X-10: When the case is transferred to the procuratorate, the defendant always says that the confession was extracted by torture. Regretfully, the court cannot accept this complaint and has to disregard this claim because there is no evidence to prove it. . . . There are two possibilities: either there is extortion of the confession or not. If no one else can supervise or oversee the interrogation, those suspects who are tortured cannot be effectively protected. On the other hand, those who were not tortured and who complain of torture blacken the reputation of the police. As a result, a supervisory mechanism is good for both parties.

A-IL-B1-09: The problem of forced confessions should be solved. . . . Lawyers should be involved in the litigation process at an earlier stage; a lawyer should be allowed to intervene from the time the investigation organ first interrogates the suspect.

M-IL-Y-03: Lawyers should witness the interrogation of the suspect and the police should not witness the meeting between the lawyer and the criminal suspect. The detention house should be independent of the police in order to prevent the extortion of confessions by torture. Evidence should be disclosed before trial so as both sides have a definite goal and to improve trial efficiency.

J-IL-S4-03: Lawyers should be allowed to attend the interrogation of the suspect. This can prevent the investigators collecting evidence unlawfully and confirm the validity, relevance and authenticity of the evidence. . . . Investigative information should be available to the public to avoid camera-like operations.

A second area of concern, evident in the views of lawyers set out earlier, relates to the risk that lawyers run in being charged with perjury should any interview they undertake with a potential witness differ from the statement that witness has provided to the police or prosecutor. For example, between 1997 and 2005, more than 300 defence lawyers were investigated on charges of perjury or sheltering the suspect.[38] In our research sample, all lawyers who spoke on this matter sought the removal of Article 306 of the Criminal Law:

> *A-IL-B1-01:* I hope that lawyers can get access to all the case materials and I hope that Article 306 of the Criminal Law will be abolished. . . . Lawyers cannot genuinely conduct the defence if Article 306 is not abolished. . . . The provisions of the Criminal Procedure Law mainly focus on the procuratorate and the courts and the Lawyers Law does not restrict either the prosecutors or the courts. Accordingly, the demonstration of the rights of lawyers by law is insufficient. What is needed is protection by law and adjusting the power of supervision.
>
> *A-IL-B1-06:* Protect lawyers who exercise their right to conduct the defence according to the law and increase the transparency of criminal cases.
>
> *B-IL-B2-05:* Many of the basic rights and professional rights of lawyers while performing their duties are not expressly stipulated in the law.
>
> *C-IL-B3-08:* Lawyers should enjoy exemption [from prosecution] in criminal litigation.
>
> *E-IL-L-02:* The provision of perjury should be deleted from the Criminal Law. It ties the hands of the defence.
>
> *A-IL-B1-05:* I hope that amendments can be made to the existing law so as to give meaning to the lawyer's right to collect evidence. Additionally, the unintended legal responsibility of the lawyers in the course of investigating and collecting evidence should be abolished. . . . The lawyer should be exempted from possible legal responsibility that may arise in the course of investigation and collecting evidence.

A third area in need of urgent reform according to lawyers is the importance of introducing a law which requires the prosecution to disclose its case at an early point in the system, early enough for the lawyer to assess the evidence and, if necessary or appropriate, prepare a defence:

> *J-IL-S4-05:* It is very necessary to implement the practice of disclosure before trial and to change the current situation of a sudden 'evidence attack' by the prosecutors so as to give lawyers more time to prepare the defence and hence improve trial efficiency. A workable evidence law should be enacted as soon as possible.
>
> *F-IL-N-07:* The exchange of evidence before the court session should be implemented. Lawyers should have the opportunity to read all evidence and material that is presented in court or should be presented in court. After reading those materials, lawyers should be given some time to collect evidence again and then exchange evidence again.
>
> *F-IL-N-02:* At the trial stage, prosecutors show some key evidence that we have not seen at the pre-trial stage, so it takes lawyers time to read and identify it. . . . So I think it is essential to exchange all evidence to avoid 'sudden attack' of evidence. . . .

---

[38] Chen and Deng (2008). According to the statistics of the *All China Lawyers Association*, more than 200 lawyers were detained on suspected perjury. See further, 'Should Lawyers' Perjury Charge be Abolished or Not?', *Jiancha Ribao (Procuratorial Daily)*, 20 June 2005; cited in Guan Yu (2008).

A fourth area in need of reform in the view of lawyers relates to the trial itself. Lawyers recognize only too clearly that there is little that can be done to undermine prosecution evidence if the evidence is confined to witness statements and if no live witnesses are called:

> *E-IL-L-05:* First, witnesses must appear in court since there are provisions in the law. Second, the police investigator should also appear in court and undergo examination and cross-examination by the prosecutor and lawyers. Third, the prosecutor should submit all the evidence they are going to present in court before the trial.

> *F-IL-N-03:* It is very important that witnesses should attend the trial. There will be fewer problems or injustice and false cases and the judgment will be more accurate if witnesses attend and are examined and cross-examined.

> *F-IL-N-04:* Key witnesses must attend the court sessions.

What is notable in all of this is that defence lawyers continue to see law as authoritative even though they consistently lose out in the competitive struggle.[39]

OUTCOME

It does not follow that lawyers have no success although obviously 'success' is by their own accounts limited and their claims subject to the usual problems of self-report studies. However, a few said that they had achieved a level of success in persuading the police to deal with cases administratively rather than through prosecution or even succeeding in getting cases withdrawn as the following examples show:

> *F-IL-N-02:* [Director of a Law Firm; part-time lawyer] In my career over the last 20 years, there have been 17 or 18 successful cases of innocence. There are about 30 if you include withdrawals of prosecution. For 2003–4, I succeeded in three cases of innocence . . . not including withdrawn prosecutions.

> *F-IL-N-03:* [The lawyer explained that police and prosecutors operated on a presumption of guilt and that it took courage to face the facts; but it sometimes happened.] For instance [taking out a case file] in a case of intentional injury, the victim, one of the gangsters, had a knife and an iron stick and broke into a house to take revenge on the suspect. The suspect had prepared a knife before they came. During the fight, the suspect was forced into a corner. He would lose his life if he did not use the knife. Finally, in the chaos, the suspect stabbed the victim and caused his death. The suspect was investigated by the police under pressure from the victim's family. As a defender, I knew the origin and course of the fight from the suspect's family and I considered his behaviour to be lawful self-defence. When I told the police, they were afraid to take responsibility for releasing the suspect. So the case was transferred to the Procuratorate. Then I exchanged my opinion with prosecutors. After research, the suspect's behaviour was considered lawful self-defence and he was not prosecuted. From this simple case, you can see how precious a prosecutor's courage is.

---

[39] See, on this, Nelken (1981)

CONCLUSION

The historic mistrust of lawyers in China continues to have resonance today.[40] It is abundantly clear that defence lawyers at the pre-trial stage are essentially passive. They do not actively construct a case by going to the crime scene, tracing and interviewing witnesses or generally engaging in evidence collection. At its most extreme, defence lawyers are not a significant factor in pre-trial preparation and have to make the best of it when they attend at trial. According to our respondents, Legal Aid lawyers are less attentive than privately-retained lawyers.[41] On lawyers' own accounts, criminal defence lawyers in China are structurally marginalized from the process and there is little they can do for a client before the case gets to trial.

---

[40] For a rich historical account, see Macauley (1998): 'Litigation loathing and "lawyer" bashing are symptomatic of the state-society power dynamic, embodied in either state building, colonial legal construction, or simple threats to draw the state into informal systems of dispute resolution' (at p. 332). See further, Bodde and Morris (1967). An edict of a Qing Emperor in 1820 warned against the growing involvement in disputes of 'litigation tricksters'. See also, Liu and Halliday (2008).

[41] As a lawyer from Site E described her defence role: E-IL-L-01: 'I get involved in a criminal case at the trial stage and seldom get involved in the investigation stage. In general the lawyers' rights are limited; they face potential risks and difficulties in collecting evidence and conducting investigation. After the judges in court review the case and think that the defendant is likely to be sentenced to death, or if the defendant is deaf or dumb or a minor offender, he or she will contact our legal aid centre and deliver a copy of the relevant evidence and materials. Then I will read those files. . . . We seldom collect evidence. . . . It is very simple for me to defend in a criminal case which comes through Legal Aid and we seldom collect evidence.'

8. Trial procedure, rules, setting and personnel

INTRODUCTION

In this chapter we describe the physical layout of criminal courts in China, provide an overview of the procedural and evidential rules that govern the criminal trial in China, explain the extent and nature of legal representation for defendants at the trial stage, and consider the qualification requirements for, and the roles assigned to, the various legal personnel involved in the conduct of the trial. We also draw upon our interview data to provide a profile of the educational and employment background of judges, prosecutors and defenders.

COURT LAYOUT

Court layout is governed by rules found in the Provisions of the Supreme People's Court and Supreme People's Procuratorate Concerning the Positions of the Judges' Bench, Prosecution's Table and Defence Table in a People's Court (Court Setting Provisions) and in the Notice of the Supreme People's Court on Questions Concerning the Names of the Courts, the Positioning of the Adjudicative Area and the Hanging of Court Emblem (Court Setting Notice).

Applying the rules set out in these two documents provides a courtroom configuration as set out in Figure 8.1.

The positioning of the court clerks is not particularly clear from the provisions in Figure 8.1, but the Court Setting Notice does provide that:

> For courts that have sufficient space, they may put the table of the Court Clerks in front of and in the middle of the Judges' Bench. The table of the Court Clerks and the Judges' Bench should form a right angle (90°). The table of the Court Clerks' should be abutted against the Judges' Bench and facing the left side of the Judges' Bench. Additionally, the seats in front of the Court Clerks' table should be 20 cm to 40 cm lower than the seats in the Judges' Bench.

The positioning of the judicial police in the diagram has been taken from Article 9 of the Rules Governing the On-Duty Judicial Police of the People's Courts. This provides that:

> When the Judicial Police are on duty, they should stand on one (or the two sides) of the courtroom, with their backs facing the Judges' Bench and their faces facing the audience. . . . The Judicial Police have to stand straight when the court delivers a judgment; they may sit down when the court is investigating a case. . . .

In respect of defenders, the Court Setting Provisions stipulate that the defenders' table should be placed on the left side of the Judges' Bench. Additionally, Article 89 of the

```
                    ┌─────────────────────────────────┐
                    │         Judges' Bench           │
                    └─────────────────────────────────┘

  ┌──────────┐              ┌──────────────┐              ┌──────────┐
  │Prosecution│              │ Court Clerk  │              │Defenders'│
  │'s Table  │              └──────────────┘              │  Table   │
  │          │                                            │          │
  └──────────┘                                            └──────────┘

         ┌──────────┐
         │Witnesses │
         │          │
         └──────────┘
                              ┌──────────────┐
                              │  Defendants  │
                              └──────────────┘
  ┌──────────────┐                                    ┌──────────────┐
  │Judicial Police│                                   │Judicial Police│
  └──────────────┘                                    └──────────────┘

  ┌─────────────────────────────────────────────────────────────┐
  │                         Audience                            │
  └─────────────────────────────────────────────────────────────┘
```

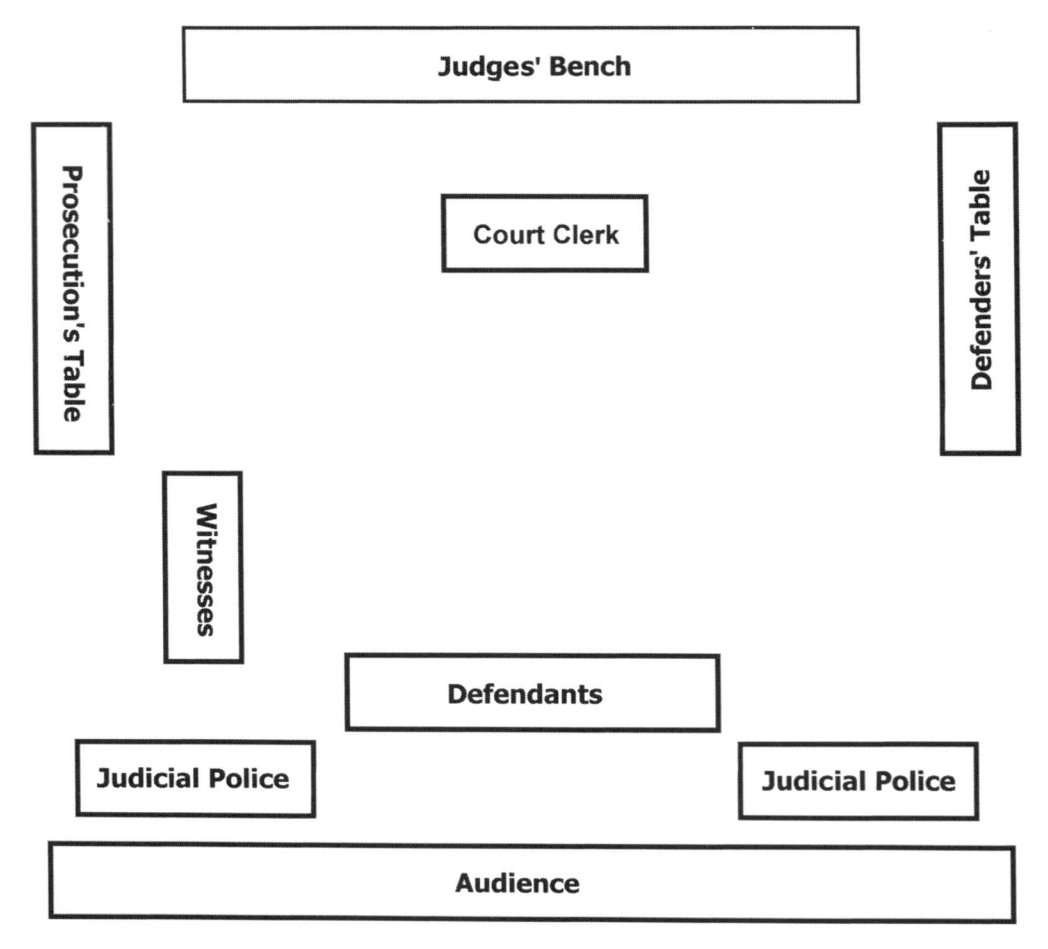

Figure 8.1   Layout of a typical criminal courtroom in China

Case Handling Standard of Lawyers' Participation in Criminal Litigation, issued by the All China Lawyers Association, provides that, in cases involving joint crimes where there are two or more defence lawyers, the defence lawyers should sit in front of the defenders' table according to the order of the defendants they represent, with the defence lawyer for the first defendant sitting nearest to the Judges' Bench.

The Court Setting Provisions also contain rules regarding the heights of the Judges' Bench, the prosecution table, the defenders' table, and the witnesses' seats. These provide that the Judges' Bench should be raised 20 cm to 60 cm from the floor, and that both the prosecution and defence tables should be at the same height as the Judges' Bench. By contrast, the Provisions require the witnesses' seat to be positioned at floor level. Not all courts followed these stipulations. In site F, for example, no seats were provided for defendants, a prosecutor explaining that defendants were required to stand so as to demonstrate the solemnity of the court and so that the impact of the adjudication would be greater.

AUDIENCE

Article 152, 1996 CPL provides that, in general, cases are to be heard in public:

> Cases of first instance in a People's Court shall be heard in public. However, cases involving State secrets or private affairs of individuals shall not be heard in public.
>
> No cases involving crimes committed by minors who have reached the age of 14 but not the age of 16 shall be heard in public. Generally, cases involving crimes committed by minors who have reached the age of 16 but not the age of 18 shall also not be heard in public. . . .

Historically, one purpose of trials in China has been educative not only of the defendant but also more generally of the community by seeing justice in action and hearing at first hand the sentencing homily as a cautionary example to all. In addition, the presence at trials of members of the public is one important mechanism by which society as a whole may be given accurate knowledge so that it is able to critically evaluate the criminal process at work and, in so doing, act as a constraint on inappropriate or unlawful activities of state officials in this regard. In this respect, we were interested to see the extent to which members of the public attended everyday trials and those which excited no more than local interest.

We found that few trials (apart from demonstration trials put on for a particular group) attracted an audience of any size apart from family and friends of the defendant or victim (most evident in cases involving a parallel civil action) although there were at least some members of the audience present in trials involving around 80 per cent of defendants.[1] In those 'open' trials where no members of the public attended, we saw no evidence of any action on the part of officials to exclude anyone from viewing the trial although it is well-established that this happens in cases deemed 'sensitive' by local or central officials.[2]

---

[1] We took a random sample of trials in five different research sites with a total of 100 defendants (excluding seven defendants in trials that were closed to the public). In 21 cases (21 per cent), there were no members of the public present at the trial. In the remainder, in 17 trials there were more than ten in the audience, the highest numbers being 65; 55; 50; 37; 30; 25; and 22. For 34 per cent of defendants (35), the audience comprised five or fewer members of the public, in all likelihood family or friends of the defendant or victim. The cases with the biggest audience were not politically sensitive in character. Thus, in I-S3-03, the audience of approximately 65 persons, mostly consisted of victims (and friends) who had been victims of a documentary fraud practised on a lot of individuals. Other cases tended to have excited local interest because they involved death/injury to a number of victims (as in I-S3-08 where there was one death and three injured victims of a knife attack with the trial attracting an audience of about 55 people; and J-S4-03 in which a village security team beat up four suspected thieves, one of whom died as a result of injuries received, in order to gain confessions with the trial attracting about 50 local people) or involved an individual defendant who was a public figure in the neighbourhood (as in M-Y-17 in which a well-known person was accused of extracting 'luck' money by blackmail).

[2] See, for example, the account in Chinese Human Rights Defenders (CHRD) (2009) available at http://chrdnet.org/wp-content/uploads/2010/04/annual-report-on-the-situation-of-human-rights-defenders-2009-online-version.pdf. In sensitive cases, people have been physically prevented from attending the trial, been told that the court is already full or been informed that they are listed as potential 'witnesses' and accordingly cannot observe the trial unless summoned.

TRIAL PROCEDURE

The main aspects of and stages in the trial procedure, as set out in the 1996 CPL and associated legal provisions may be summarized as follows:

i. Cases are heard before a collegial panel. In the Basic and Intermediate Courts the panel comprises three judges, or a combination of judges and people's assessors, with the latter having equal rights with judges (Article 147, 1996 CPL).[3]
ii. As a general rule cases must be heard in public. An exception is made for cases involving state secrets or the 'private affairs of individuals', and cases involving minors (Article 152, 1996 CPL).
iii. The trial commences with the presiding judge ensuring that all parties are present, and announcing the names of members of the collegial panel and all other persons involved in the conduct of the trial. The judge must inform the parties of their right to apply for the withdrawal of any member of the panel, the clerk, the prosecutor, expert witnesses or the interpreter. Importantly, he must inform the defendant of his right to appoint a defender (Article 154, 1996 CPL).
iv. The prosecutor reads out the Bill of Prosecution, and the defendant and the victim are given the opportunity to present statements regarding the alleged offence/s. The defendant may be interrogated by the prosecutor and the judge. If there is an incidental civil action, the victim, the plaintiff and/or *agent ad litem* and the defender may, with the permission of the judge, put questions to the defendant (Article 155, 1996 CPL).[4]
v. If the presiding judge gives permission witnesses may be questioned by the prosecutor, the parties, the defenders and *agents ad litem*. The judge is given express power to stop irrelevant questioning (Article 156, 1996 CPL).
vi. In addition to live witness testimony (if any), the prosecutor and defender 'must show the material evidence to the court for the parties to identify', and 'the records of testimony of witnesses who are not present in court, the conclusions of expert witnesses who are not present in court, the records of inquests and other documents serving as evidence shall be read out in court' (Article 157, 1996 CPL).[5]
vii. The evidence production stage completed, the parties, the defenders and the *agent ad litem* (if applicable) can request that new witnesses be summoned, new material evidence be obtained, new expert evaluation be made and/or that another inquest be held. Whether such requests are granted is in the discretion of court (Article 159, 1996 CPL).[6]

---

[3] In the Higher People's Court and the Supreme People's Court the collegial panel may consist of up to seven members.

[4] Article 155, 1996 CPL. Strictly read, Article 155 does not permit the defender to put questions to the defendant except where there is an incidental civil action and with the permission of the presiding judge.

[5] This is followed immediately by the provision that 'The judges shall heed the opinions of the public prosecutor, the parties, the defenders and the *agents ad litem*'. This presumably means that the prosecutor, the defender and the parties are allowed to make submissions on the evidence tendered in this way.

[6] It would appear from this that the procuratorate cannot seek permission to produce new evidence at this stage.

viii. If the court has doubts about any of the evidence, it can of its own motion adjourn the case to carry out an investigation to verify the evidence. The court has broad investigative powers for this purpose – it can conduct an inquest, examination, or inquiry, commission expert evaluation or order a 'freeze' (Article 158, 1996 CPL).

ix. All the evidence having been presented, the parties, prosecutor and defender may, with permission of the judge, 'state their views on the evidence and the case, they may debate with each other'. Once the presiding judge indicates the conclusion of the debate stage, the defendant is given 'the right to present a final statement' (Article 160, 1996 CPL).

x. After the final statement of the defendant, the presiding judge announces an adjournment to allow the panel to deliberate. Judgment must be pronounced publicly and delivered 'within one month or, one and a half months at the latest' (Articles 163 and 168, 1996 CPL).

xi. The verdict is in theory determined by majority vote (Article 148, 1996 CPL), and the panel are provided with a choice from three possible verdicts:

- 'if the facts of a case are clear, the evidence is reliable and sufficient, and the defendant is found guilty in accordance with law, he shall be announced guilty accordingly';
- 'if the defendant is found innocent in accordance with law, he shall be pronounced innocent accordingly';
- 'if the evidence is insufficient and thus the defendant cannot be found guilty, he shall be pronounced innocent accordingly on account of the fact that the evidence is insufficient and the accusation unfounded' (Article 162, 1996 CPL); and
- Rather than deciding the case itself, in 'difficult, complex or major case(s)' the collegial panel can pass the case to the president of the court and he may in turn refer the case for decision to the judicial committee consisting of the president and judges appointed by the standing committee at the corresponding level of the court. In such cases, Article 149, 1996 CPL provides that 'the collegial panel shall execute the decision of the judicial committee'.

xii. Withdrawal of Prosecution

The *Explanations of the Supreme People's Court on Several Questions Concerning the Implementation of the Criminal Procedure Law of the People's Republic of China* (SPC Judicial Interpretation) and the *Rules of the People's Procuratorate on Criminal Procedure* (SPP Rules) provide that a prosecution can be withdrawn at any time prior to the pronouncement of judgment. Article 177 of the SPC Judicial Interpretation provides that:

> Before the pronouncement of judgment, if the people's procuratorate requests for a withdrawal of prosecution, the people's court should examine the reasons for the procuratorate to withdraw such prosecution, and decide whether to approve the procuratorate's request.

Article 351 of the SPP Rules provides that:

> Before the people's court pronounces the judgment, if the people's procuratorate discovers . . . the facts of crime do not exist, the facts of crime were not perpetrated by the defendant or no

criminal responsibility should be investigated against the defendant, then it may request for a withdrawal of prosecution.

In addition, Article 353 of the SPP Rules requires the procuratorate to report any proposal of withdrawal of prosecution to the Chief Procurator or the Procuratorial Committee for a decision. Also, the request for a withdrawal of prosecution should be put forward to the court in writing before the judgment of the relevant case is pronounced. If a prosecution is withdrawn, Article 117(4) of the SPC Judicial Interpretation stipulates that the court must not sanction a second prosecution unless there are new facts.[7]

Some prosecutors we interviewed revealed that one of the reasons for making an application to withdraw a prosecution is where the court has indicated beforehand that the defendant is likely to be acquitted:

> *F-IP-N-01:* Maybe because of the system, we hope each case we prosecute would result in a finding of guilt by the courts. Our work for the whole year will be wasted and we will lose honour and bonus if there is one not-guilty verdict. In one case, for example, everyone in our procuratorate considered that the defendant was guilty. But the court asked us to withdraw the prosecution otherwise it would find the defendant not guilty. We had to withdraw the prosecution because there was not enough time for us to conduct supplementary investigation and our leaders were afraid of trouble.

> *F-IP-N-02:* Our tasks are fulfilled if judges find the defendant guilty. But if there is any not guilty verdict, we will risk being investigated for responsibility for causing wrongful cases, so we try to solve problems internally through methods such as not to prosecute or withdrawal of prosecution and so on . . . In fact, once a prosecution is initiated, the court should adjudicate the case and make a decision, but in some cases the court would suggest that we withdraw the prosecution, otherwise it would give a not guilty verdict.

The fear of a wrongful acquittal appears to haunt not only prosecutors, but also judges. For example, one judge (F-IJ-N-06) told us that it was difficult for a judge to give a not guilty verdict because no institution could bear the responsibility of 'causing wrongful cases'. It was much easier, therefore, to avoid making any decision at all by simply asking the procuratorate to withdraw a prosecution (Liu Jiguo, 2004), as recommended by a judge from a large eastern city:

> *H-IJ-S2-006:* In order to avoid a not guilty verdict being given, prosecutors may withdraw the prosecution. Because one not guilty verdict involves many problems such as state compensation, personal interests, etc.

A judge from a western province (D-IJ-K-05) pointed out that he would recommend withdrawal of a prosecution instead of giving a not guilty verdict when the defendant

---

[7] Article 117(4) of the SPC Judicial Interpretation provides that:
> After examination, cases should be handled in different ways depending on their particular circumstances:
> . . .
> (4) According to Article 177 of this Explanation, for cases in which the people's courts have already decided to allow the people's procuratorates to withdraw the prosecution, if the people's procuratorates re-initiate prosecution in those cases without submitting new facts, the people's courts should not handle those cases.

was likely to be acquitted to avoid causing embarrassment to prosecutors. Another judge (F-IJ-N-03) said that judges normally will not give a not guilty verdict but would rather invite the prosecution to withdraw the case.[8] The same approach was adopted by some judges we interviewed when handling cases which exhibited problems with evidence or facts. In short, although the legal provision is one which contemplates that withdrawal of prosecution will take place at the initiation of the procuratorate, the reality is that prosecutions are withdrawn mainly at the direction of the court.

We were told by defenders[9] that their lack of knowledge about a case normally made it difficult for them to ask that a prosecution be withdrawn, but if they did make such a request it was very likely to be turned down because prosecutors themselves were unable to accede to such requests as a result of external factors (protests by the victim's family and the need to seek internal approval from higher authority). It would appear that withdrawal of prosecution is used at the initiation of the procuratorate only in those cases where the concerns of an individual prosecutor are brought to the attention of higher committees:

> *F-IL-N-06:* It is relatively difficult for a court to find a defendant not guilty because, on the one hand a not guilty verdict will affect the working relationship between the court and the procuratorate; on the other hand, the court worries that the relevant decision will be protested by the prosecutor. For this reason, some cases that should have been given a not guilty verdict are solved internally, such as through withdrawal of the prosecution and so on.

APPEAL AND 'PROTEST'

Under the 1996 CPL, an appeal can be lodged by either the prosecution (referred to as a 'protest action'), the defendant, or by anyone who was a party to any incidental civil action in the trial (Article 180, 1996 CPL). In the case of an appeal by the defendant, the court is prohibited from increasing the criminal punishment on appeal (Article 190, 1996 CPL). The time limit for an appeal or a protest against a judgment is ten days and five days respectively from the day after the written judgment or order is received (Article 183, 1996 CPL).

Upon receipt of an appeal the court of second instance must form a collegial panel. The panel may refuse to hear the appeal if, having read the case file, interrogated the defendant and heard the opinions of the other parties, defenders and *agent ad litem*, it thinks the criminal facts are clear. In every other case it must open a court session and hear the appeal (Article 187, 1996 CPL). Article 195, 1996 CPL provides that the procedure adopted at second instance shall replicate the procedure at first instance. Having heard the case, the court of second instance is empowered to dismiss the appeal or protest and affirm the original judgment if satisfied that the facts were correctly determined, the law properly applied and the sentence appropriate. It can revise the judgment if there was no error in the determination of the facts but the application of the law was not correct or the punishment was not appropriate. Article 189, 1996 CPL further provides that, if

---

[8] To the same effect, judges F-IJ-N-02; B-IJ-B2-05; and L-IJ-X-02
[9] E.g., G-IL-SI-005; and L-IL-X-08.

the facts in the original judgment were unclear or the evidence was insufficient, the Court may revise the judgment after ascertaining the facts or, alternatively, it can resubmit the case to the court of first instance for retrial.

The existing research on appeals suggests that in practice most appeals in China are a paper exercise.[10] This is no doubt connected with the fact that in any case of complexity or controversy lower courts ask the court of second instance for assistance and guidance while trying the case or when determining judgment or sentence. This means that the court of second instance, having been implicated in the procedure adopted at first instance, is unlikely to open a session when seized of an appeal.[11] Some suggest that in most cases appeals are rejected after a case file review (Cohen, 2001).

There is a special procedure for reviewing all judgments and orders involving the death penalty. Generally speaking, imposition of the death penalty is subject to the approval of the Supreme People's Court. From 1 January 2007, there was a re-statement that the authority to decide life or death resides with the Supreme People's Court (SPC).[12] For this purpose, the SPC set up additional criminal courts and enrolled judges nationwide.

In order to prevent possible mistakes, reward informants and to protect pregnant criminals, Article 211, 1996 CPL allows the court to suspend execution if it is discovered that the judgment may contain error, or the criminal exposes major criminal facts or renders other significantly meritorious service requiring revision of the sentence, or if the criminal is pregnant. After verification, if the original judgment is deemed correct, or it is decided that there is no reason to reduce the penalty, execution can take place but only after a report is submitted to the President of the Supreme People's Court or a Higher People's Court and another order issued authorising execution.

CIVIL SUITS

As can be seen from the above procedural steps, one of the noteworthy aspects of criminal trial procedure in China is that any civil claim for compensation is heard alongside the criminal case (Lubman, 1999). This is because the law gives the victim the right to

---

[10] Cui Min (1998); Zhang and Tian (2001); and Li Xuekuan (1999). Chen Guangzhong's survey showed that, the open trial rate at second instance and appellate cases were 13.2 per cent/12.7 per cent, 7.5 per cent/7.2 per cent, 7.6 per cent/7.5 per cent and 4.2 per cent/3.1 per cent respectively in the Second Intermediate Court in Beijing between 2004 and 2007. In Jiangxi, the rate was 3.8 per cent/0 per cent, 2.0 per cent/0 per cent, 28.1 per cent/26.8 per cent and 39 per cent/36.6 per cent between 2004 and 2007. For details, see Chen Guangzhong (2010), vol. 3, p. 163.

[11] Xue Fei, 'Case Tried in the First Instance-Case in the Second Instance', available at http://www.legalinfo.gov.cn/xuefa/juan/susong/susongfa006.htm; Li (2002); Yue Liling (2010); Chen, Cheng and Yang (2006); Wan Yi (2005); Li and Zhen (2007); Chen Ruihua (2009); and Xu, Mao and Wu (2007).

[12] See, 'Supreme People's Court Assumes Sole Authority Over Death Penalty; a New Era of Fewer Killings Begins' available at http://www.nanfangdaily.com.cn/zm/20070104/xw/tb/200701040002.asp. Views vary as to whether this is an advance although it is often asserted that the Supreme Court removes the death penalty in one in four cases. However, in order to cope with the massive increase in case load, the Supreme People's Court is reported to have had to take on hundreds of new judges many of whom have lower qualifications than judges in the past. See, Ni Jian (2007).

file an incidental civil claim during the course of the criminal proceedings if he or she has suffered material losses as a result of the defendant's criminal act.[13] Such an action can be filed at any time between the initial filing of the criminal case and the announcement of the verdict in the criminal trial, thereby raising the potential for delay in the resolution of the criminal charges (Chen and Tang, 2002). In practice, other research suggests that when an incidental civil action is heard together with the criminal case, the procedures relating to the criminal aspects of the case predominate, and the procedures designed to adjudicate upon the civil component of the case are simplified or even ignored.[14]

Some scholars have argued that, since the incidental civil action can be initiated at the trial stage, this might provide an opportunity for the suspects or their family to transfer assets so that the judgment on the civil action will become a paper exercise (Yang Feixue, 2009). In practice, the victims or their families rarely obtain compensation awarded by the court (Zhang Yanhong, 2009; Xiao, Guo and Dai, 2009). For example, according to a survey by the Beijing First Intermediate People's Court, the enforcement rate in 2004 and 2005 was only 13.4 per cent and 6.4 per cent of the total amount that the court awarded.[15] Because their rights have not been fully protected, many complain or petition after the trial.[16] In addition, the plaintiff (victim) or their lawyer may be prevented from fully participating in the criminal trial.[17]

The law governing this aspect of criminal procedure is not altogether clear. The controlling provision is Article 78, 1996 CPL which provides:

> An incidental civil action shall be heard together with the criminal case. Only for the purpose of preventing excessive delay in a trial of the criminal case may the same judicial organization, after completing the trial of the criminal case, continue to hear the incidental civil action.

As can be seen, the term 'together with' can mean that the two matters should be dealt with at a single hearing, seriatim or that they should be heard concurrently.

Further clarification is provided by the *Interpretation of the Supreme People's Court on Several Questions Concerning the Implementation of the Criminal Procedure Law* (SPC Interpretation). This provides that, firstly, the public prosecutor will read out the

---

[13] Article 36, Criminal Law of the People's Republic of China; and Article 77, 1996 CPL. It also signifies both the traditional emphasis upon mediation and the instrumental value to the judge in helping to confirm the acceptance of responsibility on the part of the defendant.

[14] In practice, the defendant's willingness to compensate and the fulfilment of compensation are considered as important indicators of contrition in the criminal trial. Therefore, civil liability will affect criminal liability. See, Zhao and Wang (2002). See also Jing and Wang (2009). This was acknowledged by the majority of judges in our research interviews.

[15] First Criminal Court of Beijing First Intermediate People's Court, 'Survey Report on the Difficult Judicial Situation of Incidental Civil Action in the Criminal Proceedings and Solutions', (2007) 7 *Falu Shiyong (Journal of Law Application)* 76, at p. 78.

[16] Between 2004 and 2006, among petition cases in which the parties disagreed with the judgment that were accepted by the people's procuratorates at all levels, 30 per cent of the parties were victims, and it was regarded that underlying the petition was a deterioration in the financial situation arising from the crime of the defendant. See Tian (2008) at p. 130.

[17] For example, see the story in Ji (2006) at pp. 96–99, where the prosecutor challenged and requested the court to stop the *agent ad litem*'s opinion on evidence cross-examination.

Bill of Prosecution.[18] If there is an incidental civil action, the plaintiff of the incidental civil action or his or her *agent ad litem* will also read out the bill of the incidental civil action.[19] Additionally, 'the defendant and the victim may present their statements regarding the crime accused in the Bill of Prosecution'.[20] After that, as Article 133 of the SPC Interpretation provides, 'Under the direction of the presiding judge, the public prosecutor may question the defendant regarding the crime accused in the bill of prosecution. With the permission of the presiding judge, the victim and his *agent ad litem* may, based on the questioning conducted by the public prosecutor, ask supplementary questions.'[21] With the permission of the presiding judge, the plaintiff in an incidental civil action and his or her legal representative or *agent ad litem* may ask the defendant questions regarding the facts of the incidental civil action of the case. With the permission of the presiding judge, the defence lawyer and the plaintiff's legal representative or *agent ad litem* may question the defendant after the prosecution has asked the defendant a substantive question.[22] Further, with the permission of the presiding judge, the prosecution and the defence may also question the victim and the plaintiff in the incidental civil action.[23] Apart from the prosecution and the defence, 'if the judge considers it necessary, they may question the defendant, victim and the plaintiff and the defendant in the incidental civil action'.[24]

In respect of every count of the facts of the case, with the permission of the presiding judge, the public prosecutor may call witnesses and expert witnesses to testify in court. The prosecutor may also produce relevant evidence, or read out the records of statements of victims, witnesses, and expert witnesses who are not in court.[25] Similarly, with the permission of the presiding judge, the victim and his or her *agent ad litem* and the plaintiff in the incidental civil action and his or her *agent ad litem* may also do the same.[26] For the defence, with the permission of the presiding judge, the defendant, his or her defender and legal representative may call upon witnesses and expert witnesses to testify in court. Or they may read out the records of statements of witnesses and expert witnesses who are not present in court and the conclusions of expert witnesses, after the prosecution has produced evidence to prove its case.[27] According to Article 139 of the SPC Interpretation, the presiding judge may refuse to give permission if he or she considers that the witness that is going to be called or the evidence that is going to be submitted is unrelated to the case or it is unnecessary.[28]

Although Article 40 of the *Provisions on Several Questions Concerning the*

---

[18] Article 130 of the SPC Interpretation; Article 155, 1996 CPL.
[19] Article 130 of the SPC Interpretation.
[20] Article 155, 1996 CPL; and Article 132, the SPC Interpretation.
[21] A similar provision can be found in Article 155, 1996 CPL.
[22] Article 133 of the SPC Interpretation.
[23] Article 135 of the SPC Interpretation.
[24] Article 137 of the SPC Interpretation. Similar provision can be found in Article 155, 1996 CPL.
[25] A similar provision can be found in Article 157, 1996 CPL.
[26] Article 138 of the SPC Interpretation.
[27] Article 140 of the SPC Interpretation. A similar provision can be found in Article 157, 1996 CPL.
[28] Article 139 of the SPC Interpretation.

Implementation of the Criminal Procedure Law issued by the Supreme People's Court, Supreme People's Procuratorate, Ministry of Public Security, Ministry of State Security, Ministry of Justice, Legal System Working Committee of the Standing Committee of the National People's Congress (Six Departments Provisions) provides that, 'the order of questioning witnesses by the public prosecutor and the defender shall be decided by the presiding judge',[29] Articles 143 and 145 of the SPC Interpretation provide that the party who calls the witness or the expert witness concerned should question the witness or expert witness first. After that, with the permission of the presiding judge, the opposite side may also question the witness or expert witness.[30]

In this regard, Chinese judges play a dominant role in trials. Examination and cross-examination are still not regarded as legal rights of the parties to the case. Instead, both sides (the defence in particular) have to ask for the permission of the presiding judge before putting questions to the defendant and any other witness.

In questioning witnesses, there are a number of rules that need to be observed: 1) The questions being asked should relate to the facts of the case; 2) No leading question is allowed; 3) The parties cannot threaten the witnesses; 4) The parties cannot harm the personal dignity of the witnesses. These rules are also applied to the questioning of the defendant, victim, plaintiff and the defendant of the incidental civil action and expert witnesses.[31] Apart from the parties to the litigation, the judges may also question the witnesses and expert witnesses if they consider this necessary.[32] The presiding judge may stop any party from questioning if he or she considers that the content of the question is unrelated to the case or the method of questioning is inappropriate.[33]

In our research, we found wide variations in practice between different court sites and, indeed, within the same court area. In the absence of standard practice, we found considerable areas of confusion. Thus, for example, in one court observation (E-CO-L-07), a case of intentional injury in which the victim died, there were two plaintiffs and two *agents ad litem* instructed to assist with the civil claim. Invitations by the judge to put questions to the defendant during the investigative stage were declined and they expressed no disagreement with the prosecution evidence as it was adduced. Then the court moved to the civil action. Immediately after this, the court then opened the Debate Stage of the criminal trial and at this point one of the *agents ad litem* was invited to contribute:

> The *agent ad litem* expressed his opinions: First, the defendant's act broke the criminal law and caused civil infringement of the plaintiff. Second, the defendant should bear all the civil liability.

---

[29] Article 40 of the Six Departments Provisions.
[30] Articles 143 and 145 of the SPC Interpretation.
[31] Article 146 of the SPC Interpretation. It is believed that item 4 in this provision is merely a restatement of the constitutional rights of a citizen as guaranteed under Article 38 of the PRC Constitution. Article 38 of the PRC Constitution provides that:
> The personal dignity of citizens of the People's Republic of China is inviolable. Insult, libel, false charge or frame-up directed against citizens by any means is prohibited.

[32] Article 148 of the SPC Interpretation. A similar provision can be found in Article 156, 1996 CPL.
[33] Articles 136 and 147 of the SPC Interpretation. A similar provision can be found in Article 156, 1996 CPL.

After the defence lawyer entered a plea in mitigation, the plaintiff became involved, as appears from the researcher's notes:

> The plaintiff asked to make a statement. She just talked about the process of the case (i.e., how the offence was committed).
>
> *Judge:* All right, we will decide the case upon the court investigation.
> [The plaintiff wanted to talk, but the judges didn't want to listen to her.]

In other instances that we observed, when invited to put questions to the defendant, the plaintiff would embark upon a line of questioning not directly relevant to the issue and would have to be stopped by the judge, as in L-CO-X-23 (intentional homicide) and L-CO-X-24 (intentional injury) where the judge said: 'Plaintiff, you should only ask questions which are related to the case.'

In total, there were 37 criminal trials which also involved a civil action for compensation. In seven cases the court first dealt with the criminal case (six involving the death of the victim; bodily injury in the other) and, on completion of all relevant stages, then turned to the claim for compensation. In six of the cases, the plaintiff was represented by an *agent ad litem*: in the residual case, involving intentional homicide, the civil action was undertaken by the father of the deceased victim. In each case there was a clean break between the criminal and civil actions in the sense that, on completion of the criminal case, the court moved immediately to try the civil complaint. Contrary to what was permitted under the prevailing rules, the plaintiffs/*agents ad litem* were not afforded an opportunity to question the defendant and get involved in the criminal trial.

In the remaining trials (30), there was no clear demarcation between the criminal and civil proceedings. This meant different things in different trials in different areas. In many of these cases, the plaintiff or agent of the plaintiff would be invited, as the rules allow, to participate at various stages of the trial, as by putting questions to the defendant or by objecting to or agreeing with prosecution evidence or by being asked to contribute at the Debate Stage or by being asked to make a Final Statement. In five cases the offers were declined so that, for practical purposes, the criminal and civil trials were dealt with seriatim. In others, however, the plaintiff or, more usually, the *agent* was directly involved in substantive issues relating to culpability or sentence or both.

As mentioned, in a number of cases, the representative of the plaintiff in the civil action was invited to participate in the criminal trial and took an active role interrogating the defendant. Thus, for example, in J-CO-S4-09, a case of intentional homicide involving three defendants, after the prosecutor and defence lawyer had questioned the first defendant, the following exchange took place:[34]

> *Judge:* Now it is the [civil] attorneys' turn to question.
>
> *Attorney 1:* You have provided 15 statements in the police station; in 11 of these you admitted the crime while in four you did not. Just now you said the police extorted a confession. But in the file is written: the police asked you if there had been extortion, you said 'No'. What's more,

---

[34] The civil attorney made other interventions in the criminal trial including further cross-examination of defendants.

you said the police were good to you. You said they asked you if you were healthy, giving you food when you were hungry and water when you were thirsty. There is your signature on the file.

Defendant 1: I have never said that.

Judge: Bailiff, take the file to Defendant 1 for confirmation.

Defendant 1: I have never said that.

Attorney 2: When were you born?

Defendant 1: On April 18, 1982.

Attorney 2: When did this case happen?

Defendant 1: On July 23, 2001.

Attorney 2: You were 19 years old then. But just now you had said you were 17 or 18. Just now you denied that the clothes are yours. So where were your clothes?

Defendant 1: I don't know.

Attorney 2: I don't think you are telling the truth. You told the police clearly that it was on the fourth floor.

Defence Lawyer 1: Objection. She is trapping my client.

Judge: Continue.

Attorney 2: Why did you confess in the police station?

Defendant 1: Because I had been beaten up.

Attorney 2: Do you have any evidence to prove that you are innocent? For example, you had been staying in the room and you had no time to commit a crime?

Defence Lawyer 1: Objection. She is keeping trapping [my client].

Judge: It has something to do with the case. She is not trapping. Continue.

Defendant 1: . . . (silent)

Another example is case E-CO-L-15, a case of intentional injury and theft in the course of which the victim was stabbed and died. The civil agent began his involvement at the outset of the investigation stage by asking the court to punish the defendant severely and apply the death penalty. Later, the agent sought to pin the defendant down regarding his account that he was playing cards and did not kill the victim:

Legal agent: On 2 April 2006, with whom did you play cards?

Defendant: At the beginning, there were two ladies and later two men, one is tall and another was short, replaced the two women.

Legal agent: Who was the fourth person?

Defendant: My friend.

Legal agent: Was [Zhao] present at the scene?

Defendant: Yes.

Legal agent: When you fled away, did [Zhao] flee away with you?

Defendant: I don't know.

Legal agent: Did you tell the police the truth when they caught you?

Defendant: Yes. But later, I changed some content of my confession.

Legal agent: Why?

Defendant: Because of the torture.

At the conclusion of the prosecution's presentation of evidence and following an indication that there was no defence evidence, the civil agent once again interceded:

> *Civil agent:* The testimonies of the witnesses JF and XW are identical with the prosecution evidence, but we also collected the testimony of LY, which proved that the defendant stabbed the victim with the knife.
>
> [The case-responsible judge was not pleased to have the legal agent present criminal evidence.[35] He approved the legal agent's request after the legal agent's persistence.]
>
> *Judge:* Defendant, do you have any disagreement with the evidence?
>
> *Defendant:* Yes. It was perjury.
>
> *Judge:* Defence Lawyer, do you have any disagreement with the evidence?
>
> *Defence Lawyer:* No.

Civil agents tended to be vociferous at the Debate stage in calling for harsher punishment and, on occasions, expressing their displeasure over the fact that the charge was less severe than they thought justified. In L-CO-X-03, for example, where following the death of the victim the prosecution charged the defendant only with 'intentional injury', the agent told the court:[36]

> I think there is a direct relationship between the victim's death which is mentioned in the Bill of Prosecution and the defendant's act, so the charge is more lenient than we expected. The defend-

---

[35] The case-responsible judge had earlier, during the presentation of the prosecution evidence, ignored attempts by the agent to contribute by holding up his hand.

[36] To the same effect, case E-CO-L-08 and E-CO-L-13.

ant should bear civil responsibility. In the meantime, the panel should punish the defendant severely.

As a consequence, the mixing of criminal and civil proceedings[37] often introduced an element of uncertainty and confusion into the trial. In a minority of cases, the lines of demarcation were clear to all parties, but in the majority of cases the boundaries were blurred resulting either in the defendant facing additional hostile questioning, pleas for more severe punishment or role-confusion among the participants.

VARIATIONS TO TRIAL PROCEDURE

As regards criminal trial procedure, some variations are permitted to the procedure where cases are tried using 'summary procedure' or 'simplified ordinary procedure'.

SUMMARY PROCEDURE

The 1996 CPL and SPC Interpretation allows a summary procedure to be used for offences carrying a sentence of not more than three years' imprisonment; offences punishable by detention, public surveillance or fine; for cases which can only be initiated on complaint, and for cases in which the defendant may be exempted from criminal punishment.[38] Use of the procedure requires the agreement of the court and the procuratorate,[39] and the circumstances in which it can be used are further restricted by the provisions of Article 222 of the SPC Interpretation and Article 312 of the Rules of the People's Procuratorate on Criminal Procedure. The former provides that summary procedure is not available in cases where the defendant pleads not guilty, the case is complicated, the defendant is blind, deaf or mute, or where there are other circumstances which make the procedure unsuitable.[40] The latter states that the procuratorate should not give its consent to application of summary procedure where the defendant has requested application of the ordinary procedure. Only in a few cases can the defendant (have the right to) initiate summary procedure in public prosecution cases, which means they have to accept the decision by procuratorate or court passively. According to the survey by Xiao Shiwei (2008), a majority of cases were initiated under the summary procedure. When deciding on an application to use summary procedure by the court and agreed by the procuratorate, few defendants or defenders were invited to express their opinion.

In cases where summary procedure is applied the case may be heard by a single judge rather than a collegial panel (Article 148, 1996 CPL), and judgment must be rendered within 20 days of the court accepting the case (Article 178, 1996 CPL). Further, although

---

[37] It should be added that there was also confusion in a number of cases in the civil hearing when discussion/argument strayed into the area of criminal responsibility.
[38] Article 174, 1996 CPL and the SPC Interpretation Article 221.
[39] SPC Interpretation Articles 217 and 218.
[40] Article 222 of the SPC Interpretation. The translation of this provision is mainly based on Wei Luo (2000).

the procuratorate may send prosecutors to court to support the prosecution in such cases, it is under no obligation to do so (Article 175, 1996 CPL). Article 225 of the SPC Interpretation provides that in summary procedure cases where there is no prosecutor in court it is the duty of the judge to 'present or read aloud the major evidence'. More importantly, Article 177, 1996 CPL disapplies wholesale the above provisions governing the interrogation of the defendant, questioning of witnesses and expert witnesses, the production of evidence and the debate stage. Article 225 of the SPC Interpretation states that the judge may question the defendant and, in accordance with Article 177, the defendant is allowed to make a final statement before the court moves to give judgment. Article 179, 1996 CPL does, however, allow the court the option of switching from summary to ordinary procedure if in the course of trying the case the court discovers that summary procedure is not suitable.

In practice, few if any prosecutors are present during a summary trial. The judge reads the Bill of Prosecution (mostly only parts of it); helps present evidence in written form or pictures, whether it is material or documentary evidence; and asks the defendant whether the evidence is in question. When the judge reads out the evidence, he or she generally just mentions the page number in the file and states what it can prove.[41] Some commentators argue that this violates the principle of the separation of the prosecution and adjudication (Cui and Dong, 2009; Liu and Li, 2009; and Li Yanling, 2007). The judge debates with or refutes the defendant if the latter has some disagreement with the charge in the Bill of Prosecution. Because of their fear of the judge, defendants rarely challenge or cross-examine the evidence. Once the judge expresses impatience with regard to the defendant's justification, the defendant often stops speaking. In addition, if the defendant debates with the judge or disagrees with the charge, the case might be converted to ordinary procedure even if, according to the observation of Xiao Shiwei (2008), the defendant wants the court to render a judgment as soon as possible.

Not only may summary cases proceed with no prosecutor present, but they can also proceed with no defence lawyer in court, even in those cases in which the defendant has retained a lawyer. Article 226 of the SPC Interpretation provides that

> In adjudicating cases for which use of summary procedure is appropriate, after a private prosecutor reads aloud the brief of his complaint, the defendant may make a statement and defend himself concerning the criminal facts accused in the brief of the complaint. The private prosecutor shall present the major evidence. If the defendant has evidence to be presented, the judge shall permit it. With the permission of the judge, the defendant and his defender may debate with the private prosecutor and his litigation attorney.[42]

Various writers have found that few defendants can obtain the help of lawyers (e.g., Zhao and Liu, 2006; Xiao Shiwei, 2008; and Liu Jing, 2009). According to Xiao Shiwei (2008), for example, only 24.5 per cent of defendants in W Court and 11.9 per cent in P Court retained a lawyer respectively. Furthermore, defendants from a city have more chance

---

[41] Xiao Shiwei (2008), 'Criminal Summary Procedure in Practice–Demonstrative Research on the Sample of Two Grassroots Courts'. For similar views see, Zhao and Liu (2006); Gao Fei (2008); and Li Yanling (2007).

[42] Article 228, SPC Interpretation. The translation of this provision is mainly based on Wei Luo's (2000) translation.

of obtaining a lawyer than those from the countryside because of financial and cultural reasons. Zuo Weimin *et al.*'s (2009) survey on 60 sample cases also showed that the rate of suspects' obtaining lawyers in summary procedure was only 16.7 per cent, which contrasted with that in ordinary procedure (100 per cent), while the percentage retaining a lawyer in simplified procedure was 40 per cent.

When the defendant makes a final statement, Xiao Shiwei (2008) noted that the judge would often warn the defendant not to repeat what has been said before. Most defendants express remorse, pleading for leniency and a chance to make a fresh start in life. Although most written judgments are made after trial, the judge had a clear idea of the case as he or she had read the case files before trial. The only difference was that they would readjust the range of the penalty according to the defendant's justification, attitude towards the crime and repentance. Therefore, the trial in summary procedure retains a strong sense of verdict first then trial. This is challenged by some Chinese scholars as compromising the principle of judicial neutrality (Liu Jing, 2009).

In practice, decisions on the mode of adjudication, as pointed out by two judges (J-IJ-S4-06 and J-IJ-S4-08), appear arbitrary, lack transparency and there is no mechanism to separate cases that should be adjudicated according to ordinary procedure and those that should be adjudicated according to summary procedure. Having raised this problem in interview, two judges (J-IJ-S4-06 and J-IJ-S-07) called for the establishment of a mechanism to determine the mode of adjudication so as to improve the transparency of case handling.

A prosecutor (L-IP-X-02) also pointed out that the application of summary procedure in the Intermediate Courts was low. One of the reasons is said to be the complicated procedure. As one judge (L-IJ-X-09) complained, instead of simplifying their work, the application of summary procedure increased the workload of judges. For example, judges need to ask for the opinions of the defendants, prosecutors and the defence lawyers, prepare the application of summary procedure and then deliver this to the litigants. According to Geng (1998), some judges are unwilling to apply summary procedure because they lack confidence and experience, and are unwilling to bear sole responsibility, preferring to have the case adjudicated by a collegiate bench under collective responsibility. Moreover, given the poor quality of the judges, some senior officials are also unwilling to allow judges to apply summary procedure.

In addition, some procuratorates deliberately control the application of summary procedure by setting a quota. Zhan Fuliang (1997) from the People's Procuratorate of Wenshou City of Zhejiang Province reported that the procuratorate in one place restricted the number of cases that could be adjudicated according to summary procedure to 10 per cent. As a result, when the 10 per cent quota was met, all subsequent cases had to be adjudicated according to ordinary procedure, regardless of suitability.

Whilst some judges and prosecutors and even a few lawyers (I-IL-S3-05 and E-IL-L-01) called for expanding the scope of application of summary procedure, not everyone was supportive of this. As one lawyer commented:

F-IL-N-05: I think a trial should not be careless. It takes the police several months or a year to investigate a case and collect all kinds of evidence, but it takes only one or two hours for the court to try the case. It is incredible, I think. It doesn't respect the police effort and also ignores the defendants' rights. So I don't agree to the use of summary procedure very often.

SIMPLIFIED ORDINARY PROCEDURE

Although there is no provision for it in the 1996 CPL, a Joint Opinion issued by the Supreme People's Court, Supreme People's Procuratorate and the Ministry of Justice allows courts to dispose of guilty plea cases using what is described as 'simplified ordinary procedure'.[43] This can be applied in first instance cases in which the defendant does not dispute the basic criminal facts alleged and is willing to plead guilty. Where a defendant is charged with several offences, simplified ordinary procedure can be applied in respect of those offences to which the defendant is prepared to plead guilty.[44]

The procuratorate can propose to the court that simplified procedure be applied, or the court, upon examination of the case, can suggest use of the procedure. The procedure can be used only with the consent of the procuratorate and the defendant,[45] and the court is obliged to inform the defendant of the possible consequences of pleading guilty and explain the application of simplified ordinary procedure.[46] As with summary procedure, few defendants or defence lawyers are able to initiate the simplified ordinary procedure nor are their views on this solicited. The Joint Opinion encourages judges to consider leniency for those who plead guilty, but does not state in terms that judges should communicate this fact to defendants.[47]

The use of simplified procedure, however, is prohibited for certain categories of case:[48]

1) The defendant is blind, deaf or dumb;
2) The defendant may be sentenced to death;
3) Foreign defendants;
4) Cases that have great social impact;
5) Cases in which the court discovers after examination that the defendant may not be guilty despite his guilty plea;
6) Cases in which defendants are charged jointly and not all defendants plead guilty or agree to application of the simplified procedure; and
7) Other circumstances in which use of the procedure would be inappropriate.

---

[43] Several Opinions Concerning the Application of Ordinary Procedure in Adjudicating Cases in which the 'Defendants Have Pleaded Guilty' (Trial Implementation) (March 2003) (hereafter Joint Opinion).

[44] Article 1, Joint Opinion. Because we were restricted to case files and observations of open court trials, our research sheds no light on the broad question of 'plea bargaining' which has given rise to discussion among Chinese academics. See, for example, Liang Zhiping (2004); Yu Xun (2004); Cui Po and Mao Chenglin (2004); Li Wenyu (2004); Guo Jingfeng (2003). Although plea bargaining was once considered inconsistent with inquisitorial systems of justice (which traditionally employs the principle of legality and a responsibility on the authorities to seek out the truth), it has become a noticeable feature of some continental European inquisitorial systems (for example, the system of *patteggiamento* in Italy and informal arrangements (*informelle Absprachen*) in Germany.

[45] Article 3, Joint Opinion.
[46] Article 4, Joint Opinion.
[47] Article 9, Joint Opinion.
[48] Article 2, Joint Opinion.

When used, simplified ordinary procedure differs from ordinary procedure in that:

1) There are no limitations on what judges can read by way of case materials and evidence prior to the trial;[49]
2) The bill of prosecution having been read by the prosecutor, the collegial bench must ask the defendant whether his guilty plea is voluntary, whether he agrees to the application of simplified ordinary procedure and whether he understands the legal consequences of pleading guilty;
3) The defendant is not asked to respond to the bill of prosecution;
4) Questioning of the defendant by the judge, the procurator and the defence may be omitted;
5) Evidence which is not in dispute need not be read out;
6) Evidence which is in dispute can be subject to cross-examination by the parties;
7) The focus of the debate stage is on the nature of the offence, the sentence and outstanding controversial issues.[50]

The court may terminate the application of simplified ordinary procedure at any point in the adjudication process if it discovers that any of the conditions for the application of simplified ordinary procedure have not been met.[51]

In our case file analysis we were unable to record how many cases in our sample had been tried using simplified ordinary procedure. There is no systematic survey of its use in China, and a survey relying on interviews with judges in Xi'an City found that estimates varied between 7 per cent and 40 per cent as between different courts in the city.[52] The statistics of a district court in Shanghai (Xu Meijun, 2007) showed that, among the 743 cases heard in 2004, 158 were conducted under simplified ordinary procedure (21.2 per cent), 444 in summary procedure (59.8 per cent), and 141 in ordinary procedure (19.0 per cent). We did not expressly ask the judges whom we interviewed about the use of simplified ordinary procedure, but estimates that were offered by judges varied. One judge in a big eastern coastal city (G-IJ-S1-01) said that 20 per cent of cases were adjudicated using simplified ordinary procedure, whilst another from the same city (G-IJ-S1-04) said that of all the cases adjudicated using ordinary procedure (which he estimated as 50 per cent of all cases he had tried), 'most' were tried using simplified ordinary procedure.

In our interviews we asked prosecutors what changes/improvements they would like to see made to the trial stage of the process. Many prosecutors[53] and judges[54] supported the simplification of trial procedure in general, and an increase in the application of simplified ordinary procedure in particular. For example, a prosecutor from a northern

---

[49] Article 6, Joint Opinion.
[50] Article 7, Joint Opinion.
[51] Article 11, Joint Opinion.
[52] Chen Guangzhong (2004), after interviewing judges in Xi'an City, put the figure at 40 per cent in Yanta District Court, 30 per cent in Beilin District Court, but only 7–10 per cent in Lianhu District Court.
[53] E.g. K-IP-W-04, L-IP-X-06, H-IP-S2-003, A-IP-B1-11, B-IP-B2-10, D-IP-K-04, M-IP-Y-03, L-IP-X-08 and L-IP-X-11.
[54] E.g. B-IJ-B2-10, D-IJ-K-04, L-IJ-X-07, L-IJ-X-08.

big city (A-IP-B1-11) suggested that cases in which the defendant had pleaded guilty should move immediately to sentencing. One prosecutor (M-IP-Y-03) said that simplified ordinary procedure should be recognized formally in the 1996 CPL, with a procedure for regulating its use.

However, enthusiasm for simplified ordinary procedure was not universal. Thus, one judge (F-IJ-N-02) pointed out that since the educational level of many defendants was low and they lacked legal knowledge, there was a danger that they would not understand the full implications of consenting to the procedure. This view was shared by another judge from the same locality (F-IJ-N-03), who argued that as the defendant's property rights, freedom, as well as his right to life, were all at stake, the trial should be conducted carefully and for this reason simplified ordinary procedure should not be applied too often.

In addition to the concerns voiced by those whom we interviewed, existing research on the subject suggests other reasons why some judges are not keen on the use of the simplified procedure. Judges from Hainan, Shaanxi and Jiangsu Provinces interviewed by a research team complained that simplified ordinary procedure was time-consuming (Chen Guanzhong, 2004). They argued that although the procedure reduced the time taken at trial, it added to the time taken at the pre-trial stage. In this respect they pointed to the extra effort made in conducting substantive examination of the case, greater tendency to seek opinions, having to liaise with the defence to get its consent, having to deliver documents to the defence and prosecution and, in particular, the greater effort needed to seek pre-trial disclosure of evidence.

REPRESENTATION FOR DEFENDANTS

As explained above, by Article 151(2), 1996 CPL, defendants are entitled to be represented by a lawyer at the trial, and it is the duty of the court to inform the defendant of this right when it delivers a copy of the Bill of Prosecution to the defendant at the pre-trial examination stage. In some circumstances, however, the court *must* designate a lawyer for the defendant, and in these cases the lawyer is obliged to provide representation. Article 34, 1996 CPL provides that:

> If the defendant is blind, deaf or mute, or if he is a minor, and thus not entrusted anyone to be his defender, the People's Court shall designate a lawyer that is obligated to provide legal aid to serve as a defender.
>
> If there is the possibility that the defendant may be sentenced to death and yet he has not entrusted anyone to be his defender, the People's Court shall designate a lawyer that is obligated to provide legal aid to serve as a defender.[55]

---

[55] Similar provisions can be found in Article 36 of the Supreme People's Court Interpretation on Several Questions Concerning the Implementation of the Criminal Procedure Law (SPC Interpretation): 'When a defendant does not retain a defender and is in one of the following circumstances, the people's court may appoint a defender for him:
    1) Blind, deaf, mute, or a person with restricted capacity to act;
    2) A minor who is less than eighteen years old when the court opens the trial session; or
    3) A person who may be sentenced to death.

In other cases, Article 34 provides that the court *may* designate a lawyer for the defendant, and if it does so the lawyer is obliged to provide representation:

> If a case is to be brought in court by a public prosecutor and the defendant involved has not entrusted anyone to be his defender due to financial difficulties or other reasons, the People's Court may designate a lawyer that is obligated to provide legal aid service as a defender.

Some further guidance is provided by Article 37 of the SPC Interpretation as to the circumstances in which the court may exercise its discretion to assign a lawyer:

1) When the defendant qualified as economically poor according to standards set by the local government.
2) When the defendant does not have a source of income and the economic situation of his family cannot be verified.
3) When the defendant does not have a source of income and his family refuses to pay for the cost of retaining defence counsel after many attempts to persuade them to do so.
4) When the defendant is involved in a case of criminal conspiracy and the other defendants have already retained their own defenders.
5) When the defendant has foreign citizenship.
6) When the case has significant social impact.
7) When a people's court determines that the prosecution opinion and the transferred evidentiary materials of the case may influence a correct verdict or sentence.

Article 38 of the SPC Interpretation provides that the defendant can refuse to accept the lawyer assigned, in which case the court must allow him to defend himself and endorse the court transcript accordingly. However, where the court has a duty to appoint a lawyer (i.e. in cases of disability or for those who may face the death penalty), the SPC Interpretation provides that the court may accept the defendant's refusal of a lawyer only if the defendant has a 'legitimate reason to refuse the lawyer appointed by a People's Court to defend'. It further provides that in such cases a 'defendant shall retain a defender himself, or the people's court shall appoint a new defender for him'.

When a lawyer is assigned to a legal aid case in China he or she is not entitled to be remunerated (i.e. there is no guarantee that he or she will be paid from a government or other fund).[56] Despite the fact that the Legal Aid Regulations clearly state that 'legal aid is the responsibility of the government',[57] it reiterates that persons who handle legal aid

---

[56] Article 42 of the Lawyers Law 1996 provides that:
'Lawyers must undertake the obligations to provide legal assistance in accordance with the state regulations, fulfil their duties and provide those who need assistance with legal services.'
In similar fashion, the 2007 Lawyers Law provides by Article 42:
'Lawyers and law firms shall perform their obligations of legal aid according to the state provisions, provide the aided persons with standard legal services, and protect the legal rights and interests of the aided persons.'
See also Cai Peiyu (2001); Huang Chunhong (2002).

[57] Article 3, Legal Aid Regulations.

cases work for free and are not allowed to collect remuneration for providing legal aid services.[58] Any lawyer who receives money or property for handling a legal aid case may be admonished and ordered to rectify the situation by the judicial administration department. If the circumstances are serious, he or she may be suspended from practice for more than one month but less than three months. In addition, the lawyer concerned will be required to return the money and property collected. He or she may also be fined one to three times the value of the money and property collected.[59]

Lawyers who refuse to accept legal aid cases without proper reason or terminate legal aid cases without authorization may also be subjected to similar punishment.[60] Any law firm that refuses an appointment from a legal aid organ and does not assign its lawyers to handle the legal aid case may be admonished and ordered to rectify the situation by the judicial administration department. If the circumstances are serious, the firm may be ordered to cease business and engage in rectification for one to three months.[61] Individual lawyers who breach any of the rules requiring free advice and assistance may also find themselves punished for breach of professional ethics and disciplined under the Lawyers Law.[62]

Although there are some sources of funding available for legal aid, there is no unified, national system of funding and as a result coverage is patchy and resources are limited.[63] While there are some legal aid centres, in part funded by the state, many of these are reluctant to take on criminal cases.[64] There is widespread criticism within China of the haphazard nature of legal aid (Huang Chunhong, 2002), and many commentators and researchers have argued that the lack of remuneration undoubtedly undermines the enthusiasm and professionalism with which lawyers approach their task (Li Yan, 2003; Cai Peiyu, 2001; Li Baoyue, 2004). The following comment by a lawyer we interviewed suggests that there are certainly problems of motivation and professionalism when lawyers are asked to act for free:

> *F-IL-N-01:* The Legal Aid Centre requires every lawyer to make a *pro bono* defence for defendants. We don't have any remuneration and have to use our own money to pay transportation and communication fares. Some lawyers are so careless that they don't try their best to defend defendants. So if there is a guarantee of necessary expenses, the value of *pro bono* defence will be better.

In addition, according to the observation of the researchers in the sites, legal aid defence lawyers performed poorly and were inadequately prepared. Sometimes, they even could not distinguish the role of the defendant in the crime from that of other joint offenders; and what they often did was to say nothing until the end of the debate when a plea for leniency would be entered.

---

[58] Article 22, Legal Aid Regulations.
[59] Article 28, Legal Aid Regulations.
[60] Article 28, Legal Aid Regulations.
[61] Article 27, Legal Aid Regulations.
[62] Article 29, Legal Aid Regulations.
[63] Cai Peiyu (2001); Ma Mingliang (2004); Cao and Zhang (2004).
[64] Tong Lihua's Legal Aid Stations for migrant workers might be expected to take on criminal cases occasionally. Before its official dissolution, *Gongmeng* (Open Constitution Initiative) led by Xu Zhiyong took on some criminal defence cases.

RULES OF EVIDENCE

There is in China no official code setting out rules of evidence, and neither is there a sophisticated body of case law on the subject. Concepts such as the 'presumption of innocence', 'proof beyond reasonable doubt', the inadmissibility of 'hearsay', and the inadmissibility of 'confessions secured by torture',[65] are either totally absent within the Chinese legal system or given muted voice in scattered, ambiguous and sometimes contradictory legal provisions.

The 1996 CPL and the SPC Interpretation fail to address in a clear manner central issues such as the burden of proof, standard of proof and presumption of innocence. Article 12 provides that 'no person shall be found guilty without being judged as such by a People's Court according to law'. At one level this could be seen as giving voice to the presumption of innocence. However, this provision is contradicted by Article 93 of the CPL, which requires the criminal suspect to 'answer the investigators' questions truthfully', and Article 155, which allows the judge to interrogate the defendant (without any right for the defendant to refuse to answer). These provisions are supposed to be derived from the traditional Chinese practice of *'tanbai congkuan, kangju cong yan'* ('leniency for frank admission, strictness for resistance'). Although Article 43 states it is 'strictly forbidden to extort confessions by torture and to collect evidence by threat, enticement, deceit or other unlawful means', there is no rule that confessions obtained by such means must not be admitted into evidence. In fact, Article 42 appears to contain a rule that truthfulness is the sole test of admissibility ('All facts that prove the true circumstances of a case shall be evidence').

The 1996 CPL merely provides that 'if the facts . . . are clear, the evidence is reliable and sufficient . . . the defendant . . . shall be pronounced guilty accordingly'. Such a provision offers little guidance as to how reliability or sufficiency are to be judged, and neither does it say anything about how doubts are to be resolved (i.e., whether the benefit of any doubt is to be given to the accused). Further, the CPL is silent as to which party bears the burden of proof, a matter further complicated by the fact that the court can order its own investigations and thereby produce evidence independently of the prosecution.

There is similar confusion regarding admissibility of hearsay evidence. Article 47, 1996 CPL, which appears in the 'Evidence' chapter of the 1996 CPL, provides that:

> The testimony of a witness may be used as a basis in deciding a case only after the witness has been questioned and cross-examined in the courtroom by both sides, that is, the public prosecutor and victim as well as the defendant and defenders, and after the testimonies of the witnesses on all sides have been heard and verified.

This appears to be a clear rule that witness statements are inadmissible, and that the testimony of witnesses becomes evidence in the case if and only if witnesses attend trial, give live testimony, and make themselves available for cross-examination. However, Article 47

---

[65] Guidelines have recently been introduced in relation to evidence obtained by torture, for example in death penalty cases, following the wrongful imprisonment of a farmer for 'killing' a neighbour who, ten years later, returned to the village. On the guidelines see: Bai Long (2010) and Ng Tze-wei (2010a).

is contradicted by Article 157 which provides that 'the records of testimony of witnesses who are not present in court, the conclusions of expert witnesses who are not present in court, the records of inquests and other documents serving as evidence shall be read out in court'. The confusion is further compounded by Article 144 of the SPC Interpretation. Article 144(1) states that an expert witness 'should appear in court to read aloud the conclusion of his evaluation, but an exception can be made upon the permission of a People's Court'. Article 144(2) addresses non-expert witnesses, and contradicts both Article 47 of the CPL (by stating that hearsay testimony is admissible) and Article 157 (by stating that hearsay is only admissible in certain situations, whereas Article 157 requires the reading out in court of all statements as a matter of course).[66]

The ambiguity of the rules relating to evidence has been the subject of extensive analysis by Chinese legal academics and professionals. On the admissibility of witness statements, Yin Xiaoli (2002) points out that the lack of clear rules has led to an inconsistency in approach as between different courts, and sometimes even as between different judges in the same court (see also, Chen Shufen, 2004). Both Yin (2002) and Liu (2002) have argued that the current rules encourage the common phenomenon of witnesses refusing to testify in court, which in turn leads to the extensive admission of hearsay evidence in trials and Liao Haisheng (2002) argues that the lack of oral testimony is particularly worrying given that many of those who provide witness statements have a conflict of interest with either the defendant or the victim, making it all the more necessary that they should appear in court for examination.

On the burden of proof, Xu Xuefeng (2002) has pointed out that the failure of the 1996 CPL to explicitly stipulate whether a defendant should bear the burden of proof leads to continuous debate among legal academics and to a lack of consistency in judicial practice. Jiang Qi and Ye Liangfang (2002) have written that a refusal by the defendant to answer questions leads, under Article 93, 1996 CPL, to a situation in which the defendant is presumed guilty unless he provides an explanation of his innocence. In this way, the burden of proof shifts from the prosecution to the defendant, a situation criticized by some commentators as deeply unfair because of the restrictions placed on defence lawyers in collecting evidence to challenge the case as constructed by the prosecution (Luo Benqi, 1997). We should note, however, that Article 93 of the 1996 CPL is not dispositive of the issue since it discusses the interrogation of criminal *suspects* and not defendants. Feng Jie (2000) has written that only a robust guarantee of the right to silence will eradicate the tendency to presume guilt and resort to torture to secure confessions. By contrast, others have argued that these concerns are misplaced, because it is quite clear from the 1996 CPL as it currently stands that the defendant does not bear the burden of proof, there is no obligation to answer police questions, and there is no

---

[66] Article 141(2) of the SPC Interpretation provides that:
A witness who meets one of the following circumstances may, with the permission of the people's court, not be present in the court to testify:
1) He is a minor;
2) He is suffering from serious illness or his mobility is significantly impaired during the courtroom trial;
3) His testimony does not decisively affect the judgment of the case; and
4) The existence of other reasons.

duty to testify in court (He Jiahong, 2002; Li and Huang Daocheng, 1999; and Liu Yali, 2000).

There is similar confusion and controversy regarding the role of the court in collecting evidence. Feng (2000) states that Article 158, 1996 CPL, which empowers the collegiate bench to adjourn the trial to verify the evidence if it has doubts, places a burden of proof on the court. This, in her view, affects the impartiality of the bench, for proving the case should be the responsibility of the prosecution and the defence. A similar view has been expressed by Guo, Wu and Hou (2000), who argue that the provision enables the court to assist the prosecution by making the court bear the same obligations as the prosecution in respect of evidence pointing to the guilt of the defendant and in ascertaining the seriousness of the crime. Lin and Zhu (2002) point out that if a judge conducts out-of-court investigation simply because the evidence provided by the prosecution is insufficient the judge is in effect assisting the prosecution to discharge its burden of proof, in violation of the principle of 'no conviction whenever there is doubt' and in breach of the presumption of innocence.[67]

One of the lawyers we interviewed (F-N-03) said that judges might in future adopt the principle of giving defendants the benefit of the doubt:

> *F-IL-N-03:* The principle of giving the defendant the benefit of the doubt is demonstrated in contemporary trials. This shows the progress of society. When the facts are unclear and the evidence is insufficient, we would rather release the defendant than make an incorrect verdict. To achieve this, judges have to be of high standard and have the courage to make a not guilty verdict.

However, almost all others whom we interviewed were not as sanguine. One judge (F-IJ-N-06) pointed out that there had to be more positive promotion of the principles underpinning the right to silence and the principle of 'not guilty if there is doubt'. A prosecutor we interviewed (M-IP-Y-02) told us it would take a long time to change the mentality of the Chinese judicial personnel to accept such principles. The following comments of two lawyers clearly show that judges in China are still wedded to the traditional mentality of presumption of guilt:

> *L-IL-X-04:* In addition, I found judges' thinking very strange. As to the evidence which proves the guilt of the defendant, it should be for the party which produces that piece of evidence to use it to prove the guilt of the defendant. But in practice, judges will ask the defence lawyer to present counter-evidence to rebut the argument.
>
> *F-IL-N-06:* Although the law requires that the principle of presumption of innocence and giving the defendant the benefit of the doubt should be observed when the facts of the case are unclear and the evidence is insufficient, judges' thinking tends to be in line with that of the prosecution and the police. They would tend to think that the evidence collected by the police and the prosecution is more credible.

A big city lawyer (B-IL-B2-00) said that judicial personnel (including the police, procurators and judges) in China still failed to accept the principle of innocent until proven guilty, while another lawyer (E-IL-L-07) said that it was difficult to implement this principle in practice. In view of this, some lawyers we interviewed (e.g. B-IL-B2-00,

---

[67] A similar view was expressed by Yang Ming (2003) and Huang Wen (2004).

F-IL-N-05, F-IL-N-06) called for judicial personnel to change their traditional mentality and recognize and implement the principle of the presumption of innocence seriously. Two lawyers we interviewed (G-IL-S1-01 and F-IL-N-07) were of the opinion that defendants should enjoy the right to silence, whilst a judge we interviewed (H-IJ-S2-01) said the ultimate solution was the establishment of a clear standard of proof.

It should be noted that academics have sought for many years to promote the virtues of having rules of evidence. In 2002, the Center for Criminal Law and Justice and the Procedural Law Research Center produced an extensive *Criminal Evidence Law (expert Draft)*.[68] The Draft Law proposed many rules of evidence that would be familiar in their thrust to common law lawyers. Examples are set out below:[69]

> Article 4: Any person shall be presumed innocent until determined guilty with an effective judgment of a People's Court according to law.
>
> Article 13: In a public prosecution case, the public prosecutor shall be responsible for introducing evidence and proving the defendant guilty.
>
> In a private prosecution case, the private prosecutor shall be responsible for introducing evidence and proving the defendant guilty.
>
> A suspect or defendant shall not be required to prove innocence unless as otherwise provided by law.
>
> Article 15: It is strictly forbidden to compel a suspect, defendant, witness or any other person to produce self-incrimination statement or other oral evidence with the following means:
>
> (1) Torture or other means by which severe pain may be inflicted on the person;
> (2) Intimidating or cheating;
> (3) Keeping the person from being fatigued, hungry or thirsty;
> (4) Using medicine or sleep pills;
> (5) Other cruel, inhuman or degrading means.
>
> Article 16: Evidence obtained with the means forbidden by Section 15 above is illegal evidence.
> Oral evidence obtained illegally shall not be admitted as proof of the case.
> The admission of real evidence is on discretion of the court according to the degree of illegal means and other circumstances of the case. For non-prosecution cases, the prosecutor shall decide whether to use illegal real evidence.

These are mere examples drawn from a draft which includes some 193 substantive Articles covering most major topics in the law of evidence including such matters as judicial notice, real evidence, documentary evidence, witness testimony and victim statements, the statements of suspects and defendants, expert witnesses, collection and use of evidence in criminal procedure, disclosure rules and trial practice. This demonstrates at least that should China move toward the adoption of rules of evidence, there is a body of expertise available to guide policy.

---

[68] The experts working under the group leadership of Professor Chen Guangzhong and Professor Bian Jianlin of the China University of Political Science and Law included many of China's leading criminal procedure experts including Professor Fan Chongyi, Professor Song Yinghui, and Professor He Jiahong.

[69] The examples are reproduced as in the original English version.

Finally, we can note that China is in the course of introducing some guidelines relating to illegally obtained evidence especially in death penalty cases.[70] This follows the wrongful conviction of Zhao Zuohai for murder of his neighbour who, ten years after the event, turned up alive in 2010.[71]

JUDGES

Each court has a president (*yuanzhang*) and vice presidents, and each division within the court has a chief judge (*tingzhang*), deputy chief judges, and assistant judges. These various levels of judge, other than assistant judges (who are appointed by the People's Courts directly) are all appointed (and can be removed) by the people's congresses at the corresponding levels.[72]

Until 1983 there was no requirement for judges to have had any legal (or indeed any formal) education or training, and anyone over the age of 23 who was eligible to vote, eligible to stand for public office and who had not been previously deprived of any political rights could be appointed to judicial office. In 1983 the law was changed so that appointees had to have professional legal knowledge, and further amended in 1995 to require an advanced degree in law or a college degree combined with a minimum of one year work experience in a law-related field. The position is now governed by the Judges

---

[70] Regulations have been issued as a Notice from the Supreme People's Court, Supreme People's Procuratorate, Ministry of Public Security, Ministry of State Security and the Ministry of Justice regarding the issue, '*Rules Concerning Questions about Examining and Judging Evidence in Death Penalty Cases*' and '*Rules Concerning Questions About Exclusion of Illegal Evidence in Handling Criminal Cases*' (see: http://www.duihua.org/hrjournal/evidence/notice.htm). Article 1 of the Rule regarding the exclusion of illegal evidence states that illegal oral evidence includes 'statements by criminal suspects or defendants obtained through illegal means such as coerced confession as well as witness testimony or victim statements obtained through illegal means such as use of violence or threats' and Article 2 provides that, 'Oral evidence that has been determined to be illegal in accordance with the law shall be excluded and may not serve as the basis for conviction.' Commentators generally are of the view that the practical effect of these Rules will not be substantial given that the judiciary, the criminal process and the political and social forces remain unchanged.

[71] Ng Tze-wei (2010a). These were reported to have been triggered by the wrongful conviction of Zhao Zuohai who, after being tortured for one month, confessed to killing his neighbour but was freed ten years later when the neighbour re-appeared. The guidelines, issued by the Supreme People's Court, the Supreme People's Procuratorate and the Ministries of public security, state security and justice, prohibit the use of illegally obtained evidence in death penalty cases including evidence obtained through torture, violence or threats, physical evidence obtained without being properly documented and evidence obtained by unqualified organizations. For the first time, the guidelines include the fundamental principle that 'every fact must be supported by evidence' and that evidence in death penalty cases 'must be of the highest quality' with proof being absolute and to 'exclude all other possibilities'. A second guideline sets out a procedure for an accused to attempt to exclude illegally obtained evidence. This requires the defendant to provide the court with information on how the evidence was illegally obtained following which the court must begin an assessment of the claim. If the court decides that the defendant might have been tortured, prosecutors must provide the court with written records, video and audio recordings of the interview in question and witnesses who were present. If the evidence still does not rule out the possibility of torture, those who conducted the interview must be called to attend the hearing.

[72] Chow (2003) and Balme (2010).

Law of 2001, which requires that appointees who have a Masters or a PhD in law must have legal work experience of one year; those who hold such higher degrees in a non-law subject must have two years' legal work experience; law graduates must have two years' legal work experience, and non-law graduates must have three years' legal work experience. In addition the 2001 law requires that appointees must pass a national uniform judicial examination (applicable to all prospective lawyers, judges and prosecutors). The law was not, it should be noted, retroactive in effect and, whilst judges in some parts were required to take make-up examinations,[73] many judges continue to lack professional qualifications.[74]

What this means is that judges in China are career civil servants, and their role has been accurately summarized by Chow (2003) in the following terms:

> [J]udges are viewed as administrators within a system of legislative supremacy in which the NPC and its Standing Committee have the authority not only to enact laws but also have the authority to interpret them. Within such a system, judges have a role limited to the straightforward and mechanical application of the law . . . without much need for judicial discretion or legal reasoning of the type identified with judges in the United States . . . [J]udges are evaluated based upon a list of enumerated criteria, including results reached, moral character and ideology, work attitude, and judicial style. The annual examination is the basis for wage increases, adjustments in bureaucratic rank, need for further training, and dismissals. The typical salaries for judges . . . [are] . . . on a par with other mid-level bureaucrats and civil servants.

Gerard Clark (2008), in discussing the lack of judicial independence in China, states that, notwithstanding contrary assertions in the Chinese Constitution,[75] the actual position is:

> The courts, as offices or bureaucracies, maintain a status equal to the other ministries and commissions for the town or province. As employees of a quasi-executive branch, judges maintain no greater job security than any other governmental employee. Similar to those appointees, the

---

[73] This was said to have led to many judges being thrown out in some poor areas. On the other hand, there have always been suggestions that the standards for judges should be *lowered*. For some discussion see, http://www.rfa.org/mandarin/shenrubaodao/2007/08/01/judge.

[74] See, Clark (2008); Balme (2010). Stephanie Balme found that in Shaanxi Province that whilst the number of university graduates was increasing, the percentage holding law degrees is still less than 50 per cent. Grassroots courts in western China are facing shortages of judges. As far as judges' constituency is concerned, 10 per cent of judges were undergraduates who had specialized in law or other majors; 30 per cent had been mobilized from other government agencies or through the examination; 50 per cent were retired soldiers, Su Li (2000). By the first half of 2007, there were 4688 judges in courts of Guizhou Province, among whom only 40 held an LLM degree or had taken postgraduate courses (0.9 per cent), 2152 had undergraduate degree or equivalent (45.9 per cent). Of these, 44.1 per cent graduated from a Party School and 28.5 per cent in other forms of part-time education basis. See Tan Shigui (2009), p. 7. According to the survey conducted by Zuo Weimin, Huojian Tang and Weijun Wu (2001) from Sichuan University Law School in 1999, there were 61 judges and judicial police in a basic court of whom four were university graduates (three majored in law and one in Chinese), 24 studied in a local part-time three-year Court College; 28 had obtained a diploma from the four-year university or three-year colleges such as TV university, self-study college, and two majored in industry or finance. Only 4.9 per cent of judges graduated from regular law schools.

[75] By Article 126 of the Constitution, courts are required to exercise judicial power independently according to law and free of any interference by administrative agencies, social organizations or individuals.

government selects a judge because he or she is favored by the State, Provincial or Municipal Council or the State, Provincial, or Municipal Communist Party leadership, depending on who is calling the shots at that particular time. Further, the Supreme People's Court has no administrative authority over lower courts and indeed may lack appellate jurisdiction. The local government budget accounts for operating expenses, including judges' salaries. At any time, the legislature can replace or remove those judges serving in a court that corresponds with the level of that particular legislature. The local government and the party can easily express its opinion in matters before a court. The internal managerial system of the people's courts discourages independence (p. 836, footnote omitted).

We should note, however, that the law requires that *courts* not individual judges should adjudicate cases 'independently' and that since 2007 there has been a marked tendency to denounce the notion of individual judges having 'judicial independence'.[76]

Further, because the education and training requirements are of fairly recent vintage, it means that a significant (but diminishing) proportion of those who currently work as judges in China have little, if any, formal legal education or training.[77] Cai Dingjian (1999b) has observed that the judges' corps was set up after 1979 in response to the urgent need to construct a legal system, and most judges were drawn from retired military officers,[78] cadres transferred from other state organs, enterprises and institutions, and university graduates from law and non-law specialties. One expert has put it more directly, stating that 'for years, China's judges have been drawn from a pool of retired military officers with no legal background or students fresh from law school who "do what they are told"'.[79] And from time to time there is official acknowledgement that the standard of some judges is low and that there is judicial corruption.[80]

---

[76] In 2007, Luo Gan criticized the idea for China. See, New York Times report at http://www.nytimes.com/2007/02/03/world/asia/03china.html. The speech itself is available at: http://www.chinalaw.gov.cn/jsp/contentpub/browser/contentpro.jsp?contentid=co2142286068. More recently, the President of the Supreme People's Court Wang Shengjun's endorsement of the Three Supremes also had this effect. The Three Supremes require all judges to uphold the Party's cause and the people's interests as 'supreme', with the law and Constitution mentioned only as a third 'supreme'. Courts have also been ordered to follow early 1950s models of the courts under Mao (so-called 'Ma Xiwu style' justice on the revival of which see (in Chinese) http://www.nanfangdaily.com.cn/nfzm/200906110115.asp). In the 1950s and 1960s, the party-state saw courts as instruments of 'people's dictatorship', using legal processes to fight those it saw as 'the people's enemies', and to settle other disputes through mediation or coercion. See, Cohen (2008) and Pils (2009b).

[77] For an earlier and excellent appraisal of the quality of the judiciary, see: Peerenboom (2002) at pp. 290 ff.

[78] See also, He Weifang (1998). The practice of installing army veterans in the courts (*fuzhuan junren jin fayuan*) popular in the immediate post-1979 period has clearly tailed off, if not discontinued entirely.

[79] Marquand (2001). See further, Alford (1999).

[80] See, for example, Daniel Kwan (2003) reporting on the speech of Xiao Yang, President of the Supreme People's Court in which he said that public grievance against judges ran deep because 'some judges were not impartial and some did not rule on cases fairly . . . The quality of some judges is low and they behave in an appalling manner. Some are corrupt and distort justice.' A prominent example was the conviction of Huang Songyou, the former Vice-President of the Chinese Supreme People's Court (SPC), of corruption crimes for which he received a life sentence. The President of the SPC, Wang Shengjun said in March 2009 that a total of 102 court staff had been charged with crimes of corruption in the previous year. In four years prior to Huang Songyou's detention, judges at four provincial High People's Courts (just below the level of the SPC itself) had been found guilty

Comprehensive national statistics on the educational and vocational qualifications of judges who are currently in service are difficult to obtain. In 2001, according to the *People's Daily*, the former vice-president of the Higher People's Court of Beijing City, Chen Chunlong, reported that among all the presidents and vice-presidents of the courts at the basic level in China, only 19.1 per cent had undergraduate or postgraduate academic qualifications; and the equivalent percentage for judges and assistant judges was lower at only 15.4 per cent.[81] In 2002, *BBC News* reported that among over 200000 judges in China, most 'have no legal training and have traditionally being appointed for political reasons'. Additionally, it also reported that, according to the Chinese media, 'more than two thirds of judges do not even have a college degree, only a vocational training degree and not necessarily in law'.[82] This appears to have been based upon a *China Daily* report in 2002 which cited official statistics indicating that only one-quarter of China's judges had college degrees.

Randall Peerenboom (2002) describes various reforms that have been instituted with a view to raising the standards of the judiciary. These include: making promotion more merit-based; choosing judges by competitive selection; ending the practice of promoting administrative personnel; dismissing or transferring unsuitable or unqualified judges; and improving judicial training. In 2003, a Supreme People's Court official was quoted as saying that those existing judges who failed to meet the academic qualifications requirements as stated in the Judges Law 2001 would be removed from office if they could not take steps to satisfy the requirements within five years.[83] It has been reported that there has been an intensifying move away from reliance on 'army veterans'[84] with the percentage of judges with college degrees increasing considerably year on year so that Zhu (2007) has reported that by 2005, 51 per cent of judges had college degrees.[85]

We interviewed 88 judges in 13 localities in China as part of this project, and we set out below the self-reported composition of this sample by gender, age, academic qualification, prior work experience and years of experience as a judge. Our findings can be summarized as follows:[86]

- 60 per cent were male and 40 per cent were female.
- 60 per cent were below the age of 40 (with 8 per cent below the age of 30).
- 77 per cent described themselves as 'graduates',[87] with 27 per cent reporting that

---

of corruption. There were reports that the former SPC President, Xiao Yang, was also being investigated in the context of Huang's case. It is likely that this is in part an indication that corruption is being addressed and in part an indication that there is political/factional strife within the Party.

[81] To similar effect, Clark (2008).

[82] 'China Vows to Overhaul Courts', *BBC News*, 8 July 2002. See also, 'Half of Top Judges Lack Legal Training', *South China Morning Post*, 21 July 2009. See also, http://www.rfa.org/mandarin/yattaibaodao/sifa-0721200911165.8.html.

[83] 'China tightening qualifications needed to work in judiciary', *BBC Monitoring Asia Pacific*, 27 June 2003.

[84] See Upham (2005) pointing out that Zhu Suli has always opposed the liberal scholar He Weifang on this issue arguing that former soldiers were well-suited to be judges.

[85] See also, Congressional-Executive Commission on China 2005 Annual Report (2005).

[86] Percentages have been calculated excluding 'Not Knowns'.

[87] It has to be accepted that, at least in some cases, the quality and depth of education upon which the degree was based is not high, as confided to us by some respondents.

they had a postgraduate degree or were studying for such. It can be seen therefore that the proportion of judges in our sample who reported that they were graduates was much higher than has been reported by the sources cited above. In addition to graduates, ten interviewees had gained an undergraduate academic qualification by self-study, correspondence or from Party schools.[88] Eight of the remaining interviewees reported having received college education or specialized education. However, caution needs to be exercised as it is possible to acquire a 'degree' from a variety of sources.[89]

- 54 per cent of the judges in our sample had previously worked as court clerks, and 13 per cent had worked as court personnel in some capacity other than clerk (e.g., bailiff). A further 13 per cent disclosed that they did not have any working experience before becoming judges having been appointed as judges immediately after finishing their studies. Of the remainder, three had worked in the law in some capacity (prison officers, police officers, personnel in the justice bureau), but the others had no prior experience of having worked in a law-related field.
- 53 per cent of judges had 10 to 21 years' working experience; 44 per cent had less than 10 years' experience as judges, with one judge having only one year's working experience and five judges having only two years' working experience.

While our data appear on first sight to be broadly consistent with the movement in China away from appointments based solely upon party affiliation or retired military personnel and more towards graduates from universities, law school and colleges, as we have noted, caution must be exercised in drawing inferences from the proportion of judges possessing 'degrees'. Diplomas are often obtained from non-accredited institutions, at a vocational school (*dazhuan*)[90] or by part-time study which may be undemanding. Though our samples were not large enough to measure this with confidence, it is known that there are great disparities in terms of qualifications between rural and urban courts,[91] that the best judges from rural courts may be poached by courts in more affluent areas and that many rural authorities advocate reducing the required criteria in rural areas.[92] A number of judges[93] voluntarily disclosed that their qualifications had been obtained by correspondence course or at a Party School[94] and some described their educational background

---

[88] Some of our respondents told us that 'self-study' qualifications were undemanding and that the main requirement of Party schools was to attend.

[89] As Donald Clarke points out, '[A]n "LL.B." degree could come from a correspondence school, an institution with just provincial, not national, accreditation, or a university that established its law department solely to meet market demand and staffed it entirely with recycled faculty from the moribund Department of Marxist-Leninist Philosophy': Clarke (2003).

[90] See Peerenboom (2002) who reports that by 1995, 80 per cent of judges in China had at least *dazhuan* qualifications which require a minimum of two years of legal training at college level (at p. 290).

[91] With regard to rural courts, see Balme (2009b) and (2010). Stephanie Balme found that in Shaanxi Province there is evidence of an evolution towards professionalization with a substantial increase in the number of junior college graduates on court staff.

[92] See further, Congressional-Executive Commission on China 2005 Annual Report (2005).

[93] E.g., F-IJ-N-01; F-IJ-N-03; F-IJ-N-05; F-IJ-N-05; K-IJ-W-45; and L-IJ-X-10.

[94] E.g., L-IJ-X-02; and L-IJ-X-06.

as 'undergraduate at college'. In this context, it is also noteworthy that almost all respondents in our sample where the background was known had risen through the ranks, as it were, having previously worked in the courts, usually as a clerk, occasionally as a secretary or bailiff.[95] Table 8.1 covering five sites (including both rural and city areas) is illustrative.

Some judges themselves volunteered during interview that they were unhappy, in different ways, with various aspects relating to the quality and experience of the judiciary (a person can be a judge at the age of 23 years old), as the following examples illustrate:

J-IJ-S4-06: I think the Judges Law sets out only the basic qualifications required, but this is still far from the judges' qualification standard in practice. As judges, we should have not only a degree, but also professional ethics and professional skills. At present our standards for judges are too low. It takes too short a time for a law student to become a judge. I think we should reform the system of selecting judges. In the Common Law countries, the principles for judicial selection are: being old, experienced and outstanding. By adopting these principles, the high quality of judges is ensured. In order to realize the professionalism and elite-quality of judges, we should emphasize comprehensiveness in knowledge, experience and skills. . . . I hope there is a chance for training, I think we should update our professional knowledge and our outdated mentalities, improve our professional skills and professional ethics. We can study new laws and regulations, or invite experts and professors to give lectures, so as to improve our theoretical knowledge and understand the modern views of the legal profession. Further study and overseas training should also be encouraged.

K-IJ-W-03: There is no unitary standard for training judges.

M-IJ-Y-04: The expectation from society in regard to judges is very high, so it is very important to improve the quality. Further education and training is very necessary.

F-IJ-N-03: The standard required of judges is different in different ages. The educational requirement for judges was High School in the 1980s. With the development of society and development of the legal system, now we demand that judges have a bachelor's degree. And the academic qualification requirements will definitely be higher in the future. Certain educational qualifications and solid legal knowledge are the foundations for carrying out work. But it is far from enough. Sufficient experience is also required, which should be improved through practice. And surely there should be higher professional moral standards. To sum up, judges should have higher comprehensive qualifications.

M-IJ-Y-01: I think judges are specialist personnel. It is not proper to use those in administrative posts.

K-IJ-W-01: I think older judges are better because they have accumulated much experience.

E-IJ-L-07: I don't think there is a need to set up certain standards for judges. Judges are elites of the whole society, so they have the wisdom and talent which is obtained not only from theoretical study but also from the accumulation of experience in practice. There should not be too much emphasis on political performance, because judges are neutral and the persons to execute the law on behalf of the state. I think that the educational requirement for the judges to be an undergraduate at present is acceptable, but we also should consider China's national situation.

---

[95] See also, 'Half of Top Judges Lack Legal Training', *South China Morning Post*, 21 July 2009. This article reports on a survey by *Xinhua* which found that nearly half of the chief judges at provincial level did not have solid judicial backgrounds or had ever worked in the courts prior to their appointment, 14 out of 30 having worked as administrative officials before assuming their current posts.

Table 8.1 *Background characteristics of judicial respondents*

Site	Gender	Age	Education	Prior work experience	Years as judge
L-IJ-X-01	Male	38	LLB	Teacher in court	7
L-IJ-X-02	Female	40	Undergraduate Party School	Court clerk (5 years)	14
L-IJ-X-03	Male	39	Undergraduate	Court clerk (4–5 years)	10
L-IJ-X-04	Female	49	Rural cadre; factory leader	Court archive (3 years)	13
L-IJ-X-05	Male	36	LLB	Court secretary (4 years)	4
L-IJ-X-06	Male	50	Undergraduate Party School	Soldier (12–13 years); Court clerk (7–8 years)	12
L-IJ-X-07	Female	49	3-year college	Typist (10 years); Office secretary (3 years)	20
L-IJ-X-08	Female	36	Undergraduate self-study	Court clerk (8 years)	3
L-IJ-X-09	Male	32	LLM	Court clerk (8 years)	2
L-IJ-X-10	Male	47	Undergraduate by correspondence	Court clerk (3 years)	17
L-IJ-X-11	Male	38	LLM	Court clerk (7 years)	9
K-IJ-W-01	Male	33	none	Court clerk (11 years)	7
K-IJ-W-02	Male	39	Undergraduate	Court clerk (20 years)	16
K-IJ-W-03	Male	43	3 years at college	Worker (4 years); Court clerk (2 years)	18
K-IJ-W-04	Male	45	Undergraduate by correspondence	Worked in court; Court clerk (2 years)	20
F-IJ-N-01	Male	44	LLB by correspondence	Worker; clerk	19
F-IJ-N-02	Male	37	LLB	Court clerk (2 years)	12
F-IJ-N-03	Male	41	LLB by correspondence	Court clerk	18
F-IJ-N-04	Female	50	LLB by correspondence	Clerk unit; Court clerk (8 years)	17
F-IJ-N-05	Female	42	Undergraduate by correspondence	Court clerk	18
F-IJ-N-06	Male	34	LLB	Court clerk (2 years)	10
F-IJ-N-07	Male	43	LLB	Court clerk (2 years)	15
I-IJ-S3-01	Male	41	Undergraduate	Court clerk	17
I-IJ-S3-02	Female	39	Undergraduate	Court clerk (2 years)	14
A-IJ-B1-01	Female	32	Undergraduate degree	Court clerk (7 years)	2
A-IJ-B1-02	Male	28	LLB	Court clerk (2 years)	3–4
A-IJ-B1-03	Male	34	Undergraduate	Court clerk (4 years)	7
A-IJ-B1-04	Female	31	Postgraduate student	Court clerk (7 years)	2
A-IJ-B1-05	Female	35	Undergraduate degree	Court clerk (5 years)	7
A-IJ-B1-06	Female	30	Masters degree	Court clerk (3 years)	2
A-IJ-B1-07	Female	37	Postgraduate student	Court clerk (3 years)	9
A-IJ-B1-08	Female	38	Undergraduate degree	Court clerk (6 years)	12
A-IJ-B1-09	Male	33	Postgraduate student	Court clerk (5 years)	5
A-IJ-B1-10	Male	48	Undergraduate degree	Farmer (2 years); worker (10 years); Court clerk (5 years)	12

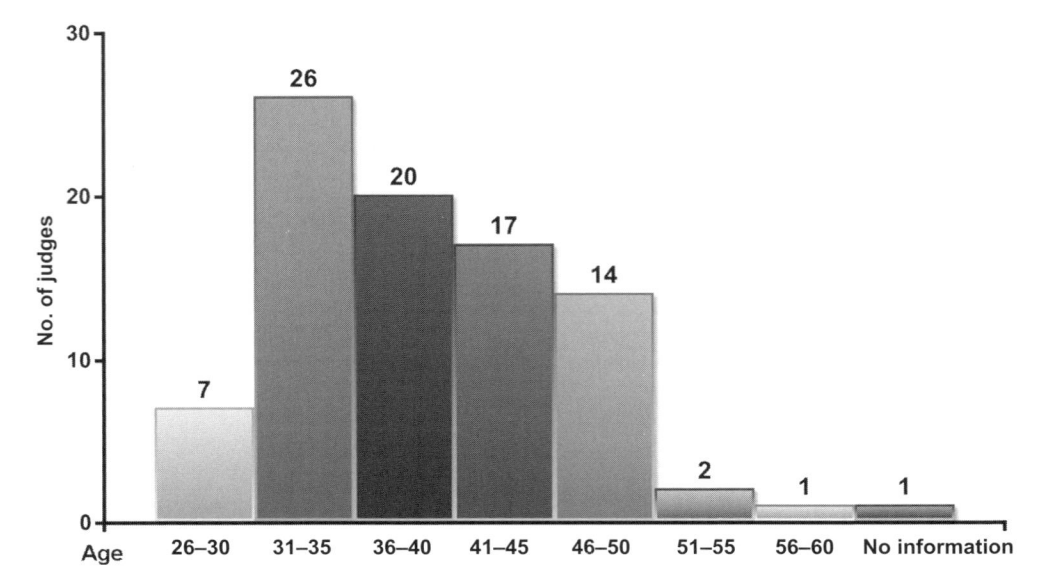

Figure 8.2   Age: profile of 88 judges being interviewed

However, the undergraduate education of those who became judges through special relationships is too low, and they are not suitable to work in court and are unworthy of the judicial title. For example, the presidents of the court should be elected from those who possess the judges' qualification. It is impractical to discuss this issue now.

J-IJ-S4-01: Being a judge, in my opinion, we need abundant social information, life experience in addition to accumulating professional knowledge. So the best age to be a judge should be 35 years old.

E-IJ-L-03: According to the Judges' Law and the reform outline of the People's Court in China, there is no cause for more criticism to have higher requirements on the judge's education. From my experience, however, I think it is better to have a higher educational level. In summary, a good judge should have certain academic knowledge, good appearance, tactful mind, good eloquence and writing skills.

F-IJ-N-07: Strictly speaking, we are outdated. According to current judicial requirements, judges shall receive at least a postgraduate degree. Undergraduate students who have passed the State Justice Examination for 2–3 years may assume the position as assistant judges. They will be familiar with handling cases after several years' practical work.

The majority of judges were male (60 per cent) with overall a fairly wide age distribution, as set out in Figure 8.2. Further details of the 88 judges are set out in Figures 8.3–8.5.

In the criminal trial, apart from the fact that the judge responsible for the case handles it completely and participates in the trial process from beginning to end, other collegial members are 'Cameo or guest actors'. This leads to the appearance of a collegial panel of judges while a sole judge hears the case in practice. The mechanism of the collegial panel making the decision is thus a formality. It is obvious that the case-handling judge under this system has replaced the independent trial by all panel members. The collegial mechanism has been simplified and formalized such that no other collegial member except

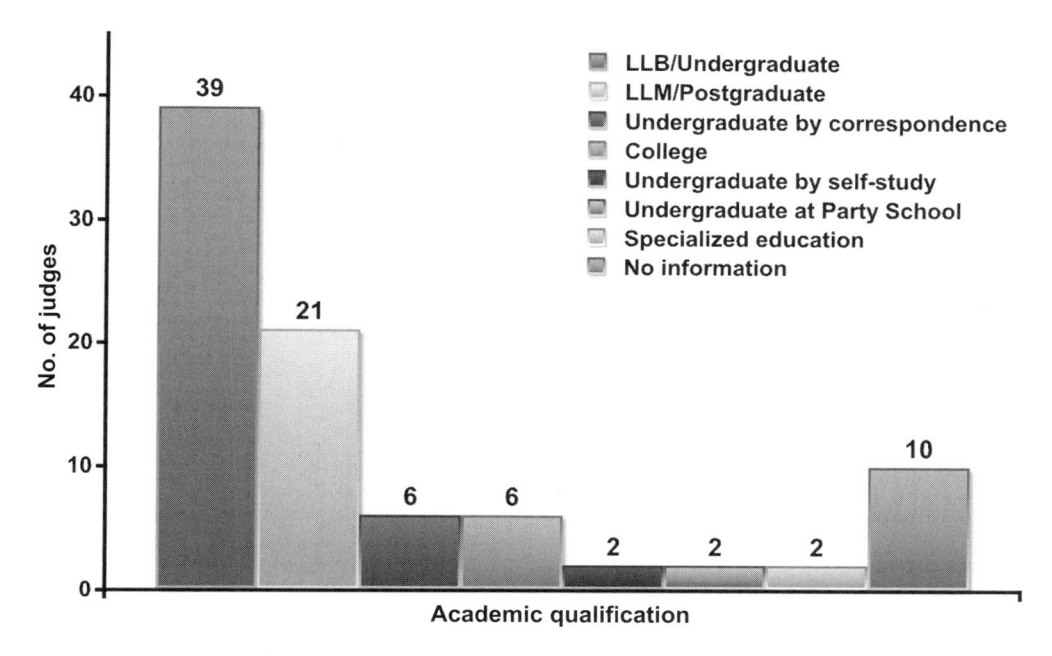

Trial procedure, rules, setting and personnel 225

Figure 8.3 Academic qualification: profile of 88 judges being interviewed

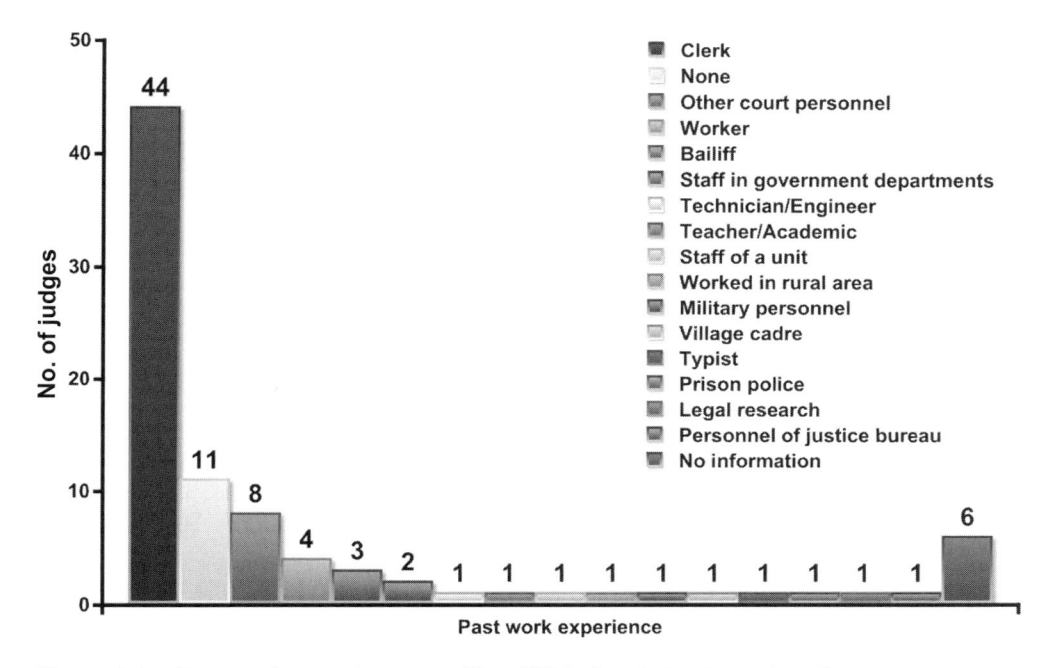

Figure 8.4 Past work experience: profile of 88 judges being interviewed

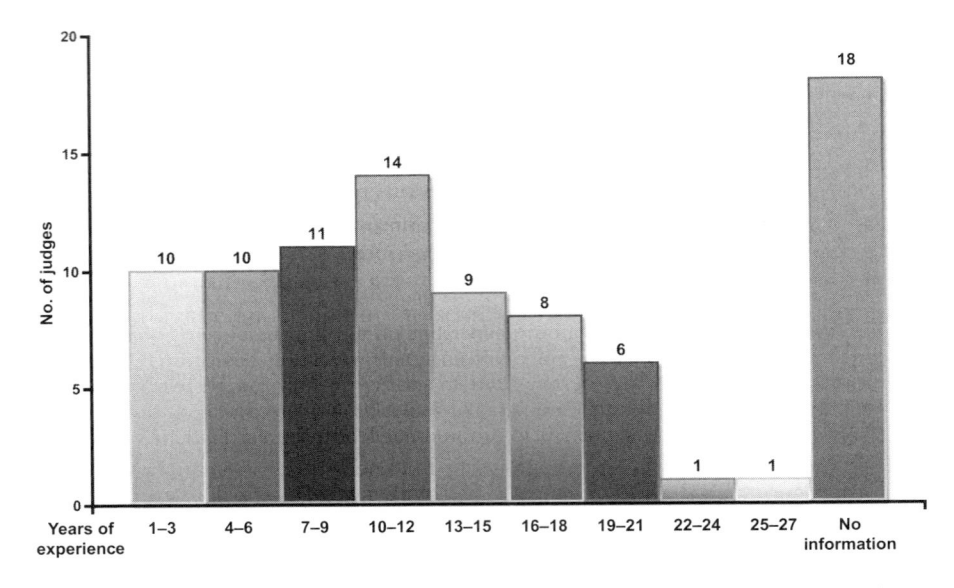

Figure 8.5   Years of experience as a judge: profile of 88 judges being interviewed

the case-handling judge will invest energy in the case nor contribute their independent understanding and judgment to the case (Qin Ce, 2006, p. 40).

Finally, it is essential to note that, while the judges we interviewed were all drawn from those who served on a collegial panel which hears the case in court, the collegial panel may refer cases which are major or complex to the political-legal committee (*zhengfawei*), a committee that operates in the shadow of the court, does not have any statutory basis but which is a key decision-making body in China's criminal justice process. The exact composition of this committee may vary in different regions but it essentially consists of the Party Secretary, the heads of the procuratorate, court, police and even local party officials. Although trials are heard before a collegial panel, they operate through a system in which one judge is responsible for the case and that judge may 'adjourn' the trial and either refer the case to the political-legal committee or seek its advice.

PEOPLE'S ASSESSORS

In China, the people's assessors system (*renmin peishenyuan*) has a long history which reflects a commitment to public participation in the judicial system. According to most scholars, if functioning well, the people's assessors system helps to resist administrative interference and the negative effect of interpersonal relationships on the trial, strengthen the independent role of judges in the trial and promotes a culture of judicial independence in China (Pang, 2009). People's assessors are elected by the people for three-year terms.[96] They have equal status with judges in evaluating cases and participating in trials

---

[96]   In practice, people's assessors may serve for many years: He Jiahong (1999).

(Baker, 1982). Like judges and procurators, assessors may be removed at any time by the people's congresses of the corresponding level if they are 'incompetent' or 'negligent' in their duties.

At present, the use of people's assessors in trying criminal cases varies from one place to another (Shen Jungui, 1999). According to Chen Weidong (2001), in Shenzhen only about 5 per cent of cases of first instance employed people's assessors in the last few years, while in Beijing, the percentage in one district court was as high as 70 per cent. There is no restriction on the educational qualification of people's assessors, and most lack legal knowledge and experience in adjudication. In practice, most people's assessors just sit in the panel chair without playing any role in the judgment: they seldom ask questions or read case files carefully after or before the trial and few express their views in the deliberation of the judgment.[97] In order to better ensure their participation in the trial, the National People's Congress made a decision to improve the current people's assessors' system in August 2004, which came into effect on 1 May 2005. Between May 2005 and June 2007, people's assessors are recorded as having participated in the trial of 644 723 cases, occupying 20.1 per cent of cases in ordinary procedure (Xu Yuezhi, 2007). The effect of the attempts to improve the system remains unclear. One judge we interviewed felt that the system was a failure:

> *A-IJ-B1-02:* There are problems with the system of people's assessors. What kind of people should be chosen to be people's assessors, their length of service should be guaranteed, their personal qualities should be improved and they should have a certain degree of understanding of the law. At this moment many people's assessors fail to insist on their opinions; they will simply follow and totally support the judge's words. This renders the system a formality.

Our research confirms this impression with assessors playing only a symbolic role in trials.

PROSECUTORS

We interviewed 96 prosecutors, randomly selected from 12 localities in China, to gain an insight into the profile of those who work for the procuratorate and prosecute cases in China's criminal courts.

In our sample, the majority were male (66 per cent) and relatively young. As Figure 8.6 shows, almost a quarter were aged 30 or less, and 60 per cent were between the ages of 31 and 40.

Excluding the 11 prosecutors who did not disclose their academic qualifications, the vast majority of prosecutors (70 out of 85) reported that they were graduates or postgraduates. This is broadly in line with the trend of professionalization, beginning in the 1990s, and noted elsewhere in the literature (Zhu Jingwen, 2007). While some of these expressly indicated that they were law graduates and others expressly indicated they had graduated in a discipline other than law, many failed to identify their subject of study. The remaining 15 respondents who provided information on their academic qualifications had obtained some form of undergraduate qualification, either by self-study, by

---

[97] Zuo, Tang and Wu Weijun (2001); and Liu Xiaoqing (2009).

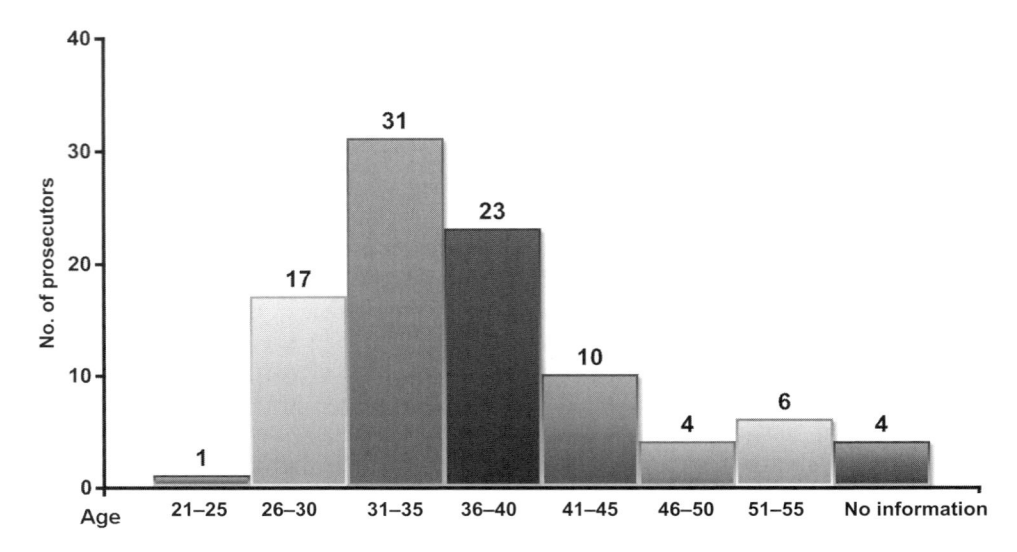

Figure 8.6 Age: profile of 96 prosecutors being interviewed

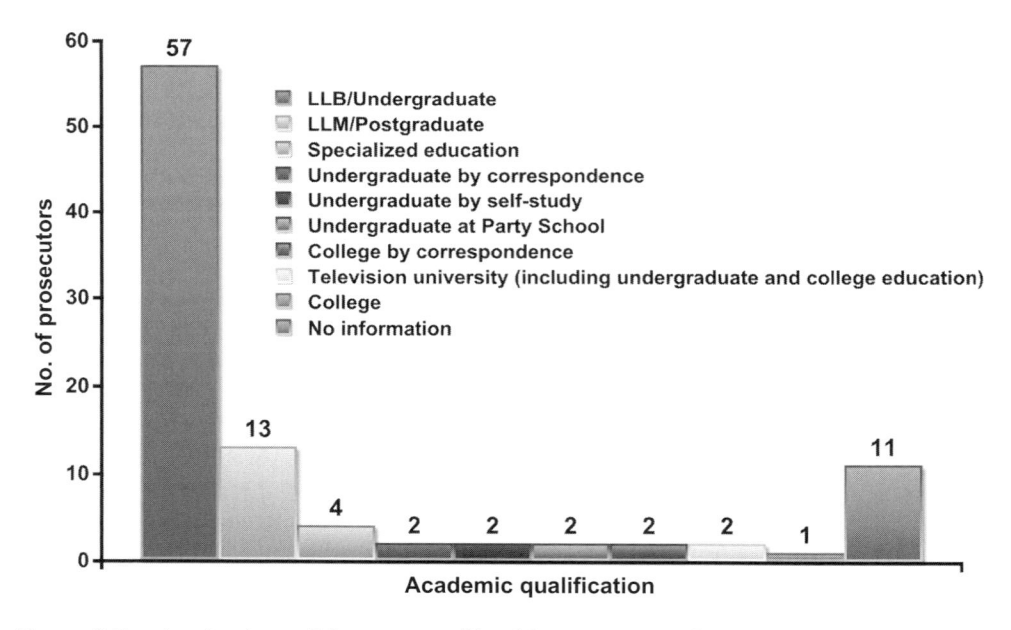

Figure 8.7 Academic qualification: profile of 96 prosecutors being interviewed

correspondence, or from Party Schools or television universities. More detail is provided in Figure 8.7.

Some 91 out of 96 prosecutors we interviewed told us their working experience prior to becoming prosecutors. Among these 91 interviewees, 38 per cent (35) said they had worked as clerks (some within the procuratorate). Seven interviewees were former

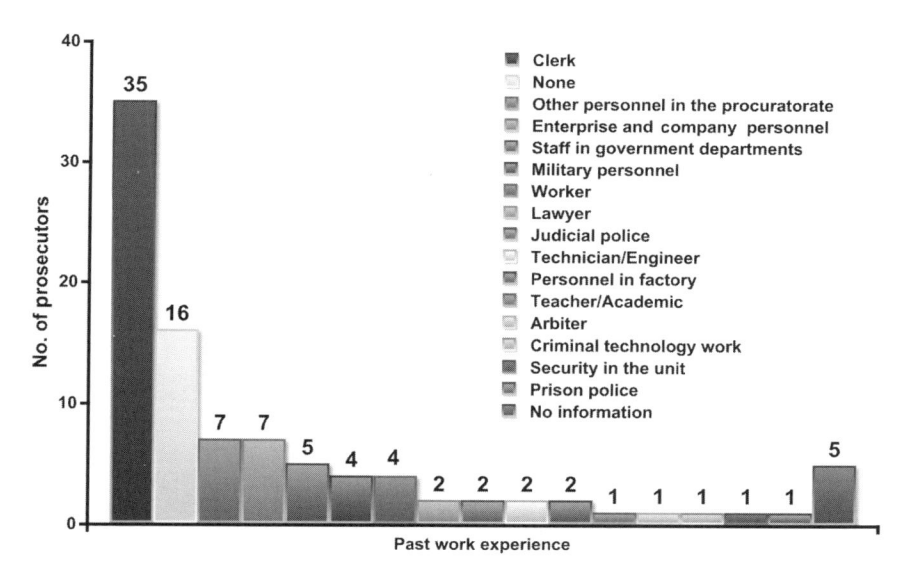

Figure 8.8 Past work experience: profile of 96 prosecutors being interviewed

personnel of the procuratorates working in departments other than the prosecution division (i.e., they had become prosecutors through internal transfer). We also found that other government departments are a source of prosecutors, with four of our interviewees disclosing that they were former personnel of other criminal justice organs, such as the judicial or prison police, and five stating that they had worked as cadres/staff of non-criminal justice-related government departments. Seven prosecutors had joined the procuratorate from a business background, while only two were former lawyers. A significant percentage (17.5 per cent) had no prior work experience, indicating that they had become prosecutors immediately upon completing their studies. Further details on work background are provided in Figure 8.8.

Among the 96 prosecutors we interviewed, 17 did not tell us how long they had been working as prosecutors. For the remaining 79 interviewees, their experience as prosecutors ranged from below one year to 26 years. A detailed breakdown by duration is shown in Figure 8.9. Almost 60 per cent of the interviewees had less than ten years' experience as prosecutors, with 16 per cent having three years or less than three years' experience. Of the 40 per cent (32) who had more than 10 years' experience, three had been working as prosecutors for over 20 years.

DEFENCE LAWYERS

The number of lawyers and law firms in China has increased dramatically in recent years so that, by 2007, it was estimated that there were 120 000 lawyers in China (Clark, 2008),[98]

---

[98] See also: Peerenboom (2002); and Yongshun and Songcai (2005).

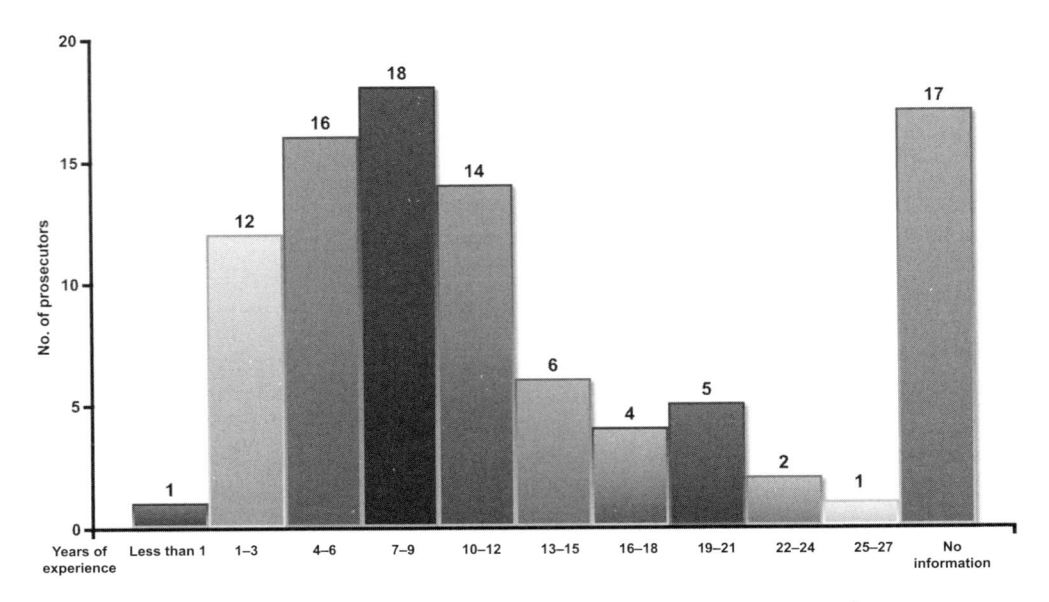

Figure 8.9 Years of experience as a prosecutor: profile of 96 prosecutors being interviewed

although many were likely to be part-time. Many avoid criminal defence work, however, not only because of the low levels of remuneration but primarily because of the risks involved to the lawyer. There have been notorious cases in which defence lawyers engaged in human rights work have been arrested and detained[99] and, as we have seen, statutory provisions provide many hazards for any lawyer who seeks to engage in active defence work. We were not able to undertake a major survey of defence lawyers in regard to their experiences but we did talk to a sample of lawyers in each research site about their day to day work in the criminal courts.[100] It should be noted, accordingly, that the lawyers in our sample were engaged in everyday cases and could not be said in any way to be *weiquan* or rights defenders.[101]

We interviewed 83 lawyers working as defence lawyers in 12 localities. We re-emphazise the limitations of self-report studies in this respect. We had, for example, no means of verifying the claims lawyers made as to their qualifications or work experience but what we were told appeared to comport with what was plausible in the circumstances. Most

---

[99] In July 2009, for example, the well-known human rights lawyer Xu Zhiyong was arrested and detained in what was seen by many as a crackdown on lawyers attempting to become independent of the state. In fact, the All China Lawyers Association and local bar associations are controlled by the state and answer to the Ministry of Justice. See the discussions in the Brookings Institution: http://www.brookings.edu./articles/2009/autumn_china_legal system_li.aspx; and Elizabeth Lynch (2010a).

[100] See also, Human Rights Watch (2008).

[101] We advert to these lawyers at appropriate points in the text. For a general appraisal, see Fu and Cullen (2007) available at http://papers.ssrn.com/so13/papers.cfm?abstract_id=1083925.

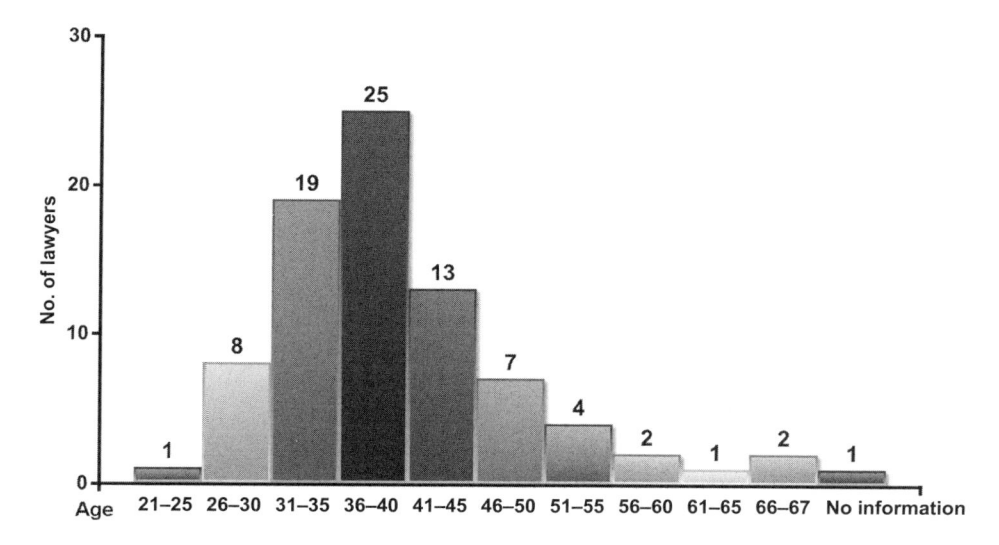

Figure 8.10 Age: profile of 83 lawyers being interviewed

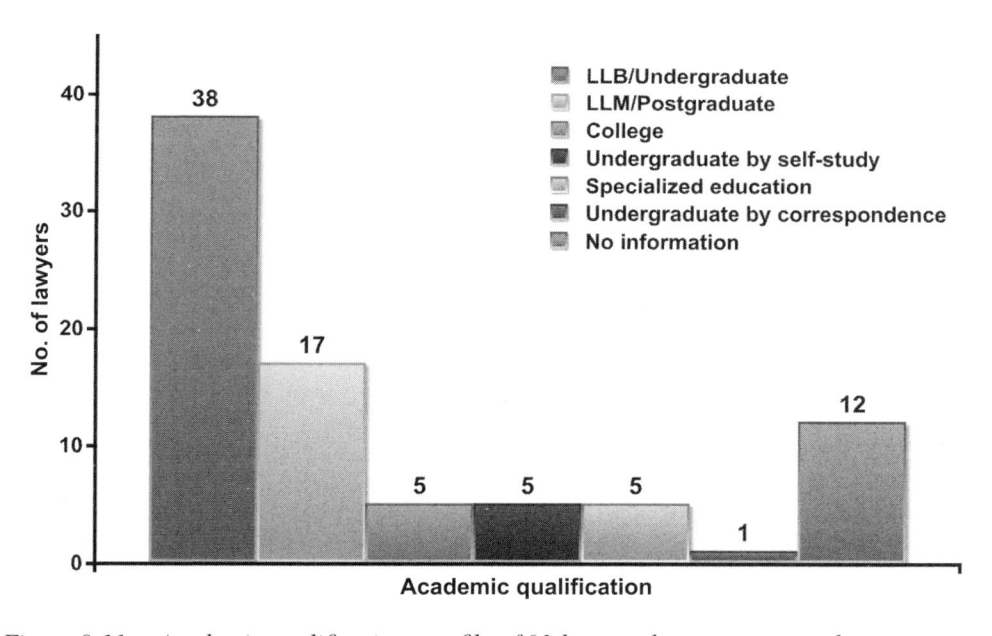

Figure 8.11 Academic qualification: profile of 83 lawyers being interviewed

respondents (80 per cent) were male, and the vast majority (almost 70 per cent) were aged between 30 and 45 (see Figure 8.10).

After excluding 12 interviewees who did not provide us with information as to their academic qualifications, 55 (almost 80 per cent) of the remaining 71 interviewees stated that they were graduates or postgraduates, with some stating that they held a law degree

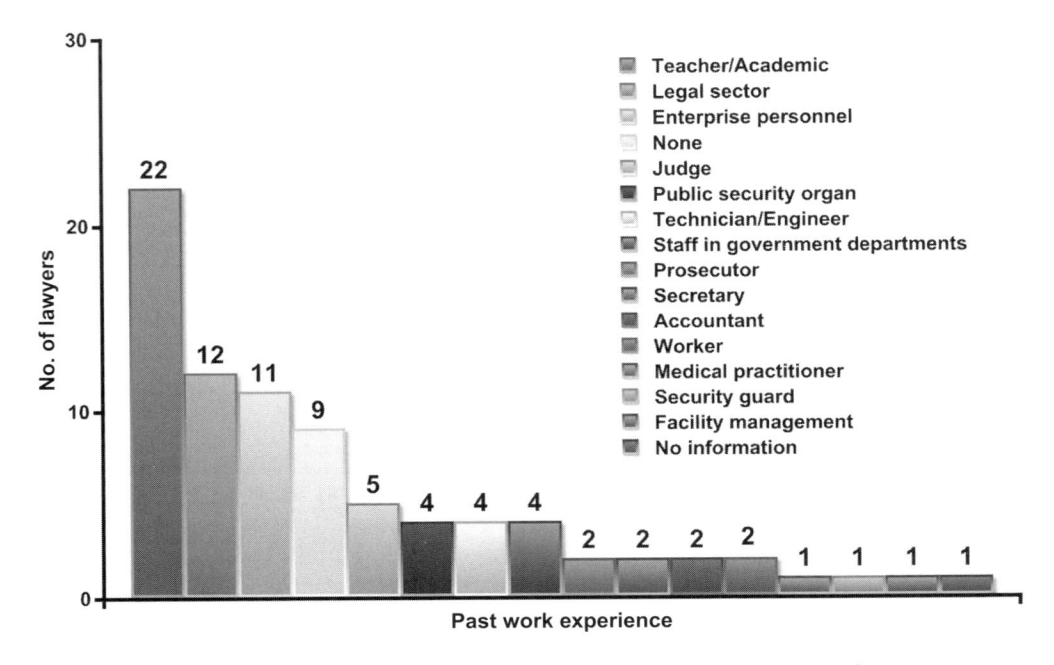

Figure 8.12 Past work experience: profile of 83 lawyers being interviewed

or law postgraduate degree. The remainder had obtained undergraduate qualifications through either self-study or by correspondence, or from a college or specialized education provider (see Figure 8.11). The value of these stated qualifications is not ascertainable by this research.

Of the 83 lawyers we interviewed, only one did not provide us with information as to his or her working experience prior to becoming a lawyer. As shown in Figure 8.12, 28 per cent of the interviewees (23) reported that they had worked in law/criminal justice-related sectors prior to becoming lawyers. Among these, 12 had formerly worked as legal consultants, lawyers' assistants, or as staff in legal aid centres, justice bureaux and judicial organs; five were former judges; four had worked in public security organs; and two were former prosecutors.

The academic sector was the next highest sector of prior experience of our interviewees: 22 (27 per cent) out of 82 interviewees reported that they had been teachers/academics before they commenced practice as lawyers. In a number of these cases, the respondent was a part-time lawyer concurrently holding a teaching post. Eleven (13 per cent) out of 82 interviewees were reported as working in business sectors before becoming lawyers. Our data showed that nine interviewees (11 per cent of our sample) did not have any work experience before they began to practise as lawyers.

Ten out of the 83 lawyers we interviewed did not provide us with information as to how long they had been working as lawyers. For the remaining 73 interviewees, 39 (53 per cent) of them disclosed that they had less than ten years' working experience; and among these 39 persons, the largest number of them (15 out of 39) had been working as lawyers for four to six years. At the same time, however, 14 interviewees were reported as having

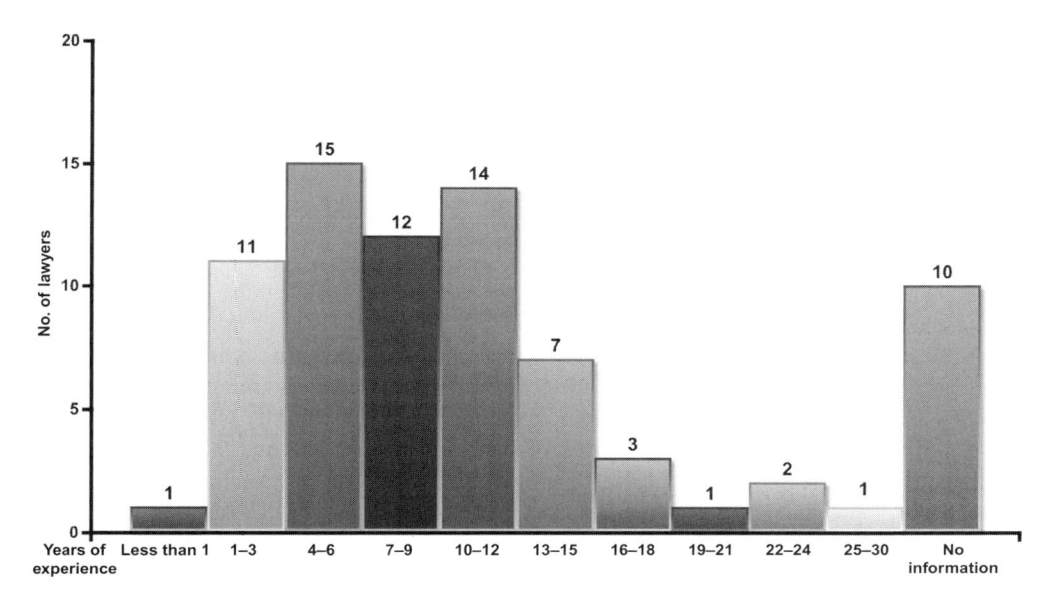

Figure 8.13   Years of experience as a lawyer: profile of 83 lawyers being interviewed

10 to 12 years' working experience, with one respondent having over 25 years' experience as a lawyer. More detailed information is set out in Figure 8.13.

CONCLUSION

Trials in China are governed by formulaic rules and procedures, and variations from the standard procedure have been introduced only on a piecemeal basis. The introduction of summary trials and simplified ordinary procedure appear to be driven by concerns over efficiency and cost-effective disposition which are commonly ascribed to the adoption of plea bargaining in common law jurisdictions although there is no concept yet in China of a plea of guilty tendered for a reduced charge. What holds the trial system together is the power of the institutions of the judiciary and the procuratorate rather than the professionalism of the courtroom actors. Lack of academic training or other professional skills does not inhibit judges and prosecutors from trying cases on a day to day basis and the trial itself faces little challenge either from within, the 'protest' system being virtually defunct, or from a generally disempowered defence bar.

9. The trial: case file analysis

INTRODUCTION

In this chapter we set out the findings generated by our case file analysis. Our researchers were provided with a 'case file analysis schedule' (see Appendix 3), and their task was to search the files in order to find answers to some 76 questions touching upon every aspect of the first instance trials. We emphasize once again that the answers we found are based on files kept by the court, and our researchers were wholly reliant on what the prosecutors/judges chose to record in these files. We found that the case files, or 'dossiers', were broadly similar across different research sites which appears to be the product of development through practice and not wholly driven by regulations (Zuo Weimin, 2008).

We were overambitious in terms of what we could discover from the files alone, and it is right to record that some of our questions failed to generate consistent and meaningful data. This was partly because the files of the procuratorate were obviously not designed for research purposes and partly because our researchers sometimes failed to understand the import of some of the questions on the schedule. Despite these shortcomings, analysis of the case files gives an important insight into what happens at the trial stage of the criminal justice process in China. What the files reveal is for the most part consistent with what our researchers observed (the subject of the next chapter), and, as we demonstrate below, what we were told by judges, prosecutors and defenders in our interviews with them.

COURT, PROCEDURE AND REPRESENTATION

As Table 9.1 shows (and as we have stated before) our case files were drawn from a Basic Court sample of cases and from an Intermediate Court sample of cases.[1]

Almost one-third of the cases in the Basic Court sample were disposed of using summary procedure, whereas this procedure was used in less than 1 per cent of Intermediate Court cases[2] (see Table 9.2).

Our finding that summary procedure is used in around one-third of cases (confined almost exclusively to the Basic Courts) is at variance with the estimate given to us by judges in our interviews with them. Although we did not question them about this specifically, three judges in one big city[3] said that approximately 50 per cent of the cases

---

[1] In this chapter we concentrate only on those cases which progressed to the trial stage. Accordingly, in the tables set out in this chapter, the column 'Not known/Not applicable' is a composite of those cases where the original case file did not reveal the answer (or our researcher failed to record the answer reliably or at all) and those cases which did not proceed to the trial stage.

[2] In addition, one case (a Basic Court case) was tried using Simplified Ordinary Procedure.

[3] G-IJ-S1-001; G-IJ-S1-002; and G-IJ-S1-004.

Table 9.1 Level of the Trial Court

	BC 7 Sites		IC 6 Sites		All Sites	
Basic Court	726	100.0	0	0.0	726	63.7
Intermediate Court	0	0.0	414[1]	100.0	414	36.3
Not known/not applicable		–	4	–	4	–
Total	726	100.0	418	100.0	1144	100.0

Note: 1. There were additionally seven cases that originally began in the Basic Court but were then transferred to the Intermediate Court for disposition.

they adjudicated each year were adjudicated according to summary procedure. One (G-IJ-S1-001) volunteered that in addition 20 per cent of his cases were adjudicated according to Simplified Ordinary Procedure. In our sample of case files only one case was adjudicated using Simplified Ordinary Procedure.

There are numerous existing surveys of the use of summary procedure, mostly conducted by procuratorates at provincial level. These suggest that while the use of this procedure varies greatly from province to province (and indeed as between different courts within a province), the overall picture is one of a low take up rate. For example, according to a commentary in *Legal Daily*, while some courts reported that they had applied summary procedure in 25 per cent of cases, others reported that summary procedure had been applied in almost 60 per cent of the criminal cases they handled (Prescott, 2003). Chen Weidong (2001) looked at the application of summary procedure by the people's courts in Zhabei, Yangpu and Pudong in Shanghai in the first half of 1998, and found the use of summary procedure to be 23 per cent, 23.7 per cent, and 40 per cent of the total number of criminal cases concluded respectively. As in these studies, the extent to which summary procedure was used in our sample of cases also varied from site to site (as low as 8 per cent in Site A and as high as 75.7 per cent in Site D).

The overall average usage of summary procedure disclosed by our case files (31 per cent) was higher than the overall national average deduced by Chen from a variety of statistical sources, who put this at 20 per cent in the Basic Courts. The two main reasons cited in the existing literature for the overall low take up rate are that courts are unclear as to when it is available, and are reluctant to use it because they are aware that more stringent deadlines apply for disposing of cases using the summary procedure.[4]

We found that whereas almost three-quarters of intermediate cases were tried before a panel of three judges, the corresponding percentage for Basic Court cases was only 15 per cent. Whereas almost 30 per cent of Basic Court cases were tried before a single judge, none of the Intermediate Court cases in our sample were tried before a one-person panel. However, there was no significant difference in the extent to which people's assessors were used in Basic and Intermediate Court cases (they featured in 29.4 per cent of Basic Court cases and in 26.8 per cent of Intermediate Court cases). With people's assessors involved in over a quarter of the cases, our research does not bear out the assertion found

---

[4] Dong Xinjian (2000); Jin Yonggang (1999); and Fu Weigao (1997).

Table 9.2 Type of procedure

	BC 7 Sites		IC 6 Sites		All Sites	
Summary procedure	212	31.3	2	0.5	214	19.7
Ordinary procedure	465	68.6	409	99.5	874	80.3
Not known/not applicable	49	–	7	–	56	–
Total	726	100.0	418	100.0	1144	100.0

Table 9.3 Composition of the collegial panel

	BC 7 Sites		IC 6 Sites		All Sites	
Cases tried with single judge	192	29.5	0	0.0	192	15.2
Cases tried with 1 judge and 2 people's assessors	15	2.3	56	13.5	71	6.7
Cases tried with 2 judges and 1 people's assessor	176	27.1	55	13.3	231	21.7
Cases tried with 2 judges	167	25.7	4	1.0	171	16.1
Cases tried with 3 judges	100	15.4	299	72.2	399	37.5
Not known/not applicable	76	–	4	–	80	–

Table 9.4 Open or closed trial

	BC 7 Sites		IC 6 Sites		All 13 Sites	
Open trial	537	81.5	359	87.6	896	83.8
Closed trial	122	18.5	51	12.4	173	16.2
Not known/not applicable	67	–	8	–	75	–
Total	726	100.0	418	100.0	1144	100.0

in the existing literature[5] that the system of people's assessors has been little used. More detailed data on the composition of the collegial panel are set out in Table 9.3.

The number of trials which were noted on the file as being closed was surprisingly high. Almost one-fifth (18.5 per cent) of the Basic Court and 12.4 per cent of the Intermediate Court trials were held *in camera* (see Table 9.4).

Overall, 54 per cent of defendants (578) had a representative, and in 553 of these cases the representative was recorded as being a qualified lawyer. In ten cases the status of the representative was unknown, in 14 cases he or she was described as a relative or friend, and in one case he or she was described as 'other'. In brief, excluding the ten cases in which we were unable to ascertain the status of the representative, 97.3 per cent of those who had a representative had one who was legally qualified. In a significant proportion of cases (one-fifth) the defendant had more than one representative (this rose to one-quarter in Intermediate Court cases and fell to 13.3 per cent in Basic Court cases). The role of the court in appointing lawyers was also significant. In 25.8 per cent of Intermediate Court

---

[5] Summarized in Chapter 8, *supra*.

Table 9.5 Defendant had a defender

	BC 7 Sites		IC 6 Sites		All Sites	
Yes	242	36.8	336	81.6	578	54.0
No	416	63.2	76	18.4	492	46.0
Not known/not applicable	68	–	6	–	74	–
Total	726	100.0	418	100.0	1144	100.0

Table 9.6 Number of defenders

	BC 7 Sites		IC 6 Sites		All Sites	
1 defender	117	86.7	144	74.6	261	79.6
2 defenders	18	13.3	49	25.4	67	20.4
Not known/not applicable	107	–	143	–	250	–
Total	242	100.0	336	100.0	578	100.0

Table 9.7 Type of defender

	BC 7 Sites		IC 6 Sites		All Sites	
Court appointed lawyer	47	20.0	86	25.8	133	23.4
Privately retained lawyer	173	73.6	247	74.2	420	73.9
D's relative or friend	14	6.0	0	0.0	14	2.5
Others	1	0.4	0	0.0	1	0.2
Not known/not applicable	7	–	3	–	10	–
Total	242	100.0	336	100.0	578	100.0

cases and 20 per cent of Basic Court cases the lawyer was appointed by the court. Further details are provided in Tables 9.5–9.7.

As can be seen from Table 9.5 there was a significant difference as between Basic and Intermediate cases in terms of the proportion of defendants who had no representation. Whereas less than one-fifth of those who appeared in the Intermediate Court were without representation, 63.2 per cent of the defendants who appeared before the Basic Courts did not have the benefit of any representation. Moreover, all 14 cases in which the representative was described as a friend or relative, as opposed to a qualified lawyer, were tried in the Basic Court.[6]

According to the case files, victims were for the most part absent from the trial process. Victims were noted as being present at the trial in only 8.7 per cent of cases (the percentage was slightly higher in Intermediate Court cases (10.2 per cent) than in Basic Court cases (8.1 per cent) (see Table 9.8).

The percentage of cases in which victims had legal representation was high in

---

[6] This is similar to the findings of Zuo Weimin et al. (2007) and Xiao Shiwei (2008).

Table 9.8 Victim was present at the trial

	BC 7 Sites		IC 6 Sites		All Sites	
Yes	45	8.1	27	10.2	72	8.7
No	514	91.9	239	89.8	753	91.3
Not known/not applicable	167	–	152	–	319	–
Total	726	100.0	418	100.0	1144	100.0

Table 9.9 Victim had a legal representative

	BC 7 Sites		IC 6 Sites		All Sites	
Yes	18	5.6	125	44.2	143	23.6
No	304	94.4	158	55.8	462	76.4
Not known/not applicable	404	–	135	–	539	–
Total	726	100.0	418	100.0	1144	100.0

Intermediate Court cases (44.2 per cent), but very low in Basic Court cases (5.6 per cent). This is probably explained by the greater seriousness of the cases in the Intermediate Courts and accordingly the greater likelihood that the cases would involve a civil element in which the victim was seeking compensation. Although there is no reason to suppose that the cases in which the file revealed whether the victim was represented are in any way atypical, it is nonetheless wise to treat the overall percentages with some caution because the 'not known' component in respect of this question was very high (in approximately one-third of Intermediate Court cases and in more than half of the Basic Court cases we were unable to ascertain from the files whether or not the victim was represented). The detailed figures are set out in Table 9.9.

ROLE OF DEFENDANTS

As explained in the previous chapter, the procedure at trial as set out in the 1996 CPL allows the defendant to challenge the participation of any member of the panel, the clerk, the prosecutor, expert witnesses or the interpreter. We found that such challenges were very rare. As Table 9.10 shows, out of a total of 1059 cases in which the case proceeded to trial and in which information on this question was available, only three defendants raised a challenge.

The 1996 CPL does not have a provision under which defendants are required to plead guilty or not guilty. Following the reading of the indictment by the prosecutor, the defendant is given an opportunity to present a 'statement regarding the crime accused in the bill of prosecution'. Our researchers looked at the statements that defendants made in response to the Bill of Prosecution, and categorized such statements into one of three categories: agree, partially agree or disagree. We categorized those cases in which the defendant disputed intent as 'disagree', as in the following example:

Table 9.10 D raised challenges after the announcement made by the judge

	BC 7 Sites		IC 6 Sites		All Sites	
Yes	3	0.5	0	0.0	3	0.3
No	648	99.5	408	100.0	1056	99.7
Not known/not applicable	75	–	10	–	85	–
Total	726	100.0	418	100.0	1144	100.0

> I personally did not have an intention to deceive, otherwise I would not return goods which only amounted to 490 000 Yuan, but not 500 000; I hope this would be taken into account when determining sentence.

Cases in which the defendant was clearly admitting to some lesser crime (e.g., unintentional homicide when charged with intentional homicide) we categorized as 'partially agree', as in the following example:

> I think I did not intend to murder. I didn't have an intention to kill at that time. I killed the victim negligently; nothing else.

The absence of a requirement that the defendant enter an unequivocal plea of guilty or not guilty meant that there were some cases in which, despite having access to the prosecutor's file, it remained wholly unclear as to whether the defendant was accepting the charges against him, partially agreeing with the indictment, or disputing the charges in their entirety. These cases we categorized as 'not known'. The following is an example of this type of case:

> *Defendant:* I wish to make two points. The Bill of Prosecution stated that I was unemployed, but I object. I was said to have been 'discovered' in a Japanese restaurant, the meaning of 'discovered' is unclear.
>
> *Judge:* The court's understanding of 'discovered' was 'discovered the use of fake currency', do you understand?
>
> *Defendant:* Yes.
>
> *Judge:* What is your actual occupation?
>
> *Defendant:* Selling electronic products.

As Table 9.11 shows, our overall finding from the case file analysis was that almost 80 per cent of defendants in the Basic Courts and almost 64 per cent of defendants in the Intermediate Courts accepted the prosecution charges in their entirety at the outset of the trial. A further 11.7 per cent (Basic Court) and 21.3 per cent (Intermediate Court) partially agreed with the charges, leaving only a very small number (9.1 per cent (Basic Court) and 14.7 per cent (Intermediate Court)) who rejected the prosecution case entirely.

Overall, therefore, it can be seen that almost 90 per cent of defendants at the trial stage

Table 9.11 Defendant's attitude towards prosecution's indictment

	BC 7 Sites		IC 6 Sites		All Sites	
Agree	512	79.1	260	63.8	772	73.2
Partially agree	76	11.7	87	21.3	163	15.5
Disagree	59	9.1	60	14.7	119	11.3
Not known/not applicable	79	–	11	–	90	–
Total	726	100.0	418	100.0	1144	100.0

Table 9.12 Victim or his/her representative made a statement

	BC 7 Sites		IC 6 Sites		All Sites	
Yes	16	3.1	62	19.2	78	9.2
No	506	96.9	261	80.8	767	90.8
Not known	204	–	95	–	299	–
Total	726	100.0	418	100.0	1144	100.0

plead guilty to some or all offences, or admit guilt to some lesser crime. This very high 'guilty plea' rate should not come as a surprise in light of the fact that around 95 per cent of suspects in our trial file sample had already been recorded as having made a full or partial confession to the police.

ROLE OF THE VICTIM

After the prosecutor has read out the Bill of Prosecution, the victim is also given an opportunity to present a statement regarding the alleged offence. As the tables above demonstrate, with the exception of victim representatives in Intermediate Court cases, victims and their representatives were present at trials in only a small minority of cases. Accordingly, the overall percentage of cases in which victims or their representatives were recorded as having made a statement was fairly low. However, as Table 9.12 shows, statements were made by or on behalf of the victim in 16 Basic Court and 62 Intermediate Court cases. These are not insignificant numbers as a proportion of those cases in which the victim had a representative in court (a representative was present in only 18 Basic Court and 125 Intermediate Court cases).

PRODUCTION OF EVIDENCE

As earlier explained, all major evidence is sent to the court prior to the trial, including copies of witness statements and any other documentary or real evidence. The procedure at trial is that this evidence, together with any evidence proffered by the defence, must be verified and read out before the court. Article 157, 1996 CPL states that both prosecutors

Table 9.13 Prosecution produced expert conclusions

	BC 7 Sites		IC 6 Sites		All Sites	
Yes	451	78.4	353	86.5	804	81.8
No	124	21.6	55	13.5	179	18.2
Not known	151	–	10	–	161	–
Total	726	100.0	418	100.0	1144	100.0

Table 9.14 Prosecution produced inquests and examinations

	BC 7 Sites		IC 6 Sites		All Sites	
Yes	212	38.2	268	66.3	480	50.1
No	343	61.8	136	33.7	479	49.9
Not known	171	–	14	–	185	–
Total	726	100.0	418	100.0	1144	100.0

and defenders 'must show the material [i.e., real] evidence to the court for the parties to identify', and that 'the records of testimony of witnesses who are not present in court, the conclusions of expert witnesses who are not present in court, the records of inquests and other documents serving as evidence shall be read out in court'.[7]

As explained in previous chapters, it is quite common for police and prosecutors in China to produce various 'expert assessments/conclusions' relating primarily to the value of stolen property or illegal drugs. In addition, in cases where there has been death or serious injury, the police file will typically contain a crime scene report supported by diagrams and photographs. In homicide and other offences against the person, forensic reports will be submitted detailing the cause of death and the nature and extent of injuries supported by photographic evidence. That these varieties of evidence feature heavily in trials is borne out by our case file analysis, which showed that so-called 'expert conclusions' were produced in court in over 80 per cent of cases, and reports of inquests and examinations in 50 per cent of cases (see Tables 9.13 and 9.14). These types of documents feature with greater regularity in the more serious Intermediate Court cases.

Table 9.15 shows that the use of audio-visual evidence is still relatively rare in China.

We found that the defence were far less likely than the prosecution to produce expert conclusions or the results of inquests and examinations. Even including material evidence (i.e., real evidence and written statements) produced by the defence, we found that the defence produced evidence in only 11.8 per cent of cases (see Table 9.16).

---

[7] This is followed immediately by the provision that 'The judges shall heed the opinions of the public prosecutor, the parties, the defenders'. This presumably means that the prosecutor, the defender and the parties are allowed to make submissions on the evidence tendered in this way.

Table 9.15 Prosecution produced audio-visual evidence

	BC 7 Sites		IC 6 Sites		All Sites	
Yes	2	0.4	11	3.6	13	1.5
No	558	99.6	297	96.4	855	98.5
Not known	166	–	110	–	276	–
Total	726	100.0	418	100.0	1144	100.0

Table 9.16 Defence produced material and/or documentary and/or inquests/examination evidence

	BC 7 Sites		IC 6 Sites		All Sites	
Yes	31	7.0	68	17.3	99	11.8
No	412	93.0	326	82.7	738	88.2
Not known	283	–	24	–	307	–
Total	726	100	418	100	1144	100

WITNESSES

One of the most striking features of criminal trials in China is the absence of witnesses.[8] With very few exceptions, we found that witness testimony took the form of witness statements read out to the court, predominantly by prosecutors – on our analysis, the defence produced witness statements in only 16 cases (ten in the Basic Court and six in the Intermediate Court). Witnesses were physically produced to give testimony in only 19 trials, involving a total of 31 defendants (24 in the Basic Court and seven in the Intermediate Court). This means that out of the 1109 defendants whose cases proceeded to trial, witnesses provided live testimony of some kind in only 2.8 per cent of cases. In all but one of these 19 trials only one witness was produced, and in 12 of these trials that sole witness was the victim.[9]

Our findings on the very low attendance of witnesses are consistent with the findings of other researchers. Chen Weidong (2001) carried out a survey in 2000 and found that the percentage of cases in which witnesses testified in court in Shenzhen Intermediate Court was about 2–5 per cent, and in Yantai Intermediate Court the percentage of witnesses who testified in court was even lower at less than 1 per cent. Li Hua (2003) has

---

[8] To the same effect: Zuo Weimin (2008). See also, Human Rights Watch (2008) at p. 78: 'According to a comprehensive survey carried out in 2004, fewer than 1 per cent of witnesses who give depositions before trial subsequently appear in court to testify' citing Li Weihua (2005). In the widely-publicized trial of Stern Hu and three others (the 'Rio Tinto' case, April 2010), the principal evidence of corrupt payments was made in a written statement by Du Shuanghua. Requests that Du be produced as a witness were unavailing.

[9] In one of the other trials, involving four defendants jointly charged with causing intentional injury, five witnesses were produced.

estimated that although witness testimony features in 80 per cent of the public prosecutions initiated by the procuratorates in China, witnesses testify in court in less than 5 per cent of cases. Other research has reported attendance rates at less than 1.0 per cent.[10]

Our interviews with judges, prosecutors and defenders supported the finding that witnesses very rarely attend trial. Prosecutors[11] and judges[12] volunteered that witnesses are very reluctant to attend court to testify. A prosecutor (K-IP-W-04) said that the percentage of witnesses testifying in criminal cases in China was estimated at less than 5 per cent. Another prosecutor (J-IP-S4-05) pointed out that very often only written statements were presented in court. A prosecutor from a big city (B-IP-B2-11) and a judge (B-IJ-B2-12) complained that the failure of witnesses to attend trial meant that it was not possible to cross-examine witnesses or for judges to verify the authenticity of witness statements. Further, it is clear that the problem of non-attendance is not confined to civilian and lay witnesses: a prosecutor (B-IP-B2-11) told us that experts routinely failed to testify in court, and a judge (D-IJ-K-03) said that police officers normally did not testify in court as witnesses.

Perhaps the most obvious reason that so few witnesses attend trial to give testimony is because in the vast majority of cases it is felt to be unnecessary to do so. As already explained, our case file analysis found that around 95 per cent of suspects make a full or partial confession to the police, and this is followed by around 90 per cent of defendants admitting their guilt wholly or in part at the outset of the trial. Assuming that many defendants know before their trial that they intend to plead guilty (a fair assumption) this would explain why the defence do not procure witnesses to attend trial. It is also likely that the prosecution know that most defendants will plead guilty – this will be clear from the fact that most of them have confessed and have further confirmed that confession at the examination for prosecution stage of the process. Against this background it should not come as a surprise that little effort is made by either prosecution or defence to ensure that witnesses are present at the trial. Strangely, however, neither our interview respondents nor Chinese researchers and commentators cite this as one of the reasons for the low attendance of witnesses.[13]

When discussing witnesses' court appearance, most Chinese scholars attribute this to defects in the law and advocate legislative improvement, such as introducing a compensation system or forced appearance.[14] Wu Danhong, Fang Baoguo and Liu Lixia

---

[10] 'Criminal litigation, why is it so difficult to request the witnesses to testify in court', *People's Court Daily*, 23 April 2000. See also, Human Rights Watch (2008) quoting a lawyer as saying that Public Security officials threaten witnesses by saying: 'We already have your testimony . . . if you change it, we will accuse you of perjury and arrest you', *ibid.*, at p. 78. See also, Sun and Liu (1998); Chen and Li (2005); Wu Danhong, Baoguo Fang and Lixia Liu (2005); Chen Guangzhong, Weiqiu Cheng and Cheng Yang (eds.) (2006); Zuo Weimin, Jinghua Ma and Jianping Hu (2007); Fang Baoguo (2010).

[11] E.g., B-IP-B2-02; B-IP-B2-07; C-IP-B3-03; J-IP-S4-05; J-IP-S4-08; G-IP-S1-04; and E-IP-L-05.

[12] E.g., M-IJ-Y-02; E-IJ-L-04; E-IJ-L-07; L-IJ-X-11; A-IJ-B1-09; J-IJ-S4-06; H-IJ-S3-02; and D-IJ-K-03.

[13] At least for serious cases, the law nominally discourages courts from relying solely upon confessions for convictions.

[14] Li Jun (2010); Chen and Li (2005).

(2001) found that fear of retaliation ranked as most important (78.3 per cent) and lack of financial incentives and that the traditional culture of non-litigation (harmony) also hinder witnesses' court appearance. The vice-president of the High People's Court of Hebei Province also pointed out that cases in which witnesses were threatened, insulted or attacked were commonplace.[15] Zhang Yi (2004) has argued that the problem is especially prevalent in important and serious cases, and such is the concern that even officials, who normally enjoy better protection than the general public, will refuse to testify in court. For example, in embezzlement and corruption cases, provincial or city officials rarely testify in court. Deng, Huang and Wu (2001) have described existing safeguards for witnesses as only remedial in nature, with no proactive system in place to prevent intimidation. In addition, news reports suggest that around 70 per cent of informants suffered retaliation from criminal suspects or defendants.[16]

Professor Chen Weidong (2001) states that as far as the personnel of the procuratorate and the courts are concerned, the lack of clear legal provisions relating to witnesses is one of the major reasons for the low number of witnesses who testify in court.[17] He has pointed out that the law fails to state clearly whether the procuratorate or the court should be responsible for reimbursing expenses and compensating for loss of wages suffered by the witnesses as a consequence of their testifying in court; the source of funding from which witnesses are to be paid is uncertain; the law fails to specify clearly whether the court or the procuratorate should be responsible for ensuring the attendance of the witnesses; and it also fails to set out the punishment for those witnesses who refuse to testify in court or to explain what power the court has to compel them to testify.[18]

In terms of responsibility for ensuring attendance, some of those we spoke to also pointed to organizational reasons as to why witnesses did not attend trial. So, for example, a judge we interviewed (C-B3-01) pointed out that it was difficult to notify witnesses that they had to attend, whilst another judge (K-W-02) said that it was difficult to locate the witnesses. Fear for personal safety, and the lack of any safeguards for witnesses in this respect, was another reason cited by both our respondents to explain why witnesses rarely testify at trial.[19] Two prosecutors we interviewed (E-IP-L-05 and J-IP-S4-05)

---

[15] 'Witness, who are you and who am I?' available at http://www.legalinfo.gov.cn/xuefa/juan/susongfa018.htm.

[16] '70 per cent Informants Suffered from the Revenge Revealed Legislative Loopholes', *Xinjing Bao*, 21 June 2010. Although the SPP officials challenged such a high rate, it is a fact that the informants' safety is not fully protected.

[17] A similar view was expressed by judges being interviewed by a research team from the Centre for Criminal Law and Justice at the China University of Political Science and Law during 2002 to 2003 and Zhang Yi from the Legal Policy Research Office of the Guilin City People's Procuratorate: Chen Guangzhong (2004), pp. 46–47, 83–85; and Zhang Yi (2004). Zhang Yi also pointed out that, in cases involving criminal gangs and violence, the victims might not have the courage to report the case to the police let alone respond positively to a request to testify in court. See also Zhang Yaowu (2001).

[18] This point was also made by Deng, Huang and Wu (2001). A similar view was expressed by judges being interviewed by a research team from the Centre for Criminal Law and Justice at the China University of Political Science and Law during 2002 to 2003: Chen Guangzhong (2004), pp. 46–47, 83–85.

[19] See, Yang Yingze (2007), pp. 261–273; and Lu Jinbao (2007), pp. 575–580. 'Witness, who are you and who am I?' available at http://www.legalinfo.gov.cn/xuefa/juan/susongfa018.htm.

said that protection for witnesses who had testified in court was insufficient, and a lawyer (J-IL-S4-04) said that fear of trouble and revenge was the major reason why witnesses were reluctant to testify in court. A big city prosecutor we interviewed (C-IP-B3-03) pointed out that some witnesses refused to testify in court because of verbal threats from the defendants and their families.

More disturbingly, it would seem that witnesses fear violence and threats not only from defendants (and possibly victims and their families if they are called as witnesses for the defence), but also from the police and other State organs such as the procuratorate. As one lawyer pointed out to us, there existed a great risk that defence witnesses, and in particular those defence witnesses who had originally given statements to the prosecution, would be the subject of revenge by public security organs and the procuratorates, who had the power of detention, arrest, and prosecution. When the evidence given by a defence witness in court was disadvantageous to the prosecution, the prosecution would often approach the defence witness again to 'verify' the evidence. Some have even suggested that the PSB and procuratorates have been known to threaten witnesses so as to extort favourable 'evidence' from them.[20] A lawyer we interviewed (L-IL-X-10) explained that in some cases the PSB will use their power to simply stop a witness from testifying in court and, as revealed in the following comments of another lawyer (M-IL-Y-04), some police officers will threaten witnesses to discourage them from testifying in court:

> *M-IL-Y-04:* Investigative organs tell witnesses that if their testimony in court is different from the statements they made originally, they will be liable for giving false testimony, and this makes the witnesses very nervous.

Concerns relating to the lack of compensation or expenses for witnesses, the fear of violence and intimidation and the general confusion over whose responsibility it is to ensure witnesses show up for trial are all predicated upon an assumption that the prosecutors and judges want witnesses to attend trial and testify. However, what is perhaps most surprising about the criminal process in China is that neither judges nor prosecutors are particularly keen on witnesses giving evidence. Indeed, the evidence suggests that they would rather that witnesses did not attend trial, and use their power and influence to keep witnesses out of the trial process.

Deng, Huang and Wu (2001) observed that the principle of using oral evidence has not been generally accepted by judicial personnel, and that the courts continue to put much more emphasis on statements. A survey published in 2004 found that some judges worried that witnesses testifying in court would make the trial more complicated, and they therefore preferred to base their decisions on witness statements.[21] Thus, Yuan Zhiqiang (2010) said:

> Many judges do not understand the importance of witnesses giving testimony in court to secure a correct judgment. In their view, the testimony obtained by the investigation organ is highly probative, oral and written testimonies are of the same legal effect, so what's the point of witness court appearance? The presence of witnesses in court would make the case more complicated

---

[20] Xu Lanting, 'Dare not to give evidence', *Nanfang Weekend*, 26 October 2000.
[21] Chen Guangzhong (2004) at pp. 46–47, 83–85.

and reduce trial efficiency as the cross-examination of witnesses is sometimes quite time-consuming. Thus, cross-examination is just a formality, since no one including the defendant and the defender will challenge its validity.

On the other hand, police and prosecutors do not want witnesses to appear in court. Once witnesses give live testimony against the prosecution, they would face an embarrassing situation in the trial. In addition, because of the low quality of police and procurators, there is a heavy reliance on the defendant's confession. If the defendant withdraws the confession, a series of negative consequences will occur (Zhu and Na, 2010).

That judges have a mentality of wanting to block live testimony from witnesses was supported by what we were told by defence lawyers, many of whom said that judicial personnel were reluctant to allow witnesses to be called and would not sanction the issue of witness summons (e.g. G-IL-S1-03, G-IL-S1-04, G-IL-S1-07, I-IL-S3-03, C-IL-B3-08 and A-IL-B1-07). For example, a lawyer (G-IL-S1-03) said that only in very few cases had witnesses been summoned because the court worried that testifying in court by witnesses would lead to 'trouble'. Another big city lawyer said that almost all the lawyers' requests for prosecution witnesses to give evidence in court were rejected by the prosecution.

The underlying reason for this reluctance to allow witnesses to enter the trial process is that judges and prosecutors cannot control what witnesses will say, and accordingly they prefer to rely on witness statements, the contents of which are settled and which they have had the ability to scrutinize in advance of the trial. Judges being interviewed by a research team from the Centre for Criminal Law and Justice at the China University of Political Science and Law during 2002 to 2003 stated that they did not want witnesses to testify in court because very often witnesses would change their evidence. A similar view was shared by two judges we interviewed (M-IJ-Y-02 and M-IJ-Y-03), as well as by many prosecutors (e.g. C-IP-B3-05, G-IP-S1-02 and G-IP-S1-04) who told us that if witnesses attended trial it would make it more difficult for them to prove the case (presumably because live witnesses held out the possibility of saying something different from that recorded in their statement). As a result, some prosecutors actively work to ensure that witnesses do not testify and will block defence requests that a prosecution witness be called to give evidence.[22] Such attitudes are evident in the following comments made by prosecutors we interviewed:

M-IP-Y-01: The witnesses are usually neighbours of the defendants and their legal consciousness is low. They usually feel nervous and are easily affected by their emotions and thus unable to hold firm to their standpoint. From the perspective of my work, witnesses' testifying in court does not help much; on the contrary more problems will arise when they withdraw their evidence.

---

[22] According to one prosecutor (M-IP-Y-05), in most cases the request for witnesses to testify in court was made by defence lawyers. A judge also said that situations where defence lawyers brought the prosecution witnesses to the court and requested them to testify in court often happened. And a prosecutor (D-IP-K-01) pointed out that when the defence summoned prosecution witnesses to testify in court, the trial would need to be adjourned. In order to ensure that the calling of the witnesses by the defence was necessary, a prosecutor (M-IP-Y-01) suggested that judges examine the purpose of the defence in summoning witnesses and the necessity for doing so.

M-IP-Y-04: Witnesses are usually nervous and their testimony in court may not be as clear as the original statements they have given earlier because their memory may fade over time and also they may be affected by other external factors. As a result, the truthfulness of their statements may be affected. For this reason, I do not want witnesses to testify in court.

M-IP-Y-05: Testifying in court by witnesses creates more problems, so I do not want any witness to testify in court.

A-IP-B1-12: If the defence lawyer requests prosecution witnesses to testify in court, normally he has done sufficient preparation for that: this may result in a change in the witness testimony.

Prosecutors we spoke to clearly worked on the assumption that prosecution witnesses who changed their mind at trial were untruthful (e.g. C-IP-B3-05, G-IP-S1-02; G-IP-S1-04; A-IP-B1-08), a viewpoint shared by at least some judges. A big city judge (A-IJ-B1-04) said he preferred to rely on evidence other than what witnesses said, while another big city judge (G-IJ-S1-01) said he would talk to witnesses after the trial. This last remark is perhaps explained by what another judge said (E-IJ-L-04), namely that, in her view, witnesses dared not tell the truth in court. A judge from a less-developed part of China (L-IJ-X-03) said that, as in other countries, the practice of witnesses being bought did exist in China. Some of the prosecutors we interviewed (e.g. K-IP-W-01, F-IP-N-03, B-IP-B2-03 and C-IP-B3-04) blamed defence lawyers for witnesses changing their evidence, arguing that witnesses were often induced or misled by defence lawyers while testifying in court.

The virtual non-existence of witnesses at trial was a cause of much frustration to some of the defence lawyers we interviewed, because it made it impossible for them to test the veracity of witnesses through cross-examination (e.g., F-IL-N-03, J-IL-S4-02, J-IL-S4-03 and E-IL-L-05). The impact of expert witnesses failing to testify in court was felt even more keenly, as revealed in the comments of a lawyer we interviewed (K-IL-W-01):

K-IL-W-01: It is a big problem that the experts who draw conclusions are absent from court sessions. We are unable to verify some issues that involve professional/technical knowledge during cross-examination. And it is very difficult to apply for another expert evaluation.

Another lawyer (E-IL-L-05) said that police officers should testify in court and be cross-examined by the parties to the litigation. Some of the defence lawyers accepted that a mandatory rule requiring all witnesses to attend trial would be unrealistic in the Chinese context (e.g., F-IL-N-06; I-IL-S3-01), but they suggested that in the case of important witness evidence, and in the case of testimony challenged by the defence, it should be mandatory for the prosecution to produce the witness in court so that he or she could be cross-examined (e.g., F-IL-N-04). A failure to produce the witness should lead to a not guilty verdict (C-IL-B3-08).

QUESTIONING THE EVIDENCE

The case files were analysed to see if any questions were asked about the evidence and if so by whom. As explained above, the evidence is in almost all cases limited to documentary evidence, whether the statement/confession of the defendant made to the police,

248   *Criminal justice in China*

Table 9.17 Questioning/challenging the statement/confession of the defendant[1]

	BC 7 Sites		IC 6 Sites		All 13 Sites	
Yes	26	7.7	65	17.6	91	12.9
No	313	92.3	304	82.4	617	87.1
Not known	387	–	49	–	436	–
Sub-total	726	100.0	418	100.0	1144	100.0
Defendant	20		38		58	
Judges	1		8		9	
Victim or victim's representative	1		1		2	
Others (including defenders)	9		25		34	

Note: 1. In a number of cases, others joined in a challenge made by the defendant.

Table 9.18 Questioning/challenging testimony of witness[1]

	BC 7 Sites		IC 6 Sites		All Sites	
Yes	69	13.3	135	34.4	204	22.4
No	450	86.7	258	65.6	708	77.6
Not known	207	–	25	–	232	–
Sub-total	726	100.0	418	100.0	1144	100.0
Defendant	57		100		157	
Judges	1		1		2	
Victim or victim's representative	0		3		3	
Others (including defenders)	23		71		94	

Note: 1. In a number of cases, others joined in a challenge made by the defendant.

statements of witnesses, expert reports on valuation, or the reports of medical personnel on autopsies or injuries. So although we asked our researchers to note whether the evidence was 'questioned'; 'questioning' does not in this context necessarily imply any form of challenge. The 'questions' may be questions of clarification, or merely observations, or even a statement confirming the contents of the documentary evidence under consideration. More details about the types of 'questions' that are asked at this stage will be provided when we present the data from trials that were observed by our fieldworkers. What the case file analysis shows is that there is little in the way of questions about any of the evidence which is read out or presented to the court.

Given that most defendants (around 95 per cent) are recorded as having confessed to the police, the statement alleged to have been made by the defendant when questioned by the police is probably the most important piece of evidence before the court in the vast majority of cases. Yet, Table 9.17 shows that in 87 per cent of cases no questions, observations or statements are made about what the defendant is alleged to have said while in police custody. In the minority of cases (12.9 per cent) where anything is said about such statements, it is usually said by the defendant himself or his defender.

Given the absence of witnesses, pre-trial statements of witnesses can be regarded as the primary evidence before the court. As Table 9.18 shows, the statements of witnesses are

Table 9.19 Questioning material evidence and/or documentary evidence by parties[1]

	BC 7 Sites		IC 6 Sites		All Sites	
Yes	35	6.8	87	21.6	122	13.3
No	480	93.2	315	78.4	795	86.7
Not known	211	–	16	–	227	–
Sub-total	726	100.0	418	100.0	1144	100.0
Defendant	26		55		81	
Judges	1		0		1	
Victim or victim's representative	2		1		3	
Others (including defenders)	14		51		65	

Note: 1. In some cases, others joined in a challenge made by the defendant.

Table 9.20 Questioning/challenging the expert conclusion

	BC 7 Sites		IC 6 Sites		All Sites	
Yes	18	3.4	44	11.8	62	6.9
No	512	96.6	329	88.2	841	93.1
Not known	196	–	45	–	241	–
Sub-total	726	100.0	418	100.0	1144	100.0
Defendant	8		12		20	
Judges	0		4		4	
Victim or victim's representative	2		1		3	
Others (including defenders)	8		29		37	

subject to greater questioning than pre-trial confessions/statements made by the defendant. However, it remains the case that nothing is said about witness statements in more than two-thirds of all cases, and when something is said it is normally by defendants or their representatives. Prosecutors and judges very rarely if ever show interest in raising questions about this evidence.

There is even less questioning of the other forms of evidence which are routinely presented during trials. One explanation of this is that much of this evidence is pro-forma in nature and does not enhance the case for the prosecution against the defendant but merely demonstrates that the relevant procedures have been followed. Audio-visual evidence, which is in any event a rarity in Chinese criminal trials, elicited questions in only two of the 13 cases in which it was produced. As can be seen from Tables 9.19–9.21, material (i.e., real) and documentary evidence, expert conclusions and reports of inquests and examinations elicit questions/observations in only 13 per cent, 7 per cent and 3 per cent of cases respectively.

In practice, the evidence entitled 'Explanation of the Situation' was often used by the prosecution, which did not go through the cross-examination process at all, but often served as an important item of evidence for judges in reaching a finding of guilt. The content of the Explanation of the Situation mainly includes such information as the process of catching the suspect, any details regarding other suspects not yet apprehended,

Table 9.21 Questioning/challenging the inquests and examinations

	BC 7 Sites		IC 6 Sites		All Sites	
Yes	6	1.8	14	4.3	20	3.0
No	327	98.2	314	95.7	641	97.0
Not known	393	–	90	–	483	–
Sub-total	726	100.0	418	100.0	1144	100.0
Defendant	5		7		12	
Judges	0		0		0	
Victim or victim's representative	0		0		0	
Others (including defenders)	0		7		7	

Table 9.22 Questioning material evidence and/or documentary evidence submitted by defence

	BC 7 Sites		IC 6 Sites		All Sites	
Questioned	13	7.0	23	9.6	36	8.5
Not questioned	173	93.0	216	90.4	389	91.5
Not known/not applicable	540	–	179	–	719	–
Sub-total	726	100	418	100	1144	100
Defendant	4		8		12	
Judges	3		2		5	
Victim or victim's representative	2		0		2	
Others (including defender/prosecutor)	4		13		17	

illicit property not found, jurisdiction, offenders' identity, statement that there was no torture in the investigation, and whether the suspect voluntarily surrendered or had meritorious performance.[23] However, none of the providers of this information would be present and testify in court. In order to minimize the negative effect of this, one scholar argued that the investigator involved should give testimony in court on the information provided through the document 'Explanation of the Situations' and be cross-examined on it before it could be admitted (Huang Jie, 2010).

Interest in material produced by the defence (insofar as interest is measured by questions asked and observations made) is significantly higher. As stated above, however, the defence proffers this type of evidence in only a few cases (12 per cent of cases overall). When such evidence was put forward, it was questioned in 13 Basic Court cases (out of the 31 in which it was introduced) and in 23 Intermediate Court cases (out of the 68 in which it was put forward) (see Table 9.22). It aroused more interest than did prosecution evidence from prosecutors and victims' representatives (as is to be expected) and also from judges although most interest actually came from the defendant or his or her representative.

---

[23] Li and Wang (2009); Huang Jie (2010).

THE DEBATE

As explained in the previous chapter, once all the evidence has been presented the parties are allowed an opportunity to state their views about the evidence and to debate with each other.

As Table 9.23 shows, the prosecution took the opportunity to present a statement in virtually all Intermediate Court cases and in 90 per cent of Basic Court cases. In a significant proportion of all cases this statement included a summary of the evidence, a statement as to the guilt of the defendant and observations about sentence.

As shown in Table 9.24, whilst defendants (or defenders in cases where they were present) were less likely to avail themselves of the opportunity of making a final statement than prosecutors, such statements were made in approximately 70 per cent of Basic Court cases and 90 per cent of Intermediate Court cases. However, these statements were more likely to focus on admitting guilt and/or asking for leniency in punishment rather than on claiming innocence or seeking to summarize the evidence.

Table 9.23 Prosecution submitted statement in court at debate stage[1]

	BC 7 Sites		IC 6 Sites		All Sites	
Yes	458	90.3	398	99.0	856	94.2
No	49	9.7	4	1.0	53	5.8
Not known	219	–	16	–	235	–
Sub-total	726	100.0	418	100.0	1144	100.0
A summary of the evidence	272		360		632	
A statement as to the guilt of the defendant	326		382		708	
A statement as to leniency or severity of punishment	226		213		439	
Others	40		19		59	

Note: 1. The prosecution often made statements in relation to guilt/innocence, the evidence and in relation to punishment.

Table 9.24 Defence submitted statement in court at debate stage[1]

	BC 7 Sites		IC 6 Sites		All Sites	
Yes	279	68.4	358	89.5	637	78.8
No	129	31.6	42	10.5	171	21.2
Not known	318	–	18	–	336	–
Sub-total	726	100.0	418	100.0	1144	100.0
A summary of the evidence	84		171		255	
A statement admitting guilt of the defendant	70		123		193	
A statement as to leniency of punishment	209		251		460	
A statement claiming complete innocence	42		15		57	
A statement claiming partial innocence	29		23		52	
Others	50		85		135	

Note: 1. The defence might make statements in relation to guilt/innocence, the evidence and in relation to punishment.

Table 9.25 There was additional debate before handing down the judgment

	BC 7 Sites		IC 6 Sites		All Sites	
Yes	119	26.2	184	46.8	303	35.8
No	335	73.8	209	53.2	544	64.2
Not known/not applicable	272	–	25	–	297	–
Total	726	100.0	418	100.0	1144	100.0

Table 9.26 Defendant/defender(s) gave a final statement

	BC 7 Sites		IC 6 Sites		All Sites	
Yes	289	55.2	309	77.6	598	64.9
No	235	44.8	89	22.4	324	35.1
Not known	202	–	20	–	222	–
Sub-total	726	100.0	418	100.0	1144	100.0
Statement as to guilt or innocence	120		118		238	
Statement as to punishment	151		183		334	
Others	137		73		210	

In about a third of all cases statements from the parties led to a further debate between the parties, with a greater likelihood of such debate in the more serious Intermediate Court cases than in Basic Court cases (see Table 9.25).

Once the presiding judge indicates the conclusion of the debate stage, the defendant is given the right to present a final statement. Although not all defendants took the opportunity to make a final statement, a significant proportion (almost 65 per cent) did so. Such statements were more likely in Intermediate Court cases, where more than three-quarters of defendants made some sort of final statement (see Table 9.26). For the most part these statements focused on punishment or on admitting or, occasionally, disputing guilt. In practice, most defence lawyers would argue for leniency based on statutory factors, or argue for mitigated or reduced punishment based on voluntary surrender, meritorious performance, actively returning the illicit goods or property, less evil intention etc.[24]

THE LAW

To date, we have said very little about the law but this is because in common law and many European continental systems, legal argument about the applicable law often involves doctrinal analysis of what the law is both in abstract terms and as it applies to the facts at hand. What, for example, is meant by 'consent' in sexual offences? When is an act 'unlawful and dangerous' in the law of manslaughter? What is meant by an

---

[24] See, for example, Jiang and Xu (2005).

'appropriation' of property for the purposes of theft? What amounts to a 'building' for the purpose of burglary? What is meant by 'intention' and 'negligence' and 'recklessness' in various offences? In China, by contrast, there is very little debate about the law.

In China, the Criminal Law is drafted in very broad terms. In place of elaborate definitions, the Criminal Law proscribes various crimes in terms which are expressed as if they are self-evident. Articles 232, 233 and 236, for example, state:

Article 232 Whoever intentionally commits homicide shall be sentenced to death, life imprisonment or fixed-term imprisonment of not less than ten years; if the circumstances are relatively minor, he shall be sentenced to fixed-term imprisonment of not less than three years but not more than ten years.

Article 233 Whoever negligently causes death to another person shall be sentenced to fixed-term imprisonment of not less than three years but not more than seven years; if the circumstances are relatively minor, he shall be sentenced to fixed-term imprisonment of not more than three years, except as otherwise specifically provided in this Law.

Article 236 Whoever rapes a woman by violence, coercion or any other means shall be sentenced to fixed-term imprisonment of not less than three years but not more than ten years.
  Whoever has sexual intercourse with a girl under the age of 14 shall be deemed to have committed rape and shall be given a heavier punishment.
  Whoever rapes a woman or has sexual intercourse with a girl under the age of 14 shall, in any of the following circumstances, be sentenced to fixed-term imprisonment of not less than ten years, life imprisonment or death:
  (1) the circumstances being flagrant;
  (2) raping a number of women or girls under the age of 14;
  (3) raping a woman before the public in a public place;
  (4) raping a woman with one or more persons in succession; or
  (5) causing serious injury or death to the victim or any other serious consequences.

The meaning of such important crimes as 'homicide' and 'rape'[25] are simply assumed. The result is that, as a matter of practice and without a strong bar, there is little, if any, room for legal argument in trials in China beyond asserting that 'intention was absent' or that the act was 'merely negligent'. An additional matter is that, constitutionally, judges in China do not have authority to interpret the law: interpretation of the law is a matter for the Standing Committee of the National People's Congress. In the rare event that genuinely 'legal' issues were to arise in court, the resolution is likely to be dealt with through the political-legal committee rather than the collegial panel. And at a practical level, for its part the court does not have to engage in an intricate account of the prevailing law and justify how the acts alleged by the prosecution or found by the court fit within it. They merely have to state that the defendant was or was not guilty of the act charged, the meaning of which is taken to be self-evident. Accordingly, and as we shall see, there is little by way of legal argument in the trials in China and almost nothing of the kind in the case files.[26]

---

[25] In the case of rape there is the qualification that sexual intercourse with a girl under the age of 14 is included within rape.
[26] See also, Max Planck Institute for Foreign and International Criminal Law (2006) which also found 'virtually no mention of doctrine at all' (p. 136).

JUDGMENT

Concern has been widely expressed in China over the practice of courts adjourning trials and handing down the judgment some days later. Prosecutors complain that this amounts to an adverse judgment on their presentation of the case as it might imply, for example, that the court has to undertake further research or investigation of its own in order to reach a conclusion. Defence lawyers, for their part, have complained that adjournments give an opportunity for others not involved in the trial to influence the outcome; while others claim that some adjournments may be needed because of a lack of competence in the judiciary.

We found in our sample, a surprisingly high proportion of cases in both Basic Courts and Intermediate Courts in which judgment was postponed until after a substantial adjournment (see Table 9.27).

Our analysis of the case files showed that once judgment was given, the outcome was almost without exception a conviction on some or all of the charges or an amended charge with only two defendants securing an acquittal, as can be seen in Table 9.28.

There did not appear to be any pattern to explain the cases in which the court amended the charge originally brought by the procuratorate or convicted the defendant on only some of the charges originally preferred except that, on the basis of the information available to us, in each case, the court decided that one or more charges were adequately covered by other charges or thought that one or more charges in a multiple-count Bill of

Table 9.27 Handing down judgment at or after trial

	BC 7 Sites		IC 6 Sites		All Sites	
Yes	652	100.0	392	100.0	1044	100.0
Not known/not applicable	74		26		100	
Sub-total	726	100.0	418	100.0	1144	100.0
Immediately	218	33.4	13	3.3	231	22.1
After short adjournment	115	17.6	60	15.3	175	16.8
After an adjournment for a number of days	319	48.9	319	81.4	638	61.1

Table 9.28 Outcome of the judgment

	BC 7 Sites		IC 6 Sites		All Sites	
D was convicted	674	99.7	390	100.0	1064	99.8
D was acquitted	2	0.3	0	0	2	0.2
Adjournment of the trial	50		28		78	
Sub-total	726	100.0	418	100.0	1144	100.0
Guilty of all charges	663		370		1033	
Guilty of some charges	3		6		9	
Guilty of amended charge	8		14		22	
Not guilty in law	1		0		1	
Not guilty due to insufficient evidence	1		0		1	

Prosecution were not made out or, in the case of amended charges, the court formed a different view of the seriousness of the facts underlying the incident as a result of such features as a compensation agreement with the victim having been reached before trial.

In only nine cases were the trial courts not in full agreement with the charges formulated by the procuratorate and convicted on only some charges. Even in these cases, all defendants were convicted. In B-CFA-B2-76, the defendant was initially charged with various acts of corruption and accepting bribes but later a further four counts were added in a supplementary Bill. The court found that there were mistakes as to times and amounts in some charges and accordingly convicted of only one of the original charges and imposed a life sentence (reduced on appeal to 14 years' imprisonment). In the other two Basic Court cases (B-CFA-B2-152 and B-CFA-B2-154), the court convicted the defendants on the original charge of theft but in each case found that not all the alleged individual incidents of thefts had been established imposing sentences of seven years' and ten years' respectively.

There was a broadly similar picture in Intermediate Court cases. In three of these cases,[27] the defendants faced two counts arising out of the same set of facts and the court decided that a conviction on one count was sufficient and that the other count was either not made out or redundant. Thus, in K-CFA-W-62, the defendant was convicted of homicide only having been charged with homicide and robbery, the court not being convinced that the motive for the killing was robbery. By contrast, in three conjoined cases (K-CFA-W-39–41), the court increased the severity of the charges by convicting of intentional homicide, the defendants having been charged originally only with intentional injury.

So far as *amended charges* are concerned, as with cases where the court convicted on only some of the charges, commonly the broad factual matrix was not disputed by the court but the facts were capable of being characterized in different ways. So, for example, in the largest group of amended charge cases involving eight cases it was not in dispute that there had been an altercation or physical confrontation leading to the death of the victim. This could be characterized as intentional injury or intentional homicide. In five cases, the court lowered the initial prosecution charge whereas in three cases (E-CFA-L-25; K-CFA-W-19; L-CFA-X-07) the original charge of intentional injury was amended by the court to intentional homicide. Another ground for differences of view lay in drugs cases: whether the defendant was trafficking in drugs or merely transporting them; and in four cases (L-CFA-X-17; L-CFA-X-18; L-CFA-X-51; K-CFA-W-57) the court formed a different view to that expressed in the original prosecution.[28] Other cases involved prostitution, bribery and misappropriation of funds.

There were two cases, by contrast, in which the court was not persuaded of the charges in the Bill of Prosecution. We shall say a little about each of these although the information drawn from the case file analysis is sketchy.

A-CFA-B1-87 (Basic Court)
This was a charge under Article 347 of the Criminal Law, trafficking in illegal drugs. The defendant, a 23-year old unskilled, unemployed migrant was apprehended as a result of a police stop

---

[27] I-CFA-S3-53; K-CFA-W-10; and K-CFA-W-62.
[28] Other cases involved charges relating to prostitution, bribery and misappropriation of funds.

and search. The suspect was subject to police detention for two months prior to the police seeking prosecutorial approval for arrest; a further month after approval had been granted before transfer to the procuratorate; and a further three months before the procuratorate made the decision to prosecute. When in police custody, the suspect was recorded as having made a complete confession and to have incriminated others. At the procuratorate, the suspect withdrew his confession. At the procuratorate he did not allege police torture and at no stage was he provided legal representation. At trial, the defendant challenged the prosecution evidence, maintained complete innocence and after adjourning for a number of days, the court decided (for reasons which are not recorded in the files) that the evidence was insufficient and the charge not substantiated.[29]

A-CFA-B1-15 (Basic Court)
An 18-year old local man was jointly charged with another defendant with robbery under Article 263 of the Criminal Law. He was held in detention for 14 weeks prior to the review of the prosecution stage. He confirmed his confession when questioned by the prosecutor at the procuratorate. The notes prepared by our researcher are annotated: 'This was a crime by a minor'; 'The circumstance of the crime was minor.' The defendant was represented by a lawyer at trial and the defendant raised questions about his confession. The lawyer urged that the defendant be treated leniently on the ground that he was a minor and only an accomplice to the principal offender (who had been convicted already in another case). The court found after an adjournment of a few days that the defendant was not guilty in law, in all likelihood because, given his age, the court was satisfied that sole responsibility rested with the adult co-defendant, the principal offender.

These cases provide some, albeit slight, evidence that courts may exercise a function that is not wholly driven by the decisions of the police and procuratorate. In the overwhelming majority of cases, the investigative file is dispositive of all that happens thereafter but there may be circumstances in which the court will vary the charge, convict of only some charges or even in exceptional cases find the defendant not guilty.

SENTENCING

One of the sacrifices that we had to make in collecting data on sentencing from the case file analysis was the decision to restrict material collected to the broad categories 'custodial' or 'non-custodial'. It would have been preferable to have gathered data of a specific kind, itemizing the actual length of any prison sentence and quantifying any fine but once the categories were initially created the accurate completion of these proved too difficult and this led us to abandon the specific in favour of the general.

Table 9.29 clearly demonstrates that, for cases where the sentence was known, the principal punishment handed down in Chinese criminal courts is imprisonment, this being the sentence in 91.6 per cent of Basic Court cases and 93.2 per cent of Intermediate Court cases.

In addition, our data show that, apart from the two not guilty cases discussed above, a 'non-custodial' sentence often (see the qualification to this in the text below) meant a suspended prison sentence. The selection of a suspended sentence could be easily

---

[29] It is possible that there was some bargain struck as a result of information supplied by the defendant about other criminals.

Table 9.29 Sentencing of the defendant

	BC 7 Sites		IC 6 Sites		All Sites	
Sentenced	669	100.0	351	100.0	1020	100.0
Not known/not applicable	57		67		124	
Sub-total	726	100.0	418	100.0	1144	100.0
Custodial penalty	613		327		940	
Non-custodial penalty	56		24		80	

understood in relation to certain offences which were deemed minor in character, such as certain traffic violations under Article 113 of the Criminal Law (one year suspended for one year: B-CFA-B2-57; B-CFA-B2-60; C-CFA-B3-163; and C-CFA-B3-164) and creating a disturbance under Article 293 of the Criminal Law (six months suspended for one year) although even in such cases there were gradations of culpability (Article 133 violations attracting two years suspended for three years in M-CFA-Y-01; M-CFA-Y-17; M-CFA-Y-18; and M-CFA-Y-32; and creating a disturbance receiving one year suspended for two years in M-CFA-Y-4). However, suspended sentences were also employed in some cases where the charge was of a more serious variety as in inflicting intentional injury contrary to Article 234 (M-CFA-Y-6; M-CFA-Y-24; M-CFA-Y-25; M-CFA-Y-33; F-CFA-N-2; C-CFA-B3-175), illegal possession of ammunition contrary to Article 120 (C-CFA-B3-170) and false imprisonment contrary to Article 238 (F-CFA-N47). Given that some 70 per cent of such cases were dealt with in Basic Court, it is possible that a view had been taken from the outset that these cases were at the less serious end of the crime continuum. Nonetheless, there was no observable pattern to the choice of sentence accountable in part, no doubt, by the fact that China does not operate a rigorous system of sentencing guidelines. In Basic Court, just over half of these suspended sentence cases were dealt with by way of summary procedure.

We could find no correlation between choosing a suspended as opposed to an immediate sentence of imprisonment nor was there any relationship between such sentences and residential status (local/migrant) or legal representation.[30] Clearly there must have been circumstances not picked up by our data collection which commended such sentences to the court in some cases. An example of a case in which a suspended sentence is perhaps readily understandable for the reasons set out in the extract from the judgment below is E-CFA-L-32:

E-CFA-L-32: The case involved a robbery in which the 16-year old local defendant played a minor part. He made a full confession and expressed remorse in court. In pronouncing judgment, the court said that, based on the principle of combining education with punishing minor

---

[30] Nor could we explain the different approaches taken towards the length of suspension. While the most common (20) was symmetry between the prison term and the length of the suspension, such as one year suspended for one year, there were considerable variations as between cases and courts in this respect, for example: M-CFA-Y-4, one year suspended two years; M-CFA-Y-6, six months suspended eight months; M-CFA-Y-65, three years suspended five years; C-CFA-B3-88, three years suspended four years).

offenders and taking into account the defendant's role in the crime, his attitude of remorse, his daily performance and the measures made available through his parents and the village committee, a non-custodial sentence would not endanger society.

In addition, there were two cases in which the court, while returning a verdict of guilty, exempted the defendant from punishment. One of those cases, L-CFA-X-23, is readily explicable. In that case, the defendant, a 16-year old male, was charged with rape under Article 236 of the Criminal Law. The court decided that although the charge was supported by evidence, because of his age, voluntary surrender and accessory status, that he should be exempted from punishment.[31]

The other case, J-CFA-S4-09, is more difficult to explain. Here the defendant, a 35-year old migrant, on a charge of intentional injury contrary to Article 234 of the Criminal Law, consistently denied involvement in the offence and refused to pay compensation to the victim on the basis that he was innocent. During the trial, the mental state of the victim was put in question and the defendant maintained his innocence. The court, however, delivered a verdict of guilty on the basis that the defendant was one of the parties involved but as an accessory. Having found the defendant guilty, the court then exempted him from punishment notwithstanding that he was an adult. It is possible, although we cannot be certain of this, that the sentence was a compromise which was designed to support the initiating actions of the police but at the same time sought to reflect the court's concern over the reliability of the victim's evidence.

Other Chinese literature shows that the probation/non-custodial penalty mostly occurs in cases heard in grassroots courts. However, the non-custodial rate is also low.[32] In 1998, for example, official figures suggest that 293 369 defendants received short-term imprisonment, of whom only 26 per cent received a non-custodial/suspended penalty.[33] In addition, local and juvenile defendants are more likely than transient and other adult defendants to be given a suspended penalty.[34]

So far as sentencing practices are concerned, however, the account does not tell the whole story because in death penalty cases, the sentence was sometimes recorded in our research as 'not-known' or 'non-custodial' without further elaboration.[35] Our analysis

---

[31] This is in line with official policy towards young offenders and the defendant would have received education in court.

[32] It varies between 5 per cent and 38 per cent in various locations and regions. E.g., see Feng Quan (2009); Wang Hongyu (2008); and Chu Weizhu (2009).

[33] Cited in Wang Hongyu (2008), p. 3, *Foreword*.

[34] See Feng Quan (2009); Wang Hongyu (2008); The First Criminal Court of Shandong High Court (2008); and Chu Weizhu (2009).

[35] The courts in China, following the precepts of the Code of Criminal Law, justify imposition of the death penalty where either the consequences or the circumstances are deemed to be 'especially serious'. While commentators have described regional variations in the use of the death penalty by courts in China, our data do not allow us to make comparisons of this sort. The number of death sentences handed down in China each year is not known with certainty, the statistics being regarded as part of 'state secrets'. In total, some 68 offences in 47 Articles in the Criminal Law of China carry the death penalty. These include seven offences involving national security, 14 of endangering public security, 15 economic crimes, five of infringing the rights of the person, two involving property crimes, eight public order crimes, two crimes against the interests of national defence, 13 involving military offences and two involving corruption: see, The Rights Practice, *The*

shows that the death penalty was imposed in at least 38 cases amounting to 3.7 per cent of known sentences.[36] Although we do not have a full record of all sentences, recourse to the death penalty tended to occur in cases regarded by the court[37] as particularly serious and all were dealt with in the Intermediate Court.[38] These were generally intentional killing/homicide or cases charged as robbery where the victim(s) had died in the course of a violent attack and property of the victim had been stolen.[39]

CONCLUSION

Analysis of case files provides a clear picture of the broad contours of criminal trials in China covering both Basic and Intermediate Courts. While most trials are open, a surprisingly high proportion of trials were closed to the public. Although there was a greater presence of defence lawyers in Intermediate Court cases, there was a significant under-representation overall with some 46 per cent of defendants being unrepresented; and of those who were represented, more than one-fifth were represented by court-assigned lawyers.

For the most part, and in line with the fact that approximately 95 per cent of defendants came to the trial with a confession recorded against them by the police, relatively few defendants contested the prosecution evidence with some 90 per cent not contesting some or all the charges or to a lesser-included crime. Whereas the prosecution case was always supported by witness statements and commonly buttressed by other evidence, including statements for expert witnesses, the defence rarely produced evidence of any kind in support of its case. Nor were witnesses, for either side, a feature in the overwhelming majority of trials, the few exceptions primarily consisting of the production of victims called by the prosecution or appearing in connection with an ancillary civil action.

Defendants or their lawyers rarely challenged the most potent item of evidence, the defendant's confession; no questions of any kind being raised about the confession in some 87 per cent of cases. There was not much more by way of questioning regarding other prosecution evidence such as witness statements and material or documentary

---

Death Penalty in China: A Baseline Document (2003). For discussion, see Cordone (2010); 'China Sees 30 per cent Drop in Death Penalty', *China Daily*, 10 May 2008; Scott (2010). Following the decision of the Supreme Court in 2007 to review all death sentences, reports suggest that up to 50 per cent of death sentences are amended to death sentence with a two-year suspension (almost all of which will not result in execution) and there are increasingly loud voices within China calling for its abolition, see: 'China Questions Death Penalty', *China Daily*, 27 January 2005. It is widely reported that China will reduce the number of death penalty offences in the near future.

[36] For more detailed investigation of death penalty cases, see, Max Planck Institute for Foreign and International Criminal Law (2006). In the case files examined in that study, 127 (58 per cent) of 219 offenders were sentenced to an unsuspended (immediate) death penalty in the first instance trial.

[37] However, a court's view of the 'seriousness' of an offence may be heavily influenced by the quality of defence representation provided to the accused: Bright (1994; 1997); and Sarat (2005).

[38] We know that in three cases the sentence was suspended following appeal.

[39] For detailed discussion of public opinion on the death penalty in China see, Oberwittler and Qi (2009).

evidence. Slightly more attention was paid to defence evidence but, again, this occurred very infrequently. There was an almost complete absence of legal argument. Defendants for the most part made statements in court admitting their guilt or pleading for leniency and only infrequently made an assertion of complete innocence. In the cases in which the defendant disputed the prosecution case, the court returned a verdict of guilty in all except two cases.

In short, once a case comes to trial in China, the confession of the defendant together with other evidence that the prosecution can muster will almost always result in conviction with few defendants placing obstacles in the path to this outcome.

10. The prosecution observed

INTRODUCTION

In the preceding chapters, we have sought an understanding of criminal justice in China through examination of data extracted from the official case files and interviews with judges, prosecutors and defence lawyers. In this and the following chapters we describe how trials actually operate in Mainland China. To begin, we deal with the presentation of the prosecution before going on in subsequent chapters to deal with the defence and the outcomes.

Our account is based upon the direct observation of criminal cases disposed of in the 13 research sites which were a mix of urban and rural settings and which varied in terms of socio-economic development. In ten of those sites, the observations were made by our three researchers and in the remaining three by selected staff drawn from within the justice system itself.[1] We did not draw a random sample but rather took any and all cases that were being handled at the time that we were undertaking field work in the relevant site.[2] As we shall see, while the sample contains a broad spectrum of criminal charges dealt with by ordinary and summary procedure and covers the less serious offences, most cases were of the more serious variety including a substantial group potentially subject to the death penalty.[3]

THE COURTROOM SETTING

The criminal trial in China is functional and bureaucratic. The trial usually starts with an announcement to set the tone of the proceedings and assert the authority of the tribunal in the following manner:

---

[1] We gave detailed instructions to these individuals about the research, its aims and objectives and we provided them with a schedule of the information that needed to be collected in each trial. The completed data schedules varied in terms of detail as between the three research sites covered in this way: although all provided the basic information we sought, most records were sparse in terms of qualitative detail.
 There was also some variance in the detail recorded by the principal researchers. The researchers operated in a pressured atmosphere: members of the audience who wrote notes were evicted from the court and a journalist had his notes torn up by the court bailiff on the judge's instruction: F-CO-N-08.
[2] We were able to see all trials, including those to which the public had no access, and were excluded from none having secured special research permission.
[3] Judges on a few occasions stopped members of the audience from making notes during a trial but this did not happen with our researchers based on the understanding that the note was taken for research purposes only and that the researchers would not misuse the data.

Court clerk: Reads out the discipline of the court.
1. No tape recording, taking photos and filming without permission.
2. Do not enter the adjudication area.
3. Do not clap, create noise, cause trouble or conduct any activities that obstruct the adjudication of the judges.
4. Do not raise questions and make submissions.
5. No smoking.
6. Switch off pagers and mobile phones.
7. If there is any opinion as to the adjudication, please raise the issues to this court in writing after the court session.

At the same time, with judges often dressed in robes with the national emblem on the front and the court officers also in uniform, there is an apparent sense of order and decorum apposite to a criminal trial.[4]

The physical structure of the courtrooms varied considerably from the austere functional rooms characterizing the big cities, to the occasional large assembly hall seating over 1000 taken over for exemplary trials, to the more dilapidated and shabby rooms in some rural areas, but the layout of the courts broadly followed the model that we have already described as that prescribed by law (see Chapter 8) with minor variations in the less developed parts of the country.[5]

There was also considerable variation in the numbers and make-up of the audience. Some trials were conducted in private according to law but most were in theory open to the public although interest in the proceedings beyond the families of those involved was limited.[6] In general, audiences tended to be noisy, with members talking to each other, some with unruly children and the frequent intrusion of mobile phones. Court officers often had to take steps to restore order and quiet. In a few cases, tensions were high where family members of the defendant and victim were in close proximity and emotions spilled over.[7]

In general, the opening of the court proceedings followed a set pattern. The judge brought order to the court by using a gavel to enforce silence and the courtroom actors sat at their designated positions. Thereafter, the judge would take steps to ascertain the

---

[4] The practice of wearing uniforms and robes varied from site to site. In some of the rural and poorer areas, judges wore robes in occasional and important cases. See, to the same effect, Stephanie Balme (2010). Stephanie Balme found that at the local Basic Court level in Gansu and Shaanxi, 'only during important trials do judges wear a robe, which they share with others' (at p. 170).

[5] In Site E, for example, the court facilities were old and shabby and the prosecutor and plaintiffs in the associated civil actions had to share a table.

[6] In a few instances, the court was relocated to a large hall in the police college to enable student officers to view an 'exemplary' or 'demonstration' trial. In general, however, the audience was small in number or non-existent.

[7] In L-CO-X-19, a case of robbery resulting in the death of the victim, the relatives of the victim physically attacked the defendant in court; and in E-CO-L-15 the court hearing had to be postponed to another day after the families of the victim and defendant fought outside the court. On re-convening the hearing, the judge spoke to both sides, drafted in additional police officers, separated the families into different seating rows and photographed and video-taped members of the audience. It is reported that members of the audience cried 'Kill, Kill' in a June 2009 Chongqing trial of Zhang Qingyang. See http://peacehall.com/news/gb/china/2009/06/200906120447.shtml.

defendant's status, set out the defendant's litigation rights and ask the defendant to confirm his or her understanding of those rights.[8] The following is a typical example as recorded by our researcher in Site F:

> When the defendant is brought into the courtroom, the case-responsible judge uses a gavel to declare the opening of the court session.
> The case-responsible judge asks the defendant relevant information, such as the name, other name, date of birth, nationality, education, occupation, family address, date of detention or/and arrest, whether the defendant has any criminal record so as to verify the status. The defendant answers one by one in the same way as in the information in the Bill of Prosecution.
> The case-responsible judge asks the defendant if he received a copy of the Bill of Prosecution ten days earlier.
> *Defendant:* Yes.
> The case-responsible judge announces the name list of the collegial panel, court clerk, public prosecutors, and stenographer. The case-responsible judge informs the defendant of his rights: right to apply for the withdrawal and the right to apply witness' appearance to testify in court, the right to defend by himself or to employ a lawyer as defender, the right to make a final statement.
> According to the Article 152 of the Criminal Procedure Law, it will be an open trial. The case-responsible judge declares the collegiate bench, court clerk and name of the prosecutor. The defendant has the following rights: First, the right to apply for a replacement of officers in the court, if you think that any of the officers in the court have a conflict of interest in this case and may affect the fairness of the trial, you have the right to replace the officers. Does the defendant apply for the replacement?
> *Defendant:* I do not apply.

Presentation appears to be important as one measure for securing legitimacy. Defence lawyers commonly wore suits or casual clothing, but when a foreigner was being tried amid intense media interest, the judge asked the defence lawyer to wear robes (Case E-CO-L-16).[9] Similarly, all courtroom actors wore their full regalia whenever an exemplary trial was held, for the benefit, in our field sites, of novitiate police officers[10] or visiting dignitaries. However, there were many indications that the image of procedural fidelity and institutional form was rather thin and that the significance of the trial and of the courtroom actors was less than that which the system sought to project.[11]

The most obvious crack in the courtroom façade was the role of the collegial panel of judges. While on paper the judgment in a case is that of the court – a panel of judges or judges and lay assessors – in practice two of the three members of the panel played no role at all, all relevant actions in court being handled by the judge who was in charge of that case – the case-responsible judge (*chengban faguan*). This case-responsible judge promulgated the rights of the defendant, controlled the actions of the prosecutor and defence lawyer, undertook the questioning of the defendant and imposed order in the court. It was exceptional for any other collegial panel member to become involved in the proceedings. Indeed, other panel members were commonly, and openly, engaged in

---

[8] The rights in question track the requirements laid down in Article 154, 1996 CPL.
[9] The robes worn by the lawyer carried the emblem of the Bar Association on the front.
[10] As in cases: D-CO-K-07 and D-CO-K-08.
[11] It is noteworthy in this context that there have been suggestions recently to remove judges' robes because they are perceived as inappropriately western. See also, Stephanie Balme (2009c).

unrelated activities such as working on their own case papers, answering telephones,[12] leaving the courtroom for periods of time, occasionally smoking or dozing off to sleep.[13]

This was not confined to minor cases but extended to serious cases as in J-CO-S4-10 (a drugs case in which both defendants received ten years in prison[14]); in L-CO-X-09 (a fraud case in which the sentence was life imprisonment); M-CO-Y-05 (intentional injury); L-CO-X-12 (bribery); and L-CO-X-22 (two defendants faced homicide charges).[15] In other cases, judges or Assessors fell asleep during the hearing, as in: E-CO-L-01 (a robbery case in which the victim had died); E-CO-L-02 (intentional homicide in which the sentence was the Death Penalty, suspended for two years); E-CO-L-03 (intentional injury in which one defendant received life imprisonment and the other 15 years). In one drug trafficking case (J-CO-S4-08), the defendant spoke throughout in Cantonese but only one of the judges was a Cantonese speaker and only occasionally did he translate what was being said for the benefit of the other judges. In a few cases, judges discarded their robes and conducted the hearing in T-shirts and in other cases the judges smoked during the trial (as in E-CO-L-14, an intentional homicide case during which the prosecutor went out of the courtroom to make telephone calls) or made or received telephone calls.

The presentational image of the courtroom was further put into question by the appearance of the defendants. In many respects, the defendant population was not unlike that seen in western criminal law courts. Of those whose information was known, some 91.0 per cent were males, mostly (61.0 per cent) under the age of 30,[16] with poor educational backgrounds (60.0 per cent having been educated only up to Junior Middle School with a full 25.0 per cent having attended only primary school), no employment[17] and with

---

[12] It was not uncommon either for prosecutors to take calls on their mobiles while the trial was in progress.

[13] See also, Stephanie Balme (2010) who found that (in Gansu and Shaanxi Provinces), although the judicial Code of Conduct prohibited smoking, drinking and the use of mobile phones in court, '[a]ctually, in almost all people's tribunals the air is suffocating from heavy smoking, and mobile phones ring during the trials simply because judges share the same lifestyle as the litigants' (p. 176). In addition, in some (not very often) cases, our researchers also witnessed the judges smoking, as in Site E's courtroom observations. In fact, there are similar reports about judges dozing off to sleep or smoking. E.g. a set of pictures was posted in a website showing 'strange phenomenon' of a court trial in Xichong County, where the presiding judge received phone calls, two other judges dressed casually and one judge smoked on 3 January 2008. See 'Xichong Court: Presiding Judge Received Phone Calls, while the Other Judges Wear Informal Dress', 4 January 2008, available at http://leaders.people.com.cn/GB/6735167.html. This also led to social criticism of the judges for treating the trial as an informal event.

[14] In this case, both the case-responsible judge and prosecutor took a telephone call during the hearing and one of the other judges left the courtroom for some three minutes while the hearing continued.

[15] In one case (E-CO-L-10) in which the victim had been killed, the family of the victim had failed to submit a civil claim for compensation in writing. Accordingly, one of the judges sat besides the family of the victim throughout the trial, spoke noisily to them and made written notes. The conversation between this judge and the family was so loud that our researcher was not able to hear all of what the defendant said during the hearing.

[16] Altogether, some 4.1 per cent were below the age of 18 and a further 31.5 per cent were between 18 and 25 years of age.

[17] Because they had been detained before trial, none were in employment at the time of the hearing. Of those who declared a status, 47.4 per cent said that they were unemployed, 14.5 per

a significant minority (25.0 per cent) being migrants.[18] Some were clearly confused when questions were put to them[19] and looked around in puzzlement when simple questions were put. Thus, in M-CO-Y-12, for example, when the defendant was asked whether he wanted any court member to withdraw, the judge had to explain what his rights were since he did not understand the meaning of the question. Most defendants adopted a subservient and compliant position throughout the trial. For example, in J-CO-S4-16 on a charge of intentional homicide, the defendant, a 31-year old male educated to primary school level was questioned by the prosecutor and the following colloquy took place:

Prosecutor: Are your confessions in the Public Security Bureau true?

Defendant: I don't know.

Prosecutor: Did you read the records?

Defendant: No.

Prosecutor: How do you explain your signature and finger print?

Defendant: I didn't know what it was about at all. I am an illiterate.

There were, however, two other significant features of the defendants that undermined the image of a neutral and objective trial system. The first, and most obvious, was the dress and appearance of defendants. In each court, almost all defendants were produced from detention, often in slippers and with shaved heads, wearing a bright orange or red vest marked 'Detention House', restricted by handcuffs and, in some instances, shackles.[20] This did not give the appearance of a system that was about to inquire into guilt or innocence.[21]

The second feature was the isolation of the defendant. Where they were represented,[22] defendants were physically separated from their lawyer giving the impression to the

---

cent said that they were self-employed or farmers and 29.6 per cent stated that they had been in employment.

[18] There may have been more migrants because the status of some defendants was not recorded by the researchers in some instances.

[19] For example, in J-CO-S4-16.

[20] In one court, the judge routinely asked the judicial police to take the handcuffs off at the start of the proceedings. It should be noted that defendants may be restrained in certain cases in other countries (e.g., USA, UK, Italy, France and Germany) but this would not be normal practice.

[21] There are occasional reports about defendants being beaten in the courtroom. One such report concerns the case of rights-defender Yang Chunlin, tried in January 2008 for subversion by Jiamusi Intermediate Court in Heilongjiang. He was hooded, handcuffed and shackled and even though his lawyers persuaded the authorities to remove the hood, handcuffs and leg irons, he was chained to an iron chair throughout the four-hour trial. At the end of his trial he was led out – again shackled, handcuffed and hooded – by the court's police officers. Just as he was turning round (perhaps to greet family members), the officers used an electric baton to knock him to the ground, according to a statement by his son. See, for example, http://www.amnestyusa.org/actioncenter/actions/uaa24007.pdf and http://www.peacehall.com/news/gb/china/2008/03/200803261114.shtml.

[22] Almost one-fifth of defendants had no legal representative.

onlooker that no one was on their side. It was even more noticeable where the lawyer was court-appointed: in such cases, the defendant might have no idea who the lawyer was. Thus, in F-CO-N-01, at the outset of the hearing, the case-responsible judge addressed the three defendants charged with robbery and the following colloquy took place:

> *Judge:* According to Article 152 of the Criminal Law, this case is not to be heard in public. [The judge then announces the name list of the collegiate panel, the court clerk, the prosecutor and the court-appointed defender, and the rights of the defendants]: '1) the right to apply for somebody's withdrawal, [Defendants 2 and 3 are looking around], that is if you think anybody I named just now has an interest in this case, and his presence may affect the impartiality of the trial, you may request the withdrawal of that person. Defendants, do you need anybody to withdraw?'
>
> *Defendant 1:* No.
>
> *Defendant 2:* Yes. [The defendant becomes silent for a while. The judge asks whose withdrawal he requests, but he doesn't say. He finally says he does not need anybody to withdraw after the judge's re-explanation.]
>
> *Defendant 3:* Yes. [He looks at everyone, and especially the defence lawyer. The judge explains that the defence lawyer is not one of the categories of persons that he can ask to withdraw. After that, he states that he does not apply for anybody's withdrawal.]

In this case, it was plain to an observer that there was not a close relationship between the defendant and the lawyer and that what insights the lawyer was able to bring in such a case derived less from the defendant and more from the prosecution file or, exceptionally, from information provided by the family of the defendant or by the defendant's unit.

SUMMARY TRIALS

As we have seen, the 1996 CPL provides that the court may apply summary procedure, in which the case will be tried by a single judge alone, in certain defined circumstances as set out in Article 174:[23]

(1) cases of public prosecution where the defendants may be lawfully sentenced to fixed-term imprisonment of not more than three years, criminal detention, public surveillance or punished with fines exclusively, where the facts are clear and the evidence is sufficient, and for which the People's Procuratorate suggests or agrees to the application of summary procedure;
(2) cases to be handled only upon complaint; and
(3) cases prosecuted by the victims, for which there is evidence to prove that they are minor criminal cases.

As can be seen from Table 10.1, in our samples, a total of 23 trials involving 24 defendants were tried according to summary procedure.[24]

---

[23] All of the cases we observed fell within Article 174(1), 1996 CPL.
[24] In nine research sites no summary trials were held during our observations.

Table 10.1 Type of procedure utilized in sample cases

Trial procedure	BC Sites		IC Sites	
	No. of cases	Percentage	No. of cases	Percentage
Summary procedure	23	17.7	0	0.0
Simplified ordinary procedure	6	4.6	1	1.0
Ordinary procedure	101	77.7	96	99.0
Total	130	100.0	97	100.0

Summary procedure is, in effect, meant to be a speedy method for dealing with individuals who accept the prosecution case and intend to plead guilty. The hearing is presided over by a single judge and provision is made under Article 175, 1996 CPL for this to be done in the absence of a prosecutor. In our cases, no prosecutors attended summary trials and only four defendants had the benefit of legal representation.

The defendants were almost exclusively drawn from the lower echelons of society. Most were unemployed males[25] whose education did not go beyond primary school.[26] In the typical case, the defendant had been caught in the act by the victim, security guards or had been captured following a 'hue and cry' by bystanders or 'the masses', as the following examples show:

D-CO-K-15 [theft of a mobile telephone]

Judge: How were you caught?

Defendant: By the victim.

D-CO-K-11 [theft of motorcycle]

Defendant: Just after I got the lock off the motorcycle, the owner came back and caught me.

While five defendants were aged 40 or over, most were young men between the ages of 19 and 25 who had engaged in opportunist theft whilst down on their luck[27] as in F-CO-N-09: 'I came to [the City] to look for a job but I couldn't find one. I didn't have any money so I stole.'

In line with expectations, judges disposed of these summary cases, both criminal and any related civil mediation, in a speedy fashion as can be seen in Table 10.2.

As Table 10.2 shows, altogether 91.3 per cent of defendants (21) were dealt with in 40 minutes or less with almost 60 per cent being disposed of in 20 minutes or less:[28] the

---

[25] One defendant was a female maid who had stolen from her employer.
[26] In three cases where information was available, the defendant had received education up to junior middle school level.
[27] We were unable to gather systematic information on residential status. Of the nine where information was available, seven were migrants.
[28] The shortest trial lasted only three minutes, the longest 65 minutes.

268 Criminal justice in China

Table 10.2 Length of the trial (cases tried under summary procedure)

Content/Site	BC Sites		IC Sites	
	No. of cases	Percentage	No. of cases	Percentage
Less than 20 minutes	13	56.5	0	0.0
21–30 minutes	6	26.1	0	0.0
31–40 minutes	2	8.7	0	0.0
41–50 minutes	1	4.3	0	0.0
51–60 minutes	0	0.0	0	0.0
More than 1 hour and less than 2 hours	1	4.3	0	0.0
Not known	0	0.0	0	0.0
Total	23	99.9	0	0.0

one case which took more than one hour to resolve was one in which the defendant was legally represented.[29] In no case was any witness produced in court: the hearings were all 'on paper'. A feature of the trials was the speed at which the dialogue proceeded with judges intent on conducting proceedings at a rapid pace so that defendants[30] barely had time to hear what was being said before a response was demanded so that the trial could move forward at its unforgiving speed.[31]

Although there was some variation in the degree of seriousness of the crimes involved, the charges were generally at the lesser end of the crime continuum. Over two-thirds (79.2 per cent) were charges of theft, three (12.5 per cent) involved drugs, one (4.1 per cent) intentional injury, one case (4.1 per cent) involved false imprisonment and another (4.1 per cent) injury caused by breach of safety regulations at a construction site. Although all custodial, the sentences handed down tended to reflect the relatively minor character of the occurrence.[32] Of the trials completed (22 involving 23 defendants),[33] the substantial majority (19 or 86.4 per cent) received a sentence of imprisonment of one year or less,[34] with no defendant receiving a sentence of three years' imprisonment at the limit of summary jurisdiction.[35]

A typical example of the hearing of a summary trial is set out below. The case involved a charge of simple theft. The defendant was not legally represented and no prosecutor

---

[29] The other three cases in which there was legal representation for the defendant were disposed of in less than 30 minutes each.

[30] It also meant that in some cases our researchers could not take an exact or verbatim note.

[31] Our findings on the length of trial in summary procedure are similar to those of Zuo Weimin (2007b) and Xiao Shiwei (2008).

[32] This is so notwithstanding that in one instance arising out of a workplace accident a death had been caused.

[33] One case arising out of an accident at a construction site in which the defective installation of scaffolding caused the death of one worker and injury to six others was adjourned after a 45-minute hearing for later judgment.

[34] Most of these (12) received six months or less.

[35] One defendant received a sentence of two years' imprisonment and two others received 18 months in prison.

appeared. No witnesses for either prosecution or defence were produced. The defendant did not challenge any of the principal allegations. The account is drawn from the notes of the researcher:

> Summary procedure is applied in this case, so there is only one adjudicator in this case. The case-responsible judge is a female around 50-years old, wearing a black judge's robe with the national emblem at the front. In addition, there is a female court clerk about 30-years old and dressed in uniform.
> There is no prosecutor.
> There is one defendant, male, about 40-years old, around 1.70 m height, dressed casually with a purple jacket and slippers. One of his hands is handcuffed.
> There is no defence lawyer.
> There are two male bailiffs, around 25–30-years old, wearing police uniforms in black with numbered badges at the front and wearing police caps.
> There are no members of the audience in the courtroom other than me.
> This case occurred on 24 October 2006, at about 1800 hours. The defendant used a pair of tweezers to take 1200 Yuan from the pocket of the victim's jacket while the victim was reading the newspaper. The defendant was discovered and was caught by the victim. The defendant is charged with theft.

Section A: Ascertain the defendant's status and announce litigation rights.

When the defendant is brought into the courtroom, the case-responsible judge asks the defendant relevant information, such as his name, other name, date of birth, nationality, education, occupation, family address, date of detention or/and arrest, whether the defendant has any criminal record so as to verify his status. The defendant answers one by one, the same as recorded in the Bill of Prosecution.

Judge: When did you receive the copy of the Bill of Prosecution?

Answer: On 14 October 2006.

Judge: According to Article 174 of the Criminal Law, this case is to be heard in public. Li will judge the case solely; Wang will be the court clerk. The defendant has: 1) the right to apply for somebody's withdrawal, that is if you think anybody I named just now has an interest in this case, and his presence may affect the impartiality of the trial, you may request the withdrawal of that person. Defendant, do you need anybody to withdraw?

Defendant: No.

Judge: Second, you have the right to conduct the defence by yourself. Apart from that, you also have the right to legal representation. Third, you have the right to apply to notify new witnesses to testify in court, submit new material evidence, and to request another identification and inquest. Fourth, you have the right to make a final statement after the court debate. The defendant has all the rights that I just mentioned, do you understand?

Defendant: Clear.

Section B: Court investigation.

Judge: The defendant may sit down. Now let's start the court investigation. Let the clerk read out the Bill of Prosecution [omitted]. Now do you wish to speak regarding the allegations stated in the Bill of Prosecution?

Defendant: No.

Judge: Why did you steal the money?

Defendant: I came to [the City] to look for a job, but I couldn't find one. I didn't have any money, so I stole.

Judge: Now, I will read out the relevant evidence materials. First, read out the report of filing the case and the statement of the victim, to prove the source of the case. [Reading omitted] Defendant, do you have any objection?

Defendant: No.

Judge: Produce the document about the process of catching the defendant to prove the time when the defendant was apprehended. Defendant, do you have any objection?

Defendant: No.

Judge: Produce the note regarding seizing the stolen goods, and the list of goods seized. Defendant, do you have any objection?

Defendant: No.

Judge: Produce the photos showing the identification of the crime scene and the goods stolen to prove the place of the crime, the goods stolen and the tools used for criminal purpose. [The bailiff shows the photos to the defendant for identification and confirmation.]

Judge: Defendant, do you have any objection?

Defendant: No.

Judge: Produce the witness statement, to prove the fact of the defendant's crime. Defendant, do you have any objection?

Defendant: No.

Judge: The evidences produced are objective and real. The court shall confirm. Defendant, do you have evidence to produce to the court?

Defendant: No.

Judge: Defendant, do you need to call any new witnesses, submit any new material evidence, or conduct any new identification or inquest?

Defendant: No.

Section C: Court debate.

Judge: Do you wish to debate this case?

Defendant: No.

The prosecution observed 271

Section D: Make a final statement.

Judge: According to Article 160 of the Code of Criminal Procedure, the defendant shall be endowed with the right of making a final statement before the judgment is made. Now, let defendant make a final statement.

Defendant: No.

Section E: Deliberation and announcement of the judgment.

Judge: The following is the judgment (Defendant stands up). The defendant committed the offence of theft and is sentenced to a fixed-term imprisonment of six months and 1000 Yuan fine. The written judgment will be delivered to the defendant within five days. If anyone refuses to accept the judgment, he may appeal to this court or directly to the Intermediate People's Court within ten days after receiving the written judgment. One original copy and two duplicates of the written judgment have to be submitted when filing a written appeal.

Judge: Defendant, are you clear?

Defendant: Yes.

Judge: Do you have any opinion on the judgment?

Defendant: No.

Judge: Now let's end the trial. Take the defendant from the court.
[The trial lasted nine minutes.]

In general, summary cases followed this pattern which was barely disturbed in those few instances where the defendant was legally represented. Thus, for example, in F-CO-N-16, where the charge was intentionally inflicting bodily injury (a minor cut to the victim's face), the intervention of the defence lawyer was confined to a plea in mitigation as set out below, the whole trial lasting 15 minutes:

> *Defence Lawyer:* First, I have no objection to the accusation of the prosecution that the defendant committed intentional injury. However, it occurred when the defendant was drunk and the defendant admitted his guilt in a good manner. Relatives of the defendant have compensated the victim. The circumstance in this case is obviously minor and has not caused any harm to society. For the above reasons, I hope the court can give the defendant a suspended sentence.[36]

Throughout, defendants expressed no objection – usually in one word – to the case for the prosecution both in terms of the overall allegation and in respect of the details contained in the statements in the files including their confessions to the police. In a few cases the defendant offered a comment on a witness statement to correct some minor point. Thus, for example, in M-CO-Y-11, on a charge of theft of various items, the defendant accepted the prosecution case in its entirety but, after the victim's statement had been read to him by the judge, said: 'I stole 1700 catties not 2000 catties'[37] and, after hearing

---

[36] The plea was not successful, the defendant receiving a term of imprisonment of eight months.
[37] A catty is a unit of weight representing in China 500 grams.

Table 10.3 Length of the trial (cases tried under simplified ordinary procedure)

Content/Site	BC Sites		IC Sites	
	No. of cases	Percentage	No. of cases	Percentage
Less than 20 minutes	1	16.7	0	0.0
21–30 minutes	0	0.0	0	0.0
31–40 minutes	1	16.7	0	0.0
41–50 minutes	0	0.0	0	0.0
51–60 minutes	1	16.7	1	100.0
More than 1 hour and less than 2 hours	3	50.0	0	0.0
Not known	0	0.0	0	0.0
Total	6	100.0	1	100.0

a witness statement, added: 'I object: the electric machine was not stolen by me.' Such interventions, in this and other cases, were not challenged when they were made or when commented upon in the judgment which invariably stated that the defendant 'does not object to the facts of the case' and that the 'evidence is clear and sufficient'.

Summary procedure cases follow a pattern in which the evidence against the defendant is elicited through the reading of the various items of evidence in the prosecution file and securing the defendant's acceptance of that evidence. For the rest, the contribution of the defendant was restricted directly or indirectly to a plea for leniency as, for example: 'I hope the court will give me lenient punishment';[38] 'I don't have any defence: I will work hard in prison and reform myself.'[39]

SIMPLIFIED ORDINARY PROCEDURE

In a few cases (seven trials involving a total of ten defendants), the court dealt with the allegation by way of simplified ordinary procedure.[40] These cases on the whole took longer than in summary cases, as Table 10.3 demonstrates.

Apart from the presence of a collegial panel, the procedure is little different from that in summary cases although a prosecutor is present and the defendant is more likely to be legally represented.[41] However, since the defendant is pleading guilty, any legal representative can only assist by tendering a plea in mitigation. An example of this procedure is the case of I-CO-S3-04 in which the 30-year old local defendant was charged with

---

[38] Case F-CO-N-05. See also, Case M-CO-Y-20: 'I have no objection to the facts but I have already paid compensation to the victim in the form of cash. This is not reflected in the Bill of Prosecution.'

[39] Case M-CO-Y-04.

[40] The authorization for this procedure is found in the Several Opinions of the Supreme People's Court, the Supreme People's Procuratorate and the Ministry of Justice on Applying Ordinary Procedure to Try Cases in Which the Defendant Pleaded Guilty, 14 March 2003.

[41] Legal representation is implied in the Opinion because under Article 5 of the Opinion the court is required to notify 'the defendant and the defendant's lawyer'.

misappropriation of public funds. As a bank teller, the defendant systematically stole money from the bank to support a gambling addiction. At trial, he indicated that he would plead guilty and did not contest any of the evidence led against him. The defence lawyer employed by the defendant's family did not challenge any prosecution evidence and confined his intervention to a few questions put to the defendant to establish lax supervisory practices in the bank:

> *Defence Lawyer:* When you were serving as a teller, normally how many people would be involved in collecting money? Are there any rules in your company governing this?
>
> *Defendant:* Normally there should be two persons, but actually it was only me alone.
>
> *Defence Lawyer:* Did that commonly exist in your unit?
>
> *Defendant:* Yes, our system was rather loose, nobody bothered.
>
> *Defence Lawyer:* You said all the money was used in soccer gambling: can you explain why you needed to participate in soccer gambling?
>
> *Defendant:* Because I had already lost a lot of money, therefore I used public funds for gambling, but I never thought that the situation would become more and more serious.

This line of questioning helped lay the foundation for the plea in mitigation:

> *Defence Lawyer:* [Case-responsible] judge, I am entrusted by the family of the defendant to defend the defendant; the following are my defence opinions: (1) the defendant admitted his guilt voluntarily during today's trial: he has a good attitude in admitting his guilt, he has frankly confessed his crime; (2) the defendant was arrested because his parents assisted the police in arresting him. While the defendant was on the run, he contacted his family by mobile phone. The defendant's parents knew the defendant's hiding place and they reported this to the police and then the defendant was arrested; (3) as a teller, the defendant committed crimes 40–50 times within a few months; such an occurrence is inconceivable in the banking sector. If the bank had strictly enforced the rules, this case could have been prevented. There are loopholes in the management of the bank which allowed this crime to take place. Also, the defendant does not have any previous criminal record. Therefore, I hope the court can take these factors into account.

The court took into account the defendant's good attitude in confessing the crime in court and accordingly imposed a sentence of 14 years' imprisonment.

As a general rule, the case-responsible judge took the lead role in handling cases dealt with by simplified ordinary procedure at least to the extent of ensuring that the basic facts of the crime were on the public record. Thus, in M-CO-Y-05, on a charge of intentional injury arising out of a dispute between farmers[42] over farm water, after the prosecutor read out the Bill of Prosecution, the case-responsible judge invited the prosecutor to begin but, being dissatisfied with the perfunctory manner of questioning, took over the interrogation:

---

[42] The defendant spoke in dialect, the judge encouraging him to try to speak Putonghua.

Judge: Prosecutor, you may question the defendant.

Prosecutor: Defendant, is your confession made during the stage of police investigation true?

Defendant: True.

Prosecutor: No other questions.

Judge: Defendant, you were competing for the farm water; was the water released by you or him?

Defendant: He released the water.

Judge: Where did the water come from?

Defendant: It came from the pool I used; he should not release the water.

Judge: [Witness Hua] said the victim chased after you for 200 to 300 metres before you threw the bowl at him: who was there at the scene?

Defendant: People from our village such as Li, Hua and Lin. Ho could also see that.

Judge: After the occurrence of the case, where did you go?

Defendant: I went to other places.

Judge: Is it true that you came back to surrender yourself subsequently?

Defendant: Yes.

Another example is provided by F-CO-N-02, a charge of robbery involving three defendants.[43] Since none of the defendants was disputing the charge of robbery, the principal task of the hearing was to identify the parts each played so as to determine who took the lead role and who acted in a subordinate capacity. In line with the usual practice, the prosecutor questioned each defendant in turn while the other defendants were taken out of the courtroom. As each defendant was produced, the prosecutor asked a few simple questions to determine who had initiated the robbery. D1 said: 'D2 proposed: I seconded.' When D2 was asked, D2 replied: 'D1.' When D3 was produced, the prosecutor stated: 'Since D3 does not dispute the facts of the crime and the amount involved, I am not going to question him.' Since the prosecutor had failed to disentangle the roles of each party, the case-responsible judge took over:

Judge: Bring D1 and D2 to the court. Let's start the cross-examination.

Judge: D3, who asked you to bring knives?

D3: D2. I brought three knives, one for myself and one for Y [the one who escaped], and I gave one to D2 before the robbery.

---

[43] A fourth individual implicated in the occurrence escaped capture.

D2: Gave one.

Judge: D1, who suggested the robbery?

D1: D2.

Judge: D2, was D1's answer true?

D2: It was D1 who asked me to rob.

D1: This is not true. It was he who made the proposal every time.

Judge: D1, who proposed the robbery?

D1: D2.

D3: D2.

D2: This is true.

This enabled the court to differentiate the responsibilities of each party and to reflect this in the sentences imposed.[44] The role of the judge in this regard was not untypical. Wherever possible, judges allied themselves with the prosecutor and, where they were able to, made good the deficiencies of the prosecutor's case presentation.[45]

This is far from saying that the adoption of simplified ordinary procedure is unproblematic particularly where the defendant is unrepresented. In M-CO-Y-05 above, for example, the unrepresented defendant did not contest the charge and confessed that he had thrown the bowl which injured the victim. His account of the circumstances giving rise to the incident was not, however, pursued by anyone. The investigative stage opened with the prosecutor reading out the Bill of Prosecution after which the hearing continued as follows:

Judge: Defendant, have you listened clearly to the Bill of Prosecution just read out to you?

Defendant: Yes.

Judge: Do you have any objection as to the facts of the crime alleged in the Bill of Prosecution?

Defendant: No.

Judge: Do you have any objection as to the pleading of the incidental civil action that was just read out by the plaintiff in the incidental civil action?
[Researcher's note: The defendant didn't know how to answer. The judge said: 'The victim asked you to pay RMB 120000 to compensate various fees and expenses, do you have any opinion?']

---

[44] In this instance, D1 received a sentence of nine years' imprisonment and RMB 5000 fine while the other defendants each received a sentence of eight years' imprisonment and RMB 5000 fine.

[45] In M-CO-Y-05, for example, the judge immediately rectified an error that the prosecutor made in the Bill of Prosecution.

Defendant: Yes, the course of the case as stated in my written record is the truth. He was carrying a hoe and rushing towards me at that time. I then threw the bowl at him. My health is poor, my left leg cannot function. I don't have so much money to pay the compensation now.

Judge: Prosecutor, you may question the defendant.

It is obvious here that on the defendant's account, which was supported by the accounts given by other prosecution witnesses, a lawyer would have argued that the defendant's actions, particularly given his state of health and his attempt to flee from the victim's aggression, laid a foundation for self-defence. In the absence of a lawyer, this line of argument was lost in the rush to judgment.

ORDINARY PROCEDURE

The vast majority of trials (197 or 86.8 per cent) were conducted according to ordinary procedure. The hearing, before a collegial panel, consists of an introductory stage during which the basic formalities are dealt with (including the names of the panel of judges, court clerks, prosecutors etc.), the court investigation stage, the court debate, the final statements of the parties and the judgment. Before looking in more detail as to what happens at each stage, we make some general observations which the reader needs to keep in mind in seeking an understanding of these trials.

These are essentially paper hearings. With limited exceptions, which will be documented later, no witnesses are produced to give evidence or to be cross-examined. The 'evidence' laid out in the hearing comprises statements taken from the defendant, victims, witnesses, records of inquests and examinations, expert conclusions, photographic evidence of the crime scene and such like as documented in Table 10.4.

In a system in which the suspect does not have a right to silence and, indeed, has an obligation to answer questions truthfully, there is a heavy reliance upon statements (usually 'confessions') alleged to have been made at the police station or before the prosecutor.

Apart from statements of defendants and of individuals said to have witnessed the

Table 10.4 Prosecution evidence led at trial[1]

Evidence species	BC Sites		IC Sites	
	No. of cases	Percentage	No. of cases	Percentage
Material or documentary evidence	76	60.3	81	85.3
Testimony of witnesses	90	72.0	92	96.8
The statement of victim	69	69.7	21	22.1
The defendant's statement	125	100.0	97	100.0
Document on expert conclusion	82	80.4	87	91.6
Record of inquest and examination	18	18.8	57	60.0
Audio-visual materials	7	7.4	2	2.1

Note: 1. This table includes all trials both summary and ordinary procedure.

crime or to have heard about the crime,[46] much of the other evidence is formalistic in nature and often contributes nothing to the resolution of the defendant's guilt or innocence.[47] Thus, the relevance of statements taken from victims in general (such as those stating that property was stolen) is directed to establishing that a crime was committed rather than pointing to the actual perpetrator of the crime. Similarly, generally records of inquest and examination are of importance only in establishing the cause of death (a blow with a blunt instrument, a stab wound and the like) or the extent of injury and do not usually implicate a particular person or, indeed, a particular weapon. In like manner, expert conclusions usually are limited to documenting the value of items stolen or damaged or the nature of the substance seized (as in drugs cases).

In many areas in China, the police do not have advanced equipment or possess modern investigative skills. Hearings are generally not forensic exercises in which the tribunal is charged with deciding upon the facts in a detailed manner. In this system, a general admission of involvement will be regarded as sufficient and allow the court to disregard inconsistencies (such as multiple statements to police which are contradictory) or challenges to details; and attempts by the defence to put the occurrence giving rise to the charge into context through reference to such matters as drink, self-defence or excessive defence, may be ignored and the various roles of accomplices may not be sorted out with any degree of care.

Where the defendant is represented, the intrusion of the defence lawyer will, in general, be directed towards mitigation of sentence rather than towards contesting the evidence or the charge. Given that the defence lawyers will have been engaged only shortly before the trial,[48] in the absence of any extensive pre-trial preparation, defence lawyers are heavily reliant upon what is in the prosecution file or upon material that by chance emerges during the hearing. In addition, almost one in five defendants does not have the benefit of legal representation and their capacity to challenge the prosecution is limited.

Given this overall structure, it is hardly surprising that hearings are rapid events. For the most part, the investigative part of trials consists of the prosecution reading out each piece of evidence (often in fact only a summary of it), ascertaining whether there is any objection to it and, whether or not any objection is registered, reading out/paraphrasing the next piece of evidence and repeating the process until the last item is concluded. In the absence of active defence representation, the hearing moves forward at speed, as is disclosed by Table 10.5 which documents the length of all trials dealt with by ordinary procedure in our sample.

---

[46] There is no rule against hearsay evidence in China.

[47] See, for comparison, the translated verdict against Hu Jia, available at http://www.cecc.gov/pages/virtualAcad/index.phpd?showsingle=107396. 'Witness Zeng Jinyan [Hu Jia's wife] testified: Zeng Jinyan and Hu Jia have two laptop computers at their BOBO Freedom City, Tongzhou District residence. Zeng Jinyan and Hu Jia each use his or her own computer; Hu Jia uses his silvery-white computer to write essays and publish them online.' See also Cohen and Pils (2008). The impression gained by Cohen and Pils was that these 'witness' statements were collected (a) to torment friends of the defendant and (b) to provide a 'reason' for excluding them from the trial audience. See further Liu Xiaobo's verdict in translation available at http://lawprofessors.typepad.com/china_law_prof_blog/2009/12/verdict-in-liu-xiaobo-case-english-translation.html.

[48] This is manifestly the case with court-assigned lawyers but is also commonly true of those instructed by the defendant's family.

Table 10.5 Length of the trial in cases disposed of by ordinary procedure

Content/Site	BC Sites No. of cases	BC Sites Percentage	IC Sites No. of cases	IC Sites Percentage
Less than 20 minutes	9	9.1	2	2.2
21–30 minutes	11	11.1	0	0.0
31–40 minutes	10	10.1	7	7.5
41–50 minutes	20	20.2	4	4.3
51–60 minutes	17	17.2	18	19.4
More than 1 hour and less than 2 hours	24	24.2	44	47.3
More than 2 hours and less than 3 hours	4	4.0	13	14.0
More than 3 hours and less than 4 hours	0	0.0	2	2.2
More than 4 hours	4	4.0	3	3.2
Not known	3	–	3	–
Total	102	99.9	96	100.0

It is clear from Table 10.5 that the overwhelming majority of trials in both the Basic Court and Intermediate Court are disposed of in less than two hours, with, in the Basic Court, a substantial majority (67.7 per cent) and, in Intermediate Court, a substantial minority (33.3 per cent) being dealt with in less than one hour.[49]

COURT INVESTIGATION STAGE

The Prosecutor

The role of the prosecutor and nature and direction of the investigative stage of the trial tends very much to be determined by the stance taken by the defence. Where the involvement of the defendant in the crime is not contested, there may be no or minimal questioning of the defendant by the prosecutor with the defendant's acceptance of guilt being elicited by means of a series of simple interrogatories.

An example of this is J-CO-S4-05, a case of intentional killing contrary to Article 234(2) of the Criminal Law. The defendant, having been called by a friend to help beat up X at a cafe, was knocked by a car door being opened by V. This incident resulted in a quarrel in the course of which V was stabbed several times and died from his wounds. The defendant was represented by a court-assigned lawyer. After the prosecutor read out the Bill of Prosecution detailing the occurrence, the following exchange took place:

Judge: Defendant, you are charged with intentional injury. Do you admit your crime?

---

[49] At least during *Strike Hard* campaigns, one measure of 'success' has been the time taken in dealing with a case from start to finish. In the campaign from 2001 to 2003, for example, the Intermediate Court was awarded an advanced collective by Anhui Higher Court for dealing with 682 *Strike Hard* cases in which no cases had been overturned in the higher court or sent for re-trial nor had any defendant appealed or prosecutor protested: see, The Rights Practice (2003) at p. 33.

Defendant: I admit the crime.

Judge: Do you have any opinion on the facts of crime charged as stated in the Bill of Prosecution?

Defendant: No.

Judge: Let the prosecutor interrogate the defendant.

Prosecutor: Why did you go to the site of the incident? What did you want to do there?

Defendant: My friend asked me to help her.

Judge: Help to do what?

Defendant: To beat the woman who was intimate with her boyfriend.

Judge: Who took the knife that was used to stab the victim?

Defendant: Another two of my friends.

Judge: How many times did you stab the victim?

Defendant: Twice.

Judge: Where did you stab?

Defendant: Buttock and legs.

Judge: Do you have any questions for the defendant, defence lawyer?

Defence Lawyer: No.

Second Judge: How did the quarrel break out?

Defendant: We were waiting for cars. The taxi stopped beside me. The victim opened the door and the door touched me. I scolded him, saying he was blind, and then we quarrelled.

Second Judge: What features did the person you stabbed have?

Defendant: The short one.

Second Judge: When were you apprehended?

Defendant: I was caught when I was at work.

Following this, the prosecutor read out (or summarized) each item of evidence including witness statements, record of the inquest, and record of site reconnaissance and photographs to all of which the defendant indicated no objection. The investigative stage was then concluded in the following manner:

Judge: Do you have the knife that was used to commit the crime, prosecutor?

Prosecutor: No.

Judge: Defendant, do you have any opinion on the evidence produced?

Defendant: No.

Judge: Defendant, do you have any new evidence?

Defendant: No.

As appears from the above, even in a serious case such as this,[50] the investigative stage of the trial can be completed very quickly where the defendant (and his lawyer) does not dispute the facts asserted by the prosecution. As also appears, cases proceed notwithstanding the fact that important items of evidence may be missing.[51]

Similarly in case M-CO-Y-07, on a charge of robbery, in which Ms Hu's handbag containing RMB 130 was taken and the defendant arrested by the masses after a hue and cry, the case for the prosecution against the unrepresented 20-year old migrant defendant was established as follows:

Prosecutor: (reads out the Bill of Prosecution).

Judge: Defendant, have you listened clearly to the Bill of Prosecution just read out by the prosecutor?

Defendant: Yes.

Judge: Do you have any objection as to the facts of the crime alleged in the Bill of Prosecution?

Defendant: Yes, I didn't threaten that female (victim); I didn't point at her head with the gun.

Judge: Do you have any objection as to the allegation that you have committed the offence of robbery?

Defendant: No.

Judge: Prosecutor may question the defendant.

Prosecutor: Defendant, the prosecutor hopes that you can frankly confess in court today. Were your previous confessions to the police true?

Defendant: True.

Prosecutor: [Reads out the defendant's first confession statement. The contents include the part to which objection was taken by the defendant, namely that a gun had been pointed at the head of the victim.]

---

[50] The defendant received a sentence of 14 years' imprisonment.
[51] This was an all too common occurrence and the failure of the police to preserve vital evidence was the subject of adverse comment by prosecutors on many occasions.

Judge: Does the defendant have any objection?

Defendant: No.

Judge: Now let the prosecutor produce evidence to prove the case.

Prosecutor: [Reads out the statement of the victim Ms Xu, which describes the course of the robbery in detail.]

Judge: Does the defendant have any objection?

Defendant: No.

Prosecutor: [Produces the photos of the illegally acquired items.]
The bailiff showed them to the defendant.

Judge: Does the defendant have any objection?

Defendant: No.

Prosecutor: [Reads out the proof of identity of the defendant, the defendant has impersonated Gu.]

Judge: Does the defendant have any objection?

Defendant: No.

Judge: Have you impersonated Gu and why?

Defendant: I didn't want my family members to know.

Judge: Were you the 'Gu' shown on that photo?

Defendant: Yes.

Prosecutor: [Reads out the Course of Arrest.]

Judge: Does the defendant have any objection?

Defendant: No.

Prosecutor: I have finished producing evidence to prove the case.

Judge: Defendant, do you have any new evidence to produce or are you going to call any witness to testify in court?

Defendant: No.

Judge: What were you thinking when you were committing the crime?

Defendant: I lost my identity card. I could not find a job. I didn't have money. I wanted to find some money for my family.

This presentation typifies that followed where the defendant, whether represented or not, does not contest the basic charge. As is also typical, neither the prosecutor nor the Court is interested in exploring detailed objections to the circumstances of the crime or facial contradictions in the evidence should these arise: what is important is the acceptance of 'guilt'. Thus, in the above colloquy, given that the defendant had admitted robbery, no one was interested in exploring whether or not the defendant had or had not pointed a gun at the head of the victim. The defendant objected to being described as having done so in the Bill of Prosecution but this was not pursued because he made no further objection after the reading out of his confession which contained an admission that he had done so.[52]

As a general rule, if the charge was admitted, prosecutors did not seek to pin down defendants to the particulars of a crime so that for an objective observer, at the end of the trial, there was no factual basis for deciding between divergent accounts. This was so even where the fact in dispute was directly relevant to such matters as premeditation, intentionality, self-defence and provocation. An example is J-CO-S4-11, a case of intentional injury leading to the death of the victim. There was no dispute that the defendant, Du (D), had gone to a market where there was an argument between his brother and the victim who was renting a market stall. The argument developed into a fight in which five or six individuals participated in the course of which the victim received injuries from a stick which led to his death. Others fled the scene: D remained and was apprehended. What was at issue was the sequence of events: who started the fight and how the weapon (a stick) had been acquired. It was alleged by the prosecution that D took the stick from a nearby building site indicating premeditation and intentionality. As soon as the Bill of Prosecution was read, however, D sought to correct this: 'The criminal weapon, the stick, was taken from the victim.' The relevant part of the prosecutor's questioning of D began as follows:

Prosecutor: Did you give the victim a punch?

Defendant: No.

Prosecutor: In the written confessions you said you gave the victim a punch.

Defendant: The victim gave me a punch first and I returned a punch back. Then the victim chased me with a stick and I snatched it and fought against him.

Prosecutor: How many people took part in the fight?

Defendant: About 4–5. There were 3–4 people on the victim's side.

Prosecutor: Did they go up to attack you?

Defendant: [silent].

---

[52] It was, in fact, common for defendants to offer a correction to the details led by the prosecution but, once having offered it, to not pursue the point further and to raise no objection to prosecution statements which repeated what they saw as an error of fact.

Prosecutor: Did they go up to attack you?

Defendant: Yes.

Prosecutor: Are your confessions in the [PSB] true?

Defendant: Some are but some are not.

Prosecutor: Did you read your written confessions?

Defendant: Yes, but too fast.

Prosecutor: Where was your stick from?

Defendant: I snatched it.

Prosecutor: Was there a building site near it?

Defendant: Yes.

Prosecutor: Were there any sticks in the building site?

Defendant: Yes.

Prosecutor: Did you pick up a stick there?

Defendant: No.

Prosecutor: That's all for my interrogation.

Later, the point was raised again by D when the case-responsible judge asked D whether he had any opinion on the evidence and D said: 'Yes. In the witness statements they said that they had seen me holding a stick but they didn't see how I came to have the stick.' It was clear, therefore, that the defendant had a consistent story: that he had not picked up the stick from the building site but had, instead, 'snatched' it from the victim. Neither the judge nor the prosecutor sought to settle this issue by further questioning. Moreover, the court-appointed defence lawyer, having made no intervention at all during the hearing, had obviously failed to grasp the significance of what had been said: his sole contribution at the Debate stage being to state: 'It was the victim who initiated the fight. The defendant *picked up the stick* for self-defence. I beg the court to give him lenient punishment (emphasis supplied).'

While many defendants are in a compliant state at the hearing stage, the case having been well-constructed in advance, the prosecutor has a number of strategies to better secure agreement with the prosecution case. Against a background in which defendants are rewarded for being 'truthful' and subject to a more severe sentence if they are not, prosecutors often warn defendants of the need to speak truthfully. A typical exchange is set out below from L-CO-X-02 (intentional homicide) on opening the investigative stage:

Judge: Now, it is time for the prosecutor to question the defendant.

Prosecutor: Defendant, you should answer my questions truthfully. Do you understand?

Defendant: Yes.

And in J-CO-S4-17, the prosecutor told a defendant who had stated that he was 'innocent', 'I hope that you will establish a good attitude in court today.' At other times, the prosecutor might underscore this admonition so that the defendant was left in no doubt of the consequences of non-compliance, as in M-CO-Y-03 where the prosecutor addressed one of the co-defendants in these terms:

> *Prosecutor:* Defendant Y, the prosecutors are going to question you in respect of the facts alleged in the Bill of Prosecution, I hope you can take this opportunity to frankly confess the facts of the crime. If your attitude is not good today, you would not be considered as having voluntarily surrendered yourself. Is that clear?

In a similar way, the prosecutor might tell an unco-operative defendant that sentence mitigation would be lost if the account at trial differed from that given at the police station: one defendant being told directly, for example, that any attempt to retract his confession would result in the loss of the 'voluntary surrender' status with adverse sentencing consequences.

Should the defendant seek to contradict a statement made by the prosecutor when reading out witness statements or the prosecutor's own interpretation of events, the defendant would be met, as in L-CO-X-09, with a curt question to which the answer would invariably be the same, as set out below:

Prosecutor: Where's your evidence?

Defendant: No, I don't have evidence.

Given a background in which many defendants conceded guilt and adopted a compliant position in court, it is difficult to make generalizations as to the professional abilities of prosecutors since they faced few challenges. There were a number of instances in which details in the prosecution case, such as dates, had to be corrected but these were for the most part easily rectified with the assistance of the judge.

The Judge

Whatever the expectations surrounding the 1996 CPL in regard to the role of judges, in particular that judges should act as neutral arbiters, our research demonstrates clearly that, in fact, judges continue to be heavily involved in the forensic arena other than as 'referees'. In this section, we document some of the ways in which trial judges actively involve themselves in the establishment of guilt so that they become, in effect, 'second prosecutors'.

Some of the judicial activism arises from their relationship with prosecutors. As was clear from our site visits, judges and prosecutors had a close relationship and although this tended not to be flaunted during the actual court setting, there were occasions on which the partnership could be seen at work. In D-CO-K-02, a case involving prolonged domestic violence leading to the death of a child, the judge met with the prosecutor immediately before the hearing started, read the case file and reviewed photographic evidence together with the prosecutor and exchanged opinions on the handling of the case. In the hearing itself, the involvement and actions of the judge were completely aligned with those of the prosecutor. On several occasions, as the defendant responded to questions in a quiet voice, each admonished the defendant to 'Speak louder!' and, following the prosecutor's questioning of the defendant, the judge subjected the defendant to a series of questions tracking what the prosecutor had asked and going beyond this to seek more detail.[53] Again, in L-CO-X-02, one member of the collegial panel drew the attention of the case-responsible judge to some matter leading to the judge calling an adjournment. During the adjournment, the case-responsible judge met with the prosecutor and exchanged opinions on how the case should be presented in court.

Judges were also helpful to prosecutors by interrogating defendants generally and, in particular, to make good deficiencies in the presentation of the prosecution case. In L-CO-X-25, a case involving intentional homicide, the prosecutor was unable to present the case in a coherent way. As part of the assistance given to the prosecution, the judge was forced to ask the prosecutor to read out the relevant part of the witness statements concerning the criminal incident on eight separate occasions, and whilst the inept prosecutor put only 14 questions to the defendant, failing to get a proper picture of the case, the questioning was completed by the case-responsible judge (34 questions) and a judge of the collegial panel (6 questions).[54]

Again, in J-CO-S4-16, on a charge of intentional injury causing the death of the victim, inept questioning by the prosecutor failed to clarify the basic issue, namely whether the defendant would clearly admit that he had stabbed the victim. Although this was implicit in some answers that the defendant was the killer, other answers (for example: 'I didn't hold a knife to stab her') amounted to a denial leading the prosecutor to state at one point: 'It is contradictory' and the matter had not been clarified at the conclusion of the prosecutor's questioning. At this point the judge stepped in to help:

Judge: Was it you who stabbed the victim with a knife?

Defendant: Yes.

Judge: Is the knife yours?

Defendant: Yes.

Judge: Did you quarrel with the victim when you stabbed her?

Defendant: I just asked her for money. She said she had no money. I said nonsense, and then she hit me. So I stabbed her with a knife and went away.

---

[53] Tao Jianjun (2002) has also observed that it is still very common for judges to examine the evidence by directly conducting questioning in court themselves, and the focus of the trials is still the questioning by judges. A similar view was shared by some prosecutors we interviewed (e.g., YK-02; BJ2-06; BJ2-07; BJ2-09).

[54] These questions were by way of cross-examination of the defendant and additional to the pro-forma questions put regarding whether objection was taken to statements etc. read out by the prosecutor.

In F-CO-N-01, a charge of robbery involving three defendants (D1, D2 and D3), it was necessary to differentiate the roles of the participants.[55] At the conclusion of the prosecutor's presentation, the matter was far from clear: D1 had remained silent when the Bill of Prosecution was read to her; D2 claimed that D1 had proposed carrying out the robbery; and D3 claimed that the robbery had been proposed by D1 and D2. The judge brought all the defendants back into the courtroom together and then sought to make good the uncertainties in the prosecution case:

Judge: Let the court examine the evidence.

Judge: Defendant 2, who proposed the robbery?

Defendant 2: Defendant 1 – that is the one sitting in the middle.

Judge: Defendant 3, who proposed the robbery?

Defendant 3: Defendants 1 and 2.

Defendant 1: It is true.

Defendant 2: It is true.

Judge: Who brought the screwdriver there?

Defendant 3: Defendant 1.

Defendant 2: Defendant 1.

Defendant 1: [Keeps silent.]

Again, in case L-CO-X-05, when the prosecutor made a mistake in reading out the Bill of Prosecution, the judge immediately intervened to correct the error.

Judges also assisted prosecutors by reproving and reprimanding defendants (and their legal representatives) and keeping them in check so that their ability to present their case was constrained, attenuated or even stopped altogether.[56] The intervention of judges in these ways and the tone many of them set had a chilling effect upon the defence so that there was little sign of any resistance to the prosecution case.[57] Although, as we shall see,

---

[55] See also F-N-02 discussed above under Simplified Ordinary Procedure.

[56] If the court believes that the evidence collected by the defence is unnecessary, it can and does refuse to admit the evidence. See, Feng Chuanping (1998). Judges will examine and verify defence evidence only if they consider that it is, in their view, really necessary to do so. See, Shao Hua (2001).

[57] Jiang and Cao (2004) have argued that the current judicial practice of only allowing the parties to raise their objections and state their disagreement instead of letting them properly debate the issues in dispute reflects the traditional belief that judges can accurately make decisions by simply relying on their own judicial knowledge, so that speculation on facts and personal experience was still at work. They argued that such practice was not only inconsistent with the requirement of due process under the contemporary criminal law but also led to unfairness in substance.

it was clear that many defence lawyers operated under a presumption of guilt, where they harboured doubts about the validity of the prosecution or the appropriateness of the charge or in regard to the details of the evidence, judges were unwilling to entertain any challenge and sought wherever possible to suppress any such line of defence.

Along with prosecutors, judges repeatedly warned defendants to speak truthfully or to confess frankly or reminded them of the significance of being designated as having voluntarily surrendered. This also occurred where, in a trial subject to simplified ordinary procedure, the initial response of the defendant to the Bill of Prosecution was to qualify the account therein and make statements which appeared to undercut the operating assumption that he had agreed to plead guilty. Thus, in M-CO-Y-08, on a charge of arson, the following exchange took place:

Judge: Defendant, have you listened clearly to the Bill of Prosecution just read out by the prosecutor?

Defendant: Yes.

Judge: Do you have any objection as to the facts of the crime alleged in the Bill of Prosecution?

Defendant: Yes, I only wanted to get back my wages; I didn't want to set fire.

Judge: [Made an explanation of the court adjudication system and then:] The key thing is you must confess frankly. I will determine your guilt and sentence according to the circumstances of your crime and your attitude in admitting your guilt. Do you have any objection as to the prosecution's allegation that you have committed arson?

Defendant: I don't object to the facts of the crime: I admit my guilt.

We see in this short exchange how the intervention of the judge immediately 'educated' the defendant as to what was expected of him and, in particular, that any dissent from the prosecution account of the events in question was not acceptable and resistance would have an adverse effect upon the sentence. Other examples below illustrate the tone set by some judges:

L-CO-X-16 (contract fraud)
Prosecutor: How did you use the 600 000 Yuan borrowed from the commercial bank?

Defendant: To pay for the interest of loan, bail and cost of the public notary.

Judge: Defendant, you answer the question directly! How did you spend that money?

L-CO-X-12 (bribery)
Judge: Defendant, can you answer the question directly and concisely?
. . . . . .
[The judge asks the prosecutor not to present the evidence which the defence lawyers don't challenge.
The judge twice asks the prosecutor to present evidence faster and concisely and briefly.]

L-CO-X-02 (intentional homicide)
Prosecutor: Can you tell us the whole story?

Defendant: xxxxx (The researcher didn't catch the answer)

Judge: Defendant, stand straight and speak loudly.

Prosecutor: Defendant, pay attention to your attitude!

Defendant: [he sobbed for a few minutes without saying anything].
. . . . . .

Judge: Defendant, do you have any disagreement with the evidence presented?

Defendant: Yes, I didn't attack her with a chair.

Judge: Defendant, do you have new evidence?

Defendant: No.
. . . . . .
The judge (somewhat impatiently) asks the defence lawyers not to bother with details which have nothing to do with this case.

L-CO-X-15 (intentional harm)
The judge asks the defendant if he wants to make a final statement.

Defendant: Yes [commencing to read from a prepared paper].

Judge: Do not read your manuscript!

Judges also showed impatience with defence lawyers and frequently interrupted them and sought to reduce their influence on the trial. In this way they enjoined the defence lawyers to be brief in their statements and cut them off when they were speaking, a feature that almost never occurred when prosecutors spoke. The manner of intervention considerably reduced the standing of defence lawyers in the eyes of their clients, their own self-esteem (which we know was already low) and their role in the trial. The following illustrate the practices of judges in respect of defence lawyers in what could hardly be called prolonged trials:

J-CO-S4-10 (drug trafficking: two defendants: trial lasted 1 hour 45 minutes)
When the defence lawyers tried to put questions, the judge interrupted twice and told them not to repeat questions and not to put any 'irrelevant' questions.

L-CO-X-01 (intentional harm: 1 hour 40 minutes)
The judge asked the defence lawyer whether he challenged the evidence.

Defence Lawyer: Yes. I challenge the conclusion of the document on the expertise of forensic appraisal and the qualification of the appraiser. In addition, the document was not sent to the defendant according to the rule . . . [At this point, the judge stopped the defence lawyer's speech and asked him to provide written evidence to support his argument].
. . . .
The defence lawyer started to reply to the prosecutor, but is stopped by the judge because she thinks the defence lawyer is repeating his opinions.

Judge: All right, you express your opinion again and again. Do you have new opinion?

. . . . . .
[The case-responsible judge and other judges interrupted or stopped the defender's speech very often].

E-CO-L-03 (intentional injury: the hearing lasted 1 hour 32 minutes)
The judge asked the defence lawyer of the second defendant if she wanted to ask the second defendant questions.

Defence Lawyer: Yes.

Judge: Do not repeat the questions that the prosecutor asked!
. . . .

Judge: Defence lawyer, because of the time, just tell us your disagreement and opinions with the prosecutor.

D-CO-K-10 (fraud: two defendants: 1 hour 25 minutes)
Defence Lawyer 2: From this evidence, in the Bill of Prosecution. . . .
(Interrupted by the judge)

Judge: Defender 2, when you make a speech, you should have a legal or factual basis, instead of imagination. There is no need to make excessive explanation.

J-CO-S4-11 (intentional injury: trial lasts total 1 hour 12 minutes)
Researcher's note: The judge is impatient and asks the defendant and defence lawyer to summarize their points.

A rather extraordinary illustration of the basis of concern over judicial 'neutrality' occurred in case I-CO-S3-01, a serious charge of robbery and intentional homicide. It was undisputed that several individuals had been involved in the fatal attack on the victim. The prosecution case was that the defendant was one of those attackers. The defence case was that the defendant did not participate in the robbery and, indeed, could not have done because he was confined to hospital on the day the crime took place. The privately-engaged defence lawyer was clearly aware of the details of the case and took objection to the prosecution evidence as it was adduced. For example, the evidence of a 'witness' was dismissed as irrelevant because it showed only that the witness was reporting what someone else had said (hearsay); and the statements relating to the crime scene were equally of no direct evidential value against this defendant as they merely showed that there had been a crime but said nothing as to the identity of those involved in the robbery. The defence lawyer also asked whether the crime scene investigation had produced any forensic evidence, such as fingerprints, relating to the defendant. This was not answered and it appeared that there was no such evidence. Shortly afterwards the following colloquy occurred:

Judge: Does the defence have any evidence to produce to the court?

Defence Lawyer: According to the fact that the defendant was admitted to the hospital, as he stated, the defence lawyer produces three witnesses to prove this.

Judge: Defence lawyer, did you defend the defendant [Yan] during the last court session?

Defence Lawyer: Yes.

Judge: According to law, one lawyer cannot act as defender for two defendants in the same case: do you know that?

Defence Lawyer: Yes.

Judge: Does the defendant agree to entrust another defence lawyer to defend you?

Defendant: Agree.

Judge: Having considered that the defender has produced new witnesses to prove the facts of the case, the court needs to review that after the court session, and the defender's procedure is illegal, it violated the relevant provisions of the Lawyers Law. He acted for two defendants in the same case therefore the court decides to postpone the adjudication. Now I announce the adjournment of the trial: take the defendant out of the court. [Bailiffs do so.]

The manner in which this case was handled, after one and a half hours of the hearing, gave the strong impression that the trial was adjourned because of the prospect of defence witnesses being produced to destroy the basis of the prosecution case rather than because the lawyer had infringed the Lawyers Law. Apart from anything else, the judge knew from the very outset that the lawyer had acted in the earlier related case and could, accordingly, have disqualified the lawyer from the outset instead of waiting until there was a real danger to the prosecution. Adjournment and replacement of the lawyer provided the court and prosecution with the opportunity to see the witnesses in private (and possibly deter them from appearing) and to assign the defendant a court-appointed lawyer who would have no knowledge of the case and perhaps little incentive or capacity to challenge the prosecution.

Finally we should mention that the involvement of judges in evidence-gathering is not confined to the court hearing. We have already described in Chapter 6 how judges, on their own admission, gather evidence in advance of trial. Additionally, it became clear in the fieldwork that judges also collected evidence *after* the court hearing had concluded when they thought it appropriate. We cannot give any indication of the frequency of this happening but some judges and prosecutors conceded that this occurred. Thus, for example, a prosecutor complained that in a particular case (identified to the researcher) the judge collected evidence that had not been before the court. In that case, the prosecutor alleged that the crime had been committed by the work unit. The judge then went to the work unit to gather evidence which was used to exonerate the unit. As the prosecutor remarked, this outcome was entirely predictable given that if the unit had been found guilty, the bonus of its staff would have been adversely affected. This simply illustrates the wider problem that evidence gathered by the judge, whether pre-trial or post-hearing, cannot be tested by either party.[58]

---

[58] Shao Hua (2001) has similarly pointed out that it is impossible for the prosecution and the defence to cross-examine evidence personally collected by judges because judges come to believe that the evidence collected by them is accurate and very often use those items of evidence as the basis of their decisions.

CONCLUSION

Although trials (except in summary cases) took place before a collegial panel, the panel did not function as a court. In almost every single case, the case-responsible judge was the only active participant of those making up the collegial panel, the other constituent members showing no interest in the hearings or engaged in other activities including sleep.

It is also quite clear from observing trials that the dominant figure in the process remains the judge rather than the other criminal justice actors. Whilst the nature of summary proceedings (where there is usually no prosecutor) and of trials by simplified ordinary procedure (another form of guilty plea) necessarily promotes the judge to the lead role in managing the court hearings, this is also true of cases dealt with by ordinary procedure. In such cases, the judge not only controls the procedure and keeps order in court but also is the dominant figure in the questioning of the defendant and giving coherence to the case for the prosecution.

The observation of the presentation of the prosecution in these hearings puts to rest a number of assumptions that have been made by some commentators. The notion that the 1996 reform initiated, at least in part, adversary practices into China's criminal justice process cannot be sustained. There is little that resembles adversary behaviour and the court actors who might assume such a role exhibit no inclination or capacity to litigate in this way. In the absence of the production of witnesses, prosecutors are restricted to reading out, in whole or in part, narratives prepared by the police or procuratorate which bear upon the crime or the defendant's alleged role in it and to eliciting, wherever possible, the defendant's agreement in whole or in substance to the overall charge. In discharging this relatively simple task, few adversary skills beyond the elementary are required but prosecutors commonly have to be assisted by or rescued by the judge in pinning down the defendant and securing acceptance of the truth of the allegation.

Our court observations also put to rest the idea that the procuratorate exercise a supervisory role over judges in criminal trials. This is the more extraordinary given the shocking behaviour of judges occasionally reported in the press and witnessed by our researchers. As we have seen above, judges may with impunity trample upon the rules of natural justice in the certain knowledge that prosecutors will adopt a supine position in the court. One can only imagine that judges themselves regard their actions as necessary to achieve outcomes which their superiors demand unless they too have internalized the presupposition of guilt and regard defendants as unworthy.

Whatever the formal position in regard to institutional balance and checks, in no case that we saw was there any evidence that prosecutors sought to contest any ruling from a judge[59] or otherwise assert an independent supervisory power. All of the evidence pointed the other way, namely that it was the judge who controlled the proceedings and who regulated and directed the prosecutors.[60] In the construction of the prosecution case, it was the judge who played the key role.

---

[59] Under Article 169, 1996 CPL, if the procuratorate 'discovers' that in handling a case a People's Court had 'violated the litigation procedure prescribed by law' it has the power to suggest to a people's court that it should be set right.

[60] Of course the prosecutor has a right to enter a protest but we know that this right is seldom exercised.

11. The defence at trial observed (1)

In this and the next chapter we report on the way in which the defence was conducted in the 227 trials involving 335 defendants that we observed. As we have already described the processing of cases in both summary and simplified ordinary procedure, the emphasis in this chapter will be upon cases tried under ordinary procedure. We begin our account by looking at cases in which the defendant did not have the benefit of legal representation before moving to those cases in which there was a lawyer appointed by the court. In the next chapter we deal with cases in which the defendant was represented by a lawyer who was privately retained.

UNREPRESENTED DEFENDANTS

Legal Representation in China: the Law

As previously stated, the right to a fair trial is widely accepted to be a fundamental human right. Chinese law allows any individual to hire a lawyer in a criminal case, but the appointment of a lawyer is required only in limited circumstances as set out in Article 34, 1996 CPL, namely in respect of juveniles, those who are deaf, mute or blind and those charged with offences carrying the death penalty. In recognition of the need to provide legal advice at a more general level China began to develop a legal aid system from 1994.[1] That system is, however, far from comprehensive and the legal service provided is of variable quality. Most criminal defendants in China are too poor to be able to afford a lawyer and many defendants in China are still without legal representation.[2] What the lawyer can do in defence of a client is limited by law. Thus, during the currency of the research, before a lawyer could collect evidence from other parties, he or she was required to obtain their consent or 'apply to the People's Procuratorate or the People's Court for the collection and obtaining of evidence, or request the People's Court to inform the witness to appear in court and give testimony'.[3]

---

[1] For an account of the emergent legal aid system, see: Smith and Gompers (2007).
[2] Statistics collected by Chen Xingliang showed that over 70 per cent of all criminal cases in China were tried without legal representation, cited for 2002 in Liu and Halliday (2009). As will appear, our figures for unrepresented defendants were considerably lower.
[3] Article 37, 1996 CPL. The 2007 Lawyers Law has changed the formal position in this regard but, as we shall see, this is not necessarily reflected in practice. And there are further restrictions placed upon the lawyer at trial, the 1996 CPL requiring the court's approval to call new witnesses, to obtain new material evidence, a new expert evaluation to be made or another inquest to be held: Article 159, 1996 CPL.

Table 11.1   Unrepresented defendants and trial format

Trial format	Number of trials	Number of defendants
Summary	23	23
Simplified ordinary procedure	7	7
Ordinary procedure	36	56
Total	66	86

Legal Representation in China: the Practice

We have already noted from our analysis of case files that many defendants appear in court without any form of legal representation. Indeed, we found overall that in 46 per cent of cases the defendant was not represented at all. As can be seen from Table 11.1, of the 227 trials we observed, in approximately 26 per cent, the defendant(s) had no legal representation at all nor, it might be added, were they represented by any other of the individuals (such as family member) allowed by law to serve in this capacity.[4]

While legal representation should always be seen as an important right, the lack of representation in summary cases and in simplified ordinary procedure cases is no doubt substantially explained by the fact that in these cases the defendant is not contesting the charge and has so indicated to the court. This does not excuse the lack of legal representation but rather places it into a context where China is struggling to establish a legal aid system and might be expected to give priority in the first stages to contested and more serious cases.[5] Nor, however, does it tell us what pressures defendants were under in order to produce the guilty plea and whether there was any bargaining that induced the compliant posture of the defendant.[6] What is much more surprising is that 56 defendants involved in 36 trials dealt with under ordinary procedure had no legal representation whatsoever. This is particularly noteworthy since the cases involved were often at the serious end of the crime continuum and the defendants from the most disadvantaged sections of the community – poor, unemployed, lacking in education with many drawn from non-local citizens (migrants).

Although we were not able to identify the residential status of many defendants in this group,[7] of the 56 unrepresented defendants dealt with by ordinary procedure, almost one-third (32.1 per cent) were known to be migrants with another two (3.6 per cent) being

---

[4] In terms of defendants, there was no legal representation for 25.7 per cent (86 out of 335) defendants.

[5] While China has rapidly expanded the number of legal aid centres, many are not serviced by qualified legal personnel or the lawyers therein concentrate on civil cases. See, Smith and Gompers (2007), *op. cit.*

[6] Negotiations over plea, charge and sentence are well-established (and contentious) features of many parts of the common law world and, indeed, are increasingly becoming part of many civil law systems. Plea bargaining has not been officially adopted in China although there are reports that it has occasionally occurred. See, for example, Xiong Qiuhong (2005).

[7] This was because of a complete failure to record relevant information in two research sites and because recordings were not consistently made in some other cases.

foreigners. Most unrepresented defendants also lacked significant education, generally only to primary or junior school level. Most were young males:[8] of those whose age was known (42), the majority (52.4 per cent) were aged 25 or below.

Some of the cases involved offences at the lower end of the crime continuum, but many were of the more serious variety with defendants potentially at risk of severe sentences. There were a number of cases involving thefts of mobile phones or handbags or were the outcome of traffic incidents caused by careless or dangerous driving,[9] but almost 27 per cent of unrepresented defendants (15) faced charges of robbery, in four of which a victim had been killed by the assailants. A further 7.1 per cent were charged with intentional injury causing death, 9.0 per cent faced drugs charges relating to smuggling or trafficking. The remaining defendants faced theft charges of varying degrees of seriousness (33.3 per cent) or kidnapping, swindling, cheating and contractual fraud. From the perspective of the sentence imposed, almost 45 per cent received a prison sentence of three years or more, 18.2 per cent receiving eight years or more and in four cases the sentence was a life term.

The Line of Defence in Unrepresented Cases

In the overwhelming majority of cases, the unrepresented defendant offered no substantive defence to the offence charged. This was consistent with the fact that they had also made statements of admission to the Public Security Bureau and to the Procuratorate, sometimes on a number of separate occasions. For the most part, defendants contributed little to the proceedings, simply agreeing with the statements of evidence read out (or summarized) by the prosecutor, not participating in the Debate stage of the trial, saying nothing when invited to make a Final Statement or pleading in a most basic manner for leniency. We set out below an example that is typical of this category of case:

D-CO-K-04: (A case of theft)
The collegial panel is made up of three judges. The case-responsible judge is a 30-year old male, medium build, wearing glasses. The other two judges include one male and one female. The male judge is short and overweight, age around 30-years old. The female judge is tall and around 35–40-years old. The three judges wear black professional robes with a red ribbon in the front. In addition, there is one female court clerk sitting beside the panel, wearing a jacket in grey, whose age is about 25-years old.

There are two female public prosecutors aged around 25–30-years old. One prosecutor has short hair and is of medium build; the other has long hair and is thin. Both wear deep blue professional uniforms with a national emblem at the front.

There is one male defendant, unemployed, aged 20 years. His hair is very short. He was a graduate of a primary school, wearing an orange vest without sleeves as the sign of a prisoner.

There is a female judicial police officer in the courtroom, whose age is around 25–30-years old, long hair, wearing a deep blue police uniform.

There are two people in the audience.

---

[8] There was only one female defendant, a foreigner aged 34.
[9] This is not to say that the incidents themselves were necessarily non-serious, some resulting in the death of other drivers: courts, however, have generally tended to treat cases involving careless or negligent driving as quasi-criminal in character at least at the sentencing stage.

9:00 am:
The case-responsible judge uses a gavel to declare the opening of court session and asks the defendant questions on relevant information such as the name, other name, date of birth, family address, occupation, date of detention or/and arrest so as to verify the defendant's status. The defendant stands up and answers the questions.

[The judge asks him if he has received the copy of the Bill of Prosecution and the time of receipt.]

Defendant: Yes.

The judge announces the name list of the panel, court clerks, and prosecutors.

[The judge informs the defendant of his right to challenge the parties concerned, and asks the defendant if he challenges the panel or other parties].

Defendant: No.

[The judge informs the defendant of his rights, such as right to defend himself or the right to employ a defender, the right to apply for witnesses to attend and give testimony and the right to apply for a new appraisal and the right to make a final statement].

[The judge asks the defendant if he has heard those rights clearly].

Defendant: Yes.

9:03 am:
[The judge announces the start of the courtroom investigation.]

Prosecutor: On 2 July 2003, the defendant opened the door of a [building] with the key he prepared beforehand and stole RMB 800, a computer screen, keyboard, the main host computer/mainframe, the mouse device, USB disk, earphones and two mobiles and a calculator from the computer room. The total value of the items taken was more than RMB 7000. When the defendant was carrying the stolen goods and leaving the scene, he was caught by a security guard and taken to the police station. The stolen goods have been returned to the victim. The defendant's act broke the criminal law, so he should be punished for theft. The defendant has the circumstance of voluntary surrender, so his punishment can be reduced or he can be given leniency. In addition, the defendant committed another crime during the period of suspended punishment. His suspended punishment should be cancelled and he should be punished concurrently for several crimes.[10]

[The judge asks the defendant if the content of the Bill of Prosecution read by the prosecutor is the same as the one he received.]

Defendant: Yes.

Judge: What's the charge in the Bill of Prosecution?

Defendant: The offence of theft.

---

[10] The defendant was already serving a suspended sentence for another offence.

[The judge asks the defendant if he has any disagreement with the facts of crime charged in the Bill of Prosecution.]

Defendant: No.

[The judge asks the prosecutors if they wish to ask the defendant questions.]

Prosecutors: No.

[The judge asks the defendant questions.]

Judge: How did you enter the computer room?

Defendant: I used a key.

Judge: How did you have a key?

Defendant: I worked there before.

Judge: You didn't return the key to the unit when you left there?

Defendant: No.

Judge: Why did you steal?

Defendant: No reason. When I have no money, I will steal.

9:08 am:
[The prosecutor presents evidence.]

I offer proof of the defendant's household registration and material on the defendant's previous criminal record, which proves the defendant's date of birth and the capacity to bear criminal responsibility as well as his criminal record.

[The judge asks the defendant if he challenges the evidence.]

Defendant: No.

Judge: Did you appeal when you received the judgment in your previous crime?

Defendant: No.

[The prosecutor presents five statements of confession of the defendant. In view of the defendant's willingness to admit his crime, there was no need to read the confessions in court.]

[The judge asks the defendant if he challenges the evidence.]

Defendant: No.

[The prosecutor presents the written record on identifying the crime scene and photos. The police present the photos to the defendant.]

[The judge asks the defendant if he challenges the evidence.]

Defendant: No.

[The prosecutor presents the victim's statement.]

[The judge asks the defendant if he challenges the evidence.]

Defendant: No.

[The prosecutor presents the written record on the site reconnaissance and photos. The prosecutor presents the photos and asks the defendant to have a look.]

[The judge asks the defendant if he challenges the evidence.]

Defendant: No.

[The prosecutor presents the document on the conclusion of price evaluation, which proved the value of stolen goods was more than 7000 Yuan.]

[The judge asks the defendant if he challenges the evidence.]

Defendant: No.

[The prosecutor presents the material on the course of catching the defendant. It showed that the security guard found one suspect, came up to question him, but that man ran away immediately. Later the guard caught that man again.]

[The judge asks the defendant if he challenges the evidence.]

Defendant: No. [The defendant sobs and wipes his eyes with his hand.]

[The prosecutor presents an explanation to prove that the defendant had the circumstance of voluntary surrender.]

[The judge asks the defendant if he challenges the evidence.]

Defendant: No.

Judge: Did you hold anything in your hand when you were caught?

Defendant: No.

Judge: Did you jump up the wall when the security guard found you?

Defendant: No.

[The judge asks the defendant if he has any evidence to present in the courtroom.]

Defendant: No.

9:24 am:
[The judge declares the beginning of courtroom debate.]

Prosecutor: All the evidence has been cross-examined in court: the evidence is effective and lawful. The defendant has admitted his crime in court. Given the fact of the crime, its nature, the attitude towards his crime and social harm, please impose punishment on the defendant by law according to the principle of the punishment suiting the crime.

[The judge asks the defendant if he would like to defend himself.]

Defendant: Yes. I did wrong, I have nothing to say.

9:25 am:
Judge: Defendant, do you want to make a final statement?

Defendant: No.

9:26 am:
The judge announces the adjournment by gavel and will make a judgment on the other day.

As is clear from this example, the defendant, having been caught near the scene of the crime in possession of the stolen items and having made confessions to the police and prosecutor, offered no resistance in court, was unable to justify his behaviour except in very basic terms and was not able to articulate a speech in mitigation of the offence.

In many other cases, the defendant's participation in the trial was equally slight. Thus, the opportunity to make a statement at the Debate Stage and to make a Final Statement was declined by many defendants and where they did speak, it was in elementary terms, as in the following illustrations:

J-CO-S4-02: (Drug smuggling)
Judge: Let the defendant defend herself.

Defendant: I didn't know that methadone couldn't be imported. But I violated this regulation. I beg the court to give me a chance to reform and start a new life.

Judge: Prosecutor and defendant, do you have any new opinions?

[Both said 'No'].

Judge: That is all for court debate. Let the defendant make a Final Statement.

Defendant: No.

In J-CO-S4-18 (intentional injury in which the victim died) the defendant, who was sentenced to ten years in prison, said nothing either at the Debate Stage or when asked if he wished to make a Final Statement; in K-CO-W-02 (robbery involving stabbing of two victims, one seriously) neither of the two defendants (migrants) said anything at the Debate Stage nor did they make a Final Statement; and in K-CO-W-03 (thefts over a long period of time) none of the four unrepresented defendants contributed at the Debate or Final Statement stage. This pattern was repeated in some other cases such as A-CO-B1-00 (theft); B-CO-B2-06 (theft); and B-CO-B2-10 (robbery).

In other cases, the defendant's contribution at the Debate and Final Statement stages was minimal, usually a simple statement admitting responsibility or requesting mercy. Thus, in L-CO-X-18 (contractual fraud) the defendant stated at the Debate Stage: 'The prosecutor's charge is true' but said nothing at the Final Statement stage. In J-S4-08 (smuggling self-use drugs), the defendant's contribution was limited to the following:

Judge: Let the defendant defend himself.

Defendant: I was wrong. The drug was for my own use. I beg the court to give me a lighter punishment.

Judge: That is all for court debate. Let the defendant make a Final Statement.

Defendant: I apply for a lighter punishment. Please give me a chance to turn over a new leaf in my life.

Again, in K-CO-W-15 (drug trafficking) the two migrant defendants said nothing at the Debate Stage but contributed an identical Final Statement each saying: 'I hope to be treated leniently' and in D-CO-K-03 on an allegation of theft the defendant, having said nothing at the Debate Stage added in his Final Statement: 'Please forgive me.' A more expansive statement at the Debate came in D-CO-K-09 (misappropriation of funds) where the defendant stated: 'I have nothing more to say. At that time, I planned to misappropriate the money first and then return it later. But I hadn't expected that I could not repay it after using it in the family. While in custody, I also learned some legal knowledge. I am quite remorseful. I hope that the panel can give me a fair judgment. I am willing to admit my crime and accept the punishment of law.'

In some cases, the defendant participated through responding to questioning by the prosecutor or judge or by offering his or her own account, in such a way as to give details of the crime that could only be known by the perpetrator, as in K-CO-W-02, a case involving a series of robberies carried out by two young migrants:

Judge: Now let's conduct the court investigation. Let the prosecutor read out the Bill of Prosecution first.

Prosecutor: (reads out the Bill of Prosecution)

Judge: Could the bailiff please leave Defendant 1 here and take Defendant 2 out of the court to wait for his trial.

Judge: Defendant Gu, are the allegations in the Bill of Prosecution that were just read out by the prosecutor true?

Defendant 1: True.

Judge: Now let the prosecutor question the defendant.

Prosecutor: Defendant Gu, you must answer the questions frankly, do you understand?

Defendant 1: Clear.

Prosecutor: On the night of 8 January 2006, did you join Defendant 2 and others to sneak to Hanchow Road of S T. . . County. . . and use violent means to rob Wen's red Toshiba mobile phone with premeditation?

Defendant 1: Yes.

Prosecutor: Were there other persons?

Defendant 1: Zhang.

Prosecutor: Did you have any premeditation?

Defendant 1: Yes.

Prosecutor: Where did [Wen] put her mobile phone?

Defendant 1: She wore it in front of her chest.

Prosecutor: Did you hit anyone?

Defendant 1: No.

Prosecutor: Who took away the things?

Defendant 1: I didn't.

Prosecutor: At about 10 p.m. on 26 January of the same year, did you and Defendant 2 join others, with premeditation, to sneak to the bridge beside a pavilion in X. . . Village of S. . . County. . ., beat the passers-by Tan, Jin and another person and stab them with knives, and steal a TCL 3188 mobile phone, a Samsung mobile phone, a Nokia mobile phone and RMB 6000 from them?

Defendant 1: Yes.

Prosecutor: Who else was there?

Defendant 1: Wang.

Prosecutor: How did you rob?

Defendant 1: Wang used a bamboo stick. . ., Defendant 2 and I went up, I hit the victim's leg, Defendant 2 hit the back of one of the persons, Wang hit one person; one person was not hit.

Indeed, in many of the cases the defendant supplied some details of the crime or the background to it in answering questions from the prosecutor or judge. Where there was disagreement, it was usually with the details. Thus, in M-CO-Y-07, in which an imitation gun had been used in a robbery, the defendant accepted responsibility for the offence but stated in response to the reading of the Bill of Prosecution, 'I didn't threaten that female [victim]; I didn't point at her head with the gun.' Similarly, in B-CO-B2-04, one of the three migrant defendants to a robbery charge stated that he had not used a knife during the robbery.

In a few cases, by contrast, the defendant expressed substantial disagreement with the prosecution case. Thus, in A-CO-B1-03, on a charge of theft of a mobile telephone from a woman at the entrance to a museum, the defendant did not accept the prosecution allegation. The prosecution evidence rested primarily upon the statements of five police officers who stated that they had seen the defendant looking for opportunities to steal when on public transport and that, at the entrance to the museum he was not interested in the museum but instead stared at the bags and waists of tourists. A mobile phone found on the defendant was consistent with that lost by the victim (but not otherwise proved to be that of the victim). The defendant insisted that he had not stolen the mobile but had picked it up in the street saying: 'I didn't steal the phone: the police beat me up.' The defendant was not able to enter a meaningful challenge beyond a denial. Because the defendant was 'unrepentant', the prosecutor requested the collegial panel to send him to prison for one year. In a hearing that lasted for 30 minutes, the defendant was convicted and given ten months in prison.

In a similar way, in case M-CO-Y-06 on a charge of robbery involving several assailants, it was clear that the defendant, a 27-year old migrant, was advancing a defence which deserved careful scrutiny. However, the account emerged piecemeal and the defendant was persuaded by the prosecutor that he was guilty anyway. The prosecution case rested primarily upon the confession of the defendant made at the police station. When, however, the Bill of Prosecution was read, the following exchange took place:

Judge: Defendant, have you listened clearly to the Bill of Prosecution the prosecutor just read out to you?

Defendant: Yes.

Judge: Do you have any objection as to the facts of the crime alleged in the Bill of Prosecution?

Defendant: I have no opinion.

Judge: Prosecutor, you may question the defendant.

Prosecutor: Defendant, the prosecutor is going to question you according to law, you just said that you didn't have any opinion on the Bill of Prosecution, does it mean that you confessed to the facts of your crime?

Defendant: Yes.

It became clear in the following exchanges that the defendant, one of three people at the crime scene, claimed that he had not participated in the robbery but had sought to discourage the others, as can be seen in the following colloquy:

Prosecutor: Who hit him?

Defendant: Fang hit him.

Prosecutor: Who did the searching?

Defendant: He also did the searching.

Prosecutor: While he was hitting and searching, were you standing on one side?

Defendant: I was standing on one side.

Judge: You found RMB 12 000. How did you dispose of the money?

Defendant: They had escaped at that time, I didn't get any money.

Judge: Was the money taken away by the two accomplices?

Defendant: Yes.

Judge: Did you hit the victim?

Defendant: I didn't hit him, not even once. They hit the victim and I asked them not to hit him.

In his closing address, the prosecutor conceded that, in the absence of the two parties who had absconded, it could not be established that the defendant had assaulted the victim but the prosecutor maintained that the defendant had instigated the plot by arranging to meet the victim in a remote area. When the prosecutor completed his case the following occurred:

Judge: Let the defendant defend himself.

Defendant: I have no opinion. Thank you for educating me. I didn't know my act was a crime.

At the least, the precise nature of what had occurred was equivocal and the young migrant did not have sufficient legal skills to put his case to the best advantage and was sentenced to four and a half years in prison.

Almost all of the cases were ones in which the prosecution case appeared to be supported by evidence (including earlier confessions by the defendant) but this was without any critical examination by a skilled adversary and, of course, without the production of any witnesses. Even so, issues of detail and sometimes of substance were raised which deserved close scrutiny. That scrutiny was not, however, given and cases were dealt with at speed. Indeed, despite the gravity of many of these cases, the average time of the hearings (including adjournments followed by judgment on the same day) was 70 minutes, with the two longest trials taking 140 minutes each (one a charge of robbery involving five joint defendants, the other a charge of robbery involving three joint defendants)[11] and the four shortest trials being disposed of in half an hour or less.

CASES IN WHICH THE DEFENDANT IS LEGALLY REPRESENTED

As we have noted, where the defendant is legally represented this may be by a court-assigned lawyer or by a lawyer engaged privately, most likely by the defendant's family. In China, as in other jurisdictions, there is often widespread scepticism of the value of

---

[11] The length of these trials was increased for the most part because of the procedural requirements involved in dealing with multiple defendants. Longer trials did not necessarily mean closer scrutiny of the evidence.

court-assigned lawyers who are generally less well remunerated, less close to the defendant and less motivated to do a good job.[12] On the other hand, empirical research in various jurisdictions has cast doubt upon the value of criminal defence lawyers in general and there are at the least substantial grounds for believing that the quality of work undertaken by lawyers in criminal cases is variable and that it would be unwise to assume that lawyers are an unqualified 'good'.[13] We begin our analysis with a short examination of cases in which the defendant was represented by a court-appointed lawyer before moving more generally to look at the strategies that defence lawyers employed in confronting the prosecution case.

Court-appointed Lawyers

It is necessary to remind the reader that the point when notice of the trial is given, i.e., ten days before the trial, is the earliest point at which appointed defence lawyers could become available during the period covered by the research[14] and have the opportunity to familiarize themselves with the case for the prosecution and prepare for trial (Article 151(2), 1996 CPL). In practice, many such lawyers will be appointed later than this, in some cases on the day of the trial itself.[15] Our researchers noted that a total of 22 defendants were represented by lawyers appointed by the court: altogether 24 such lawyers (19 men and five women) appeared for the defence, the defendant in two cases each being represented by two court-assigned lawyers. As might be anticipated, because of the legal requirement that defendants must be represented in certain grave cases (as those involving the death penalty) most of the charges were of a serious character.

Altogether, 15 trials involved intentional homicide (Article 232, Criminal Law) or intentional injury (Article 234)[16] and five involved robbery (Article 263), the residue (2) being charges of theft (in one of which one of the defendants was a minor). The crimes in question would be considered to be at the highest end of the crime continuum in any society. The gravity of the charges was reflected in the sentences handed down: five defendants received the death penalty (one suspended for two years[17]); two were given life terms; one received 14 years' imprisonment; one was given two and a half years' imprisonment; with two minors receiving 12 months and eight months respectively. Although

---

[12] See the example in Ma and Zhang (2005), pp. 166–167, where there was a great contrast between the privately-retained lawyers and the court-appointed lawyers before or during the trial. Similar views can be found in Ji Xiangde (2006).

[13] See, for example, McConville and Mirsky (1986–87); and McConville et al. (1994).

[14] As we have noted, although there is in theory opportunity to become involved at an earlier stage as the law has changed, in practice little has changed in most areas.

[15] Smith and Gompers (2007). The authors offer a number of explanations for this including the fact that a case may be assigned to a legal aid centre rather than to an individual lawyer and the centre will delay assignment because it lacks administrative capacity; courts may delay assigning a case in the hope that the defendant will hire a lawyer; or the court feels the case is so straightforward that there is no urgency in appointing a lawyer: *ibid.*, at p. 126.

[16] In some cases, there were multiple charges such as intentional injury and theft (as in K-CO-W-01).

[17] It is believed that in the majority of cases where the sentence is suspended, the sentence is later changed to life imprisonment subject to good behaviour during the term of the suspension.

trials were adjourned for judgment and sentence in the other cases, it was clear that all would be convictions and in at least a number of them the penalty would be severe given that one or more victims had been killed.

It appeared from the actions of the lawyers that they had undertaken little or no preparatory work in advance of the trial and probably most had been assigned late in the day.[18] Thus, there was no evidence that the lawyers had: prepared any papers (legal or otherwise); visited the scene of the crime; spoken to or engaged expert witnesses (with two notable exceptions); interviewed the defendant with any degree of thoroughness, if at all;[19] undertaken any investigation; or traced or spoken to any potential witness (see also, Regan, 2009). Lawyers had been assigned the case at the eleventh hour, had accepted the assignment and did the best that they could in unpropitious circumstances. They were required to be there, for the most part, to satisfy the legal requirement for representation in the most serious cases and their presence alone was deemed to meet this requirement.

Few of the lawyers assigned by the court appeared to have mastered the detailed allegations and evidence in support, had understood the account of the defendant, formed a case theory or developed a coherent strategy for raising questions on the evidence. When asked by the judge if they wished to put questions to the defendant, the typical response was: 'No questions.' Where they chose to question the defendant (there being no other witnesses to question), the questions were mundane and generally lacked purpose. In E-CO-L-10, for example, on a charge of intentional harm arising out of an incident in which the defendant had allegedly sought after and killed the victim, the lawyer, having indicated at the invitation of the judge that he wished to take the opportunity to put questions to the defendant, asked one question: 'How were you caught by the police?' The answer to this question (that he was caught while in his field) had already been given by the prosecutor and did not tie in with any case theory the defence lawyer might have had. Indeed, in making a short closing submission, the defence lawyer asserted that the defendant was entitled to leniency because he had voluntarily surrendered which elicited the following exchange:

The judge asked the prosecutors if they would like to respond to the defence lawyer's opinion.

Prosecutor: Yes. There is no evidence to prove that the defendant had the circumstance of voluntary surrender. He was caught by the police.

[The judge then asked the defence lawyer if he would like to respond to the prosecutor's opinions.]

Defence Lawyer: No.

Similarly, in L-CO-X-17, on a charge of intentional injury, the course of evidence (including the account of the defendant) made clear that the defendant had stabbed the victim to death

---

[18] We were not able to collect precise information on this but it would be consistent with other data if these lawyers had been assigned at the last moment.

[19] We deduce this from the nature of the representation provided. In a few cases, the defendant did not know that the individual in question was the defence lawyer and it would seem that in such cases at least, no interview had taken place. The exceptional cases where we are satisfied that an interview had taken place will be discussed below.

after they had been drinking together at the victim's house and a quarrel had developed. When given the opportunity to question the defendant, the following exchange occurred:

Defence Lawyer: Did you go to [the victim's] home to drink alcohol?

Defendant: Yes.

Defence Lawyer: Did you buy alcohol?

Defendant: Yes.

Defence Lawyer: Who paid for the alcohol?

Defendant: [The victim], 5 Yuan.

This exchange was the only intervention of the lawyer until the plea in mitigation during which he said that the defendant had been unable to control himself when he quarrelled with the victim during the course of drinking but, unaccountably in the light of his only questions to the defendant, that he would not argue that 'being drunk was a basis for lenient punishment'.[20]

With one exception (see below) in no case did the appointed defence lawyer proffer any evidence for the court's consideration or incorporate into the closing submission any information from any source outside of that disclosed during the presentation of the prosecution case. When asked by the judge whether there was any evidence to put before the court the answer invariably was: 'No.'[21] For all purposes, the assigned lawyer was reliant upon information in the prosecution case file and what was said in the short court hearing. There was no attempt to construct a defence. Sometimes, where the defendant had intimated that he had been assaulted first or that the victim had started the quarrel, the lawyer would add in a remark during mitigation but the foundation for this was never laid in the course of the trial. Thus, for example, in I-CO-S3-07, a case of intentional injury, the lawyer took no substantive part in the hearing until at the end of the investigative stage (see further below) when she gave her opinion on the case:

Judge: Let the defence lawyer state the defence opinion.

Defence Lawyer: There is insufficient evidence to prove the facts in the Bill of Prosecution that the defendant picked up a steel rod to beat the victim and that the lethal injury was caused by the defendant's attack. The victim also made serious mistakes. The defendant conducted self-defence as a result of a sudden attack. The defendant surrendered himself to police. He should be given lighter punishment according to the law.

Similarly, in J-CO-S4-12, on a charge of intentional homicide in which the victim was assassinated with a gun, the defendant admitted that the gun was his, that he had

---

[20] Drunkenness is not a defence to criminal responsibility in China. Under Article 18 of the 1979 Criminal Law, 'Any intoxicated person who commits a crime shall bear criminal responsibility.' However, it can be advanced as a basis for mitigation.

[21] See, for example, J-CO-S4-12, a case of intentional homicide, in which the court-appointed lawyer asked no questions of the defendant nor offered any evidence for the court's consideration.

travelled to the crime scene with accomplices but claimed that it was an accomplice (Mr Ho) who actually fired the fatal shot. The defendant claimed that his police station confession was not true and had been extracted by the police through sleep deprivation. The defence lawyer took no active part in the hearing and merely tendered a short submission at the end which was tellingly challenged by the prosecution:

> *Defence Lawyer:* First, I think the evidence is not sufficient and the facts are not objective. There is a possibility of the defendant being induced to confess by the Public Security Bureau. Mr Ho is also an accomplice in the case. It's very normal for him to shift his responsibilities. The possibility of Mr Ho shooting as the defendant claims can't be eliminated. Second, the defendant is not the principal criminal in the case.
>
> *Judge:* Prosecutor, do you want to respond?
>
> *Prosecutor:* First, the problem of inducing confessions, as the defendant claims, doesn't exist, because the defendant was arrested by the Hxxx Security organ on the basis of information placed on the Internet. But the information didn't mention the fact that the defendant shot and killed a person. Without knowing the facts how did the Hxxx Security organ induce him to give such confessions? So I think this fact doesn't exist. Second, the existing evidence is sufficient to prove the defendant's crime.

It seems clear that the defence lawyer was ill-prepared in this case and his feeble attempt at identifying doubt and displacing responsibility was badly judged. For the rest, the most that was tendered by the lawyer, typically in cases where the incident had occurred in the course of a quarrel or where the victim had also been drunk, was the observation in a number of cases[22] that 'the victim was also at fault'.

Indeed, the assigned lawyers in two cases went out of their way to assist the prosecution in disposing of the cases. In I-CO-S3-07, the defendant Zhu, a 23-year old local man,[23] educated only to primary school level, had hired a taxi claiming that he wanted to travel to the City. After travelling some distance, he took out a knife that he had brought with him and inflicted a fatal stab wound on the taxi driver, stole his mobile telephone and approximately RMB 200 in cash. The next day he put the car into a garage for repair. Later that day, he called the garage on the stolen mobile and was told that the car was ready for collection. When he arrived at the garage, he found that the police had been alerted and were waiting at the garage and arrested him. Zhu admitted the crime telling the court in his own words that he had intended to steal the money and the taxi but, when the driver resisted, he stabbed him in the chest. When the defence lawyer, a 40-year old woman dressed in a black jacket, was invited to question the defendant, the following exchange took place:

> *Judge:* Defence lawyer, you may question the defendant.
>
> *Defence Lawyer:* Defendant, did anybody assist you in committing this robbery?
>
> *Defendant:* It was committed by me alone.

---

[22] As, for example, in J-CO-S4-04 on a charge of intentional killing in which the victim had been drinking at the time of the incident.

[23] He was described as a 'farmer' but this label was commonly used in respect of anyone living in the countryside whether or not the individual was in actual employment.

Defence Lawyer: When did you form your intention to commit robbery?

Defendant: On the morning of the day of the crime.

Defence Lawyer: Why did you stab the victim?

Defendant: Even if I ran away, the victim would still pursue me. I was afraid, so I stabbed the victim.

Defence Lawyer: Presiding judge, I have finished questioning.

Later in the proceedings, the judge offered the defence lawyer a further opportunity to put supplementary questions:

Judge: Does the defence lawyer have any supplementary question?

Defence Lawyer: Defendant, did you plan to kill the driver before committing robbery?

Defendant: No.

Defence Lawyer: Did you resist when the police arrested you?

Defendant: No.

Defence Lawyer: Now, how would you describe your act?

Defendant: I admit my guilt and accept punishment.

Defence Lawyer: Presiding judge, I have finished questioning.

In the light of this line of questioning it is hardly surprising that the defence lawyer did not object to the introduction of any of the prosecution evidence. What is surprising is what happened at the conclusion of the investigative stage of the hearing, as seen in the following passage:

Judge: Does the defender of the defendant have any evidence to produce to the court?

Defence Lawyer: I am going to produce to the court the written record that I made while meeting with the defendant, which was consistent with his confession in court.

While this shows that the lawyer actually met with the defendant before the hearing, this disclosure of the confidential lawyer–client relationship is astonishing even if the lawyer had agreed to represent the defendant on the basis that he was guilty (a point that had never been intimated earlier). In the light of this, it is no surprise that the only other contribution of the court-assigned lawyer was a short pro-forma statement on mitigation[24] which the court summarily rejected in imposing the death penalty.

---

[24] The defence lawyer said that the defendant had confessed, that he did not resist when being arrested, that this was the first robbery that he had committed, that the crime was committed alone and not in a gang and that the killing was on impulse.

In the other case, two defendants were charged with intentional injury (giving rise to the death of one of the victims) and theft arising out of a fight involving two groups of youths (K-CO-W-01). When the second defendant, a 20-year old migrant, was questioned by the prosecutor and by the judge, he repeatedly denied that his confessions to the police were true and specifically denied that he had been involved in the crucial fight ('I didn't take part in the fight'). Then his court-appointed lawyer was invited to ask questions and the following exchange took place:

Judge: Does the defender have any question?

Defence Lawyer: When I interrogated you, what did you say?

Defendant 2: I said all were true, except I didn't commit theft.

Defence Lawyer: Then did you participate in the second case of intentional injury?

[Defendant 2 lowered his head, kept silence.]

Defence Lawyer: [conducted education]: If you don't confess frankly, I cannot defend you. Did you participate in the second case of intentional injury?

Defendant 2: Yes.

Defence Lawyer: Which part of the victim's body did you chop?

Defendant 2: Hands and legs.

This then allowed the judge to follow up with pointed questions, in answer to which the defendant made further admissions and also said that the first defendant had stabbed the victim in the stomach (where the fatal wound had been inflicted).

In the exceptional case referred to above, the defendant rather than the court-assigned lawyer did attempt to introduce new evidence in the trial by requesting the presence of a witness from whom the prosecution had already taken a statement. The response of the court illustrates perfectly why such requests are rarely advanced by lawyers, whether court-assigned or retained. The case, E-CO-L-10, involved a charge of intentional injury. After the prosecutor had read out the Bill of Prosecution, the following exchange took place:

[The judge asked the defendant if he had any disagreement with the facts of crime charged in the Bill of Prosecution.]

Defendant: Yes. There is no long-term conflict between the two families. I ask the witness to be present in court.

Judge: Prosecutor, is there any testimony given by the witness in this case?

Prosecutor: Yes.

Judge: Since there are testimonies, why must the witnesses appear in court?[25]

---

[25] This is another indication that judges dislike the appearance of witnesses in court, probably

Defendant: (Silence)

For the rest, the role of the lawyer was confined to submitting a plea in mitigation. These pleas were largely succinct pro-forma representations in which the lawyer sought to rest a plea for leniency upon any of the following attributes which might arguably apply: the defendant had voluntarily surrendered; the defendant had not withdrawn his earlier confession; there was no premeditation; the victim was also at fault; the defendant had displayed a good attitude; the defendant had not previously committed a crime; the defendant was only an accomplice; the defendant was young. In most cases, the mitigation was cryptic, without force and stated without conviction. A typical example is L-CO-X-19, a charge of robbery causing three deaths in which the facts were admitted by the defendant. Two defence lawyers were appointed by the court. Neither of the lawyers participated in questioning the defendant or in any other respect. At the end of the trial, one of the lawyers tendered a plea in mitigation:

> We agree with the prosecutor's charge. The defendant has no criminal record, his daily performance is good. He is willing to admit to the crime and accept the punishment of the law. We hope the panel will impose punishment at its discretion. In addition, we feel sorry for the victim's family.

In several cases, the defence lawyer's assertions did not fit with the evidence and were shot down by the prosecution, as in E-CO-L-01, a charge of robbery leading to the death of the victim, in which the likely outcome was a death sentence. The defendant, a 20-year old man, stabbed the victim to death in the course of a robbery:

> *Defence Lawyer:* I have no disagreement with the charge in the Bill of Prosecution. But I want to remind the collegial panel that the defendant has a good attitude towards his crime and shows remorse. In addition, the defendant was not over 20-years old at the time of committing the crime. As a result, I suggest that the panel impose a lenient punishment.
>
> [The judge asked the prosecutors if they would like to respond to the defence lawyer's opinion.]
>
> *Prosecutor:* Yes. The defendant was over 18-years old and was not in the category deserving of a lenient punishment.

The overall effect of this type of lawyering is that it allows the prosecution to construct the case and the defendant's role in it so that everything that thereafter occurs is an acceptance of that construction or a dialogue with it. This readily gives rise to a presumption of guilt on the part of all the courtroom actors notwithstanding the fact that there were clear opportunities for a well-planned defence to characterize the evidence

---

because of heavy caseloads, the need to improve working efficiency and to avoid unexpected difficulty where the witness's testimony in court differs from that given earlier. This further supports the findings of other Chinese observers: Yuan Zhiqiang (2010), at p. 44; and Wu, Fang and Liu (2005), at p. 111. In the prosecutors' view, once the witnesses (investigators) appear in court and their testimonies are challenged by the defence, this might affect the outcome and also impact upon the overall impression of political and legal institutions. Shen Shitao (2008), at p. 40.

(particularly relating to intention) in ways more favourable to the defendant or to construct a positive defence such as self-defence on the admitted facts.[26]

In the absence of any competing defence theory or case construction, however, attempts to de-construct the prosecution case face insurmountable obstacles for a number of reasons. Most obviously, the defendant has not been prepared as a defence witness and has not been able to put together a coherent and persuasive account. The defendant's account is that which has been extracted in a series of interrogations at the Public Security Bureau without the benefit of legal advice. And, in and of itself, that account may (as we shall see) be the words of the police rather than the words of the defendant. Thereafter, the defence lawyer makes no effort to assemble such an independent account. At the trial itself, the defendant is not given a fair opportunity to tell his or her story because the prosecution account has already achieved 'authoritative' status and any attempt to qualify or contradict the 'official' version has to be undertaken under hostile questioning which is itself tied to the official narrative.

It is the prosecutor who decides whether there was self-defence or excessive defence, whether there exists any relevant defence; and, having had unmediated access to the defendant, the defendant is often co-opted into simply going along with the prosecution account or accepting it reluctantly. Sometimes defendants seek to resist, saying, for example, in response to the reading of the Bill of Prosecution: 'I am innocent. I didn't hit the victim but he took the beer bottle to strike me first' (J-CO-S4-17) but the claim that is embedded in such an outburst, namely self-defence or excessive defence, requires careful formulation and support from the defence lawyer and, if stated in response to cross-examination by the prosecutor, is likely to be undercut in one way or another. Thus, in this case, the investigative stage started in the following way:

Judge: Now let the prosecutor question the defendant.

Prosecutor: Just now you said you were innocent, but now you said you would compensate the plaintiff. Did you do that indeed?

Defendant: I didn't do that at all.

Prosecutor: I hope you will establish a good attitude in court.

Defendant: I am innocent.

Prosecutor: Did you smash the victim in his head with a beer bottle?

Defendant: He hit me first. I surely struck back.

Prosecutor: How did you strike back?

Defendant: He took a beer bottle and tried to hit me, but he failed. Then I took a beer bottle to hit him lightly. I didn't leave then. He was not dead. I don't know why he died later.

---

[26] See also, Max Planck Institute for Foreign and International Criminal Law (2006). This study of death penalty cases in China concluded that the role of defence counsel is marginal at the investigative stage of criminal proceedings and their possible influence thereafter modest.

[Short digression on another matter]

Prosecutor: Why did you quarrel with the victim while you played Mahjong?

Defendant: He said I owed him 20 Yuan, and I said no. We were drinking beers. He took the bottle to attack me. I dodged, so he didn't hit me. I took a beer bottle and struck him gently.

Prosecutor: You began to play Mahjong from noon. Did you drink beer while playing Mahjong?

Defendant: Yes, I was muddleheaded.

Prosecutor: You were muddleheaded. How do you remember so clear that you hit the victim in the head gently?

Defendant: I remember now.

Prosecutor: Who was playing with you?

Defendant: A local person and two aunts. I don't know their names.

Prosecutor: Is the aunt the tenant of the store?

Defendant: Yes.

Prosecutor: Did you mention in your confessions that the victim hit you with a beer bottle?

Defendant: Yes, I did.

Prosecutor: Is this the confession you wrote by yourself? [Shows it]

Defendant: Not me. They wrote it and asked me to copy.

Prosecutor: Anyway, you hit the victim, didn't you?

Defendant: Yes, I hit him. But he was not dead at that time. He ran after me for a long way.

Prosecutor: That's all for my interrogation.

We see here how the defendant attempted to relate his account that he was struck first and was thereby justified in striking the victim, an issue that should have been properly pursued whatever its outcome. It is also clear that the prosecution account is based upon the police version which the defendant says was in the words of the police; only to be met with the dismissive: 'Anyway, you hit the victim, didn't you' rendering irrelevant the circumstances in which this occurred. The defendant, however, persisted. When the prosecutor then read out various witness statements, the defendant reiterated his story, saying: 'I don't agree the testimony of two aunts who played Mahjong with me. It was the victim who hit me first.' In answer to a question from the judge, 'Are your confessions in the Public Security Bureau true?' the defendant said unequivocally: 'No.'

However, despite the attempts by the defendant to relate his account in the difficult circumstances he faced, he received no assistance from the lawyer who, in his only substantive involvement in the case at the end of the case said:

Defence Lawyer: 1. I have no opinion on the prosecution and evidence. 2. It is not the only reason causing the victim's death. According to the interrogation record the defendant hit the victim's head with a beer bottle and the main cause is that the rescue time was delayed. The victim was sent to a clinic before being sent to the hospital. It's possible that there were some problems in the medicine there, because there are many illegal clinics now.

Presiding Judge: Do you wish to reply, prosecutor?

Prosecutor: I think the possibility of misuse of medicine in the private clinic as claimed by the defence lawyer can be eliminated. In this case, the medical expert conclusion said the victim died of a skull injury. There is no relevance to the private clinic. The defence lawyer emphasized that the victim died because of the delay in the rescue, but we want to emphasize why he died. That is the defendant hit the victim on his head with a beer bottle and caused his death. I think there are no legal circumstances which justify a lighter or mitigated punishment.

Whatever the merits of the defendant's account, it is clear that his account could have been formulated in a more persuasive manner with the assistance of a skilled lawyer. No lay person can be expected to tell their story in a setting where he or she is being cross-examined and treated in a dismissive manner. The more so when the defence lawyer is wholly detached from the defendant, ignores the defendant's account and confines his contribution to speculating on causes of death unsupported by facts.

Accordingly, it is the Bill of Prosecution which provides the case theory and context of the crime: L-CO-X-22 is another example. The Bill of Prosecution gives a clear picture in which the defendant quarrelled with W, his wife, struck her with a hammer and killed her, then struck M, his mother, and stole money from his mother; then finding the mother still alive, finished her off with the hammer. The defendant had a different story: but his story had to be told under interrogation from the prosecutor, a prosecutor who was not open to an alternative account. In response to the Bill of Prosecution the defendant immediately responded: 'I didn't kill my mother.' Then the judge spoke to him:

Judge: Just now, you said the charge is not correct. Say what's wrong.

Defendant: I didn't kill my mother.

When the prosecutor picked up the questioning, the following exchange took place:

Prosecutor: Did you strike her?

Defendant: She beat me.

Prosecutor: Where did you smash her with a hammer?

Defendant: Can you listen to me to know the process?

Prosecutor: All right.

Here we see that the defendant wanted to tell his story and the prosecutor indicated that he would be allowed to. But in fact cross-examination resumed immediately:

Prosecutor: When you bashed your wife, your mother called you. Did you bash her again?

Defendant: No.

Prosecutor: Since the hammer was in your hand, did your wife grab the hammer?

Defendant: No. I grabbed the hammer from her hand.

......

Prosecutor: How many times did you see her hitting your mother?

Defendant: She stopped when I went upstairs. She said that she didn't do that intentionally and then ran back into her room.

Prosecutor: Since the hammer was in your hand, why did you bash your wife?

Defendant: If a man saw his mother was bashed down on the ground, wouldn't he be angry?

Prosecutor: Who was important, your mother or your wife?

Defendant: My mother.

Prosecutor: Do you mean your wife isn't important?

Defendant: You tell me.

Judge: This question has nothing to do with the case.

Prosecutor: How many times did you hit your wife? Were your mother and your wife still alive?

Defendant: My wife was alive and my mother died at that time. I was afraid then.

Prosecutor: Why did you drag your mother into the hovel?

Defendant: I was afraid that people would find the body.

Prosecutor: And then?

Defendant: I pulled my wife into the hovel too. I cleaned the blood stains. When I saw my wife was still breathing, I hit her again.

......

Prosecutor: Was your statement in the police station true?

Defendant: No.

Prosecutor: Why?

Defendant: I wanted to die, but didn't have the courage.

Prosecutor: Why did you admit that you killed your mother?

Defendant: It was to ask for forgiveness by my mother. I killed my mother indirectly.

Prosecutor: You still admitted your crime when we interrogated you. So your withdrawal today should be reasonable.

It is obvious that, wherever the truth lay, the defendant was not able to give a free account of the events as he understood them and was placed in a hostile setting with even the judge accepting that one of the lines of cross-examination was inappropriate. And the defendant received no assistance in this regard from his lawyer whose questions were without purpose and not directed to the principal issues as can be seen from the complete record:

Defence Lawyer: How did you get to know your wife?

Defendant: By others' introduction.

Defence Lawyer: How was your relationship?

Defendant: Not good.

Defence Lawyer: Did your parents treat your wife well?

Defendant: Yes.

Defence Lawyer: How's your relationship with your neighbours?

Defendant: All right.

Defence Lawyer: How's their impression of you?

Defendant: I don't know.

The final contribution of the defence lawyer encapsulated the empty nature of his 'defence':

First, the defendant's unhealthy family environment imposed a negative influence on him. Second, the tragedy was caused by the victim. The defendant had a bad relationship with his wife and she attacked the defendant first. We suggest the panel can consider the special circumstances and impose a lighter punishment when imposing a sentence.

It is interesting in this context to note that on several occasions, when interviewed by us, judges spontaneously singled-out court-assigned lawyers for adverse comment (see to the same effect, Regan 2009), as in the following examples:

J-IJ-S4-02: Holding a court is just a procedure. It's especially simple for some cases with only one defendant, clear facts and sufficient evidence. But if the case has several defendants, this procedure is very important for learning the truth of the case. I think the most important thing in the court is to show evidence. But this part doesn't have enough attention, because judges and prosecutors are not willing to spend much time on this. It is the same with the lawyers assigned by the court. So our main work should be done after the trial.

J-IJ-S4-01: As for the defence lawyers, I will listen to their reasonable points. Some outstanding lawyers will gain my respect. But some lawyers are not so responsible for their work, especially some assigned by the court. They come here just to finish a job.

J-IJ-S4-03: Some lawyers are not so responsible for their work, especially some appointed by the court. They come here just to finish a job.

CONCLUSION

In China, there is a lack of legal representation in serious as well as in non-serious cases. In general, unrepresented defendants did not mount any challenge to the prosecution and the case for the prosecution went untested. Those few defendants who disputed the charge or some part of the evidence were not able to present their case in any coherent or persuasive way and in some cases the judge or prosecutor intervened to prevent them from doing so.

Defendants fared little better when represented by a court-assigned lawyer. These lawyers had been instructed very late in the process and had invariably not undertaken extensive defence preparation such as tracing and speaking to witnesses or visiting the crime scene. The questions they raised at trial were few and those that they advanced tended to lack purpose. In a few cases, the intervention of the lawyer assisted the prosecution. For the overwhelming majority of cases, the defence lawyer was dependent upon information provided by the prosecution in the case file and it was on the basis of this that most pleas in mitigation rested. Pleas of mitigation, in turn, tended to be stereotypical and not defendant-specific.

12. The defence at trial observed (2)

The primary focus in this chapter is on trials in which the defendant or his or her family retained a lawyer. We look at the general strategies adopted by these retained lawyers and the extent to which they engaged in pro-active lawyering. We also examine the important issue of confession evidence and, in particular, how the system responds to allegations that the defendant's confession was not reliable because of torture or some other improper behaviour on the part of investigating authorities. Confession evidence deserves this focused scrutiny because, as a matter of generality, it is the foundation-stone of the prosecution case in China and because it is, in and of itself, a test of the whole system and its willingness to comply with minimum standards of human rights.

RETAINED LAWYERS

> *E-IL-L-01 [Defence Lawyer]:* [In the Intermediate Court] we will see if there is any possibility of collecting evidence. But in general, the court is rushing through the procedures because of the time limits. Therefore, in most cases, I don't have enough time to read the files.

> *E-IL-L-02 [Defence Lawyer]:* According to the law, prosecutors should gather evidence proving the defendant's guilt or innocence. However, in practice, it is quite difficult for us to find prosecution evidence proving the defendant's lesser offence or anything advantageous to the defendant. At most, it may include some evidence to show the statutory circumstances (for leniency or severity) of the defendant's act.

Although research evidence from China[1] is equivocal, it might be expected that lawyers retained by the defendant or his or her family would be more pro-active than lawyers assigned by the court. Retained lawyers would, in general, have greater resources at their disposal, often be engaged at an earlier point in the case with accordingly greater opportunity to contact witnesses and collect ancillary evidence helpful to the defence and they would have the co-operation of family and/or friends in putting together the case for the defendant.

We stress at the outset that because our focus is upon *everyday cases*, our research does not directly address the experience of the group of lawyers, known as 'rights defenders' or the 'rights protection movement' (*weiquan yundong*)[2] whose efforts to assert the constitutional and civil rights of citizens through litigation and legal activism (including the use

---

[1] For example, Lu and Miethe (2002) found that the existence and type of legal representation had little effect on detention and release decisions, case outcome, or sentencing. In Chen Guangzhong (2004), at pp. 42–44, it was considered on an analysis of case file materials that not all court-appointed lawyers were of poor quality.

[2] 'Rights defenders' is a term used to describe lawyering activities in which lawyers represent weak parties. It is equivalent to 'cause lawyering' that emerged in the 1960s in the USA.

of the media) often bring them into direct confrontation with the state.³ As none of our sample cases involved typical *weiquan* cases,⁴ the experiences we recount are those faced by the ordinary lawyer in China.

Against this, we must reiterate the constraints operating on all defence lawyers including, but not limited to:⁵ the risk of prosecution of the lawyer if defence witnesses give evidence that is different from the statements they gave to the police; the reluctance of witnesses to become involved in criminal cases; the lack of resources available to lawyers; the exclusion of lawyers from the interrogation stage; the lack of early and full disclosure of the prosecution case; the absence of prosecution witnesses from the trial and hence the inability to cross-examine witnesses and test evidence by forensic processes; the fact that in almost all cases the prosecution will have extracted one or, frequently, more statements of confession from the defendant. For lawyers who continue to fight for their clients, there is the additional threat that the authorities may fail the lawyer at their annual evaluation or even disbar the lawyer.⁶

---

³ These lawyers, it should be noted, are court-centred and, as such, take the law and the legal process seriously whilst acknowledging the limits of what can be achieved through law in an authoritarian state. See, Hand (2006).
⁴ These are commonly (although not exclusively) cases involving such issues as the seizure of land from farmers by local officials, corrupt activities by state agents, actions on behalf of victims of torture and other ill-treatment, together with the pursuit of major scandals such as that involving tainted milk. See, Fu and Cullen (2008).
⁵ E.g., see Guan Yu (2008); Hou and Li (2003); Shen Shitao (2008); Zuo, Ma and Hu (2007); Chen Ruihua (1997); and Xu Meijun (2009).
⁶ Lawyers who defended the Falun Gong, for example, were subsequently deemed to have failed their annual evaluation and were thereby prevented from practising as lawyers. Following this, the Beijing Judicial Bureau held a hearing to determine whether the two lawyers, Tang Jitian and Liu Wei, should be disbarred for disobeying the trial judge's prohibition against arguing the nature of the Falun Gong and leaving the courtroom before the trial had concluded. It is reported that lawyers for Tang Jitian and Liu Wei have been discouraged from representing them at the hearing causing one to drop out with another being prevented from participating at the hearing: Cohen and Chen (2010b). The documentary film *Disbarment* (May 2010) about the Tang and Liu case at the end lists the following cases. 'On 10 April 2009, Guangxi lawyer Yang Zaixin was brutally beaten while handling a case of peasants deprived of their land. On 12 April 2009, Beijing lawyer Cheng Hai was illegally obstructed and beaten by street committee staff and the stability preservation office of Jinyang while trying to perform his professional duty. On 13 May 2009 while Beijing lawyers Zhang Kai and Li Chunfu were carrying out their professional duty in the home of clients in the Jiangjin district of Chongqing City, more than 20 police officers burst in, shackled them, and brutally beat them. Zhang Kai was chained to a metal cage in the police detention centre, and the police illegally seized the procuratorial files and took away key evidence. In 2003, Zheng Enchong (of Shanghai) was sentenced to three years in prison because he had taken on cases of forced evictions. In 2005, the Beijing Shengzhi Law Firm's licence was suspended for one year. In 2006 Gao Zhisheng was sentenced to three years in prison with a five-year suspension. Human rights lawyers Li Subin and Li Wusi (of Henan) have for a long time been prevented from engaging in their profession. Yang Zaixin (of Guangxi), Guo Yan and Tang Jingling (of Guangdong) in 2005 failed to pass the annual registration procedure. Wang Yonghang (of Liaoning) in 2007 had his licence confiscated and in 2009 was sentenced to seven years in prison. Liu Ruping (of Shandong) failed to pass the annual registration procedure in 2007 and in 2009 was sentenced to seven years in prison for taking on religious freedom cases. Yu Zhubiao (of Guangdong) was sentenced to two years of re-education through labour in 2007 for taking on religious freedom cases. Human rights lawyer Teng Biao (of Beijing) had his lawyer's licence cancelled in 2008. In 2009 Wang Ping (of Shandong)

On top of all of this, lawyers in China are confronted with a fundamental strategic dilemma: to submit to the inevitability of conviction and the charade of the 'trial'; or, where the client asserts innocence or there is a credible defence, to challenge the system through a genuine engagement with the prosecution case. Lawyers who adopt the former approach become complicit in state pressure on the defendant to co-operate through a confession or through repeating a confession earlier obtained by torture; but their complicity is entered into for pragmatic and caring reasons, namely, to gain the maximum reduction in sentence available to those who are 'contrite'. By contrast, those lawyers who assert innocence do so knowing that there is little or no prospect that their arguments (should they be allowed to complete them) will prevail and accordingly knowing that the client will lose the benefit of any sentence reduction otherwise available. When others judge lawyers in China, an awareness of the context of lawyering in this environment is essential.[7]

Given this background, it is hardly surprising that retained lawyers are generally inactive at the trial stage, ask few questions, make few objections and in the most usual case direct their efforts towards making a plea in mitigation.[8] A typical example is K-CO-W-11 a case in which a 46-year old primary school-educated migrant male defendant faced one count of intentional homicide. In a 52-minute trial, the prosecution alleged that the defendant, believing that he was entitled to a financial settlement from the factory where he had worked, went to see the factory director armed with a fruit knife and stabbed him in the abdomen causing his death. When questioned by the prosecutor at trial, the defendant admitted the killing and the defence lawyer declined asking the defendant any questions, as the following extract shows:

---

was sentenced to seven years in prison for taking on religious freedom cases. On 17 March 2009, the Beijing Yitong law firm had its licence suspended for six months. In 2009 the Guangdong-based lawyer Liu Shihui had his licence suspended for representing Guo Feixiong and others. In 2009 Fujian lawyer Lin Hongnan had his professional licence suspended for one year for having defended You Jingyu and others. On 28 February 2009, Heilongjiang lawyer Wei Liangyue was detained by Harbin police. On 16 April 2009, lawyer Liu Yao of Guangdong, who had represented peasants deprived of their land, was convicted and sentenced to one year in prison, suspended for two years. On 4 February 2009, famous human rights lawyer Gao Zhisheng was abducted from his home in Shaanxi and disappeared for a long time. In 2009 the following lawyers were deprived of their right to practise law for 'failing to pass the annual registration procedure': Li Heping, Li Chunfu, Li Xiongbing, Wang Yajun, Liu Wei, Wen Haibo, Xie Yanyi, Zhang Chengmao, Cheng Hai, Tang Jitian, Yang Huiwen, Tong Chaoping, Zhang Lihui, Li Jinsong, Li Jinglin, Zhang Jianguo, Wei Liangyue (some of them later regained their licences). In 2010, Shandong lawyer Wang Zhansuo was criminally detained for having taken on religious freedom cases. In April 2010, human rights lawyers Tang Jitian and Liu Wei faced the revocation of their licence to practice.' *Diao Zhao Men*, by He Yang, 1 May 2010, available at http://www.chrlcg-hk.org/?p=522.

[7] See, Cohen and Pils (2008) where such a dilemma was realized in the prosecution of the activist Hu Jia with one of his lawyers urging the court to accept his 'low level of criminality' whilst the other lawyer argued that no crime had been committed. For a general review of the ethics of lawyering in China, see: Xu Xi (2009).

[8] Others have noted that the contribution of defence lawyers to the trial is based upon the material set out in the prosecution file. See, for example, Zuo Weimin (2007). As the author puts it: 'Based on our statistics and observations in the courtroom, the defense attorneys' activities concentrate on the flaws in the dossier. . . . [I]t seldom happens that the lawyer collects and provides evidence. If they collect any, it is mainly to determine the mitigating circumstances, and it is not enough to affect the nature of the case.'

Prosecutor: Did you stab the victim?

Defendant: Yes, I stabbed twice.

Prosecutor: Which part did you stab?

Defendant: I don't know.

Prosecutor: Where is the knife now?

Defendant: I threw it away at the crime scene.

Prosecutor: Where did you go after the stabbing?

Defendant: I stayed at the crime scene to wait for the police to come and arrest me.

Judge: Does the defender have any question?

Defence Lawyer: No.

No objection was taken by the defence lawyer to the evidence introduced by the prosecutor in the form of statements: statements of various civilian witnesses; the post mortem examination report; the crime scene report; records from the factory; DNA report; the knife; and proof of household registration. The defence lawyer's principal input was to make a very basic plea in mitigation.

> *Prosecutor:* 1. The facts of this case are clear, the evidence is sufficient and reliable, the act of the defendant constituted the offence of intentional homicide. 2. The act of the defendant caused relatively great harm to society; the consequence is serious. I urge the court to punish him severely.
>
> *Judge:* Does the defendant have any defence opinion?
>
> *Defendant:* I didn't want to kill him; I only wanted to threaten him.
>
> *Judge:* Let the defender give the speech for the defence.
>
> *Defender:* 1. The defendant has voluntarily surrendered himself. 2. The defendant has frankly confessed his crime after being arrested: he has a good attitude in admitting his guilt. 3. The defendant killed the victim not out of illegal personal benefit.
>
> *Judge:* Let the prosecutor reply.
>
> *Prosecutor:* 1. As to the purpose of the defendant bringing the knife, the prosecutor argues that the defendant brought a sharp knife and used it to stab the vital part of the victim's body, this constituting the offence of intentional homicide. 2. The act of the defendant didn't constitute voluntary surrender.[9] 3. The defendant's motive to kill the victim was malicious.

---

[9] This point is unclear from the facts that emerged in court. It is not known whether the police or others caught the defendant at the scene or whether the defendant waited for the arrival of the police.

Judge: Do the prosecutor and the defender have any other opinion?

Defender: I insist on my opinion regarding the voluntary surrender of the defendant.

We see here a key feature of defence work in criminal cases in China: the personal attributes of the defendant (almost invariably poor, uneducated and oftentimes of migrant status) guide the courtroom actors (including the defence counsel) to settle the central question of criminal responsibility rather than any inquiry into the actual circumstances of the case and the actual state of mind that subsisted at the time of the criminal incident. The defendant is simply assumed to be guilty and to have the requisite state of mind and the account of the prosecution (at best a theory) is allowed to prevail without challenge. The structure of the Criminal Law in China[10] can be at best a partial explanation,[11] the presupposition of guilt deriving from an estimation of the moral worth of the defendant rather than from a fact-based analysis of the case itself. As a further consequence, the role of the defence lawyer is largely reduced to arguing that the defendant is less culpable and that punishment should be mitigated.

Another example is case M-CO-Y-13. Here, the defendant was prosecuted following his involvement in a road traffic accident which resulted in the death of the other vehicle's occupant. The driver admitted responsibility for having caused the accident and the whole event had been witnessed by a traffic police officer. Realistically, the only path open to the defence was a plea to reduce the extent of liability (which had been assessed at 90 per cent by the traffic police) and the amount of compensation that would be paid. Accordingly, the defence lawyer made no attempt to challenge the defendant's guilt but concentrated instead upon seeking a reduced liability. At the trial, the defendant had

---

[10] Criminal offences are stated rather than defined in Chinese law thereby eliminating many of the possible arguments open to defence lawyers. The Criminal Law of the People's Republic of China 1997 does draw distinctions in its General Part but these too provide great discretion to the courts and are broad in character. For example, an 'intentional' crime refers to an act committed by a person 'who clearly knows that his act will entail harmful consequences to society but who wishes or allows such consequences to occur'; whereas, a 'negligent' crime refers to an act committed by a person 'who should have foreseen that his act would possibly entail harmful consequences to society but who fails to do so through his negligence or, having foreseen the consequences, readily believes that they can be avoided, so that the consequences do occur'. (See, Articles 14 and 15 of the Criminal Law of the People's Republic of China.) While 'merely stating' but not defining the crime is a feature of Chinese traditional law (e.g. the late Qing Code), imperial law actually saw many early efforts to compile commentaries helping magistrates to determine guilt in a rational and fair way, as *Parallel Cases from Under the Pear-Tree: A 13th Century Manual of Jurisprudence and Detection* demonstrates. See, http://www.amazon.com/T%C3%ACAng-Yin-Pi-Shih-Parallel-Cases-Under-Pear-Tree/dp/0883559080. Legal literature nowadays also includes works that expound the structure (*jiegou*) of criminal offences and law students in China are required to 'learn' these. Our empirical research indicates that whatever students may have learned has little bearing on how cases are actually handled in court.

[11] Other inquisitorial systems, such as that of Germany, use abstract terms to define, for example, 'intention' but that does not lead to unjust criminal judgments. In Germany and in other similar jurisdictions, an abundance of decision-based commentaries and case materials, academic treatises etc. provides the basis for interpreting these provisions and, more importantly, the criminal process there requires intelligent engagement with this material and genuine argument.

objected to the eye-witness account of the traffic officer[12] but had conceded everything else. The defence lawyer spoke as follows:

> No objection is taken as to the facts alleged by the prosecution that the defendant has committed the traffic offence and the determination of the nature of the case. The eye-witness Zhou is a policeman, his testimony is relatively more objective. At the time, the defendant's lorry and the victim's motor car collided with each other because both of them were rushing while the traffic light was switching from red to green. Their responsibility should be equal, but according to traffic regulations, the big lorry [driven by the defendant] should let the motor car go first, therefore there is no objection that the defendant should bear the major responsibility. Now the following opinions requesting the court to give the defendant a lighter punishment are raised:
>
> (1) Although the defendant should bear the major responsibility, his responsibility should not be the 90 per cent responsibility as confirmed by the traffic police team; he should only bear 60 per cent to 70 per cent of the responsibility at most. And the victim's driving without a licence is a serious fault. The request for the defendant to undertake 90 per cent of the responsibility is obviously unreasonable; his major responsibility was just over 50 per cent.
> (2) After the accident, the defendant tried his best to pay RMB 120 000 in compensation. And the defendant has frankly confessed the facts of the crime. He has also admitted the major facts in court today. He has a good attitude in admitting his guilt and making compensation. The court should take these factors into account.[13]

In a similar fashion is the case E-CO-L-02, a charge of intentional homicide involving a twenty-five year old, thin man appearing in court wearing detention centre clothes. The defendant borrowed money from the victim when they both worked together as security officers. When the defendant sought repayment, the victim was unable to raise the amount of the original loan and the defendant decided to kill the victim. He did so by tying a rope around the victim's neck and disembowelling him. After the defendant told X that he had killed the victim and hidden his body in the defendant's house, X informed the police who immediately raided the defendant's home and arrested him. A psychiatric report concluded that the defendant was of limited capacity.[14] The defence lawyer did not ask any questions at the investigative stage and made a straightforward plea in mitigation:

> First, I have no disagreement with the charge in the Bill of Prosecution. But the defendant has limited capacity, so his punishment should be reduced or lightened. Second, the defendant has the circumstance of voluntary surrender, he actively surrendered himself to the police, stated the facts of his crime truthfully and is willing to accept punishment and has a good attitude

---

[12] The objection being that he was further away from the traffic light at the time of the incident, the defence lawyer observing that there was no other witness to corroborate the view of the officer.

[13] Throughout the mediation which immediately followed the criminal hearing, the defendant sought mercy from the victim's family. The family asked for RMB 350 000 compensation whilst the defence argued that he could afford no more than RMB 230 000. The defendant knelt in front of the victim's family throughout the mediation and plied them with cigarettes.

[14] The Criminal Law provides, *inter alia*, that 'if a mental patient causes harmful consequences at a time when he is unable to recognize or control his own conduct, upon verification and confirmation through legal procedure, he shall not bear criminal responsibility' (Article 18). However, the procedural safeguards in China for dealing with defendants suffering from mental illness are inadequate. See, for example, Zhiyuan Guo (2010). Taking as a starting point the trial and execution of Yang Jia for murdering six police officers and injuring four others, this article analyzes how mental health examinations are provided for and carried out in China and makes proposals for reform.

towards his crime and shows repentance. Therefore, he should be given a lenient or reduced punishment. Third, according to criminal policy in China, a person who shows remorse may be given a lenient punishment.

In announcing the judgment after a 59-minute trial the judge remarked on the crime and the plea in mitigation:

> There is no law in the defendant's mind. He killed the victim just because he could not repay the victim's money. His act constituted the offence of intentional homicide. The fact of the crime charged by the public prosecution organ is clear and the evidence is sufficient. Thus, the charge is established. But given that the defendant has limited capacity his punishment can be reduced by law. As for the defender's opinion and the defendant's justification that the defendant voluntarily surrendered himself to the police, after investigation, there is a lack of relevant evidence to support this argument, though the defendant may have been willing to surrender. As a result, the argument is not admissible. The court supports the civil claim because the defendant's act brought financial loss to the victim's family.
> Sentence: Death penalty with two years' suspension with deprivation of political rights for life and civil compensation of 49 000 Yuan.[15]

This is not to say that lawyers had not developed an appreciation of what might be achieved. In many instances there were simply no other avenues open to them.[16]

In some instances, the defence lawyer sought to lay a foundation for mitigation by asking appropriate questions of the defendant at the investigative stage. An example is the case D-CO-K-01. Here, during the course of a quarrel, the defendant stabbed the victim (Ling) with a knife causing serious bodily harm. The defence lawyer questioned the defendant so as to contextualize the incident:

Defence Lawyer: What is your relationship with the victim?

Defendant: Friends.

Defence Lawyer: How did the knife with which you stabbed the victim appear on the scene?

Defendant: On that night, my friends called and gave the knife to the victim. Later, the victim brought it to my room.

Defence Lawyer: What did you see when you returned to your room?

Defendant: I saw he was drunk and was going to attack others.

Defence Lawyer: Did you quarrel with him?

---

[15] In the consolidated civil action, the defendant indicated that he had no money and was content for his family to deal with the matter of civil compensation.

[16] In case E-CO-L-08, for example, a charge of intentional harm, when presented with various eyewitness accounts, the defence lawyer said in the course of argument: 'But when I read the case file, I found that Zhang's testimony showed that there was no one else at the crime scene at that time.' In a number of other cases, the nature of the lawyer's representation evidenced some knowledge of the case before the court hearing.

Defendant: Yes. He attacked me with a chair.

This broad account was supported by several prosecution witnesses who, in their statements, said that Ling had been drunk and was attacking others. This laid the foundation for mitigation:

> *Defence Lawyer:* First, I would like to say sorry and offer condolences to the victim on behalf of the defendant, and hope that the panel can make a fair judgment. The plaintiff [victim] was responsible for the occurrence of this case. The witnesses' testimonies proved that it was the victim who first made trouble on the night, then the defendant tried to stop the victim and they had an argument. It was the victim who first attacked the defendant with fists. Because both of them drank a lot of alcohol, the defendant stabbed the victim with a knife. Second, the criminal intent and subjective evilness are small. The testimony of the witness [Lo] proved that the victim brought the knife to the defendant's room, so I hope the panel can consider this circumstance at the time of sentencing. As for the consequences occurring on that night, the defendant actively sent the victim to the hospital in time and signed his name on the victim's operation notice. Afterwards, he actively negotiated with the victim's family regarding compensation. In order to show his sincerity, he didn't flee. The defendant appreciates the prosecutor's suggestion to the panel.[17] The defendant has a good attitude towards his crime; his daily performance is good; and he abided by the law and discipline before this crime. Part of the reason for causing this crime is on the victim's side.

[The judge asks the defendant if he agrees with his defender.]

Defendant: Yes.

[The judge asks the prosecutor if she wants to reply to the defender's opinion.]

Prosecutor: Yes. The defendant got the knife from his bed, not from the victim's hand.

[The judge asks the defender if he wants to reply to the prosecutor's opinion.]

Defence Lawyer: Yes. Although this will not affect the charge, but we can prove that the knife was brought to the crime scene by the victim.

[The judge asks the prosecutor if she wants to reply to the defender's opinion.]

Prosecutor: No.

A further example of an attempt to establish a factual basis for mitigation occurred in a drugs case, JCO-S4-10, which was, in fact, a police 'buy-and-bust' operation involving two defendants 25 and 31 years of age. One defendant bought 1000 pills from an undercover detective and then sought to sell them to the second defendant. Both were arrested on the spot in McDonald's where the transaction occurred. At the investigative stage, each of the retained lawyers sought information which would underpin their pleas in mitigation. In neither instance did either challenge the substantive prosecution evidence. What follows are the questions each lawyer put to his respective defendant:

---

[17] The prosecutor stated that the defendant had taken the victim to hospital and had displayed a good attitude to his crime and invited the panel to impose a punishment suited to the crime.

Defence Lawyer 1: Who contacted you to sell drugs? Do you know the buyer? Who is he?

Defendant 1: It's some fellow [Z] who called me that he wanted narcotic drug pills at the price of 3.6 Yuan each and he asked me if I could get some drugs. I said I could. I only know that he is some Mr [Z.]

Defence Lawyer 1: You were detained in the toilet of McDonald's when dealing. Did the police have a different attitude towards you? Were you both handcuffed?

Defendant 1: Their attitude was just ordinary. He (the buyer) was not handcuffed.

Defence Lawyer 2: Who was the buyer?

Defendant 1: I didn't know him.

Defence Lawyer 2: Did you get to know afterwards?

Defendant 1: They are police.

. . . .

Judge: Defence Lawyer 2, you can question Defendant 2.

Defence Lawyer 2: Have you ever sold drugs before?

Defendant 2: No.

Defence Lawyer 2: How did you come to possess 1000 pills of narcotic drugs?

Defendant 2: From G [Defendant 1].

Defence Lawyer 2: During the course of dealing, how many people were there?

Defendant 2: Four.

Defence Lawyer 2: Did you know them all?

Defendant 2: Only G [Defendant 1].

Defence Lawyer 2: When you were detained, how many people were handcuffed?

Defendant 2: I didn't see clearly.

Defence Lawyer 2: That's all for my questioning.

This was not, of course, penetrative questioning, but the lawyers made an attempt to establish that (i) the defendants had not been involved in drug dealing before; and (ii) that they had been induced to do so on this occasion by undercover police officers in a 'sting' operation. This set the scene for mitigation:

Judge: Defenders, now it is time for you to defend the defendants.

Defence Lawyer 1: I have four items of defence for my defendant: 1. Because the defendant was lured by a police informant and has thereby committed a crime, I beg the judges to give him a lenient punishment. 2. The crime hasn't caused severe damage to society, and all the drugs were recovered. 3. The defendant behaved well before this. 4. It was his first time and he was only an accessory. I beg the judges to give him leniency.

Defence Lawyer 2: 1. The defendant had been lured by a police informant. 2. The defendant hasn't sold a lot of drugs. 3. The crime wasn't actually committed. 4. The defendant confessed his crime with a good attitude. I beg the judges to give him a lenient punishment.

In other cases, defence lawyers sought to argue that their client was a secondary party (as in, I-CO-S3-10 where each of the lawyers of joint defendants argued that their own client was an accomplice rather than the principal offender); that the defendant was of weak intellect (as in I-CO-S3-08); or that the victim was only partly to blame (F-CO-N-20, a case of rape in which the defence lawyer argued that the victim did not resist, had been conscious at the time of the act and had failed to report the offence until three days later). It was rare for these arguments to persuade the court in any degree. Thus, in M-CO-Y-10, the defendant, together with others already tried and sentenced, agreed to steal metal items. Once stolen by the accomplices, the metal was left at the roadside from where the defendant collected it in his lorry and distributed it to the buyer. The defence lawyer mitigated as follows:

Defence Lawyer: Firstly, this defence lawyer does not have any objection as to the determination that the defendant Q. . . . has committed the offence of theft and the facts are as alleged by the prosecution. But I urge the court to consider the following circumstances which allow the court to give the defendant a lighter or reduced punishment: (1) The role of the defendant in this joint crime was relatively minor. First, he was not the one who proposed the crime; second, the defendant didn't perform any actual act of theft, he was only waiting nearby; after others had stolen the [metal objects], he transported these illegally acquired items to the City for sale; third, the distribution of illegally acquired money was also done by others, the amount of money he was given was only equivalent to the cost of transportation. From the three circumstances mentioned, it is clear that the role of the defendant in this case was relatively minor, other accomplices have been sentenced, and there was no distinction between principal offender and accomplices. I urge the court to take this into account in determining the sentence. (2) The defendant has voluntarily surrendered himself after committing the crime. Having considered his role, I suggest that the court reduce the sentence for the defendant. (3) The defendant has a good attitude in admitting his guilt; he deeply regrets his act. He surrendered to the judicial organ after having been persuaded by his family. (4) As to the illegally acquired items, from the judgments of the accomplices, it is clear that the victim's loss has already been compensated, the harm to the victim and the danger to society have been accordingly reduced. (5) The defendant has already paid the fine on his own initiative. I also urge that the court exercise discretion to give him a lighter punishment.

Judge: Now let's start the second round of the debate, prosecutor, do you have any supplementary opinion?

Prosecutor: I would like to add one point. As to the role of the defendant, the prosecution argues that the defendant's role in this case was average. He cannot be considered as playing a minor role or be treated as an accomplice. This is because, in the course of the crime, the defendant firstly conspired with the other accomplices to commit the crime, and after other accomplices had moved out the illegally acquired items, he actively transported the illegally acquired items and actively contacted the buyer. The prosecutor accordingly argues that the defendant has also actively participated in the crime. As to the argument that the defendant has a good attitude in admitting his guilt, the loss of the illegally acquired items has already been compensated. I have no opinion on these circumstances which allow the court to exercise discretion to give the defendant a lighter punishment.

Judge: Does the defendant have any supplementary opinion?

Defendant: I urge that I be given a lighter punishment.

Judge: Does the defender have any supplementary opinion?

Defence Lawyer: As to the issue relating to the role of the defendant, this has already been stated clearly in the first round [of Debate]. I am not going to give any supplementary opinion.

Whilst the court accepted that the defendant had expressed remorse, it did not feel able to reduce the punishment of the defendant, a recidivist, the judge saying:

Judge: The defence lawyer's arguments that the defendant has voluntarily surrendered himself and he has a good attitude in admitting his guilt and the loss of the victim has already been compensated are accepted. But her argument that the defendant should be given a lighter punishment is not accepted. In order to maintain social order and protect the legal property of citizens from being illegally infringed, the following judgment is made according to Articles 264, 25(1), 65(1), 67(1) and 52 of the Criminal Law:

The defendant committed the offence of theft: he is sentenced to 3 years' imprisonment and RMB 4000 fine.

Some of these modest efforts proved entirely misplaced. Case K-CO-W-08, for example, involved the offence of transporting narcotic drugs in circumstances where the police arrested the defendant (who had travelled from one area to another) as he got off a bus and searched him. The defendant, a thirty-two year old migrant, admitted that he had bought drugs in the past from the same supplier. The defence lawyer then questioned him as follows:

Defence Lawyer: Were the drugs you bought from him in the past taken by yourself alone or with your friends?

Defendant: Taken with friends.

Defence Lawyer: You did take drugs, but why was the result of your urine test negative [for drugs]?

Defendant: I had not taken any drugs for several days.

Defence Lawyer: Why did you buy so many drugs this time?

Defendant: To take with friends.

Defence Lawyer: Did the money used to buy drugs belong to you?

Defendant: Yes.

Defence Lawyer: I have finished questioning the defendant.

Here we see that the lawyer's questioning was designed to lay a foundation for a defence that the amount involved was not only for personal use but to share with friends (rather than trafficking in drugs) and to explain the negative urine test.

Prosecutor: 1. The facts of this case are clear and the evidence is sufficient. The act of the defendant constituted the offence of transportation of narcotic drugs. 2. The amount of narcotic drugs transported in this case was relatively large; the harm to society was big. 3. The defendant in this case is a recidivist. By taking into account the above factors, I urge the court to make a judgment according to law.

Judge: Defendant, do you have any defence opinion?

Defendant: I didn't go to [the city] often to buy drugs. I argue that the prosecution's determination of the nature of my act is incorrect. I bought drugs for consumption, but not for transportation.

Judge: Now let the defence lawyer of the defendant state his opinion.

Defence Lawyer: 1. The nature of this case should not be determined as transportation of narcotic drugs; it should be determined as illegal possession of narcotics drugs. 2. The narcotic drugs have not passed into society; the harm to society is not large.

Judge: Now let the prosecutor reply.

Prosecutor: 1. The defender failed to express clearly whether he is arguing that the defendant didn't commit the offence or his crime should be determined as illegal possession of narcotic drugs. 2. The act of the defendant in this case complied with the elements of trafficking narcotic drugs both objectively and subjectively. He could only be considered as having committed the offence of trafficking narcotic drugs.

Judge: Does the defender have any new opinion?

Defence Lawyer: The act of the defendant was only to bring his narcotic drugs from one place to another and he did that only for the purpose of consumption, but no other purpose, therefore he should be considered as having committed the offence of illegal possession of narcotic drugs.

Judge: The court has already clearly heard the arguments of both sides, if there is no new opinion, that's all for the court debate. Does the prosecutor have any new opinion?

Prosecutor: The result of the defendant's urine test is negative, and the witnesses can prove that the defendant didn't take drugs together with others in the past. There is no record of his compulsory drug rehabilitation in the drug rehabilitation centre; also he bought a large quantity of narcotic drugs on one occasion. All the evidence can prove that this case should be a case of trafficking narcotic drugs.

Judge: Does the defender have any new opinion?

Defence Lawyer: I insist on my original opinion.

It was clear, however, that this was a weak defence particularly given that the urine test showed no trace of drugs and there being no evidence other than the assertion of the defendant that he had in the past shared drugs with friends. The collegial panel accordingly rejected the defence arguments and the defendant was sentenced to life imprisonment, deprivation of his political rights and confiscation of all his property.

From time to time, the defence lawyer advanced some limited defence based upon a re-characterization of the prosecution case. Typically, this occurred in personal injury offences arising out of a fight of some kind in which the prosecution alleged that the defendant committed homicide or intentional injury and in which the defence, whilst accepting many of the basic facts, argued that it was self-defence[18] or excessive defence[19] or that the defendant was guilty of some lesser crime, such as affray. Thus, for example, in K-CO-W-12, the defendant, a 23-year old migrant, had a quarrel with the victim with whom he had been on a stealing venture and struck the victim on the head causing his death. In an unrelated incident, he and others later stole items from premises in a hostel in an industrial district. In the course of the trial the defendant gave differing accounts of the first incident: at first he told the prosecutor 'he [the victim] hit me first'; then he told the prosecutor 'we quarrelled, he pushed me once, I picked up a stone and hit his head' and said that the victim only 'hit him' and he had struck him with the stone. Asked by his defence lawyer why he had hit the victim with the stone, he replied: 'He hit me first. I had never thought of hitting him to death.' He added that when he left the victim, the victim was still alive and cursing him. Whilst the prosecutor argued for conviction of the indicted offence, the defence lawyer sought to use the defendant's account to support a lesser charge:

Prosecutor: The facts of this case are clear and the evidence is sufficient and reliable. The defendant's defence made today was that the victim pushed him first, so he hit the victim on a sudden impulse, the victim still sat on the ground and continued to curse him. From the post mortem examination, we can see that the victim suffered from a serious skull and brain injury. A person would not be able to sit on the ground if he had suffered such a serious skull and brain injury. From the examination of the crime scene, we can see that there were many bloodstains there: this could only happen if the defendant struck the fatal part of the victim's head savagely. The act of the defendant constituted the offence of intentional homicide. The defendant is a recidivist,[20] he should be punished severely.

Defence Lawyer: The prosecutor identified this case as a case of intentional homicide. The defendant and the victim quarrelled because of some argument; there was no reason for him to kill the victim. From the defendant's confession, it is clear that after the quarrel, the victim pushed the defendant first and then the defendant picked up a stone to hit him on a sudden

---

[18] Thus, by Article 20 of the 1979 Criminal Law, 'An act that a person commits to stop an unlawful infringement in order to prevent the interests of the State and the public, or his own or other person's rights of the person, property or other rights from being infringed upon by the on-going infringement, thus harming the perpetrator, is justifiable defence, and he shall not bear criminal responsibility.'

[19] Excessive defence (*fangwei guodang*) is not a defence under Chinese law but is a ground for mitigation under Article 20, 1979 Criminal Law: 'If a person's act of justifiable defence obviously exceeds the limits of necessity and causes serious damage, he shall bear criminal responsibility; however, he shall be given a mitigated punishment or be exempted from punishment.'

[20] The defendant had one prior conviction for theft.

impulse. This should be considered as intentional injury. There is no objection to the facts relating to the theft that were alleged. The defendant has a good attitude in admitting his guilt after being arrested. I urge the court to give him a lighter sentence.

Judge: Let the prosecutor reply.

Prosecutor: The distinction between intentional injury and intentional homicide is whether the act was aimed at the life or the body of the victim. The defendant picked up a stone and savagely hit the fatal part of the victim's head. This should be considered as intentional homicide. Circumstances which allow the defendant to be given a lighter sentence do not exist. I urge the court to give the defendant a severe punishment.

Judge: After the court debate, the court has already understood the opinions of the prosecution and the defence. Does the defender have anything to add?

Defender: No.

As in so many cases, the defence argument was rejected, the defendant being sentenced to the death penalty without suspension. In other similar cases the defence attempted to run a defence of excessive self-defence on a charge of intentional injury (K-CO-W-04); intentional injury instead of intentional homicide (L-CO-X-14); and excessive defence on a charge of intentional injury (L-CO-X-15).

Another indication of defence lawyer activity is seen in the making of a procedural or evidential challenge. This did not occur with any frequency but there were occasional examples. In I-CO-S3-01 on a charge of robbery and intentional homicide, the following exchange occurred:

Prosecutor: Presiding judge, I produce the testimony of witness Wang which was collected by the police according to law; it can prove the facts of the defendant's robbery and murder. It is at pp. 17–19, second volume of the case file.

Judge: OK.

Prosecutor: [Reads out the witness testimony]. . . .[content omitted].

Judge: Does the defendant object?

Defendant: Yes, he [the witness] only heard somebody say so. This is not true. I didn't do that.

Judge: Does the defender object?

Defender: This evidence was only hearsay; it cannot be used as evidence.

Here we see the retained lawyer objecting to the admission of evidence on the grounds that it was 'hearsay'.[21] Of course it is ironic that such an objection could have been made to almost all prosecution evidence in every case since the statements read out by

---

[21] A similar objection was taken in D-CO-K-06 to the relevance and persuasive value of a statement of a witness who was simply purporting to repeat what others had said.

prosecutors were hearsay, there being no live witnesses produced and almost all the statements in question were being introduced to prove the truth of their contents.

Another example arose in case D-CO-K-09 where the 22-year old defendant stood charged with inflicting intentional harm upon the victim who suffered injury to his head. This case was, it should be noted, atypical in that the trial was being used to educate student police officers and was set up more in the adversary tradition in terms of challenges to the evidence made by the defence lawyers although no witnesses were produced. In the course of initial questioning at the opening of the investigative stage, the defendant agreed with the prosecutor that his statements (confessions) at the police station were true; he agreed with his second defence lawyer that he had hit the victim once with a brick after, he said, several men had attacked him:

[The judge asks the second defender if she will ask the defendant questions.]

Defence Lawyer: Yes. Under what circumstances did you attack the victim with a piece of brick?

Defendant: They beat me down to the floor. I saw there were several pieces of brick, so I picked up one.

Defence Lawyer: Which part of his body did you attack?

Defendant: The front part.

Defence Lawyer: How many times did you attack him with the brick?

Defendant: Once.

Presiding Judge:[22] Speak with a louder voice! The panel needs to make a written record!

Defence Lawyer: Did you attack him again?

Defendant: No. His friends were chasing me.

The case-responsible judge then took over the questioning during the course of which the defendant agreed that he had struck the victim on the head. When the prosecutor introduced a confession statement,[23] the judge asked the defendant if he challenged any of the evidence. The defendant remained silent for about one minute before saying, 'Some are not true.' This sparked the following exchange:

Judge: Which are not true?

Defendant: (Silence).

Judge: You answer my question!

---

[22] These sorts of intrusions from the judge were not infrequent in our fieldwork.
[23] The defendant had made three statements of confession which, according to the prosecution, were in all essentials the same.

Defendant: I didn't use the brick to attack the victim.

Judge: You didn't use the brick to attack the victim?

Defendant: No.

Judge: Why did you say 'Yes' when the prosecutor asked you if your statement in the police station was true?

Defendant: When they made this written record at that time, my mind was not clear.

[The judge then asked the first defence lawyer whether he challenged the evidence above.]

Defence Lawyer: Yes. This evidence doesn't meet the provisions of the Criminal Procedure Law. The prosecutor didn't deliver it to the court beforehand. Since the content of this written record is not the same as the other three [confessions], it is inappropriate to present it right now.

Judge: Defenders, do you need see this written record?

Defence Lawyers: Yes.

As a result of this challenge, the judge called a ten-minute adjournment to allow the defence lawyers the opportunity to read this statement and compare it with the three other confessions made by the defendant. On the resumption of the trial, the defence lawyers argued that the victim was also at fault. They further challenged the admissibility of the document produced by the police indicating the extent of the victim's injuries on the basis that the police station is not a legal judicial appraisal organ for this purpose. Both defence lawyers, however, accepted that the defendant was at fault and the thrust of their argument was simply a plea for leniency.

Whilst the defence was almost invariably a dialogue with the case put forward by the prosecution, on a few occasions, the defence sought to introduce its own evidence into the trial. In D-CO-K-06, the defendant was charged with possession of illegal drugs. Following the presentation of the prosecution evidence, in the course of which the defendant admitted possessing illegal drugs, the following colloquy took place:

[The judge asked the defendant if he had evidence to present in the courtroom.]

Defendant: . . . . (He says nothing but looks at the defence lawyer).

Judge: You have no need to look at your defence lawyer. Do you have any evidence?

Defence Lawyer: The judge asks you if you have any evidence?

Defendant: No.

[The judge then asked the defence lawyer if he had evidence to present.]

Defence Lawyer: Yes. I have two sets of evidence. One is evidence on the defendant's being in the hospital, the log of his case history and the bill of the hospital charges.

Judge: Tell us the source and purpose of the evidence.

Defence Lawyer: They were provided by the defendant's family member and can prove that the defendant suffered from sugar diabetes and just left hospital before this crime. The defendant smoked the drug to reduce the pain of his illness.

The prosecutor said that this evidence was irrelevant as it was not reasonable to seek to justify taking drugs to relieve pain. In the debate, the defence lawyer conceded this point immediately:

First, we think the aim of illegal possession of drugs was to relieve the pain of illness. Of course, just as the prosecutor said, we cannot say it is justified that the defendant smoked drugs to relieve his pain.

A further example is case J-CO-S4-03 in which four defendants were jointly charged with intentional injury. The origin of the case lay in the activities of a village security patrol team (the defendants) who saw some people acting suspiciously, one of the individuals, Qi, running away when challenged. Qi was taken to a sentry box and beaten by various members of the security team (except, it seems, the fourth defendant) on their accounts to 'teach him a lesson' or to get him to 'admit the truth' because they believed that he was involved in dealing in drugs or some other illegal behaviour. Following the questioning of the defendants at the investigative stage to determine who did what in the beating of Qi, the judge asked whether the defendant or defence lawyers had any new evidence to present and the lawyer for the first defendant responded in this way:

Defence Lawyer: Yes. (1) The testimony of the security chief of the village to prove that the first defendant surrendered himself to the police voluntarily. (2) The medical identification of three experts to prove that the victim died because of his hypersensitive body. (3) Valid admission certificates of the security team. (4) Material to prove the first defendant is a qualified member of the security team. (5) Two letters pleading mercy by the village committee and the dead victim's father. [During the course of the reading of the letters, the fourth defendant quietly laughed because the letters were poorly written it would seem.]

The material was passed to the prosecutor who took a few minutes to read it before responding as follows:

Prosecutor: (1) The medical identification is not made by a specialist appointed by the judicial organ, so it cannot be used as valid evidence in court. (2) There is not much meaning in the letter requesting mercy. This only shows that the village committee is very concerned about this case.

Similarly, in I-CO-S3-05, the defendant was charged with two counts of fraud through the issuance of cheques. The defence argued that this was in fact a civil dispute and that the evidence of a principal witness for the prosecution was untrue. Having made appropriate challenges throughout the investigative stage, when asked whether the defence had any evidence to put before the court, the defence lawyer replied in the affirmative.

Defence Lawyer: Yes. The first piece of evidence is the development agreement between D Company and F Company; there is also a termination agreement. They can prove that the defendant's construction site was in [that province] and the facts in question related to the joint development. The second piece of evidence was the transaction account between D Company and the metal factory. From the case file we can see that the transaction account was written as [SSMD] in name. The third piece of evidence is a civil judgment: it can prove when the cheques were issued. The fourth is a part of a civil judgment that has already been executed: it can prove that this was a kind of sales and purchase but not a fraud. The fifth concerns the cheque: from the date of the cheque, we can see that the proof given by [the principal prosecution witness] was untrue. The sixth is the counterfoil of the cheque: there were words written by the financial group of the defendant on the counterfoil which can prove that the cheques were given on 21st, it can also prove that the statements of [the principal prosecution witness] were untrue and the words on another counterfoil can corroborate that the two cheques were issued before that. The seventh is the proof of reporting the case: it can prove that the statements of [the principal prosecution witness] were untrue. The eighth piece of evidence is the investigation record relating to D Company: it proves that that venture had already been cancelled.

Judge: Having considered that the defence lawyer has produced some important and relevant evidence in court today, the court needs to verify the authenticity of these. The court therefore decides to postpone the trial. Does the prosecutor agree?

Prosecutor: Agree.

In a few exceptional cases, the defence sought to introduce live witnesses to testify as to some matter relevant to the defence. Judges were usually hostile to such efforts and denied the defence request which, in any event, was not generally formulated in a procedurally correct manner.[24] Thus, in E-CO-L-07, the defendant asked that a prosecution witness be produced to give evidence in an intentional injury case but the request was ignored.[25] Similarly, in L-CO-X-16, a case involving contractual fraud, the defence lawyer sought to call a witness to prove that the defendant had not fled but was undertaking transactions in the City at the relevant time. The prosecutor objected on the ground that the individual in question was sitting in court and had been making notes during the hearing. The judge agreed and ruled that the person was disqualified from being a witness.

In three cases, however, the defence succeeded in calling one or more individuals as witnesses at the trial. Two of these cases are discussed here.[26] In F-CO-N-02, three defendants were charged with robbery, only the first defendant (D1) having a legal representative. The facts relating to the robbery were not in general disputed but D1 argued that she had been forced to participate in the crime. The relevant part of the hearing is set out below:

---

[24] This accords with earlier findings of the Human Rights Research Centre of Peking University Law School cited in Cheung Yiu-leung (2009). Referring to the earlier research (reported in 2005) Cheung writes: 'Judges generally have a negative attitude toward witnesses appearing in court. The research above, for example, found that Beijing courts rejected 82.6 percent of defense counsels' applications to call witnesses to testify at court. Likewise, 59 percent of applications to call investigating officers as witnesses were also rejected.' (*ibid.*, at p. 61). In addition to this, there are reports that defence witnesses are threatened or the subject of retaliatory attacks which increases the chilling effect on witness appearance. See, for example, an account of the trial of Tan Zouren (the Sichuan rights defender placed on trial as a result of his investigations into the reasons why so many people died in substandard buildings during the 2008 Sichuan earthquake): Reporters Without Borders (2009).

[25] Again, this further demonstrates that neither judges nor prosecutors want witnesses in court in most cases. To them, witnesses' presence in court would make the case more complicated and reduce trial 'efficiency'. See also Yuan Zhiqiang (2010), at p. 44; Wu, Fang and Liu (2005).

[26] In the third case, B-CO-B2-03, we had too little information to enable us to understand exactly the contribution that the two witnesses made to the trial on a charge of embezzlement.

Judge: Defendants and defence lawyer, do you need to call any new witnesses to testify in court, produce any new material evidence, or request any new identification or inquest?

Defence Lawyer for D1: I apply to call Xi to testify in court to prove that D1 had told her that she was forced to participate in the robbery before committing the crime.

Judge: Bring the witness to the court, examine her identity.

Witness: Gender (female), Date of birth, nationality, occupation (unemployed), address.

Judge: [Reads out the rights and obligations of a witness.] Witness, are you clear?

Witness: Yes.

Judge: Let the defence question the witness.

Defence Lawyer: Do you know what happened to D1 and D2 in May?

Witness: In May, D1 told me that D2 had forced her to tell him the whereabouts of the [victim].

Defence Lawyer: Do you know D2?

Witness: Yes.

Defence Lawyer: What did D1 tell you at that time?

Witness: At that time, D1 said that D2 asked her to do that, and wanted me to help. I said not to do that.

Defence Lawyer: What do you mean by 'do'?

Witness: Reveal the whereabouts of the [victim].

Defence Lawyer: Were you told what they had done before?

Witness: D1 said they were discussing whether to kidnap the [victim], but D2 asked her not to tell me.

Defence Lawyer: Do you know D1 had been hit?

Witness: Yes. This was about something trivial. Also, it seems that D2 asked D1 to tell him the whereabouts of the [victim], but D1 didn't tell him, so D2 hit her. I also saw the injuries of D1.

Judge: Does the prosecutor need to question the witness?

Prosecutor: No.

At the debate stage, the prosecutor argued that little weight could be given to this witness because she had originally stated that the cause of D1 being hit was over some trivial matter and, in any event, D1 had taken active steps in committing the robbery including bringing the instrument used. In the event, the court found all defendants guilty imposing a term of nine years in prison on D1 and eight years each for the accomplices.

In a second case, M-CO-Y-03, the charges of creating an affray and false imprisonment arose out of loan-sharking activities by the two local male defendants, one aged 39 (D1) the other 25 (D2), and the defence lawyers applied the day before the trial for the appearance of five witnesses (one of whom did not appear). The first witness said nothing that was material.[27] The second witness gave testimony that was favourable to D1 in answering questions from the defence lawyer. The prosecutor began questioning the witness with a warning: 'You will need to bear legal responsibility if you fabricate evidence, is that clear?' When the fourth witness gave evidence that favoured the defence, the prosecutor stated that he hoped that she would speak truthfully and reminded her that she had earlier made a statement at the police station in which she said that D1 had hit the victim contrary to what she was now telling the court:

Prosecutor: You have made written records at the police station, didn't you?

Witness 4: Yes.

Prosecutor: Have you read the written record?

Witness 4: Yes.

Prosecutor: What is your education level?

Witness 4: Junior secondary school.

Prosecutor: Could you understand the written record?

Witness 4: Yes.

Prosecutor: Have you signed it?

Witness 4: Yes.

Prosecutor: Were your previous statements true?

Witness 4: What I have said today is true.

Prosecutor: You have also said in the police station that he had hit the victim. Now let me read out the written record of [your] statement that was made on 1 June 2006 [reading omitted].

Prosecutor: The following is the statement of [witness 4] that was made with the public security organ. I hope [witness 4] will behave frankly to the court.

Judge: Witness 4, is your statement dated 1 June 2006 which has just been read out by the prosecutor true?

Witness 4: I was very angry at that time, so I spoke that way. The statements I made today should be relied on.

---

[27] The evidence of the third witness was also of no value because the witness had poor eyesight and was too far away from the incident to see what was happening.

After a few questions by the defence, the prosecutor asked to speak to the witness again initiating the following exchange:

> *Prosecutor:* I have just read out the written record of inquiry: I have also stated the legal provisions to you. A witness who conceals important circumstances in a criminal case will be sentenced to up to 3 years' imprisonment. The police also informed you of that when they were taking a written record from you. If you fabricate evidence, you will need to bear criminal responsibility. You made such statements to the police at that time, but you made this statement today: which statements are the correct ones?
>
> *Witness 4:* Today's.
>
> *Prosecutor:* Are you willing to undertake legal responsibility?
>
> *Witness 4:* Yes.

While in this case the evidence of the witnesses was not crucial, it is clear that the attitude towards witnesses and the warnings administered could have a chilling effect upon the willingness of individuals to act as witnesses in any criminal case.

Overall, retained lawyers were more active than their court-assigned counterparts. There have also been well-publicized examples of lawyers who have given rigorous defence even in politically sensitive cases.[28] In the vast majority of everyday cases in our research, however, the defence did not go beyond simple pleas in mitigation.

DISPUTED CONFESSIONS AND TORTURE

> *E-IL-L-01 [Defence Lawyer]:* In my meetings with defendants, some have complained that the police extracted a confession by torture. I asked why they made a statement in the written record at the police interrogation. They often told me that they could not bear the torture. But they dare not allege torture in court. Under such circumstances, the defence plan and apology prepared before trial is of no use in court.

On the face of it, as far as the effect of illegally obtained testimony or confessions is concerned, China takes the question of the reliability of confessions arising out of improper treatment by investigative authorities seriously. Article 61 of the *Interpretation of the Supreme People's Court on Several Questions in the Implementation of the Criminal Procedure Law of the People's Republic of China* (SPC Interpretation) provides that:

> ... If after investigation and verification, it is proved to be true the testimony of a witness, the statement of a victim, or the confession of a defendant was obtained by using torture to coerce a statement, or by threatening, fraudulent inducement, deceiving, and other illegal means, such testimony, statement, or confession shall not be used to determine a case.[29]

---

[28] For a recent account of the work of Zhang Sizhi, for example, see Mark O'Neill (2010a) in which China's most senior defence lawyer disclosed that he had not won a single case in the last 30 years.

[29] The translation of this provision is extracted from the translation by Wei Luo (2000), at p. 167.

In line with this, investigators are expressly forbidden from using unlawful means to collect evidence. Article 43, 1996 CPL provides that:

> Judges, procuratorates and investigators must, in accordance with the legally prescribed process, collect various kinds of evidence that can prove the criminal suspect's or defendant's guilt or innocence and the gravity of his crime. It shall be strictly forbidden to extort confessions by torture and to collect evidence by threat, enticement, deceit or other unlawful means. Conditions must be guaranteed for all citizens who are involved in a case or who have information about the circumstances of a case to objectively and fully furnish evidence and, except in special circumstances, they may be brought in to help the investigation.[30]

And steps have been taken to state that confessions obtained by torture would not be admissible in evidence in death penalty cases[31] including more recently the introduction of guidelines on evidence aimed at stopping the use of confessions obtained by torture being used especially in death penalty cases.[32]

As we have noted at many points, however, the Chinese criminal justice process is heavily weighted in favour of confessions which are seen to be the most persuasive species of evidence.[33] Equally, there is an incentive for a defendant not to withdraw a confession made at the police station (under whatever circumstance) since any defendant seeking to withdraw that confession will lose the benefit that the system accords those who have 'frankly' admitted their guilt. The expectation that few defendants would seek to 'retract' a confession remains true notwithstanding that there are no independent

---

[30] Similar provisions can also be found in Article 61 of the SPC Interpretation and Articles 140 and 160 of the SPP Procedural Rules.

[31] Ng Tze-wei (2009a).

[32] Ng Tze-wei (2010a). These are reported to have been triggered by the wrongful conviction of Zhao Zuohai who, after being tortured for one month, confessed to killing his neighbour but was freed ten years later when the neighbour re-appeared. The guidelines, issued by the Supreme People's Court, the Supreme People's Procuratorate and the Ministries of public security, state security and justice, were reported to prohibit the use of illegally obtained evidence in death penalty cases including evidence obtained through torture, violence or threats, physical evidence obtained without being properly documented and evidence obtained by unqualified organizations: available at: http://www.scmp.com/portal/site/SCMP/menuitem.2af62ecb329d3d7733492d9253a0a0a0/?vgnextoid=ae5e5dca3e9e8210VgnVCM100000360a0a0aRCRD&ss=China&s=News. A subsequent report has qualified this. According to Elizabeth Lynch, what is proposed is (i) giving the court a discretion to exclude oral testimony that is the result of torture; (ii) oral testimony obtained in breach of the rules (for example, with only one instead of two interrogators present) does not necessarily have to be excluded if it can be 'corrected' (the meaning of which is not yet clear); (iii) the defendant and the defendant's lawyer may request a pre-trial hearing (it is not clear whether this will be before a different judge than the trial judge) in respect of such evidence at which they can supply the names of the officers allegedly involved in the illegality and other relevant details (it is unclear who will inform unrepresented defendants of this right; and defence lawyers still confront Article 306 of the Criminal Law); (iv) once the issue of illegality is raised, the burden of proof to show that it was legally obtained switches to the prosecutor. This latter provision could give a boost to video-taping interrogations; and (v) the interrogator (police or prosecutor) must appear in court and testify. This latter provision would be a major change for China. See, Elizabeth Lynch (2010a).

[33] This, of course, was also the view taken at common law if the confession was 'voluntary' in nature. See, for example, Wills (1902): 'A voluntary confession of guilt, if it be full, consistent and probable, is justly regarded as evidence of the highest and most satisfactory nature', at p. 91.

features (such as defence counsel) in the Chinese system which assist the tribunal in giving added credibility to a confession.[34] China does not have a rule about the proof of a confession.

Frequent reports coming out of China suggests that torture remains a favoured resource for interrogators.[35] This was a conclusion, for example, of the fact-finding mission in 2005 by Manfred Nowak (2005), the Special Rapporteur of the United Nations Commission on Human Rights despite attempts to obstruct or restrict his efforts throughout his visit. In his interviews with detainees, the Special Rapporteur observed what was described as a palpable level of fear and self-censorship, which he had not experienced in the course of his previous missions. A considerable number of detainees did not express a willingness to speak with the Rapporteur, and several of those who did requested absolute confidentiality. Adverting to the fact that his predecessors had received complaints about torture, the Special Rapporteur had this to say:

> The methods of torture alleged include, among others: beatings; use of electric shock batons; cigarette burns; hooding/blindfolding; guard-instructed or permitted beatings by fellow prisoners; use of handcuffs or ankle fetters for extended periods (including in solitary confinement or secure holding areas), submersion in pits of water or sewage; exposure to conditions of extreme heat or cold, being forced to maintain uncomfortable positions, such as sitting, squatting, lying down, or standing for long periods of time, sometimes with objects held under arms; deprivation of sleep, food or water; prolonged solitary confinement; denial of medical treatment and medication; hard labour; and suspension from overhead fixtures from handcuffs. In several cases, the techniques employed have been given particular terminologies, such as the 'tiger bench', where one is forced to sit motionless on a tiny stool a few centimetres off the ground; 'reversing an airplane', where one is forced to bend over while holding legs straight, feet close together and arms lifted high; or 'exhausting an eagle', where one is forced to stand on a tall stool and subjected to beatings until exhaustion. On the basis of the information he received during his mission, the Special Rapporteur confirms that many of these methods of torture have been used in China.
>
> Although he cannot make a detailed determination as to the current scale of these abuses, the Special Rapporteur believes that the practice of torture, though on the decline – particularly in urban areas – remains widespread in China.[36]

---

[34] Experiments with tape-recording interrogations have been undertaken in a Project directed by Professor Fan Chongyi in Haidian (Beijing), Jiaozuo (Henan Province) and Baiyin (Gansu Province). See, Fan and Gu (2007). See also, Fan Chongyi (2008a). The Supreme People's Procuratorate is reported to have instituted a nation-wide system of recording interviews with defendants. Reports from some Procuratorates suggest that revocation of confession rates (against both police and prosecutors) have dropped from 15 per cent to less than 5 per cent in Nanjing; and no retractions were reported in Jinggangshan City People's Procuratorate, Jiangxi province.

[35] For example, detailed allegations of torture used over a six-month period have been disclosed by a detainee's lawyer. These allege that the suspect was repeatedly beaten, deprived of sleep and hanged from his toes with his arms shackled behind him which eventually induced a confession, the sole evidence against the defendant. See, Ng Tze-wei (2010e).

[36] The Special Rapporteur noted a number of initiatives in China directed towards reducing the incidence of torture but set out at length shortcomings of these initiatives including the lack of an exclusionary rule of evidence, the absence of a presumption of innocence or a privilege against self-incrimination, timely notice of detention and arrest, and the timely access to counsel.

The concern of many inquisitorial systems (for example, Belgium,[37] France[38] and Germany[39]) and that of the common law (for example, England and Wales[40]) about extra-judicial confessions arises from three broad principles. First, all suspects have a privilege against self-incrimination. This means that they enjoy the freedom to refuse to answer questions when the reply might incriminate them. As has been well-stated:[41] 'In formal terms, the accused's privilege against self-incrimination equates to an immunity from compulsory process directed to eliciting information on pain of penalty.' China does not recognize this principle: instead, in the Chinese understanding, suspects have a duty to answer questions and to answer them truthfully.[42]

A second principle is that evidence used in court should provide a reliable basis upon which the fact-finder can make a determination between competing accounts and, accordingly, confessions which are not wholly voluntary[43] raise serious concerns as to their reliability. China is not immune from this problem as evidenced by documented cases of miscarriages of justice and false confessions often produced by custodial confinement and torture.[44]

---

[37] Cass. 13 May 1986, *Pas.*, 1986.I.1040 cited in Pesquie (2005), p. 123.

[38] An individual placed in *garde a vue* (on the basis that there are grounds for believing that they have committed or attempted to commit an offence) must be informed of the right to refuse to answer questions: Article 63-1, para. 1, *Code de procedure penale*. See also: Garcon (1957); and Krattinger (1964).

[39] In Germany, the defendant must be informed of his or her right to silence: Article 136 I and 163a, Criminal Procedure Code 1877 (as amended).

[40] In England and Wales, the right to silence remains a cornerstone of the privileges of a suspect and defendant although statute has introduced a number of qualifications: see, Criminal Justice and Public Order Act 1994.

[41] Roberts and Zuckerman (2004) at p. 393. The overall principle has been attenuated in recent years in England and Wales as statutory changes have been made to the right to silence.

[42] By Article 93, 1996 Criminal Procedure Law, 'The criminal suspect shall answer the investigators' questions truthfully, but he shall have the right to refuse to answer any questions that are irrelevant to the case.' For historical accounts of China's condonation of torture, see: Bodde and Morris (1967); Cohen (1968); Zhou (1999); Chen Ruihua (2000b). There were many early attempts to restrain the use of torture by imperial legal rules. Ch'u Tung-tsu (1962) at p. 124 f. describes the permitted instruments, forms and limits of torture to be used by magistrates during the trial, which might be public at the magistrate's discretion at that time. Officials making unlawful use of torture faced dismissal and punishment. Manuals for magistrates and magistrates' assistants stressed that torture should be used only as a last resort to obtain a confession and warned against extorting false confessions.

[43] At common law, it had to be shown that the confession was 'voluntary'. As Lord Sumner put it: 'It has long been established as a positive rule of English law that no statement by an accused is admissible in evidence against him unless it is shown by the prosecution to have been a voluntary statement in the sense that it has not been obtained from him either by fear of prejudice or hope of advantage exercised or held out by a person in authority [or by oppression]', *Ibrahim v R* [1914] AC 599. Whilst England and Wales have moved away from the strict 'voluntariness' test, this remains the governing provision in some other jurisdictions, including Hong Kong: *Secretary for Justice v Lam Tat Ming* [2000] 2 HKLRD 431 (CFA). Of course, it must be noted that not all voluntary confessions are reliable.

[44] See, for example, cases cited by Kahn (2005). Kahn describes in graphic detail the wrongful conviction of Qin Yanhong of the rape and murder of a 30-year old woman, Jia Hairong. Qin was convicted in 1998 and sentenced to death but released in 2002 after the real culprit had turned himself in for a series of 18 killings. In detailed accounts, Qin described how the police had

A third principle is that all suspects are entitled to minimum rights and, in the custodial setting this includes an absolute prohibition on the use of oppression.[45]

While the 1996 CPL states that confessions must not be obtained by torture, and there have been attempts to reduce torture,[46] there is no explicit prohibition on a court using evidence acquired in this way[47] and no burden of proof on the prosecution to demonstrate that the confession was not so obtained. In this regard, China does not comply with the UN Convention against Torture and Other Cruel, Inhuman or Degrading Treatment or Punishment which it has ratified because Article 15 of the Convention requires State Parties to prohibit the use as evidence in court of any statement made as a result of torture.[48] In short, the Chinese system is weighted in favour of investigators and weighted against viewing positively any representation that a confession was improperly obtained. Against this background, allegations by defendants that they had been subjected to improper treatment at the police station would be expected to be few and fewer than the actual occurrence of such practices.

RELIABILITY

It emerges from our research that, setting aside the question of torture, the circumstances in which confessions are obtained raises questions as to their reliability. In China the police generally compile a statement on behalf of the suspect who is then 'invited'

---

subjected him to sleep deprivation and various forms of intense stress variously called 'tiger stool', 'taking a jet plane' and 'circling the pig'. Kahn also describes other wrongful convictions including that of She Xianglin, convicted of murdering his wife and released after serving 11 years in prison when the wife returned for a visit and disclosed that she had run away and re-married in another province; and that of a 30-year old labourer in Shanxi Province who was eventually released from custody after a boy he confessed to killing and dumping in the Yellow River came back home again having migrated to a city to find work. See also, Choi Chi-yuk (2010), reporting the wrongful conviction for murder of Zhao Zuohai who served ten years in prison (having earlier had his death sentence commuted) only for the 'victim' to re-appear in the village. Zhao was allegedly tortured by the police and made nine confessions to the 'murder'.

[45] There is no comprehensive definition of 'oppression'. In England and Wales, 'oppression' is defined to include 'torture, inhuman or degrading treatment, and the use or threat of violence (whether or not amounting to torture)': Police and Criminal Evidence Act, 1984, section 76(8).

[46] This has included efforts to restructure police departments and condemnations by leading party figures: 'Beijing Restructures Police Department in Institutional Reform', *Renmin Ribao (People's Daily)*, 23 November 2000; 'Li Peng on Implementation of Criminal Procedure Law', *Renmin Ribao (People's Daily)*, 20 November 2000. A further development is a new requirement that police interrogations in five Beijing prisons must be recorded on surveillance cameras. See, Zhong (2010). Concerns continue to be expressed regarding the scope of this experiment, the capacity for evasion and the fact that detention houses, infamous for the use of torture, are not included: *ibid*.

[47] New rules promulgated by the principal state agencies (including the Supreme People's Court, Supreme People's Procuratorate and Ministry of Public Security) are at best ambiguous, providing that oral evidence obtained by torture 'shall be excluded and may not serve as the basis for conviction'. Available at: http://www.org/hrjournal/evidence/rules_criminal.htm.

[48] Prior to the 1996 CPL reform, a 1994 regulation of the Supreme People's Court did include such a prohibition but this did not find its way into the 1996 CPL.

to sign it. In such circumstances, the words of the confession, whether inadvertently[49] or deliberately,[50] may be the words of the officers rather than those of the suspect and thereby mislead both the suspect and the court.[51] We see evidence of this in our court observations as in the following examples:

J-CO-S4-17 [a charge of intentional injury]
Prosecutor: Did you mention that the victim hit you with a beer bottle in your confessions?

Defendant: Yes, I did.

Prosecutor: Is this the confession you wrote by yourself? (Shows it.)

Defendant: Not me. *They wrote it and asked me to copy* (emphasis supplied).

Prosecutor: Anyway you hit the victim, didn't you?

D-CO-K-13 [a charge of intentional injury]
The defendant disputes details of a confession statement when questioned by the judge even though he had earlier agreed with the prosecutor that the statement was true. The contradiction was put to him by the judge:

Judge: Why did you say 'Yes' when the prosecutor asked you if your statement was true in the police station?

Defendant: When they made this written record at that time, my mind was not clear (emphasis supplied).

I-CO-S3-05 [fraud]
Defendant: 'I even signed without having a chance to read it.'

K-W-14 [intentional homicide]
Defence Lawyer: Yes. Did you say at the police station that you wanted to kill the victim?

Defendant: No, I told the police officers I didn't want to kill the victim, but the police officers refused to listen.

Defence Lawyer: Have you seen the written record: was this signature put down by you?

Defendant: I have signed it, but I had already told the police officers I didn't want to kill him, *but they didn't put it down in the record* (emphasis supplied).

These and other examples should cause a court to pause and consider the reliability of the evidence and ask questions as to its provenance: to find out, for instance, how, on the

---

[49] As Lord Devlin laconically put it in describing the former system in England, statements submitted in evidence often used 'the stately language of the police station where, for example, people never eat but partake of refreshment and never quarrel but indulge in altercations': Devlin (1960) at p. 39.
[50] The list of scandals in this regard in England and Wales is regrettably long. For an overview, see: Gudjonsson (1992).
[51] See, Softley (1980) in which, in the presence of a Home Office researcher, in two cases the interviewing officer, in effect, composed the statement for the suspect.

defendant's account, he or she was questioned and what exactly was the process used in putting the words into writing. But this never happened in any case in our sample even though many defendants were illiterate or barely educated and could hardly have constructed a statement on their own behalf.

In China, if there is a persistent challenge to the police account of the encounter with the suspect, the police might provide a statement to assert that there was no impropriety. Several judges we interviewed spontaneously acknowledged the problem of establishing the veracity of police accounts of the custodial interrogation and the helplessness, as they saw it, of the court in addressing the issue:

> *A-IJ-B1-02:* Many of my defendants said that the police only conduct the interrogations, make the records and ask questions subjectively, and they only prepare the records based on their subjective beliefs, they only record the information that is useful for them and fail to record the information that they consider useless for them. Also, they do not allow the defendants to read the written records. Since the defendants are minors, they fail to state the names and staff number of the police officers. I cannot do anything; this can only be supervised by the procuratorates.

> *D-IJ-K-03:* As you know, there is no evidence law or rules on the application of evidence. Therefore, the judge will decide the case by the evidence with more discretion. Moreover, witnesses seldom attend the court trial, including the police in charge of the investigation. The police often provide us with an explanatory document to prove the situation. This practice cannot show us the clarity and transparency of investigation methods and processes which leads to the occurrence of illegal acts of the police when enforcing the law.

As these judges recognize, even if they pressed the prosecution to provide evidence that a confession had not been obtained improperly, the outcome would be a dispositive statement refuting impropriety that, in the absence of the relevant officers giving live testimony, the court could not test.

TORTURE

If the court did not pick up on these perhaps subtle clues, one might expect it to be different were the defendant overtly to allege oppression/torture particularly because the judge or prosecutor or both[52] repeatedly enjoin defendants to answer truthfully and warn of the adverse sentencing consequences if the defendant is not compliant. In other words, because the penalties for alleging torture are made known to defendants, we might expect the court to take seriously any allegation against the police which is advanced. In fact, notwithstanding the grave disadvantages to the defendant attached to such a posture, allegations of torture[53] and other improper conduct on the part of the police occur

---

[52] And sometimes even defence lawyers at trial join in the process of 'educating' the defendant about the duty to tell the truth.

[53] See further, Zhong (2010). Zhong states that at least nine suspicious deaths of inmates have been reported by mainland media in the first half of 2010, the police seeking to explain the injuries suffered as caused by such things as sudden illness while drinking water, fainting in the toilet, drowning in a bathroom basin and falling out of bed.

regularly and the court does nothing about it.[54] This is in contrast to what judges told us during interviews.[55]

To deal with such allegations, one judge[56] told us that he would ask the prosecution to verify whether there was any evidence of forced confession and produce such evidence (if there is any), and to allow the prosecution to have sufficient time to verify the evidence, he would adjourn the trial. A similar approach was also suggested by another judge[57] who added that it was not reliable and convincing for the police to prove that they did not force defendants to confess and so normally, he said, he would ask defendants to show their wounds. A slightly different approach was claimed by two other judges:[58] the judges said they would require the prosecution to provide an explanation to prove that no forced confession had occurred. One of these judges[59] explained that he adopted such approach because 'under the current judicial system, there is no way to verify the allegation'; whereas the other judge stated in a matter of fact way that the concern would be addressed administratively:

> The defendant sometimes will withdraw his confession by alleging the phenomenon of extortion of confession by torture. Anyway, he can make such an allegation. After I hear the whole case, and if the evidence is sufficient and the facts are clear, I will ask the police *via* the procuratorate to submit one explanatory letter to prove that there was no torture in the interrogation.

By contrast to these claims, we found in our observations that when a defendant alleges police maltreatment, courts in China do not institute any separate inquiry but rather respond in one of three identifiable ways: the issue is not pursued at all; the defence is asked to produce evidence in support of the allegation; or the court will search for ways in which it can rely upon the confession without examining its provenance.[60] Each of these responses will be considered in turn.[61]

A common response by the court is to simply ignore any such allegation. In China, a representation that the suspect was subjected to oppressive treatment (whether to the prosecutor, defence lawyer or judge) is generally ignored and is not allowed to disrupt the normal business of the court. Thus, for example, in L-CO-X-09, when a 50-year old defendant charged with fraud was being interrogated by the prosecutor to ascertain how much money had been sent to another party, the following exchange occurred:

---

[54] See further, Human Rights in China (2000); and Amnesty International (2001).

[55] See also, He Jiahong and He Ran (2008). In their opinion survey of criminal justice personnel including judges, police, prosecutors and defence lawyers, He and He found that a significant proportion of respondents (45 per cent) considered that coerced confessions were a major cause of wrongful convictions.

[56] D-IJ-K-06.

[57] E-IJ-L-02.

[58] E-IJ-L-03 and E-IJ-L-07.

[59] E-IJL-07.

[60] The practice of courts is in this respect in sharp contrast to the concerns raised by judges in our interviews with them. In one province, for example, all the judges we interviewed volunteered that allegations of forced confessions were regularly encountered at trial.

[61] It is widely believed that the use of torture by the police is common in China. See, Kahn (2005).

Prosecutor: What's the amount that you confessed in the police station?

Defendant: That's the number *the police forced me to say* (emphasis supplied).

Neither the prosecutor nor the retained defence lawyers raised this issue thereafter and the court paid it no attention. Again, in L-CO-X-04, in which three defendants (Yang, his girlfriend Ms Lu and her brother Lin) were charged with trafficking in drugs, the examination of the second defendant, Ms Lu (who was unrepresented), by the prosecutor ended in this way:

Prosecutor: Did [Lin] know they were drugs?

Defendant 2: No.

Prosecutor: Why did you admit in the police station that Lin knew they were drugs?

Defendant 2: Because the police forced me to do so.

Nothing more was said on this by the prosecutor or the court. In the same case, the defence of the third defendant, Lin (who was privately represented), was that Ms Lu (the second defendant) had put 'medicines' in his room and that he was unaware of the nature of these medicines (which were in fact drugs) until the police raided his room. The questioning by the prosecutor of this defendant concluded in this way:

Prosecutor: Did the police find the drugs in your room?

Defendant 3: Yes.

Prosecutor: When did you know they were drugs?

Defendant 3: On the day the police found out.

Prosecutor: Is your confession true?

Defendant 3: Partly true. *The police tortured me for a long time* (emphasis supplied).

Once again, although Lin repeated the allegation later when questioned by the judge, no action was taken in respect of it and no further reference was made to the allegation by any party.

In like manner, several other allegations of improper police practice attracted no interest at the trial: in K-CO-W-04 (intentional injury) the migrant defendant, when asked by his defence lawyer whether his previous confessions were true, responded: 'Some of them were not: they hit me on the second occasion'; in L-CO-X-14 (intentional homicide), the second of two defendants, when asked by the judge whether he challenged the evidence, replied: 'Yes. My confession in the police station is not true because of torture';[62] in

---

[62] In relation to the same question, the first defendant merely said: 'Yes. My confession in the police station is not correct.'

K-CO-W-01 (intentional injury) the migrant defendant, when asked by the prosecutor why he had denied participating in a fight when he had earlier made an admission when interrogated by the police, replied: 'The police forced me to say so. They did not let me sleep'; and in E-CO-L-15, the defendant made reference to his treatment at the police station saying that he had changed some content of his statement 'because of torture'.[63]

A second response of the court was to ask the defendant to produce evidence to support the allegation. In China, a bare assertion or representation that the confession was improperly obtained is evidently not enough to attract the interest of the court. Thus, in L-CO-X-05, the following exchange took place on a charge of intentional homicide:

[The judge asks the first defendant whether he will make a final statement.]

Defendant: Yes. I didn't sleep (well) for more than ten days, so my confession was extorted by torture.

[The judge asks the first defendant if he has the evidence.]

Defendant: No.

Judge: Since you don't have evidence, it is not admissible. Do you have other things to say?

Again, in L-CO-X-08, on a charge of robbery, the following dialogue occurred:

[The judge requests the defence lawyer of the first defendant if he wishes to ask the first defendant questions.]

Defence Lawyer: Yes.

Defence Lawyer: Is your statement in the police station true?

Defendant: I have no other choice; so I have to sign my name on it.

Defence Lawyer: You said that a police officer beat you: who is he?

Defendant: I don't know.

Judge: Defender, please do not ask such specific questions. If you want to prove police extortion by torture, please present your evidence.

Defence Lawyer: Okay.

The intervention by the judge brought this line of inquiry to a close.[64] Similarly, in L-CO-X-06, on a charge of intentional homicide, the prosecution was confronted with

---

[63] In this case, the defence lawyer reminded the court of this allegation but it did not trigger any debate or inquiry.
[64] See also to the same effect, K-CO-W-09, in which the defendant said that he had made the first confession after being beaten up thereby casting doubt on the second confession. When the defence lawyer pointed out that the second confession's similarity to the first was not an indication of reliability because the facts in the second confession were more or less the same indicating that

12 statements taken from the defendant, the first six of which were confessions, the second six of which were denials. The defendant asserted that the confessions had been extracted by torture adding that when he was placed in the detention house after leaving police custody he could not urinate for half an hour. The following exchange closed off the issue:

> *Judge:* What do you mean?
>
> *Defendant:* I entered into there with a wound.
>
> *Judge:* Do you have any evidence to prove it?
>
> *Defendant:* No.

This placing of the burden of proof on the defendant not only is the converse of the common law position but also requires the defendant to do something which by its very nature is, in practical terms, an impossible task. The encounter with the police is entirely under police control; there are no witnesses for the defence; and the event will have occurred many months before the court appearance.

A third approach of the court and/or prosecution is to find ways in which, in their view, reliance can be placed upon the confession without inquiring into the actions of the police. Thus, in L-CO-X-08, on a charge of robbery, when the defendant said that the confession had been extracted by torture, the prosecution's answer was:

> When the police here asked the . . . defendant key questions, he didn't answer them but lowered his head. If the police had made use of torture, he would not have been able to keep silent.

The most common method used in this regard was to argue that the disputed confession(s) was consistent with other evidence such as statements by alleged accomplices or that there was some other evidence to support a conviction. This posture was captured in our interview with a prosecutor:

> *F-IP-N-01:* Generally speaking, criminal suspects who are tortured to confess will raise this issue by themselves. I will see whether they have any evidence, listen to their explanations and that of the police. I will ignore the allegation if there is other evidence to prove the facts of their crimes. I can understand investigators' work. Sometimes it is very difficult to solve a criminal case if investigators don't adopt certain measures in dealing with criminal suspects. But we cannot simply rely on defendants' confessions that are extorted by torture as the basis of prosecution.

In our courtroom observations, we found considerable evidence for this way of thinking. Thus, in J-CO-S4-15, when the defendant was asked by the privately-retained defence lawyer why his statements were inconsistent, he explained: 'I always denied it when detained. Then the police beat me, so I just said it wrongly.' At the debate stage, the prosecutor said that the evidence was sufficient and reliable and that the defendant's confession to the police was consistent with that made at the procuratorate.

---

it could have been copied from the first, the judge killed off the argument by saying: 'more or less the same does not necessarily mean that it was copied from the first'.

Similarly, in J-CO-S4-12, on a charge of intentional homicide, the defendant (represented by a court-assigned lawyer) denied shooting the victim leading to the following exchange:

Prosecutor: To what did you confess in the Public Security Bureau?

Defendant: I said I shot because they forced me to say so.

Prosecutor: That's all for my interrogation.

At the debate stage, the prosecutor addressed this point as follows:

Prosecutor: According to the court investigation, the facts are clear and evidence is sufficient. The defendant's explanation that he didn't shoot the victim was not established. The defendant's former confessions in the [PSB] are consistent with the confessions of other accomplices and the testimony of witnesses. So the defendant's former confessions in the [PSB] are true and objective. The defendant is found to have shot the victim. So the defendant is the principal and habitual criminal in the case. Please give him heavier punishment.

In like manner, in J-CO-S4-04 in which the defendant was represented by a court-assigned lawyer, after the defendant told the prosecutor in the course of questioning that his confessions at the police station had been 'extorted by torture', the prosecutor asked: 'Did the prosecutors extort your confession by torture?' to which the defendant said: 'No.' In closing, the prosecutor adverted to this exchange by saying: 'The several confessions made by the defendant in the police organs are consistent with the Bill of Prosecution. And much testimony and related evidence confirms the facts confessed by the defendant.'

In a few cases, the defence lawyer, showing considerable courage, made some attempt to support the argument of the defendant. Thus, in M-CO-Y-02, on a charge of intentional injury, the defendant, whilst admitting being at the scene of the affray, denied chopping the victim. He maintained his denial even after the prosecutor warned him on successive occasions:

Prosecutor: Defendant, the prosecutor hopes that you can frankly confess in court today. Did you chop the victim?

Defendant: No, I was standing on one side.

Prosecutor: What did you bring with you?

Defendant: A short melon knife.

Prosecutor: What about the knife that you carried before?

Defendant: It was taken away by the accomplice Wu.

Prosecutor: You insist you didn't chop the victim but what if the subsequent evidence proves that you had chopped him? You would be punished severely, do you know that?

Defendant: I know.

The prosecutor then read out the judgment of another court which had tried and convicted a large number of people who had also been present at the affray. Three of those individuals implicated the defendant in the current case and it was their 'confessions' that became of crucial importance. The defence lawyer made a clear case for the defendant:

> The allegation that the defendant participated in the gathering of others to engage in an affray and create disturbances as stated in the Bill of Prosecution, the facts are clear, but there was insufficient evidence to prove the allegation in the Bill of Prosecution that the defendant has participated in chopping the victim Zhu, the reasons are as follows: (1) From the prosecutions' producing evidence to prove the case in the course of litigation, it is clear that the evidence produced by the prosecutor is only the confession statements of the defendants [in the other case] which was used as the basis in determining this case. According to Article 46 of the Criminal Procedure Law, a case cannot be determined if there is only the confession statement of the defendant but no other evidence. The so-called 'defendant' in fact only refers to the defendant in the same case. (2) There are inconsistencies among the confession statements of the [convicted] defendants. Among the confession statements of the [convicted] defendants that were just listed out, only the third, fourth and fifth accomplices have mentioned that this defendant chopped the victim, and four other persons including the accomplice Zhang didn't say that this defendant chopped the victim. Additionally, this defendant said the third and fifth defendants were quite far away from them; they could not see clearly. Therefore, the confessions of the [convicted] defendants could not be used as the basis to determine the case. (3) In the judgment of the [other] Court, the facts were confirmed according to the confession statements of the defendants; this defendant didn't participate in the last court session. The basis confirmed by that judgment was insufficient; we cannot rely on the facts confirmed in it as the basis to determine this case.

However, the prosecutor asserted that the disputed confessions accorded with other evidence and could be relied upon notwithstanding that there had been allegations that they had been extracted by torture:

> *Prosecutor:* As to the confessions of the accomplices, *putting the issues of forced confession and inducement of evidence by the police aside*, the confession statements of all the defendants corroborate each other; this explains that their confession statements are objective and true (emphasis supplied).

After a short adjournment, the judge issued a brief oral judgment of conviction stating that the court accepted the prosecution case and that the defence was not substantiated.[65]

While there are considerable disincentives for defendants to assert malpractice on the part of the police, such allegations appear with considerable frequency and give weight to the concerns expressed by official bodies and commentators.[66] So far as courts are concerned, however, allegations of oppressive treatment are not allowed to displace the

---

[65] The judgment is set out in Chapter 13 *infra*.
[66] See, for example, United Nations Committee Against Torture, Consideration of Reports Submitted by State Parties Under Article 19 of the Convention: Concluding Observations of the Committee Against Torture: China, CAT/C/CHN/CO/4, 12 December 2008 in which the Committee expressed concern over the repeated allegations of the routine and widespread use of torture and ill-treatment of suspects in police custody.

course of the trial and are not of such moment as to deserve inquiry.[67] If the court is satisfied that the defendant is guilty, as it usually is,[68] it matters not how the evidence was obtained: it will be accepted even if it was extracted by torture. In this system, there is no room for 'process values'.

And even if a judge thought that the allegation of torture had a foundation in fact, the countervailing pressures are too great, as a judge frankly told us when explaining defects in the criminal process:

> *M-IJ-Y-01:* The investigation measure is not valid. Police are supervised by the procuratorate, but there is no unit to supervise the anti-corruption bureaux. They have to supervise themselves. That tends to be the source of problems. In court the defendant said his confession was extorted by torture. I required him to provide evidence. He said he was detained and it was impossible to provide any evidence. What were the facts? The procuratorate showed a statement written by the investigation-supervision department to prove they didn't torture the defendant. You know the leaders of two departments are the same person. You can imagine the validity of that statement! To protect the authority of the procuratorate and complete my job, I have to accept the statement.

In this understanding, institutional loyalty must take precedence in all cases over and above procedural rights.

CONCLUSION

On the basis of our courtroom observations, it appears that lawyers engaged by the defendant or his or her family, generally concentrate upon advancing simple pleas in mitigation. There is some evidence of genuine attempts to engage with the prosecution case through procedural challenges, proffering alternative case theories and the production of evidence (such as witnesses). While this is rare, it has to be set against a background in which defence lawyers may be subjected to informal harassment measures such as surveillance and violence. They do not have access to the defendant or the prosecution case file until shortly before trial where, for all practical purposes, they are denied the opportunity

---

[67] In the famous 2003 trial of Liu Yong, a mafia boss, his lawyers (including Tian Wenchang) argued that he had been tortured. He was first given a lighter punishment '*because it could not be excluded that he had been tortured (!)*' by a provincial level court, but then the SPC retried the case and sentenced him to death; the sentence was immediately executed. In an interview with Chen Guangzhong of Beijing's Chinese University of Politics and Law he stated: 'That the court *dared to mention* "that we cannot rule out the possibility of torture;" (. . .) *to dare write* this [into a court judgment] is in my opinion a good sign; it is an expression of the spirit of the rule of law.' Interview 'Special visit paid to the vice president of China's Legal Academic's Society Chen Guangzhong: the conversion into suspended death sentence was an expression of the spirit of the rule of law (*Zhuanfang Zhongguo faxuehui fuhuizhang Chen Guangzhong: gaipan sihuan tixianle fazhi jingsheng*)', 24 December 2003, available at http://www.law-thinker.com/detail.asp?id=1900. Emphases added.

[68] Fu Hualing (2003) sought to capture this reality as follows: 'There is a popular saying in China that catches the essence of the institutional relationship at work here: the police cook the rice; the prosecution carries the rice; and the court eats the rice. In fact, the court eats whatever the police have cooked.'

to question prosecution evidence because this is available only in written form and there is no access to the maker of the statements. In turn, they do not obtain defence witness statements because of the risk of criminal prosecution of the lawyer. The defence lawyer may be exposed to threats and pressure concerning the lawyer's professional status emanating from the lawyers' association, the ministry or bureau of justice often mediated via the law firm whose head(s) may be asked to put pressure on a particular lawyer or order him/her to withdraw from the case. In like manner, the linchpin of the prosecution case – the confession(s) of the defendant – is in effect bullet-proof both because there are grave sentencing consequences for any defendant who seeks to challenge the confession and because the court is not interested in allowing any exploration of what really happened during the police–suspect encounter. In truth, but for very different reasons, it is correct to say that, in China, 'the confession is the king of evidence'.

13. Trial outcomes observed

INTRODUCTION

In this chapter we discuss the outcomes of the trials that we observed in our courtroom samples. This will include a short review of the length of the trials, whether the judgment was immediate (that is, delivered on the same day immediately following the examination of evidence and the submissions of the prosecution and defence or more typically after a short adjournment of between five and 20 minutes) or delayed to another day, the overall outcome in terms of whether the prosecution was able to establish its case on some or all of the charges against the defendant to the satisfaction of the court, the content of the judgment, and a note about sentencing where relevant.

TIME OF JUDGMENT

As we have already noted, in general criminal trials in China are rapid affairs, whatever the seriousness of the charge or the number of defendants in joint trials. Not unexpectedly, summary trials are disposed of quickly, as they are effectively 'slow Guilty Pleas', with 91 per cent completed in less than 40 minutes. This is consistent with the findings of Chinese scholars. According to the survey by Xiao Shiwei (2008), in more than half of cases the trial was completed within 15 minutes. Similarly, based on 60 sample cases in Sichuan Province, Zuo Weimin (2007) found that the time of trial in summary procedure ranged from seven minutes to 75 minutes.

The same pattern is broadly true of Simplified Ordinary Procedure cases which are also another form of 'no contest'. This finding is similar to that in the small survey conducted by Guo Zhiyuan (2007) in Beijing: she found that in F Court (ten trials), trials took from ten to 80 minutes, averaging 33 minutes; in Y Court (nine trials), the shortest court trial lasted 12 minutes, the longest 55 minutes, with an average of 31 minutes; and in P Court (11 trials), the shortest trial was ten minutes, the longest 90 minutes, with an average of 40 minutes.[1]

At the same time, however, in our research samples, dispositions in Ordinary Procedure trials were also completed with considerable speed, some two-thirds of Basic Court cases and one-third of Intermediate Court cases being completed in less than one hour (including adjournments). The brevity of the hearings (as to which see below) enabled the judge to come to a speedy determination on the ultimate issue in many cases. In the Basic Court, for example, judgment was announced immediately following the trial or, usually,

---

[1] To similar effect, see: Zuo Weimin (2008) at p. 289; Xu Meijun (2007) at p. 114; and Ji Xiangde (2006) at p. 132.

after a short adjournment[2] in over half (54.0 per cent) of all cases, the equivalent figure in Intermediate Court being 15.5 per cent of all cases.[3]

In such 'instant' cases, it might be thought that the widespread concerns that have been expressed by commentators about undue or improper influence being brought to bear upon the court by the adjudicative committee or other parties in the space provided when the judgment is deferred for days at a time cannot realistically be said to apply. However, this does not account for other significant considerations. First, in summary cases, the judge is solely responsible for the trial (the outcome of which is effectively determined by the nature of the proceeding) and does not have to answer to a collegial panel. Secondly, as our researchers observed and as our interviews with judges demonstrate, the case-responsible judge would have read the case file and would have discussed it also in advance of the trial with other members of the panel or with superiors. Finally, other considerations were at work in a number of cases because they were trials staged for the benefit of particular groups such as trainee police officers or senior supervising prosecutors, ones which involved foreigners (and consequently attracted international attention) or ones which had, for reasons such as the notoriety of the crime, aroused the interest of the local populace or mass media. 'Show trials' of this kind ended with a determinative outcome in order to demonstrate the 'efficiency' of Chinese criminal justice, assuage public anger or, in some cases, to underscore its independence from external pressure.[4]

By contrast, judgments in a substantial minority of Basic Court cases (46.0 per cent) and an overwhelming majority of Intermediate Court cases (84.5 per cent) were reserved for a day subsequent to the trial. There are several reasons which explain the delay in giving judgment.[5] First, although almost every case was handled by the case-responsible judge (*chengban faguan*), with the other members taking a symbolic role, ultimate responsibility for the case lies with the collegial panel (*heyi ting*). For practical purposes, this chain of authority alone mandates some form of adjournment. But beyond that, it is

---

[2] The adjournments generally lasted for less than 20 minutes and token adjournments of a few minutes were not uncommon. Whilst these adjournments might give the impression of creating room for a deliberative process to occur, our observations showed that they served no such substantive purpose: the outcome was mostly predetermined and an adjournment was simply impression management.

[3] According to Guo Zhiyuan, of the cases she observed the rate of immediate judgment in simplified procedure cases was 30 per cent, 0 per cent and 9.1 per cent respectively. See Guo Zhiyuan (2007) at pp. 163–164. According to her, factors influencing delay include: (1) pressure of writing judgments immediately after the trial; (2) defendant needs to pay fines or compensation to victims or no mediation agreement is reached; (3) the trial involves a number of defendants or multiple offences; (4) major elements affecting the sentencing are raised in court trial; and (5) the defence lawyer may put forward some issues beyond judge's expectation.

[4] In China the purpose of the trial is not necessarily to adjudicate upon the question of guilt or innocence but to fulfil the letter of the law in procedural terms, to assist in arriving at a determination of sentence and, where appropriate, send out messages about the efficiency and reliability of the whole criminal justice system.

[5] As we have seen, an adjournment may also afford an opportunity for the civil litigants or other parties (such as the victim's family and friends) to speak to the judge to air their grievances and for the judge to remove concerns that they might have with a view to deflecting any complaint about the judgment.

Table 13.1 Time of judgment

Time of judgment	BC Sites		IC Sites	
	No. of cases	Percentage	No. of cases	Percentage
Immediate judgment	33	25.4	2	2.1
After short adjournment	37	28.5	13	13.4
Judgment on another day[1]	32	24.6	24	24.7
Judgment delayed altogether[2]	28	21.5	58	59.8
Total	130	100.0	97	100.0

Notes:
1. In these cases, judgment was delivered on another day during the currency of the researcher's stay in the field site.
2. In these cases, the judgment was not issued during the currency of the researcher's stay in the field site and we were unable to trace the record subsequently.

clear that there has to be consultation with a long line of command that includes the division chief and often the president of the court and, at least in so-called important (*zhongda*) or complex (*yinan*) cases, the adjudicative committee (*shenpan weiyuanhui*), directors of research centres, the party secretary, the local party committee and others before the judgment (in practice, the sentence) can be finalized.

In addition, the case-responsible judge in evaluating the evidence is not reliant upon the oral hearing in coming to a determination but, instead, has to become familiar with the case file and it is on the prosecution case file that the judge will make the determination. The trial hearing simply acts as a road map for the judge as to how the case file should be 'read' post-trial in order to choke off efforts that have been made by the defence to identify weak spots in the prosecution evidence. Workload is also a factor, judges constantly complaining to us that their case-load was too high.

Viewed in this way, the hearing itself may be characterized as little more than a form of compulsory disclosure of the defence which in practice, given the absence of defence witnesses or other positive evidence such as forensic or expert testimony, amounts to little more than *ad hoc* questions which barely probe the sufficiency and persuasiveness of the prosecution case. As a result, an adjournment simply serves to allow the case-responsible judge and others involved in putting together the final verdict to deal with challenges made by the defence or to cover over vulnerabilities which surfaced at the hearing and to re-assemble the prosecution evidence so as to present it in a form which appears both inevitable and beyond question.

The detailed figures on the time of judgment are set out in Table 13.1.

THE VERDICT

It will come as no surprise that most defendants in this system are likely to be convicted. Setting aside those cases where the defendant has entered a plea of guilty, in those cases subject to Ordinary Procedure the system is heavily tilted towards the prosecution.[6] As previously noted,

- the police have unmediated access to the suspect and invariably secure one or more confessions to the crime charged;
- the case for the prosecution is not made available to the defence until shortly before the trial and even at that stage it is for the prosecution to determine what constitutes the 'main evidence' upon which they propose to rely and accordingly what evidence they must disclose;
- prosecutors are under no duty to search for evidence that would be helpful to the defence or to disclose it if any has come into their possession;
- many defendants do not have the benefit of legal representation or are given court-assigned lawyers whose competence and motivation cannot be guaranteed;[7]
- defence lawyers have few if any resources to mount a positive defence for their client and are exposed to personal risk if they approach a prosecution witness;[8]
- at trial, there are limited possibilities to challenge the prosecution case since few if any witnesses are called[9] and the operative presumption of both the prosecutor and the judge (and often defence lawyers) is that the validity, completeness and truthfulness of prosecution witness statements cannot be called into question;
- the defence confronts not only the prosecutor but additionally a judge or collegial panel which is allied to the prosecution;
- every effort is made to discourage resistance through a punitive sentencing regime imposed on those who do not 'voluntarily surrender'; and
- judges are quick to cut off defence lawyers who seek to advocate on behalf of their clients.

---

[6] From an ideological perspective, outcomes are also predictable. As Fu Hualing (2003) observes: 'Criminal law is reserved to suppress the enemy. If a crime is a challenge to the political order, then a guilty verdict means more than a mere conviction: it transforms the convicted person into an enemy of the state. Consequently the police, the procuracy, and the [court] division are not there simply to enforce the law; theoretically, they also are institutions of the dictatorship. The judiciary is not supposed to be neutral in handling criminal cases.' Fu Hualing's important comment may also be understood with reference to the different kinds of contradiction (between the people/between the people and its enemies) invented by Mao Zedong as discussed by Clarke and Feinerman (1995): 'Antagonistic contradictions are those between parties with fundamentally opposed interests – "the people" and "the enemy" – while non-antagonistic contradictions occur between parties with fundamentally identical interests: the people. The former are dealt with by methods of dictatorship and compulsion, the latter by the "democratic" methods of persuasion and education' (p. 136).

[7] Chinese researchers have indicated that some lawyers appointed by the court do not prepare the case properly, do not undertake cross-examination, confining themselves to a few routine words. For example, see Ma and Zhang (2005), pp. 166–167, where there was a great contrast between privately-retained lawyers and court-appointed lawyers both before and during the trial.

[8] See, for example, 'Should Lawyers' Perjury Charge be Abolished or Not?', *Jiancha Ribao* (Procuratorial Daily), 20 June 2005; cited in Guan Yu (2008) at p. 257.

[9] Other research has given various estimates of witness appearance rates varying up to 5 per cent but generally less than 1 per cent. See, Zuo and Ma (2005). See also, Zuo Weimin (2008).

Table 13.2   Outcome of the judgment

Outcome	BC Sites		IC Sites	
	No. of cases	Percentage	No. of cases	Percentage
Convicted of all charges	101	99.0	36	92.3
Convicted of some charges only	1	1.0	3	7.7
Not known[1]	28	–	58	–
Total	130	100	97	100

Note: 1. In these cases the verdict was never really in doubt and occasionally the court inadvertently disclosed the outcome in calling the adjournment as in J-IJ-S4-16, a case of intentional homicide, in which the judge announced the adjournment in these terms: 'The sentence will be determined after discussion by the collegial panel.'

In our study, in those cases where the result was known, the outcome of cases observed in our fieldwork was a conviction of all defendants as set out in Table 13.2.

As Table 13.2 makes clear, in cases where the outcome was known, all defendants were convicted. In four trials, however, the defendants were convicted on only some of the charges and it is interesting to examine what caused this departure from routine practice and whether such an outcome would be a potential source of tension between the court and the prosecution given the 'audit' and 'performance indicator' system in place to measure the efficiency of each branch of the judicial apparatus. We start to illustrate these variants by giving an account of two of the three cases in the Intermediate Court all of which took place in the same north-western city:

> Case L-CO-X-04 was a drugs case which involved three members of the same family. The principal defendant, Yang, a man aged between 25 and 40 years of age, went to DG City, bought 600 ecstasy pills and returned to his home-town with them. He then embarked on a course of selling them by splitting them into small parcels of 20 each. The first parcel was offered to an undercover police officer and this led to his arrest. Through another person or persons,[10] the girlfriend of Yang, Ms Lu, learned of the arrest and transferred a box in which the drugs were kept to the house of her sister and then to the house of her brother, Lin, the third defendant. Yang was given bail by the police[11] but continued to sell drugs in small parcels supplied by Ms Lu and was re-arrested. The prosecution charged Yang with trafficking in drugs, Ms Lu[12] and Lin with possession of drugs. It was unclear as to when Ms Lu first became aware that the box contained drugs because she had met Yang on his return from DG City and claimed that she first knew only after Yang's initial arrest. In any event, after Yang's release on bail, Ms Lu admitted transferring drugs in small amounts from place to place. Both Yang and Ms Lu stated in court that Lin did not know that the box contained drugs and Lin was consistent in his denials at court despite having made an earlier confession to the police. However, in the confessions of both

---

[10]   There were various accounts given at the trial as to whether the message was passed by a man or a woman or more than one person.

[11]   It was accepted in the trial that Yang had received an administrative sanction from the police for this first offence. He alleged that he had given the police RMB 20 000 but that only RMB 10 000 had been recorded in the bail document.

[12]   There is a reference in the research note that Lu was charged with trafficking but the judgment makes clear that the initial charge was of possession.

Yang and Ms Lu, they stated that Lin had knowingly broken the law. When asked at the debate stage whether he had anything to say, the following exchange occurred:

Lin: Yes. I want to ask [the first defendant] and [the second defendant] how they can explain that I violated the law knowingly. [His speech was stopped by the case-responsible judge, because the judge said that the content did not meet the requirements of a 'final statement'.]

Judge: [Mr Lin], this is not the content that you should speak about in your final statement. You can ask them [Yang and Ms Lu] when we finish the trial.

The collegial panel decided that the evidence was sufficient and reliable but amended the charges and convicted Ms Lu of trafficking (with 10 years' imprisonment) and Lin of harbouring drugs rather than of possession (with 4 years' imprisonment), the principal offender, Yang, being sentenced to 15 years' imprisonment.

The second case involved offences of personal violence and robbery:

In L-CO-X-08, it was alleged that the two defendants (D1 and D2) went to the house of the victim to purchase or sell some items, tricked the victim's husband into leaving the house and then while in the house killed the victim by stabbing her, embarked on the robbery and, after being disturbed by the victim's husband returning home, fled the scene. D1 was apprehended six years later when he was detained for allegedly stealing a television in another town; and D2 was also then detained. Apart from the interval of time between the criminal occurrence and the apprehension of the suspects, the prosecution faced a number of substantial problems derived from the police investigation which no doubt contributed to a further delay of five years before bringing the suspects to trial.[13]

These investigative problems were seized on by the experienced defence lawyer retained by D1 while D2's legal aid lawyer was largely inert and ineffectual. Because of the lapse of time between the crime and catching D1, the police had lost vital evidence including photographs of the crime scene, the clothing allegedly left behind at the crime scene by D1 and the murder weapon itself. In addition, the report of the criminal investigation was written up long after the event, the police failed to gather evidence of blood at the scene, it appeared that they also arranged for someone other than the named witness to sign a witness statement and the inquest report had been altered in a number of places.

In an effort to avoid the difficulties presented, the prosecution charged both defendants with robbery rather than with murder. In addition, the prosecution charged D1 with theft of the television which had led to his initial apprehension. The prosecution sought to rely upon confessions made by the defendants, confessions that the defendants said had been extracted by torture. The retained lawyer drew attention to the deficiencies in the prosecution case and urged the court to acquit. However, against a background in which D2, while denying guilt, also admitted that he, together with D1, had been at the crime scene and that he had held the victim by the legs while D1 had grabbed her by the neck, the argument of the retained lawyer was undercut by D2's legal aid lawyer who told the court:

'We agree with the prosecutor's charge in principle. The defendant has a good attitude to guilt, his understanding of law is poor, but he is willing to undertake civil liability; so we suggest the court impose a lenient sentence.'

The court concluded that both defendants were guilty of robbery. The court agreed that the document reporting the crime could not be used in evidence but said that other

---

[13] The court made no mention of the unconscionable detention in custody between initial apprehension and trial.

evidence, such as the crime scene report, could be used since it had been copied from the original documents. The minor variation from the prosecution charges was simply that, so far as D1 was concerned, the court found that the charge of theft of the television could not be sustained because the prosecution had failed to produce any evidence from the true owner that the television had been stolen. The court imposed the death sentence on both defendants but with a two-year suspension,[14] this being a clear acknowledgement of the weakness of the police evidence while also saving the face of the procuratorate.

For reasons which are apparent, these and the other two cases[15] did not represent any significant departure from the alliance between the judges and the prosecution and would not have led to criticism of the procuratorate over 'lack of efficiency'. In each case, the prosecution achieved a conviction of the major offence charged. In each case, no direct criticism was levelled at the prosecution by the court. And, at least in one case, L-CO-X-08, the prosecution could count itself lucky that it had achieved a positive outcome in the light of the palpable deficiencies in the evidence. Indeed, the outcome in case L-CO-X-08 was practically predetermined by the way in which the trial was organized. Despite the evidential weaknesses, case L-CO-X-08 was used as an emulating trial, the courtroom being filled with police cadets who were there to witness what a 'real trial' was like, with the front row of the courtroom occupied by leaders of the procuratorate who were there to assess the professional competence of the main prosecutor. Although judges recognized structural deficiencies in the evidence, this did not prevent a conviction being returned, a situation that judges recognized in interviews with us as in the following illustration:

> *F-IJ-N-04:* Personally speaking, the common problem is that the Procuratorate does not provide enough evidence to support the criminal facts in the accusation. The underlying cause of this problem is that investigators are not careful enough to investigate and collect evidence. Some of them even adopt unlawful procedures in collecting evidence. That results in the defendants' subsequent withdrawal of their confessions and there being no other evidence to corroborate it. *The Procuratorate is in such a quandary that some cases with insufficient evidence have to be prosecuted.* But I am very strict with the standard of examining evidence. Anyhow, it is important to improve investigators' qualifications and skills (emphasis supplied).

THE JUDGMENT OF THE COURT

In conventional understanding in both inquisitorial (continental European) systems and under the common law, it may be said that the purpose of a trial is ideally encapsulated in the judge's summation of the evidence to the jury or, in non-jury cases, the judgment

---

[14] Where a death penalty is suspended, it is unlikely to be implemented.
[15] In the third Intermediate Court case (L-CO-X-12), the defendant was a Party member who faced four charges of bribery and corruption. The court convicted on three counts but concluded that the fourth could be dealt with through the Party disciplinary system. The Basic Court case (C-CO-B3-04) involved various charges against three defendants involving several thefts, possession of forged currency and the acquisition of illegal items. All the charges were established against each defendant except the possession of forged currency. The reason for the court's decision was not recorded by the researcher.

of the court. This is the occasion on which the central proposition at the heart of the criminal justice system – that the state has a right to punish one of its own citizens – is shown to have been demonstrated to the required standard through analysis of the facts and the law or shown to have failed in that regard. Typically this involves, among other things, a consideration of the persuasiveness of each item of evidence, the reliability and credibility of the testimony of witnesses, the admissibility or exclusion from evidence of controversial material, such as evidence of the character of the accused (principally any prior convictions) or evidence obtained by the investigating authorities by dubious or improper means. The court will give an assessment of the merits of each side and indicate points of strength or weakness. Where a judicial judgment is given, the court will give reasons for reaching a certain conclusion on the factual basis of its judgment and seek to apply the facts as found to the applicable law or to the law as it finds it to be where this has been put in genuine doubt.[16] Such summations/judgments are often technical and complex precisely because they are the basis for the imposition of a criminal sanction or for the release back into society of an individual whom the prosecution believe to have committed a criminal offence.

In China, researchers have found that, except for cases heard by summary procedure, the judgment in most cases tried by simplified ordinary or ordinary procedure is not announced immediately.[17] In practice, the 'presumption of innocence' is construed to mean 'presumption of lenient punishment'. Where the facts are not clear or the evidence is insufficient, the defendant will rarely be acquitted (Yue Liling, 2010; Chen Guangzhong, 2004). The court will likely dispose of the case through imposing a conviction of a lesser offence. In cases involving the death penalty, the court will generally not impose the death penalty with immediate execution, but instead life imprisonment or death penalty with suspension (Lu and Wang, 2007). Courts in China, it must be understood, are under pressure to comply with a requirement for a low acquittal rate. In one area, for example, it is known that the political-legal committee set an internal rule that the rate of acquittal was to be no more than 5 per cent (Tang Liang, 2004).

Moreover, court judgments are required to reflect not only the law but also other elements, such as the presumed social effect of the outcome, the victim's reaction and so on. Thus, Zhang Weiping, when speaking of She Xianglin's case (in which the defendant was convicted of the murder of his wife who was found to be alive ten years later), commented on this aspect of judgments:

> In the trial court, there is a slogan: Pay equal attention to both the legal and social effects of the judgment. In fact, this saying of paying attention to the social effect is more likely to cause wrongful convictions or aggrieved judgments because the so-called social effect in substance will exceed the effect provided by law. The social effect itself is a denial of the legal effect (of the

---

[16] In a jury case, the jury does not deliver a reasoned verdict. However, the judge's summation to the jury is a clear pointer as to whether the trial has been conducted according to proper procedures, whether the attention of the jury has been drawn to all material facts, whether the trial has been confined to admissible evidence and whether the jury has been directed to consider its verdict to the appropriate criminal standard, i.e., beyond reasonable doubt.

[17] According to the observations of Guo Zhiyuan (2007), of the 30 cases she observed in three Basic Courts, the rate of immediate judgment was 13 per cent on average (ranging from 0 per cent to 30 per cent).

judgment).... Pursuit of the social effect will definitely exceed legal provisions. Pursuit of both social and legal effects in essence is to pursue the social effect and deny the legal effect.... This will also make the requirement of handling cases by law an empty word.[18]

In short, the emphasis on the judge's responsibility to help restore a harmonious relationship between the plaintiff and the defendant, to take into account the effect of law enforcement (Feng Hua, 2010), and to pay greater attention to social elements and the 'national situation' when giving judgment (Kang Baoqi, 2010), increases the role of the 'social effect' in the judge's handling of cases (Zhang Yan, 2010).

Unfortunately, we are not in a position to give as complete an analysis of judgments in China of the kind that is possible in the common law or continental inquisitorial systems for a number of reasons. In the first place, we did not have access to the court's written judgment in any case where this was given: we were entirely reliant upon what was stated in court. Furthermore, while we were able to listen to the oral judgments delivered in our presence, these were in general announcements of the outcome only with limited reference, if any, to the facts. Our observations are accordingly limited.

It is clear, nonetheless, that in many cases the court was not troubled by a detailed determination of the facts because the defendant or his or her lawyer mounted no defence and the trial was simply the moment for entering a plea for leniency. In such cases, the judgment was simply an acceptance of guilt and determination of sentence without an examination of the evidence. In F-CO-N-05, for example, the defendant had been caught when fleeing the scene of a theft and the plea was for leniency: the verdict was straightforward.

> *Judge:* The defendant, for the purpose of illegal possession, used secret means to steal another's property, and the amount involved is large. His act violated Article 264 of the Criminal Law and constituted the offence of theft. The defendant was caught while he was escaping from the crime scene after committing the crime. This should be considered as an unaccomplished crime, and therefore should be given a lighter sentence when compared with accomplished crime. The judgment is made according to Article 264 and paragraph 2 of Article 23 of the Criminal Law. The allegation of the prosecution is substantiated. Now let me announce the judgment. (The defendant stands up).
>
> The defendant is guilty of theft, is sentenced to criminal detention for five months and 1000 Yuan fine. The written judgment of this case will be delivered within five days after the closure of this trial. If any party is dissatisfied with the judgment, he may file an appeal with this court or directly with the Intermediate People's Court of this City within ten days from the day of receiving the written judgment. One original copy and two duplicates of the written judgment have to be submitted when filing a written judgment.

Similarly, in J-CO-S-08 where customs officers found the defendant in possession of a small amount of heroin, the trial lasted only 55 minutes, including a ten minute adjournment following which judgment was given:

> The defendant ignored laws, violated customs regulations by avoiding customs supervision and carrying drugs into mainland. His act constituted the offence of smuggling drugs. The facts are clear and evidence is sufficient. After deliberation, the defendant is sentenced to criminal detention for two months and 15 days and a fine of 2000 Yuan according to Paragraph 4, Article 347,

---

[18] He Jiahong (2006).

Article 357 and Article 64 of the Criminal Law. The 0.27 grams of heroin found on search and the 3.40 grams of tobacco which contains the heroin are all confiscated and will be destroyed by the customs. This is an oral judgment. The written form of the judgment will be delivered within five days to the defendant. If anyone refuses to accept the judgment, he can appeal in writing or orally to this court or directly to the High People's Court of G within ten days from the date of receiving the written judgment. For a written appeal, one original copy and two duplicates of the judgments should be submitted.

There is nothing remarkable about this. At common law, for example, a judicial confession is regarded as the highest form of proof and, in and of itself, is sufficient basis to allow the court to move immediately to sentence.

This approach to fact-finding could also be found, however, in those cases where the incident itself (for example, the injury or killing) was not disputed but questions were raised as to such matters as the state of mind of the defendant or whether there was self-defence or whether the defendant intended only injury and not death. In such cases, the judgment could also be short and dispositive. Thus, in K-W-02, on a charge of robbery, the following oral judgment was delivered after a short adjournment:

> The two defendants, for the purpose of illegally obtaining property, used violent means to rob others of property and money on many occasions, the amounts involved were large, and they caused one person serious injury and another minor injury. Their acts constituted the offence of robbery. The allegation of the prosecution is substantiated. The following judgment is made according to Articles 263(4) and (5), 57(1) and 64 of the Criminal Law: 1. Defendant 1 committed the offence of robbery. He is sentenced to life imprisonment, deprivation of political rights for life and confiscation of all of his personal property. 2. Defendant 2 committed the offence of robbery; he is sentenced to life imprisonment, deprivation of political rights for life and confiscation of all of his personal property. 3. The money illegally obtained by Defendant 1 and Defendant 2 will be traced, and then returned to the victims.

Immediate judgments did occur, although exceptionally, in grave cases:

> The defendant killed a person with a stone during a quarrel. His act constituted the offence of intentional homicide; and he, for the purpose of illegal possession, secretly stole another's property, the amount involved was relatively large; his act constituted the offence of theft. According to law, all his offences should be punished together. The prosecution's allegations are substantiated. The defendant is a recidivist, he should be punished severely. After being arrested, the defendant confessed to the theft that the police had not discovered: he should be considered as having voluntarily surrendered to this theft. The defence lawyer argued that the defendant had a good attitude in admitting his guilt after arrest, but he did not provide sufficient reasons to support his request that the court should give the defendant a lighter punishment; thus his argument should not be accepted. The judgment is made according to Articles 232, 264, 57(1), 65, 69 and 67 of the Criminal Law. The judgment is as follows: The defendant committed the offence of intentional homicide. He is sentenced to death, deprivation of political rights for life; he committed the offence of theft, he is sentenced to one year's imprisonment and RMB 3000 fine. It is decided that the death penalty, deprivation of political rights for life and RMB 3000 fine will be executed.

Similarly, in M-CO-Y-02, the prosecution case that the defendant had been involved in a large-scale disturbance (which he did not dispute) and had chopped the victim (which he denied emphatically) rested in large measure upon statements made at an earlier trial involving others convicted on charges arising out of the same event, three of whom (W,

H, and Z) implicated the defendant in the chopping. The assertions of the three individuals were strongly disputed on various grounds: it was said, for example, that the identification of the defendant by the witnesses was mistaken; that two of these witnesses were too far away to have seen clearly; that the assertions of those convicted in the previous trial could not be used as a basis of fact since the defendant had not been involved in that trial and accordingly had not had the opportunity to question those witnesses or confront them; and that four other prosecution crime-scene witnesses did not implicate the defendant in any respect. However, after an adjournment of 15 minutes, the court's judgment was made in terms which did not address these objections in any way:

> *Judge:* Let's continue. After the court investigation, the court debate and deliberation by the collegial bench, it is considered that the facts of this case are clear and the evidence is sufficient and reliable. We may announce the judgment in court today: the defendant stated that he didn't chop the victim, but the confession statements of the accomplices W, H, and Z, mentioned that the defendant had chopped the victim, and the judgment of this court has also confirmed that: the defence of the defendant cannot be substantiated. This court considers that the defendant, together with others, openly ignored the law of the state and social morality, arbitrarily gathered others to engage in an affray with weapons in public places, thus causing serious injury to others: his act constituted the offence of intentional injury; and he also arbitrarily battered others; his act constituted the offence of creating disturbances. The offences alleged by the prosecution are substantiated: the opinion requesting the court to punish the defendant according to law is supported. The court does not accept the defence lawyer's argument that there is insufficient evidence to prove the prosecution's allegation that the act of the defendant constituted the offence of intentional injury. The following judgment is made according to Articles 292(2), 234, 293(1), 25(1) and 69 of the Criminal Law:
>
> The defendant committed the offence of intentional injury: he is sentenced to four years' imprisonment. He committed the offence of creating disturbances and is sentenced to one year's imprisonment. It is decided that four years and six months' imprisonment will be executed.

This is not to assert that the judgments were irrational just as it would not follow that opposite determinations would have been irrational. The point is rather that these determinations were *unreasoned*:[19] the court did not engage with the evidence except to summarily reject that of the defence.[20] While this feature that we encountered routinely in the field may be linked directly to the capacity of judges, it is not a necessary feature of inquisitorial systems.[21]

It is clear from our interviews with judges that the purpose of the court hearing is

---

[19] For an extended analysis of civil determinations in China, see, Liu Nanping (2008). Liu argues that in China, judges write their opinions within a highly corrupt environment and produce judgments that ignore the major issues raised by the parties and usually lack clear legal reasoning or analysis.

[20] Certainly, some of the reported judgments in Chinese criminal cases closely resemble our observations. See, for example, the report on the trial of Hu Jia. Here the 'reasoning' of the court is expressed succinctly and in terms which are reminiscent of what we observed: 'The facts used by the procuratorate to charge Hu Jia are clear; the evidence is reliable, and the crime as charged is established. The submissions of Hu Jia's lawyers are not tenable, and this court does not accept them. . . .'

[21] In Germany, for example, Article 267 of the Criminal Procedure Code 1877 (StPO) imposes a requirement on German courts in any conviction to set out the evidence that was before the court

limited. Judges usually evaluate a case in advance of trial and, indeed, may undertake their own investigations or discuss the case with prosecutors. After the case, further work may be undertaken by the judge in reviewing the full prosecution case file, investigating particular issues and discussing the case with superiors. For judges, the trial may still be seen as useful for gaining an overview of the case or in assessing the credibility of the defendant as the following extract from an interview shows:

> *J-IJ-S4-03:* I think the court hearing is an important stage to verify evidence, especially for cases with several defendants. Through the hearing, confrontation of both sides can be undertaken. It's very helpful to examine the veracity of the defendant. It's very common that the defendant will withdraw his confession in court, but we won't be influenced by that. Our adjudication is on the basis of evidence. If there is sufficient evidence to prove the defendant's guilt, we will still hold the defendant guilty, even without any confession. On the contrary, if there isn't any relevant evidence, we won't hold the defendant guilty, even though he admits his guilt. After the hearing in court, I will look through the files carefully, analyse the facts and the evidence, write a report on the completion of trial, organize a collegiate bench meeting and finally write a report of the judgment.

What a mass of research has shown, however, is that, even when subject to scrutiny and testing in Western systems, evidence may be unreliable notwithstanding common-sense assumptions as to its trustworthiness and the miscarriages of justice which result are often correctable, if at all, only after years of dedicated effort.[22]

Having said this, because of the way in which evidence is adduced in these hearings in China, there can be no proper forensic analysis and the absence of witnesses (other than the defendant) makes it difficult to mount any serious challenge. It is also evident that the type of lawyer, whether retained or court-assigned, can have little impact upon the issue of guilt or innocence. Against this background, it would not be surprising that miscarriages of justice occur and that innocent people are found guilty.[23]

---

and those elements which the court found persuasive. See, Spencer (2005). The same principle applies also in Italy.

[22] Early work on the issue of evidence reliability, undertaken by Borchard (1932), analysed 65 cases of false conviction, many for murder, innocence being established by, for example, the 'victim' being found alive or by the subsequent apprehension of the real culprit. Other studies have confirmed the need for extreme caution in the evaluation of evidence. See, for example, Kennedy (1961); Brandon and Davies (1973); Price and Caplan (1976); Mullin (1986); Gudjonsson and MacKeith (1988); Woffinden (1987); Bedau and Radelet (1987); Conlon (1990); Kaye (1991); May (1990); May (1992–93); May (1993–94); Jessel (1994); Hill and Hunt (1995); Rose, Panter and Wilkinson (1997); Sekar (1997); Walker and Starmer (1999); Kilias and Huff (2008); Naughton (2010).

[23] There are notorious instances in China in which innocent defendants have been falsely convicted. She Xianglin, for example, was convicted of the murder of his wife who was found to be alive ten years later; and Nie Shubin was executed for a murder to which another individual later admitted. See, Li Huizi (2009); Scott (2010); and Hayes (2006). Again, the wrongful conviction of Zhao Zuohai for the murder of his neighbour, Zhao Zhenshang, came to light almost ten years after Zhao Zuohai had been convicted when Zhao Zhenshang returned to his village in Henan Province to seek welfare support. In October 1997, the two neighbours had a fight following which Zhao Zhenshang went missing. Following the discovery in May 1999 of a headless corpse in the village, Zhao Zuohai was arrested and charged with the murder of Zhenshang. The original conviction was mainly based upon nine confessions which, it is alleged, were extracted from Zhao by

Table 13.3 Non-custodial sentencing in observed trials

Sentence	BC Sites		IC Sites	
	No. of cases	Percentage of all BC cases	No. of cases	Percentage of all IC cases
Imprisonment with suspension	17	11.0	1	1.7

SENTENCING

Given that the verdict is in practice largely predetermined, it is natural that much of the hearing is concerned, directly or indirectly, with providing information which bears upon the appropriate sentence.[24] This is true, not only of cases in which the defendant is in effect pleading guilty but also in those cases where some or all of the prosecution evidence is challenged. It is not unusual, accordingly, for assertions of innocence or reduced culpability to be made alongside pleas for leniency.

Tables 13.3 and 13.4 set out the overall sentencing patterns in our observed trial sample where the sentencing decision was known.

As can be seen, proportionately few cases were given a non-custodial sentence, 11.0 per cent in Basic Court cases and only one case (1.7 per cent) in Intermediate Court which indicates that non-custodial sentences mostly occur in cases heard in grassroots (Basic) courts. In this setting, non-custodial invariably meant a suspended prison sentence. This tended to occur in opportunistic thefts sometimes involving young people (e.g., B-CO-B2-00, theft of mobile by two defendants aged below 18 years of age; B-CO-B2-08 involving robbery of a small amount of cash by High School students) or cases of intentional injury where the victim suffered minor injuries (as in C-CO-B3-09 and M-CO-Y-05).

Our finding as to the non-custodial rate is lower than the national statistics and that of other Chinese researchers. According to statistics provided by the Supreme People's

---

torture, Zhao being forced to drink chilli-tainted water, having fireworks set off above his head and being hit on the forehead with a gun. Zhao Zuohai's then wife says that after the headless body was found, the police beat her for a month whilst asking her whether she knew that Zhao Zuohai had killed the man. It is reported that the Henan Provincial Higher People's Court has ordered an investigation into the case in which Zhao had initially been sentenced to death but had the sentence commuted to 29 years in prison. See, BBC News, 'China "murder victim" found alive', http://news.bbc.co.uk/go/pr/fr/-/2/hi/asia-pacific/8671577.stm (last visited 5 September 2010); and *China Daily News*, 'Murder convict set free after "victim" turns up', http://www.chinadaily.com.cn/china/2010-05/10/content_9826537.htm (last consulted 10 May 2010). See also: He Jiahong and He Ran (2008) reporting on a survey of police, prosecutors, judges, defence lawyers and justice bureaux personnel across 19 provinces between August 2006 and March 2007. It showed 77.7 per cent of the justice personnel think that witnesses' testimony, defendants' confessions/oral statement and victims' statement were the major reasons for wrong convictions. See also Zhang Liyun (2009).

[24] For a review of research on courts and sentencing in China, see Lu and Kelly (2008) who correctly point to a strand in all sentencing research in China, namely, the lack of statistics in the form of public, systematic and comprehensive reliable data.

Table 13.4 Custodial sentencing in observed trials

Sentence	BC Sites		IC Sites	
	No. of cases	Percentage	No. of cases	Percentage
Criminal detention	7	5.1	2	4.2
Imprisonment for less than 6 months	2	1.5	0	0.0
Imprisonment for more than 6 months and less than 1 year	28	20.3	0	0.0
Imprisonment for 1 year and less than 2 years	39	28.3	3	6.2
Imprisonment for 2 years and less than 3 years	10	7.2	2	4.2
Imprisonment for 3 years and less than 4 years	23	16.7	1	2.1
Imprisonment for 4 years and less than 5 years	6	4.3	1	2.1
Imprisonment for 5 years and less than 6 years	4	2.9	1	2.1
Imprisonment for 6 years and less than 7 years	4	2.9	0	0.0
Imprisonment for 7 years and less than 8 years	6	4.3	0	0.0
Imprisonment for 8 years and less than 9 years	6	4.3	0	0.0
Imprisonment for 9 years and less than 10 years	2	1.5	0	0.0
Imprisonment for 10 years or more	1	0.7	25	52.0
Life imprisonment	0	0.0	13	27.1
Total	138	100.0	48	100.0

Court, for example, the suspended penalty rate varied across regions, the average rate by courts at all levels being 24.4 per cent, with the lowest rate of 5.0 per cent in Guangdong and the highest (29.9 per cent) in Jiangsu.[25] A survey by the First Criminal Court of Shandong High Court showed the average rate of suspended sentences in Shandong between 2001 and 2006 to be 37.2 per cent.[26] Other Chinese researchers have shown

---

[25] Feng Quan (2009). As far as the reasons are concerned, according to Feng's analysis, firstly, courts with low rates of suspended penalty pay more attention to the punitive aims of punishment and consider that over-use may bring more social harm and fear and may not be sufficient to fight crime; secondly, the suspended penalty may cause corruption (extra income to judges) in some of the least economically developed areas (thus some courts, e.g. Chifeng Intermediate Court of Inner Mongolia Autonomous Region have an internal rule to restrict the rate of suspension to less than 20 per cent); thirdly, in considering the ability to supervise, whether the defendant is a migrant or local citizen is an important element in determining whether it is safe to suspend (*ibid*, at pp. 81–82).

[26] The First Criminal Court of Shandong High Court, 'Survey Report on the Application of Suspended Penalty by Courts in Shandong', (2008) 5 *Shandong Shenpan* (Shandong Justice) 30, at p. 30, footnote 3.

that the likelihood of migrant defendants obtaining probation is lower than for local defendants;[27] the rate of suspended penalty in negligent crimes is much higher than for intentional crimes,[28] and higher for juveniles than for adult defendants.[29] The application of a suspended penalty is closely related to the compulsory measures taken at the pre-trial stage: if the defendant is granted bail pending trial or residential surveillance, he or she is more likely to receive a suspended penalty.[30] Moreover, the defendant's attitude toward crime, voluntary surrender, meritorious performance and compensating victims are factors in making the non-custodial decision.[31]

In addition, the rate of suspended sentences is affected by criminal policies in China. For example, the 'strike hard' policies in 1983, 1996 and 2001 led to a low rate of suspended penalties in those years. During those periods, the ideology of severe punishment, the 'strike hard' policy, high crime rate and the effect of public opinion were regarded as the most important reasons for not giving non-custodial penalties.[32]

Similarly, in our research, the few cases where criminal detention was imposed were also at the less serious end of the crime continuum such as importing self-use drugs,[33] opportunistic thefts of small items[34] or where the offence was relatively minor and the defendant assisted the police as by helping trace a co-offender.[35]

Where the death penalty was applied in the Intermediate Court,[36] the defendant had been convicted of an offence such as intentional homicide or robbery in which the victim had died and the court did not accept that the plea in mitigation justified suspending the sentence.[37] Death penalty cases where the sentence was suspended for two years (and

---

[27] In Shunyi Court of Beijing, there were 267 local theft offenders between 21 December 2004 and 20 November 2007, of whom 90 were granted bail and 22 were given a suspended penalty (41.9 per cent). By contrast, of the 529 migrant (non-local) theft offenders, only 49 were granted bail and ten given a suspended penalty. 'Statistics and Analysis of Application of Non-custodial Penalty for Theft Offenders', available at http://bjgy.china.court.org/public/detail.php?id=61652, cited in Feng Quan (2009) at pp. 169–170. See also Wang Xinhuan (2010) at p. 127; Chu Weizhu (2009) at pp. 76–77.

[28] Based on his survey data in a Basic Court (Chifeng Intermediate Court) in Inner Mongolia and a Guangdong Provincial High Court, the application rate of suspended penalty in negligent crimes was 66.78 per cent and 32.06 per cent respectively; that of intentional crimes was 34.15 per cent and 3.71 per cent in turn. See Feng Quan (2009) at pp. 89–96. The population of migrants is more than 60 per cent of all the criminal populations in Guangdong, but only 29.6 per cent of the migrant population received a suspended penalty (*ibid.*, at p. 84). In Beijing 85 per cent of the defendants who received probation are local residents and the rate of juvenile defendants is triple that of adult offenders. In addition, the majority of defendants (95 per cent) who received probation were granted bail pending trial. Li Bin (2010) at p. 263.

[29] Feng Quan (2009).

[30] Feng Quan (2009). For instance, courts in Liaocheng City of Shandong Province gave suspended penalty to 375 offenders, among whom 353 had been granted bail before trial (94.1 per cent). Wu Sheng (2007). See also Zang Desheng (2005).

[31] Li Bin (2010) at p. 262.

[32] Feng Quan (2009) at pp. 87–88; and Wang Hongyu (2008) at pp. 105–106.

[33] As in J-CO-S4-02 and J-CO-S4-08.

[34] As in F-CO-N-05; B-CO-B1-06; and M-CO-Y-04.

[35] As in M-CO-Y-01, a case of minor theft.

[36] This was recorded in 11 cases in six of which the sentence was suspended for two years.

[37] There are no reliable statistics on the death penalty rate in China. Based upon public reports, Amnesty International estimated that at least 470 people were executed and 1860 people sentenced

accordingly were not likely to be implemented) also involved in four cases the killing of the victim by intentional homicide or in the course of robbery in which the court recognized mitigating factors or, in two instances, involved major trafficking in drugs.

For the record, we did not have enough discrete information about each case or sufficient numbers of cases in the relevant categories to determine whether specific factors such as legal representation or migrant/local status had an impact on sentencing decisions. As with Lu and Miethe (2002), we could find no relationship between sentence and legal representation and, as we discuss below, sentencing appeared based on such factors as the seriousness of offence, the role that each individual played in multiple-defendant cases and the extent to which the court was persuaded of mitigating factors.

In our interviews with judges, great stress was laid upon the sentencing process. Some judges showed awareness of different sentencing theories and of the need to adjust the punishment, so far as the law allowed, in order to better reflect the detailed circumstances of the case and the possible impact upon society. Commonly, judges were content to list factors that they would take into account (for example, L-IJ-X-08: 'the amount of money involved in the case, criminal circumstances, social harm, criminal record, attitude of victim, and contrition') but some were much more expansive. We set out below some illustrations extracted from our interviews to show how some judges appeared to be conscious of the competing considerations to which the sentence function gives rise:

> *K-IJ-W-04:* I adjust punishment according to the principle that the crime should equal the punishment. There is a general standard and a social standard. Punishment reflects equality within the law and produces an effect upon society. Punishment should be flexible too. For instance, in a joint kidnapping case, some defendants who were tricked to do that didn't play much part in the case. They just kept watch for the principal defendant and they didn't get any money. They were regarded as accessories and were given mitigated punishment. You know, the start of punishment for kidnap is very high, at least ten years. It is unfair to determine punishment only by it. For another instance, in a case that a defendant fought a thief to death, the thief was caught immediately when he stole in a village one evening. Villagers crowded around him and beat him to death. Three defendants were prosecuted for intentional injury causing death and they should be sentenced for fixed-term imprisonment of no less than ten years according to law. I considered that many defendants fought the thief and there was no evidence to prove which defendant's act caused light injury, serious injury or death, so the punishment should go in the defendants' favour. Moreover, it announced to thieves that stealing would be punished by authority. Certainly the human rights of thieves should be protected by law: whoever catches thieves should send them to a police station. But to a certain degree I could understand the defendants' actions in beating the thief. Considering the social consequence, I sentenced defendant No. 1 to a fixed-term imprisonment of six years, defendant Nos. 2 and 3 to three years. The Procuratorate thought the punishment was too light and lodged a protest against it. Later the Provincial High Court changed defendant No. 1's fixed-term imprisonment to ten years, and

---

to death during 2007, the true figure being almost certainly much higher: available at http://www.amnestyusa.org/annualreport.php?id=ar&yr=2008&c=CHN (last viewed 7 June 2010). In 2008 the Supreme People's Court accepted a total of 10 553 cases, a large rise from the 2007 figure of 7725. It is widely accepted that most of these cases (given that the Supreme People's Court does not have jurisdiction over many other cases) involve the death penalty see: Chinese Law Prof Blog (Ed.) Donald C. Clarke, 3 April 2009 at http://lawprofessors.typepad.com/china_law_prof_blog/. The estimate of death sentences given in the blog is around 10 000 per annum. For further information on this, see: Bakken (2000) and (2004).

defendants 2 and 3 to five years. I think it is hard to say that the final judgment is correct, but it is final.

M-IJ-Y-04: A judge's right to adjust punishment is not as large as you might imagine. There are a great number of cases in court every year. We have internal regulations and long experience in regulating the range of punishments. There is no big difference between sentences by different judges. In an offence of theft, if the amount is large, or if there are other serious circumstances, the defendant will be sentenced to fixed-term imprisonment of not less than three years but not more than ten years. Large amount means the property stolen is over RMB 10 000. That is to say, if the property is RMB 10 000 in value, the defendant will be sentenced to a fixed-term imprisonment of three years – RMB 3300 a year. Furthermore, I will consider the legal circumstances and the discretionary circumstances. Society's evaluation of whether the judgment is fair or not relies on discretionary circumstances such as the measures themselves, the social effect, the attitude towards accepting the crime and so on. Consideration of heavier punishment is to guarantee social stability.

I-IJ-S3-02: There are legal circumstances and other circumstances, such as voluntary surrender, meritorious services, whether the defendant has any criminal record, repentant behaviour like disgorging ill-gotten gains or compensation, the defendant playing a principal or an accessory role in the crime and so on. With the development of society, there is a gap in the state of the economy in different areas, so there also should be some difference in the punishment. I think it too inflexible to regulate fixed amounts in some offences.

J-IJ-S4-08: The amount of punishment is determined on the basis of clear facts. The role and function of the defendant in the case determines his corresponding responsibility in law. The judge's right to adjust punishment is limited to the range as set out in the law. I always pay particular attention to the social consequence of the judgment. I draw conclusions on which theory I should adopt: retribution; prevention; or rehabilitation. For instance, for some defendants who have deep evil minds, use cruel means to commit the crimes and whose acts cause such serious consequences as several people dying, they ought to be sentenced to death. This is the theory of retribution. Some defendants will never stop offending if they are not sentenced to a fixed-term imprisonment for several years. This is the theory of prevention. But there are still some defendants who protected themselves from the victim's unlawful offending by using excessive force. Their return to society doesn't cause any danger to society, so they can be given a suspended sentence. This is the theory of rehabilitation. The determination of punishment is also connected with personal character, preferences, experience and inference. Anyway, judges also live in society.

F-IJ-N-07: The amount of punishment determined is in accordance with the defendant's criminal circumstances, intentional malice, and the role he played in the offence if there are several defendants in the case, the consequence of the violation and whether there are any circumstances for a heavier or lighter punishment. For instance, the defendant will be given a lighter punishment according to the law if he has voluntarily surrendered or given meritorious service, or if he confesses his crime truthfully, or he returns the stolen money or property to the victim, or he pays fines, or the victim requests a lenient punishment for the defendant and so on. The defendant will be given a heavier punishment according to the law if he is a major criminal. It depends on the situation of the case. For instance, in a crime of causing a communication or traffic accident, the defendant doesn't have intentional malice. He causes the accident because of careless driving. The defendant and the victim have reached a compensation agreement. Having considered the circumstances of the defendant's crime, his demonstration of repentance, and that he definitely would not endanger society again, therefore a suspension of sentence may be granted. The standard is different at different times and in different areas. For example, a defendant who stole three bicycles would be given a fixed-term imprisonment of three years in 1988, but now even if the defendant stole 30 bicycles, he would not be given an imprisonment of more than three years.

I-IJ-S3-01: (1) In practice there are many types of voluntary surrender and meritorious service. It can be considered great meritorious service if the criminal suspect provides clues to catch other criminal suspects in the same case. Whereas, it will not be considered meritorious service if the criminal suspect asked his wife to positively co-operate with the PSO to catch the other three suspects after he had been detained. Voluntary surrender and meritorious service cannot be substituted. In one case, I sentenced an habitual criminal who should receive the death penalty to life imprisonment when considering his attitude of acknowledgement of guilt and remorse. (2) I will also consider the social consequence. The social consequence of deception of 2000 yuan to a rich boss and to a poor person is different. (3) The amount of punishment is different from area to area. . . . (4) Some Criminal Law measures should be improved. For example, students who have psychological problems should not be detained; otherwise they will form a bias against society. They should be reprieved to take part in some re-education through labour and charitable activities.

J-IJ-S4-03: It's really important that the punishment must fit the crime. I am very cautious in this respect. The features of a crime are always equivocal. It is rare that practical cases in real life have the same features described in the law, so it needs our deep analysis. For instance, in an intentional homicide case, the defendant quarrelled with his girlfriend, carried and threw her body downstairs in a temper, causing her severe injuries. When we determined his punishment, one judge thought it should be intentional injury, because the defendant just wanted to frighten his girlfriend instead of killing her, but he didn't expect to cause her severe injury. But I didn't think so. When the police asked the defendant, 'Did you know the consequence when you threw your girlfriend down from the third floor?' The defendant answered, 'I knew it was very dangerous. It would cause her severe injury at least. At the worst, she would be dead.' According to his words, I could judge that he held a reckless attitude towards the life of his girlfriend. He was aware of the possibility of his girlfriend's death, but he still persisted in his actions. So I thought it was indirect intentional homicide. Finally both the collegiate panel and the chief of the court agreed with my opinion.

Sometimes, judges suggested that sentencing caused them more anxiety than the determination of guilt or innocence:

J-IJ-S4-03: Compared with the finding of guilt, I am afraid to determine the amount of punishment. I try to make it impartial. Firstly I will consider whether there is any circumstance justifying severity of punishment, for example, the defendant had used some cruel means, his crime caused an adverse impact on society, or the defendant is an habitual criminal. Then I will analyse other factors which might justify leniency of punishment, for example, whether the defendant turned himself in or offset guilt by meritorious conduct or had a good attitude toward admission of guilt. Finally I will fix the middle number among the range of the punishment, and plus or minus according to the circumstances.

Occasionally, judges also volunteered that personal or social relationships were factors that could affect the sentence, as in the following illustration:[38]

I-IJ-S3-01: We base the sentence on the facts and the evidence. There are many factors that must be considered, such as the nature of the case, social consequence, criminal circumstances, the measure adopted and the attitude of acknowledgement of guilt. Of course it is also influenced a little by social relationships.

---

[38] In criminal cases in China, sentence determinations are a point in the procedure where personal networks (*guanxi*) and human feelings of empathy (*renqing*) may play a significant role. Certainly, in our research, we witnessed strong pressure being brought to bear upon judges by families of victims and other parties with an interest in the case.

In practice, we found that because pleas in mitigation by the defendant tend to be short and uncomplicated ('I ask for leniency'; 'I am sorry and hope for light punishment') and, as we have already seen, pleas by the defence lawyer stereotypical (emphasizing such matters as 'good attitude' to guilt, 'voluntary surrender', first offending or efforts to reach a compensation agreement with the victim or victim's family), the most important sentencing driver in many cases seemed to be the position taken by the prosecutor because it is from the prosecutor that the judge takes his or her cue.[39] It is to this part of the prosecution case that we now turn.

Before addressing the issue of sentence, prosecutors adopted one of two broad strategies in advancing their position at the debate stage. Where the case was clear and unchallenged, the prosecutor might make no reference to the detailed evidence but simply state that the prosecution would rest upon the evidence that had been led before anything, if at all, was said as to sentence. A second strategy was to remind the court of the essential pieces of evidence upon which the prosecution relied, as in M-CO-Y-10:

> *Prosecutor:* During the court investigation and cross-examination, the prosecutor has read out evidence such as the confession statements of the accomplices, the witness testimonies, the written record of reporting the case by the victim, the written record of the examination of the crime scene, etc. The procedure for collecting the evidence was legal and effective. The above [items of] evidence corroborated each other and can corroborate the confession statements of the defendant. The evidence formed a chain, the guilt and sentence of the defendant can be determined by relying on the evidence.

When they turned to address sentencing, four basic patterns dominated the approach of the prosecutor: the defendant should be punished 'according to law' or 'impartially'; the prosecutor recognized that there were circumstances which might justify leniency; the case was one in which there were both mitigating and aggravating features; the defendant should be punished severely. We illustrate each of these in turn.

Where the case was clear, the prosecution evidence being unchallenged in all material respects, and where the defendant had confessed, the prosecution would often take a neutral position on sentencing neither seeking severe punishment nor moving the court to a more merciful stance. In such cases, the crime while serious was generally not one that would excite uncontrollable passions and where there was no special need to pacify the victim's family or local anger. The following are examples of cases in this category:

> *Case NN-07 [theft]*
> *Judge:* That's all for the court investigation. Let's start the court debate. Now let the prosecutor announce the words of the public prosecution.
>
> *Prosecutor:* The prosecutor has already produced evidence that is relevant to the defendants' crime to prove that the two defendants, for the purpose of illegal possession, stole other people's property by secret means. The amount involved was relatively large. The conduct constitutes the offence of theft. The collegiate panel is urged to give an impartial judgment based on the facts of the crime, the circumstances of the case and the defendants' attitude in confessing their crime.

---

[39] This is not to say that in many cases the prosecution view went unchallenged: indeed, it could be, as we shall see, the start of an iterative process at least in cases in which there was a defence lawyer of any substance.

Case NN-02 [robbery]
Prosecutor: After the court investigation: 1) the court should consider the question whether the first defendant [D1] was forced to participate in the crime; 2) In this case, D1 took active steps in committing the robbery and provided the location of the victim and the [instrument] used in the robbery. Also D1 pretended that she was also being kidnapped by the other defendants [in order to deceive the victim]. 3) The three defendants took [compromising] photos of the victim: the circumstances of the case are serious. 4) D1 and D2 surrendered themselves voluntarily. In sum, the acts of the three defendants constituted the offence of robbery. The collegiate panel is urged to determine the defendants' sentence according to the facts of the crime and the circumstances of the case. According to the court investigation, the facts are clear and the evidence is sufficient to determine the defendants' guilt. Please punish them according to law.

This posture might also be taken even in the most serious cases if there was no doubt in the prosecutor's mind as to the actual sentence that would be imposed by the court given the absence of any defence or any substantial basis for mitigation. In the following example, the defendant's fate was sealed after he murdered one individual and seriously injured another two out of jealousy, confessed to the killing and all parties clearly accepted that he would receive the death penalty. In these circumstances, there was no need for the prosecutor to strain for a particular outcome:

I-CO-S3-12 [intentional homicide]
Judge: Let's start the court debate: let the prosecutor express the opinion of public prosecution first.

Prosecutor: The facts of this case are clear and the evidence is sufficient and reliable; they are sufficient to confirm the case. The act of the defendant [G] constituted the offences of intentional homicide and intentional injury. I urge the court to punish him according to law.

Judge: Let the legal representative of the victim express his opinion.

Victim's representative: Yes. . . . I request the court to sentence the defendant to death with immediate execution.

Judge: Let the defendant defend himself.

Defendant: Yes, I had already known the consequence at that time [of the crime]. I only feel sorry for the family of the victim.

Judge: Let the defence lawyer defend the defendant.

Defence Lawyer: The major opinions are as follows: the defendant confessed the facts of his crime on his own initiative; this was his first crime; he had no previous convictions. I urge the court to give him a lighter punishment according to law.

Judge: Does the prosecutor have any reply?

Prosecutor: No.

Judge: Does the defendant have any new opinion?

Defendant: No.

Judge: Does the defender have any new opinion?

Defence Lawyer: No.

Judge: That's all for the court debate.

The inevitability of the sentence was underscored when the defendant was asked if he wished to make a final statement and he replied:

Defendant: I hope the court will execute the punishment according to the wishes of the victim's parents.

Although the prosecutor might submit that the court should proceed to sentence the defendant according to law, in some cases this resulted in an extended discussion as to the extent of the defendant's liability and what weight should be given to certain factors in sentencing. Thus, in L-CO-X-13, the defendant stabbed the victim after the victim had dared him to do so during the course of a drinking session. It was accepted that both the victim and defendant had been drunk at the time of the stabbing. The issue of how to characterize the victim's behaviour and the relevance of the defendant's drunkenness came to the fore after the prosecutor took an initially neutral stance:

L-CO-X-13 [intentional injury]
[The judge declares the start of the courtroom debate.]

Prosecutor: The defendant could not properly deal with disputes during the course of drinking alcohol and caused the victim's death, which had serious consequences. The defendant's act constituted the offence of intentional harm . . . Please punish him by law.

[The judge asks the defendant if he wishes to defend himself.]

Defendant: No.

Defence Lawyer 1: The defendant's characteristics deserve lenient punishment, so we suggest the panel impose a lenient punishment. The defendant had no conflict with the victim, the social harm is not large, and the result of the victim's death is not what he wanted or expected. The defendant in a drunken state should be liable for his crime, but should bear a lighter responsibility. In addition, the victim had grave fault: he handed the knife to the defendant and caused the defendant to lose self-control. The defendant confessed his crime truthfully, and he tried to obtain the victim's family's understanding and pardon by positive action, so we suggest that the panel impose a lenient punishment.

Defence Lawyer 2: The defendant's subjective evilness is small and his act in causing the victim's death was beyond his expectation. In addition, the testimonies indicate that the victim was gravely at fault and bore responsibility. The defendant has a good attitude towards guilt: both his family and the victim's family have reached an agreement on civil compensation. Please combine the defendant's good daily performance with his act of crime and we suggest the panel reduce his punishment or give him a lenient punishment.

[The judge asks the prosecutor if he wishes to respond to the defenders' opinions.]

Prosecutor: Yes. The defendant's act was intentional. Although he was drunk, he is still criminally responsible. There is no legal provision that the defendant can be punished leniently under the circumstance of being drunk. The victim's act was a joke. It is improper if you classify his act as a grave fault.

[The judge requests the defendant if he will make a final statement.]

Defendant: I have nothing to say. I behaved wrongly because I had drunk alcohol.

The second sentencing strategy adopted by the prosecutor was to acknowledge factors in the case which justified leniency and to draw these to the attention of the court. Typically, this would occur where the defendant had voluntarily surrendered and confessed, where the victim could be said to have been partly at fault, where the defendant had agreed compensation with the victim's family or where it was manifest to all parties that the defendant was of limited capacity. We set out below some examples of such circumstances:

M-CO-Y-05 [intentional injury]
Prosecutor: The facts of this case are clear and the evidence is sufficient and reliable. The defendant caused the victim to suffer serious injury. His act constituted the offence of intentional injury. According to Article 234(2) of the Criminal Law of our country, he should be sentenced to imprisonment for more than three years but less than ten years. According to Article 67 of the Criminal Law, the defendant should be considered as having voluntarily surrendered himself: he might then be given a lighter or mitigated punishment.

[The court responded as follows.]

Judge: After deliberation by the collegial bench, it is considered that the facts of this case are clear and the evidence is sufficient and reliable. This court considers that the defendant injured others over a trivial matter, thus causing serious injury. His act constituted the offence of intentional injury; the offence alleged by the prosecution is substantiated; its opinion requesting the court to punish the defendant according to law is supported. Having considered that the victim was at fault to a certain extent, the defendant has paid the victim RMB 100 000 as compensation, and was forgiven by the victim, the court will exercise discretion to give him a lighter punishment. The judgment is made according to Article 234(2) of the Criminal Law, the judgment is as follows: The defendant committed the offence of intentional injury; he is sentenced to two years' imprisonment with three years' suspended sentence.

M-CO-Y-01 [theft by two defendants]
Prosecutor: (1) During the court investigation, the prosecution produced evidence such as the statement of the victim, witness testimonies and conclusion on identification of value. After cross-examination, the two defendants frankly confessed their criminal acts in court. The evidence produced by the prosecution is sufficient and reliable; the pieces of evidence corroborate each other and form a chain of evidence. (2) Defendant 1 has committed theft three times . . . and the amount stolen was huge. Defendant 2 has committed theft twice, the amount involved is . . . relatively large. The acts of both defendants violated Article 264 of the Criminal Law of the People's Republic of China, and constituted the offence of theft. (3) The two defendants had meritorious performance after being arrested: they might be given a lighter punishment according to law.

Judge: After the court investigation and the court debate, the collegial bench has conducted its deliberation on the case. It considers that the facts of this case are clear and the evidence is sufficient and reliable. The two defendants didn't object to the facts of the crime alleged by the prosecution, and evidence such as the testimonies of six witnesses . . ., the written record of obtaining items, photos, conclusion on identification of value, proof of household registration and the Course of Arrest are sufficient to prove that. This court considers that the two defendants, for the purpose of illegal possession, secretly stole others' property. The amount stolen by Defendant 1 was large; the amount stolen by Defendant 2 was relatively large. The acts of both of them constituted the offence of theft. The offence alleged by the prosecution is substantiated:

the prosecution's opinion requesting punishing the two defendants according to law is supported. After being arrested, the two defendants assisted the patrolling team in catching the accomplices and the person who bought the illegally acquired items from them and in recovering the illegally acquired items that had already been sold. They have meritorious performance: thus a lighter punishment might be given to them. Also they have good attitudes in admitting their guilt and the illegally acquired items have already been recovered and returned to the victim. The court might then exercise discretion to give them a lighter punishment. In order to maintain social order and protect the legal property of citizens from being illegally infringed, the following judgment is made according to Articles 264, 25(1), 68, 52 and 53 of the Criminal Law: Defendant 1 committed the offence of theft: he is sentenced to three years' imprisonment and RMB 5000 fine. Defendant 2 committed the offence of theft; he is sentenced to five months' criminal detention and RMB 1000 fine.

E-CO-L-02 [intentional homicide]
Prosecutor: First, the fact of crime is clear and the evidence is sufficient. The defendant admitted his murder and the witnesses [W1] and [W2] also proved this point, apart from the document of appraisal and written record of site reconnaissance. All the evidence is lawful and valid. Second, the defendant's act constituted the offence of intentional homicide. Third, the defendant has limited capacity, which deserves lenient punishment by law.

Judge: There is no law in the defendant's mind. He killed the victim just because he could not repay a debt. His act constituted the offence of intentional homicide. The fact of crime charged by the public prosecution organ is clear and the evidence is sufficient. Thus, the charge is established. But given that the defendant has limited capacity his punishment can be lighter by law.

The third approach of prosecutors, utilized in a few cases, was to draw the attention of the court to what the prosecutor saw as aggravating features and what might constitute mitigation, as in the following example:

M-CO-Y-10 [theft]
Prosecutor: (1) During the court investigation and cross-examination, the prosecutor read out evidence such as the confession statements of the accomplices, witness testimonies, the written record of reporting the case by the victim, the written record of the examination of the crime scene, etc. . . . (2) [T]he prosecutor said that the defendant . . . joined Y and others . . . and stole [metal]. The amount involved was large. His act violated Article 264 of the Criminal Law and constituted the offence of theft. (3) The prosecutor outlined the circumstances relating to the determination of the sentence: the defendant committed the crime again within five years of his release after having served his previous sentence. He is a recidivist. This is a circumstance which allows the court to give the defendant a heavier sentence according to law. The defendant has voluntarily surrendered himself after having committed the crime: this is a circumstance which allows the court to give him a lighter punishment according to law.

The final strategy adopted by the prosecution was to argue for severe punishment. This recommendation could be made on a number of grounds, for example that the defendant was a repeat offender or had shown no remorse or to distinguish between the roles of defendants in a joint trial. Some illustrative cases are set out below:

F-CO-N-14 [robbery]
Prosecutor: 1) This case has been through the process of trial and presenting the relevant evidence material. The evidence proves the defendant's act constitutes the offence of robbery. 2) Because the defendant attempted to commit the crime [and was not successful], the court may sentence leniently. 3) The defendant is a recidivist and committed a crime within five years of release from the previous sentence and he should be punished severely. 4) The defendant denied

the testimony: the attitude of admitting the crime is unsatisfactory and should be punished severely.

F-CO-N-06 [robbery by joint defendants]
Prosecutor: 1) The prosecutor has already produced evidence that is relevant to the defendants' crime to prove that the two defendants committed the offence of robbery. 2) Defendant 1, having committed new crimes within five years after serving his sentence, is a recidivist and should be given a heavier punishment.

E-CO-L-01 [robbery]
Prosecutor: First, the fact of crime is clear and the evidence is sufficient. Just now, the prosecutor has presented the defendant's statement of confession, the testimonies of witnesses, document on the conclusion of criminal technology, written record on the taking of evidence and other evidence. They can prove the existence of the crime committed by the defendant. In addition, when the police collected the evidence, the procedure was lawful and the content was true. Second, the defendant's act constituted the offence of robbery. . . . [Then the prosecutor analysed the details of the crime.] The defendant robbed the victim and looked for the money with a kitchen knife. When he found there was someone in a room on the next floor, he chopped the victim, so his act constituted the offence of robbery. Third, the social harm of this case was large. The defendant's act seriously endangered the personal safety of other citizens, a crime of the type against which the state has been striking hard. It destroyed social stability and caused serious damage to the victim's family; it should be punished severely. The defendant has [previously] been sentenced to prison, but he did not show his repentance after being released from serving his sentence in prison. He robbed again – he committed a new crime within the five years after release; as a recidivist, he should be punished severely.

We can note that, as is inherent in these broad strategies, the prosecution sought to differentiate in appropriate cases between defendants in joint trials according to their respective roles in the crime charged. In this way, the prosecution would argue that the defendants were equally responsible or that, because of their participation in the crime, their age or criminal record, they deserved to be punished differently. In Case F-CO-N-01, three defendants jointly committed a robbery but two of them were under 18 years of age when the offence was committed:

Judge: That's all for the court investigation. Let's start court debate. Now let the prosecutor announce the words of public prosecution.

Prosecutor: The prosecution has already produced evidence that is relevant to the defendants' crime to prove that the three defendants committed the offence of robbery. Because defendants 2 and 3 are still under 18, they should be punished leniently according to the law. The collegiate panel is urged to give an impartial judgment based on the facts of the crime, the circumstances of the case and the defendants' attitude in confessing their crime.

Similarly, in a drug trafficking case, the prosecution evidence was that the first defendant was the main culprit and that the responsibility of the second defendant was less both because the amount of drugs he held was smaller and because, unlike the first defendant, he exhibited remorse and did not seek to evade responsibility:

J-CO-S4-15 [drug trafficking]
Prosecutor: According to the court investigation, the facts are clear and the evidence is sufficient to determine defendants' guilt. Just now I have shown you relevant evidence: the defendants' confession statements, witness testimonies, the conclusion of the criminal examination and the

written records and photos of the site reconnaissance. Defendant 2's confessions in the court are consistent with his confessions in the [PSB] and people's procuratorate and witness testimonies. Defendant 1's fingerprint on the crime scene and his phone records all prove his explanation to be untrue. The two defendants trafficked in cocaine and committed a serious crime, which does great harm to society. The defendants violated Paragraph 4, Article 347 of the Criminal Law. Defendant 1 shall be investigated for criminal responsibility of [400] grams of cocaine, and defendant 2 of [25] grams of cocaine. Defendant 2 has a good attitude and he regrets what he has done. I beg the court to take all facts into consideration and make a determination according to law.

In all these cases, where the record was available to us, the court's judgment tracked the recommendation of the prosecutor in terms of the reasons given and the sentence handed down. The court and the prosecutor acted as one and the recommendation of the defence was reflected in the judgment only where this was congruent with or not inconsistent with that of the prosecution.

For completeness sake, we can note that the sentencing stage in China is also an opportunity for the defendant to be 'educated' as to the error of his or her ways. Typically this occurs where the defendant is a first offender and has committed an opportunistic crime such as theft. Thus, for example, in M-CO-Y-01, two young defendants were convicted of theft, the Presiding Judge having passed sentence educated them as follows:[40]

> *Judge:* [Conducts court education] Defendants, you are healthy, you are perfectly able to earn your living through work; you need not resort to theft and commit crime. I hope you can reform and return to society as soon as possible. Take the defendants back to the Detention Centre. Close the court session.

At least so far as young offenders are concerned, court education is an activity that all the courtroom actors may join in. A good example of this is Case F-CO-N-01 referred to above. Once the determination of sentence had been made, the court sought to educate the two younger defendants:

> *Judge:* Since Defendants 2 and 3 were under 18 when committing the offence, the following is a court education. Let the prosecutor give the education speech first.
>
> *Prosecutor:* Defendants 2 and 3, you participated in this crime involuntarily, but your participation constituted great danger to society. I hope you can learn law properly and go back to society soon.
>
> *Judge:* Let the defence lawyer of Defendant 2 give the education speech.
>
> *Defence Lawyer 2:* Although you are a minor, robbery not only infringes the victim's property but also threatens his life, so robbery has been a crime that is severely controlled in our country. I hope you confessed not simply because you want the court to give a lenient sentence. I hope you can learn a lesson and become a good person.
>
> *Judge:* Let the defence lawyer of defendant 3 give his educational speech.

---

[40] Similarly, in Case M-CO-Y-07, the judge in passing sentence, told the defendant that 'I hope that you can genuinely regret and redeem yourself through labour in order to seek a reduction of your sentence and a return to society as soon as possible.'

Defence Lawyer 3: Defendant 3, although you didn't rob, the fact that you accompanied others to do that is also a crime. I hope you can study more in future. Although your family is poor, your father and second brother are also willing to help you to go back to school. I hope you can study properly.

Judge: Let the legal representative [of the victim] give the education speech.

Legal representative: Defendant 3, you were a good boy before. I hope you can learn a lesson and become a good person. [Defendant 3 cries]

Judge: You should be studying in school according to your age, but you are sitting in court and receiving punishment today. Since your education level is low, you are young, so you turn from an illiterate into a person who does not know law. In court, your defence lawyers have already said that you feel remorse: is it true? The sentence for robbery is a fixed-term imprisonment of three years or above.[41] You committed the crime because you had a wrong mindset at the time of committing the crime. You didn't consider the consequence before taking action. I hope you can reform properly. Now let's end the trial. Take the defendants from the court.

CONCLUSION

In China's criminal justice system, the verdict of those cases which are prosecuted in court is never in real doubt. There may be an occasional finding of not guilty, but we did not encounter any such case and reports of such events are rare. Courts operate on a presupposition of guilt based upon the prosecution case file. What happens in the court hearing is largely incidental to verdict and the 'trial' is a trial in form only or, occasionally, functions to serve a wider social or political purpose. When set against a dossier prepared by the police and prosecutor and assisted in the presentation and management of the case by the judge, defence lawyers, whenever present and of whatever level of skill or commitment, are no match. Hearings are held with the minimum of dispatch. Compliance is expected and required. While a lawyer may tender a plea in mitigation, the sentence function is ultimately determined, with input from the prosecutor, by the court though not in most cases, it would appear, in advance of trial as was the practice in the past.

---

[41] In this case, the principal offender was sentenced to three years' imprisonment, defendant 2 to 18 months' imprisonment and defendant 3 to 12 months' imprisonment with all being additionally fined RMB 1000.

14. The process and the system

In this chapter, we examine how our respondents view the institutions of the criminal justice process, the relationship between the different components and their place within those institutions. On the face of it, the criminal justice system comprises three elements with separate but interrelated responsibilities, each combining to assist and reinforce the work of the others. Article 7, 1996 CPL states:

> In conducting criminal proceedings, the People's Courts, the People's Procuratorates and the public security organs shall divide responsibilities, coordinate their efforts and check each other to ensure the correct and effective enforcement of law.

Our concern here is to get beyond this institutional façade and gain an understanding of how the principal actors – those on the frontline of the system – see the overall architecture of the system and their own roles within it.

We begin our account by looking at three core state institutions – the police (PSB), the procuratorate and the judiciary – before turning to the lawyers for the defence, the group that sits outside the institutions listed in Article 7. We preface this analysis by reminding the reader that in China progress towards the rule of law and recognition of the importance of human rights has to co-exist with a system which demands crime control on a daily basis, intensified at critical social or political moments by 'strike hard' (*yanda*) campaigns[1] which serve to underline for state officials their own responsibility for delivering law and order.

---

[1] On strike hard campaigns, see: Huang Xiangqing (2001); and Trevaskes (2007a). See also, Verna Yu (2009) reporting on a speech by the Vice-Minister for Public Security, Yang Huanning, telling security officials across the country that they must 'strike hard against the destructive work of hostile forces inside and outside the country' that pose a threat to the government. He encouraged police to target what he described as racial separatist and terrorist forces and religious extremists such as the banned Falun Gong sect. See further, Ribet (2010) reporting on the killing of Li Shiming, Xiashuixi's village chief in Shanxi province, by a teenager, Zhang Xuping. The report details how Li Shiming and his gang terrorized the village, grabbed land and engaged in various other illegal acts all under the protective umbrella (*baohu san*) of senior officials that Li is said to have paid off with his ill-gotten gains. The trial of Zhang Xuping had to be postponed because more than a thousand people showed up to support him and tried to cram into the court building. When it went ahead three months later on 26 November 2009 there were more than 100 police in attendance. One Chinese scholar, Chen Xingliang (2006) commented: 'Because crime arises from deep social causes and special conflicts in the transitional period, "strike hard" is a facial solution to crimes, as it cures only the symptoms, not the disease.' See also Ji and Liu (2006).

POLICE[2]

> Recurring references to the legal system as a tripartite network of *Gong-Jian-Fa* organs, comprising in descending order of importance the Public Security Bureaus (*Gongan*), Procuracy (*Jiancha*) and Courts (*Fayuan*), suggest a viewpoint that the legal system is primarily about criminal law enforcement in pursuit of social control (Potter, 1999, p. 681).

We can speak of the public security bureau (PSB) only on the basis of indirect information. We did not involve the PSB in our research but Pitman Potter's characterization of the institutional hierarchy in China's criminal justice system is in our experience justifiable.[3]

Of the three institutions, the PSB is the most powerful. Its Minister is traditionally a member of the Political Bureau of the Central Committee, the key institution of the Party-state and – directly of relevance to court cases in all our research sites – the head of the PSB generally heads the political-legal committee which oversees and directs the activities of the police, procuratorate and the courts.[4] Informal overtures through various sources[5] indicated that any request to the PSB (formal or informal) for research access would not be entertained and, indeed, that the whole research project would be at risk were we to alert the PSB to what we were proposing to do.[6]

In talking to our respondents, the picture that emerges is of a major gap between the PSB and the other state organs. It is clear that the principal state actors see themselves as government officials working co-operatively, and as such, there is a vestige of the former so-called 'three workshops in the same factory'.[7] There is in general, however, a degree of

---

[2] For a general review of literature on the police see: Dai Mengyan (2008); see also, Wong (2002).

[3] Other work relating to the current research undertaken between 2007 and 2010 served only to reinforce this picture. See also Peerenboom (2002). Peerenboom argues that legal reforms have acted to increase the functional independence, professionalism and specialization of the police, procuracy and courts leading to tensions between them (*ibid.*, at p. 312) so that rather than forming one fist 'each finger is now used, often as not, to point blame at others for rising crime or to warn them that they are overreaching their authority'. This was not a marked feature in our research, although it was clear to us that discussions between the police and procuratorate directed towards co-operation collapsed at the first sign that the procuratorate might be seen to exercise 'control' in any form over the police.

[4] The fact that the chief of police tends to head the political-legal committee also places enormous pressure on courts to convict in cases that come before them. Some scholars and some people's deputies hold a negative view on this practice as it is argued to adversely affect the fairness of the Chinese criminal justice system. In practice, it is not an easy task for the procuracy to supervise the police whose leader is the head of the political-legal committee which is responsible for the leadership and coordination of the police, procuratorial and adjudicative work. For example, see Cao Jingjing et al. (2010); Shen Xinwang and Shen Haijiao (2010).

[5] This included advice from leading academics in China and friends within the judiciary and procuratorates.

[6] We recognize that it has become easier for academics within China to undertake some research on the public security bureau. See further Wong (2002).

[7] The phrase is derived from a leading judge writing in 1956: Ma Xi-wu (1956). Arguably, the relationship between the three institutions is now better captured by the 'iron triangle' label that commentators use today. Over recent years, there have been calls for a revival of Ma Xi-wu-style justice as, for example, SPC President Wang Shengjun praising it in his 2009 Court Work Report: available at, http://lawprofessors.typepad.com/china_law_prof_blog/2009/04/

closeness between judges and prosecutors which is absent so far as PSB and other state actors are concerned.

The PSB is seen as a relatively autonomous entity loyal and dedicated to the interests of the Party; an organization, led and controlled by the Party, that operates under its own rules.[8] This closer relationship between judges and prosecutors is also exacerbated by the increased educational attributes of prosecutors and judges consequent upon the introduction of the Unified Judicial examination from 2001.[9] So far as defence lawyers, judges and, to a lesser extent, prosecutors are concerned communications with the PSB are at the minimum required for instrumental reasons connected with case processing. In our discussions with respondents, notwithstanding the fact that there was strong influence from local political leaders[10] and a reputation in some areas for high-level corruption,[11] we found a remarkable degree of similarity in the views given to us across all research sites.[12]

While defence lawyers might be expected to be the most hostile to the PSB, given the high profile arrests of leading activist lawyers as well as low-level harassment,[13] we should begin by noting that not every defence lawyer had a wholly negative view of the PSB, around 30 per cent (25 out of 83 respondents) describing their relationship as 'fair' or even 'good'.

F-IL-N-05: I have a good relationship with [judges, police and prosecutors] and my work goes smoothly. Maybe I am lucky, but I have my principles and I won't do anything illegal.

J-IL-S4-04: They are polite to me; they respect me.

This is understandable because, as Ethan Michelson (2008) has noted, many defence lawyers maintain 'good relationships' precisely because the system is biased against them.

---

supreme-peoples-court-work-report.html. The new policies have included not only drives to educate judges but also to rein in lawyers. On a recent 'warning campaign' see the report available at http://english.caing.com/2010-05-11/11/100142991.html.

[8] For historical material on the role of the police and its centrality to the state, see: Tao Lung-sheng (1966); McAleavy (1962); and Pfeffer (1970).

[9] See, Liu and Halliday (2008).

[10] Fu Hualing (2005a).

[11] For an account of the recent crackdown on alleged corruption in Chongqing, see Mooney (2010). In the course of this crackdown, Wen Qiang, a former deputy police chief and head of the city's justice bureau, was found to have accepted payments for police promotions and providing a political umbrella to protect gangs or 'black societies' and received a sentence of life imprisonment. The article quotes Professor Chin Ko-lin, an expert on Chinese gangs, as saying that it is unlikely that such crackdowns are effective: 'I speak to the public security in many cities and they often talk about this – when there's a crackdown, when there's pressure, they have to come up with the numbers, the quotas', said Chin, 'Often they go after the less powerful.'

[12] We note the cautionary rebuke of Dai: 'Another weakness is the tendency of some research to generalize Chinese policing, especially in the discussions of how one strategy has been replaced by another in the history of Chinese policing. This type of research failed to realize that China is made up of many distinctive cultures, and that the economic reform has not been carried out evenly across the country:' Dai (2008) at p. 225. Despite the fact that our research was conducted in areas at quite different stages of economic development, the views on policing that we received from respondents in different research sites were remarkably uniform.

[13] Reports regularly appear on these matters. See, for example, Ng Tze-wei (2009b).

However, the overwhelming majority of lawyers spoke of a lack of trust between them and the PSB, a dislike, even fear, of the PSB and as the institution with which they had the worst relationship. It is hardly surprising that lawyers view police negatively given that the police routinely deny or delay access to clients, harass and threaten lawyers or, at its lowest, treat them with disrespect. For lawyers, the PSB is seen as an agency that mistrusts lawyers because they are identified with criminals and are thought to collude with criminals to avoid the hand of justice:[14]

> *D-IL-K-06:* Our relationship is tense, we oppose each other; they hate lawyers.
>
> *L-IL-X-08:* My relationship with the police is worse than the relationship with judges.
>
> *F-IL-N-04:* I think the police hate lawyers, they don't want to see lawyers and they think lawyers increase their workload.
>
> *J-IL-S4-02:* The quality of the police is poor and their attitude is worse.
>
> *I-IL-S3-02:* The police always guard against the lawyers, worrying that they will collude with the suspects in tallying the confessions and affect the investigation and the trial of the case, they treat lawyers as thieves.

Against this background, lawyers describe their relationship with the PSB in instrumental terms restricting their contacts to those which are necessary to enable them to function as defence lawyers. Given the choice, they would not interact with the police but they recognize that, in the best interests of their clients, they must deal with the police.

> *A-IL-B1-07:* We have an average relationship. We know each other because of work but due to the conflicts in the system, we do our own work and have no other further communication with each other.
>
> *K-IL-W-05:* [The police] don't respect lawyers subconsciously, but in order to handle the cases properly, I will be friendly with them.
>
> *K-IL-W-04:* The relationship with them can't be too remote, but at the same time can't be too close; the police still haven't changed their mentality; they still think lawyers create trouble for them.
>
> *E-IL-L-07:* We have an average relationship. We are reluctant to contact them: the nature of their job determines their working manner, but I don't like that manner.

Even at this level, however, dealing with the PSB means no more than maintaining superficial contact and (with the one exception cited below) it does not extend towards actively cultivating a relationship (through the usual channels of gifts in money or kind) because of the obvious dangers to which this would give rise:

> *F-IL-N-07:* I have a good personal relationship with [the police] but I have never made use of my relationship with them; not many people can do that in practice.

---

[14] See to like effect: J-IL-S4-01: 'They don't trust lawyers'; I-IL-S3-01: 'The police tell suspects that it is useless to hire a lawyer: they are reluctant to co-operate with lawyers.'

D-IL-K-03: There are strict requirements when we contact the police because nobody wants anything to go wrong.

E-IL-L-05: I have a poor relationship with the police. But for the sake of my work, I have to do something unhappily or reluctantly, to give some small benefit to them, for example to pay the costs when they add fuel at the gas station.

The constant message we received from defenders was that they rarely communicated with the PSB. By this lawyers meant not only did they have no dealings with police at a social level but also that their work-related interactions were slight or non-existent, an outcome that is perhaps not surprising given that the lawyer's first point of contact with the formal institutions generally occurs only after the case is transferred to the prosecutor for examination:

L-IL-X-0: I rarely communicate with the police.

D-IL-K-04: The police and I are not familiar with each other; we rarely communicate.

A-IL-B1-05: We only have basic contact with each other, no communication.

E-IL-L-01: I have no contact with the police.

E-IL-L-02: I almost don't have any contact with the police.

Behind all this lies a thinly-veiled concern, even fear, of the PSB as an institution. Lawyers did not want to spend any time talking about the police confining themselves to short remarks, even asides which do, however, convey their sense of unease and concern. One lawyer said that it was essential that defenders tolerated the police during the investigation stage, that there was no alternative but to do so even though lawyers could not exercise the rights laid down in law. Another lawyer in E-IL-L-04 remarked: 'We have an average working relationship. We will not offend them or create difficulties for them.'

It is to be expected that defence lawyers would have little contact with the police, but we also found that judges repeatedly said that they had little direct communication with the police. In one sense this can be seen as a successful product of the reforms which were intended to remove the responsibility of investigation from the judges and, accordingly, reduce their dealings with the police. The following comments illustrate the responses of judges to a question asking them to describe their working relationship with the police:

K-IJ-W-03: I seldom associate with police. It is better with prosecutors.

LIJ-X-01: My relationship with the prosecutor is harmonious: we can communicate with each other, exchange opinions and discuss the case. We seldom have dealings with the police.

A-IJ-B1-06: My relationship with prosecutors is quite good; they are very co-operative. I have comparatively fewer contacts with the police.

A-IJ-B1-08: I do not have much contact with the police.

A-IJ-B1-09: My relationship with the police is that I basically do not have direct contact with them.

D-IJ-K-03: I have few contacts with the police because we seldom communicate with them directly.

D-IJ-K-04: We seldom contact the police directly.

E-IJ-L-02: I have almost no contact with the police except when we want to find out the true facts in some cases.[15]

As pointed out by two judges (F-IJ-N-07 and E-IJ-L-04), even when they needed to return a case to the police or make an inquiry with the police about a case, normally they would only communicate with the PSB through the prosecutors. This may also be the reason why many judges described their relationship with the police as 'average': 31 out of 88 judges we interviewed described it as 'acceptable', 'average', 'a normal working relationship', or they just treated the police according to law:[16]

E-IJ-L-04: I have no contact with the police. If need be, we can contact them indirectly through the procuratorate.

Notwithstanding this, many judges said that they did co-operate with the PSB in various aspects. For example, a judge (M-IJ-Y-01) said judges would exchange opinions with the police. Similarly, another (J-IJ-S4-08) said that sometimes when the evidence was insufficient, judges might call the PSB directly and ask it to provide supplementary materials. As revealed in the following comment, one judge (D-IJ-K-05) even said that there was an annual meeting involving the police, procurators and judges:[17]

D-IJ-K-05: Every year, there is a joint meeting held by the police, the court and the procuratorate, where we meet the police and settle the problems existing in our work. Sometimes, we send judges down to the police station and provide the police with work guidance.

Eight judges expressly stated to us that they had a good, or very good, relationship with the PSB.[18]

While judges had serious criticisms concerning the quality of police investigative work, they did not confront the police and there was a clear recognition that they were on the same side as the police. As one judge put it in a matter of fact tone:

D-IJ-K-01: As you may know, the police, the judge and the prosecutor are in one family.

---

[15] This comment still exhibits trust in the police to provide the 'true facts'.
[16] The following is a list of judges who said their relationship with the police was acceptable, average or merely a working relationship, or they only treated the police according to law: C-IJ-B3-03, C-IJ-B3-04, C-IJ-B3-05, C-IJ-B3-07, B-IJ-B2-05, B-IJ-B2-06, B-IJ-B2-07, B-IJ-B2-08, B-IJ-B2-09, B-IJ-B2-10, B-IJ-B2-11, B-IJ-B2-12, B-IJ-B2-13, K-IJ-W-02, B-IJ-B1-01, B-IJ-B1-04, B-IJ-B1-05, B-IJ-B1-07, B-IJ-B1-09, D-IJ-K-01, D-IJ-K-02, L-IJ-X-09, M-IJ-Y-01, M-IJ-Y-02, M-IJ-Y-03, M-IJ-Y-04, EIJ-L-07, I-IJ-S3-01, I-IJ-S3-02, K-IJ-W-01 and K-IJ-W-04.
[17] This practice no doubt varies from area to area according to local culture.
[18] One judge (D-IJ-K-05) said he had a very good relationship with the police; seven judges (B-IJ-B3-01, K-IJ-W-03, L-IJ-X-06, L-IJ-X-11, J-IJ-S4-01, J-IJ-S4-02 and J-IJ-S4-04) said they had a good relationship with the police. Among these eight judges, one (J-IJ-S4-02) also said that there was mutual trust between him and the police.

The close relationship between judges and police and/or prosecutors, as succinctly pointed out by another judge, did not mean that judges were unaware that this might affect a defendant's right to a fair trial:

A-IJ-B1-02: Strictly speaking, judges should be impartial and independent, but in reality the police, procuratorate and the court are members of the same family; it is still not very fair to the defendants . . .

For their part, prosecutors have greater interaction with the PSB and see themselves, in general, as allied to the police. Of the 96 prosecutors we interviewed, nearly 50 per cent of them said they had a good relationship with the police.[19] The comments of these prosecutors on their relationship with the police could be summarized as, 'mutual respect, mutual co-operation and mutual supervision'. At one level, this is very much the 'three workshops in the same factory' approach which traditionally characterized the state institutions of the criminal justice system. Prosecutors are very much aligned with the police. The comments of those interviewees who said they had mutual co-operation with the police, showed that they worked closely with the police and were very satisfied with the police co-operation. For example, many of them told us that they had frequent contact with the PSB, they could discuss cases with the police, the police respected their opinions, and their requests were promptly and effectively responded to by the police. The following are some of the comments of our prosecutor interviewees:

F-IP-N-02: The relationship between the procuratorate and the police is relatively close. We often communicate with each other on cases. The police respect our advice for supplementary investigation and we support each other's work.

L-IP-X-02: We have a good relationship with the police, because we usually have a business relationship with them. They seldom pass the buck where there are problem cases. They solve problems actively.

L-IP-X-09: My relationship with the police is very good. The police in charge of cases respect me. They often ask for my guidance . . .

A-IP-B1-10: My relationship with the police is one of collaboration and co-operation, our relationship is quite smooth. Normally my requests in relation to cases will be responded to.

J-IP-S4-04: Prosecutors and police have good relationships and we support each other. With respect to some cases, we always keep communicating, and we will engage ourselves in some cases in advance. That will provide convenience for our prosecution.

F-IP-N-01: Our working relationship with the police depends on our leaders. Ours is very close. We often communicate with each other regarding cases. I will list my examination and

---

[19] The following is a list of prosecutors who told us that they had a good relationship with the police: K-IP-W-02, K-IP-W-03, K-IP-W-04, M-IP-Y-01, M-IP-Y-03, M-IP-Y-05, F-IP-N-01, F-IP-N-02, F-IP-N-03, F-IP-N-04, F-IP-N-05, L-IP-X-02, L-IP-X-03, L-IP-X-05, L-IP-X-07, L-IP-X-08, L-IP-X-09, A-IP-B1-00, A-IP-B1-02, A-IP-B1-03, A-IP-B1-06, A-IP-B1-07, A-IP-B1-08, A-IP-B1-10, A-IP-B1-12, A-IP-B1-14, B-IP-B2-04, B-IP-B2-05, B-IP-B2-09, B-IP-B2-10, B-IP-B2-12, B-IP-B2-13, B-IP-B2-17, D-IP-K-02, D-IP-K-04, J-IP-S4-01, J-IP-S4-02, J-IP-S4-03, J-IP-S4-04, J-IP-S4-05, J-IP-S4-06, H-IP-S2-01, H-IP-S2-02, H-IP-S2-07, E-IP-L-01, E-IP-L-02, E-IP-L-05 and E-IP-L-06.

prosecution suggestions and request the police to collect evidence accordingly. We co-operate with each other in relation to work.

F-IP-N-05: I can say prosecutors and police are in the same boat. We have a good relationship and co-operate with each other. Police will communicate with us whenever they encounter any problem in handling cases, and we will try to provide them with guidance and service.

Apart from the prosecutors who said their relationship with the police was good, seven prosecutors described their relationship with the police as 'acceptable'[20] while 14 prosecutors told us they only had a normal working relationship with the police.[21]

The principal concerns that prosecutors expressed in relation to the PSB are directly relevant to the 'same family' concept that is widely accepted as defining China's system. The first, echoing negative comments of judges, is the view that the quality of police investigation is poor with an over-reliance on confession evidence and a failure to seal obvious gaps in the prosecution case. This was sometimes stated to be a problem of 'communication' between the two organs:

M-IP-Y-02: Poor communication with police is because of the different understanding of standards of evidence between prosecutor and police. The evidence I think necessary is considered unnecessary by them. It seems as if I create trouble for them.

M-IP-Y-04: We often quarrel with the police over cases mainly because we have different understandings as to the standard of evidence.[22]

M-IP-Y-05: We often communicate with the police and our relationship is good. But sometimes we also argue with each other over cases mainly because of their irregular evidence-collection methods and the different understandings of evidence between us.

Indeed, a number of prosecutors made clear that their relationship with the police was not in any way social but one founded in the working environment, as the following illustrate (in all cases, emphasis supplied):

F-IP-N-4: We co-operate with each other *in work*.

F-IP-N-05: We are on the same side and we co-operate with each other *in work*.

B-IP-B2-09: We co-operate with each other *in work*.

J-IP-S4-04: We co-operate with each other *in work*.

Significantly, however, prosecutors also reported that the quality of the police was poor and individual police officers were not serious about their work:

---

[20] The following is a list of prosecutors who said their relationship with the police was acceptable: M-IP-Y-04, L-IP-X-04, L-IP-X-06, A-IP-B1-04, A-IP-B1-05, D-IP-K-01 and D-IP-K-06.

[21] The following is a list of prosecutors who said they only had working relationship with the police: K-IP-W-01, L-IP-X-01, L-IP-X-11, A-IP-B1-07, B-IP-B2-03, B-IP-B2-06, B-IP-B2-15, B-IP-B2-16, C-IP-B3-01, C-IP-B3-04, D-IP-K-03, D-IP-K-05, E-IP-L-04 and E-IP-L-07.

[22] Similarly, one prosecutor (F-IP-N-03) said that individual police officers failed to understand the standard of evidence the prosecutors requested in examination for prosecution.

A-IP-B1-06: I think the sense of evidence of the police is quite poor; the evidence they collect is not useful, but they can quickly solve the problems after some communication.

J-IP-S4-05: Our working relationship with the police is good. But the situation is different in different police stations. Some police officers are responsible and efficient, but some of them seem to be courteous but careless in work. That is because of the poor quality and low sense of responsibility of some policemen. For example, some identification records, interrogation records and examination records are not made according to the requirements; on the other hand there are too many cases but too few staff.

J-IP-S4-07: Our working relationship is close, but sometimes I am a little disappointed with them. Their standard of evidence is too low; therefore we have to supervise and instruct them on how to collect evidence. Certainly I feel sympathy for them. There is a serious shortage of personnel and lots of jobs for them. And the responsibility of maintaining public order is very important.

This view was summed up by one prosecutor who remarked: 'We need to improve the quality of the police. Their work determines whether we can prosecute criminal suspects smoothly. That is to say, only if they provide good grains can we cook good rice.'[23]

This concern was not simply abstract. Prosecutors worried about the quality of police work[24] because they ultimately lacked authority to deal with the police despite having in theory a 'supervisory' role over the PSB. Prosecutors feel subordinate to the police who may disregard their advice or ignore requests for supplementary evidence at will:

A-IP-B1-12: The relationship between the police and prosecutors is one of mutual supervision. But there are also problems in supervision. Some officers think that our supervision is targeted at them as individuals, but in fact our target is their work although supervision definitely will affect them. Sometimes police officers do not pay attention to my opinions; they simply give perfunctory responses.

C-IP-B3-03: On the surface, our relationship is one of direction, guidance and being guided, but in fact we do not play a decisive role as to whether the police officers would accept our opinions; we cannot do anything if they refuse to do so.

Forty years ago Stanley Lubman observed:[25]

> The principal decision maker in the Chinese communist criminal process has been the police. . . . Convincing proof is afforded by recalling that Procuracy and courts generally negotiated informally with the police rather than return a case for insufficient evidence.

This would appear still to be the position today. The procuratorate and the judges continue to deal with the police in private and seek to persuade the police to take a particular course of action rather than mandating them to do so.

---

[23] This is a variant on the well-known saying: 'The police cook the food; the procuratorate serves it; and the court eats it.' See, He Weifang's paper: available at: http://journals.cambridge.org/action/displayFulltext?type=1&fid=1347016&jid=CQY&volumeId=191&issueId=1&aid=1347012.

[24] It is noteworthy that, while police inefficiency was commonly referred to, respondents did not talk about police corruption or abuse of power (except in relation to torture and confessions). For a broader account of concerns over police behaviour, see: Wong (2004).

[25] Lubman (1969) at p. 563.

However, this recognition of the supremacy of the PSB and its autonomous character[26] is a clear point of tension which some prosecutors would like to see changed. A number of prosecutors, while talking about 'mutual respect' and 'mutual supervision' actually want power to direct and control the PSB:

F-IP-N-04: The right to complete the case should be handed to the procuratorate. Police officers tend to consider that criminal suspects should be prosecuted if the People's Procuratorate approve the arrest and so they will not try their best in the subsequent investigation. If the right to case-determination was given to the procuratorate, the PSB would work without delay.

D-IP-K-03: I think we should follow western countries on the supervision of the police. If the prosecutor knows how the police collect evidence, he may avoid much repetition.

A-IP-B1-16: There should be more detailed guidelines on the procurator's power of supervision of investigation and adjudication, thus making such power more substantive and more effective.

L-IP-X-11: I hope that my opinion can be made legally binding on the police. I even hope that I would be given the power of impeachment.

Outside the police, those with the strongest formal powers of 'supervision' within criminal procedure[27] – the procuratorate – do not in practice have significant influence over the police who may, with impunity, ignore advice or requests from both the prosecutor and the judge. One prosecutor set out the position clearly:

J-IP-S4-08: According to Article 7 of the Criminal Procedure Law, the People's Courts, the People's Procuratorate and the Public Security Bureau shall divide their responsibilities, coordinate their efforts and check each other to ensure the correct and effective enforcement of the law. But in practice, there is much coordination but little check. This is disadvantageous to the defendant's rights and interests.

What gives the PSB authority is not professionalism and quality of work, both of which are often put into question by judges and prosecutors. Their authority derives from the authority that they have always exercised in recent Chinese history and which does not depend upon formal allocation by law.

PROSECUTORS

Prosecutors see themselves as a key component of 'the family' that constitutes the iron triangle of the institutions of Chinese criminal justice. While they have misgivings at various levels about the PSB and, in particular, its self-directed and self-governing character, they see themselves as allied with the police in the fight against crime, a commitment that is even more marked in relation to their alignment with the judiciary. Prosecutors

---

[26] 'Autonomous', that is, with respect to the procurators. The police are not only subject to control by the Ministry of Public Security but also are heavily controlled by local political committees through their power over budget and human resources: Fu Hualing (1994a).

[27] For an account of the many layers of supervision that exist on the books, from the Ministry of Supervision to local citizenry, see: Ma (1997).

overwhelmingly spoke of their good relationship with judges in working closely together, in sharing opinions and, though less frequently, in interacting in social settings.

> *D-IP-K-03:* I have a good relationship with judges. Comparatively speaking, my relationship with judges is the best one among my relationship with judges, lawyers and police. When judges make decisions, they will consider my opinions.

> *F-IP-N-04:* Sometimes [judges] will borrow the notes that I jotted while reading the case materials in order to read my conclusion.

> *K-IP-W-03:* We support each other in our work.

> *L-IP-X-03:* We co-operate with each other.

In addition to claiming that they have a good relationship with judges, prosecutors acknowledged that judges were normally biased in favour of the prosecution:

> *M-IP-Y-05:* Judges are inclined to be on the side of the prosecutors.

It was also commented that:

> *A-IP-B1-08:* Judges and prosecutors – there are always the same cases and the same people. As time goes by, people become familiar with each other. This is natural. But once they are familiar with each other, the problem of giving 'face' will occur.

In this regard, the relationships between state actors are intensified and institutionalized in China and they share certain core values which directly bear upon how they discharge their case-related responsibilities. The relationships between state actors, however, do not depend upon the creation or evolution of common work habits or professional value-systems or on teaching defence lawyers to comply with courtroom culture or on defence lawyers learning the practices of the other institutional actors. In China, the relationships between state actors are an essential part of the architecture of the system so far as the prosecution and judges are concerned, leaving little space for lawyers to work within.

Of course, these relationships are in good measure conditioned by a disciplinary framework in which there are unwelcome consequences for disagreements. If, for example, the judge acquits a defendant, this is a black mark against the prosecutor which may lead to loss of bonus or other sanction for the prosecutor and open the possibility of state compensation for the defendant. In any disagreement about the strength of the evidence in pre-trial discussions, should the judge foreshadow this, the prosecutor will be obliged to withdraw the case:

> *K-IP-W-02:* Given the control of the acquittal rate,[28] prosecutors are very cautious and they will consult judges when they have queries.

> *F-IP-N-01:* Our relationship with judges is good. We cooperate with each other in work and sometimes we have some joint leisure activities. But there are also unpleasant things. In some

---

[28] Each area sets a target acquittal rate that would be acceptable or that would attract sanction if exceeded.

individual prosecutions, judges will consider that there is insufficient evidence. If the case is tried in the court, a not guilty verdict would be entered. So judges require us to withdraw the prosecution. From our point of view, however, the evidence we have collected is sufficient. But we have to submit in order to maintain a good relationship.

This disciplinary framework does not, of course, remove differences between prosecutors and judges over case-related issues. However, these are not differences to be aired in court: differences are 'managed' in a private setting where face may be given, face saved and conflict reduced:

> *L-IP-X-04:* We co-operate very well with the judge. After the initiation of the prosecution, if the judge has a disagreement or if he is not clear about the case, we will exchange opinions in time. Generally speaking, we can reach a common understanding.
>
> *K-IP-W-01:* We often communicate if there are any questions, such as problems with supplementary materials, whether there are circumstances of voluntary surrender and meritorious performance, etc.
>
> *L-IP-X-05:* Our relationship with judges is good. At least, judges will communicate with us beforehand, and if there is a problem, we will ask the police to supplement the missing materials, so that we will not be too embarrassed and passive.

Some prosecutors asserted that these were meaningful exchanges in which opinions could be advanced robustly, while others insisted that they would always maintain a distance from judges.

> *J-IP-S4-05:* I will communicate with judges in some cases so as to make them fully understand the case and the basis of prosecution. But what I do is not to interfere with judges' impartial judgment.
>
> *J-IP-S4-08:* I know the judges very well because of our long working relationship, but I think it is normal to keep a certain distance.
>
> *M-IP-Y-03:* My relationship with judges is good but also not too close. It is not good for supervision if our relationship is too close.

When there were divergent opinions between prosecutors and judges, some prosecutors told us that they would insist on their viewpoint. This was, we felt, in many cases an effort by prosecutors to keep their self-respect and to show the researchers that there was a degree of equivalence between themselves and judges:

> *A-IP-B1-11:* I treat the judge as a target of debate, convincing the judge to accept my opinions is the direct purpose of my appearing in court. Therefore sometimes I will co-operate with the judge, but when we have divergent opinions I will try my best to argue.[29]
>
> *A-IP-B1-12:* If judges change my decisions, I will raise my opinions, and discuss with them.
>
> *B-IP-B2-02:* I do not communicate with judges before trial; I supervise the judges during trial.

---

[29] Similarly, a prosecutor (L-IP-X-06) also said that he would not concede if his opinion on a case was different from that of the judges.

I respect judges, but I insist on the opinions of public prosecution and will reflect any problems after trial.

B-IP-B2-13: [Prosecutors and judges] cooperate with each other in work, but we insist on our own independence while handling cases.

But while prosecutors would like to project an image of authority and be objects of respect, they are in fact a subordinate class with a relatively poor self-image, ultimately lacking in the ability to monitor or control either the police or the judge.[30] As others have noted, prosecutors have no substantive control over either the police or the court and the prosecutorial supervisory powers they enjoy may be disregarded with impunity.[31]

Prosecutors believe that they are of low standing in the eyes of the general public and they suffer from low self-esteem, complaining of low salaries and oppressive case-loads:

F-IP-N-02: I think that the quality of prosecutors needs great improvement. The phenomenon of 'Three high, one low' was mentioned in an *Economic Daily* report. . . . That is to say, there were high quality judges, defence lawyers and defendants but poor quality prosecutors.

J-IP-S4-01: I personally think we should build a professional team step by step. A prosecutor cannot reach a higher level if he hasn't been engaged in prosecution work for years. But the reality is that if you are a good prosecutor you will be promoted to be leader of the prosecution department or the Procuratorate itself. When you become a leader, you will be busy doing administrative work instead of handling cases. In this system, the [prosecution] team is always young. . . .

J-IP-S4-07: The treatment we receive is far below that accorded to [defence] lawyers. The remuneration for a lawyer in a single case is more than my salary for one month. Sometimes I feel it is unfair.

M-IP-Y-03: Our workload is very heavy. Each of us has to handle about 100 cases per year on average.

C-IP-B3-01: The social recognition of the prosecutor's work is low.

L-IP-X-07: The workload of my branch is the heaviest. One person has to deal with 3–4 cases on average [at one time].

L-IP-X-11: Prosecutors receive poor treatment. Remuneration needs to be higher to foster uncorrupted officials.

---

[30] Several prosecutors saw the failure of judges to deliver a judgment at the conclusion of a trial (instead, announcing the decision days or weeks later) as an insult to prosecutors. Thus, for example, as one prosecutor said in interview: E-IP-LY-06: 'It is disrespectful to the prosecutorial organ for the court not to make an immediate judgment in court.'

[31] Thus, by virtue of Article 87, 1996 CPL, if the procuratorate considers that the reasons given by the police for not filing a case are 'untenable', 'it shall notify the public security organ to file the case, and upon receiving the notification, the public security organ shall file the case' but no mechanism for enforcing this is provided. The prosecutor's power under Article 169, 1996 CPL, exercisable if it discovers that in handling a case a People's Court has violated the litigation procedure prescribed by law, 'to suggest to the People's Court that it should set it right' is manifestly without teeth. See also: Liu and Halliday (2009) at p. 930. Of course, should the procuratorate enter a 'protest', formally there is no option but to reconsider the case in the People's Court: Fu Hualing (2000).

Some are acutely aware of the disparity between their position 'in the books' and their lack of authority in practice and of the oppressive environment within which they work:

> *E-IP-L-04:* As a prosecutor, the law in China makes us the God of Judicial Justice. However, for reasons related to legislation, the quality of prosecutors and the enforcement of the law in practice, our role has not been realized completely.

> *D-IP-K-01:* There are many pressures in my work. First, the workload is heavy. For example, we handled 30 cases per person every year five years ago. But now, I have to handle between 80 and 90 cases every year. The number of prosecutors remains the same as before. Moreover, cases today are more complex than before. In addition, the procedure and the requirements are more complicated: for example, if you make a mistake it may involve the system of state compensation. The system also causes psychological pressures.

The lack of personal self-esteem is not wholly explained by a criminal justice process in which the caseload is heavy and the procedures complex: it also derives from a lack of self-worth and self-confidence. Aside from the disciplinary system and possible sanctions for an 'incorrect' outcome, prosecutors feel strongly that they do not have a basis in professionalism which could act as a counter-weight and give them capacity to assert themselves. Prosecutors are clear about the deficits that they face in terms of professional competence: the system for training prosecutors is poor; they personally feel they lack professional skills; and the prosecution office is, through the promotion system, structured to produce an inexperienced environment.

For our respondents, the existing system for training prosecutors does not address the needs of a professional charged with handling a criminal case. Although many were not knowledgeable about foreign systems, their own training system is regarded as simplistic, unrefined, and lagging behind that found in Western counterparts. In the absence of a centralized system, such training as takes place is superficial and patchy, as prosecutors made clear:

> *A-IP-B1-08:* The existing system of training in China is primitive. There is no strict unified mechanism for recruiting candidates . . . there are no professional training institutions. Our training is scattered: talks, professional lectures – they are not specific enough. This training only aims at providing general training but many people are at different levels of expertise. . . . We should learn from Japan and Germany, putting all university students recruited through the judicial examination in unified training institutions to receive about two years of unified training and then assign positions to them based on their results and after being assigned positions the students should work there as a trainee for two to three years. A student should only obtain the qualification of being a permanent judge or prosecutor after he has completed and passed the training.

> *J-IP-S4-08:* I have just returned from America where I received training. There are not many training opportunities for us in general. I was selected out of the whole province, received three months' training in legal English in China before I received one month's training in an American university. The time was short but I benefited a lot and my horizon was broadened. The thing I feel strongest is that there is a big gulf in the judicial systems and the qualities of the judicial personnel between China and America.

Prosecutors spoke with authority not only because of their assessment of the training systems in place but, more significantly, because of their own experience. We asked prosecutors: 'Do you think that you were adequately trained when you started as a prosecutor?' Prosecutors made clear that they arrived at their current position by different routes but few regarded themselves as adequately prepared for the responsibilities they were required to assume. Several spontaneously mentioned that in-post training did not make good the deficits. The examples below illustrate their own biographies:

A-IP-B1-06: I started to do prosecution work after completing postgraduate studies and after having passed the judicial examination. I was appointed as an assistant prosecutor. I think I didn't have sufficient training in terms of practical experience.

A-IP-B1-07: The training was not sufficient because I had only studied industrial economy and only started to study law after joining the procuratorate.

M-IP-YK-05: Our training is not adequate.

A-IP-B1-03: I did not receive any training before I took up the job as a prosecutor. I was only given a brief introduction to the various departments before the commencement of my work. I mainly relied on the teachings of the masters, that is, the senior prosecutors.

A-IP-B1-05: The training we received was not sufficient. Now we have a lot of training but much of it is from a macro-perspective and is not very helpful to actual practice. I mainly rely upon accumulated experience.

J-IP-S4-05: I was a procuratorial clerk before becoming a prosecutor. I didn't receive any special and systematic training before taking up the position. I only learned from experienced prosecutors. The features of prosecution work are practical and operational, so practice is the best training. To do a good job, it is very important to accumulate practical experience.

Almost 93 per cent of the prosecutors we interviewed stated that further training and education was necessary for them.[32] But when asked whether they would be willing to receive further training and education, although the majority of the interviewees gave a positive answer, some said that their heavy workloads would make this impossible:

D-IP-K-03: We are busy with handling cases; consequently we don't have the time and energy to study.

---

[32] The following is a list of prosecutors who told us that further training and education were necessary for them: K-IP-W-01, K-IP-W-02, KIP-W-03, K-IP-W-04, M-IP-Y-01, M-IP-Y-02, M-IP-Y-03, M-IP-Y-04, M-IP-Y-05, F-IP-N-01, F-IP-N-02, F-IP-N-03, F-IP-N-04, F-IP-N-05, L-IP-X-01, L-IP-X-04, L-IP-X-05, L-IP-X-06, L-IP-X-07, L-IP-X-08, L-IP-X-09, L-IP-X-10, L-IP-X-11, A-IP-B1-00, A-IP-B1-01, A-IP-B1-02, A-IP-B1-03, A-IP-B1-04, A-IP-B1-05, A-IP-B1-06, A-IP-B1-07, A-IP-B1-08, A-IP-B1-09, A-IP-B1-10, A-IP-B1-11, A-IP-B1-12, A-IP-B1-13, A-IP-B1-14, B-IP-B2-00, B-IP-B2-01, B-IP-B2-02, B-IP-B2-03, B-IP-B2-04, B-IP-B2-05, B-IP-B2-06, B-IP-B2-07, B-IP-B2-08, B-IP-B2-09, B-IP-B2-10, B-IP-B2-11, B-IP-B2-12, B-IP-B2-13, B-IP-B2-14, B-IP-B2-15, B-IP-B2-16, B-IP-B2-17, C-IP-B3-01, C-IP-B3-03, C-IP-B3-04, C-IP-B3-05, C-IP-B3-07, D-IP-K-01, D-IP-K-02, D-IP-K-03, D-IP-K-04, D-IP-K-05, D-IP-K-06, J-IP-S4-01, J-IP-S4-02, J-IP-S4-03, J-IP-S4-04, J-IP-S4-05, J-IP-S4-06, J-IP-S4-07, J-IP-S4-08, G-IP-S1-03, G-IP-S1-04, G-IP-S1-05, H-IP-S3-02, H-IP-S3-03, H-IP-S3-04, H-IP-S3-07, E-IP-L-01, E-IP-L-02, E-IP-L-03, E-IP-L-04, E-IP-L-05, E-IP-L-06 and E-IP-L-07.

D-IP-K-04: Our training is not enough, because we have too many cases to handle. I have to handle more than 90 cases every year. Therefore, on the one hand I don't have time to study; on the other hand, I neglect studying.

K-IP-W-03: Further training and education are very necessary. But I am too busy to receive training.

L-IP-X-04: I feel very tired, because I have many cases. I am busy and tied up with cases. I don't have time to learn new knowledge.

Additionally, the following comments revealed some other factors discouraging prosecutors from receiving further training and education:

L-IP-X-05: I am eager to have a chance [to receive further training and education], but my child is too young and I don't have enough energy. . . . In addition, there are too many unfair things happening in my work,[33] so I don't want to have further education.

L-IP-X-01: Further training and education are useful, but given my age, I don't want to learn. . . . The cost of study is huge and my unit will not compensate me. . . . I don't have much interest in study.[34]

E-IP-L-07: We have very few training opportunities but lots of cases to handle, so we cannot participate in such training or education.

Given the fact that heavy workload was considered by the prosecutors as the major factor hindering their further studies, some prosecutors suggested that off-work study was necessary.

L-IP-X-04: [O]f course [further training and education are useful]. But this study should be worthy of the name. . . . Our study should be on release from the present post to other duties.[35]

E-IP-L-06: I hope the state can arrange for us to study for a period of time, which is the ideal way.

D-IP-K-01: It is better to have full-time training, for example, for around one month. But it is impossible at the moment.[36]

The lack of self-esteem and low status is magnified by the lack of personal autonomy and independence which marks the job of being a prosecutor. Prosecutors feel impotent in a prosecutorial system in which they do not take decisions themselves. Key decisions, as they were keen to point out, are made by those above them in the prosecutorial hierarchy or in some other administrative structure.[37] While this may have a protective side, insulating them to a certain degree from personal criticism, it also places them in a dependent

---

[33] The prosecutor did not elaborate on this issue.
[34] This prosecutor reported that he was 42 years old.
[35] A similar view was expressed by two prosecutors (A-IP-B1-02 and A-IP-B1-13).
[36] A similar view was shared by another prosecutor (E-IP-L-04).
[37] As we have seen, some prosecutors saw this as a necessary protection precisely because of the lack of trained prosecutors and the dangers of leaving key decisions to them.

relationship lacking that autonomy of decision-making which they associate with a professional status:

L-IP-X-05: Right now, I have to report to the chief prosecutor and then to a section meeting and then to the attorney-general in charge.

B-IP-B2-17: We obtain approval from the departmental head, the chief prosecutor in charge and submit the case to the prosecutorial committee if necessary.

E-IP-L-05: First, the system of dealing with cases should be reformed in order to avoid administrative interference with the disposition of the case by order and by the leader's prior decision on the case. . . . We should learn from the practice in ancient times – the officials were appointed to work in other areas. The system of localized leaders has tremendous dangers to society.

B-IP-B2-10: More discretion should be given to prosecutors as individuals: they should be allowed to make decisions on their own in minor criminal cases. Now, decisions must still be approved at various levels and the leader will make the final decision. . . . Now there is much interference in handling cases thus leading to a doubt about whether law or politics should be at the centre.

B-IP-B2-05: The [problem] is the independence of prosecutorial power: at this moment, there is too much administrative interference.

L-IP-X-07: External interference mainly comes from leaders.

L-IP-X-11: We should prevent external interference and influence from high-ups and exercise the power of prosecutorial independence.

The gap between the formal arrangements and prosecutorial practice is perhaps most clearly displayed in relation to appeals or 'protests'.[38] A few prosecutors told us that they did enter protests (almost invariably over sentence) and thought it important to do so as part of their monitoring and supervision of judges:

A-IP-B1-04: I have protested before; this is a means to guarantee judicial fairness. I insist on using law instead of the judges as the standard; therefore I will protest if a protest is needed.

D-IP-K-01: [Prosecutors and judges] co-operate and coordinate with each other. But when we have different opinions on the case, we will protest if we think it necessary.

B-IP-B2-09: My supervision of judges is exercised mainly in the form of a protest; this can control judges to a certain extent.

A-IP-B1-03: I have protested in about ten cases. About five were successful. Some of the protests were made because the circumstances of the cases were extremely bad but the sentences given by the courts were too lenient.

---

[38] Under Article 181, 1996 CPL, 'If a local People's Procuratorate at any level considers that there is some definite error in a judgment or order of first instance made by a People's Court at the same level, it shall present a protest to the People's Court at the next higher level.'

Our research strongly suggests that the incidence of 'protests' is not a reliable measure of court autonomy as some writers have argued. Fu Hualing[39] identifies adjudicative review (which may be triggered by the President of the second instance court, the superior courts, the procuratorate and the defendant concerned) as a crucial means to control the courts' autonomy in criminal adjudication on the basis that:[40]

> . . . the higher the number of adjudicative review cases, the stronger the external control, and hence the lower the autonomy by the courts in adjudication.

He shows that, on the basis of official statistics,[41] adjudicative review (in both the actual number of cases received by courts and its percentage in the total number of first and second instance criminal cases) has been decreasing steadily since the mid-1980s and argues this is evidence of the increase in autonomy enjoyed by the courts.

We are not persuaded that the statistics tell us very much about the 'autonomy' of the courts or, if they do, what kind of 'autonomy' it is and its importance in the criminal process. Certainly, our interviews with prosecutors did not lead us to believe that the relative absence of protests is a reflection of the prosecutors' greater confidence in the courts but is explicable more in terms of the heavy constraints that prosecutors operate under from within the procuratorate that inhibit them from entering protests.

While on the face of it, a prosecutor may enter a protest whenever he or she believes that the court has fallen into error in terms of the verdict or sentence (in reality, on sentence), in practice decisions on whether a protest should be entered are subject to a strict decision-making hierarchy. Not only does the system require approval at all levels, it also acts to discourage protests because protests are seen to be criticisms of the judges and hence expose judges to possible sanction, as prosecutors told us:

> *J-IP-S4-01:* [explaining why very few protests were entered] When I receive a written judgment, I write a written protest. At first I hand it to the chief of the department and then to the chief prosecutor. They both approve. It is then sent to the Intermediate People's Court within ten days and duplicates are at the same time sent to the Higher People's Procuratorate of a Province as well. The Intermediate People's Court receives the protest and hands the case over to the Higher People's Court of a Province. Of course, if the Higher People's Procuratorate of a Province considers the protest inappropriate, it will withdraw the protest from the Higher People's Court of a Province and notify us.

> *L-IP-X-06:* We will exchange opinions [with judges] in ordinary cases. I will insist on my views if the cases are complex. But the initiation of a protest has to be approved by the leaders of the unit.

> *A-IP-B1-00:* Normally we will not protest. We will only protest if the decision is really bad; but there is very little support from the court at the upper level.

---

[39] Fu Hualing (2010).
[40] *Ibid.*, at p. 6.
[41] Our purpose here is not to question the reliability of official statistics, though it should be noted that Fu Hualing urges caution in viewing these and, in particular, in the conflation in the statistics of, on the one hand, prosecution challenges to the decision of a trial court and, on the other, the initiation of an adjudicative review by the prosecutor against the determination of a second instance court decision.

The upshot is that very few protests are entered or proceed any further. The following are illustrative of the overwhelming majority of responses that prosecutors gave in relation to entering a protest against a decision of the court:

A-IP-B1-01: I have never protested.

A-IP-B1-02: I have never protested.

A-IP-B1-07: I have protested before but was unsuccessful because the second branch of the procuratorate did not give support.

G-IP-S1-03: There was only one case in the last six years: we wanted to protest but we did not.
...

J-IP-S4-07: There are not many protests. I have never protested.

As a result, a picture emerges of a system which, at the coalface, is staffed by individuals with low morale and self-esteem, possessing little autonomy by way of decision-making, having received inadequate training for the responsibilities which nominally fall to them and ultimately constrained in anything they do by a supervening hierarchy which includes others in the administrative or political sphere.

JUDGES

Judges, like prosecutors, identify themselves as state functionaries allied to the police and procuratorate in the fight against crime.[42] This much is also clear from the Chinese Constitution which, as Jonathan Hecht points out, does not speak of judicial independence (*sifa duli*) but of 'independent exercise of the power to adjudicate' (*duli xingshi shenpanquan*),[43] a formulation which accommodates political control at least over the selection of judges and the parameters of their work.[44] As such, judicial independence is

---

[42] This is not, of course, unique to China. In some other civil law systems, judges and prosecutors are or were part of the same organization and, indeed, may or could alternate roles. Thus, for example, in Italy, judges and prosecutors used to be both members of the judiciary (*magistratura*) with the same entrance examinations and salary and individuals could move from one role to another. The link between the two was broken by a change in the law in 2006 (Decreto Lg. April 5, 2006, n. 160): Van Cleave (2007). In France, however, while the functions of prosecutors and judges are kept separate, both are considered to be 'magistrates', there is a common training programme at the end of which candidates choose one or other branch of the magistracy; but after this, while those who choose to be judges usually remain so for life, prosecutors sometimes later switch to the judiciary and it is possible to move between the two branches: Frase (2007). For an earlier account of training regimes in various European countries see: Council of Europe (1996).

[43] Hecht (1996a) at p. 59. On the general question of judicial independence, see Peerenboom (2010a). See also Yue Liling (2010) at pp. 64–65.

[44] For a helpful discussion of judicial independence, impartiality and integrity principles, see Henderson (2010). Henderson sets out (at p. 15) 18 principles captured in a series of IFES (International Foundation for Electronic Systems) which reflect an emerging global consensus. These include: (1) guarantee of judicial independence, the right to a fair trial, equality under the

ascribed to 'the court' not 'the judge'.[45] For its part, the Constitution is defined as having 'supreme legal authority' but it also enshrines the principle of the 'leadership of the Communist Party'. Thus the inherent contradiction has been described in the following terms:[46]

> Courts are supposed to adjudicate independently, but the Party opposes the idea of an independent judiciary. Power nominally resides in government organs, yet real power rests with the Party committees that shadow those organs at every level. State organs must carry out the paramount task of protecting 'social stability' by offering legal remedies to protesters with legitimate complaints, but they must also suppress them if Party authority is being undermined.

As Fu Hualing (2003) has noted, the police, the procuratorate and the courts are not there simply to enforce the law; 'theoretically, they also are the institutions of the dictatorship'. Since April 2006, in a movement launched by Luo Gan (then head of the Party's Central Committee's Legal and Political Committee) the pressure upon judges has intensified through a campaign to crack down on rights-defenders and to strengthen the Party's control over judicial work. The import of this was neatly captured in a speech by the President of the People's Court, Xiao Yang:[47]

> The power of the courts to adjudicate independently doesn't mean at all independence from the Party. It is the opposite, the embodiment of a high degree of responsibility vis-à-vis Party undertakings.

Additionally, there has been the emergence of the 'Three Supremes' doctrine, first promulgated by Hu Jintao. Under this, judges and prosecutors are directed as to their work-priorities:

> In their work, the grand judges and grand procurators shall always regard as supreme the party's cause, the people's interests and the constitution and laws.

The importance of this, as Jerome Cohen (2010a) notes, is that the theme was developed by the head of the Supreme People's Court, Wang Shengjun, that judicial fairness and justice must be interpreted in the light of public opinion (*minyi*) and that judicial autonomy was no longer a factor that should inform the views of judges.[48]

---

law, and access to justice; (2) institutional and personal/decisional independence of judges; (4) adequate judicial resources and salaries; (5) adequate training and continuing legal education; (6) security of tenure; (8) judicial freedom of expression and association.

[45] Article 126 of the Constitution of the People's Republic of China. Jerome Cohen long ago set out how 'independence' in China did not apply to the institution of the judiciary, although it could be considered to be applicable (at least in theory) to individual decision-making: Cohen (1969).

[46] Human Rights Watch (2008).

[47] Cited in Human Rights Watch (2008) at p. 24.

[48] See, for example, Li Yumei (2008); and Zhu Daqiang (2010). Shortly after becoming President of the Supreme People's Court and in a meeting with judges in Zhuhai of Guangdong Province, Wang talked about three grounds for imposing the death penalty: 1. law; 2. the overall situation of social order; 3. the feelings of the society and the masses. See 'Wang Shengjun, President of the Supreme People's Court: Mass' Feeling Should Be One of the Bases for Sentencing

Against this background, judges are clear as to their allegiance. As they see it, they are simply one component of the criminal justice machine that has been established for the purpose of processing criminal cases – crimes sometimes seen to be a direct challenge to the authority of the governing party – through to conviction and punishment. Whilst they recognize that defence lawyers are a presence in the courtroom, they do not, for the most part, accord them any influence in the proceedings and often see them as simply allied to their clients and accordingly subject to disdain as they made clear during interview:

> *J-IJ-S4-02:* We have a better relationship with the prosecutor and police than with the defence lawyer. We won't overturn their conclusions unless there is sufficient evidence; generally speaking, we don't trust lawyers and so we won't believe their words unless there is sufficient evidence. [Police and prosecutors] often come to our office or talk by phone to talk about the situation, to review evidence and so on. After all, it's not common that the defendant is found not guilty in law. You know, judges and prosecutors and police are all paid by the government. We do our job for the benefit of our country, so our relationship is better. But lawyers are different. They get money from clients; they do jobs for clients; so they will stand on the side of clients. We will doubt their words.

> *J-IJ-S4-07:* It is hard to change the mentality of presumption of guilt of judges. All cases are investigated by the investigative organ and examined and prosecuted by the people's procuratorate. And both of these are state organs. Judges naturally presume the defendant is guilty.

Comments by many of the judges we interviewed showed that they have a much closer and much better relationship with prosecutors than with the PSB: while 30 interviewees described their relationship with the prosecutors as 'very good' or 'good',[49] a further 41 interviewees said their relationship with prosecutors was 'acceptable', 'average', 'a normal working relationship' or they simply treated the prosecutors according to law.[50] While judges were aware that both the PSB and prosecutors often lacked professionalism, they nonetheless saw themselves as part of an overall system:

> *J-IJ-S4-08:* I have a better relationship with prosecutors. We all work in state organs, get salaries from government and serve the state. We cooperate with each other in work. But they are

---

the Death Penalty', 11 April 2008, available at http://news.xinhuanet.com/politics/2008-04/11/content_7956341.htm. According to him, when making the judgment, judges are instructed to pay equal attention to the social and legal effects.

[49] The following is a list of judges who told us that they had a 'very good' or 'good' relationship with the prosecutors: D-IJ-K-05, L-IJ-X-05, E-IJ-L-02, E-IJ-L-03, E-IJ-L-06, M-IJ-Y-03, C-IJ-B3-01, K-IJ-W-03, D-IJ-K-02, A-IJ-B1-06, A-IJ-B1-10, L-IJ-X-01, L-IJ-X-03, L-IJ-X-04, L-IJ-X-10, L-IJ-X-11, E-IJ-L-01, F-IJ-N-03, F-IJ-N-04, J-IJ-S4-01, J-IJ-S4-02, J-IJ-S4-03, J-IJ-S4-04, J-IJ-S4-05, J-IJ-S4-06, J-IJ-S4-07, J-IJ-S4-08, G-IJ-S1-03 and D-IJ-K-06.

[50] The following is a list of judges who said their relationship with the prosecutors was 'acceptable', 'average', 'a normal working relationship', or they just treated the prosecutors according to law: M-IJ-Y-01, M-IJ-Y-02, M-IJ-Y-04, K-IJ-W-01, K-IJ-W-02, K-IJ-W-04, D-IJ-K-01, D-IJ-K-03, D-IJ-K-04, L-IJ-X-02, L-IJ-X-03, L-IJ-X-06, L-IJ-X-07, L-IJ-X-08, L-IJ-X-09, E-IJ-L-04, E-IJ-L-05, E-IJ-L-07, C-IJ-B3-03, C-IJ-B3-04, C-IJ-B3-05, C-IJ-B3-07, B-IJ-B2-01, B-IJ-B2-02, B-IJ-B2-05, B-IJ-B2-06, B-IJ-B2-07, B-IJ-B2-08, B-IJ-B2-09, B-IJ-B2-10, B-IJ-B2-11, B-IJ-B2-12, B-IJ-B2-13, A-IJ-B1-04, A-IJ-B1-05, A-IJ-B1-07, A-IJ-B1-09, F-IJ-N-07, H-IJ-S2-01, I-IJ-S3-01 and I-IJ-S3-02.

sometimes lazy and think their work is finished after initiating the prosecution, so they are not enthusiastic when asked to conduct supplementary investigation.

K-IJ-W-01: My relationships with prosecutors and the police are good. We try to co-operate with each other. . . . We really want them to perform their duties well. But I think they should improve their investigation skills and appreciation of evidence.

Judges also stated that there was frequent co-operation between judges and prosecutors. Many judges commented that they often exchange opinions on cases and the relevant sentence with the prosecutors before trial;[51] and when a case is unclear, the judge normally will ask the prosecutor to provide supplementary materials to avoid having to dismiss the prosecution or refer it back for supplementary investigation. Some judges further disclosed that, given that both judges and prosecutors were state functionaries, judges tended to be biased in favour of prosecutors in practice:

L-IJ-X-10: We keep a close relationship with prosecutors because nobody will blame you if you are on behalf of the state.

M-IJ-Y-03: My relationships with prosecutors are good. We support each other in work.

H-IJ-S2-04: Judges are less cautious towards prosecutors. When they have doubts, they will directly talk with the prosecutor, go to ask them, but they will not do so to the [defence] lawyers.

It would be an understatement to say that a direct consequence of this is that judges in China exhibit clear bias towards the prosecution. In fact, there is no real distinction that can meaningfully be drawn between the judge and the prosecutor: they are different parts of the same entity. As a result, judges assist the prosecutor in various ways as, for example, by privately inviting the prosecutor to withdraw a misconceived case before it gets to court thereby saving the prosecutor from the ignominy of a 'failed' case:

D-IJ-K-05: I have a very good relationship with the prosecutors. For the sake of their interests and to avoid making them embarrassed, if a defendant is quite likely to be found innocent, we will suggest that they withdraw the case. But strictly speaking, we should not do so.

F-IJ-N-04: Our relationships with prosecutors are better [than with the police]. They are afraid of us finding defendants innocent, so we often communicate with each other on cases.

F-IJ-N-02: I have more contact with prosecutors [than with police]. We often communicate our opinions about cases, mainly because they are afraid that I will find the defendants innocent.

Judges also admitted that they would assist the prosecutor at trial by supplementing the presentation of the prosecution where the prosecutor has fallen down on some aspect or by curtailing the defender's attempts to damage the prosecution case.

---

[51] As revealed in the following comment, one judge (D-IJ-K-06) admitted that they did communicate with prosecutors before trial even though they knew that this was in violation of law: 'When the prosecutor has a problem related to a case before initiation of a prosecution, he may also discuss it with us. As we know, this is unlawful, but it is just private discussion.'

B-IJ-B2-04: As a judge, my main responsibility is to control the pace of adjudication, use the law to convict the defendant, let the evidence speak for itself, *remedy the mistakes of the prosecutors* and criticize wrong viewpoints of defenders (emphasis supplied).

L-IJ-X-06: Our relationship with the prosecutor is all right. To tell you the truth, we show our inclination to them because they are representing the state. It is not good to make them feel embarrassed in court. We seldom deal with the police, but we co-operate well with each other. Our relationship with the lawyer is also alright because he will not offend the judge.

L-IJ-X-07: We are biased towards the prosecutor so we seldom stop them talking. But we stop lawyers' speeches more often. The defenders' speech is too long and they cannot focus on the key points in their defence. And in this situation, I will not allow the lawyer to speak.

Some judges recognized that their alliance with the police and prosecutors comes at a price which may involve overlooking illegal practices (such as torture)[52] on the part of the police as well as overlooking deficiencies in evidence:

A-IJ-B1-01: The various mechanisms of the system render it impossible to implement the presumption of innocence in practice. The judge's power of adjudication is not independent and sometimes it is obvious that the means used by the police and the procuratorate during investigation and collecting evidence are illegal and affect the evidence, thus embarrassing the judges during the trial.

In the larger picture, judges operate as state agents in preserving social stability which is seen to be threatened by the 'serious' crime with which they have to deal. In this context, procedural irregularity, evidentiary weaknesses or unlawful behaviour (including torture) must be subordinated to the court's mission in preserving public order and social stability, a function that has been re-emphasized in recent years.[53]

Whatever their relationship with other institutional actors, as they made clear to us, judges importantly work within a wider 'judicial-political' complex – under the supervision of superiors and of the adjudicative committee and political-legal committee – and that internal set of institutions, its rules and precepts, defines their role in the criminal justice process. The guarantee of judicial independence by many international instruments[54] has little meaning, *stricto sensu,* for judges in China where party influence is

---

[52] See also M-IJ-Y-01 (in Chapter 12) in which the judge said that he had to accept statements from the prosecution saying that the defendant had not been tortured 'to protect the authority of the procuratorate. . . .'

[53] See, for example, 'Courts Told to Create Warning System to Help Prevent Protests', *South China Morning Post,* 10 June 2009; 'Courts to Help Government Reduce Protests', *China Daily,* 9 June 2009.

[54] Judicial independence is at the heart of many well-known treaties, for example the Universal Declaration of Human Rights, Article 10 ('Everyone is entitled in full equality to a fair and public hearing by an independent and impartial tribunal, in the determination of his rights and obligations and of any criminal charge against him'); the International Covenant on Civil and Political Rights, Article 14(1) ('All persons shall be equal before the courts and tribunals. In the determination of any criminal charge against him, or of his rights and obligations in a suit at law, everyone shall be entitled to a fair and public hearing by a competent, independent and impartial tribunal established by law. . . .'); and the Beijing Statement of Principles on the Independence of the Judiciary in the LAWASIA Region (Article 2 of which provides, *inter alia,* that 'everyone should be entitled to a

regarded as legitimate not merely as a generality but also in regard, as commentators agree, to at least some important individual cases.[55] Stephanie Balme (2010) found in her study of rural courts in Shaanxi Province, that while the reason for the continuation of the adjudicative committee system might have been limited to providing authoritative guidance on problems that fundamentally and systemically impacted upon trial work, in reality 'at the local level, the system keeps young and professional judges in a situation of childish servitude'.

This does not mean that there has to be direct interference in every case by Party officials but it does mean at least that in cases regarded as politically sensitive or whenever the interests of the Party-state are seen to be at risk, the rule of law may be suspended and decisions may be dictated on a political basis.[56] This account of 'criminal procedure with Chinese characteristics' – under the Party's leadership – is further emphasized by a procurator:

> The Chinese Communist Party is the only ruling party with legal status; the operation of the state is under the leadership of the Party, any state organs must receive the Party's leadership, and the judicial organ is not an exception. Under such a leadership regime, legislative and judicial activities must not only abide by law but also carry out the criminal policies of the Party. Therefore, in criminal pre-trial procedure and its construction, it must go deep to grasp the Party's policies so as to make sure that the system will meet the requirement of the Party; or even formulation of such a system, it will not possess an everlasting life. For example, the Party's criminal policy of 'leniency for confession and resistance for severity in punishment', if reflected in the criminal pre-trial procedure, requires the accused to confess the crime truthfully; those who express their repentance will be treated in a favourable manner when deciding on compulsory measures or non-prosecution; while by contrast, those who refuse to admit the crime will be treated in a strict manner when deciding on compulsory measures or non-prosecution. Meanwhile, the judicial organ in our country is set as the 'dictatorship organ' of the state, which is the tool for the Party to rule and manage the country to realize social stability. This in turn has decided that, in treating the crime, the police, procuratorates and courts are obliged to run investigations into the crime, the only difference is that their work focus is not same.... [When we discuss criminal procedure], if we don't connect with this reality but just partially compare it with the common practice in the western countries, we will exaggerate the problems in pre-trial procedure in our country....[57]

---

fair and public hearing by a competent, independent and impartial tribunal established by law. An independent judiciary is indispensable to the implementation of this right'; and under Article 3, the 'judiciary shall decide matters before it in accordance with its impartial assessment of the facts and its understanding of the law without improper influences, direct or indirect, from any source'.

[55] See, for a defence of this, Zhu Suli (2010): '[S]ometimes CCP interference represents and promotes a local population's particular understanding of what justice and fairness demand in the handling of a particular case.... From a western constitutional perspective, such interference seems to be improper. But from a political perspective, it is hard to see why legal control over a case is always and necessarily more morally just or reasonable than political control. Why should a technocratic judicial determination always be superior to a political one?' (p. 57). On this view, the CCPC is a parallel and alternative source of constitutionalism.

[56] Some commentators see intervention in some cases in terms of the competence of the bodies originally charged with the decision-making responsibility: Peerenboom (2010a) at p. 80: 'The party's main interest in the outcome of most cases, whether commercial, criminal, or administrative, is that the result be perceived as fair by the parties and the people' (*ibid.*, at p. 80). The empirical basis for this statement is not disclosed.

[57] See for example, Chong Songzhi (2009) at pp. 236–240.

Further, as judges made clear in our study, criminal cases *par excellence* are seen to pose a threat to social stability such that convictions are required in cases that go to trial. While it has been said that there is 'limited systemic interference from party organs in routine criminal cases'[58] our respondents claim that interference occurs not only of 'sensitive cases' but also, importantly, in regard to everyday cases which were the staple of the current research.[59]

The picture that emerges in our study is of individual judges operating within a process which reposes authority and control in superiors and higher bodies and to that extent judges are subject to a dominant hierarchical legal procedure. This subordination is *general* in character in criminal trials and not, as sometimes portrayed, confined to 'politically-sensitive' cases.[60] In this setting, it is not plausible to speak of 'judicial independence': instead, judges must act with Party-defined political correctness.[61] In the political jargon of 'harmony rights' (*hexie quan*), 'harmonious adjudication' and 'The Three Supremes', judges are, as Eva Pils has pointed out,[62] 'being reintegrated into an administration of the party-state based on authoritarian centralism rather than on a separation of functions'. This is also reflected in judges' writings when talking about the making and enforcing of judgments. Judges emphasize their responsibility and obligation in helping restore harmonious relationship between the plaintiff and the defendant in the trial and in the effect of law enforcement;[63] when emphasizing the legal effect of the judgment, judges are to pay more attention to social elements and the national situation;[64] and judges should increase the social effect when handling cases.[65]

Judges are particularly susceptible to external domination because they have low self-esteem and see themselves as mere small cogs in a big machine. Constant themes which emerged spontaneously were oppressive case-loads,[66] disrespect and low remu-

---

[58] Fu and Peerenboom (2010) at p. 123.
[59] For a contrary view, see Peerenboom (2010b): 'Notwithstanding problems in politically sensitive and socioeconomic cases or institutional weaknesses particularly in lower level courts, there has been a significant increase in decisional independence of the courts overall as measured by various indicators. It is incorrect to conclude (or to assume) that the Chinese judiciary is unable to decide any case independently, especially commercial cases and many other routine civil, administrative, or criminal cases' (at p. 86). The empirical basis for the quantitative aspect of these assertions is not stated.
[60] For a different perspective, see Fu and Peerenboom (2010) who assert that party influence in political and politically sensitive cases is primarily through policy guidance rather than intervention in particular cases: *ibid.*, at p. 122.
[61] As Eva Pils notes, in quoting the exhortation of Luo Gan, a Politburo member, this means that 'they must in their politics, their thoughts and their actions preserve identity with the Party': Eva Pils (2009b).
[62] Eva Pils (2009b) at p. 150.
[63] Feng Hua (2010) at pp. 493–494.
[64] Kang Baoqi (2010) at p. 117.
[65] Zhang Yan (2010).
[66] See further, Mark O'Neill (2010b) reporting on the suicide of Judge Liu Liming in Xiangtan City, Hunan Province who left behind a note saying: 'The pressure of work is too great. I am exhausted. Death is better than this. Goodbye.' O'Neill reports on a survey of 113 judges in a county court in Beijing in 2007 which found that 94 felt they had a heavy caseload and too much work; 90 per cent said that society had a prejudice against the legal system; nearly 20 per cent said they wanted to change career; and nearly 10 per cent said they wanted to see a psychiatrist.

neration.[67] Low remuneration (and sometimes none where the local government in rural areas ran out of money)[68] defined for them their status and left the system vulnerable to corruption.[69] Their lived experiences told them clearly that they were low in the hierarchy of power, as the following quotations show:

> *J-IJ-S4-08:* Our workload is very heavy, holding court sessions, discussing cases in the collegial panel, reading files, studying cases, writing reports on the completion of trial, writing judgments and sometimes attending meetings. Normally, many of them are administrative meetings . . . The pressure is very great. As you know some evidence is judged according to common sense and experience, and this perhaps may not be logical. But judges are not supernatural beings, their knowledge is limited. It is right to adopt the evidence at such time and in such conditions, but after several months, the surrounding conditions may have changed, and the laws may have been revised, then your judgment at that moment would then seem to be wrong. What should we do? The only thing I can do is to write the report on completion of the trial and make the judgment as detailed as possible to explain clearly the reasons why I reached such a judgment. The reasons can't be explained clearly after a long time if the work is dealt with carelessly.

> *E-IJ-L-01:* Poor treatment! I feel that my dignity is not fully respected by the parties concerned, who sometimes even insult me or call me names. But I cannot avoid such embarrassment. During one period in the past, the reform carried out in our court caused upset to the judges, since no one knew which department he would be sent to next. As a result, the work efficiency was quite low. The appropriate treatment and proper entitlements were not fulfilled, which upset the judges' work efficiency. In addition, I feel great mental pressure in my work, because you are not allowed to leave any defects when you deal with cases: for example, the system of punishing judges for 'wrongful' cases. Furthermore, we also have to pay attention to the effect of the long-term effect of the case, which takes time.

Judges in China operate within an administrative hierarchy which conditions much of their work. Local judges in Basic Courts are 'elected, appointed and removed by local people's congresses, they are paid by local governments, and a large majority of them are members of the ruling party'.[70] As we have noted, the court formally functions through a collegial panel or bench of judges (*heyiting*).[71]

---

[67] Judicial salaries are known to be low in rural areas and experienced judges may be 'raided' by courts in more developed coastal areas. See, for example, Congressional-Executive Commission on China (2005). The Report discloses that rural basic level court judges in Shaanxi Province earn between 500 and 800 yuan per month whereas urban judges in Xi'an or Guangdong earn several thousand yuan per month. Low remuneration is certainly a contributory factor to problems of corruption. Balme (2010) states: 'In the case of Chinese local tribunals, inadequate salaries and the lack of transparency in the management of funds have led to institutionalised corruption' (at p. 175).

[68] See, Peerenboom (2002) who notes, at p. 294, the issue of low remuneration, the failure to pay salaries occasionally and some judges having their salaries docked 'if they perform poorly'.

[69] Balme (2010) reports that in Shaanxi and Gansu in late 2008, Basic Court judges' salaries ranged from RMB 900 to RMB 1500 monthly including housing compensation and a subsidy for children, which averaged RMB 90 per month but could be as high as RMB 150 per month. She found that: 'Yet for both provinces, a few tribunals could not even provide full salaries to judges for several months.' (*ibid.* at p. 174).

[70] Balme (2010) at p. 162.

[71] By virtue of Article 147, 1996 CPL, first instance trials may be conducted by a collegial panel comprising 'three judges or of judges and people's assessors totalling three'.

While the collegial panel comprises three judges, in practice responsibility for a case falls on the case-responsible judge (*chengban faguan*): the other two judges (or assessors) serve largely symbolic functions although their presence in the courtroom no doubt helps to enhance the legitimacy of the proceedings.[72] With respect to 'difficult, complex or major' cases on which the collegial panel considers it difficult to make a decision, the collegial panel must refer the case to the president of the court for him to decide whether to submit the case to the adjudicative committee for discussion and decision.[73] It is little surprise, therefore, that judges often drew attention to this power of referral:

B-IJ-B2-06: The difficult and complicated cases I will submit to the adjudicative committee.

B-IJ-B2-09: When encountering new types of case, given the lack of clear legal provisions, there will be difficulties in adjudication. The solution is to check with the books and, for difficult and complicated cases I will submit these to the adjudicative committee.

The referral of cases symbolized a very significant matter of concern for judges underlining, as they see it, their lack of independence and the widespread interference in their decisions by other parties.[74]

According to judges, the influences brought to bear upon their decisions by their administrative superiors or by the adjudicative committee and/or political-legal committee were much wider in scope than the referral of complex cases implies. In this regard, within each administrative section, on any case, the head of division or president of the court might make the decision (or authorize or direct it), and beyond this further 'administrative' influence was commonly brought to bear on decisions.[75] What is especially noteworthy is that the judges spontaneously drew our attention to this issue[76]

---

[72] This may be undercut in practice, as our researchers frequently noted, by the actions of the ancillary judges in reading unrelated materials, talking on mobile telephones or drifting off to sleep in the course of a trial.

[73] Article 149, 1996 CPL. The judicial or adjudicative committee includes the president of the court and high-ranking Party officials. According to Chinese scholars, the adjudicative committee is more like an administrative organization rather than a trial organization as the members often include presidents and section chiefs of the court, who may not have sufficient professional knowledge and mostly do not hear the case in dispute, given that the case is complicated or important. See He Qinhua (2009) at p. 319; Li Liangxiong (2010). For the discussion of the adjudicative committee, see also Pang (2009), at p. 14; Su (2009); Zhang and Hao (2005) at pp. 126–128; Zhao and Liu (2002); Tan Shigui (2009) at p. 6; Peng (2009) at p. 124.

[74] We are conscious that 'judicial independence' is not a term of art conceptualizing an agreed definition and set of criteria, as discussed, for example, by Peerenboom (2010b).

[75] Judges rarely directly identified the sources of influence but they made clear that the interference was both administrative and political. Informally we were told that there was repeated interference by local party officials. This, of course, is merely one symptom of a wider issue in China. As Pitman Potter notes, the political-legal committee (*zhengfawei*) 'continues to dominate the process of legal reform, although its senior leadership contains few if any trained lawyers': Potter (1999) at p. 674. See also Zuo, Tang and Wu (2001) at pp. 81–83; Chen, Cheng and Yang (2006) at p. 10; Zhang and Hao (2005) at pp. 124–126; Pang Xiaoju (2009) at p. 14; Zhao and Liu (2002) at pp. 272–273; Tan Shigui (2009) at p. 6.

[76] Interestingly, although the procuratorate has a supervisory power over the courts, judges made no complaint over interference by prosecutors: the concerns focused upon administrative officials and 'external' (i.e., political) influences.

in answering the question 'what were the main problems in the trial process?' Judges were not directed to this in any way during the interviews because we were conscious of the highly sensitive nature of the issue in China and for the respondents themselves. Judges were fully aware that they operate within a hierarchical system which, as we have noted, reposes authority and responsibility in the court rather than in individual judges but their concerns went beyond their embeddedness within a bureaucracy. Oftentimes, of course, judges were reluctant to elaborate their precise concerns[77] preferring to talk indirectly or euphemistically about 'administrative intervention'[78] or 'treatment of judges', but they left us in no doubt that this remained a significant feature of their day to day judicial experience.[79] What was surprising was the breadth and depth of the concerns, as the following examples illustrate:[80]

C-IJ-B3-03: Administrative intervention.

A-IJ-B1-02: Independence in adjudication has not been genuinely implemented. We are strongly influenced by various aspects.

B-IJ-B2-07: The judiciary is not independent. There is too much interference from various quarters.[81]

L-IJ-X-10: In China, the system is one in which the presiding judge is responsible for the case. In addition, we have to consider if the masses can accept the verdict.

L-IJ-X-05: At the outset, I was pleased with the job. I felt that it was an honour to punish guilty people. But there are too many kinds of case and many problems relating to personal relationships and interference. Some are related to the relationship between the upper and lower levels and there are also man-made influences. I am unhappy with this problem and experience a great deal of pressure, especially if the defendant is innocent. I cannot handle the case completely by law.

E-IJ-L-05: The position of the judges in charge of cases is too subordinate and there is no protective mechanism to guarantee your independence in dealing with cases. You have to report the case to the presiding judge, section leaders and presidents one by one. I think the situation is similar in the Procuratorate.

---

[77] See also Liu and Halliday (2008) who report that few of their respondents were willing to talk frankly about the political-legal committee. Whilst one part-time defence lawyer made some remarks about the committee, most of their defence lawyer respondents were very cautious when directly asked about the committee. As we have noted, we did not ask direct questions about the committee yet judges volunteered some information.

[78] Judges used this term in general to denote interference by non-judicial actors. This form of interference, by party administrative personnel in the courts, by local government officials and the like is well known to be a feature of the Chinese system.

[79] It should be re-emphasized that many judges spoke out in favour of what Peerenboom (2002) describes as 'internal independence', namely the ability 'to decide cases without regard to administrative hierarchies within the court and in particular without interference from senior judges'. This concept is specifically rejected in China.

[80] We were not able to identify systematically the sources of the concerns. For further information on this, see Peerenboom (2002) reporting on a survey in 1993 at p. 307.

[81] This judge had over 20 years' experience as a judge.

E-IJ-L-06: The judge is not the final decision-maker. There is too much administrative interference inside and outside the court, which is an old problem. It has existed for many years, but no one has been able to improve the situation.

E-IJ-L-07: The defendant in an alleged crime but lacking sufficient evidence is deemed innocent and requires the judge to make an objective and fair judgment. But, at present, if you declare the defendant innocent, both your leader and the authority demand that you consider the social and legal effects instead of only the legal impact. But if there is a conflict between the two, what can you do? . . . There is a conflict between the social and legal effect when we deal with cases. As you know, the environment for enforcing the law is not good. I have to face external interference from the leaders outside the court. Sometimes, the leader directs me to punish one person (the defendant) in order to lower the emotions of the victims who seek help from the higher authority. However, the evidence was not sufficient, so it is difficult for me to deal with such cases.

J-IJ-S4-04: The time limit is too short and the procedures are too many, especially when the adjudicative committee is involved: they have no first-hand information and have not been engaged in the trial. I think the decision is taken in an administrative way. I think it is inappropriate. . . . I think it is necessary to reform the adjudicative committee. I personally advocate a system in which the trial judge is responsible for the case.

D-IJ-K-05: The first problem is that when a judge handles a case, he is somewhat restricted or interfered with, because he needs to consider the interests of the police and the procuratorate. Second, he must consider the court's interest, since both staffing and finance are dependent on the government. Consequently, there are many kinds of external interference and restrictions. A case law system would be more persuasive for the parties concerned, but there is no case law in China.

A-IJ-B1-06: Judicial independence is a problem. . . . The National People's Congress issued a provision, empowering it to supervise individual cases. The National People's Congress is the highest organ of state power but it is also a legislative institute: it is not very appropriate if it also has the power of adjudication at the same time. Moreover, although the National People's Congress cannot intervene in the criminal justice process from the perspective of procedures, their so-called 'supervision over individual cases'[82] actually seriously affects the courts.

A-IJ-B1-07: Now independence in adjudication is required. Adjudications should not be subject to intervention by the administrative institutes. But judges are subjected to control by the administrative units; the judges' status is also subjected to control by their administrative standing, so how can they prevent the intervention of the administrative organs?

A-IJ-B1-08: Judges cannot make decisions. The decision of the collegial panel cannot be a real decision. We are subjected to various controls such as being interfered with by the administrative organs internally and the upper levels of the courts externally, all of which is shown by the system of reporting cases by judges.

---

[82] For discussion of the issue of 'individual case supervision' (*ge an jiandu*), see, Randall Peerenboom (2008). Peerenboom concludes that: 'Supervision in some form is arguably necessary given problems with judicial competence, corruption, local protectionism and the legitimacy issues arising from the expectations of citizens that the legal system will deliver substantive justice, no matter what the cost. Once these systemic issues are addressed, supervision may be eliminated.' (*ibid.* at p. 36).

E-IJ-L-05: As a state trial organ, the court cannot break away from the leadership of the local administration and the Party. It should set up a vertical leadership system and guarantee judicial independence and the budget to deal with cases independently in order to avoid such interference. . . . I feel the judge's great responsibility and the honour of this job. But, the environment for dealing with cases is poor, for example, the internal mode of administrative leadership and external interference from the Party and the government.

The successful processing of cases may bring material rewards to a judge,[83] but judges are more conscious of the fact that, in addition to the natural influence their direct superiors exercised over them, the system of judicial subordination and dependence is supported and reinforced by sanctions[84] or the fear of sanctions:[85]

J-IJ-S4-08: Our cases are checked periodically. Failed (false) cases will be investigated for responsibility; so I am very careful in handling every case.

F-IJ-N-06: Many prosecutors and judges still have the old mentality of a presumption of guilt and 'We would rather wrongfully convict an innocent person rather than wrongfully let a person escape justice.' The Public Security Bureau and the People's Procuratorate have the same task in making criminals responsible for their crimes and judges appear to assist in determining the sentence. It is not easy for a judge to find someone innocent. Every organ is responsible for a failed case.

It also means that, whatever view judges might entertain as to the persuasiveness of the evidence, ultimately they are subordinate to the views of their superiors (and other influential external influence) and this leads inevitably, in criminal trials, to one outcome – *conviction*, as the judge in E-IJ-L-03 put it:

E-IJ-L-03: According to the old criminal procedure law, the court might suggest that the procuratorate withdraw the case or conduct supplementary investigation if we thought the facts or the evidence was not clear after the [pre-trial] review. But now, in the light of the new Criminal Procedure Law, the court must make a judgment after the procuratorate has transferred the

---

[83] See Fu Hualing (2003) whose respondent judges told him that 'successful prosecution of a major criminal case often is rewarded politically and materially with the promotion of prosecutor and judge' (*ibid.* at p. 196).

[84] See Peerenboom (2002). Peerenboom describes (at p. 294) various sanctions which may be imposed on judges including dismissal; judges in China do not enjoy tenure of office. See also, Zhu Suli (2010) who, having noted that American judges, with life-time tenure and high salaries, may oppose both government and political party pressures when so inclined, states: 'In China . . . judges enjoy no such protection and are further subject to political party influence through the party's disciplinary oversight of the judiciary and individual judges' (*ibid.*, at p. 60). Zhu Suli sets out a case for these arrangements and, indeed, for their continuation as China develops and acknowledges that, apart from the influence of the Party, and other state organs, 'individual parties, the media, civil society, and others also exert direct or indirect influence on the court' (*ibid.*, at p. 67).

[85] Peerenboom (2010b) states that few judges are in fact prosecuted or subject to administrative sanctions pointing to data from the Supreme People's Court Work Reports relating to 2001 and 2002 which state that in 2001, 995 judges violated judicial personnel laws and rules with 85 being serious enough to lead to criminal prosecutions, the corresponding figure for 2002 being 45 prosecutions. These data, however, cannot in and of themselves give insight into how judges discharge their responsibilities under the *threat* of sanction or accordingly what degree of independence they see themselves as having within such a system.

case, no matter what the state of the evidence or facts is. Xiao Yang, President of the Supreme People's Court, said that the court should make a judgment of guilt or innocence after the trial. But in practice, it is very difficult for the court to declare the defendant's innocence. The leaders of the Court do not have the same opinion as the judges, which may also involve such elements as the leaders' personal qualities, consideration of the upper-level leader's opinion or instruction and the fear that the parties concerned might make trouble.

This judge (E-IJ-L-03), like some others, looked to a different future:

> I hope we can in future deal with cases by law and enforce the standard of evidence strictly. If the evidence is not sufficient and the facts are not clear, the defendant should be declared innocent. We should insist on this point, whether from the viewpoint of protecting human rights or the rights and interests of the parties concerned.

In a less robust way, one judge in Site I looked to a different future whilst acknowledging the present reality:

> *I-IJ-S3-02:* There is clear regulation of the relationships among public security organs, procuratorate and courts. When a criminal lawsuit proceeds, the three units are responsible for individual jobs co-operatively and restrictively to insure the correct and efficient implementation of laws. I can say that we have good co-operation. But I think the court should be more independent and neutral. I also have good relationships with defending lawyers. I will carefully consider their defence opinions.

One result of the system of dependence, however, is that the outcome is predictable and while the trial itself is a shell so far as guilt/innocence is concerned, the judgment will usually be made after the conclusion of the trial[86] and by parties other than the case-responsible judge as judges made clear:[87]

> *J-IJ-S4-02:* Holding a trial is just a procedure. It is especially simple in some cases where there is only one defendant, clear facts and sufficient evidence. But if the case has several defendants, this procedure is necessary to learn the truth of the case. I think the most important thing ought to be to show evidence. This part does not receive enough attention because judges and prosecutors are not willing to spend much time on this. It is the same with the lawyers appointed by the court. So our main work needs to be done after the trial.

> *J-IJ-S4-01:* The information provided through the court hearing is limited. A great amount of work needs to be done after the court hearing, including carefully reading files, analysing the facts and evidence, writing the report on the completion of the trial, taking part in the collegial panel, and finally writing a judgment. So the court hearing is just part of the job.

---

[86] Some thought that the reform would actually increase the power of the collegial panel; but this has not proved to be the case. See, Fu Hualing (1998): 'The Amendment increases the powers of the collegial panel. Article 149 states that a collegial panel has the right and duty to render its decision after trial. If the panel is unable to make a decision on a complex and important case after a trial, it should submit the case to the Judicial [Adjudicative] Committee for consideration and decision. There are two important changes. First, the collegial panel itself, not the President of the court, is to initiate the process of referring a case to the Judicial Committee for decision; secondly, such a referral occurs only after a trial is completed.' (p. 44).

[87] Judges, prosecutors and defence lawyers acknowledged that this system gave rise to opportunities for corruption.

This is all the more troubling because, as some judges told us, the system of 'case-filing' under which insupportable or weak cases may be weeded out before going to trial is in many courts no longer operating properly. As a result of staffing shortages or internal distribution of administrative functions, some courts are not implementing this screening system and simply accept whatever cases the procuratorate sends, as these judges indicate:

> *K-IJ-W-01:* Nowadays, courts basically accept all cases sent by the procuratorates. It is against the law. But we don't have enough staff. We can't spare any time examining cases carefully. Because we don't examine the details of the case materials when filing a case, some problems occur when the case is heard, for example, the defendant's identity is not clear, his age is not clear and so on.
>
> *L-IJ-X-01:* The functions of the case-filing court have not been fully realized. As a result, the relevant workload is imposed on the trial judge.[88] The examination by the case-filing court is not detailed.[89]

Judges may accordingly be confronted with a situation in which a weak or insupportable case comes before them because of failings in the case-filing system: nonetheless they are expected or required to return a conviction.

This hierarchical process also can create in judges a mindset typical of dominant hierarchies in which those at the bottom either carry out orders or make decisions that are expected to be made in order to win favour or avoid sanction from those above:

> *K-IJ-W-01:* I think the main issue is not the quality of judges but the court system, particularly the administrative management system. Some of the administration connected with the performance indicators of judges fails to let judges display their qualities and wisdom. In order to keep their job, judges perhaps think whether the judgment would be amended by the higher court when they determine the judgment. If the judgment is amended because it is said to be erroneous, judges will thereafter do their job to retain favour with the higher court.
>
> *L-IJ-X-09:* The judge's decision is restricted by the head of the section and the adjudication committee; even by pressures from outside. The second issue concerns the judge's neutrality. The judge is not neutral because he has not been converted completely from his traditional function to the present role. The judge always has to show off his position and power so he either scolds

---

[88] A similar view was shared by a judge from Site D (D-IJ-KM-04).

[89] Given the problems related to filing cases, some judges we interviewed proposed several ways to improve such procedure. Two judges, from Site K (K-IJ-W-01) and Site J (J-IJ-S4-08), called for the strengthening of the administration of the work of filing cases. Additionally, they also said that the examination during the stage of filing cases should be conducted strictly and seriously. On the other hand, a judge from Site E (E-IJ-L-04) suggested that the examination of cases should be performed by persons with legal knowledge in the case-filing courts; once problems with evidence were discovered, they should communicate with the prosecutors concerned. Similarly, a judge from Site D (D-IJ-K-05) called for the professionalization of the personnel of the case-filing courts by appointing persons with knowledge of criminal law to these courts. A judge from Site K (K-IJ-W-04) also suggested the separation of the pre-trial adjudication and the trial judge: while the pre-trial adjudication judge should be responsible for procedure such as examining the basic situation of the defendant, notifying the defendant of his rights and providing the defendant with a list of the evidence, the trial judge should be responsible for substantive examination.

the defendant or interrupts the defender's presentation. The judge has certain emotions which demonstrate his low professional quality. . . . In China, there is no difference between a judge and a government servant. In other words, the judge is a government servant; he just performs the role of an executive officer. There is no professional sense of honour.

We only found one judge who said that he had resisted pressure from his superiors in dealing with a case.[90] Perhaps, because it was a private prosecution, the judge felt more emboldened but it still appears as an extraordinary act of resistance:

M-IJ-Y-01: If a case is still unclear, I will consult books or discuss in the collegial panel. If still not sure, I will ask the adjudicative committee for instructions. In this way they can share some of the responsibility. If I can determine the matter, I won't let external pressure interfere with me. For instance, in a case of intentional injury prosecuted privately . . . the accuser had a dispute with the defendant. The defendant beat the accuser and caused damage to his leg, not a fracture, not enough to constitute light injury. But the defendant found a doctor to say that it was a slight injury. The accuser also got the director of People's Representative Congress in the city to interfere. But I still insisted to find the defendant innocent and I said it was impossible for me to find the defendant guilty if the case was retained by me. Under pressure, the President of our court moved me to another court and let other judges deal with this case. The defendant applied for re-examination again and again. After . . . various appeals, the defendant was found innocent after five years. This judgment also proved that my initial determination was right. . . .[91] I am very responsible for my work. I cannot violate laws and my conscience. Relying on my current level and conditions, I have no problems being a judge. Even if I was not a judge, I could also find a way to live.

It is also interesting to note that, while some judges referred to the need to pay attention to the views of victims and their families (which we witnessed in our observations of trials) and to the more general sentiments of society, this was greatly subordinate to their concerns over those superior to them in the bureaucratic hierarchy. This means that judges must place greater emphasis upon their accountability to their political and administrative masters than to society in general. Pitman Potter's general discussion of this mode of operation as 'patrimonial sovereignty' as emblematic of China's official regulatory culture is entirely applicable to the criminal courts: 'Under the dynamic of patrimonial sovereignty, political leaders and administrative agencies have responsibility for society but are not responsible to it.'[92]

Because of the sensitivities involved, judges naturally did not want to go into detail as to the changes, if any, they would like to see and gave non-committal responses, as in the following example:

L-IJ-X-03: I haven't thought about it, since this is not a problem that I should consider.[93]

---

[90] The judge was 57 years old, had served 15 years in the army and had worked in the court system for 25 years, six of them in criminal court.
[91] The portion omitted is the notation of the researcher: 'I was moved by his spirit in not fearing authority and insisting on justice.'
[92] Potter (2004) at p. 477.
[93] It is revealing that the judge considered that she should not be involved in considering changes to the present system.

Most contented themselves by saying that 'the system' should be reformed or that the 'authority' of judges should be enhanced or 'the treatment' of judges improved. Where they ventured a more substantive view, judges were divided on what should be done: for some, there should be an assertion of 'independence'; for most judges, however, there could be no justification for change until judges themselves were better qualified, better remunerated and corruption was removed.[94] Supervision, for some judges, was a requirement in the face of a degraded judiciary:[95]

> *J-IJ-S4-08:* The independence of judges in adjudication should be guaranteed and too much supervision should be avoided. There is supervision by the lawmaking organs of the People's Congress, supervision by the political-legal committees of the coordinating organs of the public security organs and the procuratorates. There are also adjudicative committees in courts. Such things are reasonable to a certain degree but the adjudication rights of judges have not been fully respected. It is urgent to improve the professional qualities of judges, particularly the spirit of dedication to work. . . . I think the biggest challenge is to improve public confidence in judges. On the one hand, the judicial system should be reformed to safeguard the independence of judges in trials, to strengthen administration and to improve the treatment of judges. The current situation in which judges are treated as common civil servants and judges don't take pride in their occupation should be changed. On the other hand, judges should improve their own professional qualities to convince the public that they are impartial and that the final judgment of the court is an authoritative source to prevent them from seeking redress through other inappropriate channels.
>
> *L-IJ-X-02:* A system of whole-life training will bring more repute or status to judges. Higher remuneration will remove corruption. The judge's income is unequal to his labour.
>
> *A-IJ-B1-07:* [T]here are great differences in the status and remuneration between the Western and Chinese judges. Psychological imbalance results; this may also be the reason behind many problems of corruption. Judges can only wholeheartedly invest in the work of adjudication after they have solved their living conditions.
>
> *F-IJ-N-07:* There are lots of problems involving judges. But I think the most essential is the reform of the system regarding human resources and financing judges. I have worked for almost

---

[94] Whilst judges (and lawyers) referred to judicial corruption, we have no direct information on this issue. For an analysis of corruption, see Li Ling (2010). Li Ling studied around 350 court corruption cases between 1991 and 2008 in which judges or court officials were punished for corrupt acts. Among 179 judges bribed in the adjudication phase, at least 57 took bribes in criminal cases (*ibid.*, at p. 208); the proportion of bribery is relatively greater in criminal cases than in civil cases, although the absolute number is greater in civil cases because they are more than seven times as numerous (*ibid.*, at pp. 217–218). See also, He Huifeng (2010) giving an account of the arrest of a judge for allegedly killing a businessman and dismembering the corpse. The judge is said to have admitted inviting the victim to his home for lunch and killing him after quarrelling over a disputed legal case. It is alleged that the victim offered the judge bribes of HK$1.14 million, that the money was accepted but failed to deliver the desired result.

[95] This point was also often made by defenders, as in the following example: Defender M-IL-Y-05: 'There is more disadvantage than advantage in having the adjudicative committee but it is still necessary to have such an organ because the quality of the present judges in our country is not very high. So the adjudicative committee should deal with complicated cases, cases of innocence and cases for probation.' See also Weng (1987). The view of these judges was the closest connection they made between bureaucratic discipline and corruption. Predominantly, for judges, bureaucratic discipline meant interference with their decision-making in individual cases.

20 years but my salary still remains less than 1000 Yuan [per month]. . . . Only without financial worries and career promotion can I serve the people with all my heart.

K-IJ-W-04: Judges should be neutral and free from administrative interference. First of all, personnel and finance should be independent from local government control. Otherwise ordinary people will have no confidence in law suits. Certainly, some judges of low quality are unable to uphold rights correctly. They need supervision and control. It is essential to allow the collegial panel or even the adjudicative committee to check on them. We need to improve judicial authority and the reputation of judges step-by-step.

Whatever their misgivings and concerns regarding the quality of the judiciary and the need for supervision, judges are quite clear that, whilst they are squarely within the iron triangle, defence lawyers are not and that close association with them is dangerous. Of course, whilst drawing attention to what they saw as poor defence lawyers, some judges acknowledged that there were good lawyers whom they respected, as in the following illustration:

J-IJ-S4-01: Generally speaking we will establish good relationships with prosecutors and the police. We co-operate. After the court hearing, judges will sometimes talk with the prosecutor, but we will deal with the case independently, ignoring the prosecutor's urgings. There are some cases of protest against a judgment of first instance, especially where the judgment is not guilty. Nearly every prosecutor will protest it. We are seldom in contact with the police. In order to arrest escaping suspects, sometimes they will come here to open the file of whom it may concern. We will also occasionally ask the police to collect supplementary evidence. As for the defence lawyers, I will listen to their reasonable views. Some outstanding lawyers will gain my respect. But some lawyers are not so responsible for their work, especially some appointed by the court. They come here just to finish a job. And we sometimes find other lawyers with poor professionalism and a bad attitude towards the defendant.

So far as relationships were concerned, however, corruption or concern to avoid accusation of corruption was a constant theme with judges[96] as it was with prosecutors. Corruption within the courts has been described as 'rampant'[97] and in our interviews, judge after judge spontaneously told us that they tried to avoid any social contact with defence lawyers for fear that this would give rise to suspicions of corruption and bias:

J-IJ-S4-05: I have a better relationship with prosecutors and police. We trust and co-operate with each other. As for lawyers, I insist upon one principle: never take part in a dinner organized by lawyers. Even if he has no case in front of me, I will be passive if he comes back to ask me for help

---

[96] See, Fu Hualing (2003): 'The SPC has long openly acknowledged corruption in the judiciary and the problem of adjudicating cases by means of personal relations (*guanxi' an*), favours (*renqing' an*), and bribes (*jinqian an*). Over the years, the nature of corruption in the courts has become more sophisticated' *ibid.* at p. 211. See further, Mark O'Neill (2010c). O'Neill gives a graphic account of various state officials, including a former judge from Chongqing, who are said to have taken their own lives while being investigated for corruption.

[97] See, Peerenboom (2002) at p. 295. While reliable statistics are not available, Peerenboom was of the view that 'even official accounts acknowledge that the corruption is becoming more serious and widespread' (*ibid.*, at p. 295). He also draws attention to official attempts to address corruption which include imposing personal liability on judges for wrongly decided cases (*ibid.*, at p. 297 *et seq.*). We have no data on this issue.

on a future occasion. Just now you've heard my telephone conversation with a lawyer. He asked me to have dinner with him tonight over and over again, but I found many reasons to refuse.[98]

J-IJ-S4-04: If we have a close relationship with [lawyers] we will be suspected of being biased. In order to preserve our impartiality, we should try to avoid contact with lawyers.

J-IJ-S4-06: To ensure impartiality in trying cases, I will refuse lawyers' invitations to dinner. Everything is dealt with in the office.

L-IJ-X-09: Our relationship with defence lawyers is alright. I don't like to establish a close relationship with them, because excessive connection will impair the image and status of a judge.

K-IJ-W-03: Judges should have authority. Judges are not like other civil servants: they should have better status and authority. If judges often go to places of entertainment, judgments, even impartial judgments, will arouse other people's suspicion.

L-IJ-X-01: As for the relationship with lawyers, I have a better relationship with friends or classmates who are lawyers and I will not introduce them to defend a case in the Intermediate Court because this would make others challenge my impartiality.

L-IJ-X-10: The law forbids us to be too close to the lawyers so as to prevent there being something we cannot explain.[99]

K-IJ-W-01: Compared with such big cities as Shanghai and Hangzhou, the lawyers here seldom invite judges for dinner. Perhaps defendants hope to get a lighter punishment through relationships but not lawyers. Anyway, I think defence lawyers play a limited role in the trial. On the one hand, according to the judicial system in our country, investigators should collect incriminating evidence and also exonerating evidence for criminal suspects during the investigation stage; prosecutors should perform objective obligations in the examination and prosecution; for judges, we should examine facts and make impartial judgments. We never go against defendants because they don't have defence lawyers or on the basis of how long defence lawyers speak. Certainly some lawyers have played an important role in some cases. On the other hand, outstanding law experts in our area tend to be judges and prosecutors, but not lawyers.

J-IJ-S4-07: The administration of our court is very strict. The balance will be upset if I have dinners with lawyers or victims. At the same time we cherish our jobs. It is unnecessary to spoil the ship for a halfpennyworth of tar.

J-IJ-S4-08: The relationship between judges and lawyers is very sensitive. To ensure the impartiality of the trial, lawyers can go to my office if they have any questions but I will not accept any invitation or gifts from lawyers, including some lawyers who were my former classmates. . . . As a judge, I also have some classmates who are lawyers and I have two principles in social relationships: we maintain a pure relationship as friends without the exchange of money and they cannot handle cases in my court. Otherwise we won't be close friends. My insistence on these two principles is to protect myself and my family and the impartiality of law enforcement.

It is noteworthy that working hand in glove with the procuratorate is either not seen to affect judicial independence, or if it is, it is a price deemed to be worth paying to uphold

---

[98] The presence of the researcher may have led to the judge's refusal.
[99] It appears that what this judge meant was that the law prohibits judges from having a close relationship with defence lawyers so as to prevent judges' impartial image and judgment from being undermined.

social order. By contrast, having any kind of contact with defence lawyers is viewed as potentially egregious misconduct, sufficient to call into question the neutrality and allegiance of the judge. This inconsistency makes sense perhaps in a system in which all defendants are deemed guilty well in advance of the trial process, and accordingly anyone associated with defendants, such as those who defend them, must be treated in the same way as defendants themselves.

DEFENCE LAWYERS

> The iron triangle that has existed for 50 years among the police, procuracy and judges has proved immensely difficult to fracture and to rebalance. A culture of law-enforcement collusion that is resistant to legal representation proves highly resistant to modification.[100]

Lawyers are unequally distributed across China, heavily concentrated in the big cities and eastern seaboard with comparatively few in the western and poorer regions.[101] Wherever they are situated, however, criminal defence lawyers are faced with low levels of remuneration[102] and low status. Despite the professional protocols that might be expected to finesse the arrangements, both judges and prosecutors made starkly clear that defence lawyers were not part of the inner circle of state institutions which run China's criminal justice system. At best, lawyers can expect no better than treatment according to the strict letter of the law; at worst, judges and prosecutors look with disdain upon lawyers, seeing them as no better than the 'criminals' they represent. Outside the court, the police often treat lawyers with contempt[103] and lawyers have been beaten or arrested on various charges[104] or disappeared[105] while trying to carry out their duties.[106]

In addition, lawyers are subject to state supervision and control through the seemingly innocuous Article 2 of the Lawyers Law 2007 which refers to lawyers 'who have obtained

---

[100] Halliday and Liu (2007).
[101] See, for example, Ng Tze-wei (2010b). Ng reports official figures showing that of approximately 160 000 lawyers nationwide, 12 per cent are in Beijing. This equals 12 lawyers per 10 000 residents in the capital compared with 1.43 in Chongqing, 1.0 in Xinjiang and 0.72 in Qinghai.
[102] Ng Tze-wei (2010b).
[103] See, Liu and Halliday (2008). Liu and Halliday describe how the chief of a local public security bureau in Hebei Province saw lawyers as not professional at all, people who speak nonsense and place obstacles in the way of policing: *ibid.*, at pp. 9–10.
[104] See, for examples, the 2009 trial of Tan Zuoren, a rights-defender who was brought to trial following his investigations into why so many people had died in the substandard buildings that collapsed during the 2008 Sichuan earthquake; Zheng Enchong, a Shanghai lawyer fighting against illegal land acquisition, was tried and convicted for illegally obtaining state secrets after he had made an inquiry of a reporter on an 'Internal Reference' regarding unlawful land seizures; and Chen Guangcheng, the blind rights defender, imprisoned after exposing coercive family planning policies in Linyi. The problem of violence towards lawyers is more general in character being described as an 'ever-present risk' against which lawyers feel inadequately protected by the state: Human Rights Watch (2008) at pp. 30 ff. See also Ji Xiangde (2006) at p. 194.
[105] See, for example, the case of the prominent dissident lawyer, Gao Zhisheng discussed in Cohen and Pils (2009); Cohen (2009b).
[106] See, for example, Peerenboom (1998) and Tom Kellogg (2003).

a law licence in accordance with the law'.[107] Lawyers in China are regulated by the state and they are not able to form their own professional associations.[108] The Ministry of Justice exercises its powers of supervision through the 'annual inspection' which involves an examination and approval process through which lawyers' licences are registered.[109] While this procedure enables the screening out of sub-standard lawyers, it also allows the state, by using the colour of legal process, to delay the registration of rights-defenders or to de-licence them altogether and to warn law firms that the participation by their lawyers in 'sensitive' cases would affect the firm's forthcoming licensing and approval. Managing their everyday life in this setting has proved a difficult task for lawyers[110] and it is unsurprising that lawyers have increasingly turned to the media for help in covering their stories or exposing official obstruction.[111]

Comments of the judges we interviewed showed that their relationship with defenders was generally a negative one. While one (F-IJ-N-03) said that he would safeguard lawyers' rights as long as the lawyers performed their duties according to law and 13 judges even told us that their relationship with defence lawyers was 'good' or 'acceptable',[112] the overwhelming majority of judges were negative or even hostile towards defenders. For example, more than 50 per cent of the judges we interviewed described their relationship with defence lawyers as 'average', simply a 'normal working relationship', or stated that they only treated defence lawyers according to law.[113] Additionally, some judges disclosed that they did not have much communication with defence lawyers[114] and ten judges told us that they would keep

---

[107] The body which has oversight of lawyers in China is the PRC Ministry of Justice.

[108] By Article 4 of the Law on Lawyers, 2007, the judicial administrative departments 'conduct supervision and guidance of lawyers, law firms and bar associations according to the present law'.

[109] A number of conditions have to be fulfilled in order to practice law in China. The individual must: hold a personal lawyer's licence; register this licence annually with the local bureau of the Ministry of Justice; be a member of the local lawyers' association; and be employed by a registered law firm. See Conditions for Practicing Law in China', available at http://news.9ask.cn/lvshifuwu/lsssdl/msssdl/200908/223684.html; see also Administrative Measures for Lawyers' Practitioner Note issued by Ministry of Justice, 28 May 2008, and Lawyers' Law of the People's Republic of China.

[110] See Liu and Halliday (2008).

[111] Liebman (2005). See also Ji (2006) at p. 194.

[112] Four judges said they had a good relationship with defence lawyers: C-IJ-B3-01, I-IJ-S3-02, L-IJ-X-01 and L-IJ-X-11; nine judges said their relationship with defence lawyers was acceptable: M-IJ-Y-02, M-IJ-Y-03, L-IJ-X-04, L-IJ-X-06, L-IJ-X-10, E-IJ-L-03, EIJ-L-04, E-IJ-L-07 and B-IJ-B2-13.

[113] Twelve judges said their relationship with defence lawyers was average: C-IJ-B3-04, B-IJ-B2-10, B-IJ-B2-11, B-IJ-B2-12, D-IJ-K-01, D-IJ-K-04, A-IJ-B1-09, L-IJ-X-02, L-IJ-X-07, L-IJ-X-08, L-IJ-X-09 and F-IJ-N-07. A further 27 judges said they only had a normal working relationship with defence lawyers: C-IJ-B3-03, C-IJ-B3-05, C-IJ-B3-07, B-IJ-B2-01, B-IJ-B2-02, B-IJ-B2-04, B-IJ-B2-05, B-IJ-B2-06, B-IJ-B2-07, B-IJ-B2-08, B-IJ-B2-09, K-IJ-W-02, D-IJ-K-03, D-IJ-K-04, D-IJ-K-05, D-IJ-K-06, A-IJ-B1-01, A-IJ-B1-04, A-IJ-B1-05, A-IJ-B1-07, A-IJ-B1-09, L-IJ-X-03, E-IJ-L-05, E-IJ-L-06, F-IJ-N-02, F-IJ-N-04 and J-IJ-S4-04. Additionally, four judges said they only treated defence lawyers according to law: M-IJ-Y-01, I-IJ-S3-01, I-IJ-S3-02 and B-IJ-B2-05.

[114] Judges who said they did not have much communication with defence lawyers include the following: D-IJ-K-02, F-IJ-N-07, B-IJ-B2-13, A-IJ-B1-01, A-IJ-B1-06 and A-IJ-B1-08.

a distance from defence lawyers.[115] As Wang pointed out, many defence lawyers consider that it is difficult to deal with judges, and they either have to keep a distance from the judges so as to avoid being accused of colluding with the judges, or alternatively try to establish a good relationship with judges. They cannot maintain a normal and harmonious working relationship with judges.[116] The following are broadly representative of these judicial views:

> *A-IJ-B1-02:* Strictly speaking, judges should be impartial, independent; but in reality the police, the procuratorate and the court are members of the same family. It is still not very fair to the defendants: we mainly co-operate with the prosecutor.
>
> *E-IJ-L-06:* As to my relationship with defence lawyers, to tell you the truth, I don't like them. But I can still treat them according to official rules.
>
> *L-IJ-X-05:* In general, lawyers have certain connections with the defendants and their family members. If we have a close relationship with them, people will doubt our impartiality. Some lawyers make use of their relationship with us to give their clients empty promises and charge them more money.
>
> *J-IJ-S4-02:* Generally speaking, we don't trust lawyers, so we will not believe in their words unless there is sufficient evidence.

Judges were quite blunt in speaking about the consequences of this negative relationship, namely that they would pay little heed to the representations of defenders and that there was nothing that a defence lawyer could do to secure a favourable verdict. In other words, the outcome would not be placed in doubt by the actions of the defence and the judge would not give the defence any leeway in putting the defence case:[117]

> *L-IJ-X-07:* Many lawyers think we are in the same position as the prosecutors. There is no practical value for the lawyer in defending from a subordinate position since the crime and evidence charged by the procuratorate is sufficient. The lawyer's defence is just to reassure the family of the defendant. I have been engaged in trial work for 20 years: it is seldom that a lawyer is able to establish the innocence of the defendant.
>
> *J-IJ-S4-02:* We have a better relationship with the prosecutor and the police than with the defence lawyer. . . . You know, judges and prosecutors and police are all paid by the government. We do our job for the benefit of our country, so our relationship is better. But lawyers are different. They get money from clients; they do jobs for clients; so they will stand on the side of clients. We will doubt their words.

---

[115] The following is a list of judges who said they would keep a distance from defence lawyers: M-IJ-Y-04, K-IL-W-01, D-IJ-KM-05, L-IJ-X-05, L-IJ-X-10, J-IJ-S4-03, J-IJ-S4-05, J-IJ-S4-06, J-IJ-S4-08 and H-IJ-S2-004.

[116] Wang Ying (2004).

[117] Sometimes, judges attributed their attitude towards defenders on the basis that defenders mounted arguments but lacked supporting evidence. Thus: L-IJ-X-10: 'As for the defender, a good defender can grasp key points and I feel it easy to adopt his opinion. But we cannot accept or confirm some defenders' opinions because they do not conduct investigation or collect evidence'; and L-IJ-X-04: 'Some lawyers don't make their defence on the basis of facts and evidence in order to make the defendant and his family happy. As a matter of fact, the defendant is guilty but the lawyer's insistence on innocence gives a false impression to the defendant. . . . Sometimes, when the lawyer cannot find any loophole, he will propose that the defendant is innocent.'

> *L-IJ-X-02:* The lawyer in a criminal case does not play an important role because their channels to collect evidence are restricted and their quality needs further improvement. The lawyer is a professional whose aim is to earn money. We are angry with those lawyers who only collect fees but fail to perform their duties. We sometimes will question the defendant to understand his situation so that his rights and interests can be fully protected.

For their part, while some prosecutors were in favour of greater involvement of the defence at trial, others were negative in their assessment of defenders.

> *A-IP-B1-08:* Defence lawyers are only good at teaching criminal suspects to collude in giving evidence and fabricating evidence, buying meals for prosecutors and bribing judges.

> *M-IP-Y-01:* Most of the lawyers have good professional standards but a minority of them are bad and ignore the law and facts when defending the interests of their clients.

> *D-IP-K-04:* They are like merchants, only paying attention to charging fees. In order to display themselves in the courtroom, they sometimes defend a case by disrespecting or distorting the facts. There is a lack of regulation of lawyers in China, so the lawyer's defence is simply to make the defendant's family happy. Sometimes, the defendant says that he is guilty but his defender still insists upon the defendant's innocence in his defence. Then the defendant doesn't know if he is guilty or innocent.

> *L-IP-X-06:* I treat lawyers with politeness; but my colleagues may not be like that.

For their part, defenders saw their relationship with judges and prosecutors in functional terms. Of those interviewed, nearly 25 per cent commented that they had a good relationship with prosecutors[118] while 50 per cent said their relationship with prosecutors was 'acceptable' or at least 'an average working relationship'.[119] A number of defenders said that preserving a good relationship with the prosecutors could enable them to perform their work efficiently and smoothly.

Nonetheless, defenders were fully aware that they were second-class citizens in the eyes of the state parties:

> *M-IL-Y-02:* The investigation and prosecuting organs are prejudiced against lawyers. They feel uncomfortable if lawyers lodge a claim of innocence or for leniency. The aim of prosecutors is that the defendant is convicted, even if sentenced to lesser punishment.

> *D-IL-K-05:* I have an average relationship with prosecutors, because they have a tendency to discriminate against lawyers, and most lawyers are unwilling to frequently contact prosecutors.

---

[118] The following is a list of lawyers who said they had a good relationship with prosecutors: L-IL-X-05, L-IL-X-08, M-IL-Y-01, M-IL-Y-03, M-IL-Y-04, M-IL-Y-05, B-IL-B2-00, B-IL-B2-01, B-IL-B2-05, H-IL-S2-02, K-IL-W-02, K-IL-W-03, I-IL-S3-03, I-IL-S3-04, J-IL-S4-04, J-IL-S4-05, J-IL-S4-06, D-IL-K-02, F-IL-N-02, F-IL-N-05, F-IL-N-06 and F-IL-N-07.

[119] The following is a list of lawyers who considered their relationship with the prosecutors as 'acceptable' or 'an average working relationship': L-IL-X-01, L-IL-X-03, L-IL-X-04, L-IL-X-06, L-IL-X-07, L-IL-X-09, L-IL-X-10, L-IL-X-11, L-IL-X-02, B-IL-B2-01, I-IL-S3-01, D-IL-K-01, D-IL-K-03, D-IL-K-05, F-IL-N-03, C-IL-B3-06, C-IL-B3-08, A-IL-B1-08, A-IL-B1-09, E-IL-L-01, B-IL-B2-03, B-IL-B2-04, B-IL-B2-06, G-IL-S1-04, G-IL-S1-05, G-IL-S1-06, K-IL-W-02, D-IL-K-04, D-IL-K-06, C-IL-B3-00, C-IL-B3-02, C-IL-B3-03, C-IL-B3-04, A-IL-B1-01, A-IL-B1-04, A-IL-B1-06, A-IL-B1-07, E-IL-L-02, E-IL-L-03, E-IL-L-04, E-IL-L-06 and E-IL-L-07.

J-IL-S4-01: The rights of litigation between the prosecutor and defender are unbalanced. All in all, the lawyers are not trusted or respected: their rights are limited everywhere.

K-IL-W-01: Judges do not pay much attention to the defence.

I-IL-S3-02: I am always concerned about the social and political standing of lawyers. There have been great changes and rapid progress made in the legal situation in China and people gradually realize the function of the lawyer. But there are still many problems in front of us at work, particularly the imbalance between prosecuting and defending.

F-IL-N-04: Some judges are prejudiced against lawyers. They think that since lawyers receive money from their clients, they would ignore the law and simply act in favour of their clients.

M-IL-Y-03: Not many [of my opinions are accepted by judges] because they pay little attention to the speeches of the lawyer. For judges, lawyers are only after money and defendants are considered to be guilty before the judgment comes out.

Given this background, it is not surprising that defence lawyers consider that their standing also leads judges to disregard their opinions and to treat them with contempt in court proceedings:

C-IL-B3-03: In most circumstances, judges will not consider the opinions of defenders.

D-IL-K-5: Lawyers are shut out of the trial and their attendance at court is just a formality.

J-IL-S4-06: There is no proper respect for the lawyer's opinion on defence. When I think that a particular defence opinion is very important, judges do not think so and they often interrupt when a lawyer is speaking.

A-IL-B1-09: There is inequality between the prosecution and the defence. I'm always interrupted while making my submissions. I'm not allowed to explain my viewpoint. I am not given sufficient respect: many of my opinions are quite reasonable but they are not accepted.

K-IL-W-05: Judges seldom interrupt or stop the speech of prosecutors but they often do so to defenders.

L-IL-X-02: When we have different opinions in court, we should respect each other, find out the truth and correct mistakes. The Lawyers Law in fact did not have any provision on the lawyers' position, thus the judges and prosecutors do not respect lawyers. A judge is supposed to be an impartial arbiter, but his decision is not impartial.

Following on from this, lawyers often drew attention to their low status in the legal system and called into question their very presence at trials. The lived experiences of lawyers taught them that they were bottom of the hierarchy and, more than this, that they were actually surplus to the requirements of the case-processing machine. They were only too aware of the fact, identified by other researchers, that their involvement in criminal cases has little or no impact upon outcome.[120]

---

[120] See Lu and Miethe (2002). This study of theft cases in China concluded that there was 'little indication of the effectiveness of defence attorneys in China' (*ibid.* at p. 276).

First, as defence lawyers see it there is the question of status:

A-IL-B1-01: The main problem is to enhance the status of lawyers. Our democratic legal system will reach standing when lawyers enjoy equal status with the police, the procuratorates and the courts.

A-IL-B1-04: [The main problem] is that our status is not high.

A-IL-B1-07: Our status is not high, there is difficulty in conducting investigations and collecting evidence and defence opinions are not accepted by the court.

D-IL-K-04: The lawyer lacks social security and encounters a lot of pressure, so they belong to a weak social group. In comparison with state functionaries, we do not have actual powers; thus, we cannot offend them.

I-IL-S3-05: I am always concerned how to improve the working environment and social status of defence lawyers.

Then, as they see it, there is the question of the value or effectiveness of the lawyer:

M-IL-Y-03: The lawyer's defence is just for the client not for the judge.

C-IL-B3-02: I think the major problem facing lawyers is that whether a defendant has or does not have a defender does not make any difference. Some defenders even place defendants in a more disadvantageous position. This is the sadness of China's judiciary.

E-IL-L-05: I have a feeling of helplessness. I have thought of a lot of ways and undertaken lots of work in defence which should be effective, but in practice it is in vain.

E-IL-L-06: Lawyers are facing a powerful state, so they sometimes feel that they lack any protective mechanism in this profession.

M-IL-Y-02: The trial is just a kind of formality.

Given that judges and prosecutors view defenders in negative terms and given that defenders feel that they are of low status (and experience this on a daily basis),[121] a question arises whether the negative evaluation of lawyers has any material foundation.

For their part, defenders were ready to acknowledge that many of those acting as lawyers had received inadequate training and lacked the necessary trial skills to properly represent defendants:

F-IL-N-02: Personally speaking, the standards of lawyers are quite low in China: the number is inadequate and we especially lack lawyers of high quality.

---

[121] There are regular reports of lawyers being harassed, mistreated or abducted by official state agents. For example, Chinese Human Rights Defenders (Online), 'Beijing Lawyer Cheng Hai Assaulted by Officials for Representing Falun Gong Practitioner', 14 April 2009; Cohen and Pils (2009); and Cohen (2009e).

K-IL-W-01: Certainly, some lawyers talk claptrap. Lawyers should be brief if defendants admit the crime. It is annoying that some lawyers say so many unnecessary words just to please defendants and their families.

D-IL-K-02: Comparatively speaking, the reform of the judicial system has regulated practice. But I dare not say that the level of lawyers is going up. I feel that the social status of the lawyer is lower than it was at that time the lawyers system was re-started.

L-IL-X-05: At the moment, the professional ability of some lawyers is low.

Defenders also made clear that at least some of their number (or individuals representing themselves as lawyers) had been guilty of improper or corrupt actions[122] and had thereby helped bring the profession into disrepute:[123]

F-IL-N-02: It cannot be denied that there are some black sheep in the lawyers' field but they are a minority just as there are also some corrupt judges. . . .

M-IL-Y-01: Some lawyers ignore professional ethics and charge (fees) informally. Unfair competition causes society to reproach lawyers and damages law firms.

M-IL-Y-04: Some lawyers undertake cases by using illegal means.

E-IL-L-06: Sometimes, because there is no guarantee of cases, some lawyers have to maintain a special relationship with judges. . . . I think this profession is not bad and at least is better than other professions although our status is not high. Law firms often produce false certificates for fraudulent lawyers who deal with cases which has a negative effect upon the image of regular lawyers and damage our business.

E-IL-L-07: The law should regulate what types of lawyer are allowed to deal with criminal cases and should not tolerate the phenomenon of 'one rat ruins the whole pot of soup'. The professional levels of lawyers vary, so some of the low quality lawyers may affect the image of lawyers.

I-IL-S3-02: Police worry that lawyers will engage in collusion to make confessions tally and affect the investigation and trial. Personally speaking, there really are some lawyers who are not strict in their behaviour. But this does not represent all lawyers. Those lawyers should be punished according to law and the legal rights of lawyers guaranteed.

L-IL-X-01: From the perspective of professional ethics and performance, there are quite a few low quality lawyers.

---

[122] See, Fu Hualing (2003). Fu argues, looking at court cases in general and not restricted to criminal cases, that the participation of lawyers in the legal system has led to the 'democratization of corruption' with lawyers acting as facilitators: 'Lawyers in particular have become instrumental in brokering deals and facilitating transactions between litigants and judges. Lawyers are repeat players in the system, and they tend to have a stable and close relationship with a select number of judges. With the participation of lawyers, corruption has become normalized and institutionalized; and it has become less visible' (*ibid.*, at p. 211).

[123] See also Alford (1995) where Alford noted that the increase of lawyers had given rise to increased competition, a part of which involved lawyers bribing public officials and judges to secure advantages for their clients.

> *L-IL-X-11:* Some lawyers disregard the facts and law in any circumstances and raise claims of innocence in order to make the defendant's family happy which results in a bad impact upon [defence lawyers].

Defenders explained their working environment as one based upon personal connections (*guanxi*)[124] which could give rise to the appearance of corruption. As other researchers have noted, lawyers may need to utilize personal networks in order to compensate for the weak standing of the profession and to provide protection against various forms of institutionalized, state-sponsored harassment and rent-seeking.[125] Personal relationships, defence lawyers told us, were also the means by which they received instructions and without these social relationships, friends and acquaintances,[126] they would have difficulty functioning as a lawyer:

> *M-IL-Y-01:* Most cases I get come from acquaintances. . . . Many of my cases are from friends and acquaintances.
>
> *L-IL-X-10:* Because I am a part-time lawyer, most cases are introduced by friends or acquaintances.
>
> *L-IL-X-07:* We accept a case either through the firm or friends.
>
> *L-IL-X-03:* Many clients go directly to my firm or contact me via friends and relatives.

However, the link to possible 'corruption' was not restricted to the development of a client base: some lawyers openly talked about the need to bring influence to bear upon prosecutors and judges that was not available to them in the trial setting. This mostly involved low-level meetings at dinners or the giving of unspecified gifts:

> *F-IL-N-01:* I think it is very important to strengthen the professional morality of judges and that is the key to impartial judgment. You know, judges have the right to determine the amount of punishment. Some lawyers invite judges to dinner or send gifts for judges in order to obtain a lighter or mitigated punishment for defendants. . . . Now there is the phenomenon that many judges receive invitations from lawyers to eat or accept money.
>
> *J-IL-S4-02:* I think the main problem facing us is judicial corruption. The verdict in similar cases is a little, even very, different between different judges and in different courts. Judges get many influences, so they determine the sentence based upon friendship. It is hard to guarantee judicial impartiality.
>
> *K-IL-W-03:* As a lawyer, it is necessary to socialize with [prosecutors]. Dinner parties are unavoidable: but I'll not send money to them. It is dangerous to do that. You never know when the bomb will explode.

---

[124] *Guanxi* has been described as the Chinese term for 'certain kinds of particularistic ties between pairs of people': Nathan (1993). See also Danching (1993).

[125] See in this context Michelson (2007). See also, Peerenboom (2002): 'Corruption impedes the development of the legal profession, and adversely affects the relationship between lawyers and judges. Lawyers are forced to rely on their connections rather than legal arguments to win cases and earn a living' (*ibid.*, at p. 296, footnote omitted).

[126] Family relations were occasionally mentioned in this context.

M-IL-Y-03: On the whole my relationship with [judges and prosecutors] is good. . . . It is impossible to be real friends with prosecutors and judges. Judges and prosecutors are from the government. They have a superiority complex so they do not understand working conditions of lawyers. Only when they have trouble can they think of lawyers. I will invite them for dinner and send gifts to them but I will never give them money.

The problem of personal relationships is, of course, much wider: it is a structural feature of Chinese society in which relationships underpin interactions of all kinds whether in education, housing, employment or criminal trials. Lawyers are not immune from community values and, indeed, are expected to conform to them:

K-IL-W-02: The pressure on lawyers is immense. Clients like to ask lawyers whether they have a relationship with the judge. They want the lawyer to send presents to the judge. If the judgment is not satisfactory, they will complain that the lawyer did not send a present to the judge.

K-IL-W-04: Some judges consider lawyers to be people who take money from clients and help clients. Some clients think that they have to just send gifts to judges so the judges would be willing to help them. But I refuse to do so. I will try to find opportunities to communicate with judges and influence them.

E-IL-L-02: If a lawyer doesn't have relationships, he will have fewer sources of cases and his life will be harder; lawyers care about sources of cases most. The family of the suspect or defendant would ask you if you have a good relationship with police, prosecutors and judges. . . . It is noticeable that there are many provisions in legislation beginning with 'the lawyers should not. . . .' The judges have more and more powers. Consequently, it seems that the relationship between judges and lawyers is a vital factor to determine the fate of the defence. If you don't have the relationship, you will have fewer sources of cases and your life will be harder. To lawyers who just entered this profession, they have to pay 1500 Yuan per year to the judicial administrative organs and lawyers' society. But these authorities do not provide any service to the lawyers, so the lawyers cannot get many benefits there. In one word, lawyers' duties are more than their rights.

It is little surprise that some defence lawyers who have internalized fair trial concepts, see themselves as victims of a whole system which has gone wrong and one which is not likely to be fixed in the near term:

J-IL-S4-03: The key sticking point of the current problem is this: On the one hand, when those above behave wrongly, those below will do the same. Even some court presidents and chiefs of the department will bring pressure and interfere in the judge's judgment. And there is much interference from government officials. It is not certain that all are concerned with money and presents. But it is mutual help, the exchange of power. And they gradually become common benefits. On the other hand, the cost of corruption is too low. So we must strengthen the power to fight corruption and dare them not to be corrupt.

E-IL-L-07: The law should regulate criminal defence in order to safeguard lawyers in performing their duties. Here is the problem: if the judges, prosecutors or the police infringe the rights of lawyers, who is going to supervise and correct these illegal acts? This is the imperfect aspect of our legal system. You may say that we have the People's Congress, but it does not have factual supervisory power. The Congress can show its power only when there is an election. The Chinese characteristic puts lawyers in an embarrassing situation so we sometimes have to drift with the tide. The root problem is that if there is too much corruption in the state, the law alone cannot solve the problem completely.

L-IL-X-01: The biggest problem is that, when your opinion is correct, it is not likely to be accepted by the judge. This problem concerns the system: there exists a camera-like operation. The judge has no discretion to reach a verdict: his or her opinion may not be accepted because most cases are decided by the adjudication committee. The professional quality of judges and the adjudication committee is not high. Moreover, this may involve the problem of judicial corruption. No matter how correct your opinion is, the judge will not accept it. . . . Adjudication in China is centralized, whereas it is a system of individual responsibility in Western countries.

K-IL-W-01: [When asked to identify any problems]: The problem is the whole system.

In the face of what they see as a system which is both rotten and surrounded by danger, many defenders want little to do with criminal cases[127] and would rather specialize in other areas:

K-IL-W-05: I think the risk of handling criminal cases is great and the fee is low, so the percentage of criminal cases taken by lawyers is declining. We would rather do economic and civil cases.

E-IL-L-04: Most lawyers are unwilling to deal with criminal cases, because of low fees and the potential risk.

E-IL-L-05: I don't want to receive criminal cases, because of the difficulties in the defence under the present arrangements. So far as my personal benefit is concerned, I cannot make money from criminal cases.

D-IL-K-06: The reason that I would like to learn civil and commercial law is that a lawyer can play a more important role in civil cases and have room to show his talent.

E-IL-L-03: I want to learn civil and commercial law. . . . Civil and commercial law are closely connected to economic development. As you know, China is setting up a market economy system so relevant reforms to the political system will also be carried out. A regulated market requires regulation by law. Actually, I like criminal law and procedural law but because of the factual situation, China is not a state governed by the rule of law.

L-IL-X-04: The whole legal profession is not interested in criminal defence and accordingly the development of criminal defence is in a state of atrophy. Most lawyers do not think that being a defence lawyer in a criminal case will lead to success.

Some others have found that the best way forward for them is a co-operative or compliant stance as a consequence of which potential clashes with the authorities are minimized or avoided altogether.[128]

---

[127] For a discussion of the obstacles facing Chinese lawyers, see: Wang Gong (2003); and Liu and Halliday (2009) at p. 932.

[128] See, for example, Ng Tze-wei (2010f). This is an account of two lawyers defending clients in Chongqing following the crackdown against triads that began in 2009. One lawyer, Zhu Mingyong, resorted to using the media in an effort to save his client from the death penalty publicizing detailed allegations of torture which resulted in a confession. By contrast, the other lawyer, Yang Kuangsheng, a former prosecutor turned defence lawyer, maintains a close relationship with the authorities. Yang sought approval from the Judicial Bureau before accepting the defence and he gave up the right to investigate on the basis that it would be too risky in that he could easily be accused of fabricating evidence. Yang is reported as saying: 'Under an ideal situation we should not

CONCLUSION

As Richard Pfeffer pointed out in 1970, China's criminal justice process is a community of organizations[129] and the concept of the iron triangle continues to define criminal justice in China. In this sense, relations between the different organizations are continuing in nature, based on common interests, characterized by reciprocal influence and to varying degrees manifested in face-to-face encounters.[130] However, as Pfeffer also noted, within the community there are antithetical interests and perspectives and, we would add, it is not a coalition of equals.

Although it is theoretically the case that the hierarchical organization of each state institution and their independent auditing roles offer an institutional basis for reviewing and constraining the exercise of arbitrary discretion by state actors within the criminal justice process, in practice each institution retains a high degree of autonomy and each institution is unwilling to assert a meaningful audit-role over the companion institutions because in large part their relational positions make them mutually vulnerable to cross-audit. More importantly, the shared ideological driver is not procedural regularity (although facial compliance with the rules is easily achieved in this setting) or even substantive justice (factual as opposed to legal guilt) but rather system-wide 'efficiency' and 'aggregate justice' as framed by Party ideology.

Further, the impact of the 1996 Criminal Procedure Law, in so far as it is perceived as having sought to introduce a clearer division of responsibilities between state institutions, redistribute power between them and inject a greater element of adversariness,[131] has been blunted by three factors: the principal institutions resisting any reduction in their power and authority; the continuance of a decision-making structure within the state institutions that tends towards continuity rather than institutional change; and the absence of a strong defence bar.[132]

Within the iron triangle, the dominant force remains the PSB, an institution which still exercises a controlling influence over the whole process such that the other institutions tend to go along with its decisions, themselves driven in large measure by quotas and generalized performance indicators, notwithstanding concerns over the provenance of evidence (particularly confessions) and its persuasiveness. Requests for supplementary investigation may be made but little can be done if they are ignored. A notification to the PSB from the procuratorate to file a case where it is found that the reasons offered by the police for not doing so are 'untenable' may be disregarded without the prosecutor being able to do anything to enforce the notice.

For their part, prosecutors operate within a disciplinary framework marked by quotas and performance indicators in which real power resides elsewhere so that the determinative voice on individual case decisions is that of the chief of the department, the section committee, the president of the unit or administrative or other officials. Frontline

---

give this [right to investigate] up, but if lawyers investigate, not only might we return empty-handed, we will easily get ourselves into trouble.'

[129] See further, Pfeffer (1970).
[130] *Ibid.*, at p. 265.
[131] We accept that these are all problematic 'aims' of the reforms.
[132] See also, Peerenboom (2006) at pp. 847 ff.

prosecutors suffer low morale, lack self-esteem and are always vulnerable to, if not haunted by, charges of low-level corruption.

Like prosecutors, judges are captive to the system and dependent upon the rulings of higher-level committees or political-administrators. Oftentimes, deficient in legal skills and lacking a professional sense of honour, judges preside over shell trials to later announce the decisions of their superiors in the sure knowledge that no protest will be entered except occasionally regarding sentence.

Whatever the individual merits of judges, prosecutors and lawyers (and some were experienced, intelligent and thoughtful individuals) and whatever differences there may be within each institution (and clearly there are ideological as well as personal conflicts within each of the state institutions at any given time) the individual actors who operate the criminal justice process are all *structurally* weak and this is known and made-known to them on a daily basis.

In this setting, defence lawyers have little standing, status or influence. In a system in which outcomes are pre-ordained and in which they (in general) lack respect, lawyers are powerless to do anything other than plead mercy or lenity for the defendant. Those who seek to challenge the system are dealt with in summary fashion in or outside the courtroom.

15. Conclusion

In this chapter, we draw together some thoughts emerging from this empirical study of criminal justice in China. Before doing so, we wish to enter some cautionary notes which affect both the nature of the conclusions that can be drawn and the possible wider implications to which some of our findings might give rise. The overall direction of our discussion is to stimulate further research and debate rather than to offer a definitive analysis of what all informed commentators agree are difficult issues concerning one of the world's leading economic powers and the way in which it deals with matters relating to criminal justice. We nevertheless believe that certain theoretical and policy issues are made clearer by the empirical data that we have amassed and we put forward our views to assist further debate and inform policy decisions.

INTRODUCTION

This research is not intended to and does not provide a basis for evaluating the *generality* of China's progress towards the rule of law. We have made no inventory of law reform efforts in areas (such as commercial law, intellectual property law, labour law, land ownership or environmental law) other than crime and any fair 'rule of law' assessment would ideally have this wider sweep to significantly add to existing debates. Nevertheless, in any persuasive appreciation of China's progress towards rule of law its treatment of those accused of criminal offences must, we argue, occupy a central position.

It follows, for example, that we do not seek to adjudicate between various theories commentators advance concerning the overall direction of law reform in China although we hope to contribute to the ongoing debates. Some of those arguments are neatly summarized by Ethan Michelson (2008): (i) that the legal system may undermine the Party by institutionalizing limits to its powers or by legitimizing and upholding popular grievances against its agents;[1] or (ii) that the legal system may strengthen the Party by enhancing the popular legitimacy of its rule while obscuring the subordination of law to politics and the enduring use of law as an instrument of political administration;[2] or (iii) that the Party is *trying* to maintain control over the legal system.[3] An additional and, as we will see, important perspective in the struggle for a better society is that the law in China, however imperfectly constructed, stands as a handbook providing citizens with arguments which can be used against the excesses of the party and the state, and this is so even though no

---

[1] Making reference to Diamant, Lubman and O'Brien (2005).
[2] Referring to Jones (1999).
[3] Referring to: Alford (1995); Alford (2003); Cohen (1997); Liu (2006); Lubman (1999); Potter (1994); Potter (1999); Potter (2004); and Woo (1999).

state or party institution today upholds claims and arguments advanced in accordance with the law, especially those based on fundamental human rights guarantees and even though 'the legal system' purports to de-legitimize such claims, in particular through court decisions but also in laws and regulations which stand in contradistinction to such guarantees.

Nor do we seek to intervene directly into the 'law and development' debate extensively reviewed and critiqued by Randall Peerenboom (2006),[4] although some of our findings, as we will see, bear upon the broader picture and may be seen to qualify the warning he issued:[5]

> [A]ssessment or evaluation raises issues about the proper timeframe and standard. Too often, foreign commentators jump to negative conclusions about legal reforms in China and elsewhere because they have not produced miraculous changes overnight. There is a danger of repeating the mistakes of the earlier law and development movement, when some of the movement's leaders abandoned this ship at the first sight of troubled waters. As other commentators pointed out, however, people living in developing states had no choice but to push on with reforms. As a result, many states made progress in improving their legal systems, and reformers learned valuable lessons from both their successes and failures.

In addition, we have not, as we have made clear elsewhere in this book, reviewed either 'strike hard' campaigns[6] or 'crime' in its generality because, apart from the inherent limitations of any empirical research project such as this, the criminal law that is the subject of the current research forms a relatively small part of the lives of the ordinary Chinese citizen, much smaller indeed, as we have indicated, than the 'administrative' punishments in the hands of the police.[7] And there are unknown numbers of cases in which the prosecution is 'withdrawn' after a private indication by the court that it would otherwise fail and which ought to be part of an overall assessment of the role of law in China and the ways in which critical decisions are 'managed' by the system as a whole.[8] Despite this, as we will argue, criminal justice, as opposed to administrative punishment, has greater significance than some commentators have recognized.

---

[4] One central conclusion of Peerenboom is the need for pragmatism and the importance of avoiding the attempt to identify or establish 'a single, comprehensive, unified theory able to predict both macro and micro legal system reforms in all states' (*ibid.*, p. 868). See also, Peerenboom (2002) who argues that a principal driver for the rule of law is economic development together with increased exposure to global ideas; these, it is said, will increase the demand for reliance on a law-based system of governance.

[5] Peerenboom (2006), p. 866 (footnote omitted).

[6] We have referred at various points in this book to 'strike hard' campaigns which have been used at times of actual or anticipated social or political stress. Crackdowns have also been used, for example, against citizens protesting over such matters as land grabs or health issues. See, for example, Choi Chi-yuk (2009) reporting on the incarceration of individuals jailed for protesting against lead pollution which left hundreds of children sick.

[7] See also, Clarke and Feinerman (1995).

[8] See further, Fu Hualing (2010) available at: http://ssrn.com/abstracts=1588733 who states, based upon 'reports from Guangzhou, Anhui and elsewhere' that this informal practice of judges in persuading prosecutors to withdraw cases from court might be as high as 5 per cent of prosecution cases and that there might be 'five to ten informal withdrawals of prosecution for every not guilty verdict' (p. 9) citing various reports from police or procuratorate sources.

Crime, we would argue, occupies a special role both in terms of the legitimacy of the state and in terms of its claims to be compliant with the rule of law. Market liberalization and rapidly growing prosperity have increased the need to provide social order for citizens and give them a heightened sense of personal security.[9] As Fu Hualing (2010) has remarked in a related context:

> To a government with a democratic deficit, the ruling party relies on performance-based legitimacy; a low crime rate and a high sense of safety are key components in establishing regime legitimacy.

The point put emphatically by Jerome Cohen (2010b) in discussing the treatment of dissidents in China is generalizable to the whole criminal process:

> Beijing wants the world to admire a 'rising China' not only for its phenomenal economic accomplishments and growing military prowess but also for the quality of its civilization. Yet, no matter how many Confucius Institutes the government establishes abroad to teach Chinese language and culture, the People's Republic will not win international respect for its political and social progress until it ceases locking up political dissidents and treats those currently detained in a more humane manner.

At a more fundamental level, we would argue that criminal justice is at the heart of the identity of China and the relational position of its citizens to the state. Klaus Muhlhahn's observation on China's modern history from the late Qing dynasty to the end of the Cultural Revolution that 'criminal justice lay at the heart of debates on the meaning of citizenship and the nature of social inclusion and exclusion'[10] is, we believe, equally applicable in understanding today's criminal justice process in China and its meaning for its citizens.

LEGALITY

There is little doubt that the modern era has seen the introduction of major changes to the formal law in China clearly demonstrated in the 1996 Criminal Procedure Law. As Stanley Lubman (2000) has observed, even in this politicized area there has been a tendency 'albeit slow' to:

> ... extend and increase the formal rationality of the criminal process. The differentiation of offenders on the basis of their class background, for example, no longer seems to determine their punishment.... The [1996 CPL] ... revision somewhat limited the power of the police to detain criminal suspects indefinitely, expanded the right to counsel, and enlarged the role of the court so as to make the criminal trial a review of the substance of criminal cases rather than a pro forma approval of a decision reached before the actual trial. Despite these changes, however, the extensive power of the police and the CCP over the criminal process have been only ineffectually restrained (footnote omitted).

Additionally, it is important to stress that the legal process should be viewed as it is and not as it is often assumed to be. A common analysis is to account for the condition of

---

[9] It is also used by the government to justify its widespread use of the death penalty.
[10] Muhlhahn (2009), p. 285.

criminal justice in China as a 'gap' issue under which 'problems' are attributable to a failure of courts and state officials to live up to what is assumed to be, but may not in fact be, the letter of the law.[11] On this view, it is also common to assert that the pace of reform will gather speed as capacity grows and that eventually internalization of the principles of legality and increases in capacity will close the gap. As Albert Chen (2004) put it:

> As time goes by, as more better' qualified people are recruited into the system as its operators, as the officially endorsed ideology of 'ruling the country according to law' and 'constructing a socialist *Rechtsstaat*' penetrates more deeply into the consciousness of officials and citizens alike, the gradual shortening of the gap between the law-in-the-books and the law-in-action may be expected (p. 202).

However, as we have intimated earlier, these forms of analysis often misstate, misunderstand or misrepresent the legal provisions to which they are addressed. We agree with Liu and Halliday (2009),[12] who, in engaging with the 'reform' movement, caution against 'naïve notions that more precise formal law, more training of lawyers and judges, or more refinement of purely legal institutions will suffice to produce a criminal procedure law consistent with global norms without reconstruction of the state'.[13]

In discussing 'legality', the starting point must be a clear recognition of the legal process as it is rather than what it is thought to be (legal rhetoric). Thus, some commentators believe that there was a *formal presumption of innocence* introduced in 1996,[14] deriving authority for this from Article 12, 1996 CPL which provides:

> No person shall be found guilty without being judged as such by a People's Court according to law.

They also point out in this regard that no conviction can be entered solely on the basis of a confession: Article 46, 1996 CPL. Other commentators claim that the requirement that 'the facts are clear and the evidence is reliable and ample' (Article 162(1), 1996 CPL) imposes on the prosecution a standard of proof higher than, for example, the beyond reasonable doubt standard typical of common law jurisdictions.[15] In fact, as Jonathan Hecht (1996a, p. 44) points out, neither Article 12, 1996 CPL nor any other provision in the 1996 CPL says anything directly about the standard of proof, standard of guilt or anything associated with the presumption of innocence.[16] Article 12, 1996 CPL says no

---

[11] As we make clear in the foregoing analysis, this is not to deny that there are always debates in any jurisdiction which takes the rule of law seriously about the precise meaning and character of particular legal provisions.

[12] Liu and Halliday (2009).

[13] *Ibid.*, p. 945.

[14] Hecht (1996b), at pp. 16–17; Chen Guangzhong and Duan Yan (1996) at p. 5; Buxbaum and Lin (1995) at pp. 54–55. See for disparate views: Q. Lu (1998); and Yang (1998). See also, Muhlhahn (2009): '[The CPL 1996] for the first time in the history of the People's Republic, recognized the fundamental principles of the presumption of innocence and the right to defense counsel in the pre-trial investigation process. . . .' (p. 293).

[15] Chen Guangzhong and Duan Yan (1995), p. 173.

[16] Though it can be argued that in various indirect provisions the 1996 CPL at least implies that suspects have certain 'rights'. For example, the proscription against using torture (Article 43,

more and no less than that only a court (no other institution or individual) can determine guilt. Indeed, as Hecht (1996a) points out, proposals to introduce a presumption of innocence at the time when reform was being debated were actually rejected.[17]

It is also remarked in this context that the term 'defendant' (*beigaoren*), used throughout the 1979 CPL, is in the modern era now applied only in proceedings *after* the decision to prosecute, whereas for prior proceedings the term 'suspect' (*fanzui xianyiren*) is used and by lowering the arrest standard, the former implication that all persons subject to arrest are guilty has also been weakened.[18] However, the police remain the prime arbiters of whether the suspect should be subject to detention and on what basis; the suspect/defendant has no right to remain silent; and there is no privilege against self-incrimination, the latter two subject to the qualified 'right' to refuse to answer questions that are irrelevant to the case (Article 93, 1996 CPL).

Similarly, while the 1996 CPL represents an advance in formal terms of the right to counsel the structure of the law falls far short of the benefit that some commentators imagined. Thus, Ran Yanfei (2009), for example, states:[19]

> However, the 1996 Lawyers Law is not a law that protects lawyers. Rather, it is a law to limit or even restrict the rights of lawyers. The 1996 Lawyers Law contains 53 articles. Among those 53 articles, five articles provide that 'lawyers must . . . ;' eight articles state that 'lawyers shall not . . .;' eleven articles read that 'lawyers shall . . . ;' and fifteen suggest that 'lawyers must or shall not . . .' More than seventy-three percent of those articles limit or restrict lawyers' rights. In this law that is specifically meant to govern lawyers, only nine articles say that 'lawyers may' or 'lawyers have the right'. . . . Even among those limited nine articles, some articles simply state basic principles without any practical meaning since there are no other detailed regulations to implement these rights (p. 996, footnotes omitted).

The same has been said in regard to the amended law brought in by the 2007 Law on Lawyers, Article 37 of which provides:

> The personal rights of a lawyer in practicing law shall not be infringed upon. The representation or defense opinions presented in court by a lawyer shall not be subject to legal prosecution, however, except speeches compromising the national security, maliciously defaming others or seriously disrupting the court order.

As has been pointed out, what the first part of Article 37 gives is effectively taken away by the reference to the ambiguous concept of 'national security'. The lawyer Teng Biao put the matter thus:[20]

1996 CPL) and the partial recognition of a privilege against self-incrimination (Article 93, 1996 CPL according a suspect during interrogation 'the right' to refuse to answer any questions that are 'irrelevant' to the case).

[17] This is far from denying the importance of claims advanced by rights-defenders in China that their clients are entitled to a presumption of innocence by invoking in support a generalized claim to such a principle (which they recognize is not fully spelled out in the 1996 CPL) buttressed in some instances by reference to international standards such as those incorporated into the International Covenant on Civil and Political Rights.

[18] *Ibid.*, at pp. 62–63.
[19] See to the same effect the defence lawyer (LY-02) quoted in Chapter 14 above.
[20] Cited from http://www.chrlg-hk.org/?p=292.

In order to fulfil the duties set out above, lawyers must do their best to collect evidence favourable to their client and rebut the arguments and evidence presented by the other party in the course of the litigation process. In this process of gathering evidence, challenging the other side's evidence and making a case for their client lawyers will inevitably come in conflict with the other side, and possibly even with the official ideology of the State. If a lawyer's performance of his role can be regarded as giving rise to tortious or criminal liability, this will have tremendously adverse effects on the legal profession

Many other examples can be given:[21] instead of providing that a failure to prove to the required standard should result in an acquittal, a separate category of not guilty cases has been created where the evidence is insufficient to substantiate the charge (Article 162(3), 1996 CPL) the 'clear implication is that defendants found not guilty on grounds of insufficient evidence are somehow *less* not guilty';[22] Article 38, 1996 CPL makes it an offence for a defence lawyer to 'help the suspect of a crime or defendant to conceal, destroy or fabricate evidence; collude with each other . . . etc.' (the terms 'collude', 'threaten', 'induce' etc. are not defined); while some commentators assumed that the trial judge had been converted into a neutral referee by the 1996 CPL, there is nothing in the new law to prevent a judge from reading the case materials before the trial, interrogating witnesses at trial or engaging in investigations before, during or after the trial; courts cannot quash a conviction obtained on the ground of error, the only remedy being to remand for retrial (Article 191, 1996 CPL), and the reliance upon unlawful evidence is not in any event a ground for retrial; and behind all of this lies, as we have seen, Article 306 of the Criminal Law[23] which provides, *inter alia*, that:

> If, in criminal proceedings, a defender or agent ad litem destroys or forges evidence, helps any of the parties destroy or forge evidence, or coerces the witness or entices him into changing his testimony in defiance of the facts or give false testimony, he shall be sentenced to fixed-term imprisonment of not more than three years or criminal detention; if the circumstances are serious, he shall be sentenced to fixed-term imprisonment of not less than three years but not more than seven years.
>
> Where a witness's testimony or other evidence provided, shown or quoted by a defender or agent ad litem is inconsistent with the facts but is not forged intentionally, it shall not be regarded as forgery of evidence.

---

[21] See generally Hecht (1996a) who identified many of the issues at the very point of 'reform' of the law and who remains an expert source in this regard. See also, Lynch (2010b). Lynch points out that although the Western media focused heavily on the closed commercial secrets portion of the Stern Hu trial, with some commentators arguing that it violated China's domestic law (in particular Article 152 of the 1996 Criminal Procedure Law which states that criminal trials, except those involving state secrets or personal private matters, are open to the public), Article 121 of the Supreme People's Court Interpretation of the Criminal Procedure Law provides that in cases involving 'business secrets' the court may close the trial if a party requests it. Lynch further points out that the reference to 'a party' is not restricted to the prosecutor or any of the defendants but can include any interested party including Rio Tinto, the Chinese steel companies involved or the Chinese government.
[22] *Ibid.*, at p. 65. This resembles the Scottish verdict of 'Not proven'.
[23] We have earlier discussed an equivalent chilling provision under Article 37, Criminal Law. Article 36 was relied upon to convict the defence lawyer Li Zhuang for allegedly fabricating evidence in his defence of an alleged triad boss in Chongqing by it was said 'coaching' him to falsely claim forced confession: Ng Tze-wei (2010d).

There is accordingly plenty of latitude *within the legal process* to engage in practices which critics often imagine to be not in conformity with the relevant legal provisions.[24] An illustration of how things might get worse without changes to the letter of the law is seen in figures supplied by John Kamm, who points out that more than twice as many people were arrested for 'endangering state security' in China in 2008 as compared with 2007[25] and in the conclusion of Donald Clarke that the environment for lawyers who get involved in cases or activities of any sensitivity – and it is important to remember this is not a large number – has distinctly worsened over the last several months.[26] Both of these experts are fully aware that certain practices (such as de-licensing of lawyers and firms) can be undertaken by *using* existing legal provisions, but many other commentators have assumed that practices which they regard as coercive or oppressive are in fact contrary to legal precepts.

This is not to deny that some of the most egregious practices *are* violations of existing legal provisions. Thus, although courts may turn a blind eye to confessions obtained by torture, the law is clear that it is 'strictly forbidden to extort confessions by torture and to collect evidence by threat, enticement, deceit or other unlawful means' (Article 43, 1996 CPL). State officials charged with investigating crime are fully aware of this proscription. Indeed, because of this, violations of the law are conducted in secret. This indeed seems to have happened in the 'anti-mafia' campaign in Chongqing in which state officials although using systematic torture did so in a clandestine operation.[27] Officers also know that they might, if occasionally and contingently, be sanctioned for breach should the matter become a matter of such public concern that it has to be assuaged by real or symbolic action.[28]

Nevertheless, Liu and Halliday (2009)[29] demonstrate a significant indeterminacy in the nature of 'law' in China – whether it comprises not only of laws and regulations but also of policies, interpretations and political pronouncements on legal issues – as well as the indeterminate meaning of individual provisions. Accordingly, even if we acknowledge

---

[24] A similar point is made by Trevaskes (2007a). Discussing 'strike hard' campaigns, Susan Trevaskes draws attention to the dominant court, prosecution and police discourse of 'doing justice in accordance with the law' (*yifa*).

[25] Congressional-Executive Commission on China Report, October 2009.

[26] *Ibid*.

[27] See, for example, Mooney (2010).

[28] According to a report in *Xinhua* (17 November 2009) the Baita District Court in Liaoyang City, Liaoning Province found four Henan police officers guilty of torturing to extract a confession from a suspect who died in police custody. On 3 April 2009, the four officers drove the suspect, named Zhai, from Henan to Liaoyang, where, with the cooperation of local police, they detained and interrogated him in a local hotel, a site not subject to video-taping. During the interrogation, the police tortured Zhai with electric shocks. Zhai began having trouble breathing and was rushed to a local hospital, where he died. In ruling on the case, the Baita judge noted the appraisal of medical experts at China Medical University, who stated that Zhai's underlying heart condition, and not the torture, caused his death. The warning to state officials that this case gives out, may be thought to be more symbolic than real evidenced by the fact that the officers were given short prison sentences that were immediately suspended and then they were released from custody.

[29] See, in particular, Table 1 at pp. 923–924 detailing the major regulations and notices (27) related to lawyer representation between 1979 and 2004.

that it is difficult to differentiate in terms of primacy/legitimacy between laws, regulations, edicts, official pronouncements, exhortations to justice officials,[30] it has to be emphasized that some matters of which complaint is made, including some treatment of activist lawyers, is done under the colour of law and referable to particular legal provisions. This, of course, is not meant to imply that all legal rules in China are 'lawful' in the deeper sense of 'law' or protected from constitutional challenge, difficult as that may be in China.

At a practical level, it appears that the police utilize the cloak of the law to legitimize many of their activities. They can and do choose whether to put an individual into the criminal system or into the administrative system or, indeed, to exclude the individual from both; the police can and do subject individuals to extended detention under apparent legal authority; they can and do extract evidence in secret so that false statements, crafted by the police, take on a semblance of truth by being signed by compliant civilians or suspects without these individuals necessarily adopting the contents by reason of illiteracy or otherwise; they can and do extract confessions from suspects who do not have the benefit of counsel; their theory of the incident, whether a crime should be homicide or injury for example, can be and is imposed through compliance with the law and attendant procedural rules; and, even if it is facially proscribed, the institutional structure allows the possibility of torture and reliance upon the products of torture as evidence; the police may and do at their discretion turn aside requests for supplemental investigation; and prosecutors can and do endorse police decisions even where they doubt the evidence or its completeness.

Similarly, while Article 47, 1996 CPL appears to require oral testimony by witnesses, Article 157 of the Criminal Procedure Law allows prosecutors/judges to read out the statements of any and all witnesses. Against this permissive background, prosecutors have developed an informal rule under which witnesses are not called to give evidence and judges, for their part, have adopted rules of practice which generally result in the refusal of permission to call available witnesses for either the defence or prosecution. In the result and perfectly 'lawfully', no prosecution witness will appear at court and vary his/her account under examination-in-chief or through the process of cross-examination; there is no concept of a 'hostile' witness who fails to come up to proof; no witness will come forward at trial who has given a proof of evidence to the defence lawyer which conflicts with one previously given to the police; and those witnesses who do appear (defendants), appear under compulsion to appear and compulsion to answer.

Looked at from this perspective, for state officials (but not for suspects, defendants or their lawyers) much of the law and the architecture of its institutions is in some marked degree *enabling*.

---

[30] Clark (2008), p. 834, drawing upon Albert Chen (2004).

THE CAPACITY FOR CASE CONSTRUCTION

Although the permissive character of the legal process enables state actors to construct criminal cases *using legal provisions*[31] to achieve the objectives they themselves set, it is now widely recognized that, in addition, the formal rules of an organization do not prescribe practice;[32] and that formal rules themselves generate secret *informal organizational practices* which are often there in order, as the members see it, to better realize the formal goals. Thus, police officers know the rules against torture but they are also aware that the use of torture may better secure confessions upon which the wider system places high priority. As they also know, the informal 'organizational' practices which they utilize for this purpose and to which a blind eye may be turned are necessarily subterranean in character and in no sense part of the public rules and principles which represent 'the law'.

In this setting, it is important to note that 'cases' are not objects waiting to be 'discovered': they are all *socially constructed*. In turn, the processes of construction are, depending upon the point at which the case is in the criminal process, more or less (in China, mostly less) visible to the outside observer.[33] At every point in the process, what might appear to be a constraint on state actors is less so because the legal process is fraught with inconsistencies and contradictions and because state actors have developed their own internal organizational practices to guide their everyday behaviour.

In constructing cases, the police are accorded the powers and the space in which to gather and create evidence in secret. Torture is prohibited in the letter of the law but the law does not exclude reliance upon its product at trial and the police have been accorded *de facto* freedom of action because they are not under meaningful external supervision. In these circumstances, it is not surprising that police in China, in the same way that occurred with police in England and Wales, the United States of America, Canada and elsewhere,[34] have developed their own informal rules of behaviour which better enable them, as they see it, to meet the evidential needs of the case at trial.

At the same time, police, prosecutors, and judges have developed informal practices which effectively eliminate meaningful opportunities to invoke a defence at any stage of the process. Whilst 'shelter and investigation' are no longer on the books, the defendant

---

[31] Of course, even in this system there is considerable room for illegality. The use by the police of agents, shoulder-hitters and thugs against activists and reformist counsel; the use of extended detention; the recourse to black jails; the use of alternative methods for dealing with dissidents are simply examples of egregious practices which are *outside* the law.

[32] See Etzioni (1961); and Feeley (1973). As Feeley (1973) put it, a functional systems model of criminal justice, whilst recognizing the influence of legal rules and procedures, places greater emphasis upon informal factors which shape decisions and behaviour so that 'the "rules" the organization members are likely to follow are the "folkways", or informal "rules of the game" within the organization; the goals they pursue are likely to be personal or sub-group goals; and the roles they assume are likely to be defined by the functional adaptation of these two factors' (*ibid.*, at p. 413).

[33] Of course, all the actors take part in the process of construction but, as we have seen, in China cases are almost exclusively constructed by state actors.

[34] See, for example, Bittner (1967); Black (1971); Ericson (1982); Graef (1989); Manning (1977); and Shearing (1981).

continues to be subjected to custodial detention and police interrogation, isolated from family and friends, against a background of leniency for those who confess; will generally not be allowed to see a lawyer until late in the process because of practices and 'ploys' developed by the police; and will find that the defence lawyer is disempowered to assist because he/she has not been given disclosure of the prosecution case until just before or even at the trial.

Judges (who themselves might lack adequate legal qualifications) have developed informal rules under which they become involved in the investigation under an enabling legal process. Without infringing the letter of the law, judges become partners with the prosecutor at trial in cross-examining the suspect, disallowing witnesses, attenuating speeches of defendants and defence counsel. Judges can and do impose on defendants a burden to displace prosecution evidence, including any said to have been obtained by torture. Judges can and do rely upon evidence obtained by torture because the law imposes no burden on the prosecution to disprove torture nor does it prevent a court from relying upon other evidence of dubious provenance although it must be stressed new rules relating to evidence in handling criminal cases and death penalty cases have created a forum in which it will be somewhat easier in theory for the defence to challenge illegally-obtained evidence.[35]

Additionally, even if they privately entertain doubts about the persuasiveness of the evidence or the correctness of the prosecution, organizational rules have been developed so that judges can and do refer cases for decision to committees the members of which may have no legal qualification, have not been parties to the trial and may have motivations unrelated to evidence sufficiency. In making determinations themselves, courts can operate sub-organizational rules which reflect generalized policy choices (not only where there is a 'strike hard' campaign but more generally in compliance with internally-set quotas and targets) so as to affect the verdict and the sentence imposed on individual defendants.[36]

There should be nothing surprising about this overall architecture of the criminal process because it has been produced by design and not by accident. As Fu Hualing (1998) has observed, for example, the 1996 CPL is the product of power struggles between different state entities: the Supreme People's Court was the most liberal, supporting early intervention by lawyers which would provide it with an indirect mechanism for imposing some control on police and prosecutors (since the court is reliant on the official records prepared by police and prosecutor). A similar view held by the Ministry of Justice, the body which regulates the legal profession, proposed early defence representation whenever compulsory measures (such as detention or arrest) were imposed. For their part, the Supreme People's Procuratorate were agreeable to earlier legal representation but took the position that involvement should be different at different stages and defence

---

[35] See, Ng Tze-wei (2010a); and Jacobs (2010).
[36] According to news reports, during the 2010 World Soccer Cup, in order to fight against the online soccer gambling, the banker would be charged with opening a gambling site and upon conviction would receive up to 10 years in prison, the previous maximum being 3 years. The Criminal Law of the People's Republic of China (Sixth Amendment) set up such a named offence in 2006 to 'strike hard' at online soccer gambling activities. See Zhu Yan (2010).

lawyers should not be allowed to 'interfere with the normal investigation'.[37] Against this, the Ministry of Public Security opposed lawyers' involvement at the investigation stage (Liu and Halliday, 2009).

Accordingly, as described by Liu and Halliday (2009), it was no accident that the legal process 'incorporated contradictory concepts and ideologies' (p. 929). As these authors argue, these contradictions included: (i) striking at crimes versus protecting human rights; (ii) substantive versus procedural law; (iii) efficiency versus justice; and (iv) rights of victims versus rights of defendants. Thus, for example, both striking crime (Article 1, 1996 CPL) and protecting rights (Article 2, 1996 CPL) were incorporated as basic principles.

Nor should there be any surprise by the parallel finding that the principal institutions (police, procuratorate and courts) are interlocking mechanisms held in a more or less state of equilibrium by various forms of internal and intra-institutional forms of audit and accounting related to such matters as the detection rate, the speed of detection rate, the rate of prosecutorial approvals of arrest, the rate of bail, the rate of summary procedure cases and allowable rate of acquittals. The institutions, to paraphrase Article 7, 1996 CPL, coordinate their efforts but do not check each other to ensure the correct and effective enforcement of law: it is a system of co-operation without restraint.

This too is a result of design not accident. While, for example, the procuratorate can 'supervise' it cannot do this over either the investigation or the trial since substantively the police and the court respectively are actually in control of these forums. Although the procuratorate has the right to request that the police undertake supplementary investigation, if the police choose not to the procuratorate may renew the request but the outcome is usually equally fruitless. Moreover, while the procuratorate has a power to question police decisions on such matters as failing to file a case or on court procedure which has violated litigation procedure by issuing a correcting opinion (*jiuzheng yijian*) to which the police or court must respond (Articles 87 and 169, 1996 CPL), if the police or courts stick to the original decision there is nothing that the procuratorate can do.[38] And, despite the prediction that the legal system would become more forensic in character, with judges having to master a more substantial body of law and to rule on evidentiary issues,[39] criminal trials in China remain largely unsophisticated, devoid of substantive or evidentiary issues and in which the naked assertion of authority through the judge always prevails.[40]

---

[37] Fu (1998), p. 41 quoting LAC, submission of Supreme People's Procuratorate on the Amendment of the 1996 Criminal Procedure Law.

[38] See, Liu and Halliday (2009) at p. 930.

[39] Peerenboom (2002): 'Reforms to the trial process have put pressure on judges to improve their performance. After twenty years of legal development, there is a much more substantial and technical body of law for judges to master. The move away from an inquisitorial to an adversarial system requires judges to rule on evidentiary issues in response to the objections of legal counsel. Judges must also deal with well-trained lawyers who make increasingly sophisticated and complex legal arguments' (p. 293).

[40] We say 'through' rather than 'of' given that, as we have detailed earlier, judges cannot be said in general to exercise authority in their own right.

WHAT DRIVES CASE CONSTRUCTION

The constructionist perspective provides a framework for action not a straitjacket on the actors. In other words, the constructionist theory tells us only what the state actors *may* do within the legal process and within the institutional frameworks established through law: it does not prescribe what they should do or what they choose to do in fact. By way of illustration, although the legal process confers on the police considerable licence in dealing with suspects, it does not demand that they behave in particular ways as, for example, by using blandishments or threats or resorting to torture in order to secure confessions. Although it is a matter of legitimate interest to ask why the legal framework bearing upon state actors is in this sense permissive, in order to understand the actions of the police, prosecutors, judges we need to look at the underlying values, ideologies, motivations and structures that enable, encourage or determine actual behaviour.

THE SETTING

According to some commentators, one important factor bearing upon the structure of the institutions and the behaviour of actors within them is the background of crime in Chinese society. It seems that, in the post-reform era after 1979, crime rates in China (although possibly considerably lower than in Western developed states)[41] have risen substantially along with industrialization, urbanization and the transition to a market economy together with an extraordinary increase in social mobility, migration, and social and economic inequality.[42] Contrary to the old-style rhetoric that crime is a product of a class-based society, it is widely accepted in China that crime will be a continuing social phenomenon and that fear of crime, however engendered, will remain an influence on public policy.[43] This context it is said provides a sense of legitimacy to the actions of state officials in behaving as they do. Accordingly, in this perspective, it is hardly surprising

---

[41] Caution needs to be exercised in relation to crime figures in China for many reasons. Apart from the fact that so-called minor infractions may be classified as misdemeanours rather than 'crimes', there is no reason to believe that reported crime accurately reflects actual crime since under-reporting is likely to be high and it is widely accepted that official police records document crimes that can be solved rather than crimes that have been reported.

[42] For accounts, see Dutton (1992); Tanner (1999); Bakken (2000); Bakken (2005).

[43] On 13 June 2010, Vice Minister of Public Security, Zhang Xinfeng, deployed the 'strike hard action in 2010' via tele-conference in Beijing, thereby starting a seven-month long 'strike hard' nationwide campaign. Zhang emphasized the action as a way to implement the central leaders' instructions and fight against a complex internal security situation. Public security organs were told to stick to the policy without any hesitation, strike hard and suppress by law various serious violent crimes, increase the case detection rate, so as to create social order in China. The focus of the strike hard action in 2010 included: individual violent personal crime with extreme impact on the public's sense of safety, crimes involving explosives and guns, mafia and gangsters, fraud through telecommunications, abducting and trafficking children and women, theft and burglary and robbery, crimes related to drugs, pornography and gambling. The police were called upon to work hard and use their own practical actions to submit a piece of paper in the 'examination' to satisfy the Party and the people. See, 'The Ministry of Public Security Convened Tele-conference

that public support for government 'strike hard' campaigns[44] or specific drives against corruption[45] or in favour of the death penalty[46] appears strong and that state actors might feel considerable freedom to dispense justice with a strong hand.

Add to this the widely-held view that in China people are said to have a strong preference for social stability and favour group interests over the individual, it is argued that high-level state actors feel no pressure to adopt a 'rights-based' approach to criminal justice policy (law-formulation) and that low-level state actors are averse to operating criminal justice in ways that would be more rights-sensitive (as by renouncing extended detention or eschewing torture or providing early and full prosecution disclosure). In a thoughtful discussion of whether the Party in China actually supports the rule of law, Randall Peerenboom (2004) states:

> Repeated appeals to rule of law raise expectations among people that the government will act accordingly. As a result, the large gap between the ideal of rule of law and actual practice could undermine the authority of the government. However, in the case of criminal defendants, the public seems willing to tolerate a considerable gap between law on the books and actual practice (p. 1063).

Peerenboom makes the point that calls for removal of the Party from criminal justice in China are unlikely to have the effects desired by many reformers because, *inter alia*, there is little reason to believe that a democratic government will take the 'rights of criminals' (*sic*) seriously. He argues that while judges (anywhere in the world) tend not to get too

---

to Deploy its "Strike Hard Action in 2010"', available at http://news.sohu.com/20100613/n272785675.shtml.

[44] See, for example, the evidence collated in Peerenboom (2004) at pp. 1049ff. See also, Trevaskes (2007a). Trevaskes, having critically examined major *yanda* campaigns, points out that there have been numerous smaller 'specialized offensives' using the *yanda* policy and rhetoric since the end of *yanda* in 2003 including, *inter alia*, a province-wide *yanda* campaign in Liaoning that began in September 2005.

[45] The well-publicized drive against black societies (*dahei*) in Chongqing spearheaded by a chief of police (Wang Lijun) brought in from Liaoning province by the Chongqing Party Secretary, Bo Xilai, is reputed to have attracted widespread public support within Chongqing and brought Bo Xilai national fame. See, Mooney (2010). The focus of the crackdown, said to have been on high-ranking officials, had by early 2010 led to dozens of officials sentenced to prison terms, the confiscation of thousands of weapons and some nine death sentences passed. However, serious doubts have now emerged on this campaign, particularly the revelations of lawyer Zhu (who defended Fan Qihang) regarding systematic torture used to obtain confessions.

[46] See, Hu Yunteng (2002) where it is reported that over 99 per cent of Chinese citizens support the death penalty and a significant fraction (around 20 per cent) believe that there should be more executions. See also Bakken (2000) reporting on a survey of 15 000 people in China which showed that almost 60 per cent of respondents thought that the state's handling of criminals was too lenient while only 2 per cent thought it too strict: *ibid.*, at p. 395. But see also Oberwittler and Qi (2009). This survey shows a good deal of indifference and ignorance towards the death penalty with only about 25 per cent of respondents being interested in the subject and only slightly more claiming some or much knowledge. Overall, the survey suggests, in line with Western studies, that when confronted with concrete cases, respondents become more cautious and that accordingly support for the death penalty among the Chinese population is more likely to be expressive or symbolic. Nevertheless, even in cases where the offender was below 18 years of age at the time of commission of the crime (for whom the death penalty is not available under Chinese law) only 33 per cent of respondents supported such a limitation.

much out of step with public sentiment, clearly in China the lack of judicial independence means that the Party's calls to 'strike hard' are likely to have a greater impact on Chinese judges than similar appeals to wage war on crime would have on more established and independent judiciaries.

In seeking to explain, as he puts it, the failure to implement reforms, Peerenboom (2006) rejects Western news accounts which locate the problem in political ideology ('the repressive state out to persecute criminal defendants and repress political dissidents'):

> Political ideology is at best only a small factor. Most cases are run-of-the-mill criminal cases involving theft, murder, rape, drugs, and the like. While crime disrupts social order, criminals do not directly challenge the Party's right to rule. . . . [W]hat distinguishes criminal law from other areas of law is the lack of public support for criminal law reforms; the majority of the citizenry see such reforms as harming, rather than furthering, their interests. At the same time, there is little support for criminals. The government has responded to the fears of the public by acceding to demands to crack down on crime. Thus, interest group politics explain much of China's harsh approach on crime . . . (p. 845).

Echoing the points made earlier, Peerenboom (2006) further argues that the harsh treatment of criminals also results from cultural factors, including preferences for social stability, group rights over the individual, the lack of a strong tradition of individual rights and the traditional emphasis in China on substantive justice over procedural justice; and economic/social factors including rising crime rates which have resulted in a popular backlash against liberal reforms. To all of this he adds institutional factors:

> China's weak legal institutions have been unable to resist the combined pressure from an angry public demanding heavy punishments to deter criminals, and a political regime seeking to shore up its legitimacy by pandering to the public's attitude for vengeance. Indeed, key institutions have not fully committed to reforms. Not surprisingly, perhaps, given their law and order orientation, the police and procuracy in particular have resisted many of the changes. Even the judiciary has been at best lukewarm (pp. 846–7).

Peerenboom concludes that notwithstanding the relatively short time frame and marginal improvements for some suspects, the criminal reforms have for the most part been a failure at the basic level of compliance.

These and similar arguments while outwardly persuasive seem on further reflection to have differential explanatory power depending upon what issue – for example, reform of the law or the actions of state officials on the ground – is being addressed. Thus, while the apparent hostility of public opinion to 'criminals' and by association 'suspected criminals' might influence (or be encouraged by) those charged with the task of formulating a code of criminal procedure or rules of evidence (e.g., in considering whether to abolish the death penalty), it is less obvious that this would routinely impact on the behaviour of police (whose significant actions and conduct often occur in private settings),[47] prosecutors and judges in *everyday criminal cases* many of which are low-profile, localized and lacking an audience in court. Given this, it is necessary to unpack the issues being addressed in order to better appraise the argument that external factors shape issues in particular ways.

---

[47] Where egregious conduct on the part of the police, or indeed other state officials, becomes notorious, the public can become hostile.

So far as *law reform* is concerned, proposals to change the formal law, as by introducing a right to silence, may run up against public opinion in China which may see or be persuaded to see such 'reforms' as soft on crime. And this no doubt goes some way to explaining the relatively weak character of the modern reforms and the contradictions built into the 1996 CPL. Law is after all a product of political power and this often has a direct relationship to public opinion, itself susceptible to influence by the party-state.[48] In China, law is not meant to constrain official action. In China, due process principles have never been dominant ideologies. The state does not revere law for the inherent qualities which are assumed in liberal democracies but rather sees law as one key method by which power is exercised under a system of autocratic central control. As one official put it,[49] 'There is no question about where legal departments should stand. The correct political stand is where the Party stands.'

Similarly, policy pronouncements, as in 'strike hard' campaigns are likely to have some direct impact upon the actions of state actors such as the police, procuratorate and judges. Indeed, during our fieldwork at times when there was an official crackdown on crime, the court made direct reference to its role in serving the interests of the state when delivering judgment. In Case L-CO-X-44 on a charge of bribery, for example, the court said in convicting the defendant: 'In order to maintain the order of the socialist market economy and strike hard at crimes in the economic area, the court makes the award by law.' Similarly, in Case L-CO-X-35, the court stated: 'In order to strike hard at crimes of robbery, to protect people's persons and property, the court makes the award by law.' However, this does not appear to be a matter bearing heavily upon state actors in everyday cases and may often amount to little more than paying lip-service to a concurrent campaign.[50]

Nor do state actors regularly utilize the trial as a means of overtly promoting state policy. Whilst conceding that the trial may retain a didactic function in educating the defendant and the masses,[51] this tends to be muted (except in demonstration trials and high-profile cases) because it is ordinarily achieved through denunciation and sentence, features which are less evident when cases are so commonly disjunctive with many adjourned for judgment on another unspecified day and many lacking an audience.[52]

Finally, it is at least arguable that the social and political environment has a direct and negative impact upon defence lawyers. Michelson (2008) notes that while economic

---

[48] The link between public opinion and legitimacy (of both the courts and the party) are important issues on which we have no direct empirical evidence. See, Liebman (2005).

[49] Luo Gan, a then member of the Politburo Standing Committee reported in Kahn (2007).

[50] See also, Fu Hualing (2010). Fu Hualing argues that, with a significant re-orientation away from counter-revolutionary cases since the 1980s, criminal cases are becoming less important because they are no longer political in the sense that everyday cases for courts are crimes against property, inter-personal violence and crimes against public order.

[51] The early legal education campaign was at the time seen as an important social movement in China. See, for example, Eliasoph and Grueneberg (1981) reporting on a four-day visit to China in 1980 and a visit to a major exhibition, 'Socialist democracy and legal education' (*Shehui zhuyi minzhu yu fazhi jiaoyu zhanlan*).

[52] In many of the cases we observed in our fieldwork, few members of the public were present in court except where a parallel civil action was being undertaken or where a particularly egregious crime had stirred up emotions in the locality.

disincentives often encourage lawyers to 'cool out' their clients by concealing or obscuring viable legal options that may exist in the books,[53] in China '*politics* represents an additional operative logic: Just as the media remains beholden to state interests, political disincentives to advocate against state interests, too, remain palpable at the Chinese bar.'

CRIMINAL JUSTICE AS PROCESS AND SYSTEM

If we stand back, however, it becomes clear that much of the argument assumes that criminal justice in China operates as a legal *system* which comprises identifiable segmental parts: investigation, examination, adjudication. Thus, some commentators assert that many of the problems in China derive from weak institutions – lack of an effective mechanism to deal with legislative inconsistency; a weak and inadequately-trained judiciary; the lack of a constitutional court; a poorly trained, poorly equipped and poorly educated police force; and a procuratorate that is beset with problems of competency, unable to adjust to its new role in an adversarial system.[54]

Our evidence, however, overwhelmingly shows that in China the investigation, examination and adjudication functions in criminal cases operate as a *process*. The appearance of separate procedural stages belies a reality in which each unit reinforces the actions of the other such that there is a seamless process from approval of arrest to conviction. The common scenario, underpinned by audits and performance indicators, is for prosecutors to assist the progression of the police case by moving it forward with or without supplementary investigation and despite misgivings or concerns that they might entertain over the quality or provenance of the evidence; and for judges to assist by carrying out their own investigations, cross-examining the defendant, and making good deficits in the police case before, during or after the trial. Despite the surface fissures or tensions between these state institutions (undeniably real and of importance in the political arena), the ties that bind are deep and overarching so that all the parts are interlocking and interdependent, moving cases inexorably, though not always smoothly,[55] to a single conclusion – *conviction*.

For their part, and typical of bureaucratic institutions, Chinese judges (whether experienced or not) are able to assert and exude authority over other courtroom actors and the defendant notwithstanding that key decisions may lie in the hands of others. Indeed, in this way, judges seek to project an authority that they do not in fact possess. Judges can and do impose rules and procedures on other courtroom actors by stopping prosecutors from addressing the court; stopping defence lawyers questioning prosecution evidence; stopping defendants from speaking; stopping prosecutors/defence lawyers from bringing witnesses to court; relieving lawyers of case responsibility when the progress of a case

---

[53] Referring to Blumberg (1967). There is an extensive literature on plea bargaining in particular which discusses the role of defence lawyers in 'managing' clients. For an analysis of defence solicitors in England and Wales, see, McConville, Hodgson, Bridges and Pavlovic (1994).

[54] See, for example, Peerenboom (2004), p. 1069.

[55] In isolated cases, the process may be disrupted by defendants or criminal defence lawyers who refuse to co-operate.

is threatened; and, generally, curtailing discussion/debate/proceedings. For this reason, the relative lack of appeals and protests is a product of a process which has created the outcomes rather than as evidence of increasing judicial autonomy.[56]

There is truth in Donald Clarke's observation that the courts are only 'co-ordinate' with other bureaucratic agencies rather than in any way superior to them, but in criminal trials courts serve the important function of *coordinating* the work of other institutions. This is most clearly seen in the roles of the adjudicative committee and the political-legal committee[57] – the body that ultimately manages all the state criminal justice institutions – and it is acted out on a day-to-day basis by the courts themselves in their interactions with the procuratorate[58] and defence lawyers. It is the judges who manage the trial proceedings and, although often directed by and subservient to external forces, ultimately give apparent coherence and public legitimacy to the prosecution case. In China, what is at work is not a set of shared values among all courtroom actors (though there is a widespread assumption of guilt and co-operation in the establishment of officially prescribed guilt) but a clear differential distribution of power which, though usually subterranean, emerges in open court from time to time and is further evidenced in our interviews.

Common values are not necessarily shared by or motivating all the actors but this does not mean that the actors lack personal values or, indeed, estimable personal values. As our research shows, many respondents (judges, prosecutors as well as defence lawyers) espoused values and articulated aspirations that would be considered worthy and progressive in any setting. These, however, struggle to find a voice within the process. In Chinese criminal courts there is no room for what Fuller famously described as 'reasonable argument' (about values etc.) as a central characteristic of the adjudicative process evidenced both by the fact that in the ordinary case the defence lawyer is virtually silent except so far as his or her co-operation is required to move the process along and, in the extraordinary case, defence lawyers who speak up are silenced by the judge or removed from the case.[59]

Despite this, the criminal justice process in China, as in other inquisitorial systems and those in the common law, is not insensitive to securing 'reliability' in everyday cases (reliability being an attribute fixed to cases by the process rather than being an inherent

---

[56] Compare Fu Hualing (2010). In a thoughtful and rich account, Fu Hualing argues that courts are becoming more assertive in mobilizing legal power including behaving aggressively in dealing with horizontal relations with the police and procuracy: *ibid.*, pp. 6–7. While some judges no doubt have secured authority over individual prosecutors (as our research shows), we found no evidence that courts confront the police in any meaningful way and the authority of individual judges over individual prosecutors should not be confused with the relational position of courts and the procuratorate, the latter increasingly seeking to gain authority over police investigations and to assert itself more in the court.

[57] Where, of course, judges may not have the decisive voice.

[58] Whilst the near-certainty of conviction in criminal cases demonstrates that the requirements of state policies have subverted rule of law precepts, not all judges have internalized the demands of the ruling elite setting out in our interviews claims for greater independence of the courts and standing and status as legal professionals.

[59] As reported earlier, one defence lawyer was removed from a case in our research sample and there are other examples of lawyers being prevented from raising issues concerning such matters as the legal nature of the Falun Gong (Tang Jitaian and Liu Wei) or punished for raising the issue of torture (Li Zhuang).

attribute) and seeks to achieve an accommodation between reliability and efficiency. In China, however, the accommodation that has been sought resides in good part in out-of-sight investigations and out-of-court determinations. Investigations which 'fail' through lack of sufficient evidence or palpably illegal action on the part of the police are 'managed' wherever possible outside the courtroom environment and have affixed a 'lawful' administrative tag. Similarly, cases advanced by the procuratorate which are too weak to continue may be quietly winnowed out of the process and hidden from view or finessed into the administrative track. Those which make it into the criminal process are managed in such a way that weaknesses are masked by the process itself so that no 'failures' are allowed to appear, a process that is buttressed by the various sanctions that can be imposed within each of the state institutions by the relevant bureaucratic superiors.

We noted earlier in assessing China's move towards the rule of law that some commentators have tended to underplay the importance of the criminal process because crime, it is said, forms a relatively small part of the lives of Chinese citizens and because most criminal cases anyway are everyday matters that do not involve an overt political challenge to the dominance of the Party. There is an element of truth in this but the conclusion drawn is far from obvious.

Whereas in the broader political economy accountability in liberal understanding is based upon the notion that political superiors and state institutions are responsible to society,[60] China's criminal process operates on the understanding that accountability is ultimately a matter for the Party while those at the front line (police, prosecutors and judges) are called to account in the event of any departure from the Party line embodied in part by performance indicators and the co-ordinates of inter-institutional auditing grids. It is for this reason that criminal justice becomes a process and it is for this reason that it is *a process within a system*, a Party-centred system which demands certainty of outcome (conviction).[61]

High-profile dissident and criminal cases may be the litmus test of any country's claims regarding the rule of law and respect for human rights, but the state also depends upon the courts to process everyday cases in an 'efficient' and 'reliable' manner, with the minimum cause for concern and unwelcome external attention.[62] In order to secure this outcome, the state needs to have official actors (police, prosecutors and judges) upon whom it can rely and actors (defence lawyers) about whom it does not need to worry (because they are powerless).[63] Even though criminal transgressions may not directly touch the lives of proportionately many of its citizens, the state's management of, disposition towards and use of the criminal justice process is central to an understanding of the wayward history of the modern 'reforms'.

---

[60] This is, of course, relative autonomy as Isaac Balbus noted (1977).

[61] We accept that the Party-state, even when utilizing the most extreme rhetoric, recognizes and, indeed, encourages a degree of local autonomy, particularly in cases which excite public interest. Indeed, the 'Three Supremes' doctrine, by weakening the importance of the rule of law, consciously empowers local officials and agencies at the expense of the courts.

[62] It has become increasingly clear that a major concern of the Party-state is less the legal threat posed by activist lawyers, rights-defenders and other critics and more the media attention that these groups and individuals have been able to mobilize in support of their concerns.

[63] See further, Sheskin (1981).

In this context, it is no surprise that courts need little reminding of what is expected of them. As Pitman Potter (1999) has remarked, in an environment of formalism that conflates policy ideals with the interpretation and enforcement of law, China's institutions function largely according to policy priorities imposed on them by the Party machine so that, where the requirements of regime policies (the system) conflict with the requirements of rule according to law, as in criminal cases, the capacity of legal institutions suffer.[64]

Even if reminders are not needed, the institutions in China still get reminders. Courts, in general, are expected to respond positively to policy pronouncements by state officials as with the warning noted earlier issued against the importation of Western ideas. Indeed, the promulgation of the 'Three Supremes' policy, specifically designed to direct the work of courts, prescribes the guiding considerations which are, in order: the cause of the Party; the interests of the people; and the constitution and law.[65] This formulation represents a reversion to mass-line, populist justice based around notions of substantive rather than procedural justice and a conscious falling away in commitment to relatively autonomous technocratic institutions such as 'independent courts'.[66]

Similarly, whether the reduction in the frequency and intensity of 'strike hard' campaigns is evidence of the courts having greater autonomy is at least an open question. For some experts, this is a sign that the courts are less vulnerable to a politically-oriented arbitrary process. For Fu Hualing, the smaller scale and less aggressive *ad hoc* campaigns against crime are now largely contained within the legal framework:[67]

> Courts in particular keep a degree of distance from the politics of crime, and in their institutional and procedural design, the courts are able to factor-in, internalize and absorb the arbitrariness of the political process. Because of the ability to capture political intrusions, criminal trial is much less volatile and more predictable.

Our research suggests that rather than being contained by the legal process, the Party continues to control the legal process and the criminal courts act according to the proclaimed ideologies of the state which thereby seeks to secure legitimacy in perhaps less overt ways.[68]

Throughout the process, courts pay 'symbolic homage'[69] to the slender tenets of criminal procedure and individual rights that exist within the 1996 CPL. On opening the trial, the judge will ask when the defendant received the Bill of Prosecution so as to ensure that it had been received at least ten days before the trial; the judge will advise the

---

[64] Potter (2004), p. 472.
[65] See, 'Supreme People's Court Wang Shengjun: In Meeting the Needs of the People and Work Hard', available at http://news.xinhuanet.com/politics/2008-06/16/content_8378100.htm (last viewed 16/05/2010).
[66] An alternative view is that this is simply an attempt to rehabilitate the judiciary in the face of clear loss of public confidence in the courts. In the view of a leading Chinese expert, this will fail because the independence of the judiciary has been undermined by interference from Party officials: He Weifang, 'Difficult Position of Judicial Reform and Paths', available at http://blog.sina.com.cn/s/blog_488663200100b0nw.html.
[67] Fu Hualing (2010).
[68] See, Sheskin (1981), p. 92.
[69] Ibid.

defendant that he or she can ask for the withdrawal of a member of the collegial panel; will advise the defendant that he or she can submit proof of innocence or reduced liability, conduct the defence personally or with the assistance of a lawyer and make a final statement at the conclusion of the debate; and at various points in the trial invite the defendant to introduce evidence (such as evidence of torture) or make a statement.

In this sense, the projection of an image of legitimacy is highly regarded by the court if not always faithfully reflected in practice.[70] Western legal norms associated with the role of law as a restraint upon state power may remain anathema to Chinese legal culture, but many of the trappings of foreign trials are readily embraced. Judges request lawyers to don lawyers' robes in cases that have attracted media interest and judges will attempt to comply with legal formalities in 'demonstration or emulation trials'. Judges also seek to secure legitimacy with the families of victims by seeing them either publicly or privately, before, during or after the trial, to reassure them that justice will be or is being done and to deflect any later challenge, particularly to the sentence. Similarly the increased emphasis upon recruiting 'qualified' personnel into the judiciary and procuratorate gives colour to the claim of legitimacy.[71]

Indeed, the 1996 reforms were in and of themselves an attempt to enhance the legitimacy of the criminal process rather than to displace the way in which state actors conduct their business. It was necessary for the state to remove the old system under which cases could go before a court only where 'the facts were clear and the evidence ample' because this was essentially the same standard required for conviction and accordingly led to 'verdict first, trial second', an image of trials which undercut any sense of trial legitimacy. What the reforms achieved, however, was to give an apparent sense of legitimacy while actually preserving the right of judges to investigate before trial and to receive evidence after trial, to examine and cross-examine witnesses and to continue with the transfer of major evidence to the judge before trial so that judges could still decide upon the verdict first. As our research shows, the differentiation of roles between judges and prosecutors in this regard was in fact a difference without distinction.[72]

Of course, as we have sought to make clear, it does not follow that courts are uninterested in 'truth' or 'reliability' as they see it. On the contrary, there are many instances where the prosecution case appears overwhelming or unchallenged and in

---

[70] As we have noted, courtrooms in China very commonly engage in practices which undercut the image of 'legitimacy'. This includes disorder on the collegial panel where judges not interested in the actual case before them will read papers or answer mobiles during the course of the hearing or even walk out of the court and take telephone calls and where judges are forced to silence lawyers or defendants who seek to challenge the case for the prosecution.

[71] The local study of a civil court in Hebei Province by Sida Liu suggests that there is a move away from recruiting army personnel into the judiciary and instead an emphasis upon recruiting college graduates. This suggests a functional transformation of the court from a military instrument of the proletarian dictatorship to a professional legal institution, 'or at least the image of a professional legal institution'. See, Sida Liu (2006) at p. 83.

[72] See also Hecht (1996a). Hecht argued that the reforms sought to enhance the status of courts by avoiding a situation in which they were reduced to announcing a decision made by others and avoiding a situation in which the court, having reviewed the evidence itself before trial, could come into conflict with the prosecutor thereby damaging its ability to project an image of independence.

which courts do seek to secure what they deem to be an accurate outcome. And if they have not screened out the case by persuading the prosecutor to drop it or divert it into the administrative system, there has been a decision from the outset that, on the material in the dossier, the defendant is probably guilty.

But in many cases, as they know, the prosecution is in some material respect flawed or may suffer badly under close scrutiny. In such cases, judges assist or come to the rescue of (less than competent) prosecutors and they (sometimes less than competent judges) close down or attenuate speeches of defence lawyers or defendant presentations because they realize that the threat to the integrity of the prosecution case is real. Similarly, they make inquiries or receive evidence after the trial in order to cement a necessary outcome – conviction. And when the case is to be discussed before the adjudicative committee, they are concerned to ensure beforehand that no stones have been left unturned so that they can escape internal criticism or censure. At this stage, before the adjudicative committee or before the president of the court, or before the political-legal committee, the die is already cast and any residual doubts over the validity of the charge or the defendant's guilt cannot prevail. This only goes to underscore the accuracy of the observation of Jerome Cohen (1968) made more than four decades ago when he wrote:

> At every stage of the criminal process the fate of the defendant depends entirely on the degree of conscientiousness and ability of government and Party officials, and he seldom has an opportunity to see and persuade the most authoritative of these officials (p. 50).

It is also important to remember that criminal courts in China, as elsewhere, deal with those regarded as the lowest stratum of society that fall into the criminal dragnet and that criminal courts for this reason attract, with notable heroic exceptions, lower quality legal representation[73] or neutralize or render impotent those lawyers who do appear. In this setting, it is the task of the courts to achieve or balance three often contradictory functions that emerge clearly from our research:[74] to maintain social order; to secure formal rationality; and to perpetuate the organization itself.[75]

In convicting defendants the courts in China help to maintain social order. They seek to do this by *ex facie* adherence to procedural rules and by paying lip-service to the demands of legal rationality.[76] Cases are presented as if the weight of evidence against the accused is overwhelming without a viable legal defence but this is a *result* of the process applied to the cases rather than a quality that the cases inherently possess, as our research and research elsewhere demonstrates in courts which have a defendant population similarly constructed and represented by impotent defence lawyers.[77] Together with

---

[73] See McConville and Mirsky (1986–87). It is also the case in China that lawyers are discouraged from getting involved in criminal cases because of the real threat of criminal action being taken against them as discussed at various points in this book.
[74] See Balbus (1971).
[75] See Sheskin (1981). See also Heydebrand (1979).
[76] The police, by contrast, occupy such a position in Chinese society that they can flout legal rationality in carrying out 'law and order' tasks on the street and continue to be the dominant legal institution.
[77] See, for example, McConville and Mirsky (1995).

throughput and 'efficiency' (i.e., cost-effectiveness),[78] it is these factors which help to perpetuate the organization itself.

The raw materials of the court, the defendant population, are highly significant in this regard. While 'crime' in and of itself gives rise to anger in Chinese society and a feeling that malefactors should be dealt with harshly, the admixture of indigents, illiterates and migrants who are seen as socially inferior generates a collective sense of unworthiness in state actors and even in low-level criminal defence lawyers. It is the combination of the assumption of guilt *and unworthiness* that defines the responses of the courtroom actors. Indeed, this combination of presumed guilt and unworthiness has a general importance in lowering the expectations of all courtroom actors so far as what is considered as deserving for defendants. In particular, the attributes of the defendants, as Jerome Skolnick[79] observed in another context, are brought into play in answering the question that is central to many of the cases which come before courts in China where the occurrence of the event itself (the injury or death) is not in dispute, namely: was the requisite intent present for the purpose of attributing criminal responsibility? It is precisely against this background that, as we have seen, stereotypical thinking on the part of courtroom actors comes to the fore.

REFORM

It should be abundantly clear by this stage that there is plenty of scope for reforming the criminal process, removing constraints on defence lawyers, strengthening the rights available to suspects, preventing the abuse of those who fall into the hands of the police as criminal suspects and reducing the probability of process error for those who are prosecuted. Candidates for reform might include: imposing strict controls and time limits on police powers of detention; giving criminal suspects the right to see a lawyer before and during police interrogation; requiring all police-suspect interrogations to be videotaped; providing full disclosure of prosecution evidence long in advance of trial; giving defence lawyers adequate powers and resources to engage in pre-trial investigations without fear of prosecution; establishing clear and enforceable rules of evidence in regard to such matters as the burden and standard of proof and the admissibility of evidence obtained unlawfully or by torture; requiring witnesses to turn up to court and be examined and cross-examined at trial; and strengthening the ability of judges to try cases without external interference and undue pressure to produce convictions.

It is necessary, however, to draw a distinction between those who believe that change will come about by changing the rules ('law reformers') and those who seek more fundamental change ('system reformers'). We first address the law reform movement.

---

[78] The introduction of such things as 'simplified ordinary procedure' and 'summary procedure' have to be seen, not as in any way related to the needs or interests of defendants, but rather as a direct response to the fiscal concerns of the state (whether local or central). As case load increases and as the demands upon the court correspondingly increase, so the courts have to respond by becoming more and more 'cost-effective' which is then represented as 'efficient'. See Heydebrand (1979). This has already paved the way in China for extensive discussions of plea bargaining.

[79] Skolnick (1966).

The 'law reform' agenda as we term it is open to various concerns at both theoretical and practical levels. As we have seen, calls for reform of the law are often based upon false assumptions about what the legal process actually is and accordingly put the focus on the wrong issue. Also, as we have seen, over-concentration on the formal rules misses the point that those rules do not necessarily condition let alone describe human behaviour. The effects of changing a rule are accordingly unpredictable and contingent. This means that while a change in a legal rule *may* lead to changed behaviour, the change may not be that which was intended but may, for example, simply result in a change in *accounting for* behaviour which otherwise remains unaffected by the 'reform'.[80] To some degree this is a feature of all legal systems although in many jurisdictions outside China there is greater opportunity to challenge and (ultimately) change the system through law reform and to insist that formal rules be obeyed in a comparatively transparent, public legal process.

This is not to downplay the work of law reformers but to contexualize their well-intentioned efforts.[81] It is also to make the important point that the efforts of these law reformers frequently run the risk of missing the real drivers of human action. To take but one example, China is in the process of introducing an exclusionary rule of evidence by virtue of which statements extracted from defendants by torture, inhuman or degrading treatment would be rendered inadmissible in evidence at trial.[82] The introduction of these rules into China's criminal justice process will not be of benefit to a defendant if, as now, once a representation is made that a confession had been extracted by torture, judges require defendants to prove that the alleged torture had in fact occurred. Nor would it be of benefit if judges continue to accept that any such challenge is trumped by a mere assertion by the police or prosecutor that no impropriety occurred. Moreover, so long as the audit, sanction and bonus culture remains a part of the 'supervision and sub-ordination' system legitimated in turn by 'performance indicators', it would be astonishing if judges were to routinely rule that the police had in fact engaged in torture. Such findings would, in short, threaten the whole institutional edifice upon which the criminal justice process rests and cast grave doubts upon the overarching system to which it pays tribute.

The challenges facing a law reform strategy are neatly captured in the proposals of Randall Peerenboom (2004) for improvements to administrative detention. Having dismissed the position taken by scholars and human rights activists who advocated abolishing administrative detention, Peerenboom, accepting that dramatic changes may not be possible, advances the following:

(i) limit the use of non-custodial sentences;
(ii) introduce national legislation with clear limits on the length of detention;
(iii) grant due process rights to all those subject to detention;
(iv) reform provisions relating to torture;
(v) increase transparency and accountability for detainees;

---

[80] This was pointed out many years ago by Banton (1964).
[81] See in this regard, Cohen (2009a).
[82] The exact definition of any such rule, given that there are great variations in different jurisdictions, is not relevant for the purposes of this argument.

(vi) instigate institutional reforms including increasing the authority of the courts;
(vii) educate the public over such matters as the actual rates of crime and the effectiveness of the various forms of detention; and
(viii) encourage local experimentation as by, for example, subjecting the death penalty to testing.

This is a formidable agenda but what is of more interest is not the merit of the proposals (many of which look wholly estimable) but what, in Peerenboom's view, would be needed to give them any chance of success. This set of enabling conditions deserves spelling out and the following is but a selection of the changes needed that are embedded in Peerenboom's argument:

(i) Since strike-hard campaigns encourage harsher treatment, the government should make greater efforts to ensure that police and prosecutors do not use their discretion to impose custodial sentences when not appropriate by, among other things, heightened supervision by external bodies. To achieve this, special committees might need to be set up to provide greater supervision of Re-education through Labour. Additionally, the procuratorate could be given the power to review custodial sentences considered too severe;
(ii) A new law should establish and clarify the scope and duration of the various forms of detention as well as the rights of detainees;
(iii) A new law should make clear that local regulations should not be able to impose greater restrictions on personal freedom beyond that set out in national laws;
(iv) Plea bargaining should be introduced on an experimental basis;
(v) All detainees should be allowed prompt review by a custodial judge;
(vi) Laws and regulations defining torture and cruel and inhuman treatment should be clarified and should be made to apply to private contractors that assume public law enforcement functions;
(vii) Training the PSB so that they do not engage in torture;
(viii) Providing that interrogations be videotaped and undertaken by two police officers;
(ix) Permitting family members and lawyers to have access to suspects during the investigation phase, and allowing detainees to challenge any police claims to 'state secrets' before a judge if this is used as a basis for denial of access;
(x) Where torture is alleged, there should be a mandatory investigation preferably by a committee whose members should include private citizens and members of the media;
(xi) Where state secrets is advanced by the state, detainees should be able to challenge the claim in a hearing held in camera;
(xii) Independent consultative citizen review boards should be established;
(xiii) The authority of the courts should be substantially increased with judges assuming the role of neutral arbiters rather than as state functionaries;
(xiv) The independence and authority of the procuratorate, police and legal profession should all be enhanced;
(xv) A change in the attitudes of the citizenry, the police, and other state-actors will be necessary;

(xvi) Sustained economic growth is a prerequisite to substantial improvements in the criminal justice.

Our purpose here is not to engage with the set of preconditions outlined although it must be said that it is somewhat alarming to see substantial improvements in human rights being tied to economic advancement and it has not been evident that economically-advanced areas of China have any more rights than those areas yet to reap the benefits of sustained economic growth. Setting that aside, it is obvious, as he concedes, that Peerenboom's proposals cannot succeed unless there are massive structural, social and political changes to Chinese society which include: introducing new and radically different laws, including protection of freedom of expression; creating new institutions to control the actions of state officials; making judges trained, independent (but supervised), actors; holding hearings in public with families and local and foreign press present; strengthening the police, procuratorate and the legal profession; re-educating the public; and changing attitudes among the citizenry, the police, and other state-actors.

This challenging agenda draws attention to a number of matters related to the law reformist movements. It follows from Peerenboom's analysis that changes to the legal rules will not, in and of themselves, be sufficient to institute changes that would be beneficial in the sense of improving rights and increasing system reliability. It is also clear that law reform cannot be divorced from state interest. Every proposal Peerenboom advances would require action on the part of the Party-state: to introduce constraining laws; to establish supervisory committees; to mandate open hearings and transparency; to authorize social experimentation; and to educate state actors and the public in such a way that they will discard existing prejudices and adopt new and liberal values. This is 'system reform' not 'law reform'.

One obvious problem with this approach is that there is no clear Party – or government – interest in making the changes proposed. The present meta-system has been established consciously and deliberately, not by chance or as part of an ill-thought out experiment, to assist the Party in securing social control through the form of law. The judiciary, though lacking independence and in many instances technical legal expertise, is not weak and in need of strengthening but assertive in court and dutiful to Party interests. So far as the state is concerned, the police and procuratorate do not need to change their values because those values – internal solidarity, the need to control the weak and powerless in society and fidelity to the Party – are the very values sought by the state. The problem is not so much the law as the context within which the law is situated and, of which, accordingly, it is only a part.

Basically, 'law reform' proposals assume and depend upon a state interest in 'reform' and assume system failure. However, it is not easy to see why the state should have an interest in fundamental as opposed to cosmetic reform since, for its purposes, the present criminal justice process and the master-system which directs it works. The downsides of the present arrangements (including mistaken verdicts, the creation of dissidents, the criticisms of international organiszations, bad publicity in the foreign press and an increasingly active local media) appear, so far as the state is concerned, of less consequence than the upsides (a cost-effective, loyal and reliable instrument for social control of the under-classes).

By contrast, 'system reformers' have no illusions about the possibility of achieving meaningful change under the existing political structures. They do not seek mere amendments to the rules but fundamental political change including freedom of the media and the abolition of political censorship. In this light, the *weiquan* movement or rights-defenders in China,[83] are fully aware of the magnitude of the problems they confront and their proposals call for deep-seated change directly arising out of their lived experiences. As they know only too well, rights-defenders in China are not simply fighting individual *cases*: they are taking on a *master-system* organized on aggregate lines expressed in terms of directives, quotas and performance indicators. In this context, 'reform' is not primarily about changing individual values of state actors, though that needs to be done, but about confronting institutionally-embedded cultures which create, generate and sustain such values. Similarly, the overhaul of legal, procedural and evidential rules, even if 'successful' (in the sense of becoming incorporated into non-porous legal provisions), would leave untouched the centres of power and influence from which all else derives personality and force. To grasp that nettle takes system reformers away from a focus on rules, regulations and laws and toward a genuine engagement with the state and its various agencies.

CONCLUSION

Criminal justice in China cannot be understood by studying the Criminal Procedure Law, the Criminal Law, the Lawyers Law or any of the other Laws that bear upon the process. Nor can it be understood by viewing trials and documenting the public actions of courtroom actors. The usual analytical grids which help define and delineate the structure, motor-force and direction of criminal justice systems prove of little value in this setting. In China, it is the larger socio-political context within which the criminal justice apparatus operates that gives it its character, infuses it with particular values, determinants and performance indicators – which are necessarily largely systemic and non-individuated – and directs the conduct of those who run it on a daily basis.

There is no doubt that the legal framework introduced by the 1996 Criminal Procedure Law differs in many respects from its predecessor and that the 2007 Lawyers Law and new rules relating to illegally-obtained evidence are welcome introductions. There are, as we have noted, traces of due process in the procedures and rules and in the aspirations of individual courtroom actors. Equally, actual or proposed amendments to official policies augur for enhanced protections for those who fall under criminal suspicion. As we have seen, a review system has been introduced in death penalty cases, there is a move to reduce reliance on illegally obtained evidence and videotaping of interrogations is being introduced into some procuratorates and prisons. These advances have limitations but they are nonetheless advances.

However, the new legal architecture, whatever the intentions of its authors, remains an *enabling* structure, not penetrating the underlying political economy and its core value system, which allows state actors to conduct business in ways that differ little from past practices sometimes under the colour of the law but also, in what Floria

---

[83] See the rich account given by Eva Pils (2007b). See also Fu and Cullen (2007 and 2008).

Sapio has termed 'zones of exception', carried out during investigation, detention, trial decision-making over verdict and sentencing, in clear violation of legal precepts. While 'counter-revolutionary crime' may have been consigned in a formal sense to history, defence lawyers are reported to continue to be detained,[84] dissidents are reported to continue to be arrested,[85] 'petitioners' and 'protesters' are sometimes harassed or detained and dumped in psychiatric wards,[86] even physically or mentally tortured.[87] In the result, criminal justice in China takes on a particular inflection precisely because it is the forum within which direct challenges to the state may be seen to be mounted.[88]

It is a mistake to see the practices of police, prosecutors and judges as aberrational or simply unlawful. Changing the law has not in any significant way changed the behaviour of courtroom actors in ordinary everyday cases, let alone those infused with clear political overtones. They remain able, and indeed may be said to be required, to construct cases to achieve particular outcomes that are deemed appropriate. Violations of the law's public rules and principles, weak as the latter may be, has become systematic and entrenched in the sense that they have also become internalized: from the 'inside' perspective of a state official – police officer, prosecutor or judge – the rules to be followed are quite different from the rules in the formal rules set out in the Criminal Procedure Code or other such codes. The most obvious impact of the 'reform', accordingly, is less on the actions of state officials than on the fact that they have to *account for* their actions in ways that comport with the new requirements.

A development with potentially greater theoretical and practical significance is a state-centred movement to lay siege to the idea of legality as an attribute of the way in which courts in China should operate. As Eva Pils (2009b) points out in her analysis of the promotion by the state of 'harmony rights', 'The Three Supremes' and 'harmonious adjudication', state officials are openly asserting their authority and power rather than, as in the past, resorting to the artifice of charging rights-defenders with implausible and improbable crimes. This is seen in the various forms of 'advice' given to lawyers to avoid 'sensitive' cases and participate in harmonious litigation mediation; but also in various

---

[84] See, for example, Stacey Mosher and Patrick Poon (2009).

[85] See, for example, Jerome Cohen (2010b), discussing the detention of the activist-critic, Hu Jia, on the grounds that his support for environmental reform, Aids victims and civil rights had 'incited subversion of state power'. Cohen points to various forms of low-visibility harassment that have been used against dissidents including threats, illegal house arrest, loss of employment, repeated brief detentions and beatings.

[86] See, for example, Fiona Tam (2010). Tam reports on the case of Peng Baoquan who had earlier helped expose a county leader's misconduct and was later detained by Shiyan police for taking photos outside a hotel during a rally by 20 petitioners who were protesting about illegal land grabs and unpaid severance wages. According to the report, Peng and another passer-by who photographed the petitioners were sent to a mental hospital for a check-up. Tam further points out that state media have reported that many petitioners seeking redress for perceived wrongs are thrown into illegal 'black jails' or mental hospitals where they can face abuse, beatings or rape.

[87] See, for example, Peter Sharp (2009).

[88] This remains true even though, as Peerenboom correctly observes, political ideology is only a very small part of the criminal scenario: 'While crime disrupts social order, criminals do not directly challenge the Party's right to rule': Peerenboom (2006) at p. 845.

forms of harassment undertaken to discourage activist lawyers.[89] And judges are coming under even more pressure to preserve 'social harmony' and advance the interests of the Party.

In a highly stratified and bureaucratic process the collegial panel that sits in court is itself subject to supervision and subordination outside the courtroom. Even where judges have doubts or hesitations about the correctness of a prosecution and even where they believe that a prosecution is altogether misplaced, the system that lies behind ('the leaders', local government officials, Party representatives and the political-legal committee) would not readily allow a verdict of innocence in a case that has reached the trial stage.[90]

The structural goals of the state and its criminal justice agencies sustain only those who comply with its goals by providing a dependable and cost-efficient means of social control, just as it disciplines those within the structure who deviate from the central mission (subjecting 'deviant' police officers, prosecutors or judges to forms of sanction from reprimand, loss of bonus, demotion, loss of job to prosecution based upon performance indicators and quotas which are themselves manifestations of a system of aggregate justice) as it disciplines those outside (primarily rights-defenders) who seek to invoke the formal process to test the state's case or to protect the weak and vulnerable in society.

Looked at overall, the architecture of criminal justice in China remains inhabited by state officials many of whom have internalized the values of social control, the ideologies of the Party or have decisions imposed on them by others higher in the bureaucratic chain of command, who are not confronted by a strong defence bar because steps have been taken to emasculate and marginalize activist lawyers,[91] and who operate under the general direction of state political figures largely unabashed by international outcries over sensitive topics such as the harassment of lawyers in politically charged cases, the death penalty,[92] and miscarriages of justice.[93]

---

[89] For example, Eva Pils describes an incident in which two lawyers, who had travelled to Chongqing to assist the family of a man who had died in suspicious circumstances in police detention, were detained, taken to the police station for questioning, beaten and sent back to Beijing. All of this was carried out by officers in their uniforms rather than having recourse to hired thugs: Eva Pils (2009), pp. 152–153.

[90] Explanations for the few acquittals that occur may need to be sought outside a rational-legal framework.

[91] See, for example, Stacey Mosher and Patrick Poon (2009).

[92] We say 'largely' because there are some indications that, so far as the death penalty is concerned, China may be moving towards a reduction in the crimes punishable by the death penalty. See, 'Crimes that carry death penalty to be cut', *South China Morning Post*, 26 July 2010. Some 68 crimes (44 of which do not involve personal violence) currently carry the death penalty and, while the Supreme People's Court must since 1 January 2007 approve all death sentences, court statistics suggest that only about 10 per cent of those reviewed are reduced to suspended sentences or life terms.

[93] Reference has been made in Chapter 13 above to notorious miscarriages of justice. It is believed, however, that these are the tip of an iceberg. For further information, see; Song Yuansheng (2008) who discusses miscarriages of justice (wrongful convictions) in 17 death penalty cases in China. See the excellent discussion by Thomas Stutsman, 'Culture, Psychology, and Criminal Justice Reform: Reforming Eyewitness Interview Procedures to Reduce Wrongful

In an increasingly evidence-based world, the starting-point of reform of criminal justice institutions for any state is critical self-awareness. As recent history in China has demonstrated, changing the formal rules does not in and of itself lead to predictable changes in human behaviour and does not necessarily alter the inflection and direction of official institutions to which these formal changes are supposedly addressed.

In an exemplary way, the operation of the criminal courts in China demonstrates that law and its institutions cannot be isolated from embedded social and cultural practices or from the larger political economy from which these, in turn, are derived. In a top-down system, the glue that holds the criminal justice process together in China seeps down the hierarchy in the form of policies, addresses, performance indicators and coded discourse defining in aggregate rather than individual terms the work of the day-to-day institutions which, in turn, seek legitimacy through the appearance of formal rationality in serving the state's interest in securing the stability and continuation of its institutions and a particular form of social control.

Convictions and Protect Human Rights in China' (on file with authors as at 2010). Stutsman points to various systemic causes of wrongful conviction in China: (i) a lack of procedural protections for suspects and defendants and a highly attenuated role for defence attorneys; (ii) coerced confessions; (iii) inaccurate eyewitness testimony; (iv) intense pressure on police to solve cases involving serious offences; and (v) the politicization of criminal justice and a lack of judicial independence.

Appendix 1. Chinese criminal procedure: an overview

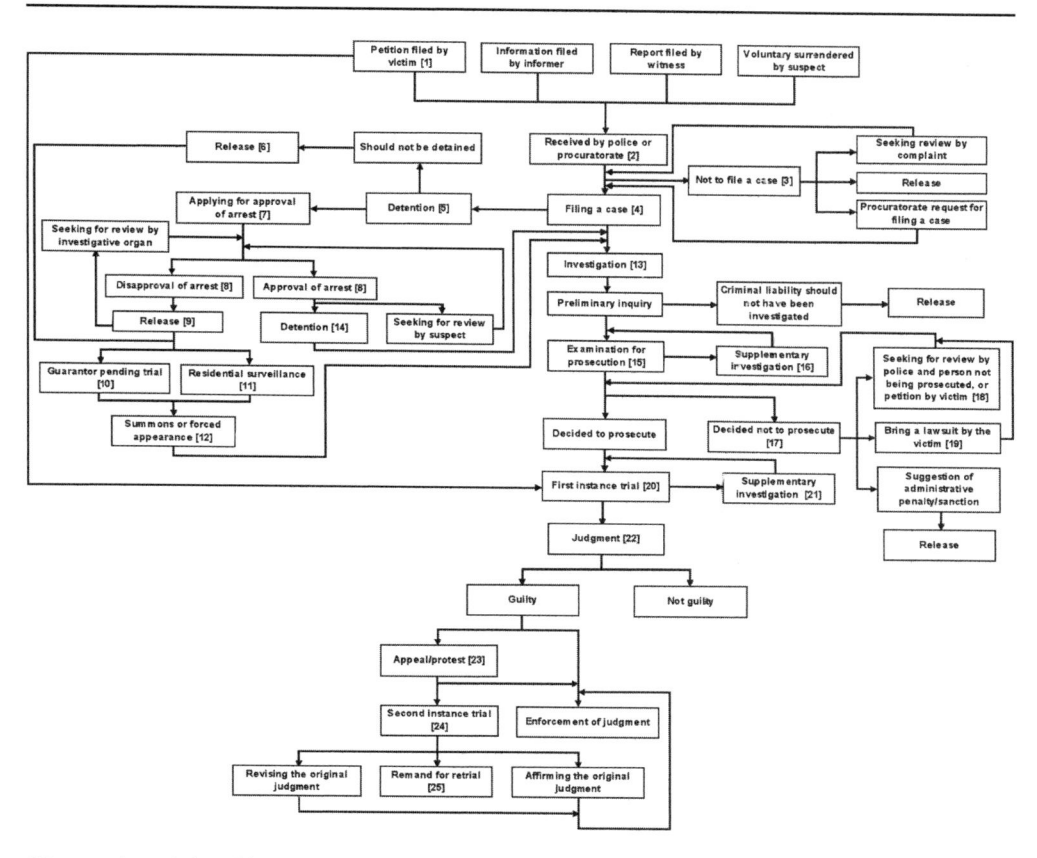

Figure App. 1.1 Chinese criminal procedure flowchart

EXPLANATIONS OF THE CHINESE CRIMINAL PROCEDURE FLOWCHART

[1] The victim may also bring a lawsuit directly to a people's court without presenting a petition first (Art. 145). But such kind of private prosecution may be initiated only in the following circumstances: 1) cases to be handled only upon complaint; 2) cases for which the victims have evidence to prove that those are minor criminal

455

cases; and 3) cases for which the victims have evidence to prove that the defendants should be investigated for criminal responsibility according to law because their acts have infringed upon the victims' personal or property rights and the public security organs or the people's procuratorates have not investigated the criminal responsibility of the accused (Art. 170).

[2] Ordinary criminal cases are handled by the public security organs, while crimes of embezzlement and bribery, crimes of dereliction of duty committed by State functionaries, and crimes involving violations of a citizen's personal rights such as illegal detention, extortion of confessions by torture, retaliation, frame-up and illegal search and crimes involving infringement of a citizen's democratic rights – committed by State functionaries by taking advantage of their functions and powers – are directly handled by the procuratorates (Art. 18).

[3] If the public security organ or the people's procuratorate believes that there are no facts of a crime or that the facts are obviously incidental and do not require investigation of criminal responsibility, it shall not file a case (Art. 86).

[4] If the public security organ or the people's procuratorate believes that there are facts of a crime and criminal responsibility should be investigated, it shall file a case (Art. 86).

[5] Public security organs may initially detain an active criminal or a major suspect under any of the following conditions: 1) if he is preparing to commit a crime, is in the process of committing a crime or is discovered immediately after committing a crime; 2) if he is identified as having committed a crime by a victim or an eyewitness; 3) if criminal evidence is found on his body or at his residence; 4) if he attempts to commit suicide or escape after committing a crime, or he is a fugitive; 5) if there is likelihood of his destroying or falsifying evidence or tallying confessions; 6) if he does not tell his true name and address and his identity is unknown; and 7) if he is strongly suspected of committing crimes from one place to another, repeatedly, or in a gang (Art. 61). Within 24 hours after a person has been detained, his family or the unit to which be belongs shall be notified of the reasons for detention and the place of custody, except in circumstances where such notification would hinder the investigation or there is no way of notifying them (Art. 64). A public security organ shall interrogate a detainee within 24 hours after detention. If it is found that the person should not have been detained, he must be immediately released and issued a release certificate (Art. 65). A detainee in a case directly accepted by a people's procuratorate shall be interrogated within 24 hours after the detention (Art. 133).

[6] If an arrest is necessitated but the evidence is insufficient, the detainee may be allowed to obtain a guarantor pending trial or be subjected to residential surveillance (Arts 65 and 133).

[7] Where there is evidence to support the facts of a crime and the criminal suspect or defendant could be sentenced to a punishment of not less than imprisonment, and if such measures as allowing him to obtain a guarantor pending trial or placing him under residential surveillance would be insufficient to prevent the occurrence of danger to society, thus necessitating his arrest, the criminal suspect or defendant shall be immediately arrested according to law (Art. 60). If the public security organ deems it necessary to arrest a detainee, it shall, within three days after the detention, submit a request to the people's procuratorate for examination and approval. Under special circumstances, the time limit for submitting a request for examination and

Appendix 1 457

approval may be extended by one to four days. As to the arrest of a major suspect involved in crimes committed from one place to another, repeatedly, or in a gang, the time limit for submitting a request for examination and approval of arrest may be extended to 30 days (Art. 69).

[8] The people's procuratorate shall decide either to approve or disapprove the arrest within seven days from the date of receiving the written request for approval of arrest submitted by a public security organ. If the people's procuratorate disapproves the arrest, the public security organ shall, upon receiving notification, immediately release the detainee and inform the people's procuratorate of the result without delay (Art. 69). If a case is directly accepted by the people's procuratorate and it deems it necessary to arrest a detainee, it shall make a decision within ten days after detention. Under special circumstances, the time for deciding on an arrest may be extended by one to four days (Art. 134).

[9] If further investigation is necessary, and if the released person meets the conditions for obtaining a guarantor pending trial or for residential surveillance, he shall be allowed to obtain a guarantor pending trial or subjected to residential surveillance according to law (Art. 69).

[10] Guarantor pending trial may be granted to criminal suspects or defendants under any of the following conditions: 1) they may be sentenced to public surveillance, criminal detention or simply imposed with supplementary punishments; or 2) they may be imposed with a punishment of fixed-term imprisonment at lease and would not endanger society if they are allowed to obtain a guarantor pending trial (Art. 51). The period granted to a criminal suspect or defendant for awaiting trial after obtaining a guarantor shall not exceed 12 months (Art. 58). If a criminal suspect or defendant who should be arrested is seriously ill or is a pregnant woman or a woman breast-feeding her own baby, he or she may be allowed to obtain a guarantor pending trial (Art. 60).

[11] Criminal suspects or defendants may be placed under residential surveillance under any of the following conditions: 1) they may be sentenced to public surveillance, criminal detention or simply have imposed supplementary punishments; or 2) they may be given a punishment of fixed-term imprisonment at least and would not endanger society if they are placed under residential surveillance (Art. 51). The period for residential surveillance shall not exceed six months (Art. 58). If a criminal suspect or defendant who should be arrested is seriously ill or is a pregnant woman or a woman breast-feeding her own baby, he or she may be placed under residential surveillance (Art. 60).

[12] A criminal suspect who need not be arrested or detained may be summoned to a designated place in the city or county where the criminal suspect stays for interrogation, or he may be interrogated at his residence. The time for interrogation through summons or forced appearance shall not exceed 12 hours. A criminal suspect shall not be detained under the disguise of successive summons or forced appearance (Art. 92).

[13] After the criminal suspect is interrogated by an investigative organ for the first time or from the day on which compulsory measures are adopted against him, he may appoint a lawyer to provide him with legal advice and to file petition and complaints on his behalf (Art. 96). Originally, if a case involved State secrets, the criminal suspect had to obtain the approval of the investigation organ for appointing a

lawyer (Art. 96) but under the Lawyers Law 2007 lawyers may *in theory* meet with their clients after the first interrogation without being monitored by public security personnel and without having to obtain prior approval in any case (including those involving 'state secrets') and once the procuratorate begin to examine a case for prosecution, the lawyer has the right to consult, extract and duplicate documents and materials related to the case.

[14] Within 24 hours after an arrest, the family of the arrested person or the unit to which he belongs shall be notified of the reasons for arrest and the place of custody, except in circumstances where such notification would hinder the investigation or there is no way of notifying them (Art. 71). The time limit for holding a criminal suspect in custody during investigation after arrest shall not exceed two months. If the case is complex and cannot be concluded within the time limit, an extension of one month may be allowed with the approval of the people's procuratorate at the next higher level (Art. 124). With respect to the following cases, if investigation cannot be concluded within the time limit, an extension of two months may be allowed upon approval or decision by the people's procuratorate of a province, autonomous region or municipality directly under the Central Government: 1) grave and complex cases in outlying areas where travel is most inconvenient; 2) grave cases that involve criminal gangs; 3) grave and complex cases that involve people who commit crimes from one place to another; and 4) grave and complex cases that involve various quarters and for which it is difficult to obtain evidence (Art. 126). If in the case of a criminal suspect who may be sentenced to fixed-term imprisonment of ten years at least, investigation of the case can still not be concluded upon the expiration of such an extended time limit, another extension of two months may be allowed upon approval or decision by the people's procuratorate of a province, autonomous region or municipality directly under the Central Government (Art. 127). If due to special reasons, it is not appropriate to hand over a particularly grave and complex case for trial even within a relatively long period of time, the Supreme People's Procuratorate shall submit a report to the Standing Committee of the National People's Congress for approval of postponing the hearing of the case (Art. 125). If during the period of investigation a criminal suspect is found to have committed other major crimes, the time limit for holding the criminal suspect in custody during investigation shall be recalculated from the date on which such crimes are found. If a criminal suspect does not tell his true name and address and his identity is unknown, the time limit for holding him in custody during investigation shall be calculated from the date on which his identity is found out (Art. 128).

[15] A criminal suspect in a case of public prosecution shall have the right to entrust persons as his defenders from the date on which the case is transferred for examination before prosecution. A people's procuratorate shall, within three days from the date of receiving the file record of a case transferred for examination before prosecution, inform the criminal suspect that he has the right to entrust persons as his defenders (Art. 33). Defence lawyers may, from the date on which the people's procuratorate begins to examine a case for prosecution, consult, extract and duplicate the judicial documents pertaining to the current case and the technical verification material, and may meet and correspond with the criminal suspect in custody. Other defenders, with permission of the people's procuratorate, may also consult,

extract and duplicate the above-mentioned material, meet and correspond with the criminal suspect in custody (Art. 36). A people's procuratorate shall make a decision within one month on a case that a public security organ has transferred to it with a recommendation to initiate a prosecution; an extension of a half month may be allowed for major or complex cases (Art. 138).

[16] In examining a case that requires supplementary investigation, the people's procuratorate may remand the case to the public security organ for supplementary investigation or conduct the investigation itself. In cases where supplementary investigation is to be conducted, it shall be completed within one month. Supplementary investigation may be conducted twice at most (Art. 140).

[17] If a criminal suspect is found to be under one of the following circumstances, the people's procuratorate shall make a decision not to initiate a prosecution: 1) if an act is obviously minor, causing no serious harm, and is therefore not deemed a crime; 2) if the limitation period for criminal prosecution has expired; 3) if an exemption of criminal punishment has been granted in a special amnesty decree; 4) if the crime is to be handled only upon complaint according to the Criminal Law, but there has been no complaint or the complaint has been withdrawn; 5) if the criminal suspect or defendant is deceased; or if other laws provide an exemption from investigation of criminal responsibility. Besides, with respect to a case that is minor and the offender need not be given criminal punishment or need be exempted from it according to Criminal Law, the people's procuratorate may decide not to initiate a prosecution (Art. 142).

[18] If a person against whom a people's procuratorate decides not to initiate a prosecution still refuses to accept the decision, he may present a petition to the people's procuratorate within seven days after receiving the written decision (Art. 146).

[19] If the victim refuses to accept the decision, he may, within seven days after receiving the written decision, present a petition to the people's procuratorate at the next higher level and request the latter to initiate a public prosecution. The people's procuratorate shall notify the victim of its decision made after re-examination. If the people's procuratorate upholds the decision not to initiate a prosecution, the victim may bring a lawsuit to a people's court. The victim may also bring a lawsuit directly to a people's court without presenting a petition first (Art. 145).

[20] The people's court may apply summary procedure to the following cases, which shall be tried by a single judge alone: 1) cases of public prosecution where the defendants may be lawfully sentenced to fixed-term imprisonment of not more than three years, criminal detention, public surveillance or punishment with fines exclusively, where the facts are clear and the evidence is sufficient, and for which the people's procuratorate suggests or agrees to the application of summary procedure; 2) cases to be handled only upon complaint; and 3) cases prosecuted by the victims, for which there is evidence to prove that they are minor criminal cases (Art. 174). Defence lawyers may, from the date on which the people's court accept a case, consult, extract and duplicate the material of the facts of the crime accused in the current case, and may meet and correspond with the defendant in custody. Other defenders, with permission of the people's court, may also consult, extract and duplicate the above-mentioned material, and may meet and correspond with the defendant in custody (Art. 36).

[21] During a trial, if the procurator finds that a case for which public prosecution has

been initiated requires supplementary investigation, he may make a proposal to that effect (Art. 165). But the supplementary investigation shall be completed within one month (Art. 166).

[22] A people's court shall pronounce judgment on a case of public prosecution within one month, or one and a half months at the latest, after accepting it. However, the period may be extended by one more month upon approval or decision by the higher people's court of a province, autonomous region or municipality directly under the Central Government if any of the following conditions is satisfied: 1) grave and complex cases in outlying areas where travel is most inconvenient; 2) grave cases that involve criminal gangs; 3) grave and complex cases that involve people who commit crimes from one place to another; and 4) grave and complex cases that involve various quarters and for which it is difficult to obtain evidence (Art. 168). For a case to be tried through summary procedure, the people's court shall conclude it within 20 days after accepting it (Art. 178).

[23] The time limit for an appeal or a protest against a judgment shall be ten days and the time limit for an appeal or a protest against an order shall be five days (Art. 183).

[24] After accepting a case of appeal or protest, a people's court of second instance shall conclude the trial of the case within one month, or one and a half months at the latest. Under any of the following circumstances, the period may be extended by one month upon the approval or decision by the higher people's court of a province, autonomous region or municipality directly under the Central Government: 1) grave and complex cases in outlying areas where traffic is most inconvenient; 2) grave cases that involve criminal gangs; 3) grave and complex cases that involve people who commit crimes from one place to another; and 4) grave and complex cases that involve various quarters and for which it is difficult to obtain evidence. However, with respect to cases of appeal or protest accepted by the Supreme People's Court, the matter shall be decided by the Supreme People's Court itself (Art. 196).

[25] If a people's court of second instance discovers that when hearing a case, a people's court of first instance violates the litigation procedures prescribed by law in one of the following ways, it shall rule to rescind the original judgment and remand the case to the people's court which originally tried it for retrial: 1) violating the provisions of the Criminal Procedure Law regarding trial in public; 2) violating the withdrawal system; 3) depriving the parties of their litigation rights prescribed by law or restricting such rights, which may hamper impartiality of a trial; 4) unlawful formation of a judicial organization; or 5) other violations against the litigation procedures prescribed by law which may hamper impartiality of a trial (Art. 191).

ADJUDICATION BY THE COLLEGIAL PANEL

In China, except for those simple cases for which a sole judge is sufficient, the collegial panel system is adopted in adjudicating all criminal cases in China,[1] the composition of the collegial panel may vary according to the nature of the case.

---

[1] Article 10, Organic Law of the People's Courts.

POLITICAL-LEGAL COMMITTEE

Apart from the collegial panel, the political-legal committee (*zhengfa wei*) is vested with the power to make final decisions on cases.

Appendix 2. A note on research methodology*

The project's main aim was to provide reliable, empirical information about the operation of the Chinese criminal justice process since the reforms introduced by the Criminal Procedure Law of 1996. Informed policy making requires reliable information collected in a systematic fashion. Currently, the debate about whether China's criminal justice process is working well or badly is swamped by anecdotal evidence of questionable worth together with limited, but very useful, methodologically-sound studies in various localities or reliant upon limited data, some official or disclosed officially. When we began our research, there was no systematic information of a substantial character available on the workings of the criminal justice system in China subsequent to the 1997 reforms.[1] This research is an attempt to begin to fill that gap.

The main project lasted for four years (2002–2006) during which all the main data were collected with follow-up visits undertaken up to and including 2009.[2] At the initial stage, three researchers drawn from Mainland China were trained in Hong Kong for between four and six months before undertaking the fieldwork.[3] At intervals during the fieldwork, the researchers were brought back to Hong Kong (together with Chinese colleagues who assisted in the research) to review progress and, in the early stages, to make adjustments wherever needed to the research instruments or to have discussions about access. The initial phase included a period of intensive training for the researchers in fieldwork skills as well as a period of immersion and acceptance in the fieldwork sites. The training of the researchers was essential because clearly the accuracy of the data collected depended in large part upon their skill and reliability. In the final phase, Professor Satnam Choongh joined the project and helped draft a number of chapters.

It is important to note that for three research sites we accepted the offer of assistance from researchers drawn from a key state institution. This decision was not taken lightly but the research department of the institution in question was headed by an individual trained outside China with close knowledge of research methodologies. The research instruments had been designed in such a way as to limit the possibility of bias and subsequent analysis gave us confidence that all the quantitative data thus collected were reliable and consistent with the findings of other research sites. The principal shortcoming that this element of the research presented was that the data collected in some cases, particularly in courtroom observations, lacked rich detail that generally characterized the other

---

* All research instruments were originally in both Chinese and English. In this book, Chinese characters have been removed.

[1] See, for example, Liang and Lu (2006).

[2] The 'follow-up' visits involved informal conversations with prosecutors and judges and were data-gathering exercises.

[3] The training was undertaken in various phases by the Project Director, Professor Carol Jones, Professor Eric Chui Wing Hong and Professor Ian Dobinson.

research sites.[4] It is also possible of course that some material discovered in the course of the research was not documented or passed to the Project Team, but we have no way of knowing this.

RESEARCH SITES

In devising our research strategy, we sought to provide a broad cross-section of cases, in both the Basic and Intermediate Courts, in different parts of China taking in both cities and rural regions, developed and less-developed provinces and regions containing differing socio-economic and ethnic (migrant/local) mixes. China is a country of such immense size and contrasts that one project could not hope to provide a fully representative sample of cases. Accordingly, we had to do the best that we could in extracting data from quite different areas of the country to see whether there were commonalities which could be identified and differences which stood out.

We initially decided upon four areas but we were able in the end because of the hard work of the researchers and the co-operation of courts and prosecutors to spread the net more widely. Ultimately, the research took in regions of China that were geographically spread, socially and economically diverse containing different mixes of locals and migrants. The inclusion of rural courts was seen as imperative if the project was to gain a clearer picture of how the legal system operates outside the major cities where court personnel and lawyers may be more aware of reform initiatives and have better access to the resources required to implement change. We reasoned that examining the rural courts would allow us to observe the 'reach' of the reforms to criminal justice. It is, indeed, in these rural areas that the leadership itself exhibits most concern over shortcomings in the operation of the criminal justice system.

We were also conscious that after the reforms brought in at the end of the 1970s there was a gap in economic development between the eastern coastal areas and central and western regions. Whilst the provinces, regions and municipalities in western and central areas[5] occupied 91 per cent of the country and 62 per cent of the total population in China[6] there were clear disparities in development between the regions. Indeed, in order to reduce the gap and to hasten development in the western area, the State Council set up a Working Group on the Development of Western Areas of China in 2000. We accordingly decided that it was important to include western parts of China within the research.[7]

Another reason was that, at the start of our project, the vast area in western and mid-China had been a 'forgotten corner' to most Chinese researchers in the past. For

---

[4] Having said this, it should also be noted that there was variance in some aspects between the three principal researchers with two of these providing richer detail and completing more data-sets than the other researcher.
[5] The nine provinces, regions and municipalities in mid China cover Heilongjiang, Jilin, Shanxi, Hebei, Henan, Hubei, Hunan, Anhui and Jiangxi. The twelve provinces, autonomous regions and municipalities in the western areas include: Shaanxi, Gansu, Qinghai, Ningxia, Inner Mongolia, Xinjiang, Chonqing, Sichuan, Guizhou, Yunnan, Tibet and Guangxi.
[6] Yu and Guo (2003).
[7] See, for a similar observation, Liang and Lu (2006).

instance, while a few scholars conducted research on the implementation of the Criminal Procedure Law in China,[8] most research involved theoretical aspects of the problems[9] and no doubt ran up against access issues. As Liang and Lu (2006) noted:

> A review of . . . published fieldworks in China shows that almost all researchers chose small convenience samples rather than random probability samples. In a few studies that managed to use semi-random or random samples, their population was nevertheless regional and lacked generalizability to China.[10] The majority of these studies were conducted in major cities in China, such as Beijing, Shanghai, Chengdu, Wuhan, Tianjin, and Nanjin. One's *guanxi* appeared to be critical in site selection, research access, and quality of data obtained. (p. 161)

One indicative empirical study had been undertaken by Chen Weidong (2001), who led four students and visited public security bureaux, judicial bureaux, law firms, courts and procuratorates in Beijing, Shenyang, Shenzhen and Yantai between April and December 2000. Their research methods mainly involved questionnaires, group discussion, reading of case files and individual interviews. While this study assisted legislators to understand some practical problems in the operation of criminal procedure, these research efforts were located in economically advanced areas and may not have been representative of the much more extensive economically-developing areas. Yet most scholars assumed that the situation in the west of China was similar to that in the eastern areas. For instance, although there were some empirical data on the appearance of witnesses in court in eastern areas such as Beijing, Shangdong, Shanghai, Guangdong, Zhejiang and Jiangsu,[11] one scholar reasoned: 'the data on the rate of witnesses' appearance is low in the courts of provinces in eastern and southern China; the situation in the mid and western regions can well be imagined'.

As a result, our research also focused on mid- and western areas in an attempt to supply information on the implementation of the Criminal Procedure Law, to enrich the data researchers had obtained in the eastern region and provide a basis for comparison with other parts of China. Furthermore, given that most minorities are located in western and mid-China, one by-product of the data might reflect whether minorities are equally treated with other nationalities.

We are satisfied that, although the research sites cannot be said to be a technically representative sample, the picture that emerges offers a good general account of the workings of the criminal justice process across China. The research sites not only cover those economically-developed areas such as Guangdong, Zhejiang, Beijing and Shanghai, but also those less or least economically developed areas in China. In other words, it covers almost all the regions in China: Northeast, Northwest, Southwest, Southern, Northern, Eastern and Central China.

What we are unable to do, however, is supply that deep local research which is so necessary in all jurisdictions and may have considerable play in certain parts of China.

---

[8] For example, the research conducted by Chen Guangzhong, Fan Chongyi, He Jiahong and Chen Weidong.
[9] Chen Guangzhong and Song Yinghui (2000); and Fan Chongyi (2001).
[10] Referring to Zhang and Messner (1995); and Zhang et al. (2000).
[11] Liu and Wu (2004); He Jiahong (2004); Wu (1999a); Zhang Zetao (2001); and Cheng (2003).

Our general view, nevertheless, is that the forces at work in criminal justice are generally greater than those exerted by local culture; but that remains to be tested by other research.

We cannot give detailed accounts of the actual courts studied in the areas of our research sites because, in addition to having given undertakings of confidentiality and anonymity to the respondents who helped us, in this sensitive area we believe that it is imperative for all researchers to take into account variables which might present risks for the individuals who co-operated in the research. We also emphasize here that, in discussing individual cases in the text, we have used conventional social science techniques to disguise events or persons where the data are so distinctive that identification might otherwise be possible.[12]

We reiterate that it is a limitation of the research that we were unable to include other sites and consequently are not able to say with any certainty whether other regions, not included in the research, were similar or different to the research sites in their courtroom practices or their approach to criminal justice. We remain confident that the central propositions arising from our data are probably generalizable but it is also likely that there will be variations that we did not pick up and that other local studies will better determine. Our research claims no more than being an effort to provide systematic empirical data on a large-scale basis across a broad spread of regions within a vastly diverse country.

RESEARCH INSTRUMENTS

The basic research strategy was to employ a process of data triangulation using both quantitative and qualitative research instruments. Although it might ideally be desirable to gain access to other stages and institutions of the criminal justice process (such as the investigative practices of the police) this project focused principally on the pre-trial acquisition of evidence and the trial of first instance cases. Our research did not involve appeal cases. A pragmatic decision was taken that we would not seek the co-operation of the Public Security Bureau on the basis that any such approach would be denied and that the request might result in wholesale project failure. Our focus, accordingly, was upon getting access to the procuratorate, the courts and courtroom actors (judges, prosecutors and defence lawyers).

After their period of training in Hong Kong, the researchers undertook fieldwork in the research sites, being stationed in courthouses or prosecution offices of the procuratorates at the various locations. Whilst observation of policing and detention practices would be insightful, such research was regarded as premature and unrealistic. Instead, the main focus of the research was upon the court system, with some ancillary data collection focusing upon the availability of legal aid and assistance in the areas of the research.

Each researcher was assigned at least one rural and one urban court.[13] It was anticipated that in the initial phase of the research they would each spend up to five months in

---

[12] Thus, for example, we have changed names or amended the value of property lost or altered the detailed description of the criminal incident.
[13] Exceptionally, one researcher undertook fieldwork in two urban courts and was unable to study a rural court.

these areas, building up their relationship with local legal personnel, an essential aspect to successful ethnographic research, and observing the conduct of criminal cases in the courts. The researchers were equipped with fieldwork protocols and data schedules as well as a detailed schedule for court observation. These were developed by the Project Director and the team of experts involved in the research.

The kind of data which the researchers sought to collect was intended to include items such as whether or not the accused was represented by a lawyer, whether oral evidence from witnesses was led in court or whether the case was a 'paper trial' only, how many witnesses were called, to what did they testify, whether they were cross-examined and by whom, whether the questioning of prosecution witnesses by the defence indicated that the defence lawyer had prepared a foundation for the questioning, whether the defence produced witnesses and if so how many, whether they were cross-examined and if so, on what basis, whether any of the parties produced tangible evidence, forensic evidence or expert witnesses and if so how such evidence was presented and dealt with at trial, whether a case was subject to adjournments and if so how many/how long, whether the judge adopted a supervisory or interrogatory role at trial, whether the defence had been given reasonable time to prepare case/access to prosecution file, length of time suspect had been held in detention pre-trial, length of the trial itself, whether the court had a system for summoning witnesses and if so how this operated, whether the court had expert administrators, whether courts provided separate waiting areas for suspects/witnesses, what involvement the judge had in the progress of the trial e.g. by ruling on questions of admissibility and other questions of law, by questioning witnesses, how judgment is delivered/what judgment was delivered, whether reasons were given.

We stated at the outset of the research project design that systematic data collection in the court would hopefully provide rich insights not only into the workings of the courts themselves but also into the pre-trial criminal process and, further, that the research would also attempt to gain access to case files held by the courts. We said:

> These data are extremely sensitive as they might constitute 'state secrets'. As such, they are not accessible to Chinese researchers and are specifically banned to foreigners. Nonetheless, case files . . . contain invaluable information on how the prosecution case is structured and on the actions of the investigating authorities (including the Public Security, or police) prior to the involvement of prosecutors. Attempts will be made to gain access to some of these case files.[14]

In the event, with the help of our Chinese colleagues, we were successful in securing access to the procuratorate and the courts in all research sites and, in addition, we secured a range of interviews from courtroom actors in each site.

The data-set which forms the basis of this research accordingly comprises: analysis of first instance case files; direct observation of first instance court trials; interviews with judges; interviews with prosecutors; and interviews with defence lawyers. This was

---

[14] What is or is not included in the concept of 'state secrets' or, in the parallel notion of 'internal' (*neibu*) material is far from clear. See, for example, the analysis by Human Rights in China (2007) which concludes: 'The state secrets system continues to seriously deny the right to freedom of expression and information by classifying too much information as secret and maintaining a culture of secrecy that has a chilling effect on the rule of law and independent civil society, and undermines any reform efforts towards these goals.' (*ibid.*, at p. 57).

Table App. 2.1 Fieldwork data from 13 sites

	Case File Analysis	Courtroom Observations	Interviews with Judges	Interviews with Prosecutors	Interviews with Defence Lawyers
Site A	157	10	10	15	10
Site B	141	22	14	18	7
Site C	153	10	4	5	6
Site D	70	15	6	6	6
Site E	65	16	7	7	7
Site F	65	20	7	5	7
Site G	70	33	5	5	4
Site H	53	10	6	7	4
Site I	70	12	2	0	5
Site J	60	19	8	8	6
Site K	70	15	4	4	5
Site L	100	25	11	11	11
Site M	70	20	4	5	5
Total	1144	227	88	96	83

supplemented wherever possible by field notes compiled by our researchers. The principal data-set is listed in Table App. 2.1.

We collected our samples in the same way with the same set of the research instruments in each site in order to ensure comparability between areas. The research instruments devised and used to undertake the fieldwork comprised two data-gathering instruments and three interview schedules. We conducted the empirical research in these ways to ensure that our sample of cases was reasonably representative of different types of cases and different types of official decision-making so that generalization was possible. Data collection went over a three-year period beginning in spring 2003 and ending in 2006.

Case File Analysis

The basic idea of the research was to gain access to *case files* and subject them to close and systematic analysis. The most significant limitation to such research anywhere in the world is that the respondent organization might create or modify the files in order to influence the findings of the research or, at least, to fillet the files so that material regarded as detrimental to the organization is likely to be removed. To circumvent that danger, we decided to focus on first instance trials that had just been completed and for which the case files had already been sealed. To accomplish this, we collected the most-recently completed or 'dead' criminal cases going back at least until our pre-set totals (50) were reached.

One limitation of the research is that those who prepared the case files did so to fulfil the remit of the organization itself and not with any research interest in mind. Material that a research project might have considered important may have been systematically omitted or not collected on a systematic basis. There is also a risk that information which might be considered detrimental to the organization itself or to a sister organization or, indeed, to the individual who compiled the file would be left out of account. We are confident, however, that the focus of the study upon 'dead' cases reduced to a minimum these problems.

An additional problem is that we were dependent upon the case flow of each court to form the basis of the samples. Among other things, this meant: that we took whatever cases had been most recently processed rather than a random sample of cases or a sample drawn to include certain species of case (such as homicide or robbery); that in busy courts the period covered by the sample might be a matter of a few months whereas in less busy areas (particularly rural courts) the sample might be drawn over half a year or so; and that the time frames covered by each research site differed as the researchers moved from area to area. Having said this, one major advantage of our approach is that the research can be said to have focused upon 'everyday' trials and thereby gives a broad account of the staple diet of courts in China rather than, say, focusing upon high profile causes célèbres which might give an insightful but unbalanced view of the system at large.

A self-generated problem of the case file analysis resulted from the complexity and technicality of the research instrument.[15] Having been given some sample case files through confidential contacts, we realized that these included a vast amount of information on all stages of the criminal justice process from initial report of the crime to disposition. And we accordingly set out to extract as much of this information as was possible in a systematic quantitative form. Although we had a number of intensive workshops in the training period, the *Case File Analysis Form* that resulted proved so complex in some respects that the researchers were not able to get out all that we could have hoped for. We decided, however, that we would sacrifice some detail in order to draw the wider picture and we stayed with the Form as devised. To give one example of our over-ambition in this respect: We asked the researchers to provide various details on prosecution witnesses: whether the prosecutor produced the testimony of any witness or the live witness and how many prosecution witnesses there were; but we also asked (Question 50) to categorize the witnesses into: (i) occurrence witnesses; and (ii) post-occurrence witnesses because this may be one indicator of the nature and strength of the prosecution case. However, in practice, it was not possible for the researchers to make such distinctions or to do so in consistent ways. The answers to such questions were accordingly untrustworthy and unusable.

A second example relates to information regarding the sentence passed by the court. It would have been valuable to have recorded the actual sentence passed in relation to each convicted defendant. There were concerns expressed about the sensitivity of this information in the hands of researchers. Accordingly, following initial trials, we decided to limit this part of the data collection to the binary divide: custodial or non-custodial. In doing so we are conscious of what we had thereby lost.

---

[15] The Case File Analysis Schedule was also difficult to complete in a timely manner. The material in the files was not organized in the same way as the Form and, accordingly, to complete the lengthy questions involved the researcher in going back and forth through the case file and doing this time and again for each case. This caused some researchers to give preference to the quantitative aspect of the Form with some considerable sacrifice to qualitative information that would have taken much longer to extract.

Courtroom Observations

We set out to observe actual first instance trials in different level of courts in each area with the *Courtroom Observation Forms* as the data-gathering instruments used to record the information on live first instance trials observed in a systematic fashion. Our pre-set totals were ten cases for each of the 13 sites. The research instruments were completed by researchers in all sites but with varying degrees of detail.

Our researchers were successful in gaining access to any and all cases that they had time to observe during the currency of their stay in each research site. Distinguished professors from China paved the way for their entry and the researchers themselves were able to capitalize on this by establishing good relationships with key court/procuratorial personnel. In this way, the researchers became accepted into the courts and their presence was not the subject of concern. Nor was it the subject of knowledge or interest to the other parties: the defendants, prosecutors and defence lawyers.

Observations of this kind quite clearly run the well-documented risk that the presence of the observer will affect the behaviour of those who are being observed. The traditional way of overcoming this problem is to spend a period of immersion in the field site so that those who are being observed revert to natural behaviour after a period of assimilation. The objective, as Bottoms (2000) put it, is to make sense of the world of the respondents as they themselves understand it:

> First and most obviously, its preference is for carefully-nuanced reportage on deep immersion in the life-worlds of the subjects being studied; hence ethnography as a preference (usually a strong preference) for qualitative rather than quantitative data. Secondly and relatedly, ethnography places much more emphasis than does positivism on the meaning of social actions to actors, and on their detailed understandings of particular social contexts. Thirdly, therefore, the ethnographic approach emphatically rejects the view that social science can be studied in the same way as natural science, for the phenomena studied in natural science do not attribute meaning to their life-worlds as human beings do. These three attributes . . . lead, collectively, to a particular strength in the ethnographic tradition, . . . namely, its ability to uncover some of the deep cultural meanings and normative bonds which are often so important in everyday social life.

This was not possible to the extent desirable in the current research, because researchers needed to take advantage of viewing trials which were in progress during their stay in the field and could not delay observing cases until such time as they were sure that they had become accepted by respondents. It is possible, accordingly, that there was some research-effect as, for example, respondents being more punctilious in observing procedural rules. Whilst we do not think that this occurred to any degree or, where it might have happened, was significant, the possibility cannot be discounted, and is a factor to be taken into account in evaluating our findings.

Another limitation of our research is that, unlike full ethnographic studies, our court observations are for the most part, restricted to cataloguing what was said by the courtroom actors during the course of the trial. None of the researchers had received sufficient training to enable them to document in discrete and systematic ways the behavioural characteristics of the courtroom actors. Of course, the researchers supplied from time to time, annotations and behavioural observations, which sought to give a flavour of the atmosphere in court, such as, for example, noting that the judge acted in an authoritative manner towards the defendant or the defence lawyer or that a defendant smiled throughout the process or adopted a defiant stance. However, this was not systematically done, nor was it possible for the researchers to note down everything that was said in court. It is a tribute to the researchers that they in fact were able to document the key interactions and they were helped in this regard by the fact that many trials were disposed of in a short time period but what they achieved could not be said to be close ethnographic observations.

Interviews with Judges/Prosecutors/Defence Lawyers

We need to start with a general comment on interviewing respondents in the field in China. We begin by noting that China presents particular, if not unique, challenges to the field researcher. This primarily arises from various features of Chinese society: first, in China, there is a striking emphasis upon the collective as opposed to the individual; second, much of the material relating to prosecutions and trials is of a sensitive character or may even be classified as state secrets or 'internal'; and third, there is in consequence, little incentive for an individual respondent to go outside normal procedures and confide in an outsider on any matter bearing upon the institution, which may bring trouble for them.[16] One example illustrates the difficulty. We asked judges and prosecutors what, in their opinion, were the 'main problems' relating to criminal justice in China. We realized that this was sensitive and that it placed the respondents in a difficult position as insiders criticizing their own system but we thought it important to provide respondents with the opportunity to express their views. Most respondents did answer the question but some immediately saw the potential danger and provided diplomatic answers, for example: 'I have never thought about this before.'

All this is on top of the normal protective screen that institutions put up (namely, to keep any and all information about the organization within the institution itself or to pass out only information which will portray the organization in a particularly favourable light) in order to secure their own autonomy and independence, a tendency that may be exaggerated in China.

Additionally, gaining the confidence of respondents (not without hazard in the field anywhere) may be more difficult in China unless supported by having good interpersonal relations, such as *guanxi*, with the respondents.[17] In this regard, we were reliant upon our researchers benefiting from introductions supplied by Chinese professors, developing good relationships themselves with targeted respondents and, where necessary, the use of small incentives (such as taking respondents for lunch or dinner) to encourage cooperation. While this was, in general, successful, a few potential respondents turned down invitations to be interviewed, many preferred interviews away from the office environment and, in all cases, we were unable to tape-record the interviews which did take place.

In the institutions (procuratorate and courts), our presence at the outset was a cause of interest and in some cases overt suspicion. We found that good relationships established with one key respondent did not always extend beyond the individual contact and into

---

[16] See further, Liang and Lu (2006).
[17] Yang (1994). See also, Kipnis (1997). In no case did our researchers give direct payment in return for co-operation and in no case was this ever solicited.

the institution itself. There was, accordingly, a lot of work for each researcher to do in striking up the relationships needed to gain trust and confidence enough to grant interviews. In line with our policy, no attempt to do this took place until after the researcher had been in the field site for 3-4 weeks so that a process of 'assimilation' had a chance to take root.

After a period of assimilation, we contacted judges, prosecutors and defenders (defence lawyers) in each site and sought interviews with each independently. We avoided in all instances 'group interviews' which have been favoured by some researchers on the basis that it would be difficult in such settings for anyone whose views did not accord with the others or the Party line or official policy to give voice to their opinions and it avoided the views of individual respondents being 'contaminated' by the views offered by other respondents.

Each interviewee was given a guarantee of confidentiality and anonymity. All interviews were undertaken according to semi-structured interview schedules. These sought to tease out various strands relating to the general work, perspectives, aspirations and values of the target respondents rather than trying to persuade them to talk about specific cases, again because of the potential danger to the individuals and because this might arouse suspicion or antagonism which might be fatal to the rest of the research in that site. We found that many respondents did nonetheless refer to specific cases but these were at their choosing and could not be said to be representative in any way; and for the most part we do not rely upon such data.

The semi-structured *interview schedules* employed for interviews with judges, prosecutors and defence lawyers sought details of the operational duties for which the interviewee was responsible; of the problems encountered at pre-trial review stage and trial stage; of encounters with other parties, namely police, judges, prosecutors, defence lawyers at different stages of the penal process; of comments regarding continuing education and training; of problems encountered under the current penal process. Our pre-set totals were five interviews with judges, five interviews with prosecutors and five interviews with defence lawyers for each of the 13 sites.

RESEARCH SITES

The selection of the research sites was heavily reliant on securing in-principle access obtained through the relationship and ability of each researcher to gain the trust of relevant officials in the selected research site. As we have earlier noted, the selection of the sites was mainly based on geographical variation, so that the study would cover a wide range of regions in China taking into account socio-economic structure, population size and rural-urban mixes.

Sites A, B and C

Sites A, B and C are all located in a North China City which is a political, economic, research and cultural and international exchange centre. The city comprises 18 districts and counties, covering an area of more than 16 000 square kilometres. Its resident population is almost 17 million, including more than 4.5 million migrants.

Table App. 2.2   Abbreviations and brief introduction of the research sites

Site	Court Level	About the Site
A	BC	A provincial city located in northern China (Eastern District).
B	BC	A provincial city located in northern China (North East).
C	BC	A provincial city located in northern China (between suburbs and downtown).
D	BC	A provincial major city located in southwest China.
E	IC	A city of an agricultural province in central China.
F	BC	A regional major city of the agricultural based region which has a large non-Chinese minority in southern China.
G	BC	An international economic centre with its own legal tradition.
H	IC	An international economic centre with its own legal tradition.
I	IC	A provincial major city of an industrial base province in north-eastern China.
J	IC	A city in China's booming southern coastal economic zone.
K	IC	A coastal opening city and major trade centre of a province situated on the eastern coast of China.
L	IC	A provincial major city of an inland province located at the north-western part of China.
M	BC	A county-level city of the province located on China's eastern coast.

*Court Level: Basic Court (BC); Intermediate Court (IC)

There are social, geographical and economical variations among these three research sites. Site A is located on the east side of the city, representing one of the core areas, in which there are many historical relics or famous sites. It covers an area of more than 25 square kilometres, with a population of over 625 000 people. Site B is located in the northeast suburb of the City, 30 kilometres away from the downtown of the City covering an area of 1021 square kilometres with a population of 550 000 people. Site C, lying between the centre and suburbs, covers an area of 470 square kilometres, with a permanent population of almost 3 million.

Site D

Site D is a small/medium-size capital city in the southwest region of China famous for tourism and business. The city covers an area of more than 21 100 square kilometres, and comprises 13 districts/counties. The population of the city is over 4 million including more than 20 minorities who together make up almost 14 per cent of the whole population. The province where the city is located can be viewed as an economically developing area with a significant migrant population having relocated from other cities of the province.

Site E

Site E is a city in an agricultural province in central China. The city is located in the western part of the province, covering an area of over 15 200 square kilometres with a population of almost 7 million people in 2009. This city is characterized by having a local medium-sized population in an economically less-developed area.

Site F

Site F is a regional major city of an agriculturally-based region which has a large non-Chinese minority. This local city, in a remote western part of the southern China region, covers an area of near 22 300 square kilometres with a population of over 6 million people, including a diverse group of minorities. The city is among the least economically developed.

Sites G and H

Sites G and H are located in the same city. Site H is a district of Site G. Site G is in the eastern region of China. It is a major international economic centre with its own legal tradition, a comprehensive industrial centre and trade port and an important centre for science and technology, trade, finance and information businesses. Of the more than 19 million people living in this city, some 5 million are migrant workers.

Site I

Site I is a provincial medium/large city of a province in north-eastern China. It is located in the middle of the province, covering an area of almost 13 000 square kilometres, with a population of around 7.7 million people. It comprises 14 districts and counties. A local and less-economically developed area of (northeastern) China, it is characterized by state-owned enterprises and various forms of heavy industry.

Site J

Site J is a relatively new city, located in the southern coast area of a southeast province in China. As one of the main exporting cities in China, its population is around 14 million dominated by migrant workers. Site J represents an economically developed but non-capital city area in southeastern China.

Site K

Site K is a coastal city and major trade centre of a province situated on the eastern coast of China. It has a permanent population of almost 8 million people (in 2008) and, in addition, some 2 million migrant workers staying in the city. It is located in the southeastern part of the province in eastern China. It is characterized by a developing private economy.

Site L

Site L is a provincial major city of an inland province located in the north-western part of China. It had a population of over 8 million by the end of 2009. It is a local but medium economically developed area in China.

Site M

Site M is a county-level city of the province located at China's eastern coast. It is located in the central part of the province with a registered population of over 560 000 people and additionally a migrant population of more than 300 000 people. In an underdeveloped province, it is a developing but not yet advanced area.

Appendix 3. Case file analysis schedule

Location: ☐☐   Case Number: ☐☐☐

Part A: Information on Offence(s)/Offender(s)

1. Number of the accusation(s):   a) Single ☐   b) Multiple ☐
   If multiple, comment: (number of charges)

2. Principal accusation by the Police
   (Article no of the Law and Name of the charge):

   Comments:

3. Offender
   1) Gender: a) Male ☐   b) Female ☐

   2) Age: ☐☐

   3) Occupation: a) Professional ☐   b) Skilled ☐
                    c) Semi-skilled ☐   d) Unskilled ☐

   * Notes   If the offender is a *Farmer*, please tick Option d '*unskilled*'. If the offender is a *Student*, please tick Option d '*unskilled*'.
   Please write down the actual occupation of the offender here:

   Comment:

   4) Education: No education ☐   Primary school ☐
                   Junior middle school ☐   Senior middle school ☐
                   College ☐   Postgraduate or above ☐

   5) Status: a) Local ☐   b) Migrant ☐

   * Notes   The status of the offender should follow the classification laid down in the case file;

   6) Employment Status: a) Employed ☐   b) Unemployed ☐
                           c) Self-employed ☐

   * Notes   If the offender is a *Farmer*, please tick Option b '*unemployed*'; b)
             If the offender is a *Student*, please tick Option b '*unemployed*'; b)
             Please mark down here if the offender is a *Farmer* or *Student*:

   Comment:

Part B: Decision to File a Case

4. When was the case first reported?
   ☐☐☐☐☐☐☐☐ (yyyy/mm/dd)

5. How did the offence(s) *first* come to the attention of the police?
   *Choose **ONE** option only
   a) Victim reported crime
   b) Victim's family reported crime
   c) Other civilian reported crime
   d) On-the-spot detection by police
   e) Police discovery after investigation
   f) Information provided by another suspect
   g) Anonymous report
   h) Transferred from other judicial organs
   i) Others
   Comments:

5A. On what date was the suspect caught? (yyyy/mm/dd)?
   ☐☐☐☐☐☐☐☐ (yyyy/mm/dd)

6. How was the suspect *first* identified?
   *Choose **ONE** option only
   a) Caught in the act
   b) Directly identified by victim/witness
   c) Description provided by victim/witness
   d) Police stop and search
   e) Forensic identification
   f) Others
   Comments:

7. Was the suspect detained under the Criminal Procedure Law?
   Yes ☐   No ☐   No Info ☐

   If Yes, give the date: ☐☐☐☐☐☐☐☐ (yyyy/mm/dd)

8. Did the suspect apply for bail or surveillance?
   Yes ☐   No ☐
   Note: Option 'No' should be chosen if the file does not expressly indicate the outcome.
   Comments (Note outcome of application, if any):

Appendix 3   477

Part C: Interrogation

9. What was the outcome of the interrogation?
   a) Full confession ☐   b) Partial admission ☐   c) Denial ☐   d) No Info ☐

10. Did the suspect provide other evidence of his/her involvement in the crime(s)?
    Yes ☐   No ☐   No Info ☐
    Details:

11. Did the suspect incriminate others?
    Yes ☐   No ☐   No Info ☐

12. When was the request for the authorization ☐☐☐☐☐☐☐☐ (yyyy/mm/dd)
    of arrest made by the procuratorate?

13. What was the outcome of the request for the authorization of arrest?
    a) Approved ☐   b) Disapproved ☐   c) No Info ☐
    Comments (e.g. Reasons for disapproval and outcome):

14. How was the evidence collected (provide details for each option where different methods were used, you can choose more than 1 option)?
    *Choose *AS MANY OPTIONS AS APPLICABLE*
    a) Search Person ☐
       Details: _____
    b) Search Property ☐
       Details: _____
    c) Questioning defendant/witness*/victim ☐   *co-defendant is not a witness
                                                   *expert is not a witness
       Details: _____
    d) Scientific investigation ☐
       Details: _____
    e) Inquest and examination ☐
       Details: _____
    f) Others ☐
       Details: _____
    g) Expert Conclusion ☐
       Details: _____
    Comments:

15. What was the outcome of recommendation by the police?
    a) Prosecute ☐   b) Not to prosecute ☐   c) Others ☐   d) No information ☐

    Note: If Option b is chosen, skip Q.16
    Comments:

16. What was the date of transferal of prosecution?   ☐☐☐☐☐☐☐☐ (yyyy/mm/dd)

Part D: Prosecution Stage

17. When did the prosecution stage commence?   ☐☐☐☐☐☐☐☐ (yyyy/mm/dd)

18. How many times (if any) was the suspect questioned by the prosecutor?
    No. of Times ☐☐

19. Did the prosecutor inform the suspect of his/her rights?
    Yes ☐   No ☐   No Info ☐

20. Did the suspect......
    a) Confirm his/her confession?
    b) Withdraw his/her confession?
    c) Partially withdraw his/her confession?
    d) No Confession?
    e) No Information

21. Did the suspect allege police torture?
    Yes ☐   No ☐
    Note: Option 'No' should be chosen if the file does not expressly indicate the outcome.
    If Yes, give details:

22. Did the suspect request legal advice/defender?
    Yes ☐   No ☐
    Note: Option 'No' should be chosen if the file does not expressly indicate the outcome.
    If Yes, outcome:

23. Was the victim questioned on the following aspects?
    a) Crime details
    b) Own evidence
    c) Preferred Outcome
    d) No victim identified

Appendix 3

24. a) Were other witness statements*, material evidence and documentary evidence reviewed?
    *witness statements should not include statement of co-defendant in the same trial; *Expert conclusions are excluded
    Yes ☐   No ☐   No Info ☐
    b) If yes, were questions raised about any witness statement, material evidence and documentary evidence?
    Yes ☐   No ☐   No Info ☐
    If Yes, give details:

25. Did the prosecutor change the compulsory measures?
    Yes ☐   No ☐   No Info ☐
    If Yes, give details:

26. When was the review of prosecution completed? ☐☐☐☐☐☐☐☐ (yyyy/mm/dd)

27. a) Did the prosecutor request supplementary investigation?
    Yes ☐   No ☐
    Note: Option 'No' should be chosen if the file does not expressly indicate the outcome.
    Comments:

    b) If yes, how many times?   1 time ☐   2 times ☐
    Comments:

28. What was the outcome of the review?
    a) Prosecute
    b) Not to prosecute
    c) No Information
    Comments:

29. If the decision was *To prosecute*, what was the charge?
    (Article no of the Law and Name of the charge):

    Comments:

30. If the decision was *Not to prosecute*, was it due to?
    a) Insufficient evidence
    b) Article 15 of the CPL
    c) Prosecution's discretion/minor offence
    Comments:

Part E: The Trial

31. Level of Court: a) Basic ☐   b) Intermediate ☐   c) Higher ☐

32. Type of procedure: a) Summary ☐   b) Ordinary ☐
    Comments:

33. How many judges/people's assessors/prosecutors were there?
    a) Number of judges present
    b) Number of people's assessors present
    c) Number of prosecutors present
    Comments:

34. Was there a defender?   Yes ☐   No ☐
    If Yes, please give the number of defenders:
    If no, go directly to Q.36 and leave Q.35 Blank

35. If there was a defender, was he/she____?
    a) A lawyer appointed by the court ☐   b) A lawyer privately retained ☐
    c) Relative/friend ☐   d) Others ☐
    Note: Can choose more than one option
    Comments:

36. Was the victim present at the trial?
    Yes ☐   No ☐   No Info ☐
    If Yes, please give the number of victims:

37. Did the victim(s) have a legal representative?   Yes ☐   No ☐   No Info ☐
    Comments:

38. Was the trial_____?   a) Open ☐   b) Closed ☐
    Comments:

39. After the announcement by the presiding judge, did the defendant(s) raise any challenges?
    Yes ☐   No ☐   No Info ☐
    Details:

Appendix 3 481

40. After the indictment had been read by the prosecutor, did the defendant(s)?
    a) Agree ☐   b) Partially agree ☐   c) Disagree ☐   d) Others ☐
    Note: If the defendant claimed himself innocent, please tick option d '**Others**' and write down the details in '**Comments**'
    Comments:

41. Did the defendant or his/her defender make a statement?
    Yes ☐   No ☐   No Info ☐
    Details:

42. Did the victim or his/her representative make a statement?
    Yes ☐   No ☐   No Info ☐
    Details:

43. Was the defendant questioned?
    Yes ☐   No ☐   No Info ☐
    If yes, was the defendant questioned by:
    a) Prosecutor   ☐
    b) Judges   ☐
    c) Victim or victim's representative   ☐
    d) Others (including defender(s))   ☐
    Comments:

44. Did the prosecution case consist of the file only?   Yes ☐   No ☐   No Info ☐
    If Yes, go to Part H.

45. Did the prosecutor produce material evidence and/or documentary evidence?
    *Witnesses statements are excluded as documentary evidence
    Yes ☐   No ☐   No Info ☐
    If Yes, give details:

46. Were questions raised about this evidence?
    Yes ☐   No ☐   No Info ☐
    If yes, who raised these questions?
    a) Defendant   ☐
    b) Judges   ☐
    c) Victim or victim's representative   ☐
    d) Others (including defender(s))   ☐
    Comments:

47. What was the outcome of this questioning?
   Comments:

48. Did the prosecutor produce the testimony of witnesses?
   Yes ☐   No ☐   No Info ☐
   If Yes, did it consist of?
   a) Reading of statement
   b) Producing the witnesses in court
   c) Others
   Comments:

48A. Did prosecution produce any witness in court?
   Yes ☐   No ☐   No Info ☐
   Note: If 'No/No Info' is chosen, please go to Q.51
   Comments:

49. How many prosecution witness(es) was/were produced in court?
   Actual No. ☐
   Comments:

50. What types of prosecution witnesses were produced in court? (give number for each type)
   a) Occurrence/Direct
   ai) No. of prosecution witnesses (occurrence/direct) produced in court?
   b) Post occurrence/Indirect
   bi) No. of prosecution witnesses (post occurrence/indirect) produced in court?
   Comments:

51. Were questions/challenges raised about the testimony of prosecution witnesses?
   Yes ☐   No ☐   No Info ☐
   If yes, who raised these questions?
   a) Defendant
   b) Judges
   c) Victim or victim's representative
   d) Others (including defender(s))
   Comments:

Appendix 3 483

52. Did the prosecution produce the statement of the victim(s)?
    Yes [ ]   No [ ]   No Info [ ]
    If Yes, did it consist of?
    a) Reading of statement
    b) Producing the victim in court
    c) Others
    Comments:

53. Were questions/challenges raised about the statement of the victim(s)?
    Yes [ ]   No [ ]   No Info [ ]
    If yes, who raised these questions?
    a) Defendant
    b) Judges
    c) Victim or victim's representative
    d) Others (including defender(s))
    Comments:

54. Did the prosecution produce the statements/confessions of the defendant(s)?
    Yes [ ]   No [ ]   No Info [ ]
    If Yes, did it consist of?
    a) Reading of statement only
    b) Reading of statement and testimony by the defendant(s)
    c) Others
    Comments:

55. Were any questions/challenges raised about the statement/confession of the defendant(s)?
    Yes [ ]   No [ ]   No Info [ ]
    If yes, who raised these questions?
    a) Defendant
    b) Judges
    c) Victim or victim's representative
    d) Others (including defender(s))
    Comments:

56. Did the prosecutor produce expert conclusions?
    Yes [ ]   No [ ]   No Info [ ]
    If Yes, give details:

57. Were questions raised about the expert conclusions?
    Yes ☐   No ☐   No Info ☐
    If yes, who raised these questions?
    a) Defendant   ☐
    b) Judges   ☐
    c) Victim or victim's representative   ☐
    d) Others (including defender(s))   ☐
    Comments:

58. Did the prosecutor produce records of inquests and examinations?
    Yes ☐   No ☐   No Info ☐
    If option 'No'/'No Info' is chosen, then go to Q.60
    If Yes, give details:

59. Were questions raised about these records of inquests and examinations?
    Yes ☐   No ☐   No Info ☐
    If yes, who raised these questions?
    a) Defendant   ☐
    b) Judges   ☐
    c) Victim or victim's representative   ☐
    d) Others (including defender(s))   ☐
    Comments:

60. Did the prosecutor produce any audio-visual evidence?
    Yes ☐   No ☐   No Info ☐
    If option 'No'/'No Info' is chosen, then go to Q.62
    If Yes, give details:

61. Were questions raised about the audio-visual evidence?
    Yes ☐   No ☐   No Info ☐
    If yes, who raised these questions?
    a) Defendant
    b) Judges
    c) Victim or victim's representative
    d) Others (including defender(s))
    Comments:

Appendix 3 485

61A. Was there an adjournment of the trial at this stage for further investigation?
Yes ☐   No ☐   No Info ☐

61Aa) If yes, who requested it?
a) Prosecutor ☐   b) Defender ☐
c) Others (Specify: _____) ☐   d) No Info ☐
Comments: (e.g. what reasons were given in support of the request?)

61Ab) If yes, was the request agreed to or not?
a) Agreed ☐   b) Not agreed ☐   c) No Info ☐
Commends: (e.g. What reasons were given for agreeing or disagreeing with the request?)

Part F: Defence

62. Did the defence produce material evidence and/or witnesses and/or others in court?
Yes ☐   No ☐   No Info ☐
If Yes, did it consist of?
a) Material evidence
b) Witnesses
c) Others
    (Specify: _____)
Comments:

63. If material evidence was produced in court? What was it?

64. Were any question/challenges raised about this material evidence?
Yes ☐   No ☐   No info ☐
If yes, who raised these questions?
a) Defendant
b) Judges
c) Victim or victim's representative
d) Others (including defender(s))
Comments:

64A. Did defence produce any witness in court?
Yes ☐   No ☐   No Info ☐
Note: If 'No'/'No Info' is chosen, please go to Q.68
Comments:

65. How many defence witnesses were produced in court?
    Actual No. ☐
    Comments:

66. What types of defence witnesses were produced in court? (give number for each type)
    a) Occurrence/Direct
    ai) No. of prosecution witnesses (occurrence/direct) produced in court?
    b) Post occurrence/Indirect
    bi) No. of prosecution witnesses (post occurrence/indirect) produced in court?

67. Were any questions/challenges raised about the evidence of these defence witnesses?
    Yes ☐   No ☐   No Info ☐
    If yes, who raised these questions?
    a) Defendant
    b) Judges
    c) Victim or victim's representative
    d) Others (including defender(s))
    Comments:

Part G: Debate Stage

68. Was the prosecution's statement given in court?
    Yes ☐   No ☐   No Info ☐
    If yes, did the prosecution statement include?
    a) A summary of the evidence
       Details: _____
    b) A statement as to the guilt of the defendant
       Details: _____
    c) A statement as to leniency or severity of punishment
       Details: _____
    d) Others
       Details: _____

69. Was the defence's statement given in court?
    Yes ☐   No ☐   No Info ☐
    a) A summary of the evidence
       Details: _____
    b) A statement admitting guilt of the defendant
       Details: _____
    c) A statement as to leniency of punishment
       Details: _____

Appendix 3 487

    d)   A statement claiming complete innocence
         Details: _____
    e)   A statement claiming partial innocence
         *including accepting one charge but not the others
         where option e) is chosen, please indicate the nature of the defendant's disagreement with the prosecution case
         e.g. disputing one charge, disputing type of charge, disputing the amount stolen or whether force was used)
         Details: _____
    f)   Others
         Details: _____
    Comments:

70. Did this lead to further/additional debate?
    Yes ☐   No ☐   No Info ☐
    Comments:

71. Did the defendant(s)/defender give a final statement?
    Yes ☐   No ☐   No Info ☐
    If yes, did the defendant(s)/defender final statement include:
    a)   Statement as to guilt or innocence
         Details: _____
    b)   Statement as to punishment
         Details: _____
    c)   Others
         Details: _____
    Comments:

Part H: Judgment

72. Was the judgment given?
    Yes ☐   No ☐   No Info ☐
    If yes, when was the judgment given?
    a)   Immediately
    b)   After short adjournment
    c)   After an adjournment for a number of days
    Note: please note down any discussion and decision made by the adjudication committee
    Comments:

73. What was the outcome of the judgment?
    a)   Guilty of all charges
    b)   Guilty of some charges
    c)   Guilty of amended charge

       d) Not guilty in law
       e) Not guilty due to insufficient evidence

74.   Did the judge give reasons for his judgment?
       Yes [ ]   No [ ]   No Info [ ]
       If Yes, give details:

75.   What was the nature of the penalty given?
       a) Custodial penalty
          Details: _____
       b) Non custodial penalty
          Details: _____
       Comments:

76.   Did the judge(s) address issues as to the punishment given, for example, the need for deterrence?
       Yes [ ]   No [ ]   No Info [ ]
       If Yes, give details:

77.   Did the defendant/defender lodge an appeal?
       Yes [ ]   No [ ]   No Info [ ]
       If yes, what was the outcome? (details)
       a) Sustained   b) Amended
       c) Remitted for retrial   d) No Info
       e) Others (specify: _____)
       Details: _____

Appendix 4. Courtroom observation schedule

Case Identification Number:

Date of Court Session:

Offence(s), Number and Type:

Defendant(s) Number:

Guidelines:

I   Do a diagram of the physical layout of the courtroom and where the parties were located.

II   Describe parties present – judges, prosecutors, defendants, police and others. Include number and their physical appearance.

III   Outline the main factors in the prosecution's case.

IV   How did the trial open?

        Section A: Ascertain the defendant's status and announce litigation rights.

        Section B: Court investigation.

        Section C: Court debate.

        Section D: Make a final statement.

        Section E: Adjournment.

V   Did any prosecution witnesses give evidence at court? If yes, describe it.

VI   If there was a defence, outline the arguments. If the defendant had representation, provide details of whom this was and what was said.

VII   Did any defence witnesses give evidence at court? Describe it.

VIII Describe what the judge did? Did he/she ask questions or seek clarification?

IX Describe the giving of the judgment (note the verdict). What were the main factors stressed by the judge in deciding whether the defendant(s) was guilty or not? Did he comment the prosecution or defence?

X   What was the sentence? Outline the main points stated by the judge imposing the punishment.

XI How long did the trial take? Note details and reasons for any adjournments.

XII Note any other important factors or things that happened.

Appendix 5.   Interview schedule for judges

Section A: Pre-trial Stage

1   Describe how you prepare for trial.

2   What common problems do you encounter at this time?

3   What improvements would you like to see at this stage?

Section B: Trial Stage

4   Describe a typical day in court.

5   What are the main problems that you see in the trial process? And how do you deal with them?

6   What improvements do you think are necessary to solve these problems?

7   What are the most important factors for you in determining whether the defendant is guilty or not guilty?

8   When you sentence a defendant, what are the most important factors for you in determining the amount of punishment?

9   How is your working relationship with the prosecutor, police and defence lawyer?

Section C: Training and Education

10   In your opinion, what education and training should judges have?

11   Do you think that additional education and training would be helpful for judges?

12   Would you like to have continuing education and training opportunities? If so, what do you think this should include? How would this help you?

Section D: Overall

13   What do you think are the main issues and problems facing you as a judge in China's criminal justice process?

14 Is there anything else that you would like to tell me?

Section E: Background

Note: You remind the person that the information is completely confidential. There is nothing in this interview which will identify you in any way. However, I would like to ask you some very basic questions about your background concerning your age, qualifications and professional experience.

15 Gender: 16 Age:

17 Academic and Professional qualifications:

18 Employment prior to becoming a judge (Type of job and number of years):

19 Years of experience as a judge:

Appendix 6. Interview schedule for prosecutors

Section A: Pre-trial Review Stage

1 What do you do at this stage?

2 What factors do you take into account when deciding: 1) To prosecute 2) Not to prosecute?

3 What are the main problems you face at this stage? For example, do you have to send matters back to the PSB on a regular basis?

4 How would you describe your working relationship with the PSB?

5 How would you describe your working relationship with the defence lawyer?

6 What changes/improvements would you like to see at this stage?

Section B: Trial Stage

7 How do you prepare for trial?

8 What are the problems that you face during the trial?

9 How would you describe your working relationship with the judges?

10 What changes/improvements would you like to see at this stage?

11 Have you ever formally protested against a judgment? If so, what were the details?

Section C: Training and Education

12 Do you think you were adequately trained when you started working as a prosecutor?

13 Do you think that additional education and training would be helpful for prosecutors?

14   Would you like to have continuing education and training opportunities? If so, what do you think this should include? How would this help you?

Section D: Overall

15   What do you think are the main issues and problems facing you as a prosecutor in China's criminal justice process?

16   Is there anything else that you would like to tell me?

Section E: Background

Note: You remind the person that the information is completely confidential. There is nothing in this interview which will identify you in any way. However, I would like to ask you some very basic questions about your background concerning your age, qualifications and professional experience.

17   Gender: 18   Age: 19   Academic and Professional qualifications:

20   Employment prior to becoming a prosecutor (Type of job and number of years):

21   Years of experience as a prosecutor:

Appendix 7. Interview schedule for defenders

Section A: Pre-trial Stage

1. Describe how you prepare for the defence.

2. Have you experienced any problems in this respect?

3. What improvements would you like to see at this stage?

Section B: Trial Stage

4. What are the main problems that you encounter when defending a case? And how do you deal with them?

5. What improvements do you think are necessary to solve these problems?

6. Will your opinions be accepted by the judge when deciding upon sentence?

7. How is your working relationship with the prosecutor, police and judges?

Section C: Training and Education

8. In your opinion, what qualifications should a defender have in terms of education and training?

9. Do you think that additional education and training would be helpful for lawyers and other defenders?

10. Would you like to have continuing education and training opportunities? If so, what do you think this should include? How would this help you?

Section D: Overall

11. What do you think are the main issues and problems facing you as a lawyer and defender in China's criminal justice process?

12. Is there anything else that you would like to tell me?

Section E: Background

Note: You remind the person that the information is completely confidential. There is nothing in this interview which will identify you in any way. However, I would like to ask you some very basic questions about your background concerning your age, qualifications and professional experience.

13 Gender: 14 Age:

15 Academic and Professional qualifications:

16 Employment prior to becoming a lawyer or defender (Type of job and number of years):

17 Years of experience as a lawyer:

Appendix 8. A note on administrative punishment in China[1]

DEMARCATION BETWEEN CRIMINAL PUNISHMENT AND ADMINISTRATIVE PUNISHMENT[2]

This is a short note on an important area of punishment regimes that fall outside our research and for which we have no original data. It is necessary to understand, however, that in China, a large proportion of what might be ordinarily seen as 'criminal' acts do not come before the courts and are dealt with instead by the police. Thus, Article 15(1) of the Criminal Procedure Law 1996 (CPL 1996) provides that 'no criminal responsibility shall be investigated if an act is obviously minor, causing no serious harm, and is therefore not deemed a crime'. Similarly, Article 2 of the Security Administration Punishment Law (SAPL) also provides that:

> With regard to an act of disrupting public order, encroaching upon the right of the person, the right of property or impairing social administration, if it is of social harmfulness and constitutes any crime as provided for in the Criminal Law of the People's Republic of China, it shall be subject to criminal liabilities. If it is not serious enough to be subject to a criminal punishment, it shall, in accordance with this law, be subject to public security punishment by the public security organ.

In other words, unlawful acts are not necessarily dealt with by the formal judicial process in China. Depending on their circumstances/seriousness, they can be either disposed of by the police administratively according to the SAPL or handled according to the procedures as set out in the CPL 1996. The power to decide which of these two case disposition methods should be adopted is vested with the police. For example, where a person intentionally inflicts personal injury on another person, if the circumstances of the case are considered as not serious enough to constitute a crime (a police decision),

---

[1] For an authoritative account of administrative punishment, see Sarah Biddulph (2007). Much of our understanding here is derived from her insightful research. See also, Peerenboom (2004). For critical accounts see: United Nations Working Group on Arbitrary Detention (1998); Amnesty International (2002); Human Rights in China (2001a); Yu Ping (2002). See also, Flora Sapio (2010). Examining the co-existence of arbitrary detention and a transition towards a rule of law, Sapio argues that behind the law in China there lies a sovereign power premised on the choice to handle certain issues that derogate from rights.

[2] For the demarcation between criminal control and administrative control in China, see for example, Sarah Biddulph (1993). See also, Peerenboom (2004) making the valid point that there are significant differences between the various forms of detention available in terms of the purposes, justifications, the targets of detention, the nature and seriousness of the offence(s), the punishment or length of detention and the effectiveness and recidivism rates: *ibid.*, at p. 1010.

the police may impose on him/her administrative punishment ranging from not more than five days' administrative detention, a fine of RMB 500, to administrative detention for not less than five days but not more than ten days and a fine of not less than RMB 200 but not more than RMB 500.[3] However, if his act is considered by the police as serious enough to constitute a crime, according to Article 234 of the Criminal Law 1997 (CL 1997), he is punishable by imprisonment for less than three years, criminal detention or public surveillance; and if severe injury was caused, he may be sentenced to imprisonment for not less than three years but not more than ten years.[4] Many other forms of administrative punishment are available in various circumstances including: 'Re-education through labour'; compulsory drug treatment; and forced detention in psychiatric hospitals.[5]

It must not be assumed that 'administrative' punishment is a diluted form of punishment although the stated aim is to combine education with punishment. Conditions in detention centres are varied and historically many have been shown to be very poor.[6] Researchers and reformers have documented that detainees often sought escape or committed suicide. The period in detention was not simply a form of restraint: it also represented an opportunity for the police to use torture on detainees with a view to extracting confessions.[7]

Apart from the public security organs, depending on the nature of the unlawful acts and the relevant legislation, the Administrative Punishment Law (APL) also empowers other administrative organs in China to impose administrative punishments on the perpetrators of certain unlawful acts instead of investigating their criminal responsibility according to the CPL 1996. For example, instead of initiating prosecution according to the CPL 1996, the tax authorities and the land administration authorities may impose administrative punishments on those who evade tax and those who illegally transferred land-use rights to make profits respectively. But for the purpose of this Note, the following discussion will only focus on the administrative punishment imposed by the police, the major administrative punishment-imposing organ in China.

REASONS FOR GIVING POLICE THE ADMINISTRATIVE PUNISHMENT POWER

As pointed out by Professor Biddulph (1993), the official purpose of the administrative punishment system is to complement the criminal justice system.[8] Police administrative punishment power played a significant role in crime control in the early 1980s when China first started its economic reform. The rapid economic reform led to a series of

---

[3] Article 43, SAPL.
[4] Article 234, CL 1997.
[5] As to psychiatric hospitals, see Munro (2000).
[6] Human Rights in China (2001b).
[7] See further, Biddulph (1993); and Fu (1994a).
[8] See also, Peerenboom (2006) who describes the various forms of administrative detention available and how their use has changed substantially from dealing with political offences towards dealing much more with petty criminals: *ibid.*, at pp. 853 ff.

problems such as the influx of rural migrants to the cities, a breakdown in the household registration system, and a drastic increase in the crime rate (crimes committed by rural migrants in particular).[9] The Security Administration Punishment Regulation (SAPR), the predecessor of the SAPL, was enacted in such a social context, aiming at 'strengthening the administration of public security, maintaining social order and public safety, protecting the lawful rights of citizens and guaranteeing the smooth progress of the socialist modernization'.[10] The SAPR was the legal basis for the police imposition of administrative punishment. By empowering the police to punish public order offences and misdemeanours administratively, not only could the caseload of the courts be reduced, but disposition of cases could be speeded up.

CATEGORIES OF ADMINISTRATIVE PUNISHMENT

According to Articles 10 and 11 of the SAPL, administrative punishments include warning, fine, administrative detention, revocation of licences issued by the public security organs, confiscation of tools of the crime and proceeds of crime. There is no clear guideline in the SAPL stipulating the appropriate administrative punishment that should be imposed in a particular situation. The decision is solely vested in the police officers concerned.[11]

In respect of administrative detention, although the maximum duration as stipulated in the SAPL was 15 days, the Decision of the State Council Concerning Questions about Re-education through Labour (issued on 3 August 1957), the Supplementary Provisions of the State Council Concerning Re-education through Labour (issued on 29 November 1979), and the Trial Measure of the State Council on Re-education through Labour (issued on 21 January 1982) (Trial Measure) empower the police to put any person who satisfies any of the following conditions under *re-education through labour* (*laodong jiaoyang*) for a term between one year to three years, with the possibility of a one year's extension in case of necessity:[12]

> Counter-revolutionaries, anti-Party and anti-socialism elements whose crimes are minor and short of being investigated for criminal responsibilities;
> Persons who have committed offences such as murder, robbery, rape and arson in gang but are short of being investigated for criminal responsibilities;
> Persons who have committed crimes such as hooliganism, prostitution, theft and fraud; refuse to mend despite repeated admonition; and short of being investigated for criminal responsibilities;
> Persons who disrupted social order by acts such as gathering others to engage in affray, causing nuisance, inciting troubles and disturbances but short of being investigated for criminal responsibilities;
> Persons who have a job but persistently refuse to work; disrupt work discipline; continuously causing nuisances unreasonably; disrupting production order, work order, teaching or research order, and life order; obstructing public work; and refuse to listen to advice; and

---

[9] See also, Zhou (1989).
[10] Article 1, SAPR.
[11] Biddulph (1993); Ma Yue (1997).
[12] See further, Human Rights in China (2001b).

Persons who instigated others to commit crime but are short of being investigated for criminal responsibilities.[13]

Paragraph 4 of the Decision of the Standing Committee of the National People's Congress on Strict Prohibition Against Prostitution and Whoring 1991 also provides that prostitutes and their clients who are apprehended by the police may be put under shelter for education for a duration between six months and two years;[14] and for prostitutes and peoples who visited prostitutes who had been apprehended by the police and apprehended by the police again for engaging in prostitution, they should be put under re-education through labour.[15]

IMPOSITION OF ADMINISTRATIVE PUNISHMENT BY THE POLICE

We do not have original research data on the use of administrative punishment by the police and we are accordingly reliant on official statistics and the work done by others, in particular, Sarah Biddulph. In practice, it would appear that the imposition of administrative punishment by the Chinese police is very frequent. This situation is clearly reflected in Tables App. 8.1 and App. 8.2.

As can be seen in Table App. 8.1, it is clear that with the exception of years 1989 and 1990, the number of public security cases accepted by the police has been much higher than the number of criminal cases they filed for the past 20 years since 1986. Additionally, during the same period, the number of cases accepted by the police each year has been between 3.7 times and 12.5 times greater than the number of first instance criminal cases received by the courts. Similarly, as shown in Table App. 8.2, between 1986 and 2008 the number of public security cases concluded by the police has also risen from three times as many to more than ten times as many the number of first instance criminal cases concluded by the courts.

The most common categories of public security cases handled by the police, as reported in the *China Law Yearbooks*, were petty theft, assault, gambling, violation of the administration of household registration and citizens' identity cards, disruption of social order, prostitution and hooliganism.[16]

---

[13] Article 10 of the Trial Measure. There is no doubt that 're-education through labour' was widely used historically to oppress political dissent. It has been argued that this function is now much less prominent: Chen Ruihua (2002).

[14] Shelter for education is another kind of administrative detention that can be imposed by the police, but the targets of such kind of administrative detention are mainly prostitutes and their clients, and the former in particular.

[15] Except prostitutes and their clients, other categories of misdemeanants who are targets of re-education through labour include misdemeanants who are rural migrants and offenders of minor crimes who have previous criminal records, etc. For the details of the functions of re-education through labour, see Fu (2005b).

[16] *China Law Yearbook* (1987–2008).

Table App. 8.1 Public security cases accepted by the police and first instance criminal cases filed by the police and received by the courts (1986–2008)

Year	No. of public security cases accepted by the police	No. of criminal cases filed by the police	No. of first instance criminal cases received by the courts
1986	1 115 858	547 115	299 720
1987	1 234 910	570 439	289 614
1988	1 410 044	827 594	313 306
1989	1 847 625	1 971 901	392 564
1990	1 965 663	2 216 997	459 656
1991	2 414 065	2 365 709	427 840
1992	2 956 737	1 582 659	422 991
1993	3 351 016	1 616 879	403 267
1994	3 300 972	1 660 734	482 927
1995	3 289 760	1 609 407	495 741
1996	3 363 636	1 600 716	618 826
1997	3 227 669	1 613 629	436 894
1998	3 232 113	1 986 068	482 164
1999	3 356 083	2 249 319	540 008
2000	4 437 417	3 637 307	560 432
2001	5 713 934	4 457 579	628 996
2002	6 232 350	4 336 712	631 348
2003	5 995 594	4 393 893	632 605
2004	6 647 724	4 718 122	647 541
2005	7 377 600	4 648 401	684 897
2006	7 197 200	4 744 136	702 445
2007	8 709 398	4 807 517	724 112
2008	9 411 956	4 884 960	767 842

Sources: China Law Yearbook (1987–2006), China Statistical Yearbook (2007–2009).

REASONS BEHIND THE HIGH NUMBER OF PUBLIC SECURITY CASES

Whilst there may be valid arguments in favour of retaining administrative detention in some form in China,[17] it is generally agreed that there are identifiable factors which explain the low number of cases that might be truly 'criminal' transferred by all the public security bureaux to the judicial organs. The principal factors are: the reluctance of the

---

[17] See, Peerenboom (2004). Whilst recognizing the deficiencies of China's elaborate system of detention, Peerenboom argues that '[A]dvocating the elimination of all forms of administrative detention is overly simplistic, politically infeasible, and likely to harm those who are supposed to benefit from their abolishment.' (ibid., at p. 1103) One main strand of Peerenboom's argument is that the argument for absorbing administrative offences into the criminal system will become stronger as the formal criminal system begins to more fully deliver on its promises with respect to the procedural protections for criminal suspects.

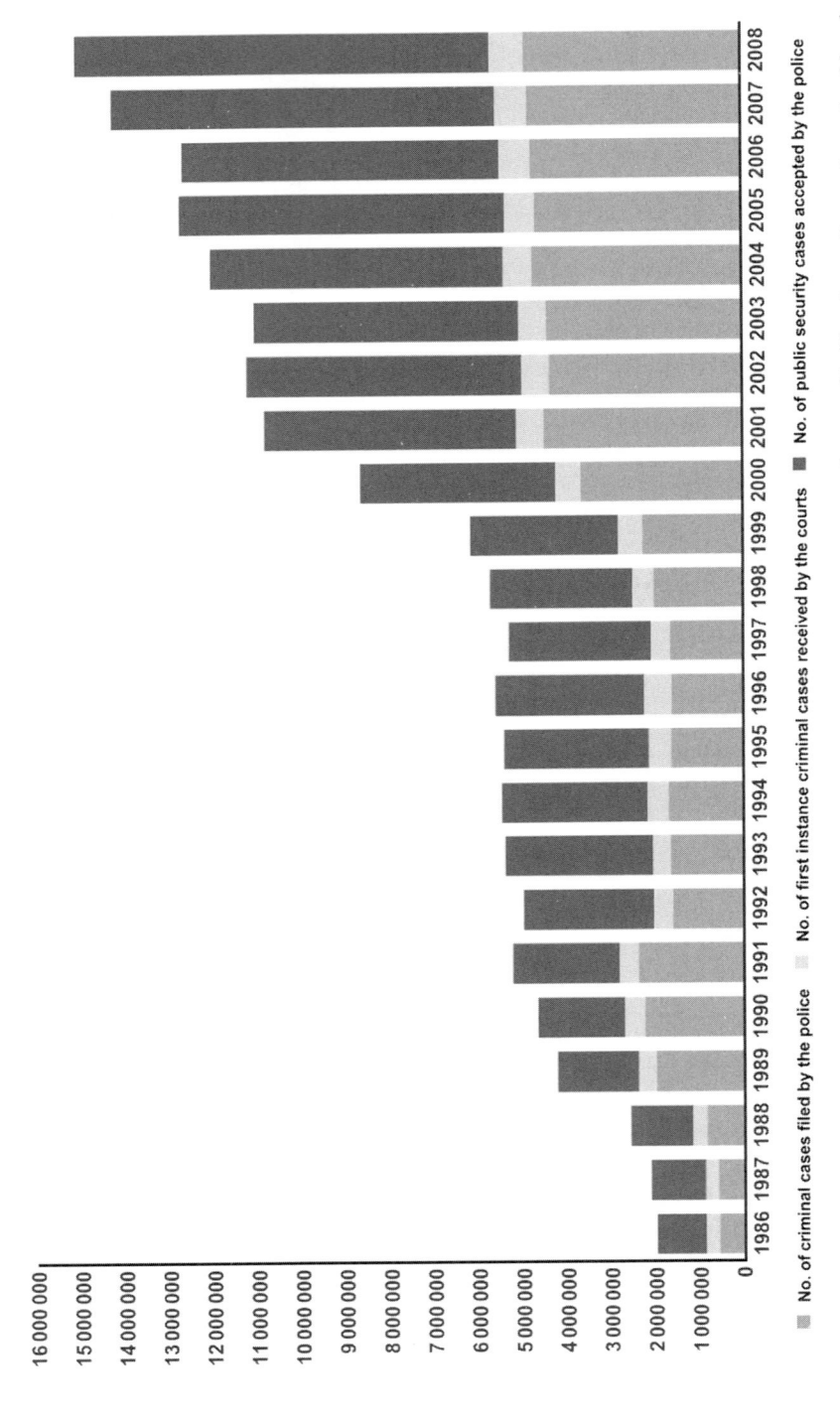

Figure App. 8.1 Public security cases accepted by the police and first instance criminal cases filed by the police and received by the courts (1986–2008)

Table App. 8.2 Public security cases concluded by the police and first instance criminal cases concluded by the courts (1986–2008)

Year	No. of public security cases concluded by the police	No. of first instance criminal cases concluded by the courts
1986	1 004 203	298 291
1987	1 125 949	292 136
1988	1 301 277	312 475
1989	1 719 110	389 597
1990	1 835 779	457 552
1991	2 240 648	427 607
1992	2 529 614	424 440
1993	2 839 124	403 177
1994	2 865 754	480 914
1995	2 968 220	496 082
1996	3 117 623	616 676
1997	3 003 799	440 577
1998	2 994 282	480 374
1999	3 105 940	539 335
2000	3 823 011	560 111
2001	4 851 600	623 792
2002	5 196 998	628 549
2003	4 869 591	634 953
2004	5 365 787	644 248
2005	6 300 772	683 997
2006	6 153 699	701 379
2007	7 649 785	720 666
2008	8 772 299	768 130

Sources: China Law Yearbook (1987–2006), China Statistical Yearbook (2007–2009).

PSB to relinquish control over cases; the retention of budgetary control; and the lack of professional skills of the PSB. Each of these will be shortly noted.

RELUCTANCE OF THE ADMINISTRATIVE ORGANS TO RELINQUISH THEIR AUTHORITY OVER CASES[18]

As mentioned above, the decision as to whether to have a case handled administratively or have it dealt with in the formal judicial process is solely in the hands of the police concerned. Accordingly, the police are reluctant to transfer cases to the judicial organs because such a transfer is seen as compromising their control over their administrative punishment powers. And in fact, as Ma Yue succinctly remarked, the police also consider the administrative punishment power crucial to their work:

---

[18] Wu and Hong (2005).

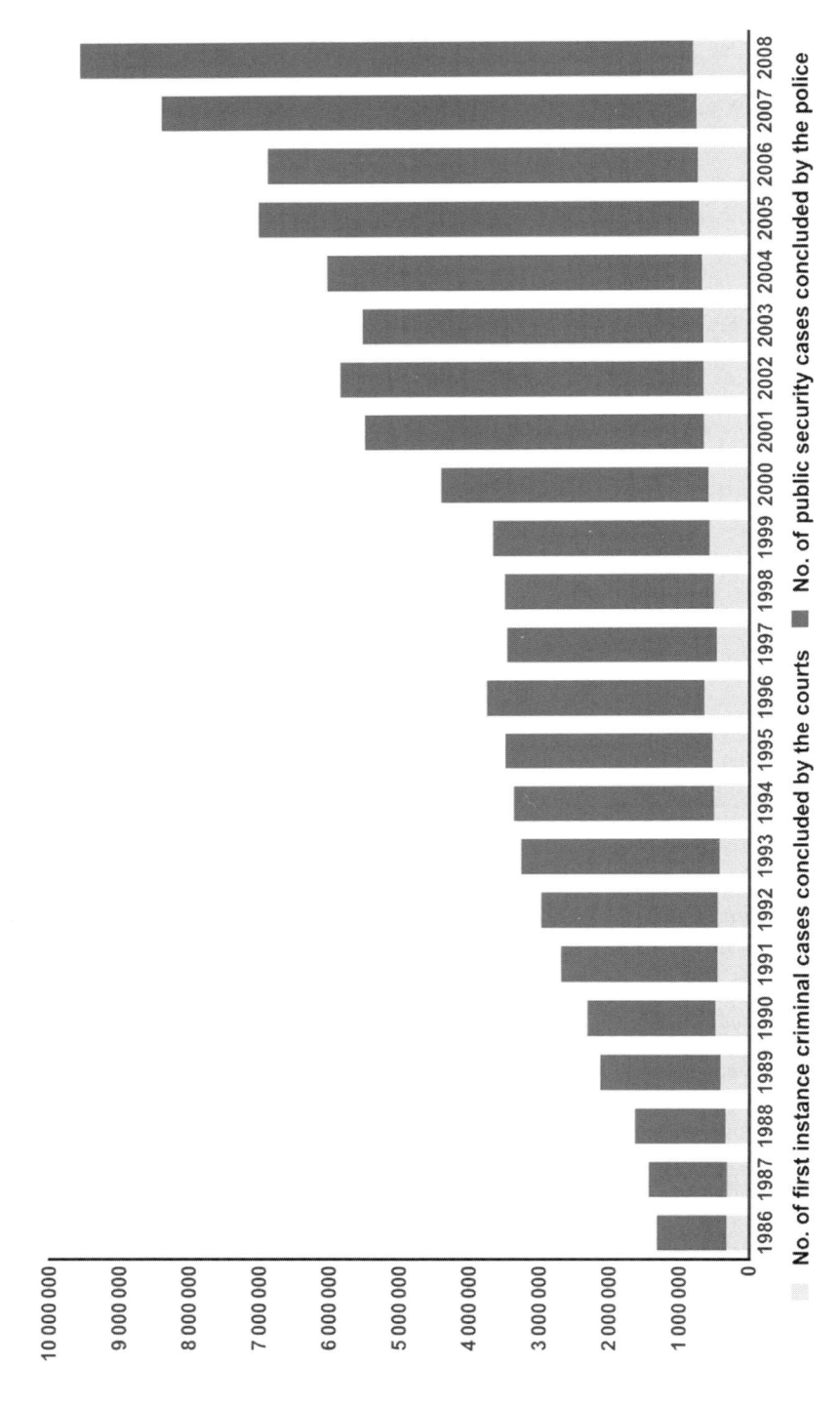

Figure App. 8.2 Public security cases concluded by the police and first instance criminal cases concluded by the courts (1986–2008)

The Chinese police are granted powers to impose a wide range of administratively coercive or punitive measures. These administrative measures, which largely lie outside the control of the court, have long been considered by the police to be among the most effective weapons in their arsenal.[19]

BUDGETARY SHORTFALL OF THE ADMINISTRATIVE ORGANS[20]

In practice, the police have often been ready to exercise (or even abuse) the wide administrative punishment power they enjoy to extract personal and/or institutional benefits. For example, instead of filing a case according to the 1996 CPL, some police officers may impose fines (in order to extract personal gain) on the perpetrators of what they are able, in their discretion, to characterize as an 'unlawful act' notwithstanding that it is serious enough to warrant criminal punishment. Moreover, even in handling cases that are not serious enough to constitute crimes, given the wide range of administrative punishment and the great discretion enjoyed by the police in determining what kinds of administrative punishment should be imposed, very often the police are able to impose a fine on the perpetrators in lieu of punishment. Similarly, because of insufficient police budgetary resources, some public security organs may also resort to such tactics in order to collect funds so as to maintain the normal operation of the institution.

IGNORANCE OF EVIDENCE AND POOR INVESTIGATION SKILLS OF THE ADMINISTRATIVE ORGANS' PERSONNEL[21]

Given poor investigation skills of many police officers and their failure to appreciate the importance of evidence requirements, the police may fail to collect relevant evidence, the evidence collected by them may be of poor quality or have been improperly obtained. The lack of sufficient evidence and/or the poor quality of evidence definitely has an impact on having a case disposed according to the formal judicial process. Accordingly, for reasons of expediency, administrative punishments may be imposed by the police in cases in which they do not have sufficient evidence to initiate a prosecution.[22]

---

[19] Ma Yue (1997).
[20] Wu and Hong (2005).
[21] Ibid.
[22] Congressional-Executive Commission on China 2005 Annual Report (2005).

Bibliography

Ai, Jianguo and Junying Yan (2006), 'Improvement of the Review and Approval of Arrest Mechanism under the Perspective of Harmony – Survey Analysis of the Application of Arrest in the Cases of Public Prosecution of Minor Offences', *Renmin Jiancha (People's Procuratorate Semi-monthly)*, cited in Sun Changyong (ed.), *Zhencha Chengxu yu Renquan Baozhang – Zhongguo Zhechan Chengxu de Gaige he Wanshan (Investigation Procedure and Protection of Human Rights – Reform and Improvement of Chinese Criminal Investigation Procedure)*, (2009) Beijing: China Legal System Publishing House, at p. 35.

Alford, William (1995), 'Tasselled Loafers for Barefoot Lawyers: Transformation and Tension in the World of Chinese Legal Workers', *The China Quarterly*, **141**: 22.

Alford, William (1999), 'A Second Great Wall? China's Post-Cultural Revolution Project of Legal Construction', *Cultural Dynamics*, **11**: 193.

Alford, William (2003), 'Of Lawyers Lost and Found: Searching for Legal Professionalism in the People's Republic of China', in A. Rosett, L. Cheng and M. Woo (eds), *East Asian Law: Universal Norms and Local Culture*, London: Routledge.

Amnesty International (2001), *Torture – A Growing Scourge in China – Time for Action 2*, New York: Amnesty International.

Amnesty International (2002), *Amnesty International Report 2002, China*, New York: Amnesty International.

Amnesty International (2008), *Death Sentences and Executions in 2008*, Amnesty International Publications, available at http://www.amnesty.org./en/library/info/ACT 50/003/2009/en.

Anderlini, Jamil (2009), 'Punished Supplicants', *Financial Times (online)*, 5 March.

Ashworth, Andrew (1994), *The Criminal Process: An Evaluative Study*, Oxford: Clarendon Press.

Ashworth, Andrew (1996), 'Human Rights, Legal Aid and Criminal Justice', in Richard Young and David Wall (eds), *Access to Criminal Justice*, London: Blackstone.

Ashworth, Andrew and Mike Redmayne (2005), *The Criminal Process: An Evaluative Study*, Oxford: Oxford University Press.

Bai, Long (2010), 'Supreme People's Court: The Strictest Evidentiary Rules Must be Implemented in Death Penalty Cases', available at http://politics.people.com.cn/GB/1026/11820740.html.

Baker, Beverly G. (1982), 'Chinese Law in the Eighties: The Lawyer and the Criminal Process', *Albany Law Review*, **46**: 757.

Bakken, Borge (1998), *Migration in China*, Copenhagen: NIAS Press.

Bakken, Borge (2000), *The Exemplary Society*, Oxford: Oxford University Press.

Bakken, Borge (2004), 'Moral Panics, Crime Rates and Harsh Punishment in China', *The Australian and New Zealand Journal of Criminology*, **37**: 67.

Bakken, Borge (ed.) (2005), *Crime Punishment and Policing in China*, Lanham, MD: Rowman and Littlefield Publishers Inc.
Balbus, Isaac (1971), *The Dialects of Legal Repression*, New York: Russell Sage.
Balbus, Isaac (1977), 'Commodity Form and Legal Form: An Essay on the "Relative Autonomy" of the Law', *Law & Society Review*, **11(3)**: 571.
Baldwin, John (1993), 'Legal Advice at the Police Station', *Criminal Law Review*, 371.
Balme, Stephanie (2009a), 'Ordinary Justice and Popular Constitutionalism in China', in Stephanie Balme and Michael Dowdle (eds), *Building Constitutionalism in China*, New York: Palgrave Macmillan.
Balme, Stephanie (2009b), 'Local Courts in Western China', in *Judicial Independence in China: Lessons for Global Law Promotion*, available at http://www.amazon.com/Judicial-Independence-China-Lessons-Promotion/dp/0521137349.
Balme, Stephanie (2009c), 'Judicial Independence in China', available at http://www.amazon.com/Judicial-Independence-China-Lessons-Promotion/dp/0521137349.
Balme, Stephanie (2010), 'Local Courts in Western China', in Randall Peerenboom (ed.), *Judicial Independence in China*, Cambridge: Cambridge University Press.
Banton, Michael (1964), *The Policeman in the Community*, London: Tavistock.
Bedau, Hugo and Michael Radelet (1987), 'Miscarriages of Justice in Potentially Capital Cases', *Stanford Law Review*, **40**: 21.
Belkin, Ira (2007), 'China', in Craig Bradley (ed.), *Criminal Procedure: A Worldwide Study*, Durham, NC: Carolina Academic Press.
Biddulph, Sarah (1993), 'Review of Police Powers of Administrative Detention in the People's Republic of China', *Crime & Delinquency*, **39(3)**: 337.
Biddulph, Sarah (2007), *Legal Reform and Administrative Detention in China*, Cambridge: Cambridge University Press.
Bittner, Egon (1967), 'The Police on Skid Row: A Study in Peacekeeping', *American Sociological Review*, **32**: 699.
Black, Donald (1970), 'Production of Crime Rates', *American Sociological Review*, **35**: 733.
Black, Donald (1971), 'The Social Organization of Arrest', *Stanford Law Review*, **23**: 1087.
Blumberg, Abraham (1967), 'The Practice of Law as Confidence Game: Organizational Cooptation of a Profession', *Law & Society Review*, **1(2)**: 15.
Bodde, Derk and Clarence Morris (1967), *Law in Imperial China*, Cambridge, MA: Harvard University Press.
Borchard, Edwin (1932), *Convicting the Innocent: Sixty-Five Actual Errors of Criminal Justice*, Golden City, NY: Doubleday.
Bottomley, A. Keith and Clive Coleman (1976), 'Criminal Statistics: The Police Role in the Discovery and Detection of Crime', *International Journal of Criminology and Penology*, **4**: 33.
Bottoms, Anthony (2000), 'The Relationship between Theory and Research in Criminology', in Roy King and Emma Wincup (eds), *Doing Research on Crime and Justice*, Oxford: Oxford University Press.
Bottoms, Anthony and John McClean (1976), *Defendants in the Criminal Process*, London: Routledge Kegan Paul.
Box, Steve (1981), *Deviance, Reality and Society*, New York: Holt, Rinehart & Winston.

Brandon, Ruth and Christie Davies (1973), *Wrongful Imprisonment*, London: George Allen & Unwin.

Bridges, Lee and Satnam Choongh (1998), *Improving Police Station Legal Advice*, London: Law Society.

Bridges, Lee, Ed Cape, Asif Abubaker and Chris Bennett (2000), *Quality in Criminal Defence Services*, London: Legal Services Commission.

Bridges, Lee, Ed Cape, Paul Fenn, Anona Mitchell, Richard Moorhead and Avrom Sherr (2007), *Evaluation of the Public Defender Service in England and Wales*, The Stationery Office: London.

Bright, Stephen (1994), 'Counsel for the Poor: The Death Sentence Not for the Worst Crime but for the Worst Lawyer', *Yale Law Journal*, **103**: 1835.

Bright, Stephen (1997), 'Neither Equal nor Just: The Rationing and Denial of Legal Services to the Poor when Life and Liberty are at Stake', *NYU Annual Survey of American Law*, 783.

Brown, David, Tom Ellis and Karen Larcombe (1993), *Changing the Code: Police Detention under the Revised PACE Codes of Practice*, Home Office Research Study No. 129, London: HMSO.

Burrows, John (2000), 'Bail and the Human Rights Act 1998', *New Law Journal*, **150**: 677.

Buxbaum, David C. and Gordon C. Lin (1995), 'Criminal Law Regime Sees Progress After 17 Years', *China Law & Practice* (May, 1995), 54.

Cai, Dingjian (1999a), *Lishi yu Biange: Xin Zhongguo Fazhi Jianshe de Licheng (History and Change: The Process of Construction of Legal System in New China)*, Beijing: China University of Political Science and Law Press.

Cai, Dingjian (1999b), 'On the Reform of the System of Court', *Zhanlue yu Guanli (Strategy and Management)*, **1**: 97.

Cai, Peiyu (2001), 'Reflections on China's Legal Aid System', *Zhengfa Xuekan (Journal of Political Science and Law)*, **6**: 23.

Cao Jingling *et al.* (2010), 'NPC Deputy Wu Xiaoling: Secretary of the Political-legal Committee should not take the position of Head of the Public Security Bureau', *Xinmin Wanbao (Xinmin Evening Newspaper)*, 13 March.

Cao, Wubin and Xianto Zhang (2004), 'Legal Aid is the Responsibility of the Government but Not an Obligation of the Lawyers – Also on the Legislative Defects in the legal liabilities under Chapter 5 of the Legal Aid Regulations', *Keji Chuangye Yuekan (Pioneering with Science & Technology Monthly)*, **12**: 116.

Cape, Ed (1997), 'Sidelining Defence Lawyers: Police Station Advice after Condron', *International Journal of Evidence & Proof*, 386.

Cape, Ed (2006), *Defending Suspects at Police Stations* (5th Edition), London: Legal Action Group.

Cham, Minnie (2010), 'Intercepting Petitioners is a Thriving Business', *South China Morning Post*, Saturday, 3 April.

Chatterton, Michael (1976), 'Police in Social Control', in J.F.S. King (ed.), *Control Without Custody*, Cropwood Papers No. 7, Cambridge Institute of Criminology.

Chen, Albert (1998), *An Introduction to the Legal System of the People's Republic of China*, Hong Kong: Butterworths (3rd Edition of this book, Hong Kong: LexisNexis, 2004).

Chen, Guangzhong (1992), *Xingshi Susongfa de Xiugai yu Wanshan (Revision and Improvement of the Criminal Procedure Law)*, Procedural Law Research Association of the China Law Society, Beijing: China University of Political Science and Law Press.

Chen, Guangzhong (ed.) (1999), *Xingshi Susong Faxue Wushi Nian (Fifty Years' Criminal Procedure Law)*, Beijing: China Police Education Press.

Chen Guangzhong (ed.) (2004), *Shenpan Gongzheng Wenti Yanjiu (A Study on Issues of Fair Trial)*, Beijing: Press of China University of Political Science and Law.

Chen, Guangzhong (2010), 'Survey Report on the Operation of Criminal Procedure at the Second Instance in Our Country', in Guangzhong Chen (ed.), *Xingshifa Luntan (Di San Ji) (Criminal Justice Forum (Vol. 3))*, Beijing: China People's University of Public Security Press.

Chen, Guangzhong and Duan Yan (eds) (1995), *Zhonghua Renmin Gongheguo Xingshi Susongfa Xiugai Jianyigao yu Lunzheng (Annotated Proposed Draft of the Revised Criminal Procedure Law of the People's Republic of China)*, Beijing: China Fangzheng Press.

Chen, Guangzhong and Duan Yan (eds) (1996), *Zhonghua Renmin Gongheguo Xingshi Susongfa Shiyi yu Yingyong (Explanation and Application of the Criminal Procedure Law of the People's Republic of China)*, Jilin: Jilin People's Press.

Chen Guangzhong and Song Yinghui (2000), *Xingshi Susongfa Shishi Wenti Yanjiu (Research on the Issues in Implementation of the Criminal Procedure Law)*, Beijing: China Legal System Publishing House.

Chen, Guangzhong, Weiqui Cheng and Cheng Yang (eds) (2006), *Xingshi Yishen Chengxu yu Renquan Baozhang (Criminal Trial of the First Instance and Protection of Human Rights)*, Beijing: China University of Political Science and Law Press.

Chen, Jianxin (2002a), 'Some "Irregularities" in the Application for Bail', *Fazhi Ribao (Legal Daily)*, 23 March.

Chen, Jianxin (2002b), 'Investigation and Revisit to the Current Situation of Implementing the Domicile Surveillance Measures', *Renda Yanjiu (People's Congress Studying)*, **1**: 40.

Chen, Jicai and Zhonghua Deng (2008), 'On the Improvement and Reinforcement of Right to Defence in the Investigation Proceedings', cited in Guan Yu, *Xingshi Shenqian Chengxu Lushi Bianhu (Criminal Pre-trial Defence)*, Beijing: Law Press, at p. 190.

Chen, Junmin (2010), 'Reflections on High Rate Compulsory Measures as Detention for Non-local Resident Criminals', *Tiedao Jingguan Gaodeng Zhuanke Xuexiao Xuebao (Journal of Railway Police College)*, **1**: 88.

Chen, Lianyi (2000), 'A Brief Analysis of the Phenomenon of "Six Too Many and Six Too Few" in Bail System', *Renmin Jiancha (People's Procuratorial Semi-monthly)*, **7**: 49.

Chen, Lunzhao (1999), 'Survey of Sending Back for Supplementary Investigation Since the Implementation of the New Criminal Procedure Law', *Zhongguo Xingshifa Zazhi (Criminal Science)*, **3**: 62.

Chen, Ruihua (1997), *Xingshi Shenpan Yuanli Lun (On the Theory of Criminal Trial)*, Beijing: Peking University Press.

Chen, Ruihua (2000a), *Kandejian de Zhengyi (Justice Observable)*, Beijing: China Legal System Publishing House.

Chen, Ruihua (2000b), *Xingshi Susong de Qianyan Wenti (The Frontier Issues of Criminal Proceedings)*, Beijing: China People's University Press.

Chen, Ruihua (ed.) (2001), 'Citizens' Rights in Criminal Litigation', in Human Rights Research Centre of the School of Law of the Beijing University, *Sifa Gongzheng Yu Quanli Baozhang (Judicial Fairness and Protection of Rights)*, Beijing: China Legal System Publishing House.

Chen, Ruihua (2002), 'Survey of and Reflections on the History of Re-education Through Labour', in Huaizhi Chu, Xingliang Chen and Shaoyan Zhang (eds), *Lixing yu Zhixu: Zhongguo Laodong Jiaoyang Zhidu Yanjiu (Rationality and Order: Research on China's Re-education Through Labour System)*, Beijing: Law Press.

Chen, Ruihua (ed.) (2005), *Xingshi Bianhu Zhidu de Shizheng Kaocha (Empirical Investigation of the Criminal Defence System)*, Beijing: Peking University Press.

Chen, Ruihua (2009), 'Diagnose the Problem of the Case Instruction System in China', *Falu Xinxi (Legal Information)*, **5**: 55.

Chen, Shufen (2004), 'Reflections on the Establishment of the Rules of Hearsay Evidence', *Luojixue Yanjiu (Sun Yatsen University Forum)*, **2**: 146.

Chen, Weidong (ed.) (2001), *Xingshi Susongfa Shishi Wenti Tiaoyan Baogao (Survey Report on the Problems in the Implementation of the Criminal Procedure Law)*, Beijing: Zhongguo Fangzheng Press.

Chen, Weidong (ed.) (2002), *Xingshi Susongfa Shishi Wenti Duice Yanjiu (A Study of Countermeasures on the Problems Relating to the Implementation of Criminal Procedure Law)*, Beijing: China Fangzheng Press.

Chen, Weidong (ed.) (2004), *Xingshi Shenqian Chengxu Yanjiu (A Study of Criminal Pre-trial Procedure)*, Beijing: Renmin University of China Press.

Chen, Weidong and Jihua Liu (1998), 'Changes in the Judicial Investigation Power of Judges in China's Criminal Litigation', *Faxue Pinglun (Law Review)*, **2**: 51.

Chen, Xingliang (2006), 'A Study of the Criminal Policies of Temper Justice with Mercy', *Faxue Zazhi (Law Science Magazine)*, **2**: 27.

Chen, Xinsheng and Shi Jin (2008), 'Thoughts on Regulated Application of Non-Prosecution because of Doubt', *Xibu Faxue Pinglun (Western Law Review)*, **3**: 58.

Chen, Yongsheng (2004), citing 'Comments on the Case of Wu Liusuo who was in Custody for 14 Years Illegally with Charge of Intentional Homicide', *Guangzhou Qingnian Bao (Guangzhou Youth Daily)*, 20 August 1998 in 'Dilemma of the System of Custody Pending Trial and Solutions', in Chen Ruihua (ed.) (2004), *Weijue Jiya Zhidu de Shizheng Yanjiu (Empirical Study on the System of Custody Pending Trial)*, Beijing: Peking University Press.

Chen, Yongsheng and Xiaolin Li (2005), 'Empirical Survey and Analysis of Difficulties Defence Lawyers Encountered in Cross-examination', in Ruihua Chen (ed.), *Xingshi Bianhu Zhidu de Shizheng Kaocha (Empirical Investigation of the Criminal Defense System)*, Beijing: Peking University Press.

Chen, Yuwen and Weiming Tang (2002), 'Problems in the Incidental Civil Action which are Urgently in Need of Being Solved', available at http://www.chinacourt.org/public/detail.php? id=14082.

Cheng, Dewen (2003), 'Problems on the Witness Appearance and its Solutions', *Nian Susongfa Yanjiuhui Nianhui Lunwenji (Collection of Academic Papers of 2003 Annual Conference of Procedure Law)*, China Law Society, 441.

Cheng, Fei and Ming Cheng (2006), 'Several Thoughts on the Application of the Supplementary Investigation System', *Hubei Caijing Gaodeng Zhuanke Xuexiao Xuebao (Journal of Hubei College of Finance and Economics)*, **6**: 6.

Cheng, Guoping (1998), 'Pretrial Examination May Include Necessary Substantive Examination', *Renmin Jiancha (People's Procuratorate Semi-monthly)*, **2**: 51.

Cheung, Yiu-leung (2009), 'Between a Rock and a Hard Place: China's Criminal Defence Lawyers', in Stacey Mosher and Patrick Poon (eds.), *A Sword and a Shield: China's Human Rights Lawyers*, Hong Kong: China Human Rights Lawyers Concern Group, pp. 57–68.

Chi, Weihui (2002), 'A Brief Discussion on the Problems in the Provisions Regarding Supplementary Investigation in Criminal Litigation and the Relevant Remedies', *Jiancha Shijian (Procuratorial Practice)*, **4**: 12.

China Labor Bulletin (2010), *The Children of Migrant Workers in China*, available at http://www.china-labour.org.hk/en/node/100316 (last viewed 22 May 2010).

Chinese Human Rights Defenders (CHRD) (2009), *Annual Report on the Situation of Human Rights Defenders in China* (2009), available at http://chrdnet.org/wp-content/uploads/2010/04/annual-report-on-the-situation-of-human-rights-defenders-2009-online-version.pdf (last viewed 21 May 2010).

Choi, Chi-yuk (2009), '"Murderer" Freed after Victim Found Alive', *South China Morning Post*, 10 May 2010.

Chong, Songzhi (2009), *Zhongguo Xingshi Shenqian Chengxu Zhidu Goujian (Construction of Criminal Pre-trial Procedure of China)*, Beijing: China People's University of Public Security Press.

Choongh, Satnam (1997), *Policing as Social Discipline*, Oxford: Clarendon Press.

Choongh, Satnam (2002), 'Police Investigative Powers', in Mike McConville and Geoffrey Wilson (eds), *The Handbook of The Criminal Justice Process*, Oxford: Oxford University Press, pp. 43–57.

Chow, Daniel C.K. (2003), *The Legal System of the People's Republic of China*, London: Thomson West.

Ch'u Tung-tsu (Qu Tongzu) (1962), *Local Government in China under the Ching*.

Chu, Weizhu (2009), 'Observation on the Current Situation of Application of Suspended Penalty for Migrant Population in Shanghai', *Fazhi Luncong (The Rule of Law Forum)*, **2**: 76.

Cicourel, Aaron (1968), *The Social Organization of Juvenile Justice*, London: Wiley.

Clark, Gerard (2008), 'An Introduction to the Legal Profession in China in the Year 2008', *Suffolk University Law Review*, **41**: 833.

Clarke, Donald (2003), 'Empirical Research into the Chinese Judicial System', in Erik Jensen and Thomas Heller (eds), *Beyond Common Knowledge: Empirical Approaches to the Rule of Law*, Stanford, CA: Stanford University Press.

Clarke, Donald (2009a), 'Evidence to Congressional-Executive Commission on China Report', *Human Rights and the Rule of Law in China*, available at http://www.cecc.gov/pages/hearings/2009/20091007/index.php?PHPSESSID.

Clarke, Donald (2009b), 'Lawyers and the State in China: Recent Developments', prepared statement for Congressional-Executive Commission on China, 111th Congress, First Session, 7 October, *Human Rights and the Rule of Law in China*, available at http://www.cecc.gov/pages/hearings/2009/20091007/index.php?PHPSESSID.

Clarke, Donald and James Feinerman (1995), 'Antagonistic Contradictions: Criminal Law and Human Rights in China', *China Quarterly*, **141**: 135.
Cohen, Jerome (1968), *The Criminal Process in the People's Republic of China, 1949–63: An Introduction*, Cambridge, MA: Harvard University Press.
Cohen, Jerome (1969), 'The Chinese Communist Party and Judicial Independence', *Harvard Law Review*, **5**: 966.
Cohen, Jerome (1970), *Contemporary Chinese Law: Research Problems and Perspectives*, Cambridge, MA: Harvard University Press.
Cohen, Jerome (1997), 'Reforming China's Civil Procedure: Judging the Courts', *American Journal of Comparative Law*, **45**: 793.
Cohen, Jerome (2001), 'Going on Trial in China', *The Washington Post*, 14 July.
Cohen, Jerome (2003), 'The Plight of China's Criminal Defence Lawyers', *Hong Kong Law Journal*, **33**: 231.
Cohen, Jerome (2005), 'Law in Political Transitions: Lessons from East Asia and the Road Ahead for China', 26 July, available at http://www.cecc.gov/pages/hearings/072605/Cohen.php.
Cohen, Jerome (2008), 'Body Blow for the Judiciary', *South China Morning Post*, 18 October.
Cohen, Jerome (2009a) 'China's Human Rights Lawyers: Current Challenges and Prospects', in Stacey Mosher and Patrick Poon (eds), *A Sword and a Shield: China's Human Rights Lawyers*, Hong Kong: China Human Rights Lawyers Concern Group.
Cohen, Jerome (2009b), 'Beijing Must Reveal Fate of Human Rights Lawyer', *South China Morning Post (Online)*, 19 March.
Cohen, Jerome (2009c), 'Key decisions', *South China Morning Post*, 3 September.
Cohen, Jerome (2009d), 'The Struggle for Autonomy of Beijing's Public Interest Lawyers', 1 *China Rights Forum*, available at http://hrichina.org/public/PDFs/CRF.1.2009?CRF-2009- 1_Cohen.pdf.
Cohen, Jerome (2010a), 'Body Blow for the Judiciary', available at http://lawprofessors.typepad.com/china_law_prof_blog/2008/10/jerome-cohen--1html (last viewed 26 May 2010).
Cohen, Jerome (2010b), 'Sage Advice', *South China Morning Post*, Wednesday, 14 April.
Cohen, Jerome and Eva Pils (2008), 'Hu Jia in China's Legal Labyrinth', *Far Eastern Economic Review* (April), 43.
Cohen, Jerome and Eva Pils (2009), 'The Disappearance of Gao Zhisheng', *Wall Street Journal (Online)*, 9 February.
Cohen, Jerome and Yu-jie Chen (2010a), 'China's Criminal Defense Lawyers – An Endangered Species', *South China Morning Post*, 28 April 2010, available at http://www.usasialaw.org/?p=3536 (last visited 20 May 2010).
Cohen, Jerome and Yu-jie Chen (2010b), 'Don't Argue', *South China Morning Post*, 28 April.
Congressional-Executive Commission on China 2005 Annual Report (2005), available at http://www.cecc.gov/pages/annualRpt/annualRpt05/2005_3b_criminal.php> (last visited 12 June 2007).
Conlon, Gerry (1990), *Proved Innocent*, London: Hamish Hamilton.
Cordone, Claudio (2010), 'Rough Justice', *South China Morning Post*, 31 March.
Corker, David (1996), *Disclosure in Criminal Proceedings*, London: Sweet & Maxwell.

Council of Europe (1996), *The Training of Judges and Public Prosecutors*, Strasbourg: Council of Europe Publishing.
Criminal Law Revision Committee (1971), *Eleventh Report Evidence (General)*, Cmnd 4991.
Cui, Min (1998), 'Problems in the Implementation of the Criminal Procedure Law and the Suggested Solutions', *Xiandai Faxue (Modern Law Science)*, **1**: 18.
Cui, Peng and Guiwu Dong (2009), 'On the Improvement of Criminal Summary Procedure in Our Country', *Falu Shiyong (Journal of Law Application)*, **1**: 96.
Cui, Po and Chenglin Mao (2004), 'Analyzing the System of Plea Bargaining and its Transplantation into China', *Jiancha Shijian (Procuratorial Practice)*, **5**: 65
Cui, Shixin (2000), 'How Can the Law Enforcers Violate the Law – An Examination of a Serious Case Concerning Extended Detention in Dongguan of Guangdong', *Renmin Ribao (People's Daily)*, 19 July.
Cutler, Brian and Steven Penrod (1995), *Mistaken Identification*, Cambridge: Cambridge University Press.
Dai, Mengyan (2008), 'Policing in the People's Republic of China: A Review of Recent Literature', *Crime Law and Social Change* **50**: 211.
Danching, Ruan (1993), 'Interpersonal Networks and Workplace Controls in Urban China', *Australian Journal of Chinese Studies*, **29**: 89.
Dell, Susan (1971), *Silent in Court*, London: Bell.
Delmas-Marty, Mireille and John R. Spencer (2005), *European Criminal Procedures*, Cambridge: Cambridge University Press.
Deng, Shengtao, Jinbo Huang and Ruyu Wu (2001), 'The Reasons for the Witnesses' Refusal to Testify in Court and the Relevant Solution', *Renmin Sifa (People's Judicature)*, **11**: 32.
Dervieux, Valerie (2005), 'The French System', in M. Delmas-Marty and J.R. Spencer (eds), *European Criminal Procedures*, Cambridge: Cambridge University Press, pp. 218–291.
Devlin, Lord (1976), *Report to the Secretary of State for the Home Department of the Departmental Committee on Evidence of Identification in Criminal Cases*, London: HC.
Devlin, Patrick (1960), *Criminal Prosecution in England*, Oxford: Oxford University Press.
Diamant, Neil, Stanley Lubman and Kevin O'Brien (eds) (2005), *Engaging in Law in China: State, Society and Possibilities of Justice*, Stanford, CA: Stanford University Press.
Dicks, Anthony (1995), 'Compartmentalized Law and Judicial Restraint: An Inductive View of Some Jurisdictional Barriers to Reform', *The China Quarterly*, **141**: 82.
Ding, Xingyu and Xiangqian Lu (2004), 'Study and Reflection on the Bengbu Procuratorate's Work of Prevention and Rectification of Extended Detention – And Discussion on Perfecting the Law on the System of Extended Detention in Our Country', *Zhongguo Xingshifa Zazhi (Criminal Science)*, **2**: 102.
Dixon, David, A. Keith Bottomley, Clive Coleman, Martin Gill and David Wall (1990), 'Safeguarding the Rights of Suspects in Police Custody', *Policing and Society*, **1(2)**: 115.
Dobinson, Ian (2002), 'The Criminal Law of the People's Republic of China (1997): Real Change or Rhetoric', *Pacific Rim Law & Policy Journal*, **11**: 1.
Dong, Lili (2007), 'Reflections on Several Problems Related to Domicile Surveillance System in Practice', *Fazhi yu Shehui (Legal System and Society)*, **10**: 827.

Dong, Qihai (2008), 'Comment and Analysis of Empirical Study of Bail Pending Trial in the Zhangjiagang Municipal Procuratorate', *Guojia Jianchaguan Xueyuan Xuebao (Journal of National Prosecutors College)*, **3**: 26.

Dong, Qihai and Qingfeng Zhang (2008), 'Exploration on the Application of Bail Pending Trial for Non-Local Suspects', *Guojia Jianchaguan Xueyuan Xuebao (Journal of National Prosecutors College)*, **3**: 98.

Dong, Xinjian (2000), 'Analysis of the Survey of the Application of Summary Procedure', *Renmin Jiancha (People's Procuratorate Semi-monthly)*, **7**: 51.

Driver, Edwin (1968), 'Confessions and the Social Psychology of Coercion', *Harvard Law Review*, **82**: 42.

Dutton, Michael (1992), *Policing and Punishment in China*, Cambridge: Cambridge University Press.

Ede, Roger and Anthony Edwards (2008), *Criminal Defence: The Good Practice Guide*, London: The Law Society.

Eisenstein, James and Herbert Jacob (1977), *Felony Justice*, Boston, MA: Little Brown.

Eliasoph, Ellen and Susan Grueneberg (1981), 'Law on Display in China', *The China Quarterly*, **88**: 669.

Ericson, Richard (1982), *Reproducing Order: A Study of Police Patrol Work*, Toronto: Toronto University Press.

Esser, Robert (2004), 'Germany', in Craig Bradley (ed.), *Criminal Procedure: A Worldwide Study*, Durham, NC: Carolina Press.

Etzioni, Amitai (1961), *A Comparative Analysis of Complex Organizations*, Glencoe, IL: Free Press.

Evans, Roger (1993), 'The Conduct of Police Interviews with Juveniles', Research Study No. 8, The Royal Commission on Criminal Justice, London: HMSO.

Fan, Chongyi (ed.) (2001), *Xingshi Susongfa Shishi Wenti Yu Duice Yanjiu (A Study on the Problems relating to the Implementation of Criminal Procedure Law and Countermeasures)*, Beijing: China People's University of Public Security Press.

Fan, Chongyi (ed.) (2004), *Xingshi Susong Faxue (Criminal Procedure Law)*, Beijing: Law Press.

Fan, Chongyi (2008a), 'A functional analysis of positive research on investigations of questioning procedure reform', paper delivered at a seminar in the Kennedy School of Government, Harvard at: www.hks.harvard.edu/.../jsw_china_seminar_oct2008.html.

Fan Chongyi (2008b), *Maixiang Lixing Xingshu Susong Faxue (Marching Towards a Rational Path of Criminal Procedure Law Study)*, Beijing: China People's University of Public Security Press.

Fan, Chongyi and Yongzhong Gu (eds) (2007), *Zhencha Xunwen Chengxu Gaige Shizheng Yanjiu (A Positive Research on the Investigative Interrogation Procedure Reform)*, Beijing: Chinese People's Public Security University Press.

Fan, Cindy (2008), *China on the Move: Migration, the State, and the Household*, London: Routledge.

Fang, Baoguo (2010), *Xingshi Zhengju Guize Shizheng Yanjiu (The Demonstrative Research on Criminal Evidence Rule)*, Beijing: Renmin University of China Press.

Fang, Ming and Zhen Wang (2009), 'Research on the Improvement of the Re-education through Labour and the Supervision System', *Xi'nan Zhengfa Daxue Xuebao (Journal of the Southwest University of Political Science and Law)*, **5**: 112.

Fang, Sheng, Jiang Lian and Xing Hong (1997), 'Problems with Bail Pending Trial', *Renmin Jiancha (People's Procuratorial Semi-monthly)*, **9**: 20.
Feeley, Malcolm (1973), 'Two Models of the Criminal Justice System: An Organizational Perspective', *Law & Society Review*, **10**: 407.
Feng, Chuanping (1998), 'Imbalance in the Power of Cross-examination in Court and their Solutions', *Falu Shiyong (Journal of Law Application)*, **2**: 17.
Feng, Hua (2010), 'Promoting the Excellent Tradition of People's Justice, Practicing the Mode of Judicial Activism, and Insisting on the Road of Judicial Professionalization and Popularity', in An Dong (ed.), *Xibu Faguan Luncong (Di 10 Juan) (Forum for Judges in West China (Vol. 10))*, Beijing: People's Court Press.
Feng, Jie (2000), 'On the Allocation of Burden of Proof in Criminal Proceeding', *Zhejiang Zhengfa Guanli Ganbu Xueyuan (Journal of the Zhejiang Administrative Cadre Institute of Politics and Law)*, **4**: 67.
Feng, Quan (2009), *Zhongguo Huanxing Zhidu Yanjiu (Study on System of Suspended Sentence in China)*, Beijing: China University of Political Science and Law Press.
First Criminal Court of Shandong High Court (2008), 'Survey Report on the Application of Suspended Penalty by Courts in Shandong', *Shandong Shenpan (Shandong Justice)*, **5**: 30.
Fisher, Stanley (2000), 'The Prosecutor's Ethical Duty to Seek Exculpatory Evidence in Police Hands: Lessons from England', *Fordham Law Review*, **68**: 1379.
Flood, John A. (1983), *Barristers' Clerks: The Law's Middlemen*, Manchester: Manchester University Press.
Foster, Janet (1989), 'Two Stations: An Ethnographic Study of Policing in the Inner City', in David Downes (ed.), *Crime and the City*, London: Macmillan.
Foster, Peter (2010), 'Leading Chinese dissident claims freedom of speech worse than before Olympics', *Telegraph*, 11 May, available at: http://www.telegraph.co.uk/news/worldnews/asia/china/5230707/Leading-Chinese-dissident-claims-freedom-of-speech-worse-than-before-Olympics.html.
Frase, Richard (2007), 'France', in Craig Bradley (ed.), *Criminal Procedure: A Worldwide Study*, Durham, NC: Carolina Academic Press, pp. 201–242.
Fu, Hualing (1994a), 'A Bird in a Cage: Police and Political Leadership in Post-Mao China', *Policing and Society*, **4(4)**: 277.
Fu, Hualing (1994b), 'A Case for Abolishing Shelter for Examination: Judicial Review and Police Powers in China', *Police Studies*, **17(4)**: 41.
Fu, Hualing (1998), 'Criminal Defence in China: The Possible Impact of the 1996 Criminal Procedure Reform', *The China Quarterly*, **153**: 31.
Fu, Hualing (2000), 'Procuracy', in Freshfields (ed.), *Doing Business in China*, Huntington, NJ: Juris Publishing.
Fu, Hualing (2003), 'Putting China's Judiciary into Perspective: Is It Independent, Competent, and Fair?' in Erik G. Jensen, and Thomas C. Heller, *Beyond Common Knowledge: Empirical Approaches to the Rule of Law*, Stanford, CA: Stanford University Press, pp. 193–219.
Fu, Hualing (2005a), 'Zhou Yongkang and the Recent Police Reform in China', *The Australian and New Zealand Journal of Criminology*, **38(2)**: 241.
Fu, Hualing (2005b), 'Re-education Through Labour in Historical Perspective', *The China Quarterly*, **184**: 811.

Fu, Hualing (2007), 'When Lawyers are Prosecuted: The Struggle of a Profession in Transition', *Social Science Research Network*, available at http://papers.ssrn.com/sol3/papers.cfm?abstract_id=956500.

Fu, Hualing (2010), 'Institutionalizing Criminal Process in China', 13 April, available at http://ssrn.com/abstract=1588733.

Fu, Hualing and Richard Cullen (2007), 'Weiquan (Rights Protection) Lawyering in an Authoritarian State: Toward Critical Lawyering', available at http://papers.ssrn.com/sol3/papers.cfm?abstract_id=1083925.

Fu, Hualing and Richard Cullen (2008), 'Weiquan (Rights Protection) Lawyering in an Authoritarian State', 15 January, available at: http://ssrn.com/abstract=1083925.

Fu, Weigao (1997), 'On Several Problems in the Operation of Summary Procedure in Criminal Litigation', *Faxue (Legal Science Monthly)*, **6**: 51.

Fu, Yulin and Randall Peerenboom (2010), 'A New Analytic Framework for Understanding and Promoting Judicial Independence in China', in Randall Peerenboom (ed.), *Judicial Independence in China*, Cambridge: Cambridge University Press, available at SSRN: http://ssrn.com/abstract=1336069.

Gao, Fei (2008), 'Research on the Reform and Improvement of Criminal Summary Procedure', *Zhongguo Xingshifa Zazhi (Criminal Science)*, **3**: 88.

Gao, Jingfeng and Hongmei Wu (2001), 'Studies on Problems of Wrongful Arrest', *Zhongyang Zhengfa Guanli Ganbu Xueyuan Xuebao (Journal of the Central Political Science and Law Cadres Institute)*, **2**: 21.

Garcon, Maurice (1957), *Defense de la liberte individuelle*, Paris: Librairie Artheme Fayard.

Gelatt, Thomas (1991), 'Lawyers in China: The Past Decade and Beyond', *New York University Journal of International Law and Politics*, **23(3)**: 762.

Geng, Jingyi (1998), 'Studies on the Application and Problems of Criminal Summary Procedure', *Dangdai Faxue (Contemporary Law Review)*, **5**: 26.

Gold, Thomas, Doug Guthrie and David Wank (eds) (2002), *Social Connections in China: Institutions, Culture and the Changing Nature of Guanxi*, New York: Cambridge University Press.

Graef, Roger (1989), *Talking Blues*, London: Collins Harvill.

Greenwood, Peter, Jan Chaiken and Joan Petersilia (1977), *The Criminal Investigation Process*, Lexington: Heath.

Gu, Zhaosen, Qiaoquan Wang and Yongsheng Tan (1999), 'Survey of the Situation of Enforcement of Bail Money in Several Counties and Cities', *Jiangsu Gongan Zhuanke Xuexiao Xuebao (Journal of Jiangsu Public Security College)*, **6**: 60.

Guan, Yu (2008), *Xingshi Shenqian Chengxu Lushi Bianhu (Criminal Pre-trial Defence)*, Beijing: Law Press.

Guang, Yan (2007), 'Legislative Defects on the System of Criminal Compulsory Measures in China and its Improvement', *Guangxi Daxue Xuebao (Zhexue Shehui Kexue Ban) (Journal of Guangxi University (Philosophy and Social Science Edition))*, **29**: 210.

Gudjonsson, Gisli (1992), *The Psychology of Interrogations, Confessions and Testimony*, London: Wiley.

Gudjonsson, Gisli (2002), *The Psychology of Interrogations and Confessions: A Handbook*, London: Wiley.

Gudjonsson, Gisli and N. Clark (1986), 'Suggestibility in Police Interrogation: A Social Psychological Model', *Social Behaviour*, **1**: 83.
Gudjonsson, Gisli and James MacKeith (1982), 'False Confessions: Psychological Effects of Interrogation. A Discussion Paper', in A. Trankell (ed.), *Reconstructing the Past: The Role of Psychologists in Criminal Trials*, Deventer, the Netherlands: Kluwer, pp. 253–269.
Gudjonsson, Gisli and James MacKeith (1988), 'Retracted Confessions', *Medical Science and the Law*, **28**: 187.
Guo, Jingfeng (2003), 'Analyzing the Necessity of the System of Plea Bargaining in Our Country', *Journal of Tianzhong* (December), 60.
Guo, Qing (2001), 'Why Can't the Problem of "Extended Detention" Be Resolved', *Guangming Ribao (Guangming Daily)*, 6 February.
Guo, Youjia (2007), 'Why Does the Discretion Become Comfortless? – Analysis on the Reality of Discretionary Non-Prosecution in Our Country', *Fazhi yu Shehui (Legal System and Society)*, **11**: 819.
Guo, Yunzhong, Chunfeng Wu and Huaiqun Hou (2000), 'On the Transformation of the Criminal Litigation Mechanism and the Establishment of the Ancillary Arrangements – Using the Connection between the System of Allocation of Burden of Proof and the Criminal Litigation Mechanism in China as an Example', *Hebei Faxue (Hebei Law Science)*, **4**: 117.
Guo, Zhiyuan (2007), 'Problems and Countermeasures "Demonstrative Analysis of Reforms on the Simplified Ordinary Procedure"', *Sifa (Journal of Justice)*, 157.
Guo, Zhiyuan (2010), 'Approaching Visible Justice: Procedural Safeguards for Mental Examinations in China's Capital Cases', *Hastings International and Comparative Law Review*, **33(1)**: 21.
Halliday, Terence and Sida Liu (2007), 'Birth of a Liberal Moment? Looking Through a One-Way Mirror at Lawyers' Defense of Criminal Defendants in China', in Terence Halliday, Lucien Karpik and Malcolm Feeley (eds), *Fighting for Political Freedom: Comparative Studies of the Legal Complex and Political Liberalism*, Oxford: Hart Publishing, pp. 65–108.
Hand, Keith (2006), 'Using Law for a Righteous Purpose: The Sun Zhigang Incident and Evolving Forms of Citizen Action in the People's Republic of China', *Columbia Journal of Transnational Law*, **45**: 114.
Hartley, Aidan (2007), 'The Secrets of Beijing's "Black Jails"', *The Spectator*, 13 October.
Hayes, Rupert (2006), 'China's New Wealth and Old Failings', *BBC News*, 12 October, http://news.bbc.co.uk/1/hi/programmes/from_our_own_correspondent/6041524.stm.
He, Huifeng (2010), 'Shockwaves as Top Judge Detained over Dismembered Body', *South China Morning Post*, 31 July.
He, Jiahong (1999), 'Thoughts on the Reform of the System of People's Assessors', *Zhongguo Lushi (Chinese Lawyer)*, **4**: 12.
He, Jiahong (2002), 'My Views on the Allocation of Burden of Proof in Criminal Litigation', *Zhengzhi yu Falu (Political Science and Law)*, **1**: 68.
He, Jiahong (ed.) (2004), *Zhengren Zhidu Yanjiu (A Study on Witness System)*, Beijing: The People's Court Press.
He, Jiahong (ed.) (2006), *Zhengjuxue Luntan (Evidence Forum) (Vol. 11)*, Beijing: Law Press.

He, Jiahong and Ran He (2008), 'Evidentiary Problems in the Wrongful Criminal Convictions: Empirical and Economic Analysis', *Zhengfa Luntan (Tribune of Political Science and Law)*, **2**: 3.

He, Qinhua (ed.) (2009), *Shehui Zhuyi Falu Tixi Yanjiu: 1949–2009 (Studies on the Socialist Legal System: 1949–2009)*, Beijing: China Law Press.

He, Weifang (1998), *Sifa de Linian yu Zhidu (Concepts and Systems of the Judicature)*, Beijing: China University of Political Science and Law Press.

He, Weifang (n.d.), 'Difficult Position of Judicial Reform and Paths', available at http://blog.sina.com.cn/s/blog_488663200100b0nw.html.

Hecht, Jonathan (1996a), *Opening to Reform? An Analysis of China's Revised Criminal Procedure Law*, New York: Lawyers Committee for Human Rights.

Hecht, Jonathan (1996b), 'PRC: Editorial Hails Amendments to Criminal Procedure Law', Foreign Broadcast Information Service: China, 28 March.

Henderson, Keith (2010), 'Halfway Home and a Long Way to Go', in Randall Peerenboom (ed.), *Judicial Independence in China*, Cambridge: Cambridge University Press, pp. 23–36.

Heydebrand, Wolf (1979), 'The Technocratic Administration of Justice', in S. Spitzer (ed.), *Research in Law and Sociology*, Greenwich, CT: Jai Press.

Hill, Paddy and Gerard Hunt (1995), *Forever Lost, Forever Gone*, London: Bloomsbury.

Hodgson, Jacqueline (2005), *French Criminal Justice: A Comparative Account of the Investigation and Prosecution of Crime in France*, Oxford: Hart Publishing.

Hodgson, Jacqueline (2006), 'Conceptions of the Trial in Inquisitorial and Adversarial Procedure', in Anthony Duff, Lindsay Farmer, Sandra Marshall and Victor Tadros (eds), *Trial on Trial (vol. 2): Judgment and Calling to Account*, Oxford: Hart, pp. 223–242.

Hou, Xiaoyan and Cui Li (2003), 'Puuting into Effect Lawyers' Involvement in Human Rights', *Beijing Qingnian Bao (Beijing Youth Daily)*, 6 July.

Hu, Guojian (2004), 'In between Theory and Practice – Analysing the Reasons for the Ignorance of Bail', *Gansu Xingzheng Xueyuan Xuebao (Journal of Gansu Institute of Public Administration)*, **2**: 96.

Hu, Yunteng (2002), 'Application of the Death Penalty in Chinese Judicial Practice', in Chen Jianfu et al. (eds), *Implementation of Law in the People's Republic of China*, The Hague: Kluwer Law International.

Hu, Zhifang and Zhihui Hu (2009), 'Supplementary Investigation During the Review and Approval for Prosecution', *Zhengfa Xuekan (Journal of Political Science and Law)*, **2**: 70.

Huang, Changxing and Chen Ye (2006), 'Reflection on the "Five Rates" Evaluating Non-Prosecution in the Public Prosecution', *Zhongguo Jianchaguan (The Chinese Procurators)*, **6**: 68.

Huang, Chunhong (2002), 'Situation of Legal Aid in Criminal Cases in Our Country and Some Reflections on This Issue', *Shanghai Zhengfa Guanli Ganbu Xueyuan Xuebao (Law Journal of Shanghai Administrative Cadre Institute of Politics and Law)*, **4**: 88.

Huang, Jie (2010), 'Analysis of "the Explanations on the Conditions" from Evidentiary Nature – Also on the Construction of System of Investigators' Testimony in Court', *Zhongguo Xingshifa Zazhi (Criminal Science)*, **5**: 7.

Huang, Wen (2004), 'The Judge's Right to Investigate Outside the Court: A Rational Approach?', *Dangdai Faxue (Contemporary Law Review)*, **2**: 127.

Huang, Wensheng (2009), 'Thoughts on the Problems of Re-education through Labour in our Country and Countermeasures', *Wuhan Gong'an Ganbu Xuebao (Journal of Wuhan Public Security Cadre College)*, 65.

Huang, Xiangqing (2001), 'Mastery of the Criminal Policy of Strike Hard', *Zhengzhi yu Falu (Political Science and Law)*, **6**: 23.

Hucklesby, Anthea (1994), 'The Use and Abuse of Conditional Bail', *Howard Journal of Criminal Justice*, **3**: 258.

Human Rights in China (2000), *Impunity for Torturers Continues Despite Changes in the Law: Report on the Convention Against Torture in the People's Republic of China*, New York: Human Rights in China.

Human Rights in China (2001a), *Empty Promises: Human Rights Protections and China's Criminal Procedure Law in Practice*, New York: Human Rights in China.

Human Rights in China (2001b), *Reeducation Through Labor (RTL): A Summary of Regulatory Issues and Concerns*, available at http://iso.hrichina.org/ download_repository /A/rtl1%2002.01.doc.

Human Rights in China (2007), *State Secrets: China's Legal Labyrinth*, New York: Human Rights in China.

Human Rights Watch (2008), *Walking on Thin Ice: Control, Intimidation and Harassment of Lawyers in China*, New York: Human Rights Watch, available at http://www.hrw.org/en/reports/2008/04/28/walking-thin-ice.

Human Rights Watch (2009), *An Alleyway in Hell: China's Abusive Black Jails*, New York: Human Rights Watch.

Inbau, Fred, John Reid and Joseph Buckley (1962), *Criminal Interrogation and Confessions*, Baltimore, MD: Williams and Wilkins.

Irving, Barrie (1980), *Police Interrogation: A Study of Current Police Practice*, Royal Commission on Criminal Procedure, London: HMSO.

Irving, Barrie and Linden Hilgendorf (1980), *Police Interrogation: The Psychological Approach*, Royal Commission on Criminal Procedure Research Paper No. 1, London: HMSO.

Jacobs, Andrew (2009), 'Seeking Justice, Chinese Land in Secret Jails', *New York Times (Online)*, 8 March.

Jacobs, Andrew (2010), 'Chinese Courts to Bar Confessions Obtained by Torture', *New York Times (Online)*, 31 May.

Jessel, David (1994), *Trial and Error*, London: Headline.

Ji, Gang and Jing Liu (2006), *Gongsu Gaige de Lilun yu Shijian (Theory and Practice of the Reform on Public Prosecution)*, Beijing: China Procuratorial Press.

Ji, Xiangde (2006), *Jianli Zhongguo Kongbian Xieshang Zhidu Yanjiu (On the Construction of Plea Bargaining System in China)*, Beijing: Peking University Press.

Jiang, Jianping and Jiesheng Cao (2004), 'On Constitution of Pledge Evidence Mode in Our Criminal Procedure', *Nanchang Daxue Xuebao (Journal of Nanchang University)*, (July): 77.

Jiang, Qi and Liangfang Ye (2002), 'The Inapplicability of the Placement of the Proof Burden upon the Defendant', *Guojia Jianchaguan Xueyuan Xuebao (Journal of National Procurators College)*, **3**: 61.

Jiang, Shimei and Xing Hong (2008), 'Current Situation on the Operation of Bail Pending Trial System and Reflections – Survey on the Operation of the Bail System of

Public Security Organ of L District, H City', *Xiangnan Xueyuan Xuebao (Journal of Xiangnan University)*, **6**: 31.
Jiang, Tao and Lanting Xu (2005), 'The End-result of the Claims – Report on the Adoption of Criminal Defence Lawyers' Opinion in Our Country', in Ruihua Chen (ed.), *Xingshi Bianhu Zhidu de Shizheng Kaocha (Empirical Investigation of the Criminal Defense System)*, Beijing: Peking University Press.
Jiang, Xianyong (2004), 'Several Reflections on the Issues in the Protection of Human Rights During the Investigative Stage in Criminal Litigation', *Xingzheng yu Fa (Public Administration and Law)*, **3**: 55.
Jiang, Yong (2009), 'Residential Surveillance: Its Alienation and Abolition', *Jiangsu Jingguan Xueyuan Xuebao (Journal of Jiangsu Police Officer College)*, **4**: 9.
Jiao, Allan (2001), 'Police and Culture: A Comparison between China and the United States', *Police Quarterly*, **4(2)**: 156.
Jin, Yonggang (1999), 'Analysing Several Problems Concerning the Application of Summary Procedure in Public Prosecution Cases', *Renmin Jiancha (People's Procuratorate Semi-monthly)*, **12**: 31.
Jing, Lizhong and Xuyan Wang (2009), 'Puzzles on Incidental Civil Action in Criminal Proceedings in Practice and Institutional Improvement', *Shandong Jingcha Xueyuan Xuebao (Journal of Shandong Police College)*, **5**: 38.
Jones, Carol (1999), 'Politics Postponed: Law as a Substitute for Politics in Hong Kong and China', in Kanishka Jayasuriya (ed.), *Law, Capitalism and Power in Asia: The Rule of Law and Legal Institutions*, London: Routledge, pp. 38–57.
Jones, Carol (2005), 'Crime and Criminal Justice in China 1949–1999', in James Sheptycki and Ali Wardak (eds), *Transnational & Comparative Criminology*, London: GlassHouse Press, pp. 179–210.
Juy-Birmann, Rodolphe (2005), 'The German System', in M. Delmas-Marty and J.R. Spencer (eds), *European Criminal Procedures*, Cambridge: Cambridge University Press, pp. 292–347.
Kahn, Joseph (2005), 'Deep Flaws and Little Justice in China's Court System', *New York Times*, 21 September.
Kahn, Joseph (2007), 'Chinese Official Warns Against Independence of Courts', *New York Times*, 3 February.
Kang, Baoqi (2010), 'Seeking for the Truth and Beijing Practical, Constructing a Scientific and Rational Mechanism of Communication with Public Opinion', in An Dong (ed.), *Xibu Faguan Luncong (Di 10 Juan) (Forum for Judges in West China (Vol. 10))*, Beijing: People's Court Press.
Karpik, Lucien (1999), *French Lawyers: A Study in Collective Action 1274 to 1994*, Oxford: Clarendon Press.
Kassin, Saul and Karlyn McNall (1991), 'Police Interrogations and Confessions', *Law and Human Behaviour*, **15**: 233.
Kaye, Tim (1991), *Unsafe and Unsatisfactory? The Report of the Independent Inquiry into the Working Practices of the West Midlands Police Serious Crime Squad*, London: Civil Liberties Trust.
Kellogg, Tom (2003), 'A Case for the Defense', *China Rights Forum*, **2**: 101.
Kennedy, Ludovic (1961), *Ten Rillington Place*, London: Berkley.
Kilias, Martin and C. Ronald Huff (eds) (2008), *Wrongful Conviction: International*

Perspectives on Miscarriages of Justice, Philadelphia, PA: Temple University Press.
King, Michael (1981), *The Framework of Criminal Justice*, London: Croom Helm.
Kipnis, Andrew (1997), *Producing Guanxi: Sentiment Self and Subculture in a North China Village*, Durham, NC: Duke University Press.
Krattinger, Peter (1964), *Die Strafverteidigung im Vorverfahren im deutschen, französischen und englischen Strafprozess und ibre Reform*, Bonn: Rohrscheid.
Kwan, Daniel (2003), 'Judiciary Ordered to Clear Backlog of Court Cases', *South China Morning Post*, 26 August.
Lambert, John R. (1970), *Crime, Police and Race Relations: A Study in Birmingham*, London: Oxford University Press.
Lan, Jian (2000), 'Problems on Implementing the Compulsory Measures by Public Security Organ in Criminal Cases and Countermeasures', *Fujian Gong'an Gaodeng Zhuanke Xuexiao Xuebao (Journal of Fujian Police College)*, **6**: 37.
Langer, Maximo (2004), 'From Legal Transplants to Legal Translations: The Globalization of Plea Bargaining and the Americanization Thesis in Criminal Procedure', *Harvard International Law Journal*, **45**: 1.
Leng, Roger (2002), 'The Exchange of Information and Disclosure', in Mike McConville and Geoffrey Wilson (eds), *The Handbook of the Criminal Justice Process*, Oxford: Oxford University Press.
Lewis, Anthony (1964), *Gideon's Trumpet*, New York: Random House.
Li, Baoyue (2004), 'On Fair Trial – A Perspective of the Defence and Representation', in Chen Guangzhong (ed.), *Shenpang Gongzheng Wenti Yanjiu (A Study on Issues of Fair Trial)*, Beijing: Press of China University of Political Science and Law.
Li, Bin (2010), 'On the Construction of Conditional Non-prosecution System by Referring to the Probation System – Taking the Probation Cases of Dongcheng District of Beijing in 2005 and 2006', in Sun Li and Zhenfeng Wang (eds), *Buqisu Shiwu Yanjiu (A Study of Non-Prosecution)*, Beijing: China Procuratorial Press.
Li, Changlin (2006), *Cong Zhidushang Baozheng Shenpan Duli: Yi Xingshi Caipanquan de Guishu Wei Shijiao (Safeguard Institutional Adjudicative Independence: From the Ownership Perspective of Criminal Adjudicative Power)*, Beijing: Law Press.
Li, Chungang and Kai Wang (2009), 'Reflection on the Explanation Relating to Case Handling Information from Evident Science', *Zhengju Kexue (Evidence Science)*, **2**: 192.
Li, Fujin (2002), 'Problems Concerning Open Trial', *Beijing Fazhi Bao (Beijing Legal Daily)*, 31 March.
Li, Hong (2010), 'On the Abnormal Occupational Hazards for Chinese Defense Lawyers', *Jiancha Fengyun (Procuratorial View)*, 3.
Li, Hua (2003), 'My Views on the Testifying in Court by Witnesses in Criminal Cases', *Renmin Sifa (People's Judicature)*, **11**: 41.
Li, Huizi (2009), 'Senior Prosecutor Calls for Better Evidence System to Improve Justice', *Xinhuanet*, 8 August, http://news.xinhuanet.com/english/2009-08/08/content_11848717.htm.
Li, Jian (2003), 'On Reform and Perfection of the Pretrial Procedure in Criminal Procedure – Also on the Establishment of the Mechanism of Pretrial Conference', *Hengyang Shifan Xueyuan Xuebao (Shehui Kexue Ban) (Journal of Hengyang Normal University (Social Science Edition))*, **1**: 15.

Li, Jian (2005), 'It is Necessary to Revise Article 306 of the Criminal Law', *Zhongguo Qingnian Bao (China Youth Daily)*, 19 January.

Li, Jianling and Xiuchun Yang (2009), 'Empirical Study on the Situation of Discretionary Non-Prosecution by the Procuratorial Organ', *Zhengfa Luncong (Journal of Political Science and Law)*, **4**: 109.

Li, Jiya (2001), 'A Preliminary Exploration of the Scope of Bail Applications', *Lushi Shijie (Lawyer World)*, **2**: 39.

Li, Jun (2010), 'Preliminary Discussion on the Improvement of the Court Appearance System of Witnesses in the Criminal Proceeding', *Lilun Jianshe (Theory Research)*, **2**: 77.

Li, Junjie and Shihui Zhen (2007), 'Analysis on the Abolition of Case Instruction System in Our Country', *Shehui Kexue Luntan (Social Science Forum)*, **7(ii)**, 83

Li, Liangxiong (2010), 'Thoughts on Reforming the Adjudication Committee System', *Zhongguo Jiti Jingji (China Collective Economy)*, **2(ii)**: 76.

Li, Ling (2010), 'Corruption in China's Courts', in Randall Peerenboom (ed.), *Judicial Independence in China*, Cambridge: Cambridge University Press, pp. 196–220.

Li, Raymond (2010a), '4 Officials Sacked for Locking Up Petitioner in Mental Hospitals', *South China Morning Post*, 29 April.

Li, Raymond (2010b), 'Nation Rapt by Detained Petitioner's Story', *South China Morning Post*, 22 May.

Li, Sha (2008), 'A Study on the Problem of the Rate of Non-Prosecution in Criminal Procedure in Our Country – Also Comparison with that in Germany', *Sichuan Jingcha Xueyuan Xuebao (Journal of Sichuan Police College)*, **2**: 90.

Li, Weihua (2005), 'Today No Witness Will Appear in Court – An in depth analysis', *Democracy and Law*, No. 4.

Li, Weiju (2004), 'Causes and Solutions of the Overflow of Criminal Detention', *Tiedao Jingguan Gaodeng Zhuanke Xuexiao Xuebao (Journal of Railway Police College)*, **1**: 41.

Li Wenyu (2004), 'Thinking of the Chinese Style Plea Bargaining System', *Journal of Southwest University of Nationalities, Humanities and Social Sciences* (April), 263.

Li, Xuekuan (1999), 'Problems of Trial Method in Second Instance Criminal Cases and Solutions', *Zhongguo Faxue (China Legal Science)*, **1**: 28.

Li, Yabin (1999), 'A Brief Analysis of the Debate in Cross-examination of Evidence during the Examination of the Case by the Court', *Hebei Faxue (Hebei Law Science)*, **3**: 50.

Li, Yan (2003), 'Reflection on the Perfection of Legal Aid System in Criminal Cases in Our Country', *Qianyan (Forward Position)*, **7**: 60.

Li, Yanling (2007), 'Problems on the Criminal Summary Procedure in Our Country and Recommendations for Improvement', *Jilin Gong'an Gaodeng Zhuanke Xuexiao Xuebao (Journal of Jilin Public Security Academy)*, **4**: 89.

Li, Yimin and Daocheng Huang (1999), 'The Allocation and Transfer of Burden of Proof', *Hebei Faxue (Hebei Law Science)*, **5**: 63.

Li, Yumei (2008), 'Wang Shengjun: The Work of Courts Must Insist on the Guiding Thoughts of "Three Supremes"', 16 June, available at http://www.cnfdzqq.com/article/show.asp?id=997.

Li, Zan and Fengjun Zhang (2007), 'Empirical Analysis of Non-Prosecuted Cases', *Guojia Jianchaguan Xueyuan Xuebao (Journal of National Prosecutors College)*, **5**: 25.

Lian, Yingting (2007), 'Lawyers' Investigation and Evidence Collection Encounters "System Bottleneck", Seeking for Legislative Breakthrough', *Fazhi Ribao (Legal Daily)*, 29 July, cited in Pinxin Liu (ed.), *Xingshi Cuo'an de Yuanyin and Duice (Reasons of Criminal Wrong Convictions and Countermeasures)*, Beijing: China Legal System Publishing House, at p. 99.

Liang, Bin and Hong Lu (2006), 'Conducting Fieldwork in China: Observations on Collecting Primary Data Regarding Crime, Law, and the Criminal Justice System', *Journal of Contemporary Criminal Justice*, **22(2)**: 157.

Liang, Zhiping (2004), 'Exploring and Analyzing Whether Plea Bargaining Should be Adopted in Criminal Litigations in China', *Dazhong Kexue (Mass Science)*, **3**: 63

Liao, Haisheng (2002), 'Research on the Rules of Hearsay Evidence', *Guojia Jianchaguan Xueyuan Xuebao (Journal of National Procurators College)*, **6**: 70.

Liebman, Benjamin (2005), 'Watchdog or Demagogue? The Media in the Chinese Legal System', *Columbia Law Review*, **105(1)**: 1.

Lin, Jinhui (2002), 'On the Rules of Evidence in Criminal Litigation in Our Country', *Guojia Jianchaguan Xueyuan Xuebao (Journal of National Procurators College)*, **6**: 74.

Lin Jinsong and Jue Zhu (2002), 'Reflections on Judge's Power of Out-of-court Investigation: An Analysis from the Perspective of the Value of Criminal Litigation', *Zhongguo Xingshifa Zazhi (Criminal Science)*, **3**: 43.

Lin, Lihong, Fengzhen Zhang and Qihui Huang (2009), 'Survey Report on the Situation of Social Cognition of Extortion of Confession by Torture (Questionnaire for Prison Detainees)', *Faxue Pinglun (Law Review)*, **3**: 119.

Liu, Chunlan and Qingyu Zhang (2010), 'Study on the Mechanism of Reviewing the Necessity of Pre-trial Detention and Remedies to the Rights – Take People's Procuratorate of Hedong District of Tianjin City as the Research Sample', *Zhongguo Xingshifa Zazhi (Criminal Science)*, **5**: 85.

Liu, Fangquan (2007), 'Treat the Investigation and Interrogation Seriously', in Zuo Weimin *et al.*, *Zhongguo Xingshi Susong Yunxing Jizhi Shizheng Yanjiu (Empirical Study on the Operation Mechanism of Criminal Procedure in China)*, Beijing: Law Press.

Liu, Fangquan (2008), 'Empirical Study on the Methods of Bail Pending Trial', *Fazhi Yu Shehui (Shuang Yue Kan) (Law and Social Development) (Bi-monthly)*, **2**: 23.

Liu, Genju (1999), 'Reforms on the Criminal Trial Mode and Transfer of Case Files', in Chen Guangzhong (ed.), *Xingshi Susong Faxue Wushi Nian (Fifty Years' Criminal Procedure Law)*, Beijing: China Police Education Press.

Liu, Genju and Lijun Li (2009), 'Comparative Study of Criminal Summary Procedure', *Bijiaofa Yanjiu (Journal of Comparative Law)*, **5**: 65.

Liu, Jiguo (2004), 'Studies on Questions concerning the Withdrawal of Public Prosecution in Criminal Litigation', *Renmin Jiancha (People's Procuratorate Semi-monthly)*, **1**: 37.

Liu, Jing (2001), *New Interpretations and New Explanations of the Criminal Procedure Law and Relevant Regulations*, Beijing: People's Court Publishing.

Liu, Jing (2009), 'Analysis of Criminal Summary Procedure', *Fazhi yu Shehui (Legal System and Society)*, **1**: 71.

Liu, Lina, Ying Wang and Jing An (2010), 'Study on the Situation of Theft and Intentional Harm Cases that Were Not Prosecuted after Arrest by Haidian

Procuratorate in 2007', in Li Sun and Zhenfeng Wang (eds), *Buqisu Shiwu Yanjiu (A Study of Non-Prosecution)*, Beijing: China Procuratorial Press.
Liu, Lixia and Danhong Wu (2004), 'An Empirical Analysis of the Witness System', in Jiahong He (ed.), *Zhengjuxue Luntan (Forum on Evidence)* Vol. 7, Beijing: China Procuratorial Press.
Liu, Nanping (2008), 'Trick or Treat: Legal Reasoning in the Shadow of Corruption in the People's Republic of China', *North Carolina Journal of International Law & Commercial Regulation*, **34**: 179.
Liu, Sida (2006), 'Beyond Global Convergence: Conflicts of Legitimacy in a Chinese Lower Court', *Law & Social Inquiry*, **31(1)**: 75.
Liu, Sida and Terence Halliday (2008), 'Dancing Handcuffed in the Minefield: Survival Strategies of Defense Lawyers in China's Criminal Justice System', available at http://ssrn.com/abstract=1269536.
Liu, Sida and Terence Halliday (2009), 'Recursivity in Legal Change: Lawyers and Reforms of China's Criminal Procedure Law', *Law & Social Inquiry*, **34(4)**: 911.
Liu, Weifa and Jun Yang (2009), 'Problems on the Review and Evaluation System of Non-Prosecution Cases and its Improvement', *Renmin Jiancha (People's Procuratorial Semi-monthly)*, **14**: 41.
Liu, Xiaojun (2002), 'A Legal Reflection on the Formulation of Rules against Hearsay Evidence in Our Country', *Wanxi Xueyuan Xuebao (Journal of Wanxi University)*, **3**: 61.
Liu, Xiaoqing (2009), *Zhongguo Peishen Zhidu Yanjiu (A Study of Jury System in China)*, Chengdu: Sichuan University Press.
Liu, Yali (2000), 'On the Burden of Proof in Criminal Litigation', *Jiangsu Gong'an Zhuanke Xuexiao Xuebao (Journal of Jiangsu Public Security College)*, **5**: 111.
Liu, Zhong and Yansheng Zhang (2005), 'Allocation of Lawyers' Right to Conduct Investigation in the Criminal Proceedings', in Ruihua Chen (ed.), *Xingshi Bianhu Zhidu de Shizheng Kaocha (Empirical Investigation of the Criminal Defense System)*, Beijing: Peking University Press.
Liu, Zhongfa, Jinsong Qi and Jingyin Zeng (2008), 'Survey on the Current Operation of Bail Pending Trial System', *Guojia Jianchaguan Xueyuan Xuebao (Journal of National Prosecutors College)*, **2**: 106.
Loftus, Elizabeth (1979), *Eyewitness Testimony*, Cambridge, MA: Harvard University Press.
Long, Zongzhi (1998), 'On China's Trial Approach', *Zhongguo Faxue (China Legal Science)*, **4**: 88.
Long, Zongzhi (2000), 'On the System of Cross-examination in China's Criminal Trial', *Zhongguo Faxue (China Legal Science)*, **4**: 81.
Lu, Hong and Kriss Drass (2002), 'Transience and the Disposition of Theft Cases in China', *Justice Quarterly*, **19(1)**: 69.
Lu, Hong and Bridget Kelly (2008), 'Courts and Sentencing Research on Contemporary China', *Crime, Law & Social Change*, **50**: 290.
Lu, Hong and Bin Liang (2008), 'Legal Responses to Trafficking in Narcotics and other Narcotic Offences in China', *International Criminal Justice Review*, **18(2)**: 212.
Lu, Hong, Jianhong Liu and Alicia Crowther (2006), 'Female Criminal Victimization and Criminal Justice Response in China', *British Journal of Criminology*, **46**: 859.

Lu, Hong and Terance D. Miethe (2002), 'Legal Representation and Criminal Processing in China', *British Journal of Criminology*, **42**: 267.

Lu, Hong and Terance D. Miethe (2003), 'Confessions and Criminal Case Disposition in China', *Law & Society Review*, **37(3)**: 549.

Lu, Hong and Terance D. Miethe (2007), *China's Death Penalty: History, Law and Contemporary Practices*, New York: Taylor & Francis Group.

Lu, Jianhong and Peizhong Wang (2007), 'Interpretative Analysis of "Two Basics" and "Leave Adequate Leeway" – Analysis of One Sample Case of Death Penalty', in Jiahong He (ed.), *Zhengjuxue Luntan (Evidence Forum)*, Beijing: Law Press, **12**: 45.

Lu, Jinbao (2007), 'Improvement of the Witness Protection System in China', in *Proceedings of the International Conference on Criminal Procedure Law: Challenges in the 21st Century*, Centro de Formacao Juridica e Judiciaria, pp. 575–580.

Lu, Q. (1998), 'Exploring the Issues Concerning the Establishment of the Presumption of Innocence in China', *(Law Science)*, **1**: 36.

Lu, Weiju (2004), 'Causes and Solutions of the Overflow of Criminal Detention', *Tiedao Jingguan Gaodeng Zhuanke Xuexiao Xuebao (Journal of Railway Police College)*, **1**: 41.

Lubman, Stanley (1969), 'Form and Function in the Chinese Criminal Process', *Columbia Law Review*, **69(4)**: 535.

Lubman, Stanley (1991), 'Studying Contemporary Chinese Law: Limits Possibilities and Strategy', *American Journal of Comparative Law*, **39**: 293.

Lubman, Stanley (1999), *Bird in a Cage: Legal Reforms in China after Mao*, Stanford: Stanford University Press.

Lubman, Stanley (2000), 'Bird in a Cage: Chinese Law Reform after Twenty Years', *Northwestern Journal of International Law and Business*, **20(3)**: 383.

Luo, Benqi (1997), 'The Scope of the Burden of Proof of a Criminal Defendant', *Anqing Shifan Xueyuan Xuebao Shehui Kexueban (The Social Science Journal of Anqing Teachers College)*, **3**: 71.

Lynch, Elizabeth (2010a), 'A Paper Tiger? China Issues New Regulations to Exclude Illegally Obtained Evidence', available at: http://chinalawandpolicy.com/2010/06/02/a-paper-tiger-china-issues-new-regulations-to-exclude-illegally-obtained-evidence/.

Lynch, Elizabeth (2010b), 'The Rio Tinto Trial in China: A Miscalculation about Rule of Law?', *Foreign Policy Digest*, April, available at http://www.foreignpolicydigest.org/Asia?April-2010/the-rio-tinto-trial-in-china-a-miscalculation-about-rule-of-law.html.

Lynch, Elizabeth (2010c), 'A Bit Too Much Pollyanna? Brookings' Report on Legal Development in China', available at http://chinalawandpolicy.com/tag/all-china-lawyers-association/.

Macauley, Melissa (1998), *Social Power and Legal Culture: Litigation Masters in Late Imperial China*, Stanford, CA: Stanford University Press.

McAleavy, Henry (1962), 'The People's Courts in Communist China', *American Journal of Comparative Law*, **11**: 52.

McBarnet, Doreen (1981), *Conviction: Law, State and the Construction of Justice*, London: Macmillan.

McConville, Michael and John Baldwin (1981), *Courts, Prosecution and Conviction*, Oxford: Clarendon Press.

McConville, Michael and John Baldwin (1982), 'The Role of Interrogation in Crime Discovery and Conviction', *British Journal of Criminology*, **22(1)**: 165.

McConville, Michael and Chester L. Mirsky (1986–87), 'Criminal Defense of the Poor in New York City', *New York University Review of Law & Social Change*, **xv(4)**: 581.

McConville, Michael and Chester Mirsky (1995), 'Guilty Plea Courts: A Social Disciplinary Model of Criminal Justice', *Social Problems*, **42(2)**: 216.

McConville, Mike and Dan Shepherd (1992), *Watching Police Watching Communities*, London: Routledge.

McConville, Mike and Geoffrey Wilson (eds) (2002), *The Handbook of the Criminal Justice Process*, Oxford: Oxford University Press.

McConville, Mike, Andrew Sanders and Roger Leng (1991), *The Case for the Prosecution*, London: Routledge.

McConville, Mike, Jacqueline Hodgson, Lee Bridges and Anita Pavlovic (1994), *Standing Accused: The Organisation and Practices of Criminal Defence Lawyers in Britain*, Oxford: Clarendon Press.

McKenzie, Ian, Rod Morgan and Robert Reiner (1990), 'Helping the Police with their Inquiries: The Necessity Principle and Voluntary Attendance at the Police Station', *Criminal Law Review*, **22**.

Ma, Haixian (2003), 'Exploring the Issue of Raising the Quality of Arrest Application Examination', *Renmin Jiancha (People's Procuratorate Semi-monthly)*, **8**: 32.

Ma, Jingrui, Xuemei Jin and Heng Liu (2005), 'Survey Analysis of High Rate of "Returned Criminal Cases for Supplementary Investigation" in the Nanguan District Procuratorate of Changchun', *Jiancha Shijian (Procuratorial Practice)*, **4**: 79.

Ma, Lifeng (2009), 'Difficulties of Non-Local Citizens in Bail Pending Trial and Solutions', *Ningbo Guangbo Dianshi Daxue Xuebao (Journal of Ningbo Radio and TV University)*, **1**: 73.

Ma, Mingliang (2004), 'Legal Aid: The Bottleneck of Developing the Criminal Justice System in China', *Xinan Zhengfa Daxue Xuebao (Journal of Southwest University of Politics and Law)*, **6**: 69.

Ma, Mingliang and Xingshui Zhang (2005), 'Empirical Analysis of Legal Aid in Criminal Cases in China – Concurrent Statement of the Impact of Legal Aid on Model Procedural System', in Ruihua Chen (ed.), *Xingshi Bianhu Zhidu de Shizheng Kaocha (Empirical Investigation of the Criminal Defense System)*, Beijing: Peking University Press.

Ma, Xi-wu (1956), 'On Several Problems in Adjudication Work at the Present Time', *Zhengfa Yanjiu (Political-Legal Research)*, **1**: 3.

Ma, Yue (1997), 'The Police Law 1995: Organization, Functions, Powers and Accountability of the Chinese Police', *Policing: An International Journal of Police Strategy and Management*, **20(1)**: 113.

Ma, Yue (2003), 'The Powers of the Police and the Rights of Suspects under the Amended Criminal Procedure Law of China', *Policing*, **26(3)**: 490.

Manning, Peter (1977), *Police Work*, Cambridge, MA: MIT Press.

Marquand, Robert (2001), 'New for China's Courts: Trained Judges, Standard Rules', *Christian Science Monitor*, 16 August, 93.

Mawby, Rob (1979), *Policing the City*, Farnborough: Saxon House.

Max Planck Institute for Foreign and International Criminal Law (2006), *Strengthening the Defence in Death Penalty Cases in the People's Republic of China*, Frieborg: Max Planck Institute.

May, Sir John (1990), *Report of the Inquiry into the Circumstances Surrounding the*

Convictions Arising out of the Bomb Attacks in Guildford and Woolwich in 1974, HC 556, 1989–90, London: HMSO.

May, Sir John (1992–93), *Second Report on the Maguire Case*, HC 296, 1992–93, London: HMSO.

May, Sir John (1993–94), *Report of the Inquiry into the Circumstances Surrounding the Convictions Arising out of the Bomb Attacks in Guildford and Woolwich in 1974*, Final Report HC 449, London: HMSO.

Meng, Deping and Guo Wei (2001), 'On Perfecting the Pretrial Examination Procedure of Our Country', *Guangxi Zhengfa Guanli Ganbu Xueyuan Xuebao (Journal of Guangxi Administrative Cadre Institute of Politics and Law)*, 104.

Michelson, Ethan (2007), 'Lawyers, Political Embeddedness and Institutional Continuity in China's Transition from Socialism', *American Journal of Sociology*, **113(2)**: 352.

Michelson, Ethan (2008), 'Dear Lawyer Bao: Everyday Problems, Legal Advice, and State Power in China', *Social Problems*, **55(1)**: 43.

Mooney, Paul (2010), 'The "Hotpot" Culture that gives Chongqing its Murky Image', *South China Morning Post*, 11 April.

Mosher, Stacey and Patrick Poon (eds) (2009), *A Sword and a Shield: China's Human Rights Lawyers*, Hong Kong: China Human Rights Lawyers Concern Group.

Muhlhahn, Klaus (2009), *Criminal Justice in China: A History*, Cambridge, MA: Harvard University Press.

Mullin, Chris (1986), *Error of Judgment: The Truth About the Birmingham Bombs*, London: Chatto & Windus Ltd.

Munro, Robin (2000), 'Judicial Psychiatry in China and Its Political Abuses', *Columbia Journal of Asian Law*, **14**: 1.

Nathan, Andrew (1993), 'Is Chinese Culture Distinctive? – A Review Article', *The Journal of Asian Studies*, **52(4)**: 923.

Naughton, Michael (2010), *The Criminal Cases Review Commission: Hope for the Innocent?*, London: Palgrave Macmillan.

Nelken, David (1981), 'The "Gap Problem" in the Sociology of Law: A Theoretical Review', *Windsor Yearbook of Access to Justice*, **1**: 35.

Ng, Tze-wei (2009a), 'Anti-torture Measures in Works, Paper Says', *South China Morning Post*, 11 August.

Ng, Tze-wei (2009b), 'Police Detain Lawyers Who Sought to Meet Obama', *South China Morning Post*, 21 November.

Ng, Tze-wei (2010a), 'Evidence Guidelines Ban Torture in Capital Cases', available at http://www.scmp.com/portal/site/SCMP/menuite m2af62ecb329d3d7733492d9253a0a 0a0/?vgnextoid=ae5e5dca3e9e8210VgnVCM100000360a0a0aRCRD&ss=China&s= News.

Ng Tze-wei (2010b), 'CPPCC Member Urges More Help for Lawyers from Ethnic Minorities', *South China Morning Post*, 15 March.

Ng, Tze-wei (2010c), 'Respect Those who Fight for Rights, Says American Don', *South China Morning Post*, 20 May.

Ng, Tze-wei (2010d), 'Lawyer Jailed for Creating Fake Evidence', *South China Morning Post*, 9 January.

Ng Tze-wei (2010e), 'Lawyer Reveals Grim Details of Client's Torture', *South China Morning Post*, 29 July.

Ng Tze-wei (2010f), 'A Tale of Two Defence Lawyers: Similar Challenges and Big Risks', *South China Morning Post*, 31 July.

Ni, Jian (2007), 'A Cold Hard Look at the Supreme Court's "Expansion of the Ranks" of Criminal Judges', *Beijing News* 21 November, posted by the Dui Hua Human Rights Foundation, 25 November 2007, available at: http://www.duihua.org/hrjournal/2007/11/will-death-penalty-review-overwhelm.html.

Niblett, John (1997), *Disclosure in Criminal Proceedings*, London: Blackstone.

Note (1985), 'Concepts of Law in the Chinese Anti-Crime Campaign', *Harvard Law Review*, **98(8)**: 1890.

Nowak, Manfred (2005), *Special Rapporteur on Torture Highlights Challenges at End of Visit to China*, available at: http://www.unhchr.ch/huricane.nsf/0/677C1943FAA14D67C12570CB0034966D (last viewed 25 May 2010).

O'Connor, Patrick (1992), 'Prosecution Disclosure: Principle, Practice and Justice', *Criminal Law Review*, 464.

O'Neill, Mark (2010a), 'Losing Hope: The Defence Lawyer Who Always Loses', *South China Morning Post*, 28 February.

O'Neill, Mark (2010b), 'Genuine Cases Often Caused by Too Much Pressure at the Office', *South China Morning Post*, 18 April.

O'Neill, Mark (2010c), 'High "Suicide" Rate Among Officials Tells its Own Story', *South China Morning Post*, 18 April.

Oberwittler, Dietrich and Shenghui Qi (2009), *Public Opinion on the Death Penalty in China: Results from a General Population Survey Conducted in Three Provinces in 2007/08*, Friborg: Max Planck Institute for Foreign and International Criminal Law.

Ofshe, Richard and Richard Leo (1997), 'The Decision to Confess Falsely: Rational Choice and Irrational Action', *Denver Law Review*, **74**: 979.

Packer, Herbert (1968), *The Limits of the Criminal Sanction*, Stanford, CA: Stanford University Press and Oxford University Press.

Pan, Diaohua and Daqing Lai (2004), 'Survey and Reflection on the Problems in Sending Back Cases for Supplementary Investigation', *Jiancha Shijian (Procuratorial Practice)*, **2**: 37.

Pang, Xiaoju (2009), 'Significance of Improving the People's Assessors System in Adjudicative Independence', *Nanjing Gongcheng Xueyuan Xuebao (Shehui Kexue Ban) (Journal of Nanjing Institute of Technology (Social Science Edition))*, **2**: 12.

Peerenboom, Randall (1998), *Lawyers in China: Obstacles to Independence and the Defense of Rights*, New York: Lawyers Committee on Human Rights.

Peerenboom, Randall (2002), *China's Long March Toward the Rule of Law*, New York: Cambridge University Press.

Peerenboom, Randall (2004), 'Out of the Pan and into the Fire: Well-intentioned but Misguided Recommendations to Eliminate All Forms of Administrative Detention in China', *Northwestern University Law Review*, **98(3)**: 991.

Peerenboom, Randall (2006), 'What Have We Learned About Law and Development? Describing, Predicting and Assessing Legal Reform in China', *Michigan Journal of International Law*, **27(3)**: 823.

Peerenboom, Randall (2008), 'Judicial Independence and Judicial Accountability: An Empirical Study of Case Supervision', available at http://ssrn.com/abstract=1300840.

Peerenboom, Randall (2010a), *Judicial Independence in China*, Cambridge: Cambridge University Press.
Peerenboom, Randall (2010b), 'Judicial Independence in China: Common Myths and Unfounded Assumptions', in Randall Peerenboom (ed.), *Judicial Independence in China*, Cambridge: Cambridge University Press.
Peng, Dongfang (2009), 'On the Feasibility of Abolishing the Adjudicative Committee System', *Xibu Faxue Pinglun (Western Law Review)*, **1**: 118.
Peng, Jianming (2010), 'Difficult Situation of the Non-Prosecution System and its Way-out', *Guizhou Jingguan Zhiye Xueyuan Xuebao (Journal of Guizhou Police Officer Vocational College)*, **1**: 29.
Pepinsky, Harold (1970), 'A Theory of Police Reaction to Miranda v Arizona', *Crime and Delinquency*, **16**: 379.
Perrodet, Antoinette (2005), 'The Italian System', in M. Delmas-Marty and J.R. Spencer (eds), *European Criminal Procedures*, Cambridge: Cambridge University Press, pp. 348–412.
Pesquie, Brigitte (2005), 'The Belgium System', in M. Delmas-Marty and J.R. Spencer (eds), *European Criminal Procedures*, Cambridge: Cambridge University Press, pp. 81–141.
Pfeffer, Richard (1970), 'Crime and Punishment: China and the United States', in J. Cohen (ed.), *Contemporary Chinese Law: Research Problems and Perspectives*, Cambridge, MA: Harvard University Press.
Phillips, Coretta and David Brown (1998), *Entry into the Criminal Justice System*, Home Office Research Study No. 185, London: Home Office.
Pils, Eva (2007a), 'Citizens? The Legal and Political Status of Peasants and Peasant Migrant Workers in China', in Xiangmin Liu (ed.), *Zhidu, fazhan yu hexie (System Development and Harmony)*, Hong Kong: Ming Pao Press, pp. 173–243.
Pils, Eva (2007b), 'Asking the Tiger for his Skin: Rights Activism in China', *Fordham International Law Journal*, **30**: 1209.
Pils, Eva (2009a), 'Yang Jia and China's Unpopular Criminal Justice System', *China Rights Forum*, **1**: 60.
Pils, Eva (2009b), 'The Dislocation of the Chinese Human Rights Movement', in Stacey Mosher and Patrick Poon (eds), *A Sword and a Shield: China's Human Rights Lawyers*, Hong Kong: China Human Rights Lawyers Concern Group, pp. 141–159.
Pizzi, William and Luca Marafioti (1992), 'The New Italian Code of Criminal Procedure: The Difficulties of Building an Adversarial Trial System on an Adversarial Foundation', *Yale Journal of International Law*, **17**: 1.
Potter, Pitman (1994), 'Riding the Tiger: Legitimacy and Legal Culture in Post-Mao China', *The China Quarterly*, **138**: 325.
Potter, Pitman (1999), 'The Chinese Legal System: Continuing Commitment to the Primacy of State Power', *The China Quarterly*, **159**: 673.
Potter, Pitman (2004), 'Legal Reform in China: Institutions, Culture, and Selective Adaptation', *Law & Social Inquiry*, **29(2)**: 465.
Prescott, Jeffrey (2003), 'Efficiency and Justice in Summary Criminal Trials', *Fazhi Ribao (Legal Daily)*, available in <http://www.legaldaily.com.cn/bm/2003-07/24/content_39533.htm> (last visited 25 July 2003).
Price, Christopher and Jonathan Caplan (1976), *The Confait Confessions*, London: Marion Boyars.

Qian, Xuetang (2005), 'Application of Domicile Surveillance and its Improvement', *Zhongguo Renmin Gong'an Daxue Xuebao (Journal of China People's Public Security University)*, **5**: 83.

Qiao, Qiuzhen (2009), 'On the Defects of the Bail Pending Trial System in China', *Fazhi yu Shehui (Legal System and Society)*, **1(1)**: 58.

Qin, Ce (2006), 'On the Independence of the Trial at the First Instance', in Guangzhong Chen, Weiqiu Cheng and Cheng Yang (eds), *Xingshi Yishen Chengxu yu Renquan Baozhang (Criminal Trial of the First Instance and Protection of Human Rights)*, Beijing: China University of Political Science and Law Press, p. 46ff.

Qin, Zongwen (2001), 'On the Reform of Examination Procedure before Trial in China', *Academic Exchange*, November, 55.

Raifeartaigh, Una (1997), 'Reconciling Bail Law with the Presumption of Innocence', *Oxford Journal of Legal Studies*, **17**: 1

Ran, Yanfei (2009), 'When Chinese Criminal Defense Lawyers Become the Criminals', *Fordham International Law Journal*, **32**: 989.

Redmayne, Mike (2004), 'Disclosure and its Discontents', *Criminal Law Review*, 441.

Regan, Francis (2009), 'Going to court in China: Observations on a Minor Criminal Case', *Alternative Law Journal*, **34(2)**: 111.

Reiner, Robert (1985), *The Politics of the Police*, Brighton: Wheatsheaf Books.

Reiner, Robert (2000), *The Politics of the Police*, Oxford: Oxford University Press.

Reporters Without Borders (2009), 'Defence witnesses and journalists held in hotel while blogger's trial takes place', 13 August, available at, http://www.rsf.org/Defence-witnesses-and-journalists.html.

Ribet, Steven (2010), 'Death of a Tyrant', *South China Morning Post Magazine*, 10 January.

Roberts, Andrew (2004), 'The Problem of Mistaken Identification', *International Journal of Evidence & Proof*, **8**: 100.

Roberts, David (1993), 'Questioning the Suspect: The Solicitor's Role', *Criminal Law Review*, 368.

Roberts, Paul and Adrian Zuckerman (2004), *Criminal Evidence*, Oxford: Oxford University Press.

Rose, Jonathan, Steve Panter and Trevor Wilkinson (1997), *Innocents: How Justice Failed Stefan Kiszko and Lesley Molseed*, London: Fourth Estate.

Ru, Yaguo (2007), 'Protection of the Suspect's Rights and Interests in the Review for Prosecution', *Jiangsu Jingguan Xueyuan Xuebao (Journal of Jiangsu Police Officer College)*, **2**: 645.

Sanders, Andrew and Lee Bridges (1991), 'Access to Legal Advice and Police Malpractice', *Criminal Law Review*, 494.

Sanders, Andrew and Lee Bridges (1999), 'The Right to Legal Advice', in Clive Walker and Keir Starmer (eds), *Miscarriages of Justice*, London: Blackstone Press, pp. 83–99.

Sanders, Andrew, Lee Bridges, Adele Mulvaney and Gary Crozier (1989), *Advice and Assistance at Police Stations and the 24 Hour Duty Solicitor Scheme*, London: Lord Chancellor's Department.

Sapio, Flora (2010), *Sovereign Power and the Law in China*, Leiden: Brill.

Sarat, Austin (2005), 'Innocence, Error, and the "New Abolitionism": A Commentary', *Criminology & Public Policy*, **4(1)**: 45.

Savadove, Bill (2006), 'Lawyers at Risk Trying to Apply the Law', *South China Morning Post*, 25 December.

Scott, Kandis (2010), 'Why Did China Reform its Death Penalty?', *Pacific Rim Law & Policy Journal*, **19(1)**: 63.

Sekar, Satish (1997), *Fitted In: Cardiff 3 and the Lynette White Inquiry*, London: The Fitted In Project.

Sellin, Thorsten and Marvin Wolfgang (1964), *The Measurement of Delinquency*, New York: Wiley.

Shao, Hua (2001), 'The Defects and Theoretical Breakthrough in the Examination System at Court in China', *Gansu Zhengfa Xueyuan Xuebao (Journal of Gansu Institute of Political Science and Law)*, March, 62.

Sharp, Peter (2009), 'Chinese Protesters Tortured in "Black Jails"', *Sky News*, available at http://news.sky.com/skynews/Home?World-News/Chinese-Civil-Rights-Protesters-Du.

Shearing, Cliff (ed.) (1981), *Organizational Police Deviance: its Structure and Control*, Toronto: Butterworths.

Shen, Jungui (1999), 'Rejectionist Thoughts about China's System of People's Assessors', *Zhongguo Lushi (The Chinese Lawyer)*, **4**: 14.

Shen, Shitao (2008), *Xingshi Shenqian Chengxu Qianyan Wenti Yanjiu (Studies on the Frontier Issues in Criminal Pre-trial Procedure)*, Beijing: Intellectual Property Press.

Shen, Xinwang and Shen Hijiao (2010), 'Head of the Public Security Bureau Taking the Position of Secretary of the Political-legal Committee May Cause Dispute and Lead More "Iron" Cases', available at http://www.chinanews.com.cn/gn/news/2010/03-25/2190487.shtml.

Sheskin, Arlene (1981), 'Trial Courts on Trial: Examining Dominant Assumptions', in James Eisenstein and Herbert Jacob, *Felony Justice*, Boston, MA: Little Brown.

Shu, Huaide (1996), 'Strike Hard at Severe Criminal Activities to Ensure a Peaceful Life for the People', *Seeking Truth (Qiushi)*, 13 June, **11**: 12.

Simpson, Peter (2003), 'Murder Trail', *South China Morning Post Magazine*, 12 October.

Skolnick, Jerome (1966), *Justice Without Trial*, New York: Wiley.

Smith, Jennifer and Gompers, Michael (2007), 'Realizing Justice: The Development of Fair Trial Rights in China', *East Asian Law Review*, **2(2)**: 108.

Softley, Paul (1980), *Police Interrogation: An Observational Study in Four Police Stations*, Royal Commission on Criminal Procedure, Research Study No. 4, London: HMSO.

Song, Jidong (2005), 'Challenge on the Legislative Appropriateness of Article 306 of the Criminal Law', *Hubei Chengren Jiaoyu Xueyuan Xuebao (Journal of Hubei Adult Education College)*, 6.

Song, Yinghui and Yongsheng Chen (2002), 'Study on Pretrial Examination and Procedure of Preparation for Criminal Cases', *Zhengfa Luntan (Journal of Political Science and Law)*, **2**: 65.

Song, Yinghui and Wu Hong Yao (2002), *Xingshi Shenpanqian Chengxu Yanjiu (A Study of Pre-trial Criminal Procedure)*, Beijing: China University of Politics and Law Press.

Song, Yinghui and Zhe Li (2007), 'A Study of Current Situation of Application of the Bail Pending Trial in China and Reforming Countermeasures', *Renmin Jiancha (People's Procuratorial Semi-monthly)*, **12**: 22.

Song Yinghui and Haimin Luo (eds) (2007), *Qubao Houshen Shiyong Zhong de Wenti yu Duice Yanjiu (A Study on the Problems of Bail Pending Trial in Application and Countermeasures)*, Beijing: China People's University of Public Security Press.

Song, Yuansheng (2008), 'Comparative Studies on Wrongful Verdict Criminal Cases', *Fanzui Yanjiu*, **1**: 73.

Spencer, J.R. (2005), 'Evidence', in M. Delmas-Marty and J.R. Spencer (eds), *European Criminal Procedures*, Cambridge: Cambridge University Press.

Steer, David (1980), *Uncovering Crime: The Police Role*, Royal Commission on Criminal Procedure, Research Study No. 7, London: HMSO.

Stephens, Otis, Robert Flanders and J. Lewis Cannon (1972), 'Law Enforcement and the Supreme Court: Police Perceptions of the Miranda Requirements', *Tennessee Law Review*, **39**: 407.

Stutsman, Thomas (2010), 'Culture, Psychology, and Criminal Justice Reform: Reforming Eyewitness Interview Procedures to Reduce Wrongful Convictions and Protect Human Rights in China' (on file with authors as at 2010).

Su, Kaijian (2009), 'Study on the Connection between the Collegial Panel and the Adjudication Committee', *Zhongguo Sifa (China Trial)*, **1**: 72.

Su, Li (2000), 'On the Issue of Judges' Professionalization in the Grassroots Courts – Current Situation, Reasons and Solutions', *Bijiaofa Yanjiu (Comparative Law Study)*, **3**: 4, cited in Yihong Hu (2009), 'The Plight of Judges' Professionalization – From the Perspective of Western Grassroots Courts', *Xibu Falu Pinglun (Western Law Review)*, **5**: 139.

Su, Xiaochuan (2001), 'Concerns Have to be Given to Problems of Bail Pending Trial', *Fazhi Ribao (Legal Daily)*, 3 March.

Subin, Harry I., Chester L. Mirsky and Ian Weinstein (1993), *The Criminal Process: Prosecution and Defence Functions*, St. Paul, MN: West Publishing Co.

Sun, Changyong (ed.) (2009), *Zhencha Chengxu yu Renquan Baozhang – Zhongguo Zhechan Chengxu de Gaige he Wanshan (Investigation Procedure and Protection of Human Rights – Reform and Improvement of Chinese Criminal Investigation Procedure)*, Beijing: China Legal System Publishing House.

Sun, Fei and Ying Liu (1998), 'Witnesses Court Appearance: What are the Difficulties?', *Jiancha Ribao (Procuratorial Daily)*, 22 August.

Sun, Qian (2000), 'Some Thoughts on Perfecting the Law of Arrest in Our Country', *Zhongguo Faxue (China Legal Science)*, **4**: 93.

Sun, Xiaoyu (2009), 'On the Supplementary Investigation in Our Country', *Fazhi yu Shehui (Legal System and Society)*, **1(1)**: 28.

Sun, Yuan (2009), 'Revisit to the Reform of Transferring the Case Files', *Zhengfa Luntan (Tribune of Political Science and Law)*, **1**: 167.

Suo, Zhengjie (1998), 'Studies on the Approach of Criminal Trial in China', *Zhengfa Luntan (Tribune of Political Science and Law)*, **4**: 58.

Tam, Fiona (2010), 'Mental Hospital for Man who Exposed Official', *South China Morning Post*, 13 April.

Tan, Hua (2010), 'Empirical Study on the Current Situation of Application of Criminal Detention in China', *Jinka Gongcheng (Jingji yu Fa) (Golden Card Project (Economics and Law))*, **5**: 68.

Tan, Shigui (2009), 'On the Obstacles of Open Trial and Solutions – From the Perspective of Criminal Trial', *Zhejiang Gongshang Daxue Xuebao (Journal of Zhejiang Gongshang University)*, **1**: 5.

Tang, Liang, (2001), 'Analysis of the Facts Relating to Pre-trial Detention in China', *Faxue*, **7**: 29.
Tang, Liang (2004), 'Report on Custody Pending Trial – A Comparison between the Two Cities', in Ruihua Chen (ed.), *Weijue Jiya Zhidu de Shizheng Yanjiu (Empirical Study on the System of Custody Pending Trial)*, Beijing: Peking University Press.
Tang, Xuelian and Weimin Zuo (2007), 'Lawyers in the Investigation', in Weimin Zuo et al., *Zhongguo Xingshi Susong Yunxing Jizhi Shizheng Yanjiu (Empirical Study on the Operation Mechanism of Criminal Procedure in China)*, Beijing: Law Press.
Tanner, Harold (1985), 'Concepts of Law in the Chinese Anti-Crime Campaign', *Harvard Law Re*view, **98(8)**: 1890.
Tanner, Harold (1999), *Strike Hard! Anti-Crime Campaigns and Chinese Criminal Justice, 1979–1985*, Ithaca, NY: East Asia Program, Cornell University.
Tao, Jianjun (2002), 'Examination of the Structure of the System of Cross-examination in Criminal Cases', *Jiancha Shijian (Procuratorial Practice)*, **1**: 42.
Tao, Lung-sheng (1966), 'The Criminal Law of Communist China', *Cornell Quarterly*, **52**: 43.
The Rights Practice (2003), *The Death Penalty in China: A Baseline Document*, New York: Amnesty International.
Tian, Siyuan (2008), *Fanzui Beihairen de Quanli yu Jiuji (Rights and Reliefs of Criminal Victims)*, Beijing: Law Press.
Tian, Yuan (2006), 'On the Problems of Extended Custody Arising from the Supplementary Investigation', *Henan Gong'an Gaodeng Zhuanke Xuexiao Xuebao (Journal of Henan Public Security Academy)*, **2**: 70.
Toborg, Mary (1981), 'Pre-trial Release: A Rational Evaluation of Practices and Outcomes', cited in Yale Kamisar, Wayne LaFave and Jerold Israel, *Advanced Criminal Procedure*, St. Paul, MN: West Publishing Co. (1994) at p. 860.
Trevaskes, Susan (2003), 'Public Sentencing Rallies in China: The Symbolizing of Punishment and Justice in a Socialist State', *Crime Law & Social Change*, **39**: 359.
Trevaskes, Susan (2007a), 'Severe and Swift Justice in China', *British Journal of Criminology*, **47**: 23.
Trevaskes, Susan (2007b), *Courts and Criminal Justice in Contemporary China*, Lanham, MD: Lexington Books.
Turack, Daniel C. (1999), 'The New Chinese Criminal Justice System', *Cardozo Journal of International & Comparative Law*, **7**: 49.
United Nations Working Group on Arbitrary Detention (1998), *Report on the Visit to the People's Republic of China*, 54th Session, Agenda Item 8, U.N. Doc. E/CN.4/1998/44/Add.2.
Upham, Frank (2005), 'Who will Find the Defendant if he Stays with his Sheep? Justice in Rural China', *Yale Law Journal*, **114**: 1675.
Van Cleave, Rachel (2007), 'Italy', in Craig Bradley (ed.), *Criminal Procedure: A Worldwide Study*, Durham, NC: Carolina Academic Press, pp. 303–350.
Vera Institute (1977), *Felony Arrests: Their Prosecution and Disposition in New York City's Courts*, New York: Vera Institute Monograph.
Wald, Michael, Richard Ayres, David W. Hess, Michael Schantz and Charles H. Whitebread (1967), 'Interrogations in New Haven: The Impact of Miranda', *Yale Law Journal*, **76**: 1519.

Walker, Clive and Keir Starmer (eds) (1999a), *Justice in Error*, London: Blackstone.
Walker, Clive and Keir Starmer (1999b), *Miscarriages of Justice*, London: Blackstone.
Walkley, John (1987), *Police Interrogation: A Handbook for Investigators*, London: Police Review Publications.
Wan, Yi (2005), 'Case Instruction System Harassed by History and Reality', *Faxue (Legal Science Monthly)*, **2**: 9.
Wang, Chunwang (2000), 'Several Problems in the Implementation of Bail by the Public Security Organs', *Henan Gong'an Gaodeng Zhuanke Xuexiao Xuebao (Journal of Henan Public Security Academy)*, **4**: 36.
Wang, Fei-ling (2004), 'Reformed Migration Control and New Targeted People: China's Hukou System in the 2000s', *The China Quarterly*, March, 115–132.
Wang, Gao (2000), 'Examining the System of Bail Pending Trial', *Renmin Jiancha (People's Procuratorial Semi-monthly)*, **5**: 4.
Wang, Gong (2003), *Wei Zhongguo Lushi Bianhu (Defending for Chinese Lawyers)*, Beijing: Democracy and Construction Press.
Wang, Guangjing and Longtian Wang (1998a), 'The Situation and Analysis of Lawyers' Participation in the Earlier Stage of the Criminal Process', *Minzhu Yu Fazhi (Democracy and Law)*, **262**: 30.
Wang, Guangjing and Longtian Wang (1998b), 'Criminal Defence: Pillars that are Indispensable for the Construction of the Building of Judicial Fairness', *Chinese Lawyer*, **1**: 14.
Wang, Hangbin (1996), 'PRC: Ren Jianxin, Wang Hanbin on Amended Criminal Procedure Law', *Beijing Xinhua Domestic Service in Chinese*, 19 April, translated text.
Wang, Heyan (2010), 'Lawyers Sweat in Heat of New Judicial Orders', *Caixin Wang (Caixin online)*, 25 May.
Wang, Hongyu (2008), *Fei Jianjinxing Wenti Yanjiu (A Study of Issues on the Non-Custodial Penalty)*, Beijing: China People's University of Public Security Press.
Wang, Jiancheng and Yang Xiong (2002), 'Reform of the Procedure of Pretrial Examination in Criminal Cases from a Comparative Law Perspective', *Zhongguo Xingshifa Zazhi (Criminal Science)*, **6**: 52.
Wang, Minyuan (2003), 'On the Improvement of Bail System in China', in Chen Weidong (ed.), *Huanxing yu Qubao Houshen (Probation and Bail Pending Trial)*, Beijing: China Procuratorial Press.
Wang, Vivian (2006), 'The "Conscience of Chinese Lawyers" Will Fight to the End', *South China Morning Post*, 28 December.
Wang, Xin'an (2004), 'Empirical Analysis of the Problem on Custody Pending Trial', in Ruihua Chen (ed.), *Weijue Jiya Zhidu de Shizheng Yanjiu (Empirical Study on the System of Custody Pending Trial)*, Beijing: Peking University Press.
Wang, Xinhuan (2010), 'Thinking of the Reform of the Sentencing Procedure', in Guangzhong Chen (ed.), *Xingshifa Luntan (Di San Ji) (Criminal Justice Forum, Vol. 3)*, Beijing: China People's University of Public Security Press.
Wang, Yanxue (2010), 'On Recessive Custody – Study on Dissimilated Application of Compulsory Measures Outside the Detention House', *Zhongguo Xingshifa Zazhi (Criminal Science)*, **5**: 56.
Wang, Ying (2004), 'Informal Report of the Survey Results of the Work Situation of Criminal Defence Lawyers', *Shiji Jingii Baodao (21st Century Business Herald)*, 11 August 2004.

Wang, Yu (2002), 'On Perfecting the Procedure of Pretrial Examination in Public Prosecution Cases', *Zhongguo Shiyou Daxue Xuebao (Shehui Kexue Ban) (Journal of the University of Petroleum, China (Social Sciences Edition))*, **2**: 76.

Wang, Yue, Guo Han and Hua Bi (1999), 'Deviations in the Application of Criminal Detention', *Renmin Jiancha (People's Procuratorial Semi-monthly)*, **3**: 55.

Wei, Hong (2000), 'Re-studying the System of Criminal Trial in China', *Gansu Zhengfa Xueyuan Xuebao (Journal of Gansu Political Science and Law Institute)*, **3**: 67.

Wei, Luo (2000), *The Amended Criminal Procedure Law and the Criminal Court Rules of the People's Republic of China: with English Translation, Introduction, and Annotation*, Buffalo, NY: William S. Hein & Co., Inc.

Wei, Zujian (2000), 'Exploring the Problems Relating to Returning a Case for Supplementary Investigation', *Shanghai Zhengfa Guanli Ganbu Xueyuan Xuebao (Law Journal of Shanghai Administrative Cadre Institute of Politics and Law)*, **2**: 72.

Wells, Gary and Elizabeth A. Olson (2003), 'Eyewitness Testimony', *Annual Review of Psychology*, **54**: 277.

Weng, Byron (1987), *Essays on the Constitution of the People's Republic of China*, Hong Kong: Chinese University Press.

Whitfort, Amanda (2007), 'The Right to a Fair Trial in China: The Criminal Procedure Law of 1996', *East Asian Law Review*, **2(2)**: 141.

Whyte, Martin King (1983), 'On Studying China at a Distance', in Anne Thurston and Burton Pasternak (eds), *The Social Sciences and Fieldwork in China*, Boulder, CO: Westview Press, pp. 63–80.

Wills, William (1902), *An Essay on the Principles of Circumstantial Evidence*, A. Wills (ed.), 5th edition, London: Butterworths.

Wilson, James Q. (1968), *Varieties of Police Behavior*, Cambridge, MA: Harvard University Press.

Witt, James W. (1973), 'Non-coercive Interrogation and the Administration of Criminal Justice: The Impact of Miranda on Police Effectuality', *Journal of Criminal Law and Criminology*, **64**: 320.

Woffinden, Bob (1987), *Miscarriages of Justice*, London: Hodder & Stoughton.

Wong, Kam (2002), 'Policing in the People's Republic of China', *British Journal of Criminology*, **42**: 281.

Wong, Kam (2004), 'Govern Police by Law in China', *The Australian and New Zealand Journal of Criminology*, **37(4)**: 90.

Wong, Kam (2007), 'Studying Police in China: Some Personal Reflections', *International Journal of the Sociology of Law*, **35**: 111.

Woo, M. (1999), 'Law and Discretion in the Contemporary Chinese Courts', *Pacific Rim Law & Policy*, **8**: 581.

Wrightsman, Lawrence and Saul Kassin (1993), *Confessions in the Courtroom*, London: Sage Publications.

Wu, Aihua (2010), 'Preliminary Analysis of Several Problems on the Application of Domicile Surveillance', *Fazhi Yu Shehui (Legal System and Society)*, **2(1)**: 291.

Wu, Danhong, Baoguo Fang and Lixia Liu (2005), 'Talks on the Reform of Witness System', in He Jiahong (ed.), *Zhengjuxue Luntan (Evidence Forum)*, Beijing: China Procuratorial Press, **9**: 111.

Wu, Dingzhi (1999a), 'What are Good Measures to Solve the Witness' Refusal to Give

Testimony – A Study of Improving the System of Protecting Witness' Rights in China', *People's Procuratorial Semi-monthly (Renmin Jiancha)*, **3**: 6.

Wu, Dingzhi (1999b), 'Witnesses Refuse to Testify, What are the Best Methods to Resolve this Problem – Ideas for Perfecting the System in Relation to the Protection of the Rights of the Witnesses in China', *Procedural Law and Legal System*, **7**: 23.

Wu, Sheng (2007), *Huanxing Zhidu Yanjiu (A Study of Suspended Penalty)*, Beijing: China University of Public Security Science Press.

Wu, Yihuo and Jun Hong (2005), 'Too Few Administrative Law Enforcement Cases Transferred to the Judicial Organs', *Jiancha Ribao (Procuratorial Daily)*, 31 January.

Xiao, Nianhua (1998), 'The Existing Situation of the System of Public Prosecution Examination in China and its Reconstruction', *Zhengfa Luncong (Journal of Political Science and Law)*, **3**: 57.

Xiao, Qianli, Jian Guo and Song Dai (2009), 'Thoughts on the Difficult Situation of Incidental Civil Action in Criminal Proceedings – Based on the Empirical Study of Incidental Civil Action in Criminal Proceedings in Yibin City (of Sichuan Province)', *Xihua Daxue Xuebao (Zhexue Shehui Kexue Ban) (Journal of Xihua University (Philosophy & Social Sciences))*, **2**: 90.

Xiao, Shiwei (2008), 'Criminal Summary Procedure in Practice – Demonstrative Research on the Sample of Two Grassroots Courts', *Yibin Xueyuan Xuebao (Journal of Yibin University)*, **7**: 21.

Xie, Cheng (2004), 'On Perfecting the System of Bail – From the Perspective of the Judicial Practice of the Public Security Organs in Criminal Cases', *Zhejiang Gong'an Gaodeng Zhuanke Xuexiao Xuebao (Journal of Zhejiang Police College)*, **2**: 53.

Xie, Mangen (2004), 'A Brief Analysis of the Pretrial Examination Procedure of Our Country from the Perspective of Litigation', *Lingling Xueyuan Xuebao (Journal of Lingling University)*, **2**: 42.

Xie, Youping and Xianwen He (2010), 'On the Improvement of Criminal Compulsory Measures in Our Country', *Fazhi Yanjiu (Research on Rule of Law)*, **5**: 3.

Xiong, Jiangning (2001), 'An Analysis of the Law Related to the Problems of Extended Detention', *Zhongguo Lushi (Chinese Lawyer)*, **4**: 39.

Xiong, Qiuhong (2005), 'Deciphering the First Case of "Plea Bargaining"', *Zhongguo Faxue Wang (Chinese Legal Studies Net)*, available at http://www/iolaw.org.cn/shownews.asp?id=598> (last visited 16 September 2005).

Xu, Jianxin, Jianging Mao and Cuidan Wu (2007), 'Problems and Analysis on the Practice of Case Instruction System', *Falu Shiyong (Journal of Law Application)*, **8**: 7.

Xu, Lanting (2000), 'Dare Not to Give Evidence', *Nanfang Zhoumo (Nanfang Weekend)*, 26 October.

Xu, Meijun (2007), 'Empirical Study of the Simplified Ordinary Procedure in Criminal Proceeding', *Xiandai Faxue (Modern Law Science)*, **2**: 113.

Xu, Meijun (2009), *Zhenchaquan de Yunxing yu Kongzhi (Operation and Control of Investigative Power)*, Beijing: Law Press.

Xu, Xi (2009), 'A Comparative Study of Lawyers' Ethics in the US and PRC: Attorney-Client Privilege and Duty of Confidentiality', *Tsinghua Law Review*, **1**: 1, 46.

Xu, Xuefeng (2002), 'Analysing the Burden of Proof of the Defendant in Criminal Proceeding', *Renmin Jiancha (People's Procuratorate Semi-monthly)*, **3**: 9.

Xu, Yongjun and Xiaolu Cheng (2008), 'Unscrambling and Interpreting the Guidelines on the Relationship between the Police and the Procuratorate (for Trial Implementation)', *Guojia Jianchaguan Xueyuan Xuebao (Journal of National Procurators College)*, 1.

Xu, Yuezhi (2007), 'People's Assessors System Goes into New Development Stage', *Jingji Ribao (Economics Daily)*, 7 October.

Xue, Fei (n.d.), 'Case Tried in the First Instance-Case in the Second Instance', available at http://www.legalinfo.gov.cn/ xuefa/juan/susong/susongfa006.htm.

Xue, Shuanliang and Yonghong Lu (1999), 'On the Court Questioning in Criminal Lawsuit', *Lanzhou Daxue Xuebao (Shehui Kexue Ban) (Journal of Lanzhou University (Social Sciences Edition))*, **2**: 93.

Yan, Xiufang (2009), 'Demonstrative Analysis Report on the Non-prosecution System', *Fazhi yu Jingji (Legal System and Economy)*, **11**: 80.

Yan, Ying (2001), 'The Design of the Pretrial Examination Procedure in Criminal Litigation', *Beijing Fazhi Bao*, 31 August.

Yang, Cheng (2007), 'Legislative Defects on the System of Criminal Compulsory Measures in China and its Improvement', *Qiannan Minzu Shifan Xueyuan Xuebao (Journal of Southern Guizhou Normal University for Ethnics)*, **4**: 49.

Yang, Feixue (2009), 'Problems on the Incidental Civil Action in Criminal Proceedings in Judicial Practice and Countermeasures', *Fazhi Lunheng (Journal of the Provincial Level Party School of CPC Sichuan Province Committee)*, **1**: 58.

Yang, Jun (2009), 'Preliminary Discussion on the Defects of the Bail Pending Trial System in China and Improvement', *Fazhi yu Shehui (Legal System and Society)*, **2(1)**: 262.

Yang, Mayfair Mei-hui (1994), *Gifts, Favors and Banquets – The Art of Social Relationships in China*, Ithaca, NY: Cornell University Press.

Yang, Ming (2003), 'The Reconstruction of the Power of the Court to Investigate Cases Out of It', *Liaoning Daxue Xuebao (Zhexue Sheke Ban) (Journal of Liaoning University (Philosophy and Social Sciences Edition))*, **1**: 130.

Yang, Yingze (2007), 'Thoughts on Improving the System of Chinese Witness Protection', in *Proceedings of the International Conference on Criminal Procedure Law: Challenges in the 21st Century*, Centro de Formacao Juridica e Judiciaria, at pp. 261–273.

Yang, Zhengwan (1998), 'Analyzing the Procedure of Pretrial Examination', *Guizhou Minzu Xueyuan Xuebao (Shehui Kexue Ban) (Journal of the Guizhou Ethnic Institute (Social Sciences Edition))*, **2**: 61.

Yang, Ziyu (2003), 'Study on Basic Rules of Criminal Cross-examination', *Guangxi Zhengfa Guanli Ganbu Xueyuan Xuebao (Journal of Guangxi Administrative Cadre Institute of Politics and Law)*, **2**: 34.

Ye, Qing (2006), 'Pre-trial Preparation Procedure', in Guangzhong Chen, Weiqiu Cheng and Cheng Yang, *Xingshi Yishen Chengxu yu Renquan Baozhang (Criminal Trial of the First Instance and Protection of Human Rights)*, Beijing: China University of Political Science and Law Press.

Yin, Xiaoli (2002), 'On the Rules of Hearsay Evidence', *Guizhou Gongye Daxue Xuebao (Shehui Kexue Ban) (Journal of Guizhou University of Technology (Social Science Edition))*, **3**: 40.

Yongshun, Cai and Songcai Yang (2005), 'State Power and Unbalanced Legal Development in China', *Journal of Contemporary China*, **14**: 117.

Yu, Ping (2002), 'Glittery Promise vs. Dismal Reality: The Role of the Criminal Lawyer in the People's Republic of China after the Revision of the Criminal Procedure Law', *Vanderbilt Journal of Transnational Law*, **35**: 827.

Yu, Verna (2009), 'Warning Police will "Strike Hard at Hostile Forces"', *South China Morning Post*, 29 December.

Yu, Xinan and Shucheng Guo (2003), 'To Accelerate Development in Mid and Western China and to Build an Overall Well-off Society', *Renmin Ribao (People's Daily)*, 20 April.

Yu, Xun (2004), 'A Rational Analysis of Transplanting the Plea Bargaining System in China', *Journal of Zhejiang Shuren University*, **7**: 52.

Yuan, Ling (2003), 'Judicial Difficulties Behind Zero Extended Detention in Chongqing', *Xinjing Bao*, 30 December.

Yuan, Zhiqiang (2010), 'Defects of the Legal Systems in Witnesses' Testimony in Our Country and Measures for Improvement', *Fazhi yu Shehui (Legal System and Society)*, **2**: 44.

Yue, Liling (2010), *Xingshi Shenpan yu Renquan Baozhang (Criminal Trial and Human Rights Protection)*, Beijing: Law Press.

Zang, Desheng (2005), 'Statistics and Analysis of Current Situation on the Application of Suspended Penalty', *Zhongguo Xingshifa Zazhi (Criminal Science)*.

Zeng, Yabo (2001), 'Problems Concerning the Execution of Bail Pending Trial', *Fazhi Ribao (Legal Daily)*, 29 September.

Zhai, Huaimin (2003), 'All cases of extended detention in the public security organs in China have been rectified in 2003', reported in the *Legal Daily*, 20 January 2004, available in China Internet Information Centre, http://www1.china.com.cn/chinese/law/484606.htm.

Zhan, Fuliang (1997), 'Problems in the Application of Summary Procedure and their Solutions', *Renmin Jiancha (People's Procuratorate Semi-monthly)*, **10**: 21.

Zhang, Chao (2010), 'Survey Report on the Period of Criminal Detention by the Public Security Organs', *Zhongguo Xinshifa Zazhi (Criminal Science)*, **5**: 98.

Zhang, Jun and Yinzhong Hao (2005), *Xingshi Susong Tingshen Chengxu Zhuanti Yanjiu (Special Studies on Criminal Court Trial Procedure)*, Beijing: China University of Political Science and Law Press.

Zhang, Jun, Wei Jiang and Wenchang Tian (2001), *Xingshi Susong: Kong, Bian, Shen Sanren Tan (Criminal Litigation: Three Men Talking about Prosecution, Defence and Adjudication)*, Beijing: China Law Press.

Zhang, Lening and Steve Messner (1995), 'Family Deviance and Delinquency in China', *Criminology*, **33**(3): 359.

Zhang, Lening et al. (2000), 'Organization of Ownership and Workplace Theft in China', *International Journal of Offender Therapy and Comparative Criminology*, **44**(5): 581.

Zhang, Linlin (2005), 'On the Abnormal Occupational Hazards for Chinese Defense Lawyers', *Shandong Jingcha Xueyuan Xuebao (Journal of Shandong Police College)*, 3.

Zhang, Liyun (ed.) (2009), *Xingshi Cuo'an yu Qizhong Zhengju (Criminal Wrong Convictions and the Seven Types of Evidence)*, Beijing: China Legal System Publishing House.

Zhang, Lizhao (1999), 'Two Questions Relating to the Application of Recalculating the Duration of Detention', *Hebei Faxue (Hebei Law Science)*, **1**: 54.

Zhang, Minyou and Denang Zhong (2007), 'Several Thoughts on the System of

Non-Prosecution because of Doubt in Our Country', *Zhongguo Jianchaguan (The Chinese Procurators)*, **11**: 18

Zhang, Qingshan and Xinqi Qu (2010), 'On the Model of Judicial Review on the Conditions of Necessary Arrest', *Faxue Zazhi (Law Science Magazine)*, **5**: 93.

Zhang, Qiyuan and Qian Ma (2003), 'Study on Process of Pre-examination of Criminal Trials', *Guangxi Zhengfa Guanli Ganbu Xueyuan Xuebao (Journal of Guangxi Administrative Cadre Institute of Politics and Law)*, **5**: 106.

Zhang, Rujin (2009), 'Preliminary Discussion on the Current Situation of Domicile Surveillance and the Countermeasures', *Fazhi Yu Shehui (Legal System and Society)*, **9**: 104.

Zhang, Yan (2010), 'Exploration and Practice of the Mass Participation in the Trial Work', in Dong An (ed.), *Xibu Faguan Luncong (Di 10 Juan) (Forum for Judges in West China (Vol. 10))*, Beijing: People's Court Press.

Zhang, Yanhong (2009), 'Several Thoughts on the Compensation Problems in the Incidental Civil Action in Criminal Proceedings', *Keji Xinxi (Science and Technology Information)*, **13**: 772.

Zhang, Yaowu (2001), 'Reasons for the Witnesses' Refusal to Testify in Court and its Solution', *Zhongguo Lushi (Chinese Lawyer)*, 22.

Zhang, Yi (2004), 'Considering the Perfecting of the System of Testifying in Court by Witnesses in Criminal Litigations', *Shehui Kexuejia (Social Scientist)*, 111.

Zhang, Ying and Xidong Shang (2009), 'Analysis of the Root of "Confession Complex"', *Xibu Faxue Pinglun (Western Law Review)*, **4**: 139.

Zhang, Yuxiang and Jinglin Men (2007), 'Rational Analysis about Article 306 of Criminal Law', *Hebei Faxue (Hebei Law Science)*, 2.

Zhang, Zetao (2001), 'An Analysis of Present Situation on the Witness Court Appearance in China and Discussion of Countermeasures', in He Jiahong (ed.), *Zhengjuxue Luntan (Forum on Evidence)*, Vol. 2, Beijing: China Procuratorial Press.

Zhao, Deqiang and Xiaoli Wang (2002), 'Problems in the Incidental Civil Action which can not be Ignored', available at http://www.chinacourt.org/public/detail.php?id=16715.

Zhao, Gang and Xuezai Liu (2002), 'Preliminary Criticism on the Administrative and Enterprising Tendency of the Court in Our Country', in Guangzhong Chen and Wei Zhou (eds.), vol. 7, *Susongfa Luncong (Procedural Law Review)*, Beijing: Law Press.

Zhao, Hui and Jianye Liu (2006), 'Problems on Criminal Summary Procedure and Countermeasures', *Xinxiang Shifan Gaodeng Zhuanke Xuexiao Xuebao (Journal of Xinxiang Teachers' College)*, **1**: 97.

Zhao, Liming, 'Article 306 of the Criminal Law in a Lawyer's Eye', available at http://www.law-lib.com/lw/lw_view.asp?no=6137&page=1.

Zhen, Zhen and Jiancheng Wang (eds) (2007), *Zhongguo Xingshi Susong Diyishen Chengxu Gaige Yanjiu (Research on the Reform of First-Instance Trial of the Criminal Procedure in China)*, Beijing: Law Press.

Zhiyuan, Guo (2010), 'Approaching Visible Justice: Procedural Safeguards for Mental Examinations in China's Capital Cases', *Hastings International and Comparative Law Review*, **33(7)**: 21.

Zhong, Daisy (2010), 'Interrogations to be Videotaped', *South China Morning Post*, 12 August.

Zhong, Jingmin (2008), 'On the Safeguard of Lawyers' Right at the Investigation Stage of Criminal Proceedings', *Lushi Shidian (Lawyers Viewpoint)*, **4**: 59.

Zhong, Shikai (2004), 'Human Rights Society Outlines China's Progress in Judicial Reform', *BBC Monitoring Asia Pacific*, 16 April.

Zhou, Cuifang (2002), 'Survey Report on the Situation of Supplementation Investigation during the Review and Approval for Prosecution by the Procuratorial Organs in Beijing', *Zhongguo Xingshifa Zazhi (Criminal Science)*, **3**: 70.

Zhou, G. (1999), 'Exploring Certain Issues Concerning the Prohibition of Extracting Confessions by Torture', *Zhengfa Luncong (Journal of Political Science & Law)*, 1.

Zhou, Guojun (1989), 'On Whether Shelter and Investigation Should Be Abolished', *Zhengfa Luntan (Forum of Politics and Law)*, **1**: 35.

Zhou, Guojun (1994), 'Discussion on the Time when Lawyers' Intervention is Allowed', *Zhongguo Lushi (China Lawyer)*, 32.

Zhou, Shimin (1998), 'A Comparison on Several Basic Issues of Criminal Procedure between Mainland China and Macao', *Comparative Law (Bijiao Fa)*, **3**: 313.

Zhou, Wei (2000), 'Several Problems on Residential Surveillance', *Dangdai Faxue (Contemporary Law Review)*, **4**: 27.

Zhu, Daqiang (2010), 'Wang Shengjun: Courts Should Pay More Attention to the Safeguard of People's Livelihood, Smooth the Expression Mechanism of Public Opinion', 23 June, available at http://news.xinhuanet.com/legal/2008-06/23/content_8420389.htm.

Zhu, Guobin (2004), 'China Regulates Extension of Custody to Safeguard Human Rights', *China Law*, **49**(4): 28–31, 90–96.

Zhu, Jingwen (ed.) (2007), *Zhongguo Falu Fazhan Baogao: Shujuku he Zhibiao Tixi (Report on China Law Development: Database and Indicators)*, Beijing: Renmin University of China Press, cited in Sida Liu and Terence Halliday, 'Dancing Handcuffed in the Minefield: Survival Strategies of Defense Lawyers in China's Criminal Justice System', (2008) http://ssrn.com/abstract=1269536.

Zhu, Suli (2010), 'The Party and the Courts', in Randall Peerenboom (ed.), *Judicial Independence in China*, Cambridge: Cambridge University Press, pp. 52–68.

Zhu, Wenping and Na Zhang (2010), 'On the System of Witnesses' Appearance and Testimony in Court in the Criminal Procedure', *Fazhi yu Shehui (Legal System and Society)*, **1**(3): 42.

Zhu, Yan (2010), 'Bankers in an Online Gambling Game will be Sentenced up to 10 Years During the World Cup', *Xinjing Bao (New Beijing Newspaper)*, 18 June.

Zimbardo, Philip (1967), 'The Psychology of Police Confessions', *Psychology Today*, **1**: 17.

Zuo, Weimin (2008), 'An Empirical Study of the Chinese Criminal Dossier System – Focusing on the Evidence Dossier', paper delivered at the Kennedy School of Government, Harvard, at www.hks.harvard.edu/.../jsw_china_seminar_oct2008.html.

Zuo, Weimin, Huojian Tang and Weijun Wu (2001), *Heyi Zhidu Yanjiu – Jianlun Heyiting Duli Shenpan (A Study of Collegial Panel – And Discussion of Independent Trial by the Panel)*, Beijing: Law Press.

Zuo, Weimin and Jinghua Ma (2005), 'The Rate of Criminal Witness Appearance in Court – an Empirically-based Theoretical Discussion', *Xiandai Faxue (Modern Law Science)*, 6.

Zuo, Weimin (2007), 'Reform on Chinese Criminal Summary Procedure – A Preliminary Observation and Reflection', in Zuo Weimin *et al.*, *Zhongguo Xingshi Susong Yunxing Jizhi Shizheng Yanjiu (Empirical Study on the Operation Mechanism of Criminal Procedure in China)*, Beijing: Law Press.

Zuo, Weimin, Jinghua Ma and Jianping Hu (2007), 'Survey Report on the Pilot of Witnesses Court Appearance and Giving Testimony in Criminal Cases', in Weimin Zuo *et al.*, *Zhongguo Xingshi Susong Yunxing Jizhi Shizheng Yanjiu (Empirical Study on the Operation Mechanism of Criminal Procedure in China)*, Beijing: Law Press.

Zuo Weimin *et al.* (2009), *Zhongguo Xingshi Susong Yunxing Jizhi Shizheng Yanjiu (Er): Yi Shenqian Chengxu Wei Zhongxin (Empirical Study on the Operation Mechanism of Criminal Procedure in China (II): Focus on the Pre-trial Procedure)*, Beijing: Law Press.

Index

access to client
  following police interrogation 174–6
  on initial detention 166–74
access to legal advice 67–70, 71, 76, 168–71
accomplice
  defendant as 325–7
  evidence against 97–9
acquittals 79, 142, 196–7, 254, 358, 452
  rate target 387
activists
  human rights activists 13–14, 41, 318, 433, 451
  lawyers, dangers to 166, 171, 432, 452
adjudication committee 2–4, 7, 10, 352, 399–400, 403, 405, 408, 410, 422, 441, 445
  see also political-legal committee
administrative cases 497–505
  authority over 503–5
  and budgetary shortfall 505
  categories of 499–500
  and criminal punishment, demarcation between 497–8
  imposition by police 500–501
  investigation skills, poor 505
  police powers of detention and arrest 42
  police punishment power, reasons for giving 498–9
  public security cases, reasons behind high number of 501–3
admission of guilt 72–5, 213, 277, 282, 294, 345
  see also confessions
adversarial system 8–13, 19–20, 291, 330
  and pre-trial involvement of judges 150, 156, 435
age of judges 224
age of suspects 32–4, 36
  juvenile offenders 56, 149, 258, 292, 365
agent ad litem 146, 180, 194, 197, 199–200, 201–2, 430
aggregate justice 423, 450, 452
Ai, J. 46
alcohol use 305, 371–2
Alford, W. 18, 219, 419, 425
Anderlini, J. 45

appeals and protests 3, 4, 109–10, 142, 197–8, 291, 389, 393–5, 411, 460
approval of arrest 49–51, 54–6, 59
  see also police powers of detention and arrest
Ashworth, A. 27, 165, 167
audio-visual evidence 66, 184, 217, 241–2, 249, 276, 448
  see also evidence
audit and performance indicators 111, 355, 423, 435, 440, 442, 447

Bai, L. 213
bail
  and Basic and Intermediate Courts 62–4
  and Criminal Procedure Law (1996) 41–2, 47, 58, 64
  and defence lawyer role 60–61, 62
  granted inappropriately 57, 60
  guarantee money 41–2, 59, 60
  internal approval process, discouragement of 59
  low success rate for 56–7, 61, 63
  and migrants 64
  and People's Procuratorate 58
  and police powers of detention and arrest 41–2, 43, 44–5, 47, 60, 63
  and residential status 63–4
  used for material gain or private favour 57–8, 61
Baker, B. 227
Bakken, B. 36, 366, 436, 437
Balbus, I. 442, 445
Baldwin, J. 29, 30, 31, 68, 71, 72, 97, 99, 168
Balme, S. 217, 218, 221, 262, 263, 264, 400, 402
Banton, M. 167, 447
Basic Courts
  age of suspects 33, 36
  and bail applications 62–4
  criminal jurisdiction 2, 3, 15–16, 29
  evidence review 126
  interrogation and confession 72, 73–4, 75–6, 124
  judges' robes 262
  legal advice requests 116–17
  non-prosecution rate 136

police mistreatment complaints 120
and pre-trial detention 49, 50, 51–3
pre-trial interrogation 123
trial procedure 194
see also Intermediate Courts; Supreme People's Court; trial and case file analysis; trial outcome observations
Bedau, H. 172, 362
Belgium 150, 339
Belkin, I. 4
Biddulph, S. 497, 498, 499
'big stick', and defence lawyers 181
Bill of Prosecution
  and major evidence 145
  and pre-trial judicial activism 147, 148, 151, 152, 157, 158, 161
  prosecutors' presentation 2, 10, 28, 135, 269, 275
  and summary procedure 206
  time constraints 7
  and trial procedures 194, 199, 200, 206, 209
  see also pre-trial preparation of prosecutors
Bittner, E. 433
Black, D. 27, 433
black jails 45, 59, 173, 451
black societies 379, 433, 437
Blumberg, A. 440
Bodde, D. 190, 339
Borchard, E. 172, 362
Bottomley, A. 27, 71
Bottoms, A. 469
Brandon, R. 172, 362
bribery 2, 28, 32, 90, 92, 129, 173, 255, 357, 456
  by defendant 111
  judicial 410, 411
Bridges, L. 165, 167, 168
Bright, S. 259
Brown, D. 167, 168
burden of proof 9, 19, 120, 213–16, 337, 346
  see also trial procedures
Burrows, J. 56

Cai, D. 5
Cai Dingjian 5
Cai, P. 211, 212
Cao, J. 286, 378
Cao, W. 212
Cape, E. 165, 167
Caplan, J. 362
case construction
  capacity for 433–5
  informal organizational practices 433
  and institutional setting 436–40
  and legal form 14–15
  see also defence case construction; police case, construction of
case file analysis
  failings of system 408
  and Ordinary Procedure 236, 267, 351–2, 354, 358
  prosecution, bias associated with 152–3, 155–6, 157–8, 159, 160
  research methodology 467–8
  schedule 475–88
  and trial *see* trial and case file analysis
case withdrawal 175–6, 189
  see also defence case construction
case-responsible judge
  and criminal justice system 2, 403
  prosecution presentation 263–4, 266, 269, 273–5, 330–31
  and trial outcome observations 352–3
  see also judges
charges *see* Bill of Prosecution
Chatterton, M. 27, 167
Chen, A. 11, 428, 432
Chen, G. 21, 45, 185, 198, 209–10, 243–5, 316, 349, 358, 403, 428, 464
Chen Guangcheng case 185, 413
Chen, Jianxin 58, 59
Chen, Jicai 188
Chen, Junmin 54, 63
Chen, Lianyi 57
Chen, Lunzhao 132
Chen, R. 46, 47, 170, 171–2, 180, 184, 198, 317, 339, 500
Chen, S. 214
Chen, W. 26, 46, 55, 68, 69, 142, 154, 227, 235, 242, 244, 464
Chen, Xingliang 292, 377
Chen, Xinsheng 130, 133
Chen, Ye 142
Chen, Yongsheng 24, 45, 154, 243
Chen, Yu 170
Chen, Yuwen 199
Cheng, D. 464
Cheng, F. 53, 133
Cheng, G. 154, 160
Cheng, M. 53, 133
Cheng, X. 186
Cheung, Y. 181, 185, 333
Chi, W. 132, 133
Chin, K. 379
Chinese Communist Party 7, 15–16, 24, 57, 171, 219, 220, 357, 425, 437, 449
  influence and supervision 396, 399–402, 403–7, 409, 410, 411, 413–14
  and party-state 171, 219, 378, 400, 401, 439, 442

Public Security Bureau (PSB) *see* Public Security Bureau (PSB)
 strike hard campaign 7, 16, 141, 278, 365, 377, 426, 431, 434, 436–8, 443, 448
 see also Criminal Procedure Law
Choi, C. 340, 426
Chong, S. 400
Choongh, S. 56, 168
Chow, D. 110, 144, 217, 218
Ch'u, T. 339
Chu, W. 37, 258
Cicourel, A. 14
civil suits for compensation 198–205
Clark, G. 218, 220, 229, 432
Clark, N. 68
Clarke, D. 23–4, 68, 166, 221, 366, 426, 431, 441
Cohen, J. 1, 24, 57, 166, 170, 172, 198, 219, 277, 318, 339, 396, 413, 418, 425, 427, 445, 447, 451
Coleman, K. 27, 71
collegial panel
 and prosecution presentation 263–4, 266, 272–3, 276–8
 responsibilities and adjudication 2, 6–7, 10, 236, 402–3, 460
 and trial outcome observations 352–3, 356
 trial procedures 224–6
 see also political-legal committee
compulsory measures, review of 127–9
confessions
 admission of guilt 72–5, 213, 277, 282, 294, 345
 and Basic and Intermediate Courts 72, 73–4, 75–6, 124
 and detention 47
 extortion of 6, 16, 68–9, 70–71, 213, 337, 340
 false, and police under pressure 172–3
 forced, concern over 187
 illegally-obtained 336–7
 innocence claims after 76–97
 and leniency 17
 and police case construction 68–9, 70–79
 reliability of 340–42
 and statement, contradictions between 75, 77
 and torture *see* torture
 withdrawal of 123–4, 130, 337–8
Conlon, G. 362
Cordone, C. 259
Corker, D. 177
corruption 18, 379, 410, 411–12, 419–21
counter-revolutionaries 3, 12, 14, 451, 499
court layout 191–2

court observations
 research methodology 469–70
 schedule 489–90
 see also defence at trial observations; trial outcome observations
court-appointed lawyers 303–15
crime control 14, 105, 141–2, 498–9
 see also criminal justice system and institutional process
crime detection *see* evidence
crime figures 436
crime reporting 26–8, 101–2, 120–21, 127
criminal justice system and institutional process 377–424
 acquittal rate target 387
 adjudication committee *see* adjudication committee
 and adjudicative review and court autonomy 394
 case-filing system *see* case-file analysis
 case-responsible judge *see* case-responsible judge
 chief of police, political influence of 378
 collegial panel *see* collegial panel
 and corruption crackdown 18, 379, 410, 411–12, 419–21
 and defence lawyers *see* defence lawyers
 'iron triangle' 378–9, 383, 386, 413
 and judges *see* judges
 judgment after trial 407–8
 and legal conditions to practice 414
 and legal reforms 436–40
 and Party influence and supervision 396, 399–402, 403–7, 409, 410, 411, 413–14
 police role 378–86
 and prosecutors *see* prosecutors
 and Public Security Bureau (PSB) *see* Public Security Bureau (PSB)
criminal procedure
 flowchart 455–60
 overview 1–5
Criminal Procedure Law (1979)
 defendant, use of term 429
 drunkenness and criminal responsibility 305
 and pre-trial investigation 9, 144
 and requests for arrest 43
 self-defence and excessive defence claims 328
Criminal Procedure Law (1996)
 and adjudicative committee 403
 and appeal and protest 197–8
 arrest conditions 43–4
 Article 306, call for abolition of 180–81, 182–3, 184, 185–6, 188
 bail conditions 41–2, 47, 58, 64
 basic objectives 15–16

and burden of proof 9, 19, 120, 213–16, 337, 346
confessions, extortion of 70, 213, 337, 340
crime proscription 253, 320
and crime reporting 26
criminal detention 14, 15–16, 42–3
criminal justice system, elements of 377
defence lawyers and collection of evidence 180–81, 182–3, 184, 185–6, 188, 303, 430
and defendant's plea 238–40
defendant's rights 263, 269
evidence collection by court 215
evidence, definition of 66–7, 100
evidence, production of 240–41
extended detention 46, 47
first instance trials 3–5, 402
forced appearance summons 41
and incidental civil action 199, 200
interrogation and access to legal advice 67–8, 70, 71, 76, 100, 168–71
and legal assistance rights 165
legal impact and background culture 12–13, 24
legal impact and legal reality (gap problem) 13–15
legal representation rights 292
migrants and bail 64
Notice Concerning Strict Enforcement 47
People's Court violation of litigation procedure 291
and pre-trial detention 49, 53, 55
and pre-trial involvement of judges *see* pre-trial involvement of judges
and pre-trial preparation of prosecutors *see* pre-trial preparation of prosecutors
and presumption of innocence 428
procuratorate powers and duties under 106–7, 389, 393
and public hearings 193, 266, 430
and recommendation for prosecution 104–5
reforms 5–15, 154, 161–2, 427
and representation for defendants 210–11
residence interrogation 41
residential surveillance 42, 47, 59–60
and right of access to lawyer at time of detention 168–71
and rules of evidence 213–14, 429–30
and search powers 100–101
shortcomings of 10–12
standard of proof and presumption of innocence 213, 216, 428–9, 446
Summary Procedure 205–6, 266–7
and superstitious material 76
suspect, use of term 429

suspect's duty to answer questions 339
witness statements 432
and young offenders 258
see also Chinese Communist Party
criminal procedure overview, political-legal committee 2–3, 4, 7, 110, 111, 226, 253, 358, 378, 403–4, 441, 461
cross examination 12, 21, 71, 186, 189, 201, 206, 246, 247, 310
Cui, M. 46, 56, 198
Cui, Peng 206
Cui, Po 208
Cui, S. 46
Cullen, R. 230, 317, 450
Cultural Revolution 1, 5, 427
Cutler, B. 29

Dai, M. 378, 379
Danching, R. 420
Davies, C. 172, 362
death penalty cases 7, 17, 210, 217, 258–9, 310
and confessions by torture 217, 337
grounds for imposing sentence 210, 396–7
reduction in crimes punishable by 452
sentencing 258–9, 365–6, 370–71
September 2 Decision 7
support for 437
and Supreme People's Court 198, 366
suspended sentences 365–6
trial and case file analysis 258–9
debate stage 76, 77, 85, 201–5, 209, 251–2, 298–9, 334, 346–7, 369
decision not to prosecute 108–12
see also pre-trial preparation of prosecutors
defence at trial observations 292–350
annual evaluation and disbarment 317–18
confessions, reliability of 340–42
confessions, withdrawal of 337–8
constraints on defence lawyers 317
court-appointed lawyers 303–15
defence lawyer assisting the prosecution 306–9
defendant as accomplice 325–7
defendants' disagreement with prosecution case 300–302
defendants' participation 298–300
and defendants' personal attributes 320–21
disputed confessions and torture 336–40
evidence produced by defence lawyer 331–3
hearsay evidence 213–14, 277, 329–31
lack of involvement in case 318–19
lack of knowledge of case 304–6
legal aid system 68, 71, 211–12, 292
legal representation rights and practice 292, 293–4, 302–15, 434–5

and perjury 181, 182, 184, 187–8, 204, 243
pleas in mitigation *see* mitigation pleas
prosecution case challenge 318
retained lawyers 316–36
self-defence and excessive defence claims 310–14, 328–9
Simplified Ordinary Procedure *see* Simplified Ordinary Procedure
Summary Procedure *see* Summary Procedure
torture allegations, dealing with 342–9
unrepresented cases 292–302
victim's family, defendant seeking mercy from 321
and witnesses *see* witnesses
defence case construction 165–90
　access to client following police interrogation 174–6
　access to client on initial detention 166–74
　and 'big stick' 181
　case materials, access to 176–9
　and case withdrawal 175–6, 189
　collection of evidence 180–86, 188, 303, 430, 433–4
　confessions, forced, concern over 187
　and Criminal Procedure Law (1996), Article 306, call for abolition of 180–81, 182–3, 184, 185–6, 188
　defence evidence status 186, 445
　identification evidence, problems with 176–7
　interrogation, no access before or during 172–3
　interrogation, request for access to 187
　and Lawyers Law (2007) 169–71, 180, 181, 186
　and lawyers' reforms 186–9
　legal representative powers and responsibilities 165–6
　limitations of contact with suspect 175–6
　and non-disclosure of evidence 177–9
　and police authority over lawyer 173–4
　and police interrogation tactics 167, 187
　and police monitoring 174–5
　problems facing lawyers 171–3
　prosecution case, request for early access to 188
　and psychological pressures of confinement 166–7
　and witnesses *see* witnesses
　see also trial and case file analysis
defence lawyers
　and bail 60–61, 62
　compliant stance of 422–3
　corrupt 419–21
　interview schedule 495–6

and judges, relationship between 397–9, 414–17
low self-esteem of 417–19
and personal relationships 420–21
and prosecution presentation 271, 273, 277, 283, 318
and PSB, relationship between 379–81
role of 7–8, 9, 12, 16, 17, 413–22
state supervision of 413–14
training standards 418–19
as victims of system 421–3
defendants
　bribes by 111
　meritorious performance 98–9, 119, 130, 133, 198, 250, 367–8, 372–3
　plea, and Criminal Procedure Law (1996) 238–40
　representation for, and Criminal Procedure Law (1996) 210–11
Delmas-Marty, M. 19
Deng, S. 244, 245
Deng, Z. 188
Dervieux, V. 150, 166
detention
　access to client on initial 166–74
　access to legal advice at time of 168–71
　apprehension and detention 5–6, 11–12
　and Criminal Procedure Law (1996) 14, 15–16, 42–3
　and defence access to client 166–74
　extended 45–9, 51, 54, 119, 131, 432, 433, 437
　extra-judicial 14
　police powers of detention and arrest *see* police powers of detention and arrest
　pre-trial detention, and residential status 17
　and right of access to lawyer, and Criminal Procedure Law (1996) 168–71
Devlin, R. 177, 341
Diamant, N. 425
Dicks, A. 18
Ding, X. 47
disclosure *see* evidence
discovery of crime 27, 29
dissidents 413, 427, 433, 438, 442, 449, 451
DNA evidence 98, 102, 104, 166, 177
　see also evidence
Dobinson, I. 12, 14
documentary evidence 125–7, 145, 240–42, 247–50, 276
　see also evidence
Dong, G. 206
Dong, Q. 37, 56, 57, 59, 63
Dong, X. 235

dossiers *see* case construction; case-file analysis
Drass, K. 17, 62, 63, 64
due process rights 8, 14, 286, 439, 447
  see also suspects' rights
Dutton, M. 436

Ede, R. 165
education
  defence lawyers 231–2
  defendants 264–5
  judicial 217–18, 219–21
  prosecutors 228
Edwards, A. 165
Eliasoph, E. 439
equality of arms principle 20, 165
Ericson, R. 167, 433
Esser, R. 144
Etzioni, A. 433
European Convention on Human Rights 19–20, 177
Evans, R. 71
evidence
  against accomplices, and interrogation 97–9
  audio-visual 66, 184, 217, 241–2, 249, 276, 448
  collection by court 215, 292
  collection of, and defence case construction 180–86, 188, 303, 430, 433–4
  collection other than through interrogation 100–104
  confession *see* confession
  conflicting 282, 283
  defence evidence status 186
  deficiencies, and judges 399
  definition of 66–7, 100
  documentary 125–7, 145, 240–42, 247–50, 276
  exclusion of 66, 217, 358, 447
  Explanation of the Situation 249–50
  forensic 103, 277
  hearsay 213–14, 277, 329–31
  identification, problems with 176–7
  investigative officers' imperfect understanding of 132–3
  involvement in other crimes, and interrogation 99–100
  major 145–6, 152–4, 155, 161, 162
  material 40, 100, 105, 125–7, 194, 241, 249–50
  medical 104, 248, 312, 332, 431
  missing 177–9, 280
  non-disclosure of 177–9
  photographic 10, 102, 104, 241, 279, 285
  pre-trial verification of 121–2
  production of 240–42
  questioning 247–50
  review, Basic and Intermediate Courts 126
  rules of 213–17, 429–30
  sufficiency 108, 112, 113
  supplementary 157, 160
  through torture *see* torture
  unchallenged, and sentencing 369–70
  verification 195
  witness *see* witnesses
examination for prosecution 48, 112–13, 131, 136–42, 243
  see also pre-trial preparation of prosecutors
exclusion of evidence 66, 217, 358, 447
expert witnesses 7–8, 66, 166, 194, 200–201, 206, 214, 238, 241, 247
  see also witnesses
extended detention 45–9, 51, 54, 119, 131, 432, 433, 437
  see also detention
extortion of confessions 68–9, 70–71, 213, 337, 340
  see also confessions
eyewitnesses 100–101, 176–7, 322
  see also witnesses

Falun Gong 76, 170, 317, 377
Fan, C. 36, 68, 69, 176, 338, 464
Fang, B. 133, 243–4, 309
Fang, M. 104
Fang, S. 57
Feeley, M. 433
Feinerman, J. 426
Feng, C. 286
Feng, H. 359, 401
Feng, J. 214, 215
Feng, Q. 258, 364, 365
final statements 195, 202, 207, 271, 298–9
  see also trial procedures
fingerprints 102, 104, 149, 375
  see also evidence
first instance cases 3–5, 402
Fisher, S. 177
Flood, J. 23
forensic evidence 102, 103, 104, 149, 375
  see also evidence
Foster, J. 167
France 150, 168, 339, 395
Frase, R. 395
Fu, H. 7, 8, 9, 10, 12–13, 15–16, 168, 181, 230, 317, 349, 379, 386, 389, 394, 396, 406, 407, 411, 419, 426, 427, 434, 435, 439, 441, 443, 450, 498
Fu, W. 235
Fu, Y. 401

Gao, F. 206
Gao, J. 55
Gao Zhisheng case 317, 318, 413
'gap' problem 13–15
Garcon, M. 339
Gelatt, T. 7
gender
　of judges 220
　of suspects 18, 32, 56, 63–4, 76
Geng, J. 207
Germany 27, 144, 150, 208, 320, 339, 361–2
Gold, T. 24
Gompers, M. 11, 13, 292, 303
Graef, R. 167, 433
Greenwood, P. 27
Grueneberg, S. 439
Gu, Y. 338
Gu, Z. 57
Guan, Y. 188, 317
Guang, Y. 57
guanxi (personal networks) 368, 411, 420, 464, 470
guarantee money 41–2, 59, 60
　see also bail
Gudjonsson, G. 68, 166, 341, 362
Guo, J. 208
Guo, Q. 46
Guo, S. 463
Guo, W. 162
Guo, Youjia 142
Guo, Yunzhong 215
Guo, Z. 153, 351, 352, 358

Halliday, T. 17, 166, 172, 174, 181, 190, 292, 379, 389, 404, 413, 414, 422, 428, 431, 435
Hand, K. 317
Hao, Y. 144, 403
harmony rights 401, 451
　see also suspects' rights
Hartley, A. 45
Hayes, R. 362
He, H. 410
He, J. 215, 226, 343, 359, 363, 464
He, Q. 6, 403
He, R. 343, 363
He, W. 219, 220, 385, 443
He, X. 41
hearsay evidence 213–14, 277, 329–31
　see also evidence
Hecht, J. 6, 9, 11, 12, 13, 42, 395, 428, 429, 430, 444
Henderson, K. 395–6
Heydebrand, W. 445, 446
Higher Court 2, 7, 278, 408
Hilgendorf, L. 68, 166

Hill, P. 362
Hodgson, J. 19, 168
Hong, J. 503
Hong Kong, *Secretary for Justice v Lam Tat Ming* 339
Hong, X. 56, 63
Hou, X. 317
household registration 36, 126, 152, 296, 372, 499, 500
Hu, G. 57, 58
Hu, Y. 437
Hu, Z. and Z. 53, 133
Huang, Changxing 142
Huang, Chunhong 211, 212
Huang, D. 215
Huang, J. 133, 250
Huang, Q. 32, 69
Huang, Wen 215
Huang, Wensheng 104
Huang, X. 377
Hucklesby, A. 56
Huff, C. 362
human rights 13–14, 41, 54, 171, 230, 317–18, 366, 377, 435, 447–9
　see also suspects' rights
Hunt, G. 362

identification of suspects 5, 27, 29–32, 176–7
illegally-obtained confessions 336–7
　see also confessions
Inbau, F. 173
incidental civil action 199–201
innocence, presumption of 12, 358, 428–9
inquests 66, 100, 103, 144, 194–5, 241–2, 249–50, 276–7, 356
inquisitorial system 10–11, 19–20, 144–5, 150, 168, 339, 441–2
institutional process *see* criminal justice system and institutional process
institutional setting, and case construction 436–40
Intermediate Courts
　age of suspects 34, 36
　and bail applications 62–4
　criminal jurisdiction 2, 3, 15–16, 29, 31
　evidence review 126
　interrogation and confession 72, 73–4, 75–6, 124
　legal advice requests 116–17
　non-prosecution rate 136, 137–8
　police mistreatment complaints 120
　and pre-trial detention 49, 50, 51–3
　pre-trial interrogation 123
　and summary procedure 207
　supplementary investigation requests 129

trial procedure 194
  see also Basic Courts; Supreme People's Court; trial and case file analysis; trial outcome observations
International Covenant on Civil and Political Rights 40–41
interrogation
  and confession, Basic Courts 72, 73–4, 75–6, 124
  and confession evidence 68–9, 70–97
  and Criminal Procedure Law (1996) 67–8, 70, 71, 76, 100, 168–71
  and defence, no access before or during 172–3
  defence request for access to 187
  and denial of charges 76, 78–96
  and evidence against accomplices 97–9
  and evidence of involvement in other crimes 99–100
  legal advice access 67–70
  length 69–70
  and multiple interviews 72–4
  police tactics 42–3, 44, 167, 187
  pre-trial preparation of prosecutors 122–4
  relevance of questions to case 100
  residence 41
  and surveillance cameras 340
  tape-recorded 338
  third degree 69
  and trial procedures 194
'iron triangle' 378–9, 383, 386, 413
Irving, B. 68, 166
Italy 10, 150, 208, 361–2, 395

Jacobs, A. 45, 434
Jessel, D. 362
Ji, G. 53, 132, 133, 377
Ji, X. 153, 170, 172, 176, 199, 303, 351, 413, 414
Jiang, J. 286
Jiang, Q. 214
Jiang, S. 56, 63
Jiang, T. 252
Jiang, X. 46
Jiang, Y. 60
Jin, S. 130, 133
Jin, X. 133
Jin, Y. 235
Jing, L. 199
Jones, C. 8, 14, 425
judges
  case-responsible *see* case-responsible judge
  and defence lawyers, relationship between 397–9, 414–17
  and evidence deficiencies 399

interview schedule 491–2
judicial bribes 410, 411
and judicial corruption 410, 411–12
judicial education 217–18, 219–21
judicial independence 395–7, 399–401, 403–7, 408–11, 412–13
pre-trial involvement *see* pre-trial involvement of judges
presiding 2, 7, 22, 158, 194–5, 200–201, 252, 404
and prosecutors, alliance between 378–9, 387–9, 397, 411, 412–13
and PSB, relationship between 381–3
robes 262
role of 395–413
salaries 401–2
sentencing *see* sentencing
  see also trial and case file analysis
Judges Law (2001) 217–18, 220
Junying, Y. 46
jury role 358
  see also trial outcome observations
juvenile offenders 56, 149, 194, 210, 214, 258, 292, 365
Juy-Birmann, R. 150

Kahn, J. 339–40, 343, 439
Kamm, J. 431
Kang, B. 359, 401
Karpik, L. 168
Kassin, S. 71, 173
Kaye, T. 362
Kellogg, T. 413
Kelly, B. 18, 363
Kennedy, L. 362
Kilias, M. 362
King, M. 56
Kipnis, A. 470
Krattinger, P. 339
Kwan, D. 219

Lai, D. 132–3, 134
Lambert, J. 72
Lan, J. 59
Langer, M. 144
lawyers
  licence 169, 170, 171, 317–18, 414
  reforms, and defence case construction 186–9
  weiquan (rights-defenders) 396, 414, 429, 442, 450, 451–2
  see also defence lawyers; prosecutors
Lawyers Law (2007) 10, 68, 169–71, 180, 181, 186
  and collection of evidence 292

and defence case construction 169–71, 180, 181, 186
Law on Lawyers amendment (2007) 170, 171, 414, 429
and representation for defendants 211, 290
and state supervision of lawyers 413–14, 429–30
legal aid 68, 211–12, 292
legal reforms
  agenda 447–8
  agenda, enabling conditions 448–9
  assumptions about 427–8
  case construction, capacity for 433–5
  case construction, and institutional setting 436–40
  and case reliability 441–2
  challenges 447–8
  contradictions in 435
  criminal justice as process and system 440–46
  Criminal Procedure Law (1996) 5–8, 154, 161–2, 427
  and cultural factors 437, 438
  defence lawyers, and political and social environment 439–40
  institutional accountability and legitimacy 442–5
  institutional interdependency and coordination 435, 441
  judicial role 440–41
  legal provisions and CPL reform, tensions between 154, 161–2
  perceived legality of 427–32
  and policy pronouncements 439
  previous research 16–18
  and public opinion 439
  scope of 446–50
  and social order, maintenance of 445–6
  and state input 449
  and system reformers 449–50
legal representation
  of defendants, and prosecution presentation 265–6
  practice and rights 292, 293–4, 302–15, 434–5
  and sentencing, links between 366
  victims with 237–8
legal rhetoric 14, 428, 436, 442
legality, police actions 118–20, 427–32, 433–4
legitimacy 17, 211, 263, 400, 403, 425–6, 427, 432, 436–8, 444
  and institutional accountability 442–5
Leng, R. 14, 29, 30, 31, 32, 71, 72, 167, 174, 177
Leo, R. 172
Li, Baoyue 212

Li, Bin 365
Li, Chunfu 317
Li, Chungang 133, 250
Li, Heping 170
Li, Hong 180
Li, Hua 242–3
Li, Huizi 362
Li, Jian 154, 160, 180
Li, Jianling 111, 142
Li, Jiya 57, 59
Li, Jun 243
Li, Junjie 198
Li, Liangxiong 403
Li, Lijun 206
Li, Ling 410
Li, S. 142
Li, Weihua 242
Li, Wenyu 208
Li, Xiaolin 243
Li, Xuekuan 198
Li, Yan 212
Li, Yanling 206
Li, Yimin 215
Li, Yumei 396
Li, Z. 142
Li Zhuang case 170, 181, 430
Lian, Y. 172
Liang, B. 17, 462, 463, 464, 470
Liang, Z. 208
Liao, H. 214
Liebman, B. 414, 439
lien 41
Lin, J. 215
Lin, L. 32, 69
Liu, C. 172, 181
Liu, F. 72
Liu, G. 153, 206
Liu, H. 133
Liu, Jihua 154
Liu, Jing 53, 132, 133, 174, 206, 207, 377
Liu, Lina 46
Liu, Lixia 243–4, 309, 464
Liu, N. 361
Liu, S. 17, 18, 166, 172, 174, 181, 190, 292, 379, 389, 404, 413, 414, 422, 425, 428, 431, 435, 444
Liu, W. 142
Liu, Xiaojun 214
Liu, Xiaoqing 227
Liu, Xuezai 206, 403
Liu, Y. 215, 243
Liu Yong case 349
Liu, Zhong 54, 184
Liu, Zhongfa 55, 56, 57, 59, 63, 141
Loftus, E. 29

Long, Z. 154, 163
Lu, H. 16–17, 18, 62, 63, 64, 316, 363, 366, 417, 462, 463, 464, 470
Lu, Jianhong 358
Lu, Jinbao 244
Lu, W. 46
Lubman, S. 24, 198, 385, 425, 427
Luo, B. 214
Luo, G. 219, 439
Luo, H. 57, 59, 63
Lynch, E. 337, 430

Ma, H. 55
Ma, J. 53, 133
Ma, L. 56
Ma, M. 212, 303
Ma, Q. 163
Ma, X. 378
Ma, Y. 40, 41, 386, 499, 503–5
McAleavy, H. 379
Macauley, M. 190
McBarnet, D. 14
McConville, M. 29, 30, 31, 68, 71, 72, 97, 99, 167, 168, 174, 303, 445
MacKeith, J. 68, 362
McKenzie, I. 167
McNall, K. 173
major evidence 145–6, 152–4, 155, 161, 162
   see also evidence
Manning, P. 167, 433
Mao, C. 208
Marafioti, L. 10
Marquand, R. 219
mass-line justice 443
material evidence 40, 100, 105, 125–7, 194, 241, 249–50
   see also evidence
Mawby, R. 27, 71
May, J. 362
medical evidence 104, 248, 312, 332, 431
   see also evidence
Men, J. 180
Meng, D. 162
mental hospitals 97, 321, 451, 498
meritorious performance 98–9, 119, 130, 133, 198, 250, 367–8, 372–3
Messner, S. 464
Michelson, E. 16, 379–80, 420, 425, 439–40
Miethe, T. 16–17, 18, 316, 366, 417
migrants 36, 42, 64, 76, 265, 365
Ministry of Justice 170–71, 181, 201, 208, 217, 230, 414, 434
Mirsky, C. 303, 445
miscarriages of justice 339–40, 358, 362–3, 452–3

mitigation pleas 208, 305, 309, 319–20, 321–5, 446, 448
   and prosecution presentation 272–3, 277, 284
   and sentencing 369, 371–4
Mooney, P. 379, 431, 437
Morris, C. 190, 339
Mosher, S. 451, 452
Muhlhahn, K. 427
Mullin, C. 362
Munro, R. 498

Na, Z. 246
Nathan, A. 420
National People's Congress, indefinite detention 44, 46
national security 12, 19, 170, 181, 258, 429
Naughton, M. 362
Nelken, D. 14, 189
Ng, T. 213, 217, 337, 338, 379, 413, 422, 434
Ni, J. 198
Niblett, J. 177
non-prosecution see under pre-trial preparation of prosecutors
Nowak, M. 338

Oberwittler, D. 259, 437
O'Connor, P. 177
Ofshe, R. 172
Olson, E. 29
O'Neill, M. 336, 401, 411
Ordinary Procedure 205–10, 227, 272, 276–8
   and case file analysis 236, 267, 351–2, 354, 358
   and defence case 293
   and pre-trial involvement of judges 146, 147, 152, 153
   see also Simplified Ordinary Procedure; Summary Procedure

Packer, H. 14
Pan, D. 132–3, 134
Pang, X. 226, 403
party-state 171, 219, 378, 400, 401, 439, 442
Peerenboom, R. 4, 10–11, 13, 16, 24, 219, 220, 221, 229, 378, 395, 400, 401, 402, 404, 405, 406, 411, 413, 420, 423, 426, 435, 437–8, 440, 447–9, 451, 497, 498, 501
penalty system 15
Peng, D. 403
Peng, J. 111, 142
Penrod, S. 29
people's assessors system 226–7, 235–6, 402
People's Courts 2, 3, 4, 109
   and cases accepted for trial 146–7

and public hearings 193
violation of litigation procedure 291
People's Procuratorate 2, 5–6, 9, 12
  and bail 58
  and confessions, extortion of 70–71
  detention times 44, 46, 51–6
  powers and duties under CPL 106–7
  and pre-trial involvement of judges *see* pre-trial involvement of judges
  requests for arrest 43, 44
Pepinsky, H. 72
performance indicators 111, 355, 423, 435, 440, 442, 447
perjury 181, 182, 184, 187–8, 204, 243
Perrodet, A. 150
personal networks (*guanxi*) 368, 411, 420, 464, 470
Pesquie, B. 150
petitioners 451
Pfeffer, R. 379, 423
Phillips, C. 167
photographic evidence 10, 102, 104, 241, 279, 285
  see also evidence
Pils, E. 64, 166, 219, 277, 318, 401, 413, 418, 450, 452
Pizzi, W. 10
pleas in mitigation 305, 309, 319–20, 321–5, 446
ploys used by police 167, 171, 434
police
  administrative cases, imposition by 500–501
  mistreatment complaints 120
  punishment power, reasons for giving 498–9
  stop and search 30–31
  third degree interrogation 69
police case, construction of 66–105
  and authority over lawyer 173–4
  and confessions, extortion of 16, 68–9, 70–71, 213, 337, 340
  confessions and statement, contradictions between 75, 77
  crime scene report 26–8, 101–2
  evidence collection other than through interrogation 100–104
  evidence, sources of 66–7
  forensic evidence 103
  innocence claims after confession 76–97
  interrogation *see* interrogation
  monitoring, and defence case construction 174–5
  and recommendation for prosecution 104–5, 106, 113, 177, 459
  and search powers 100–101, 102

police cases, sources of 26–39
  age of suspects 32–4, 36
  charging and offence type 28–9
  crime reporting 26–8, 101–2
  education of suspects 34, 37
  identification of suspects 5, 27, 29–32, 176–7
  and inaccurate recording 31
  profile of suspects 32–7
  residential status of suspects 36, 38
Police Law of the People's Republic of China (1998) 26, 41
police powers of detention and arrest 40–65
  administrative detention 42
  applications for approval of arrest 49–51, 54–6, 59
  arrest 43–4
  and bail *see* bail
  criminal detention 42–3
  extended detention beyond legal time 45
  internal evaluation mechanism problems 59
  interrogation 42–3, 44
  legality of 118–20, 427–34
  ploys used 167, 171, 434
  at police station 40–44
  pre-trial detention problems 44–54
  requests for arrest 43
  residential surveillance 42, 43, 45, 47, 59–60, 63, 64
  restrictions 9
  risk prevention systems, lack of 59
  summons 41, 67, 457
  time lapse after transfer for prosecution 51–4
  time lapse between date of arrest and transfer for prosecution 51
  time lapse between initial detention and application for approval of arrest 5–6, 11–12, 49–51
  see also Public Security Bureau (PSB), detention
political-legal committee
  and acquittal rates 358
  PSB involvement 378
  responsibilities and adjudication 2–3, 4, 7, 111, 226, 253, 403–4, 441, 461
  see also adjudication committee; collegial panel
Poon, P. 451, 452
post-trial, trial outcome *see* trial outcome observations
Potter, P. 18, 24, 378, 403, 409, 425, 443
pre-trial detention 49, 50, 51–3, 55
  see also detention
pre-trial involvement of defence *see* defence case construction

pre-trial involvement of judges 144–64
  anticipatory nature of 150–51
  and attitude towards case 150
  case-filing and assignment 158
  and criminal injuries compensation cases 151
  defence, contact with 156
  examining judge conducting trial 154
  and familiarisation with case information 151–63
  information gathering and meeting with defendants and victims 148–9, 151
  and judge quality and ability 160–61
  legal provisions and CPL reform, tensions between 154, 161–2
  and major evidence 145–6, 152–3, 154, 155, 161, 162
  and Ordinary Procedure 146, 147, 152, 153
  pre-trial judicial activism 147–60
  pre-trial procedure of 1996 CPL 145–7
  preliminary examination 150, 152
  prosecution case file, bias associated with 152–3, 155–6, 157–8, 159, 160
  reasons for pre-trial activism 160–63
  and Summary Procedure 146, 147, 162–3
  and supplementary evidence 157, 160
pre-trial preparation of prosecutors 106–43
  Bill of Prosecution *see* Bill of Prosecution
  case material examination 120
  challenge to decision to prosecute 107, 109
  compulsory measures, review of 127–9
  confession withdrawal 123–4, 130
  crime scene, visiting 120–21, 127
  criminal records, checking 114–15
  decision not to prosecute absolutely 109–12
  decision-making interference 112
  decision-making levels 111–12, 113
  discretionary decision not to prosecute 108–9
  evidence, investigative officers' imperfect understanding of 132–3
  evidence and witness statements 125–7
  examination for prosecution 48, 112–13, 131, 136–42, 243
  identity of suspects, confirming 114–15
  key tasks 113–14
  law examination and verification of facts and evidence 121–2
  legal advice/defence lawyer for suspects 115–18
  legality of police actions, examination of 118–20
  non-prosection as performance indicator 111
  non-prosecution because of doubts 107–8, 113
  non-prosecution controversies 107
  non-prosecution rate 136, 137–42
  police decisions, prosecutors' tendency to follow 128–9, 136
  and police mistreatment of suspects 119–20, 121
  and police performance, criticism of 129–30, 134–5
  pre-trial activities in practice 112–13
  procuratorate powers and duties under CPL 106–7
  prosecution review period 135–6
  punishment for mistaken cases 111
  report stage and preparation of documentation for trial 135
  right of appeal against decision not to prosecute 109–10
  and sufficiency of evidence 108, 112, 113
  supplementary investigation and communication problems 133–4
  supplementary investigation request 129–35, 142–3
  suspect, interrogation of 122–4
  time limits 106, 130, 135–6
  and victims *see* victims
  see also prosecution headings
preliminary examination 150, 152
Prescott, J. 235
presentation, prosecution *see* prosecution presentation
presiding judge 2, 7, 22, 158, 194–5, 200–201, 252, 404
  see also case-responsible judge
presumption of innocence cases 12, 358, 428–9
Price, C. 362
private affairs of individuals, cases involving 194
procuratorate *see* Supreme People's Procuratorate
prosecution presentation 261–91
  and Bill of Prosecution *see* Bill of Prosecution
  case defence challenge 318
  case, defence request for early access to 188
  case-responsible judge 263–4, 266, 269, 273–5, 330–31
  collegial panel of judges, role of 263–4, 266, 272–3, 276–8
  court investigation 269–70, 278–90
  court proceedings, opening of 262–3
  courtroom setting 261–6
  defence lawyer role 271, 273, 277, 283, 318
  defence lawyers, judges' relationship with 288–90
  defendants' appearance and isolation 265–6

and defendants' plea in mitigation 272–3, 277, 284
and defendants' rights 263, 264–5, 269, 275–6
deliberation and announcement of judgment 271
and determination of guilt 9
evidence, conflicting 282, 283
evidence, missing 280
final statement 271
forensic evidence, lack of 277
and judges, alliance between 378–9, 387–9, 397, 411, 412–13
judges' role 284–90
judges smoking and falling asleep 264
judicial activism and relationship with prosecutor 284–8
legal representation of defendants 265–6
ordinary procedure 276–8
ordinary procedure, length of 277–8
prosecutor role 278–84
public audience 193, 261, 262
robes, wearing of 262, 263, 264
simplified ordinary procedure 272–6, 286, 287
summary trials 266–72, 276
summary trials, speed of 267–8, 272
and witness statements 268–9, 271–2, 276–7
see also trial and case file analysis
prosecutors
appeals and protests, dealing with 393–5
defence lawyer assisting 306–9
interview schedule 493–4
limited powers and lack of self-esteem 389–93
and PSB, relationship between 383–6
recommendation, and Criminal Procedure Law (1996) 104–5
role of 386–95
training system 390–92
protests 3, 4, 109–10, 142, 197–8, 291, 389, 393–5, 411, 460
public hearings 193, 261, 262, 266, 430
public opinion, and legal reforms 439
Public Security Bureau (PSB)
and criminal justice system and institutional process 378–86
and defence lawyer access 68
interview practice 72, 74
responsibilities 1, 66–7, 100
and supplementary investigation 129, 130–31
and witness threats 245

Qi, S. 259, 437
Qian, X. 59

Qin, C. 226
Qin, Z. 160, 162
Qu, X. 54

Radelet, M. 172, 362
Raifeartaigh, U. 56
Ran, Y. 166, 171, 429
recommendation
for non-prosecution 112
for prosecution 104–5, 106, 113, 177, 459
see also pre-trial preparation for prosecutors
Redmayne, M. 165
Re-education through Labour 1, 14, 55, 104, 171, 317, 368, 448
reforms
lawyers, and defence case construction 186–9
legal *see* legal reforms
system 449
see also criminal justice system and institutional process
Regan, F. 304, 314
Reiner, R. 27, 167
reliability of confessions 340–42
see also confessions
reporting crime 26–8, 101–2, 120–21, 127
research methodology 462–74
case file analysis 467–8
case file analysis schedule 475–88
courtroom observation schedule 489–90
courtroom observations 469–70
defenders' interview schedule 495–6
fieldwork 20–25, 40
interviews with judges, prosecutors and defence lawyers 470–71
judges' interview schedule 491–2
limitations of 425–6
project practice and theory 18–20
prosecutors' interview schedule 493–4
research instruments 465–71
research sites 463–5, 471–4
residence interrogation 41
residential status of suspects 17, 36–7, 38, 63–4
residential surveillance 42, 43, 45, 47, 59–60, 63, 64
retained lawyers 316–36
Ribet, S. 377
rights *see* suspects' rights
Rio Tinto case 242, 430
Roberts, A. 29
Roberts, D. 168
Roberts, P. 339
Rose, J. 362
Ru, Y. 53, 133
rule of law 13, 24, 46, 110, 171, 349, 377, 400, 427–8, 437, 442, 466

rules of evidence 213–17, 429–30
  see also evidence

Sanders, A. 14, 29, 30, 31, 32, 71, 72, 167, 174
Sapio, F. 497
Sarat, A. 259
Savadove, B. 24
Scott, K. 259, 362
search powers 100–101
Security Administration Punishment Regulations (1986) 15
Sekar, S. 362
self-defence and excessive defence claims 310–14, 328–9
self-incrimination, accused's privilege against 339, 429
  see also suspects' rights
Sellin, T. 27
sentencing
  and aggravating circumstances 373
  custodial 364
  death penalty cases 258–9, 365–6, 370–71
  and education of first offenders 375–6
  factors involved in 366–70
  grounds for imposing, and death penalty 210, 396–7
  and joint trials 374–5
  and legal representation, links between 366
  and leniency, justifiable 372–3
  non-custodial 363–4
  and pleas of mitigation 369, 371–4
  severe punishment argument 373–4
  suspended 303, 364–6
  in trial and case file analysis 256–9
  trial outcome observations 363–76
  and unchallenged evidence 369–70
  verdict and majority vote 195
  verdict procedure and conviction 353–7
September 2 Decision 7
Shang, X. 69
Shao, H. 286, 290
Sharp, P. 451
She Xianglin case 340, 358–9, 362
Shearing, C. 433
shelter and investigation 6, 9, 11, 14, 433–4
Shen, H. 378
Shen, J. 227
Shen, S. 172, 309, 317
Shen, X. 378
Shepherd, D. 167
Sheskin, A. 442, 443, 445
Shu, H. 16
Simplified Ordinary Procedure
  defence at trial observations 294
  prosecution presentation 272–6, 286, 287

trial and case file analysis 235, 236
trial procedures 208–10, 446
  see also Ordinary Procedure; Summary Procedure
Simpson, P. 97–8
Skolnick, J. 446
Smith, J. 11, 13, 292, 303
Softley, P. 71, 97, 99, 341
Song, J. 180
Song, Yinghui 27, 45, 57, 59, 63, 154, 464
Song, Yuansheng 452
Songcai, Y. 229
Spencer, J. 19, 362
standard of proof 213, 216, 428–9, 446
Starmer, K. 362
state secrets 3, 14, 68, 169, 172, 194, 431, 448
Steer, D. 27
Stephens, O. 99
stop and search 30–31
strike hard campaign (yanda) 7, 16, 141, 278, 365, 377, 426, 431, 434, 436–8, 443, 448
Stutsman, T. 452–3
Su, K. 403
Su, L. 218
Su, X. 56
Summary Procedure 4, 146, 147, 162–3
  and Bill of Prosecution 206
  Criminal Procedure Law (1996) 205–6, 266–7
  defence at trial observations 294
  and Intermediate Courts 207
  and judicial neutrality 207
  and lack of lawyer 206–7
  number limitation 207
  and pre-trial involvement of judges 146, 147, 162–3
  prosecution presentation 266–72, 276
  speed of, prosecution presentation 267–8, 272
  Supreme People's Court 205–6
  trial and case file analysis 235, 236
  trial procedures 205–7, 209, 446
  see also Ordinary Procedure; Simplified Ordinary Procedure
summons, and police powers of detention 41, 67, 457
Sun, C. 46, 55, 59, 69, 71, 141, 144, 166
Sun, F. 243
Sun, Q. 45
Sun, X. 53, 133
Sun, Y. 162
Suo, Z. 163
superstitious material 76
supervised residence 9, 42, 43, 45, 47, 59–60, 63, 64

Supreme People's Court 3–4
  and court layout 191–2
  and death penalty 198, 366
  and evidence through torture 217, 340
  and incidental civil action 199–201
  and judicial impartiality 219–20
  and judicial independence 396–7, 406
  and prosecution withdrawal 195–6
  and representation for defendants 210, 211
  and rules of evidence 214
  and simplified ordinary procedure 208
  SPC Interpretation and illegally obtained confessions 336–7
  SPC Interpretation and major evidence 145–6, 153–4
  SPC Interpretation and pre-trial judicial activism 160
  summary procedure 205–6
  and Three Supremes doctrine 219, 396, 401, 442, 443
  trial procedure 194
  see also Basic Courts; Intermediate Courts; trial and case file analysis; trial outcome observations
Supreme People's Procuratorate 2–6, 9
  and arrest, applications for approval of 54–6
  and bail conditions 57–8
  and court layout 191–2
  and defence evidence status 186
  and detention period 46, 47, 48–9
  discretionary decision not to prosecute 108–10
  and evidence through torture 70–71, 217
  and legal representation conditions 434–5
  non-prosecution cases, evaluation of 141–2
  pre-trial activities in practice 112–13
  pre-trial powers and duties under 1996 CPL 106–7
  and prosecution recommendation 104–5
  and prosecution withdrawal 195
  recording interviews 124
  and requests for arrest 43, 44
  and Simplified Ordinary Procedure 208
  and sufficiency of evidence 108
  and tape-recoded interrogations 338
  and time lapse between arrest and prosecution 51–3
suspects
  age of *see* age of suspects
  duty to answer questions 339
  education levels 264–5
  residential status 17, 36–7, 38, 63–4
  use of term 429
suspects' rights 40–41, 47, 115
  and Criminal Procedure Law (1996) 263, 269

  defendants' rights, and prosecution presentation 263, 264–5, 269, 275–6
  due process rights 8, 14, 286, 439, 447
  harmony rights 401, 451
  human rights 13–14, 41, 54, 171, 230, 317–18, 366, 377, 435, 447–9
  legal assistance rights 165
  legal representation rights 292
  practice and rights, legal representation 292, 293–4, 302–15, 434–5
  right to silence 100, 214, 215–16, 439
  rights protection movement 316–17, 396, 414, 429, 450
  rights-defenders 396, 414, 429, 442, 450, 451–2
  self-incrimination, accused's privilege against 339, 429
suspended sentencing 303, 364–6

Tam, F. 451
Tan, H. 46
Tan, S. 218, 403
Tan Zuoren case 413
Tang, L. 55, 56, 104, 358
Tang, W. 199
Tang, X. 172
Tanner, H. 7, 16, 436
Tao, J. 285
Tao, L. 379
Teng, B. 170, 429–30
third degree interrogation 69
  see also interrogation
Three Supremes doctrine 219, 396, 401, 442, 443
Tian, S. 199
Tian, W. 198
Tian, Y. 142
Toborg, M. 56
torture
  allegations, defence dealing with 342–9
  and confessions 5, 119–21, 187, 213, 217, 336–40, 430–31, 433, 437, 448
  confessions by, and death penalty cases 217, 337
Trevaskes, S. 7, 18, 377, 431, 437
trial and case file analysis 234–60
  adjournments 254, 434
  and collegial panel *see* collegial panel
  court, procedure and representation 234–8
  death penalty cases *see* death penalty
  debate stage statements 76, 77, 85, 201–5, 209, 251–2, 298–9, 334, 346–7, 369
  defence material, questioning 250–51
  defendant, questioning 248
  defendant's representative 236–7

defendants' role 238–40
evidence *see* evidence
and expert assessments 241
Explanation of the Situation evidence 249–50
judgment 254–6
law and legal argument 252–3
open or closed trial 236
and people's assessors 235–6
probation/non-custodial penalty 258
sentencing *see* sentencing
Simplified Ordinary Procedure *see* Simplified Ordinary Procedure
summary procedure 235, 236
victims *see* victims
witnesses *see* witnesses
see also case file analysis; defence headings; judges; prosecution headings
trial outcome observations 351–76
and case-responsible judge 352–3
and collegial panel 352–3, 356
court judgment 357–62
custodial sentences 364
death penalty *see* death penalty
and defence, lack of 359–60, 362
judges and prosecution, alliance between 357, 375, 434
judgment, immediate 360–61, 407–8
judgment time and adjournment 351–3
jury role 358
and miscarriages of justice 339–40, 358, 362–3, 452–3
presumption of innocence cases 358
sentencing *see* sentencing
social effects of judgment 358–9, 368–9
trials, speed of 351–2
trial procedures 191–233
appeal and protest 197–8
and Bill of Prosecution 194, 199, 200, 206, 209
and burden of proof 9, 19, 120, 213–16, 337, 346
civil suits for compensation 198–205
collegial panel *see* collegial panel
court layout 191–2
and Criminal Procedure Law (1996) 194–8, 200, 205–6, 210–11, 213–15
and death penalty *see* death penalty cases
defence lawyers, profile of 229–33
and evidence *see* evidence
evidence collection by court 215
evidence verification 195
final statements 195, 202, 207, 271, 298–9
interrogation 194
judges' role 217–26

judicial independence, lack of 218–19, 226–7
and legal aid cases 68, 71, 211–12, 292
mitigation pleas *see* mitigation pleas
Ordinary Procedure *see* Ordinary Procedure
people's assessors system 226–7, 235–6, 402
prosecution withdrawal 175–6, 189, 195–7
prosecutors, profile of 227–9
public audience 193, 261, 262
representation for defendants 210–12
rules of evidence 213–17
sentencing *see* sentencing
Simplified Ordinary Procedure *see* Simplified Ordinary Procedure
Summary Procedure *see* Summary Procedure
variations 205
witness testimony 194, 200–201, 206, 214
Turack, D. 12

UK
access to suspect in police custody 174
defence lawyers' role 440
defence lawyers, shortcomings of 168
detentions in custody 167
Ibrahim v R 339
identification parades 177
Police and Criminal Evidence Act (PACE) (1984) 167, 174
police interrogation 71, 72, 97, 99
R v Parris 168
search powers 101
self-incrimination, accused's privilege against 339
suspect identification 29–30, 31
suspects not told of rights 167–8
UN Commission on Human Rights 338
UN Convention against Torture 340, 348
unrepresented defendants 292–302
unworthiness and low self-esteem of state actors 224, 389–93, 417–19, 446
Upham, F. 220
US 29, 71, 97, 99

Van Cleave, R. 395
victims
family of, defendant seeking mercy from 321
informing of rights 114–15
with legal representation 237–8
meeting with, and information gathering 148–9, 151
present at trial 237, 238
questioning of 124–5
role of 240

Wald, M. 97, 99
Walker, C. 362
Walkley, J. 173
Wan, Y. 198
Wang, C. 56
Wang, F. 64
Wang, Gao 57
Wang, Gong 422
Wang, Guangjing 56
Wang, Hanbin 5
Wang, Heyan 181
Wang, Hongyu 258, 365
Wang, J. 154, 163, 178
Wang, K. 133, 250
Wang, L. 56
Wang, M. 57
Wang, P. 358
Wang, V. 24
Wang, Xiaoli 199
Wang, Xin'an 45, 49
Wang, Xinhuan 365
Wang, Ying 415
Wang, Yu 154, 162, 163
Wang, Yue 45, 46
Wang, Z. 104
Wei, H. 154, 163
Wei, L. 70, 205, 206, 336
Wei, Z. 132–3
weiquan lawyers (rights-defenders) 396, 414, 429, 442, 450, 451–2
Wells, G. 29
Weng, B. 410
Whitfort, A. 8–9
Whyte, M. 16
Wills, W. 337
Wilson, J. 167
withdrawal of prosecution 175–6, 189, 195–7
witnesses
 cooperation, and defence case construction 185–6, 189
 in court observations 333–5
 cross examination 12, 21, 71, 186, 189, 201, 206, 246, 247, 310
 expert witnesses 7–8, 66, 166, 194, 200–201, 206, 214, 238, 241, 247
 eyewitnesses 100–101, 176–7, 322
 interviews, safer strategies for 183–4
 low attendance of 16, 242–7
 questioning 248–9
 threats to 245
witnesses' statements
 consequences of changes to 181–2, 187–8
 Criminal Procedure Law (1996) 432
 and prosecution presentation 268–9, 271–2, 276–7

 review of 125–7
 and trial procedures 194, 200–201, 206, 214
Witt, J. 97
Woffinden, B. 362
Wolfgang, M. 27
Wong, K. 378, 385
Woo, M. 425
Wrightsman, L. 71
Wu, Danhong 243–4, 309
Wu, Dingzhi 464
Wu, Hong 27
Wu, Hongmei 55
Wu, S. 365
Wu, Y. 503

Xiao, N. 154, 163
Xiao, Q. 199
Xiao, S. 206, 207, 237, 268, 351
Xie, C. 58
Xie, M. 163
Xie, Y. 41
Xiong, J. 47
Xu, J. 198
Xu, L. 245, 252
Xu, M. 53, 133, 153, 317, 351
Xu, Xi 318
Xu, Xuefeng 214
Xu, Yongjun 186
Xu, Yuezhi 227
Xue, F. 198

Yan, D. 428
Yan, X. 111
Yan, Y. 162
yanda (strike hard campaign) 7, 16, 141, 278, 365, 377, 426, 431, 434, 436–8, 443, 448
Yang, C. 46, 198, 243, 403
Yang, F. 199
Yang, J. 63, 142
Yang, Mayfair 470
Yang, Ming 215
Yang, X. 111, 142, 154, 163
Yang, Y. 244
Yang, Z. 154, 162
Ye, L. 214
Ye, Q. 154
Yin, X. 214
Yongshun, C. 229
Yu, P. 166, 497
Yu, V. 377
Yu, X. 208, 463
Yuan, Z. 245–6, 309
Yue, L. 198, 358, 395

Zang, D. 365
Zeng, Y. 57
Zhai, H. 45
Zhan, F. 207
Zhang, C. 45, 49
Zhang, F. 32, 69, 142
Zhang, H. 5
Zhang, J. 144, 170, 198, 403
Zhang, Lening 464
Zhang, Linlin 180
Zhang, Liyun 363
Zhang, Lizhao 46
Zhang, M. 141
Zhang, Qingfeng 57, 59
Zhang, Qingshan 54
Zhang, Qingyu 181
Zhang, Qiyuan 163
Zhang, R. 59
Zhang, W. 358
Zhang, X. 212, 303
Zhang Xuping case 377
Zhang, Yan 359, 401
Zhang, Yanhong 199
Zhang, Yansheng 54, 184
Zhang, Yaowu 244
Zhang, Yi 244
Zhang, Ying 69
Zhang, Yuxiang 180

Zhang, Z. 464
Zhao, D. 199
Zhao, G. 206, 403
Zhao, L. 180
Zhao Zuohai case 217, 337, 340, 362–3
Zhen, S. 198
Zhen, Z. 178
Zheng Enchong case 41, 317, 413
Zhong, Daisy 340, 342
Zhong, Denang 141
Zhong, J. 169
Zhong, S. 47
Zhou, C. 133, 134
Zhou, G. 339
Zhou, Guojun 7, 499
Zhou, S. 26
Zhou, W. 59
Zhu, D. 396
Zhu, G. 46
Zhu, J. 215, 220, 227
Zhu, S. 4, 220, 400, 406
Zhu, W. 246
Zhu, Y. 434
Zuckerman, A. 339
Zuo, W. 41, 53, 69, 72, 100, 113, 144, 166, 172, 184, 207, 218, 227, 234, 237, 242, 243, 268, 317, 318, 351, 403